THE MUSIC OF BILL MONROE

MUSIC IN AMERICAN LIFE

A list of books in the series appears at the end of this book.

The Music of
BILL MONROE

NEIL V. ROSENBERG
AND CHARLES K. WOLFE

University of Illinois Press • Urbana and Chicago

Library of Congress Cataloging-in-Publication Data
Rosenberg, Neil V.
The music of Bill Monroe / Neil V. Rosenberg and Charles K. Wolfe.
p.   cm. — (Music in American life)
Includes bibliographical references and index.
ISBN-13: 978-0-252-03121-2 (cloth : alk. paper)
ISBN-10: 0-252-03121-0 (cloth)
1. Monroe, Bill, 1911–1996—Discography.
I. Wolfe, Charles K. II. Title.
ML156.7.M66R72   2007
016.781642092—dc22   2006018802

On February 9, 2006, not long after the final manuscript of this book went to the Press, my coauthor Charles K. Wolfe died. Charles was a prolific researcher, a widely published writer, and a charismatic teacher. He was often honored for his work in documenting the vernacular music of the American South. He loved talking with the people who made this music, and he told their stories with grace and wit. It was a privilege and a pleasure to work with him on this project. *The Music of Bill Monroe* is dedicated to his memory.

—NEIL V. ROSENBERG

Contents

Acknowledgments

The Music of Bill Monroe is the result of decades of collaborative research. There are many people to thank. The first version of this book, *Bill Monroe and His Blue Grass Boys: An Illustrated Discography,* acknowledged the help of Owen Bradley, Chick Doherty, Tom Ewing, Carl Fleischhauer, Douglas B. Green, Danny Hatcher, Bill Ivey, Bill Monroe, Bob Pinson, Robert Ronald, and Sandy Rothman. Because that book formed the foundation for our work on this book, we are happy to renew our thanks.

We are particularly indebted to Richard Weize of Bear Family records for his decision to reissue virtually all of Monroe's studio recordings in five elegant boxed sets. Much of the detail and accuracy of this book's data would not have been possible without Weize's own research at Columbia, MCA, and elsewhere. Working on the notes for those boxed sets' booklets made both Charles and I better aware of the fascinating stories, sounds, and images in Bill Monroe's music. We are grateful to Richard for encouraging us to draw upon the texts and data we developed for the notes for our work on this volume.

We are also grateful to former Blue Grass Boy, author, and researcher Tom Ewing for his considerable research and commentary as an editorial consultant. Over the years Tom responded with grace and good humor to our frequent requests for assistance and clarification, drawing upon his own research and his contacts among the bluegrass community to make valuable contributions to the narrative and discographical content of our work. He also provided helpful suggestions as one of the two readers of our final manuscript for the Press. John Wright, the other reader, also gave useful advice and was a valuable consultant during the period of final revisions.

During the long process of assembling this book we drew upon the knowledge and experience of many others in interviews, correspondence, and conversation. We want to extend our gratitude for this help to Robert Akeman, Mary Katherine

Aldin, Hugh Ashley, Walter Bailes, Kenny Baker, Butch Baldessari, Byron Berline, Bob Black, Harold Bradley, Michael Brooks, Richard J. Brooks, Steve Buchanan, Carl Butler, Jimmy Campbell, Boyden Carpenter, Kathy Chiavola, Hugh Cherry, Jackie Christian, Norm Cohen, Larry Cohn, Brenda Colladay, Tabby Collins, Ed Davis, Hank Edenborn, Tony Ellis, Colin Escott, Peter Feldman, Eberhard Finke, Jim Fogelsong, Charles Freeland, David Freeman, Bob Fulcher, Vic Gabany, Alice Gerrard, Don Ginnings, Patricia Glen, Frank Godbey, Tommy Goldsmith, Emory Gordy Jr., Doug Green, Clarence H. Greene, David Grisman, Peter Hackman, David Haerle, John Hartford, Kerry Hay, Walter Haynes, Mark Hembree, Jack Hicks, Bill Holden, Doug Hutchens, Jo Inguanti, Doyle Jones, Bill Keith, R. J. Kelly, Christopher King, Larry Klein, Henry Koretzky, Pete Kuykendall, Matt Levine, Ralph Lewis, Rachel Liebling, Don Lineberger, Wade Mainer, Frank Mare, Del McCoury, Brad McCuen, Bill Monroe, James Monroe, Tom Morgan, Lynn Morris, Paul Morris, Alan Munde, Jocelyn Neal, Jim Nelson, Bruce Nemerov, Richard Nevins, Robert Nobley, Charley Pennell, Reinhard Pietsch, Bob Pinson, Jeff Place, Joel Price, Nolan Porterfield, Ronnie Pugh, Gary Reid, Don Rhodes, Ralph Rinzler, Butch Robins, John Rossbach, Sandy Rothman, Peter Rowan, Don Roy, Tony Russell, Earl Scruggs, Chris Skinker, Jim Skurdall, Charlie Smith, Hazel Smith, Richard D. Smith, Eugenia Snyder, Steve Spence, Harold (Red) Stanley, Alan Steiner, Edward L. Stubbs, Gwen Taylor, Gordon Terry, Jack Tottle, Tony Trischka, Stephen Wade, Saburo Watanabe, Sharon Watts, Paul Wells, Bill Wesbrooks, Roland White, Blake Williams, Otto Willwood, Stacey Wolfe, and Johnnie Wright. We wish there was space to say more about the contributions of each of these people, for that in itself would reveal the many musicial and cultural connections Bill Monroe forged during his long career.

Our work on this book began in 1996. It was supported from the beginning by the University of Illinois Press. Acquiring editor Judith McCulloh, our old friend from the worlds of bluegrass and folklore studies, gave essential support and advice over the many years when we were doing the research needed to produce it. The work of Rebecca Crist and Mary Giles of the Press's editorial department transformed a very complicated manuscript into a finished book; Copenhaver Cumpston and Paula Newcomb made it a visual treat.

Finally, we're grateful to the many fans of Bill Monroe who've talked to us, encouraged us, and given us information. We've learned that these people were very important to Bill Monroe. The respect he gave his fans has helped us tell better this part of his story.

"Walls of Time": Assembling the Bill Monroe Discography

NEIL V. ROSENBERG

Since the death of the longtime Grand Ole Opry star and "Father of Bluegrass Music" in September 1996, the many recordings that Bill Monroe made over more than sixty years enable us to continue hearing him "through the walls of time."[1] Since 1997 Charles Wolfe and I have been working on this book, *The Music of Bill Monroe,* a catalog of Monroe's published recordings. We started with the album notes we did for the German company Bear Family's three comprehensive boxed sets of Monroe's Decca/MCA recordings between 1950 and 1979. We've expanded it to cover Monroe's entire amazing sixty-year recording history. Charles has been in charge of the narrative, and the discography has been my bailiwick. There's been considerable exchange of information and assistance in both directions, and we've depended upon the knowledge and resources of many others. I'll say more about this later.

In 1961 I came to Bloomington, Indiana, to begin graduate work in folklore at Indiana University. Within a week of my arrival, I'd gone to nearby Bean Blossom and seen Bill Monroe for the first time there at his Brown County Jamboree park.[2] At just about the same time I learned about what I now call a "research discography" when I discovered *Disc Collector* ("The Country Record Collectors Bible") and its research spin-off *Country Directory,* mimeographed country and folk music record journals published occasionally by Lou Deneumoustier. The research discographies included a few bluegrass ones by Pete Kuykendall that inspired me to start compiling a series of bluegrass discographies.[3] This was my way of making sense of the music—trying to understand its history, to distinguish fact from assertion. I wanted to *hear* recordings others spoke of as "definitive," *name* the musicians making the sounds I heard, and *know* who had done what first.

In the case of Monroe, it was also a way to learn his repertoire, which was necessary because I played his music as a member of the house band at Bean Blossom and occasionally as a substitute banjoist in his band. I began with partial Monroe research discographies published by Brad McCuen and Pete Kuykendall in *Country Directory* and *Disc Collector* that listed his Victor and Columbia recordings made between 1940 and 1949.[4] But for Decca recordings made since 1950 there was only Kuykendall's list of singles—just numbers and titles.

Using that list I started building my own Decca research discography. I dug through personal collections and record store bins, looking at copies of published singles and noting master numbers and other label information. I also sent "want lists" of the titles for which I needed master numbers to bluegrass and country record collectors. Soon I was ready to start typing my first list organized by master numbers, and eventually I had a rather complete outline. But recording dates and musicians' names were missing. Also missing was anything not released on a single (singles have master numbers on their labels) because I didn't have master numbers for the unissued cuts and the recordings released only on LP. Such information could only be gotten from the companies, and they didn't answer my letters.

What are "master numbers"? When Bill Monroe began his recording career he sang into a microphone that converted sound waves into an electrical signal fed to a needle that created grooves on a wax disc (the "master"). From it, a metal casting (a "stamper" or "matrix") was made. The 78-rpm records that the companies marketed were "pressed" using these stampers. In order to keep track of recordings during this process, companies assigned numbers to masters at the time of recording. These numbers ("matrix" or "master" numbers) were written, or stamped, onto the wax disc on the blank space between the end of the grooves and the edge of the label. Because numbers enabled companies to identify individual recorded performances in their files, the practice of assigning numbers in this way continued even after newer recording technologies replaced that of the wax disc. The *master* is, in most cases, the same as one *side* of a single, one *band* on an LP album, or one *track* on a CD album. Each of the three companies to which Monroe was under contract assigned master numbers to his recordings in this way. The numbers that record companies assigned were sequential within each recording session; hence, master numbers are the starting point for studying recording sessions.

In the spring of 1963 Ralph Rinzler moved to Nashville to work as Monroe's manager. We met at Bean Blossom when Monroe next played there, and at the end of June Rinzler hired me to work for Monroe as manager of the Jamboree. Rinzler

was working to revitalize Monroe's career by booking him at folk venues, suggesting innovative recording projects, and writing articles. We often spoke about this, sharing as we did an interest in the history of this music. He soon told me he had gotten access to the Decca files, thereby gaining a complete list of masters with dates and personnel for each recording session. He had thus been able to compile the complete research discography for the Decca sessions. I was very excited about this and immediately asked for a copy, but he demurred, saying he was saving it for a songbook to be published soon.[5] During the next few years, bits and pieces of that discography appeared in the liner notes of reissues that Ralph edited for Decca, but the songbook never appeared. I continued to build my own version from Ralph's reissue notes, new releases, and anecdotal information from Blue Grass Boys I'd met at Bean Blossom.

In 1973 Bill Ivey, a former academic and music colleague from Indiana University who had recently become director of the Country Music Foundation, asked if I would be interested in doing a publication on bluegrass for the Foundation. I was already under contract with the University of Illinois Press for the book that would appear in 1985 as *Bluegrass: A History,* so I suggested a complete and illustrated Monroe discography. He agreed that it was feasible and appropriate given Monroe's recent induction into the Hall of Fame and the popularity of bluegrass festivals, so the project began. Ivey introduced me to his board member, Owen Bradley, the Nashville musician, producer, and recording studio owner, who gave me access to the Decca/MCA files. These did not, I discovered, include files on the first six or seven years of Decca sessions from which Rinzler had drawn most of the recordings on his reissues. I was only able to complete the Decca research discography after obtaining a copy of Rinzler's version covering those early Decca years. It came from David Grisman, who'd obtained it in the mid-1960s from Rinzler.[6]

The information thus cobbled together from many sources I mixed and poured together, with considerable help and direction from former Blue Grass Boy Douglas Green, into a slim volume published in 1974 as *Bill Monroe and His Blue Grass Boys: An Illustrated Discography*. It received enthusiastic reviews in the bluegrass, old-time, and folk music press and polite notice in a few academic journals. The first and only printing of 2,100 was gone by about 1981, but I still receive letters and calls from people looking for copies. In 1973, while conducting research at MCA for that book, I tried to talk Owen Bradley into doing a reissue album of the many pieces Monroe had put on singles only. I also pointed out that there were many unreleased cuts from the previous fifteen years. Unimpressed, he said, "We already have too much product out on Monroe."[7]

MCA's lack of interest notwithstanding, within the next year several foreign reissues appeared that took advantage of the information in *Bill Monroe and His Blue Grass Boys.* Two albums, apparently produced in Europe, pirated thirty-two songs and tunes recorded between 1950 and 1954 that had not previously appeared on LP.[8] They included complete information on recording dates and personnel taken from my book. And from Japanese Victor, which owned the rights in that country to the MCA masters, came a three-LP set with thirty-eight songs and tunes that included, in addition to everything not on LP, seven previously unissued masters. The twelve-page book of notes that accompanied the set contained the entire Decca discography in tabular form, in addition to a number of photographs. Both were taken without credit from the discography.[9] Toru Mitsui translated a part of the introduction to these notes for me; my work had, Japanese Victor indicated, enabled them to "trace all the unidentified recordings of Bill Monroe."[10]

That was just the beginning. Ultimately, I saw the book widely quoted, copied in part or whole, and its format was borrowed for other discographies. Often, secondhand copies were offered in record auction lists. Although I didn't see Monroe until some six or seven years after it appeared, on more than one occasion his comment to my friends, acquaintances, and relatives who mentioned my name to him was to ask how much I'd made on the book. I'd made nothing—it was done without a contract.

When Bear Family decided to reissue the complete recordings of Bill Monroe in sequence and include previously unissued material, they began at 1950 and invited Charles Wolfe and me to do the notes. This was my first experience with Bear Family. Charles, however, had done many interesting and substantial projects for them before urging the initially wary Weize to try the bluegrass market. Officially, I led the work on the discography while Charles did the work on the song notes. For the first BF set, which included all of Bill's Decca recordings from 1950 to 1959, Charles drew heavily from the Decca/MCA chapter in *Bill Monroe and His Blue Grass Boys,* adding new material from his research. With the basic discography, Richard Weize and Eddie Stubbs added new information as the booklet was followed by an errata sheet and then a revised reprint.

Notes for the second set, covering the years between 1960 and 1969, were written in a somewhat similar way. By the time of the third set for 1970–79 the contents of my discography had

been exhausted, and Eddie Stubbs and Weize provided additional data, along with help from Blue Grass Boys Dana Cupp and Tom Ewing as well as by Don Roy and Charles.

By this time Charles had done a considerable amount of new research that was reflected in those final notes. Throughout, we'd been helped considerably by Richard Weize, whose reissue activities have given him access to and made him familiar with the archives of many record companies as well as the activities of a wide circle of collectors and discographers. In October 1996, just a few weeks after Bill Monroe's death, Charles and I met backstage at the Riverfront Center in Owensboro, Kentucky, during the International Bluegrass Music Association's annual awards show. He was there as a member of the IBMA's board of directors; I was there to play banjo along with Byron Berline, Vince Gill, Bobby Hicks, Billy Rose, and Ricky Skaggs in a Blue Grass Boys' tribute number to Monroe. Charles suggested that we put together a book about Monroe's recordings based on our Bear Family material and the Monroe Brothers project on which he was working with Rounder. I agreed, and that was the beginning of our work on this volume.

Sound recordings have played a central role in shaping the canons of twentieth-century vernacular musicology. What I learned in assembling the first version of the Monroe discography is that the data discographers distill become valuable knowledge. Once it is published, most people for whom it has meaning immediately forget that someone created it. It is no longer research and ceases to be speculation; it becomes, like a map, reality in shorthand. Discographies become an aspect of the marketing and consumption of the music they represent. People who compile and read discographies consult them before buying or selling "historic" sound recordings. Both directly and indirectly, they shape ideas about recordings as historical musical performances. Discography is a potent form of contemporary musicology.

What discographers seek to do is contextualize sound recordings by describing them as artifacts. We call this artifact, the original recording from which the commercial reproductions are copied, the "master." The creation of each artifact is a historical event. What I call "research discography" is not just a list of published recordings—that's a reference or citation discography.[11] Rather, it's a list of masters or "artifact-events." We create artifact-event descriptions by synthesizing from data published with the recording; from information contained in company, recording studio, and musicians' union files; from trade publications; from the testimony of individuals involved in the recordings; and from whatever other useful straws come within our grasp.

This is a specialized type of ethnography in which aspects of the artifact-event are discovered by asking questions: Who played and sang what instruments and parts? When and where did the recordings take place? What are the specifics of their publication on various media (from 78s to CDs)? What are the proper titles of the pieces and their composer credits? Who was the producer?

Any discography brings together multiple artifact-events around some kind of organizing theme. Each theme is, in essence, arbitrary and reflects the agendas of the discographers. Among the recurrent discographical themes are region, genre, company, and era. Many discographies combine these parameters, and each theme raises its own problems about inclusion and exclusion. That is true as well for the entire discography of one performer.

Early on in our work on this book Charles and I decided to include commercially released videos of Monroe's performances in the discography. That created some research challenges, but it also enabled us to better represent the documentaries of Monroe's work created in the late 1980s and early 1990s, several of which released the same performances on both video (now republished on DVD) and albums.

We also considered including set lists from Monroe's live shows, something in which we're both interested. People began recording Monroe's broadcast and personal appearance performances in the late 1940s, and hundreds of these recordings are scattered in many private collections and large public collections such as the Archives of Traditional Music at Indiana University, the Archive of Folk Culture at the Library of Congress, the Smithsonian/Folkways Archive, the John Edwards Memorial Collection at the University of North Carolina, and the Country Music Foundation in Nashville. Over the years, many of the recordings have been copied and traded among private collectors. Eventually, we hope, it will be possible to bring together these fugitive recordings and create a definitive list.[12] Such a document would allow us to study the life of a repertoire. With it, one could explore many questions about how a master musician like Monroe conducted his art business.

Ultimately, however, we agreed that constructing a definitive list was a more substantial research task than we could attempt now. And yet that dimension of Monroe's music is

still present in this more limited research discography, for it includes commercial reissues of recordings of broadcasts and personal appearances. The earliest was made in 1939 before Monroe made his first studio recordings with the Blue Grass Boys.

It's significant that I could not make this statement about Monroe's non-studio recordings in the introduction to my 1974 Monroe discography. What, you may ask, has happened? What changed in Monroe's last two decades of recording activity? When I look now at the 1974 discography I see that several significant changes had already begun to take place in Monroe's career. The first is his recording with persons other than the Blue Grass Boys. The first example came in 1962 when he played mandolin on part of Rose Maddox's bluegrass album.[13] That Monroe was on that album was, at the time, an open secret, but he was not credited on the album itself.

Decca probably did not know he had appeared, for the company did not believe it was a good idea for its artists to be guests on recordings of others. Rinzler, who was traveling with Monroe as his manager, and I spoke regularly by telephone in 1963 when I managed Monroe's Brown County Jamboree, and he often discussed his experiences in the crusade to bring Monroe the recognition we thought he deserved. In July, for example, they'd been in New York City to record a folksong radio show transcription with Oscar Brand. Ralph had gone to the MCA offices for a meeting with Milt Gabler of Decca Records. Ralph then managed Doc Watson as well as Monroe, and earlier that year Doc had emerged as a star in Tom Clarence Ashley's band. Ralph had gotten Doc and Bill together to sing duets in the style of the Monroe Brothers when the two of them were booked into the same venue. Doc had a recording contract with Vanguard, and Ralph asked Decca executive Gabler for permission to let Bill do a duet album with Doc. Gabler, Ralph told me, was offended that he'd even asked. "I wouldn't ask you to loan me your toothbrush," he said, "you shouldn't ask me to loan you a Decca artist."

Ralph enjoyed telling that story, but the album didn't get made.[14] Not until the mid-1970s did Bill begin to appear as a credited guest on others' albums, a reflection of his growing stature as a Nashville icon and also a general trend in the country music recording business toward such guest appearances as well as entire albums with prominent "friends." This, in turn, reflected a trend in the business toward a higher degree of artist involvement in the generation of concepts and the production processes.

The second of the changes in Monroe's later recording

career is the release of albums of live performances. The 1974 discography ended with Monroe's first Bean Blossom album. His festivals at Bean Blossom began in 1967, and by the early 1970s they were massive events that received considerable national popular press coverage. The two-LP set of recordings from his 1973 festival was not only a live event but also included guest performers. Its success inspired a second Bean Blossom album in 1979. A live Grand Ole Opry album came in the late 1980s. But beyond these most live Monroe recordings that have been released were archival retrospectives taken from the many personal-appearance and air-check recordings that exist. Some have come from "official" recordings like those made at the Opry and at the Newport Folk Festival, while others come from unofficial recordings made by Monroe's friends and fans.

As a consequence, discographers face difficult problems in organizing the total Monroe discography. In 1974 I followed a chronology shaped by Monroe's career, putting (in chronological order) the Victors first, then the Columbias, and finally the Deccas. After that came a brief section with several guest and live recordings on other labels. Now that last section would be very much longer and contain material that overlaps with the entire chronology. Consequently, in this book we've elected to place the basic discography in chronological sequence, identifying each session by the company for which it was recorded or that released it.

Most information in the basic discography is finite. It describes a specific time, place, and performance and specific performers. For the discography to be a useful research tool, however, the information has to be tied to an infinitely expanding body of data—the list of commercial publications on which performances are marketed. That boils down to a list of singles (mostly published on ten-inch, 78-rpm or seven-inch, 45-rpm discs) and a list of long-playing albums (from LP to CD and beyond), videos, and DVDs. In the basic discography, numbers and letters refer the reader to, or interlock with, what we call "the numerical," a list organized alphabetically by company (at its beginning is a list of abbreviations for the company's name as used in basic discography references). This list, always growing, sets forth the numbers and names of various recordings, along with their release dates where known.

Thus, this version of the Monroe discography is, unlike previous ones, thoroughly chronological. Monroe relished trying new musicians or combinations of old and new ones and was constantly composing and seeking new compositions from others. To help provide a sense of the flow of his music and the continually shifting configurations of his bands, we've divided the basic discography into historical segments and placed a prefatory essay at the beginning of each. Chapter 1, "'What Would You Give in Exchange for Your Soul?': 1936–38," introduces Monroe and presents his RCA Victor Bluebird recordings made with brother Charlie. Chapter 2, "'Mule Skinner Blues': 1939–41," deals with Monroe's first recordings with the Blue Grass Boys on the Victor label. Chapter 3, "'True Life Blues': 1942–45," covers Monroe's activities during the war years and his first recording session with Columbia. Chapter 4, "'Heavy Traffic Ahead': 1946–49" focuses upon the rest of Monroe's Columbia recordings, most of which were made with his famous "original" Blue Grass Boys: Lester Flatt, Earl Scruggs, Chubby Wise, and Howard Watts. Chapter 5, "'Uncle Pen': 1950–56" presents his first Decca recordings, including many of his most famous pieces such as "Raw Hide" and the second version of "Blue Moon of Kentucky." Chapter 6, "'Gotta Travel On': 1957–62," takes us into the sessions that led to Monroe's first albums for Decca. Chapter 7, "'Devil's Dream': 1963–72," covers the folk revival era and the emergence of bluegrass festivals—a time of revitalization for Monroe's music and reputation. Chapter 8, "'Jerusalem Ridge': 1973–80," presents recordings made at Monroe's Bean Blossom festivals as well as many others, including a number with son James and brother Birch. Chapter 9, "'My Last Days on Earth': 1981–96," takes us through times of illness and celebration as Monroe entered the digital age and became the first to win a bluegrass Grammy. His final recordings were made within a few days of sixty years after his first recordings. All in all, these chapters contain references to more than a thousand separate performances.

At this point we have brought together almost all of the information about Monroe's many recording sessions. To be sure, a few puzzles and gaps remain, and it's probable that we won't be able to solve or fill all of them before the book is published. But there is another dilemma to be faced: what to do about unissued recordings. When the science of discography began, an unissued recording was a completed master because everything had been done at one time—records were mixed as they were recorded. But since the 1970s master recordings have had more and more tracks and not all recorded at one time. Monroe preferred live (or "from the floor") recording to overdubbing, but he became involved in that practice on a few occasions. Even without overdubbing, the more separate tracks there are on a master recording, the more critical becomes its postrecording production aspect: mixing. Unissued masters are often unmixed masters—hence, they're really incomplete or unfinished recordings. To include them in a list is to perpetuate a half-truth, for if they are not mixed the recordings really only half exist.

Digital recordings present a further problem. Because it is possible to separate tempo and pitch—something impossible with analog recordings—digital technology enables engineers to mix not just separate tracks from a single master but to borrow and electronically splice in material from different masters of the same song. What results are recordings that can become like oil paintings—products of many different efforts over an extended period.

Thus a contemporary research discography must somehow reflect the contemporary realities. The masters of old, issued or unissued, contain a finished performance from one time, one place, and one auditory standpoint. The masters of today represent an additional act (or layer or level) beyond the performance, or, in the case of overdubs, performances; mixing represents an infinity of second steps. A published recording represents possibilities chosen from that infinity. It's only with our research on Monroe's final years and our education from Vic Gabany and Emory Gordy Jr. about his recording work of that era that we've come to conclude that Monroe worked as diligently to control the shape of his recorded representation at the end of his career as at its beginning.

I've dated Monroe's first stereo session as occurring in 1959. But throughout the 1960s and into the 1970s some of his recordings were published in mono only, whereas others were published in both mono and stereo. Alternate mixes have been around for several decades, but we haven't dealt with that issue in a complete way. Reissues raise a related question. The Bear Family reissues have, in some cases, been remixed and differ in various auditory details from the Decca/MCA originals. We haven't paid much attention to this new aspect of discographical research, so in that sense we're not finishing the Monroe discography but rather just starting it.

After thinking and writing much about the details of Bill's recording history during the past several years, what's become clear to me is that while the technology (wax to digital), business environment (major labels to independents and the birth of BMI), production environment (from A&R man to producer), and cultural environment (from hillbilly to country to bluegrass to folk to roots) all were changing, Bill Monroe stubbornly, single-mindedly, and with seemingly little counsel beyond a few trusted friends consistently strove to maintain control of his musical vision. He did so in all his enterprises—onstage, radio, and at festivals—throughout his career. What we've found

seems to me to underscore what the many biographical pieces and reports seem to say in various ways. While it's not hard to find critical comments about Monroe's behavior offstage, few people have anything negative to say about his music. No one has accused him of selling out.

With the completion of this book a full listing of Bill Monroe's recorded repertoire, along with extensive annotations, will allow scholars to begin studying his music in a close and systematic way. I think of this volume as a favor to Monroe's memory, rescuing from obscurity that which lies beyond the walls of time and thereby helping tell the story of an important American musical artist.

Notes

1. Monroe co-wrote "Walls of Time" with Peter Rowan, who played guitar and sang lead with the Blue Grass Boys from 1965 to 1967. It is a variation on a recurrent theme in Monroe's songs: the contemplation of connections with a dead loved one. Of this genre it differs from most of his others in its focus on a dead lover rather than a dead daughter, and in the metaphor that became its title, the "Walls of Time." I suspect the metaphor reflects Rowan's mystic touch. Musically, it is distinguished by a vocal duet whose melody lines were polyphonic as well as harmonic, with as much as an octave between them at points.

The song was frequently performed during Rowan's tenure with the Blue Grass Boys. Today three live performances by Monroe and Rowan of "Walls of Time" are in print on the Vanguard (sessions 650724.1 and 650724.2) and Smithsonian/Folkways (session 650905) labels. But in 1966–67, when Monroe recorded for Decca while Rowan was a Blue Grass Boy, it was not recorded. This omission was much commented upon at the time, for fans considered the song a highlight of Rowan's tenure with the band. Two years later Monroe did record it in the studio for Decca, with Roland White singing the lead part (session 681114). The first version to be published was the last one Monroe recorded, done in 1972, with his son James singing the other half of the duet (session 720321). It was issued by MCA on the *Bill Monroe and James Monroe: Father and Son* album in 1973, and Rowan received no credit for co-composing.

2. I've written about this in "Picking Myself Apart: A Hoosier Memoir," *Journal of American Folklore* 108 (1995): 277–86.

3. I subsequently published Osborne Brothers and Flatt and Scruggs discographies—one in *Bluegrass Unlimited* and the other in the *Journal of Country Music*.

4. Brad McCuen, "Bill Monroe on Records," *Country Directory* 2 (April 1961): 16. Pete Kuykendall included some of the Columbia data in his "Lester Flatt and Earl Scruggs and the Foggy Mountain Boys," *Disc Collector* 14 (1960): 37–44; the remainder and some Decca information appeared in his "Bill Monroe," *Disc Collector* 15 (1961): 29–33.

5. Rinzler can be heard talking about this on session 630727.

6. In 2003 Tom Ewing found the original discographical data, upon which this early version of the discography was based, in Rinzler's papers at the Smithsonian/Folkways Archive. As a result, a number of inconsistencies and conflicts have been discovered for material from

1954 through 1961. These are discussed in notes to the relevant sessions in the discographies.

7. Quotation in Neil V. Rosenberg to Jim Peva, Dec. 7, 1974.

8. Both albums were entitled *Bill Monroe, Blue Grass Special;* on the first album, BS-1, there is no publication data whatsoever. On the second, BS-3, is "Manufactured in France."

9. *Bill Monroe and His Blue Grass Boys,* vol. 2: *Recorded 1950–1972* (MCA 9269–71)

10. Toru Mitsui to Neil V. Rosenberg, July 2, 1976.

11. A very good discographical resource of this type for bluegrass recordings is Charley Pennell's Web site at http://www.ibiblio.org/hillwilliam/BGdiscography/index.html.

12. Stewart Evans's Web site contains work-in-progress toward this end: http://doodah.net/bgb/index.html.

13. Sessions 620319.1 and 620319.2.

14. Ultimately, Rinzler made it himself in 1994 using live recordings; performances from sessions 630514.1, 630517, 640418, 641031, 660826, and 800807 were issued on Smithsonian/Folkways SF 40064.

"I Live in the Past": A Rationale for Methodology

CHARLES K. WOLFE

In the early 1940s, about the time Bill Monroe was popularizing "Mule Skinner Blues" on the Grand Ole Opry, a curious story was being told in the halls of Vanderbilt University, about a mile west from downtown Nashville. It concerned a veteran professor of English literature, an Old South maven who had taught the same course, and from the same lecture notes, for more than thirty years. On the day in question he offered to his class a lecture on Marvell's classic "To His Coy Mistress." He began by dating the poem and went into a sketch of the historical turmoil in England during the time the poet lived. He then offered a lengthy account of Marvell's life, talked about the morals of the time, explained about the tension between the Roundheads and Cavaliers in the court, explained the role of a mistress among British nobility, and speculated whether Marvell had a mistress and who she might be. By now his hour was up, and he closed his notebook, saying, "So there you have it students: the famous 'To His Coy Mistress.' Are there any questions?" Finally, one brash new student timidly raised his hand. "But professor—what about the *poem?*" "Oh yes," the professor said as he was going out the door. "Damn fine poem."

It was a question that might have been expected at Vanderbilt in those days. A new generation of poets and critics had arisen—people like Robert Penn Warren, Cleanth Brooks, and John Crowe Ransom—and they were getting tired of the old nineteenth-century method of understanding a poem through biographical and historical background alone. They wanted to focus on the actual work of art the poet had produced, the poem itself. A great poem, they argued, should be understandable as an artifice in itself with no outside information. They wanted to know in detail what made "To His Coy Mistress" a "damn fine poem," and they set about forging a new methodology that would soon become known as "new criticism."

Modern poets have been notorious for refusing to provide detailed answers about what their poems mean. A good poem, they argue, has many valences and can be interpreted a number of different ways by a number of different readers. But most agree that their poetry, not their life or letters or literary influences, is their central artistic product. It is the statement they put before their public, the creative work they will leave behind, and the basis on which future generations will judge them.

So it is with the subject of this book, William Smith Monroe. Although his life was colorful and complex, his personal relationships had a mysterious chemistry that left many friends and enemies alike puzzled, his fascination with his past was both a trap and an inspiration, and legends have grown around him since the 1950s, the one thing to which he always came back was his music. To begin with, he was a naturally private man; for many years he avoided interviews and didn't like seeing his name in print. When Linnell Gentry was working on his *History and Encyclopedia of Country, Western, and Gospel Music,* the first real reference book on the music, Monroe refused to answer even the most basic biographical questionnaire. When Gentry approached him in person backstage at the Opry, Monroe told him that he would break his mandolin over Gentry's head if his name appeared even once more in that book. In later years that attitude mellowed and Monroe gave a number of revealing interviews, but there was always a wall around certain parts of his life. When approached with questions about them, Monroe could still be vague or evasive or say, "That story doesn't need to be told."

The one thing he did want to talk about, and often was eager to talk about, was his music and his recordings. In the early 1990s I was asked to attend a series of meetings at Monroe's office along with James Monroe, members of Monroe's booking company, and a publisher's agent. There was concern about an "unauthorized" biography that was being planned, and the Monroe camp wanted to head this off by sponsoring an "as-told-to" autobiography by Monroe himself. One of the first questions Monroe asked me was how much time it would take to do the long series of interviews that would be needed for a firsthand account. He was visibly dismayed when I said it might require a series of interviews over several months to do a complete job. Discussions continued, and the enthusiasm of the staff and the publisher's agent mounted. Monroe responded by falling asleep in his chair.

When the group took a break to look at something in the bus, Monroe and I were left alone. When he awoke from his nap he walked to a cooler to get a bottle of Gatorade, and I saw my chance to have a word with him privately. "Mr. Monroe, I get the impression that you aren't too enthusiastic about this book

idea." He thought for a moment and then said, "I guess I've always thought that I've said what I wanted to say in my music." In other words, his team was on the court, and he was going with it. Like the poets at Vanderbilt, like Shakespeare, like modern writers such as Salinger and Pynchon, he was willing to let his work stand on its own. That was his real legacy, and that would be the foundation of his reputation in years to come. Thus the rationale for this present book: a definitive listing of Monroe's collected works, a complete descriptive catalog of his art, and a detailed account of how one man and one vision altered the face of American music.

Systematic studies of a composer's compositions are not all that uncommon in classical music, but they are rare in popular and vernacular music. One of the first such studies I encountered—and one that had a profound effect on me—was Howard J. Waters Jr.'s *Jack Teagarden's Music: His Career and Recordings,* published by the jazz scholar Walter J. Allen in 1960. Teagarden was the remarkable Texas trombonist and vocalist whose career spanned from the 1920s to the heyday of Louis Armstrong to the 1960s. A second major effort was Russell Connor's study of Benny Goodman, *B.G. on the Record: A Bio-Discography of Benny Goodman* (1978). More recent works that have in various ways served as models for this book are Ernst Jorgensen's *Elvis Presley: A Life in Music, the Complete Recording Sessions* (1998) and Will Friedwald's superb *Sinatra: The Song Is You, a Singer's Art* (1995). All of these have full discographies as well as commentary on sessions, sources of repertoire, musicians and their backgrounds, producers and arrangers, various release formats (including reissues), and what impact the work had on the music and the artist's career.

We have decided not to interrupt the data for each individual record session with passages of text on its background. We felt it would be far more readable and logical to create chapters about the various stages of Monroe's recording career and then gather all discographic details for each period into separate listings that follow the chapters, cross-referencing from the former to the latter. There are thousands of Bill Monroe recordings, including many informal ones done at concerts, off the air, in clubs, or at jam sessions. We intend, however, to confine this discography to recordings made for public consumption—pieces either released commercially to the public or unissued performances that originally had been intended as part of a commercial session. Monroe lived well into the age of video so we also decided to include videotapes and DVDs as long as they were at some point sold commercially.

Our basic intent, then, has been to create a complete catalog of Bill Monroe's recorded work, one that can be used as a reference by both Monroe's longtime admirers and also artists just coming into the fold. If possible, it needs to be used with the recordings themselves. We hope that by the time this book is in print the complete commercial recordings of Bill Monroe will be available on a series of compact disc sets by Bear Family Records. To paraphrase the old Vanderbilt professor, "It's damn fine music."

Format of the Discographies

The discographies that follow each chapter are organized chronologically to present the details of Bill Monroe's commercial recording career from his first recording session in February 1936 to his final session in February 1996. We define *commercial recording* as any recording, audio or video or film, which was made available to the general public. The principle unit of organization is the session, by which we mean a single period of time at the recording venue on a specific day. Each session unit is arranged as follows:

I. Session data

A. The number of the session is at the left-hand margin of the first line of the unit. This is a number we have created for this book. Session numbers are based on the date of the session. The first two digits represent the year; the next two, the month; and the final two, the day. When more than one session took place on a single day, a decimal point followed by a number indicates the sequence of sessions on that day. For example, session 900615.2 was the second session on June 15, 1990.

B. On the same line to right of the session number is the name of the company associated with that session, followed by the names, where known, of the individuals associated with the session: producer(s), session leaders, and so forth.[1]

C. On the line below is the recording venue and the names of the city and state in which that venue is located. Most often, the venue is a recording studio, but it can also be a radio station, a festival, or some other performance location. Following this are the names of the city and state in which the venue is located.

D. On the next and final line is the date of the session and, following that (where known) the time of day at which it took place.

Within each session is a list of songs or tunes. Here the fundamental descriptive unit is the *master,* by which we mean a recording of a single musical performance. Historically, the master number(s) is (are) the number or numbers assigned by the recording company for their own internal filing systems.

II. Master data, line one:

A. The master number is at the left-hand margin. Master numbers enable record companies to identify individual recorded performances in their files. As pointed out in Rosenberg's introduction, the *master* is, in most cases, the same as one side of a "single," one band on an L.P. "album," or one track on a C.D. Each of the three companies to which Monroe was under contract assigned master numbers that are combinations of numbers and letters. The Columbia master numbers include some "alternate takes."[2] These are master numbers that append a hyphen, and a number or letters after it, in order to identify multiple versions of the same song or tune recorded at the same date. Decca/MCA has two sets of master numbers, the first assigned in Nashville and the second assigned by the New York office. In sessions where that occurs, the Nashville number is on the first line and the New York number is directly below (indented one space) on the next line.[3] For sessions where company master numbers are not known or were not assigned, we created our own numbers and placed them inside brackets. These numbers are, like the numbers assigned by the record companies, sequential within each session. This reflects the chronology of recording at the session if it is known; otherwise the sequence is arbitrary.

B. Following the master number comes the title of the song as given on the record label or album container, in capital letters.

C. Directly after the title, and in parentheses, is the composer credit as published on the record label or album container or, in the case of unreleased masters, as listed in company files. There may be occasions where this information is incomplete or erroneous, but we have elected to reproduce it for bibliographical accuracy exactly the way it appears on the original issue. It is important to note, however, that, especially in the 1930s and 1940s, the prevailing attitude about composer credits for country and gospel songs differed from today's practice. For many performers and writers, a song was seen merely as a commodity, to be bought and sold like a guitar or mandolin. In many cases the legal copyright owner of the song was not necessarily its composer but one

who purchased the song outright from a songwriter. In other cases it was standard practice for an artist to ask for his or her name to be added to a song as co-composer before agreeing to record it. Monroe did this himself a few times and also admitted to buying a couple of songs. He also recorded others—especially gospel songs—that had already been "branded" by someone other than the composer. Where such songs have a traceable history, we have discussed them in the text but have allowed the credits in the discography to stand as they were on the original record.

D. Next comes the listing of single record catalog descriptors (a set of symbols, either numbers or a combination of letters and numbers, used by the recording company to identify the published recording in their catalog). By *single* we mean any publication that includes no more than two masters. That means 78-rpm, ten-inch and 45-rpm, seven-inch discs (see "Numerical Listing of Releases" for additional information about the records referred to here). If there are more than two single record numbers for a master, the list continues immediately below, indented by one space, in the same column. Releases outside the United States are not included.

E. Finally comes the listing of album catalog descriptors. By *album* we mean any publication, either on vinyl or compact disc, that includes more than two masters (see "Numerical Listing of Releases" for additional information about the records referred to here). If there are more than three album catalog descriptors for a master, the list continues immediately below, indented one space, in the same column. Releases outside the United States are not included except for those on the Bear Family, Country Roads, and Rebel of Canada labels—all of which are, or were, widely available to U.S. consumers.

F. A lack of catalog descriptors in both the singles and albums listing spaces indicates that the master has not been published. Some masters have been simply shelved becauses they were considered flawed. Others have been lost, while still others, particularly those made after the advent of multiple-track recordings and, later, digital technology, were never mixed and are thus unfinished.

III. Master data, line two:

On the second line, directly below the title, are vocal part identifications or an indication that the master is an instrumental. Here, abbreviations are used that follow standard bluegrass terminology for harmony parts.

A. First comes the last name of the singer. The full name is given only when the singer does not play an instrument. Otherwise it is given in the personnel data (IV.), along with instrument identification.

B. Separated from the name by a hyphen is a capital letter or letters indicating the part sung: L, the lead vocal part (the melody line); T, the tenor vocal part (that part sung in harmony) above the lead part or melody line); B, baritone vocal part (that part sung in harmony below the lead part or melody line); and BS, the bass vocal part (the lowest harmony part in vocal quartets).

A slightly more complicated set of abbreviations is necessitated by Monroe's practice from the 1950s on of singing lead on the verse of a song and tenor on the chorus, whereupon the lead part is sung by another singer: LV/TC, the lead vocal part on the verse, tenor vocal part on the chorus; and LC, the lead vocal part on the chorus.

We used a number of guidelines in determining vocal part identifications, including aural recognition based on our knowledge of the sounds of various singers' voices, statements by musicians, and educated guesses based on the fact that certain vocal roles in the Blue Grass Boys were usually taken by certain instrumentalists. Guitarists sang lead, Monroe sang tenor or lead, and banjoists and fiddlers sang baritone. Some attributions may be incorrect, especially the baritone parts, which are difficult to hear because they are overshadowed by the higher parts.

IV. Personnel and instruments are listed at the bottom on the session units.

A. The first time the name of a musician appears, we have endeavored to give his or her full name, along with a nickname if widely used. Subsequent listings of that individual use a standard name. Both names are given in Appendix A, "Performers' Names in the Discographies."

B. Separated from the name by a colon is a lower-case letter or letters indicating the standard bluegrass instruments played: m, mandolin; g, guitar; f, fiddle; b, banjo; and sb, string bass. All other instruments are identified in full. These names are placed in a standard arrangement that generally takes up two lines. On the first, the mandolinist (invariably Bill Monroe) is at the left, the guitarist in the center, and the fiddler on the right. On the second line, the banjoist is at the left, the bassist in the center, and additional instruments on the right. Where there is more than one individual playing an instrument, as happens frequently with fiddlers, the listing for that instrument carries on directly below on the next line, as it does with the singles and albums lists (II., D and E). Where there are variations in who plays what from one master to the next in the session, that information is noted in parentheses that include the last two digits of the master numbers where that occurs.

Notes

1. The term *producer* does not seem to have come into common usage in the music recording industry until the mid 1950s. See Charlie Gillette, *The Sound of the City: The Rise of Rock and Roll* (London: Souvenir Press, 1983), 413. For purposes of clarity, we have used the word to describe workers who supervised the recording session. They were most often called A&R (artist and repertoire) men in the early years of commercial recording. An alternative definition comes from Emory Gordy Jr., who wrote, "Nashville's most current and popular definition of a producer is someone who doesn't know what he wants and definitely knows how to get it!" In "Recording a Bluegrass Album: Part 4," *International Bluegrass* 2 (Sept.–Oct. 1987): 12.

2. Take numbers (but not alternate takes) appear on a few masters by Decca, Capitol, and other companies. There are also two alternate takes in Monroe's first RCA Victor session.

3. Columbia also assigned two sets of master numbers when it began recording in Nashville. These appear on just one Monroe session, his last for Columbia in 1949. Here the standard numbers come first, and the Nashville numbers are on the second line.

THE MUSIC OF BILL MONROE

"WHAT WOULD YOU GIVE IN EXCHANGE FOR YOUR SOUL?": 1936–38

In the spring of 1933 the American record industry was in shambles. The Great Depression was at its depth, and newly elected president Franklin Roosevelt had just declared a bank holiday. Few people had money to buy luxuries like Victrola records. The various record companies had seen their total sales plummet from a high of 106 million in 1921 to 16.9 million in 1931; by 1933 they were seeing sales of a mere five million. The newly developed country music market, started only ten years before with the recording of Fiddlin' John Carson, had never sold as well as mainstream or pop music. Now sales were so low that they were scarcely worth recording in company ledgers. The releases of Jimmie Rodgers, the biggest country record star of the 1920s, routinely sold four to five hundred thousand copies in 1928 and 1929; in May of 1933 his new release, "Old Love Letters," managed only a little over a thousand. Columbia's all-star band the Skillet Lickers dropped from selling two hundred thousand copies in 1927 to as few as five hundred in 1931. And these were sales from the biggest stars and the biggest labels. Minor labels were even worse. The independent Superior label, for example, had release sales as low as thirty-five or forty copies.[1]

The big record stars of the 1920s had also seen their fortunes plummet. Rodgers still had a contract, but a bout with tuberculosis would cause his death in May 1933; banjoist and singer Charlie Poole died tragically in 1931; and Carson, who started it all, now found his singing and fiddling too rough for modern tastes. Okeh dropped his contract in 1931. Banjoist and Grand Ole Opry star Uncle Dave Macon lost his longtime contract in 1930. The Skillet Lickers, the most famous string band of the time, had split up and were spread out far from their original Atlanta base. Al Hopkins, leader of the Hill Billies, "the band that named the music," had been killed in a car accident, and his splendid band dissolved.

Record companies were also experiencing a bewildering round of mergers and consolidations. As early as November

1926, two of the major companies, Okeh and Columbia, had merged. The Radio Corporation of America (RCA) had taken over the Victor Talking Machine Company in January 1929. Several smaller independent labels were merged into the American Record Corporation (ARC) in 1929 and were in turn bought out by Consolidated Film Industries in 1930. Soon thereafter the CFI company added Brunswick, Vocalion, and Melotone to its holdings and then Columbia and Okeh in 1933, making ARC one of the two largest companies of the 1930s.[2]

Small wonder that up at the RCA Victor headquarters in New York the mood was gloomy and apprehensive. To make matters worse, the company had just lost the services of the man who pioneered and developed their country and blues lines: Ralph S. Peer. Sensing there was more money to be made in pop music publishing, Peer bought the Southern Publishing Company from Victor and went out on his own. His last southern field trip was in February 1932. At the company's insistence, though, Peer passed some of his knowledge about southern music and how to market it to another man at Victor, Eli Oberstein.

At first it seemed an unlikely choice. Oberstein (1901–60) was an urbanite whose personal tastes ran to dance bands. Peer had known him since Oberstein worked in the bookkeeping department of Okeh and brought him to Victor to work in sales and accounting. He did so in order to "have someone on staff to protect his interests."[3] Peer took Oberstein on some of his field trips and tutored him not only in the nature of southern music per se but also in the way publishing and copyrights could be used to make money.

Oberstein learned his lesson well—too well. He soon began trying to out-Peer Peer, trying to steal artists who had signed personal management contracts with him and cash in on the publishing aspect of the business. But where Peer had one big, legitimate publishing house (Southern) that paid the composers decent royalties, Oberstein created a network of shadowy publishers and bogus composer credits. "Where Peer tried to dignify the music and the whole field trip business," a colleague at Victor remembered, "Eli gave them a bad name. As late as the 1950s, we were still locating phony names and publishing companies he had set up as dummies to receive extra royalties."[4] To his credit, though, Oberstein was an irresistible salesman, a smooth-talker and artful persuader. He soon put those skills to use. By the end of 1932 he had taken over Peer's old job, and he embarked on his first southern field trip in March 1934.

This spring of 1933 also saw serious changes in the way Victor marketed its country and blues product. The standard Victor records were still selling for 75 cents each, pretty much what they had been during the happier 1920s. Now, however, 75 cents was an impossible sum, especially in the working-class South, where it often represented a day's wages for a coal miner and even more for a farmer. As early as June 1931 the company started cutting costs, mandating to its producers that all recordings were to be done on a single take "unless defective."[5]

They also took note of the one bright spot in the record business: the mail-order initiative by the catalog giant Sears. From 1930 to 1932, *Variety* noted in February 1933, Sears's sales of "hick disks" tripled. Would there be some way that Victor could get a better piece of that? Moreover, word was out that the English giant Decca was preparing to enter the American market (which it did in 1934) and would sell its discs at 35 cents each. The new company had already signed the nation's best-known pop singer, Bing Crosby, and was aggressively moving into the blues and country fields. That, too, was a threat to Victor and a challenge to create some sort of budget label.

Victor began by working out a deal with Montgomery Ward, Sears's biggest rival in the mail-order business. In the 1930s Ward issued regional editions of its catalogs to more efficiently direct products to those who needed them. There was no sense, for instance, in devoting a page to tobacco planters in a catalog going to Maine, and customers in Texas had little need of snowshoes. The listings for Victrola records could also be customized to specific audiences—those in the South and those in the rural Midwest.

In earlier catalogs Ward's featured customized records on the Broadway label, which was produced by the Paramount Company of Grafton, Wisconsin. Aside from a number of blues singers, however, Broadway's roster of country or hillbilly stars was slim. Ward's thus approached Victor to see about reprinting some of their better-sellers on a custom, Montgomery Ward label. It seemed like a good idea for all concerned, and the fall 1933 Ward's catalog listed dozens of titles by the likes of Jimmie Rodgers, the Carter Family, Bob Miller, and others under the heading "Popular Hill Country Hits." Generally, the records sold at the bargain rate of ten for $2.09, and with luck a customer would get all ten of the fragile 78s through the mail with only one or two broken. Throughout the 1930s the Ward's label would continue to be an outlet for Victor's country recordings; its last appearance in the catalog was in 1941. Although it began as a reprint label, many recordings were issued through

Ward's almost simultaneously with their regular release as the decade progressed.

The more important change Victor made to create a marketable product was to form a new label that they decided to call Bluebird. The name had been used a year earlier for a short-lived, eight-inch children's record series, but now Victor was determined to make it the name of the new budget label. Attractively designed with a soaring bluebird against a buff-colored background, the new records were designed to sell for 35 cents, about half the price of a regular Victor-label record. Although Bluebird would later include sides by jazzmen like Louis Armstrong and dance band great Glenn Miller, at first its audience was mainly southern: blues and country. "Bluebird, Bluebird, take a letter down South for me," sang bluesman Sonny Boy Williamson in 1937, an indication of how well the southern strategy eventually worked for both races.[6]

In the spring of 1933 the very first of the new Bluebirds was issued as B-5000, two cuts by Jimmie Rodgers, and the next ten included songs by the Allen Brothers, Reece Fleming and Respers Townsend, Jimmie Davis, and the Carter Family. Throughout the 1930s the label would release some 2,950 records, many done under the supervision of Eli Oberstein. Resuming Peer's practice of traveling throughout the South to record on location, he discovered and recorded dozens of acts, both known and unknown. In a 1938 *Collier's* article a reporter wrote of the effect of Oberstein's field trips on local musicians: "A hint from New York that . . . Eli Oberstein of Victor is heading South will find the tidings flying over mountains and the result will be that when the city slickers arrive they will be unable to get into their hotels for the presence of mouth-organ virtuosos, yodelers, blues singers, and specialty bands."[7]

Oberstein's early finds included string bands like J. E. Mainer's Mountaineers, duet singers like the Delmore Brothers and the Blue Sky Boys, western swing pioneers like Bill Boyd and Milton Brown, radio stars like Fiddlin' Arthur Smith, veterans like the Carter Family, and two brash kids from Kentucky, Bill and Charlie Monroe. The sales curve began to turn upward again, and by mid-1937 Oberstein could brag that he had real hits on the label and that some, like the Delmore Brothers' "Brown's Ferry Blues," were selling in excess of a hundred thousand copies. The Bluebird was flying high.[8]

About the time Oberstein was launching his Bluebird label, a twenty-three-year-old working at the WLS National Barn Dance in Chicago was making a momentous decision about his life. He was going to become a professional country musician—something bold and almost unheard of in these days when most radio singers and recording artists still had day jobs to feed their families. His name was William Smith Monroe, and he worked as a dancer on the Barn Dance's theater shows and sang in a duet with his older brother, Charles. It would be three more years before his path would cross that of Oberstein, but the two were set upon an inexorable course that would change the face of American music. It would also begin a line of music that would endure for more than seven decades and define a genre that would, in time, be called bluegrass.

⌐

William Smith Monroe was born on September 13, 1911, near Rosine in Ohio County, Kentucky. His brother Charles had been born on July 4, 1903. Bill was the youngest child of the eight children born to Malissa Vandiver and James Buchanan "Buck" Monroe, a farmer, coal miner, and timber cutter. Rosine, far from the rugged mountains of eastern Kentucky, was set in the rolling hills at the western end of the state, only a few miles from the Ohio River. Young Bill, like the rest of his family, grew up doing hard physical chores on the family's 653-acre farm—an experience that instilled a work ethic that would dominate his life.

The Monroe children relaxed with music. Buck Monroe, an especially fine flat-foot dancer, often featured a move called the Kentucky back-step, and three of his sons—Birch, Charlie, and Bill—would begin their careers by doing such dancing onstage. The brothers learned music from their mother, who sang the classic ballads; from their Uncle Pen Vandiver, the region's best-known square dance fiddler; from the shape-note singing schools that local churches and traveling teachers held in the summers; from local black musicians like Arnold Shultz, who played a blues-tinged, thumb-picking guitar style; and from the stars of the National Barn Dance such as Mac and Bob (Lester McFarland and Robert A. Gardner), two blind musicians who used mandolin and guitar, and the Prairie Ramblers, a hot string band from western Kentucky that featured a mandola. Bill—along with thousands of others—also admired the Victrola records of Vernon Dalhart, Jimmie Rodgers, and Bradley Kincaid.

It was the younger of the Monroe children who became most involved with music. Older brother Birch took up the fiddle, and Charlie and Bertha began playing guitar. When Bill was eight or nine he began to fool with instruments, mainly the guitar and mandolin; he wanted to specialize in the fiddle or guitar, but as the youngest and smallest he was stuck with the mandolin in family music sessions. In later years Bill liked to tell how his brothers would only let him use four strings on the mandolin instead of the usual eight so he wouldn't sound too loud.

On October 21, 1921, Malissa Monroe died, and it was several years after that Bill started to play seriously. He began by playing guitar back up for his Uncle Pen at dances and later spoke of Pen as "the father that I learned to play from."[9] He also began to play dances with Arnold Shultz, who was comfortable with the blues, traditional Anglo tunes, pop music, and even jazz. (Friends recall that Shultz used to spend winters in New Orleans where he picked up a fondness for "passing" chords.) In 1927, when Bill was only sixteen, his father, Buck Monroe, also died, and Bill was sent to live with his Uncle Pen because his older brothers and sisters had already moved away. Bill continued to learn music from him as well.

Birch and Charlie Monroe, like so many young men in the late 1920s, had left the farm and gone north to work in the new factories supplying the auto industry. For a time they were in Detroit and then they moved to the East Chicago area, first to Hammond and then to Whiting, where they found jobs in oil refineries. Bill, eighteen, came north to join them around 1929. His first job was in the barrel house at the Sinclair refinery, where he moved huge and heavy oil drums all day. The bruising labor gave him the build of a weight lifter, but the job was the best available during the Great Depression and Bill kept it for five years. Some of his brothers who had "lighter" employment were often out of work, so young Bill was the sole support for parts of the family.

The brothers continued their music while working and living in the East Chicago area, playing at dances and house parties much as they had back in Rosine. But the urban setting also had other important advantages, one of which was the Chicago radio station WLS owned by the catalog giant Sears, Roebuck ("WLS," they said, stood for "World's Largest Store"). Since 1924 WLS had broadcast the National Barn Dance, a pioneering country music show originally built around the music of Tommy Dandurand, a sixty-year-old fiddler from Kankakee, Illinois, and the square dance calls of Tom Owens. Owens was now organizing a "Barn Dance tour" in which some of the stars of the radio show would embark on a series of live stage shows. He needed dancers, and one night in 1932 he "discovered" the three Monroe brothers at a square dance in Hammond, Indiana. Would they, he asked, be interested in dancing professionally for the WLS tour? They accepted the offer, and for the next two years the three brothers, along with their girl friends, toured the Upper Midwest as dancers. Between shows

the brothers had a chance to practice their own music and listen to established WLS stars like Karl and Harty (Karl Davis and Hartford Connecticut Taylor), the Prairie Ramblers, and Chubby Parker.

Eventually they began to find work as musicians, not dancers, and for four or five months they broadcasted over WAE in Hammond and then moved on to a weekly show at WJKS in Gary ("Where Joy Kills Sorrow" Monroe joked about the call letters' meaning.)[10] Bill continued to work at Sinclair, but as dates with the Barn Dance tours increased he was having to take more and more time off from the refinery. By 1934 the brothers had attracted the attention of a company interested in sponsoring promising young acts in the new world of professional country music. In these early days, such sponsors were often patent medicines. For the Monroes, it was a company called Texas Crystals, a cathartic similar to the more widely known Crazy Water Crystals. The company, interested in sponsoring radio programs in the Midwest, first approached Charlie about working as a soloist for a new show at Shenandoah, Iowa. A Texas Crystals boss named Thompson had heard them broadcasting at Gary, Indiana. Although not a large town in itself, Shenandoah was the home of the Henry Field Seed Company, known throughout rural America for its catalog, and was becoming a national mail-order center.

Charlie liked the idea but did not want to go by himself and asked Bill, who had performed with him since at least 1928, to go along. Birch, whose fiddle had been a key part of the Monroe Brothers' string band, had gotten a better job at a refinery and preferred to stay and work because he had to help support their sister.

Thus the Monroe Brothers' duet act was formed. After a two-week vacation the brothers boarded the Big 4 train out of Chicago to Omaha. "We landed in Omaha," Charlie recalled, "we went to Shenandoah, and we worked there three months. Then we went to Omaha."[11] The Shenandoah station was KFNF, and the bigger Omaha station was WAAW. The Omaha engagement lasted about six months, and the brothers began to develop their repertoire. Charlie remembered, "We done a lot of hymns. Like 'I Dreamed I Searched Heaven for You.'" Others included "spirituals" like "Ain't Gonna Study War No More," Carter Family favorites like "When I'm Gone," and pieces like "No Place to Pillow My Head" from Karl and Harty. "We just had a lot of stuff that we'd copied from records and learned ourselves," Charlie observed. "We just had a lot of old stuff. Neither one of us had ever written a song."[12]

While they learned about music they also learned something of the economics of mail-order patent medicine. Omaha was the headquarters for Texas Crystals, and Charlie never forgot the day he stumbled into the basement of the building and watched dozens of youngsters working to put "crystals" (which arrived loose from the manufacturer) into boxes, which were then sold for a dollar each. Nor did he forget the time he and Bill dropped by the station to carry more than a thousand letters to their boss—"a dollar bill in every letter, for a box of Texas Crystals! Couldn't live without them!"[13]

In 1935 Texas Crystals decided to try the brothers in the South and sent them to WIS in Columbia, South Carolina, and then a little later to WBT in Charlotte, where the company sponsored them on its Tennessee Barn Dance show. Before long, though, Texas Crystals went head to head with Crazy Water Crystals, an older, more established company, and lost. Texas Crystals dropped the Monroes, who wasted no time in going over to see if they could sign on with Crazy Water Crystals. They could. In fact, they soon became the talk of the Carolinas. In addition to live radio and touring shows, the company let the brothers make transcribed shows that allowed them to be heard over several stations at once. For a time the Monroes were being heard on at least four stations, those in Charlotte, Greenville, Atlanta, and Raleigh. It was a hectic but rewarding life and would yield the first Monroe recordings.

BLUEBIRD 1: FEBRUARY 1936

With their precision harmonies, driving instrumental virtuosity, and penchant for dressing up old gospel and sentimental songs, the Monroe Brothers were soon the talk of the Carolinas. In a music dominated by string bands and Jimmie Rodgers–styled yodelers, such a duet act was something special. It was, in fact, the harbinger of an entirely new style in country music, one not built so much around the square dance or the vaudeville stage but on the new medium of radio and the new technology of the microphone. Radio allowed young musicians to make a living with their music and play it full time. The stations seldom paid a living wage, but performers quickly found they could use air time to advertise personal appearances in small theaters and country schools. By charging 25 to 50 cents a head admission, they could earn enough to support their families, and the new microphones allowed for softer singing, more complex arrangements, and more sophisticated harmony. Indeed, in the Southeast, the 1930s has been called the great age of duet singing, with names like Karl and Harty, the Blue Sky Boys, the Delmore Brothers, the Dixon Brothers, and

Asa Martin and James Roberts joining the Monroe Brothers in radio listings and on records.

The basic instrumentation of duet singing was by no means new with the Monroes or any of their contemporaries. Country songs featuring mandolin and guitar duets dated back as far as 1926, when a duo named McFarland and Gardner (Mac and Bob) had a huge hit with "When the Roses Bloom Again." In gospel music the tradition went even further back. One of the first gospel records was one on the Rainbow label by a Texas team named Nymar and Kim, guitar and mandolin doing "Keep on the Firing Line." By 1912 the composer of "What Would You Give in Exchange for Your Soul?" was traveling to revivals with his wife, singing the song as a duet with mandolin and guitar. And throughout the 1890s formal instruction books for guitar and mandolin duets appeared, suggesting that the combination was a familiar one.

Thus as Eli Oberstein was trying to guess what direction his "hill country" music was taking he soon began to suspect that the Monroe Brothers might well have some answers. He probably first heard of the Monroes in August 1935 when he made a field trip to Atlanta to record several North Carolina acts such as Mainer's Mountaineers and Dick Hartman's Tennessee Ramblers. Knowing he was setting up a session the following February in Charlotte, Oberstein began trying to contact the Monroes.

By this time the brothers were working at stations in both Greenville and Charlotte, and it was to Greenville that Oberstein sent a telegram: "WE MUST HAVE THE MONROE BROTHERS ON RECORD STOP WE WON'T TAKE NO FOR AN ANSWER STOP ANSWER REQUESTED." "We just sort of ignored it," remembered Charlie. Victrola records didn't seem all that important to an act that had all the radio and tour work it could handle. Receiving no answer, the next day Oberstein called them at the station. "And I never got talked to so straight," said Charlie. "And I couldn't get a word in edgewise. He had the answers and the questions."[14] Three hours later Oberstein met with them and a contract was signed. He even promised to interrupt his recording schedule to let the Monroes record any time they wanted and accommodate their hectic schedule. The session would only take a couple of hours he said.

The first sessions were held in Charlotte on the third floor of the Southern Radio Building at 208 South Tyron Street, just down from the WBT studios and right in the center of town. Bill recalled, "It was a warehouse, where they handled their records in Charlotte. And it was just right back; they had two mikes set up in this place where they kept the records. Looked just like a warehouse, wasn't nothing fancy. So we went back in the middle of this warehouse and recorded there." True to his word, Oberstein let them record as soon as they could get there. "When we got there," Bill said, "the Delmore Brothers was recording with Arthur Smith. Our time was short, we had to get back in time to play a school that night, and they made the Delmore Brothers and Arthur Smith sit down, and they let us record right quick and get back to our playing the school that night."[15]

This first session, as would every other Bluebird session, included ten titles. Only four were gospel songs, but Oberstein decided to release them first—and with sensational results. "What Would You Give in Exchange for Your Soul?" backed by "This World Is Not My Home" came out first, on Bluebird 6309, in April, barely two months after the session. "What Would You Give?" immediately started selling and eventually became the brothers' biggest hit—what modern music analysts would call a "career song." It did much to define the classic Monroe Brothers' style and repertoire for the next three years, and its success assured a continuing contract with Bluebird. In view of its importance, it seems justified to consider the provenance of "What Would You Give?" and the circumstances surrounding its recording.

To begin with, "What Would You Give?" was neither an old "hymn" nor a modern gospel song; in 1936 it was twenty-five years old and had been around for a generation. It came from the pen of James H. Carr (music) and F. J. Barry (words). Little is known about Barry, but Carr (1892–1976) was an important figure in early gospel publishing. A native of Arkansas, he soon became affiliated with the popular Trio Publishing Company headquartered at Waco, Texas. Carr traveled as a singing teacher, like so many other early gospel songwriters, but also performed a good deal. His wife Jessie was an accomplished mandolin player, and Carr played guitar and violin. They soon had the reputation as outstanding instrumentalists of the 1910–20 era.

In 1911 "What Would You Give?" first appeared in a Trio songbook, *Hosannas to the King.* This was not a sacred harp–type book but one of the newer volumes that used the system of seven shape notes that would dominate the southern gospel field until the 1940s. Trio, one of the most influential of these early publishers, was a training ground for early gospel writers. In its original appearance "What Would You Give?" was numbered zero in the book—a spot usually reserved for very new songs or ones that had attained some unexpected or intense popularity. The song would become a standard in later Trio books—testimony to how popular it was even in the early days—and even be reprinted by other publishers. In fact, its popularity was such that Trio printed the song as sheet music with a cover photograph of the Carrs and their instruments. "What Would You Give?" became one of the Carrs' most requested pieces, and as they traveled about the South they not only spread the song but also the idea of singing it to the mandolin and guitar.[16]

It is unlikely that either of the Monroes knew much about the early history of the song; Bill would have been only a baby during its first flowering. In a 1978 interview he recalled "What Would You Give?" as "a song I learned in church. Where I was raised at Rosine, they had a little Methodist church there, and a Baptist church to start with, and later a Holiness church. But I learned to sing 'What Would You Give' when I was fourteen-fifteen years old. They used to have singing conventions and each church would have a choir and they would meet at a certain church in Kentucky and have a singing convention. And 'What Would You Give' was great there."[17]

The singing conventions of the 1920s in western Kentucky were strongly influenced by one particular songbook company, the James D. Vaughan Publishing Company out of Lawrenceburg, Tennessee. A surprising number of Monroe Brothers' songs came from these little paperback books. Vaughan was a fine composer himself and often reprinted favorite older songs in his annual songbooks of the 1920s and 1930s—always with permission from their original owners.

"What Would You Give?" was featured in a Vaughan book called *Millennial Revival* that dated from 1926—the very year Bill Monroe would have turned fifteen. Because the song was not published in many other songbooks from that era, it is quite likely that the brothers knew *Millennial Revival* and might, in fact, have sung directly from it at the recording session. Two other songs from *Millennial Revival* were part of later Monroe Brothers' recordings. There is a good chance, indeed, that the Monroes had the book with them in the studio at Charlotte. (In later years, Monroe was often seen taking out of his mandolin case pages of old gospel songs torn from old paperback shape-note books.) Even more telling is the fact that the words sung on the Bluebird recording were virtually identical to the text in the Vaughan book. There were none of the slight alternations one might expect had the brothers remembered the song from childhood and maintained it via oral tradition.

Due to the time limits of the 78-rpm disc (about three minutes) the duo sang only the first three stanzas of the four printed in *Millennial Revival*. The famous "echo" in the Monroe arrangement, in which Bill sings a high "in exchange" to complete Charlie's lead, is also found in the original printed arrangement. The only difference is that Bill sings it an octave higher than the book arrangement. In his own 1939 songbook, Charlie noted that the brothers "brought this hymn from Kentucky with them, re-arranged the tune to suit their voices, then recorded it. The RCA Victor company has [said] that this song out-sold any song ever put on record by an 'oldtime' group.'"[18] Because the biggest Bluebird hit until then ("Brown's Ferry Blues") had sold more than a hundred thousand copies, we may assume that sales from "What Would You Give?" were somewhat higher.

Why did Eli Oberstein choose "What Would You Give?" as the premier release by the Monroes? One possibility was that they featured it on the radio and it was pulling in a lot of mail. He and other A&R men were beginning to understand that there was emerging a strong relationship between a song performed on the air and the number of records that song would sell. Radio was a proving ground for new songs. The same year the Monroes recorded, Oberstein's counterpart at ARC, W. R. Calloway, was talking a young Knoxville singer named Roy Acuff into recording one of his radio audience favorites, "The Great Speckled Bird." In fact, the Monroes were not the only group using the song in the Carolinas. Wade Mainer and Zeke Morris had been doing "What Would You Give?" on the air and even recorded it for Oberstein just three days before the Monroe session. As Mainer recalls, the Monroes became angry when they learned of the Mainer-Morris recording. "They felt it was their song, that they had made it popular, and Oberstein didn't want to upset them."[19] Thus the Mainer-Morris recording of the song went into the vaults and was not issued until 1939 or 1940, after the Monroe Brothers had split.

Bill called "What Would You Give?" a "powerful hit in the Carolinas" but remembered that "we didn't make much money off of it."[20] In fact, it seems to have sold like wildfire all over the South and even in the Midwest. As early as June 26, just a few weeks after the Bluebird release, a Chicago band, the Prairie Ramblers, was rushed into the studios to cut a cover version of it for RCA's arch-rival, the American Record Company. And on June 21, just five days earlier, the Monroes themselves were hurried back to Charlotte to cut more gospel tunes. Everyone seemed startled at the intense reception of the Monroe disc, and the Victor people were moving as fast as they could to capitalize on it. Not only did the song become a standard with duet singers but the Monroes also recorded three follow-ups to it during the next three years.

The song on the other side of that fabled first release had an equally complex history. "This World Is Not My Home" had roots deep in the African American gospel tradition and had been recorded several times by black singing groups in the 1920s. In 1932 it was also recorded by a white gospel duo from West Virginia, Frank Welling and John McGhee. Although it is certainly possible that the Monroes heard the song from older oral sources, it is far more plausible that they got it from a string band they often heard at WLS in Chicago: the Prairie Ramblers.

Members of the Ramblers (who originally first called themselves the Kentucky Ramblers) were from a region of western Kentucky not far from where Bill and Charlie grew up. When the Ramblers first came to Chicago and the National Barn Dance in the early 1930s, they were a hot fiddle band with a taste for the blues. By 1935, though, they had begun backing popular new singers like Gene Autry and Patsy Montana and were honing their vocal harmonies to a fine edge. A number of their songs appear in later Monroe Brothers' sessions.

In February 1935, a year before the Monroe Brothers' first session, the Ramblers recorded a version of "This World Is Not My Home" (for which they later claimed composer credits). Their company was the American Record Company, and the cut was released on at least seven different dime-store labels, including Sears's Conqueror. By the time the Monroes did their session the song was familiar to listeners around the South and Midwest because other radio entertainers had been forced to add it to their repertoire. When the Monroes issued their first songbook in 1936, "This World" was the first item in the book, ahead even of "What Would You Give?" A comparison of the Ramblers' text with the Monroes' recorded text shows only superficial differences and one transposed stanza. It seems likely that the Monroe version was derived from the Prairie Ramblers' hit recording. Even the tempo and harmony voicing are similar. And though "What Would You Give?" is doubtless the main reason for the spectacular success of Bluebird 6309, the proven appeal of "This World" certainly added to the excitement.

The response to the first Monroe Brothers' release was as sudden and spectacular as anything the Bluebird bosses had seen. Noting that both sides of Bluebird 6309 featured southern gospel songs done at rather relaxed tempos, Oberstein wasted no time in following it up with something similar. Looking over the list of the eight remaining titles from the session, he saw that he had only two other gospel songs and scheduled them for the second Monroe Bluebird, to be released in July 1936: "What Is a Home without Love?" and "Drifting Too Far from the Shore."

"What Is a Home?" had a rather odd history. Most scholars credit the words and music to the famed tunesmith Charles K. Harris, but the basic idea of the song—what modern Nashville writers would call the hook—came from Septimus Winner, later to win fame as composer of "Listen to the Mocking Bird" and "Whispering Hope." About 1850 Winner enjoyed success with "What Is a Home without Mother?" a song so popular it generated numerous parodies such as "What Is a Home without a Baby?" and "What Is a Home without Brother?" Two generations later a similar idea occurred to Charles K. Harris (1867–1930), a banjo player and songwriter in Milwaukee. Harris, who never learned to read or write music, composed by humming melodies to music transcribers. A native of New York state, he began to write songs with a "southern" flavor by quizzing a fellow office worker—who was actually from the South—about the region's customs and geography. Predictably, his sentimental portraits of the region won favor not only on northern vaudeville stages but also with buskers and small-town singers south of the Mason-Dixon line. Harris's most enduring hit, "After the Ball," became widely popular in the South and was a record hit for the white bluesmen Tom Darby and Jimmie Tarlton.

"What Is a Home?" also appealed to the early generation of country singers. Under the name "What Is a Home without Babies?" it became a favorite of North Carolina singer and banjoist Charlie Poole, who recorded it for Columbia in 1928. It was also featured by the early WLS Chicago singer Walter Peterson (the "Kentucky Wonder Bean") and found in a 1931 songbook he published through M. M. Cole. The Monroe text, however, is a little different from either the Poole or Peterson ones. The opening phrase "sad and lone in a mansion" appears in neither printed versions although the balance of the text is similar. That suggests either an unknown third source or that one of the two versions had undergone considerable variation via oral tradition. When the Monroe version was released in July, this second coupling began selling almost as fast as the first one. Charlie Monroe, in fact, remembered that "What Is a Home?" also became a best-seller. He called it a "love song" and said it was nearly as big as "What Would You Give?"[21]

This is in marked contrast to "Drifting Too Far from the Shore." Here the Monroe arrangement and text is a letter-perfect copy of a text printed in numerous southern gospel songbooks. The composer, Charles E. Moody, a singer, composer, and guitarist from Gordon County, Georgia, was also a well-trained musician who began composing gospel songs after attending singing schools in North Carolina. He is known today for another song, "Kneel at the Cross," which

like "Drifting" dated from 1923. A few years later Moody would become a member of the Georgia Yellow Hammers, one of the most-recorded string bands of the time and Victor's rival to Columbia's popular Skillet Lickers. With the Yellow Hammers, Moody wrote the country standard "No One to Welcome Me Home." Although it did not sell as well as "What Would You Give?" "Drifting" became increasingly popular as a radio song. Indeed, it showed up in the Stamps-Baxter Music Company's songbook *Favorite Radio Songs Number Two* (1939), a collection designed for radio country and gospel singers. That same year it was even recorded in a cover version by the young Roy Acuff. With "What Is a Home without Love?" and "Drifting Too Far from the Shore" the Monroe Brothers almost overnight established themselves as the record industry's most popular duet. For the rest of the year Bluebird tried to issue a new Monroe record at monthly intervals.

In August 1936 Oberstein released the first two secular songs from the session: "My Long Journey Home" and "Nine Pound Hammer Is a Little Too Heavy." It was that record that introduced the public to the blistering speed and instrumental virtuosity for which the Monroes were to become famous. Historian and singer Doug Green, who interviewed both Bill and Charlie for a 1975 RCA/Bluebird reissue, has commented, "Bill's mandolin playing even then far surpassed anything that had been previously done on the instrument, and the effect was electrifying both to musicians and general listeners. Before the Monroe Brothers entered the scene, the mandolin generally played short, gentle turnarounds between verses, but Bill's fiery virtuosity on the instrument, both in his ability to play fast and his use of slurred, bluesy phrasing, made a featured and popular instrument out of what had been a simply used and thought-of tool."[22]

In 1936 there were few models for this kind of blinding speed and aggressive style—at least on records. Ted Hawkins, the Georgia mandolin player with the Skillet Lickers, had recorded a handful of mandolin solos, but Bill, when asked about Hawkins, replied that he could never hear him well enough to emulate him.[23] One player able to knock off similar runs was Chick Hurt of the Prairie Ramblers. Hurt, also from western Kentucky, as early as 1933 was using his instrument—it was actually a mandola—to add tasty accents to recordings like "Shady Grove" and "Tex's Dance." Given the interest the Monroes had in the Ramblers, it would not be surprising that young Bill would also pay attention to Chick Hurt's style.

"My Long Journey Home" appeared in the Victor files as "arranged by Charles Monroe," which suggests that the brothers considered it traditional. "Nine Pound Hammer" was one of the very few Monroe Brothers' songs that bore a publisher's credit—in this case "Joe Davis Music." In fact, the song was a unique mixture of two earlier hillbilly recordings of the same tune. One was by the east Tennessee singers G. B. Grayson and Henry Whitter (Victor, 1928) and the second by a Galax, Virginia, string band, Al Hopkins and His Buckle Busters (Brunswick, 1927). The Monroes seemed to combine both versions and added a new element, a reference to the John Henry legend ("Ain't one hammer in this tunnel / That rings like mine, that rings like mine"). A full account of the song's complex history—which later included a re-writing by Merle Travis—is found in Archie Green's *Only a Miner: Studies in Recorded Coal-Mining Songs*.

The remaining four sides from this first session were temporarily shelved and not released until 1937. One reason was a second session in June that yielded a new supply of material. Oberstein was anxious to release more gospel material and scheduled the June session after only three Bluebirds had been issued. On the shelf went "On Some Foggy Mountain Top," a breakneck version of the Carter Family hit, and "In My Dear Old Southern Home," the Jimmie Rodgers favorite from 1928, when it was called "Dear Old Sunny South by the Sea." The Bluebird version of the Rodgers version was still in print in 1936, and Oberstein may not have liked the idea of having competition for it.

The last pairing was "Little Red Shoes," a version of the traditional lyric "Who's Gonna Shoe Your Pretty Little Feet" and "New River Train," another traditional piece that probably refers to the branch line of the New River Division railroad that was built into Galax in the 1890s. Many singers from southwest Virginia knew and recorded the song, including Ernest Stoneman, Henry Whitter, and Kelly Harrell. It was widely gathered by folksong hunters as well.

BLUEBIRD 2: JUNE

Following the spectacular success of the first session in February 1936, Victor rushed the Monroes back into the studio barely four months later, on June 21. This session, too, was not set up exclusively for them but was part of the annual summer field trip to Charlotte that Bluebird director Eli Oberstein was making. The sessions were for the most part quick and dirty, seldom more than one take and with no way to make corrections or repairs on the old wax master discs. In later years Bill Monroe recalled vividly just how primitive conditions were:

"We sang on the same mike, I remember. But one thing—if Charlie said one word and I said it different, why they never did correct us. I was real young, and we let a few things like that get by that should have been corrected. I guess it was balanced pretty good; they brought the mandolin out, and the guitar; it wasn't a bad set-up. I guess if we had to do it over, some of the songs would be pitched higher than we did back in those days."[24]

In contrast to a session in the 1960s of, say, Elvis Presley, when as many as fifteen or twenty takes would be laid down, Oberstein seldom permitted more than one take—not only with the Monroes but also with everyone else he recorded in the field. "Good enough for jazz" he would say, reflecting his willingness to overlook small imperfections in the records. The original recordings were done on heavy wax discs that were then shipped to the Victor plant at Camden, New Jersey, where they were made into metal stampers. These were pressed onto shellac discs and adorned with a Blue Bird (later, Montgomery Ward) label, put into paper sleeves, and shipped to record dealers.

The June 1936 session in Charlotte was a typical Oberstein affair. During the eight days he spent in town he recorded an astounding 223 masters—an average of almost thirty a day. On June 21 he recorded the Monroe session of ten sides in a little over three hours, from 1 to 3:15 P.M. The rest of the day he did some twenty-one other masters by a local dance band, Bob Pope and His Charlotte Orchestra, and the Bright Moon Quartet, a black gospel group from Durham. On other days the schedules included J. E. Mainer's Mountaineers, Norwood Tew, the Blue Sky Boys, Cliff Carlisle, the Dixon Brothers, Dick Hartman's Tennessee Ramblers, and a popular black group called the Heavenly Gospel Singers. Most were emerging as major figures in the new world of country music radio.

Although its gospel sides made such a success of the first session, the brothers only produced four new gospel sides for this session. One was "You've Got to Walk That Lonesome Valley," which had been, and would continue to be, a favorite for string bands and (in later years) bluegrass acts. It has no clear lineage, and everyone from the black singing preacher F. W. McGhee to white gospel pioneers such as the Jenkins Family had recorded it. It was a hit for the Carter Family, who recorded it twice, and was even covered by the aerated Vernon Dalhart. It has been assumed that the Monroes got their version from the Carters, but even a casual comparison shows that cannot be. The Monroe version is slower, more stately, and much more white-sounding than the Carters'. With rhetoric like "the field is plowed and harvest falling," the Monroe version sounds like another gospel songbook product.

There's little doubt that the flip side of "Valley," "God Holds the Future in His Hands," also came directly from a James D. Vaughan songbook. It dates from 1922 and features words by the prolific James Rowe, a remarkable Englishman who often worked with Vaughan and is credited with writing words to thousands of songs. Here again, Bill's echo refrain was written out in the shape-note songbook as part of Vaughan's original arrangement.

The other gospel pairing was shelved temporarily. One, "Do You Call That Religion?" had roots almost exclusively in black gospel, where it was known variously as "Drinking Shine," "God Don't Like It," and "Scandalous and a Shame." Guthrie T. (Gus) Meade discovered that there were more than a dozen commercial recordings of the song before "Do You Call That Religion?" by performers such as Blind Willie McTell, the Kentucky Jubilee Singers, the Birmingham Jubilee Singers, and F. W. McGhee. The Monroes, in their age of repealed Prohibition, substitute the word *beer* for *shine*. Bill liked the song and would in later years feature it with his Blue Grass Quartet on the Grand Ole Opry.

"I'm Going Through" (mistakenly listed on the label title as "I'm Going") came from the pen of an odd gospel writer named Herbert Buffum. A native of Indiana, Buffum published many of his songs in sheet music editions rather than gospel songbooks and not in the South but through a company in Topeka, Kansas. It is possible that the Monroes ran into him and his songs when they did their stint in the Midwest. Buffum's other big favorite was "When I Take My Vacation in Heaven," which the Monroes sang but did not record. It appears in their first and self-produced songbook.

"Watermelon Hangin' on the Vine," which Oberstein credited for some reason to J. E. Mainer, is a familiar old minstrel song that had been a favorite with southern fiddle bands since the Skillet Lickers recorded it in 1926. W. K. McNeil has noted that the song's ultimate origins were in the work of the popular nineteenth-century Indiana composer Thomas P. Westendorf (1848–1923), who wrote "I'll Take You Home again Kathleen." He published a version called "Watermelon Smilin' on the Vine" in 1888, and on the Bluebird record it became a showcase for Bill's flying mandolin. "Watermelon Hangin' on the Vine" survived in the Monroe repertoire of later years. From at least the mid-1950s he used it to open his live shows, and as late as the 1990s he used it as the closing theme for his segment of the Grand Ole Opry. In later years it was routinely played as an instrumental, and Monroe seldom announced the title. "On the Banks of the Ohio," the familiar Native American murder ballad, also stayed in the later repertoire. In 1963 Monroe would re-record it with Doc Watson (Doc taking Charlie's part) and again in 1972 with his son James.

In October, Bluebird released the fifth Monroe Brothers' pairing, "Six Months Ain't Long" and "Darling Corey" (Bluebird B-6512), both familiar favorites of old-time music even then. "Six Months" had been popularized by a team of wandering musicians from Monticello, Kentucky, named Dick Burnett and Leonard Rutherford. The duo had traveled the South long before the recording era, busking and selling their song sheets on street corners and courthouse lawns and at railway stations. Bill Monroe recalled hearing them as a boy and especially remembered the smooth, long-bow fiddling of Leonard Rutherford. About 1930 Rutherford temporarily split with Burnett and made some recordings with singer-guitarist John Foster of Elgin, Tennessee. One of these was "Six Months," and it became one of the more popular old-time releases. "Darling Corey" was collected as early as 1918 by the fabled folksong collector Cecil Sharp and had also been commercially recorded by eastern Kentucky banjoists Buell Kazee and B. F. Shelton, both in 1927. The Monroes smoothed out the lonesome modal melody preferred by the mountain banjoists but retained much of the lyric structure. The song also remained in Bill Monroe's later repertoire; he recorded a new version in 1962 at the height of the folk music revival.

The November single was "Just a Song of Old Kentucky" backed by "Don't Forget Me." The former was apparently original and played off the brothers' Kentucky heritage. The frontispiece of their first songbook was a drawing of "the Old Homestead in Old Kentucky" where the brothers were supposedly born ("a small cozy home, surrounded by a white fence and plentiful shade"). "Don't Forget Me" is one of the few Monroe Brothers' songs that seems to have been deliberately done as a cover of what was already a major radio hit. Between 1927 and 1935 no fewer than nine old-time acts recorded it, including the Carter Family. The song itself goes back to the 1870s, where it was copyrighted by C. W. Vance and Thomas P. Westendorf.

BLUEBIRD 3: OCTOBER 1936

The third Monroe Brothers' session in nine months took place, as did the earlier ones, in the Southern Radio Building in Charlotte. It was now early October, and the brothers were doing a number of things to take advantage of their new fame. They were sending out photographs identifying themselves as "Exclusive (BLUE BIRD) record artists" and noting that they were heard both on WPTF Raleigh and on an "RCA-Victor Broadcast" at 10:15 A.M., presumably a network show. On the reverse of the picture was a list of their Blue Bird (the company early on spelled its name with two words) releases from the first two sessions. It was also during this period that Victor released all ten sides from the first session on the Montgomery Ward label, and these were listed in the fall 1936 Ward's catalogs that went to thousands of households in the South and Midwest. This gave the Monroe music even wider distribution. Collectors still find Montgomery Ward issues more often that the original Bluebirds. In later years all Monroe Bluebirds would be also released on the Ward label.

It was during the fall of 1936 that the brothers put together their first souvenir songbook. *The Monroe Brothers, Favorite Hymns and Mountain Songs,* custom-printed in Raleigh, was a slim, sixteen-page affair that contained the words only to seventeen songs, a sketch of the "Old Homestead," and a one-page biographical sketch. "Please allow us to express our heartfelt appreciation for the marvelous way you have received us over the radio and in your community," the sketch reads. "We owe you more than thanks, and to try to show our appreciation we will endeavor to give you bigger and better programs." No where is there mention of Bluebird records. At this point, it would seem, the brothers were still most concerned with their radio and personal appearances. At the bottom of the sketch appears a motto: "Give them your request, and they will give you their best."

The songs in the book included most of their record hits in addition to a number of songs the brothers had not recorded. The table of contents listed "This World Is Not My Home," "Drifting Too Far from the Shore," "When I Take My Vacation in Heaven," "What Would You Give in Exchange?" "Working and Singing," "Happy Day," "I Couldn't Hear Nobody Pray," "Joy Bells in My Soul," "What Is a Home without Love?" "Going Back to Texas," "My Loving Kathleen," "Down in Arkansaw," "I Left My Gal in the Mountains," "Traveling Man," "Smoky Mountain Bill," "My Alabama Home," and "All Night Long."

Because the Monroes themselves compiled this collection, it might well represent a better indication of their "core repertoire," songs routinely done at shows and on radio, than a listing of their recordings. Indeed, they had recorded only four of the songs in this collection. They did "Smoky Mountain Bill" on the air and at personal appearances, but Bluebird might have

been hesitant to record it because the company had two other versions of it as well, one by composer Carson J. Robison and a second by the Delmore Brothers. "Going Back to Texas," a fairly new song by Robison, had been recorded on Bluebird by Bill Boyd in 1935, so there was little need for another version of it. "Down in Arkansaw" was an old rube song from vaudeville days that had sold well for Victor for more than twenty years. "I Left My Gal in the Mountains" had been a hit record for Robison in 1929.

The other unrecorded pieces in the songbook include the gospel numbers "Joy Bells in My Soul," "When I Take My Vacation in Heaven," and "Happy Day"; comic songs like "All Night Long" and "Traveling Man"; and sentimental fare like "My Alabama Home" and "My Loving Kathleen." "Joy Bells in My Soul," which was new, was later featured and recorded by Charlie Monroe after the brothers split. (It is not the same "Joy Bells" later featured by Flatt and Scruggs.) And "I Couldn't Hear Nobody Pray" is not, as the title might suggest, an early version of Dorsey Dixon's song "Wreck on the Highway" that Roy Acuff popularized. Although its refrain is the same as that of Dixon's song, this seems to be an older, camp-meeting song and perhaps derived from black gospel tradition.

The third session began with the up-tempo call and response pattern of "My Savior's Train" and quickly moved to "I Am Thinking Tonight of the Old Folks." The latter, not to be confused with the modern bluegrass favorite "I Wonder How the Old Folks Are at Home," was also known as "My Dixie Home" and had earlier been recorded by two other Kentuckians, Asa Martin and James Roberts. It, too, remained in the Monroe repertoire; Bill routinely performed it on the Opry, doing it at a much faster tempo and as a showcase for Earl Scruggs. Del McCoury also recorded it in the 1980s as an up-tempo number for Rebel. "I Dreamed I Searched Heaven for You" is another from the printed gospel songbook tradition and another written by the famed Lawrenceburg, Tennessee, published-composer James D. Vaughan. His co-composer was Mary Ethel Weiss, and "Dreamed I Searched Heaven for You," which first appeared in a 1931 Vaughan songbook, had earlier been recorded by the WLS duo of Karl and Harty. "The Old Cross Road" is also from a Vaughan songbook dating from 1920.

"The Forgotten Soldier Boy" is one of the rare topical songs the brothers recorded. It refers, albeit in rather vague terms, to the "bonus army" that marched on Washington, D.C., in the summer of 1932—World War I veterans demanding their promised bonus pay. When Congress refused, the U.S. Army dispersed the group. A text very close to this one appeared in a 1934 songbook by Asher Sizemore and Little Jimmie, popular radio entertainers of the day. There, "The Forgotten Soldier Boy" is dated 1930 and credited to Bert Layne, a former member of the Skillet Lickers and part-time song writer. "We Read of a Place That's Called Heaven," better known under its correct title "How Beautiful Heaven Must Be," was composed by a north Alabama native, A. P. Bland, about 1912. Uncle Dave Macon popularized it as his theme song over the Grand Ole Opry. "Will the Circle Be Unbroken?" is not the familiar version heard in country circles today but the earlier gospel song that was the basis for that. This version, which dates from 1907, was the product of two veteran hymn writers, Ada Habershon and Charles H. Gabriel. The song was a radio and record favorite of a South Carolina duet, the McCravy Brothers, as the Monroes were beginning their careers. For some reason the session sheets for "Will the Circle Be Unbroken?" credit it to Zeke Morris, duet partner of Wade Mainer.

"The Saints Go Marching In" is the familiar Dixieland piece, while "Roll in My Sweet Baby's Arms" was probably derived from a 1931 record by two Virginia singers, Buster Carter and Preston Young, and in later years it was associated with Monroe's two best pupils, Lester Flatt and Earl Scruggs. Another more recent entry was "Where Is My Sailor Boy?" (more properly entitled "What Does the Deep Sea Say?"). It came, as did so many hillbilly hits in the 1930s, from the pen of the prolific Memphis songwriter Bob Miller ("Eleven Cent Cotton and Forty Cent Meat"). The composer himself had recorded it, as did Mac and Bob, one of Monroe's favorite acts on WLS.

BLUEBIRD 4: FEBRUARY 1937

For much of 1936 and early 1937 the brothers were associated with a local announcer named Byron Parker, who billed himself as the "Old Hired Hand." He was a native of Iowa, and the Monroes met him years earlier while they were at WAAW in Omaha. Parker had started his radio career as a gospel singer but switched over to announcing and doing commercials. "That man could sell water," remarked Charlie. "Put it in a bottle, he could sell it! And get cash for it! But he had a voice you could understand and he talked nice and he wasn't excited and he could talk you right out of it!"[25] It was a perfect skill for hawking something like Crazy Water Crystals. In addition, Parker would occasionally sing bass on the brothers' gospel songs although he never recorded with them.

By now the Monroes were being heard often over WBT Charlotte. They had a daily morning show at 7:15, a mid-day

show at 12:15, and a regular spot on the Crazy Barn Dance from 8 to 9 on Saturday nights. Crazy Water Crystals also helped cover travel expenses as the brothers spent their week nights making the rounds of country schoolhouses and local meeting halls. As their popularity increased so did their audiences, and by the end of 1936 they were attracting as many as a thousand fans to their shows.

All this was putting a strain on the brothers' repertoire—a problem common enough to early radio performers but made worse by the Monroes' need for songs that would fit their style and have a gospel flavor. "I myself worked it hard," Charlie observed. "I would get numbers. I rode a mule one time, nine miles it was, to buy a songbook—an old songbook—had one song in it we wanted. And I give the man a dollar for it. And that was the only song in there we used. . . . It was 'I'm Guided by Love.' We wanted it. It sounded good to us, we liked the wording."[26]

For the first session in 1937—almost a year to the day after their first session—Eli Oberstein moved his studio out of the warehouse and into the Charlotte Hotel, where he reserved a block of three rooms (1050–52–54). This time the Monroes completed their customary ten sides in two hours, from 2:30 to 4:30 P.M. On that day more gospel songs were waxed than at any other of the sessions—seven out of the ten.

"I Am Ready to Go" led things off and is noteworthy today for Bill's mandolin breaks as much as anything. It was an up-tempo songbook product replete with Bill's familiar echo refrain. On many of the earlier records he played his mandolin turnarounds and solos pretty straight—that is, he generally followed the melody line of the song. Here he started pushing the envelope a little, adding, especially on the second and third breaks, a subtle blues touch to the solo. It was a precursor of things to come.

Another Vaughan songbook product is "What Would the Profit Be?" by an obscure writer named John M. Freeman and found in the 1923 songbook *Awakening Praises*. "Some Glad Day" came from the pen of Arkansas writer and publisher Will M. Ramsey although it was based on an earlier black spiritual. "I Have Found the Way" was in one of R. E. Winsett's Tennessee gospel books, with credits going to the Rev. L. A. Green (words) and Adger M. Pace (music). "I Am Going That Way" dates to before 1921 and is credited to the prolific James Rowe (words) and L. B. Register (music). "I'll Live On" is one of the older gospel songs in the session, dating from 1914 when Thomas J. Laney wrote both words and music; it had been recorded once previously before the Monroes did so. "Oh, Hide You in the Blood," which in later years emerged as a popular church hymn, dated from 1902, when it was penned by the Rev. L. McHan (words) and John P. Ballew (music). It had been previously recorded in 1928 by the Taskiana Four, a black quartet.

The three "secular" songs from the session were all familiar to the country music world of the 1930s. "Weeping Willow Tree" is the folk lyric made so popular by the Carter Family in the late 1920s. "Katy Cline," dating from printed sources as far back as 1853, was popularized in the late 1920s by records of Ernest "Pop" Stoneman and others. "Roll On, Buddy" is partly related to the familiar coal-mining song "Nine Pound Hammer," and the title phrase refers to what Norm Cohen calls "the tasks of hauling and rolling (wheelbarrows) rather than hammering."[27] Parts of the song were collected as far back as 1891 from a black levee-camp worker in Texas. On the Bluebird session sheets, the composer credit is to Charles Bowman, the east Tennessee fiddler who had won fame with a Virginia band, the Hill Billies.

BLUEBIRD 5: AUGUST 1937

In April 1937 Byron Parker left the Monroe Brothers to start his own band at WIS in Columbia, South Carolina. Although the brothers took over most of their own booking work they did feel it necessary to replace Parker in some way—and that way was to hire a comedian. The person they chose was a twenty-eight-year-old native of Sparta, North Carolina: Boyden Carpenter. Billed as the "Hillbilly Kid," Carpenter had worked with the blind singer Ernest Thompson, made records in 1930 and 1932, and been a regular on numerous radio shows, including *The Crazy Water Barn Dance* in Charlotte. It was there that he met the Monroes. "We made a lot of show dates," he recalled:

> Mostly in schoolhouses, on the stage, sponsored by the Parent-Teachers Association or some church. We'd be invited by the fans to come home and eat chicken or country ham with them. A lot of times I'd eat so much . . . I'd have to belch a little bit between numbers. People liked that. The sponsors would also invite us out a lot of times. I lived out of Raleigh, in the country, and Charlie and Bill would come out and get me . . . I was kindly the rube, I did comedy. I did a possum hunt sketch, and I had a deal about how I got on radio—got a big laugh. Just the three of us did the show; they'd come on and play and sing their numbers and I'd come on and they'd introduce me. I'd tell 'em my life story for about twenty minutes, then they'd come back. At the end, I'd come out and thank 'em and Godbless 'em, the people. They did a lot of gospel songs. One of their numbers, it wasn't a Christian song, was "Footprints in the Snow." "This

World Is Not My Home." "He Will Set Your Fields on Fire." They never sold records that I knew of. They had a songbook, and they did sell their pictures. A lot of times they liked to play ball before the shows.[28]

By 1939 Carpenter stopped playing music, and eventually he went to work at a shipyard. He left behind with Bill, however, a huge box of old lyrics, some typed from unknown sources and others folios from concerns like M. M. Cole. Many were cowboy songs, and others were more like pop songs; they might well have been the main source for the songs of this sort in the Monroe repertoire. Bill cherished the tattered box of material and in later years wrote on it, "Old Songs. Do Not Throw Away." Many of the song sheets were stamped with Boyden Carpenter's name.

It was about this time, the fall of 1937, that the brothers issued their second songbook, *The Monroe Brothers: Their Life, Their Songs,* which was custom-printed for them by the Mitchell Printing Company in Raleigh. It is was a larger and more sophisticated affair than their earlier one, *The Monroe Brothers, Favorite Hymns and Mountain Songs,* and the biographical sketch ("Meet Charlie and Bill") is longer and more polished, reflecting the hand of a professional writer. Even the dedication waxes poetic:

DEDICATED TO
Those hundreds of thousands of our friends whose support and encouragement have helped us to continue from year to year providing the world with songs from our beloved Kentucky hills. Dedicated also to that old home back in Kentucky which saw us grow to manhood and taught us to sing to forget sorrow and play to banish grief.

The contents reveal more songs that had been recorded and also a number of unrecorded ones.

"He Will Set Your Fields on Fire" (rec. 8–37)
"What Would the Profit Be?" (rec. 2–37)
"He Will Open the Gate"
"Help the World to Smile and Sing"
"Smiling Sea"
"I'm Going That Way" (rec. 2–37)
"What Would You Give in Exchange?" no. 2 (rec. 8–37)
"On My Way to Glory" (rec. 8–37)
"I Have Found the Way" (rec. 2–37)
"God Holds the Future in His Hands" (rec. 6–36)
"Will the Circle Be Unbroken?" (rec. 10–36)
"I'll Live On" (rec. 2–37)

"The Round-Up in Cheyenne"
"The Girls Don't Worry Me"
"Brown's Ferry Blues"
"Blue Railroad Train"
"The Old Man's Story" (rec. 1–38)
"The Quilting Party"
"Lonesome Jailhouse Blues"
"Let's Be Lovers Again" (rec. 8–37)
"Sippin' Cider"
"Polly-Wolly-Doodle"
"The Rambler's Yodel"

Eleven of the twenty-two songs in the book either had been or would be recorded by the brothers. Eleven texts, fully half, were gospel songs. Four had been borrowed from the Delmore Brothers, who had earlier recorded them: "Brown's Ferry Blues," "Lonesome Jailhouse Blues," "Blue Railroad Train," and "The Girls Don't Worry Me" (which the Delmores called "The Girls Don't Worry My Mind").

By the time of this session—August 1937—the Monroes were seeing their reputation expand beyond the Carolinas. They were among a handful of country artists listed in the annual *Variety* guide to radio shows that year. In the annual *Blue Bird Catalogue of Race and Hillbilly Records* the Monroes now had their own section, replete with their photograph, just like the Carter Family and Mainer's Mountaineers. Even Ward's catalogs had a specific section dedicated to their releases. Their radio station work was being amplified by important new developments in broadcasting; many Crazy Water Crystals groups got their music over several stations by cutting fifteen-minute electrical transcriptions that were then sent to other stations in lieu of a live show. It is possible that the Monroes made such transcriptions, but none are known to have survived. What the Monroes apparently did to allow them to appear on several different stations many miles apart was take advantage of NBC's plan to create a series of "regional networks." One of these was the NBC Southeastern Group, which linked five stations in the Carolinas: WPTF Raleigh, WIS Columbia (S.C.), WSOC Charlotte, WFBC Greenville, and WWNC Asheville. If they performed live on one of those stations then hook-ups would permit them to be heard on any of the others. Transcriptions became unnecessary.[29]

By now the Bluebirds were fanning out all over the South and Midwest, but the brothers were not making much money from them. The standard Bluebird royalty rate in those days was an eighth of a cent per side sold; a sale of ten thousand

would net the performer the munificent sum of $25. The later songbook states, "Right now they have no way of knowing how many thousands of their recordings have been sold all over the country, but a safe guess would be far above ten thousand." That implies that the brothers had taken lump-sum payments for their earlier recordings; it also implies that they had not allowed Oberstein to copyright their songs and give them song royalties. Today it is hard to figure out just what Oberstein was doing, but by 1935 he seems to have formed a secret alliance with publisher Joe Davis whereby he fed Davis new songs in exchange for under-the-table royalties. Davis often copyrighted country songs under the name John Hancock, and those included some of the biggest-sellers Oberstein recorded, such as "Maple on the Hill," "Greenback Dollar," and "Honey, Where You Been So Long?" None of the actual Monroe Brothers' songs appear on "Hancock's" list of compositions, and it is unclear whether they in fact protected their songs or whether they just intimidated Oberstein into leaving them alone. Had they published the songs with, say, Peer-Southern, they would have gotten publisher's royalties and sales statements every month and would have a much clearer idea of what things were selling.[30]

Also in the fall, the brothers were featured in the new edition of the nationally distributed Gibson instrument catalog. For several years Bill had been using a Gibson instrument although it was not the Loar model he would make so famous. He recalled specifically that all Monroe Brothers' recordings were done with an F-7 "Artist-model" instrument that sold in the 1937 catalog for $125. It had a rich, chocolate-brown finish and sunburst shading on its top. The neck was a little shorter than the Loar model's, which might have had an effect on Bill's ability to explore the higher ranges during his turnarounds and solos. All the publicity photos of the Monroes show Bill holding this instrument (although a very early candid shot from 1928 shows him holding an older, A-model Gibson). The presence of the instrument is not heard as strongly on the first session, but that might have been because the engineers miked it too far back, Bill lacked experience with recording, or a combination of both.

Because the brothers appeared in the Gibson catalog (listed as "radio-records" artists from "Norfolk, Virginia") it might seem likely that Gibson either gave them instruments or sold them a set at discount. Charlie, however, denied that. "I bought a Gibson, and Bill had a Gibson mandolin. But the Gibson guitar never did do what the Martin could do. Never had the bass, never had the volume, and that big Martin I had, that jumbo-size that was before the D-45, it had an awfully good sound when you was mashing down on it."[31] Whatever the case, their presence in the Gibson catalog—again, as one of the few country performers—reflected their increasing acceptance as more than regional artists.

Several Monroe Brothers' classics came from session five. The breathtaking "He Will Set Your Fields on Fire," with its Pentecostal imagery, was written by H. M. Ballew and Mrs. L. L. Bracket and popularized in songbooks issued by the Winsett Company in Tennessee. "Sinner You Better Get Ready" had been published in a book called *Cabin and Plantation Songs* in 1877 and was recorded by a black gospel group, Bryant's Jubilee Singers, in 1931. "On That Old Gospel Ship" is familiar to both white and black gospel traditions, and "On My Way to Glory" appears to be a Pentecostal song that features driving string instruments.

"Let Us Be Lovers Again" is a nineteenth-century love song more commonly known as "Jack and May." It was written in 1893 by a popular African American composer from Cincinnati, Gussie Davis, who was earlier responsible for "Maple on the Hill" and "Good-Night Irene." The song had been commercially recorded by the Golden Melody Boys, Darby and Tarlton, the Blankenship Family, the Carter Family, the Dixon Brothers, and others. "All the Good Times Are Passed and Gone," which showed an ownership of "Joe Davis Music" on session sheets, had been early recorded by the Georgia team of Fred and Gertrude Gossett (Columbia 15572). "My Last Moving Day" sounds like another product from Herbert Buffum, but it does not appear in any of the standard gospel songbooks. Its provenance remains somewhat of a mystery.

The last three sides from this session were devoted to capitalizing on the success of "What Would You Give?" In the 1930s this kind of thing was best accomplished by what the industry called "answer songs"—those that were essentially extensions of already proven hits. Whenever an artist had a major hit, recording companies encouraged them or some other performer to create a sequel and take advantage of sales momentum. Thus in 1936 the Dixon Brothers wrote and recorded "Answer to Maple on the Hill" as a response to the J. E. Mainer classic; Roy Acuff did a "Great Speckled Bird No. 2" as a follow-up to his successful 1936 original. Seldom did follow-up songs sell as well as the originals, but the ever-hopeful A&R men kept trying.

The Monroes created not one but three answer songs to their career song and recorded them all at the same session. "What Would You Give in Exchange for Your Soul Part 2" uses the same melody as the original on the verses but with a dif-

ferent melody and phrasing on the echo refrain. The motif "o weary soul" is powerful and effective but does not appear in the original source; its origin is a mystery. The song was interesting enough that it was covered by the popular WLS band the Westerners. "What Would You Give in Exchange for Your Soul Part 3" returns to the format of the original, with Bill singing the high echo on "in exchange" and even playing turnarounds similar to those on the first recording. Both Part 2 and Part 3 were released back to back on a Bluebird single (Bb 7122) in October 1937, just two months after the session. Why Oberstein waited that long to try an answer song on one of his biggest hits is a puzzle.

"What Would You Give in Exchange for Your Soul Part 4" follows the same pattern as the other two and was released in February 1938. The Monroes were the only ones ever to record it. Two days after the Monroe session finished, however, the Dixon Brothers came into the same studio and recorded "What Would You Give in Exchange for Your Soul Part 5." It's not clear whether either Monroe had anything to do with writing Part 5, which was also copyrighted "John Hancock," generally accepted as a pseudonym for Oberstein. The Dixon version was released in January 1938 and was followed on cover versions by the Philyaw Brothers (ARC) and Edith and Sherman Collins (Decca).

BLUEBIRD 6: JANUARY 1938

The final Monroe Brothers' session was also held in the Charlotte Hotel on January 28, 1938. The brothers were barely weeks away from an event that would have an immeasurable impact on the rest of their careers: their break up as a brother duo. Friction had been building for some time and probably centered on Bill's increasing desire to get out from under his role as the junior partner, or younger brother, in the act. As he recalled years later, "If we had had a manager, you know, no telling how far we could have gone. But so many times brothers can't get along good. One wants to be the boss, and the other's mad because he does, and so it was better that we split up."[32]

Charlie Monroe said that the break up was also a matter of finances and personal style. At many of their schoolhouse concerts, he recalled, "We couldn't get half the people in the building. And at the same time we got together and I told Bill, 'Bill, we either need a manager, or else we need to separate, and get a band apiece. We'll make more money.' The money was what we were worried about. And he told me, Bill told me, said, 'Well, no man will ever manage me!' He didn't like the idea of being told what to do, so we separated. . . . Bill and I never see business alike. I never wanted to be late; Bill always wanted to make 'em wait."[33]

The last session was as varied and eclectic as the first and, like it, contained key gospel songs. "Pearly Gates," more properly known as "Open Up Them Pearly Gates," was another pseudo-gospel song by the Kansan Carson J. Robison, who wrote it in 1929 and recorded it with Frank Luther both for Victor and ARC. Carson was one of the "citybilly" performers of the age, an artist who spent much of his time in New York doing studio work and writing songs, many of which had a strong appeal to more traditional singers. Another song from the session from his pen was "The Old Man's Story," which Robison wrote in 1928. It had been recorded several times by Robison's friend Frank Luther and even been waxed by Jimmie Rodgers and Sara Carter under the title "Why There's a Tear in My Eye." "A Beautiful Life" was created by William Golden around 1918 and widely published in shape-note songbooks; it had also been recorded by the Westerners the year before. "On My Way Back Home" combines what would emerge as two key Bill Monroe ideas: returning to the old home place and finding religious salvation. "When Our Lord Shall Come Again" is more of a church congregational song, with composer credits to the Rev. Johnson Oatman (words) and R. L. Ferguson (music). It began appearing in songbooks about 1910 and had been a favorite of the WLS's Mac and Bob.

"Goodbye Maggie," one of the more effective pieces from the session, came from the singing of Karl and Harty, the two men from eastern Kentucky who had known the Monroes since their days on the WLS National Barn Dance. It appeared in the M. M. Cole songbook that Karl and Harty issued with the Cumberland Ridge Runners, and except for the added echo the Monroes' version is word for word like the printed text. Composer credits in the Cole book were to "J. Guest," of whom nothing is known. "Little Joe" was a major radio favorite of the era and had already been recorded by groups ranging from the Carter Family to the Prairie Ramblers. It dated from 1876, when it was first set to paper by Maj. Charles E. Addison.

"I've Still Got Ninety-Nine" represents the end of a long recording history of a Native American ballad sometimes called "Poor Boy," "Ninety-Nine Years," or "Cold Penitentiary." Discographer Gus Meade has identified at least twenty-seven commercial recordings of the piece, including ones by Darby and Tarlton, B. F. Shelton, Tom Ashley, Steve Ledford, Mac and Bob, and Robison and Luther. "Have a Feast Here Tonight" is

the Monroes' blistering reading of an old minstrel tune, while "Rollin' On" was currently in fashion with western swing bands.

CONCLUSION

The last of the Monroe Brothers' Bluebirds was released in July 1938—a coupling of "Little Joe" and "Rollin' On." They had done some sixty sides in all—none remained in the vaults. All were also released on the Montgomery Ward label, giving the body of work an even wider circulation. But by the early 1940s, most of the Bluebirds were out of print. Victor, after all, now had new recordings by Charlie and his band and Bill and his band. (Indeed, Victor had started recording Charlie and his new band at Rock Hill, S.C., in September 1939; Bill would have to wait another year for his shot.) In 1941 the brothers' "Darling Corey" was reissued in the 78-rpm album *Smoky Mountain Ballads* edited by John A. Lomax; as such, it was one of the first old-time 78s to be reissued as "folk music." In 1964 an expanded version of the album was issued on LP.

Although the Monroe Bluebird legacy would have a major influence on later duet singers such as James and Martha Carson and early bluegrass bands, the body of material itself was in large part inaccessible. Because of its 1933 cutoff date, no Monroe cuts appeared in Harry Smith's important *Anthology of American Folk Music*. In 1964 RCA Victor released a set on their budget Camden label, produced by one of the most knowledgable producers, Brad McCuen. The set mixed Monroe Brothers' cuts with ones done by Charlie Monroe, but it was widely circulated and helped maintain the Monroes' influence. In 1975, as part of its Bluebird reissue series, RCA hired Doug Green to program and annotate a two-LP set, *Feast Here Tonight*. It contained no fewer than thirty-two tracks—more than half the output—with informative notes and fine sound. About this time as well, RCA in Japan issued a five-LP box containing all the Monroe Brothers' titles as well as fifteen or so titles by Charlie's first band. Some copies of the set were available in the states, but it was generally very hard to find; it was reissued on CD in 1998.

The CD era saw new initiatives on the reissue scene. Billy Altman's Victor anthologies *Are You from Dixie?* and *Something Got a Hold of Me* each had several well-mastered cuts from the Bluebird repertoire. In 1997 the company—now BMG—produced *The Essential Bill Monroe,* which included six Monroe Brothers' sides, and in 1999 Rounder Records, leasing the rights from RCA/BMG, began a four-CD set that would restore, for the first time domestically, all the Monroe Brothers' Bluebirds to print. In 2002 Bear Family reissued all sixty cuts.

The songs that compose the Bluebird repertoire are an interesting and varied lot, and many would be picked up and added to the later repertoires of both brothers. From 1963 to 1980, when Bill picked a lot and made informal recordings with guitarist Doc Watson, their work was full of the old duets. Although it is impossible at this date to know exactly how the brothers learned their songs—the conduits through which the songs were passed—it is possible to identify the ultimate source for many of them. Using these sources (most of which have been detailed), we can attempt a rudimentary classification of the pieces. The list that follows provides the categories of the Monroe Brothers' repertoire and the number of songs in each (which total sixty).

Nineteenth-century printed sources: five
Gospel songbooks (shape-note): nineteen
Traditional or African American gospel: seven
Current compositions or recordings: twelve
Traditional folksongs and ballads: nine
Originals or unidentified: five
Minstrelsy: two
Topical: one

One of the things most apparent from the list is the number of gospel songs in their repertoire: twenty-six. That is well over a third of the repertoire and supports the popular image of brothers who specialized in "old hymns." Equally surprising is the number of songs taken from 1930s' music scene, from newly minted songs by the likes of Carson Robison to Jimmie Rodgers pieces. The Monroes had a personal aesthetic about what made a good song, but they also functioned in a competitive and commercial world and had to respond to it as best they could. Like the Carter Family, the Monroes reworked a number of nineteenth-century parlor and sentimental songs, seldom learning the names of composers like Gussie Davis. Only nine of the songs—fewer than a sixth—were actually traditional ones that folklorists had collected and studied "on the ground." The Monroe repertoire thus fits to some extent the popular image (e.g., the gospel); in other ways, however, it is more complex than folksong enthusiasts have assumed.

Notes

1. Sales of Rodgers's records are given in a document from the RCA files that is reproduced in the notes to *Jimmie Rodgers: The Singing Brakeman* (Bear Family BCD 15540, 1994), 59; other sales figures for the Victor 40000 and 23500 series are from unpublished notes by Tony Russell, who gathered them from RCA files.

2. The most dependable record company histories of the 1930s are found in the introduction to *Blues and Gospel Records, 1890–1943*, compiled by Robert M. S. Dixon, John Godrich, and Howard Rye (New York: Oxford University Press, 1997), as well as Dixon and Godrich's *Recording the Blues* (New York: Stein and Day, 1970).

3. Nolan Porterfield, *Jimmie Rodgers: The Life and Times of America's Blue Yodeler* (Urbana: University of Illinois Press, 1979), 315.

4. Charles K. Wolfe, notes to *Bill Monroe: Blue Moon of Kentucky* (Bear Family BCD 16399, 2002), 4.

5. Blue Bird source material from vertical file on the company consisting of dealers' lists and sales promotional material, Country Music Hall of Fame.

6. Sonny Boy Williamson, "Blue Bird Blues," Bluebird 7098, recorded May 5, 1937.

7. Kyle Crichton, "Thar's Gold in Them Hillbillies," *Collier's*, April 30, 1938, 24–25.

8. Information on Oberstein from CKW interview with Brad McCuen, Nashville, Feb. 17, 1989; obituaries in *New York Times*, June 14, 1960, and *Billboard*, June 22, 1960; Nolan Porterfield, *Jimmie Rodgers: America's Blue Yodeler* (Urbana: University of Illinois Press, 1979); George A. Blacker, "Eli Was an Operator," *Record Research* 149–50 (Oct. 1977): 2, and 151–52 (Jan. 1978): 12.

9. CKW conversation with Bill Monroe, Madison, Tenn., Oct. 1984.

10. Bill Monroe conversation with CKW, Nashville, fall 1989.

11. Wolfe, notes to *Blue Moon of Kentucky*, 8.

12. Ibid.

13. Douglas B. Green, "Charlie Monroe's Story: Part 2, the Monroe Brothers," *Muleskinner News* 4 (Feb. 1973): 8–11, 18.

14. Wolfe, notes to *Blue Moon of Kentucky*, 8.

15. Charles K. Wolfe, "Bluegrass Touches: An Interview with Bill Monroe," *Old Time Music* 16 (Spring 1975): 7–8.

16. Harlan Daniel to Charles K. Wolfe, Dec. 1988.

17. Wolfe, "Bluegrass Touches," 7–8.

18. Charlie Monroe, *The Songs You Have Requested by Charlie Monroe and the Boys* (n.p.: n.p., 1939), 3.

19. Wolfe, notes to *Blue Moon of Kentucky*, 11.

20. James Rooney, *Bossmen: Bill Monroe and Muddy Waters* (New York: Dial Press, 1971), 31.

21. Wolfe, notes to *Blue Moon of Kentucky*, 12.

22. Douglas B. Green, notes to *Feast Here Tonight: Monroe Brothers* (Bluebird AXM2–5510, 1975).

23. Wolfe, "Bluegrass Touches," 6.

24. Ibid., 8.

25. Wolfe, notes to *Blue Moon of Kentucky*, 17.

26. Ibid., 18.

27. Norm Cohen, *Long Steel Rail: The Railroad in Folksong* (Urbana: University of Illinois Press, 1981), 574.

28. Boyden Carpenter interview with Charles K. Wolfe, Winston-Salem, N.C., Sept. 18, 1978.

29. *Radio Annual 1938*, Archives of the Center for Popular Music, Middle Tennessee State University, Murfreesboro.

30. Bruce Bastin, *Never Sell a Copyright: Joe Davis and His Role in the New York Music Scene, 1916–1978* (London: Storyville, 1990), 70–85.

31. Wolfe, notes to *Blue Moon of Kentcky*, 21.

32. Rooney, *Bossmen*, 32.

33. Ibid.

DISCOGRAPHY, 1936–38

360217   RCA Victor Bluebird Monroe Brothers session; producer, Eli Oberstein
Southern Radio Building, 208 S. Tyron St., Charlotte, N.C.
Feb. 17, 1936, 3:30–5:45 P.M.

99193-1	MY LONG JOURNEY HOME (-) C. Monroe-L, B. Monroe-T	BB-6422, MW-4747	AXM2-5510, RCX 7193, MCAD 4-11048, Rdr 1073, BF 16399
99194-1	WHAT IS HOME WITHOUT LOVE? (-) C. Monroe-L, B. Monroe-T	BB-6363, MW-4746	AXM2-5510, Rdr 1073, BF 16399
99195-1	WHAT WOULD YOU GIVE IN EXCHANGE? (-) C. Monroe-L, B. Monroe-T	BB-6309, MW-4745	AXM2-5510, BMG 2100-2-R, RO 25, MCAD 4-11048, OC-1001, Rdr 1073, TLCW-05, BF 16399, C4K 90628, NH 8061-2
99196-	LITTLE RED SHOES (-) C. Monroe-L, B. Monroe-T	BB-6645, MW-4748	AXM2-5510, RCX 7103, Rdr 1073, BF 16399
99197-1	NINE POUND HAMMER IS TOO HEAVY (-) C. Monroe-L, B. Monroe-T	BB-6422, MW-4747	AXM2-5510, RD 7870, RCX 7103, RCA 8417-2-R, LPV 532, Rdr 1073, RVN 211, BF 16399
99198-1	ON SOME FOGGY MOUNTAIN TOP (-) C. Monroe-L, B. Monroe-T	BB-6607, MW-4749	AXM2-5510, Rdr 1073, BF 16399
99199-1	DRIFTING TOO FAR FROM THE SHORE (-) C. Monroe-L, B. Monroe-T	BB-6363, MW-4746	AXM2-5510, Rdr 1073, BF 16399
99200-1	IN MY DEAR OLD SOUTHERN HOME (-) C. Monroe-L, B. Monroe-T	BB-6607, MW-4749	AXM2-5510, Rdr 1073, BF 16399
99201-1	NEW RIVER TRAIN (-) C. Monroe-L, B. Monroe	BB-6645, MW-4748	CAL-774, AXM2-5510, RCX 7103, RCA 07863-67450-2, RDR 1073, BF 16399
99202-1	THIS WORLD IS NOT MY HOME (-) C. Monroe-L, B. Monroe-T	BB-6309, MW-4745	SHA 604, Rdr 1073, BF 16399

Bill Monroe: m   Charlie Monroe: g

360621   RCA Victor Bluebird Monroe Brothers session; producer, Eli Oberstein
Southern Radio Building, 208 S. Tyron St., Charlotte, N.C.
June 21, 1936, 1–3:15 P.M.

102739–1	WATERMELON HANGIN' ON THAT VINE[1](-) C. Monroe-L, B. Monroe-T	BB-6829, MW-7010	AXM2-5510, Rdr 1073, BF 16399
102740-1	ON THE BANKS OF THE OHIO (-) C. Monroe-L, B. Monroe-T	BB-7385, MW-7010	CAL-774, AXM2-5510, Rdr 1073, BF 16399, RCA 07863-67450-2
102741-1	DO YOU CALL THAT RELIGION (-) C. Monroe-L, B. Monroe-T	BB-7055, MW-7143	Rdr 1073, BF 16399
102742-1	GOD HOLDS THE FUTURE IN HIS HANDS (-) C. Monroe-L, B. Monroe-T	BB-6477, MW-5026	AXM2-5510, Rdr 1073, BF 16399
102743-1	YOU'VE GOT TO WALK THAT LONESOME VALLEY(-) C. Monroe-L, B. Monroe- T	BB-6477, MW-5026	Rdr 1073, BF 16399
102744-1	SIX MONTHS AIN'T LONG (-) C. Monroe-L, B. Monroe-T	BB-6512, MW-7012	Rdr 1074, BF 16399
102745-1	JUST A SONG OF OLD KENTUCKY (-) C. Monroe-L, B. Monroe-T	BB-6552, MW-7011	CAL-774, RCA 07863-67450-2, Rdr 1074, BF 16399
102745-1	DON'T FORGET ME (-) C. Monroe-L, B. Monroe-T	BB-6552, MW-7011	CAL-774, RCA 07863-67450-2, Rdr 1074, BF 16399
102746-1	I'M GOING (-) C. Monroe-L, B. Monroe-T	BB-7055, MW-7143	Rdr 1074, BF 16399
102747-1	DARLING COREY (-) C. Monroe-L, B. Monroe-T	BB-6512, MW-7012, 27493	LPV 507, AXM 2-5510 Rdr 1074, BF 16399

Bill Monroe: m   Charlie Monroe: g

361012   RCA Victor Bluebird Monroe Brothers session; producer, Eli Oberstein
Southern Radio Building, 208 S. Tyron St., Charlotte, N.C.
Oct. 12, 1936, 2–4:40 P.M.

02538-1	MY SAVIOR'S TRAIN (-) C. Monroe-L, B. Monroe-T	BB-6729, MW-7086	Rdr 1074, BF 16399

| 02539-1 | I AM THINKING TONIGHT OF THE OLD FOLKS (-) | BB-6773, MW-7141 | CAL-774, RCA 07863-67450-2, |
| | C. Monroe-L, B. Monroe- | | Rdr 1074, BF 16399 |

| 02540-1 | DREAMED I SEARCHED HEAVEN FOR YOU | BB-6729, MW-7086 | Rdr 1074, BF 16399 |
| | C. Monroe-L, B. Monroe-T | | |

| 02541-1 | THE OLD CROSS ROAD (-) | BB-6676, MW-7087 | Rdr 1074, BF 16399 |
| | C. Monroe-L, B. Monroe-T | | |

| 02542-1 | THE FORGOTTEN SOLDIER BOY (-) | BB-6829, MW-7140 | Rdr 1026, NW 287, Rdr 1074, |
| | C. Monroe-L, B. Monroe-T | | BF 16399 |

| 02543-1 | WE READ OF A PLACE THAT'S CALLED HEAVEN (-) | BB-6676, MW-7087 | Rdr 1074, BF 16399 |
| | C. Monroe-L, B. Monroe-T | | |

| 02544-1 | WILL THE CIRCLE BE UNBROKEN (-) | BB-6820, MW-7142 | AXM2-5510, Rdr 1074, BF 16399 |
| | C. Monroe-L, B. Monroe-T | | |

| 02545-1 | THE SAINTS GO MARCHING IN (-) | BB-6820, MW-7142 | AXM2-5510, Rdr 1074, |
| | C. Monroe-L, B. Monroe-T | | BF 16399 |

02546-1	ROLL IN MY SWEET BABY'S ARMS (-)	BB-6773, MW-7145	AXM2-5510, RCA 8417-2-R,
	C. Monroe-L, B. Monroe-T		Rdr 1074, BMG 75517 43600 2,
			BF 16399

| 02547-1 | WHERE IS MY SAILOR BOY (-) | BB-6762, MW-7140 | AXM2-5510, LPV 507, |
| | C. Monroe-L, B. Monroe-T | | Rdr 1074, BF 16399 |

Bill Monroe: m   Charlie Monroe: g

370215   RCA Victor Bluebird Monroe Brothers session; producer, Eli Oberstein
Field studio, rooms 1050-52-54, Charlotte Hotel, Charlotte, N.C.
Feb. 15, 1937, 2:30–4:30 P.M.

| 07019-1 | I AM READY TO GO (-) | BB-6866, MW-8453 | BF 16399 |
| | C. Monroe-L, B. Monroe-T | | |

| 07020-1 | WHAT WOULD THE PROFIT BE? (-) | BB-6912, MW-8454 | BF 16399 |
| | C. Monroe-L, B. Monroe-T | | |

| 07021-1 | SOME GLAD DAY (-) | BB-6866, MW-8453 | AXM2-5510, BF 16399 |
| | C. Monroe-L, B. Monroe-T | | |

| 07022-1 | I HAVE FOUND THE WAY (-) | BB-6912, MW-8454 | BF 16399 |
| | C. Monroe-L, B. Monroe-T | | |

07023-1	I AM GOING THAT WAY (-) C. Monroe-L, B. Monroe-T	BB-7007, MW-7141	BF 16399
07024-1	KATY CLINE (-) C. Monroe-L, B. Monroe-T	BB-6960, MW-8455	AXM2-5510, BF 16399
07025-1	ROLL ON, BUDDY (-) C. Monroe-L, B. Monroe-T	BB-6960, MW-8455	AXM2-5510, BF 16399
07026-1	WEEPING WILLOW TREE (-) C. Monroe-L, B. Monroe-T	BB-7093, MW-7145	CAL-774, AXM2-5510, RCA 07863-67450-2, BF 16399
07027-1	I'LL LIVE ON (-) C. Monroe-L, B. Monroe-T	BB-7007, MW-7144	BF 16399
07028-1	OH, HIDE YOU IN THE BLOOD (-) C. Monroe-L, B. Monroe-T	BB-7093, MW-7144	BF 16399

Bill Monroe: m   Charlie Monroe: g

370803   RCA Victor Bluebird Monroe Brothers session; producer, Eli Oberstein
Field studio, Rooms 1050-52-54, Charlotte Hotel, Charlotte, N.C.
Aug. 3, 1937, 2–4:20 P.M.

011875-1	WHAT WOULD YOU GIVE IN EXCHANGE FOR YOUR SOUL—PART 2 C. Monroe-L, B. Monroe-T	BB-7122, MW-7312	BF 16399
011876-1	ON THAT OLD GOSPEL SHIP (-) C. Monroe-L, B. Monroe-T	BB-7273, MW-7312	AXM2-5510, BMG 2100-2-R, BF 16399
011877-1	WHAT WOULD YOU GIVE IN EXCHANGE— PART 3 (-) C. Monroe-L, B. Monroe-T	BB-7122, MW-731	BF 16399
011878-1	LET US BE LOVERS AGAIN (-) C. Monroe-L, B. Monroe-T	BB-7191, MW-7316	BF 16399
011879-1	ALL THE GOOD TIMES ARE PASSED AND GONE (-) C. Monroe-L, B. Monroe-T	BB-7191, MW-7316	ACLI-0535(e), LPV 569, AXM2-5510, BF 16399
011880-1	WHAT WOULD YOU GIVE IN EXCHANGE— PART 4 (-) C. Monroe-L, B. Monroe-T	BB-7326, MW-731	BF 16399

011881-1	ON MY WAY TO GLORY (-) C. Monroe-L, B. Monroe-T	BB-7145, MW-7313	BF 16399
011882-1	MY LAST MOVING DAY (-) C. Monroe-L, B. Monroe-T	BB-7273, MW-7314	BF 16399
011883-1	HE WILL SET YOUR FIELDS ON FIRE (-) C. Monroe-L, B. Monroe-B	BB-7145, MW-7315	AXM2-5510, BF 16399
011884-1	SINNER YOU BETTER GET READY (-) C. Monroe-L, B. Monroe-T	BB-7326, MW-7315	AXM2-5510, BMG 75517 43600 2, BF 16399, DD01

Bill Monroe: m   Charlie Monroe: g

380128   RCA Victor Bluebird Monroe Brothers session; producer, Eli Oberstein
Field studio, Charlotte Hotel, Charlotte, N.C.
Jan. 28, 1938, 2:15–3:15 P.M.

018808-	HAVE A FEAST HERE TONIGHT (-) C. Monroe-L, B. Monroe-T	BB-7508, MW-7447	AXM2-5510, RCA 8417-2-, BF 16399
018809-	GOODBYE MAGGIE (-) C. Monroe-L, B. Monroe-T	BB-7508, MW-7447	AMX2-5510, BF 16399
018810-	ROLLING ON (-) C. Monroe-L, B. Monroe-T	BB-7598, MW-7451	AMX2-5510, BF 16399
018811-	THE OLD MAN'S STORY (-) C. Monroe-L, B. Monroe-T	BB-7425, MW-7448	BF 13699
018812-	I'VE STILL GOT NINETY-NINE (-) C. Monroe-L, B. Monroe-T	BB-7425, MW-7448	BF 13699
018813-	LITTLE JOE (-) C. Monroe-L, B. Monroe-T	BB-7598, MW-7451	AMX2-5510, BF 16399
018814-	A BEAUTIFUL LIFE (-) C. Monroe-L, B. Monroe-BS	BB-7562, MW-7450	AMX2-5510, BF 16399
018815-	PEARLY GATES (-) C. Monroe-L, B. Monroe-T	BB-7460, MW-7449	AMX2-5510, BF 16399
018816-	ON MY WAY BACK HOME (-) C. Monroe-L, B. Monroe-T	BB-7460, MW-7449	BF 16399

018817-	WHEN OUR LORD SHALL COME AGAIN (-)	BB-7562, MW-7450	AMX2-5510, BF 16399
	C. Monroe-L, B. Monroe-T		

Bill Monroe: m   Charlie Monroe: g

Note

1. The title on AXM2-5510 is given as "Watermelon Hanging on the Vine."

2

"MULE SKINNER BLUES": 1939–41

Just weeks after the final Monroe Brothers session in late January 1938 the brothers had gone their separate ways. Charlie, who had done all the lead singing, formed a band called the Kentucky Partners and found a job at WNOX in Knoxville. Bill went to Memphis, where he hired fiddler Robert Jamieson, singer-guitarist Willie "Bill" Wesbrooks, and bassist Charles "Chuck" Haire. He formed a new band and, finding no radio jobs in Memphis, went to Little Rock, where he got on KARK, in company with such acts as Curly Fox and Texas Ruby and the Stamps-Baxter Melody Boys. According to Jamieson, Monroe called his band the Blue Grass Boys from the beginning. But the band was listed in the newspaper as "Bill Monroe and the Kentuckians." Years later, Bill referred to the band by that name, and he was listed under it in the 1939 *Radio Daily Annual* yearbook of radio shows. But by that time Bill's first band, whatever its name, was no more, although one member, Wesbrooks, would rejoin him in 1940. In late fall, after fiddler Jamieson decided against continuing as a professional musician, he had dissolved it and hauled his house trailer back to Atlanta.[1]

In the meantime, Charlie continued to record for Bluebird and did so in a way that confused fans for years. His first session was in Rock Hill, North Carolina, just across the state line from Charlotte, on September 29, 1938. For his band he had hired Zeke Morris to sing and play mandolin and Bill Calhoun to sing in trios and play guitar. None of the songs had been recorded by the brothers, but some were quite likely performed by them on the air; one was a unique version of "Great Speckled Bird." Many of the sides were issued under the name "Charlie Monroe's Boys," a oddly vague term that could easily confuse record buyers.

On February 5, 1939, Charlie did a second Rock Hill session, and this one featured only Charlie and Zeke Morris playing the mandolin and singing harmony—an even more obvious attempt to sound like the Monroe Brothers. The sides from that session include "Is She Praying There?" "Joy Bells," "Oh Death," "Just One Year," "Black Sheep," "Guided by Love," "If You See My Savior," and "From Ship to Shore." These records, which sound amazingly like Monroe Brothers sides, were in some cases issued under the name "Monroe's Boys," leading to even more confusion among listeners.[2] In later years, RCA, in several key reissues, mistakenly included sides from the second Rock Hill session in collections of Monroe Brothers' originals. Even a 1998 CD reissue of Bill Monroe's Victor sides includes some of these Charlie Monroe sides on which Bill is not present.[3]

Determined to form another band, Bill advertised in the *Atlanta Journal* for a new singing partner, and through this hired a trucker named Cleo Davis. Rehearsing with Davis in the back of a service station near his trailer, Bill taught him most of Charlie's parts, and the two began to audition for local stations.[4] Nobody wanted duet singers anymore; bands, especially with a swing or western flavor, were in. Frustrated, Bill and Davis left Atlanta and went to WWNC in Asheville. By then, Bill was again using the name Blue Grass Boys. He was still getting fan mail addressed to the "Monroe Brothers," and he needed some way to let fans know that he indeed had a different band.

His first move was to hire a fiddle player. He had always looked at the fiddle as the most important of the traditional instruments; "I think the fiddle is the king instrument of string music," he said in 1974.[5] Some of his earliest memories were of his mother playing fiddle at local dances, and he came of age admiring his uncle, Pendleton Vandiver (Uncle Pen). For a time Monroe himself had tried to play the fiddle. "Bill took up fiddling, and see-sawed around," Charlie remembered, "and he could make the sourest notes of anybody you ever heard in your life. He could make the sourest! So he finally kind of give up the fiddle."[6] At Asheville, Bill found himself in a mountain region full of good fiddlers who played with a driving, aggressive "short bow" style, and by the spring of 1939 he hired one for his new band—a versatile young man named Art Wooten. He was to become the first of a long line of superb fiddlers to pass through the ranks of the Blue Grass Boys.

Wooten had been born in 1906 in Sparta, North Carolina, due east of Asheville near the Virginia–North Carolina line, and grew up and learned his fiddling in his native Allegheny County. By 1937 he was good enough to compete in the Galax fiddlers' contest and had rigged up a one-man-band contraption that attracted a lot of attention. According to a friend who

watched it, Wooten used "a guitar and banjo set in a box with pedals. It was rigged so that Art could play with one foot and chord with the other while he played the fiddle and sang."[7] Such goofy devices were by no means uncommon in the days of busking musicians. Fate Norris, the banjo player for the Skillet Lickers, had such a thing, and it won him a write-up in *Variety*. Art could also sing and double on harmonica; later he refined his one man band so it would run from an electric motor.

Novelty instruments helped the Blue Grass Boys on personals, but Bill was most interested in Wooten's fiddling. After the war, Wooten, who died in 1986, would play for both the Stanley Brothers and Flatt and Scruggs—two of Monroe's most serious competitors at the time. The Stanleys expressly hired Wooten to replace Leslie Keith in order to achieve a sound that was more bluegrass. Like most mountain fiddlers, Wooten was used to racing through old breakdowns like "Katy Hill" and "Grey Eagle," but like some of Asheville-area fiddlers, including Luke Smathers and John Rector, his back-up and fill-ins had a nice bluesy tone. "Art was a wonderful old-time fiddler," Bill recalled. He was also skilled enough and young enough (thirty-three when he joined) to respond to the new style Monroe was experimenting with. Often he would take Wooten aside and show him on the mandolin a phrase or lick he wanted, and Wooten was able to oblige.

For a time Monroe added a fourth member, Tommy Millard, who created a bass effect by blowing on a jug in a style reminiscent of the great black street bands of a generation earlier such as the Memphis Jug Band. Millard also played spoons and bones and tried blackface comedy. Indeed, sometimes comedy onstage was so broad that Monroe and Cleo Davis would come out dressed as women and do a round of old vaudeville jokes. Thankfully, Millard was soon replaced by Amos Garren, a skilled string-bass player.

After about three months of this Monroe heard that the Delmore Brothers were leaving station WFBC in Greenville, South Carolina, and managed to get his band a job replacing them. Here he continued to hone the quartet, rehearsing them daily in an old service station near his trailer. By that fall it seemed that the Blue Grass Boys were about where Monroe wanted them to be. The time was right, in the words of John Rumble, "to grab the brass ring." Cleo Davis recalls the day of the decision: "He told me to go back and tell the other boys to get their toothbrushes ready. We were going to Nashville."[8]

As Monroe explained to Jim Rooney years later, "When I started on the Grand Ole Opry, I had rehearsed and we was ready. Our music was in good shape. We had a good fiddler with us—for bluegrass in them days—Fiddlin' Art Wooten. And my singing was high and clear, you know, and I was in good shape, and we was ready to go on the Grand Ole Opry."[9]

The actual audition occurred in October 1939. The Opry had just lost one of its veteran old-time string bands, the Binkley Brothers' Dixie Clodhoppers. Although a newly arrived singer named Roy Acuff was showing that audiences were turning to vocalists, the Opry managers felt there was still need for bands as well. The story of the audition is a familiar one but just what numbers the band played is not. At one time Monroe said they played "John Henry," "Bile Them Cabbage Down," and "another one" that has been identified as "Katy Hill." The one song on which all accounts agree, however—the one that made bosses say that Monroe had "the music that National Life needed"—was a remarkable vehicle named "Mule Skinner Blues."[10]

"Mule Skinner" was by many accounts the most popular song Monroe did on the early Opry and on tours. "Bill didn't sing too much at that time," recalled fellow Opry performer Pete Pyle. "He'd come in with 'Mule Skinner Blues' every now and then and knock the house down."[11] It was what Music Row today calls a career song for Monroe's new band, one that would stay in his repertoire throughout the rest of his life. As such, it deserves close inspection.

Almost certainly, Monroe's immediate source for "Mule Skinner" was the classic recording by Jimmie Rodgers, done in, of all places, Hollywood in 1930. It was released as "Blue Yodel No. 8" with the "Mule Skinner Blues" subtitle and with composer credit to Rodgers. Many of the Rodgers blue yodels have demonstrable roots in black folk tradition, and "Mule Skinner" is no exception.

Although the exact circumstances of how Rodgers created or arranged the verses cannot be known, historians have identified a number of commercial blues recordings with "Mule Skinner" stanzas that predate Rodgers's 1930 recording. These include the "Good Morning, Captain" stanza that appears in "Labor Blues" (Okeh, 1928) by an obscure singer named Tom Dickson; the "water boy" stanza found in "Section Gang Blues" by Texas Alexander (Okeh, 1927); and the "turn your damper down" stanza by Papa Harvey Hull (Gennett, 1927). Rodgers's fifth verse (Monroe's third), about going to town and the John B. Stetson hat, does show up in slightly different form in another recording by Texas Alexander.[12]

Monroe used four of the six Rodgers stanzas. On his Victor recording he dropped Rodgers's stanzas four ("working on the railroad") and six ("turn your damper down)." This was one of a number of Rodgers songs Monroe would do as solos in his recording career; his admiration of Rodgers's work was deep-seated but not unconditional. In 1974, when talking about records he liked as a boy, he said, "People like Jimmie Rodgers touched me—with some of the songs they sang. Like 'Mule Skinner Blues.'"[13]

Some historians have noted that Monroe's new fellow Opry star Roy Acuff beat him with a recorded version of "Mule Skinner Blues." Indeed, Acuff recorded a version in 1939 that was released in mid-1940, and on it his guitarist Lonnie Wilson does the same introductory guitar run that Monroe uses. Acuff like Monroe had the ability to do a high, keening, falsetto yodel, and his text is close to that of both Rodgers and Monroe. What is different—radically different—is Monroe's charging, train-shuffle rhythm. Acuff played the song in an easy boom-chuck two-beat like it was any other country lament. Monroe uses a driving guitar that sounds to the contemporary ear more like rockabilly than anything else. "Charlie and I had a country beat I suppose," he told Jim Rooney, "but the beat in my music—bluegrass music—started when I ran across 'Mule Skinner Blues' and started playing that. We didn't do it the way Jimmie Rodgers sung it. It's speeded up, and we moved it up to fit the fiddle and we have that straight time with it, driving time. And then we went on and that same kind of time would work with 'John Henry,' and we put it on that."[14]

It was because of this new hard and driving time, Monroe felt, that they so impressed the Opry bosses George D. Hay and Harry Stone. He auditioned for the show with "Mule Skinner" and was almost certainly singing it when he came to Nashville. A recently discovered air check from November 1939 proves he played it on the radio that early. Thus it now seems likely that instead of Monroe being inspired by the Acuff recording, the opposite was true: Acuff borrowed Monroe's arrangement even though the latter had not gotten around to recording it.[15]

The initial version of the Blue Grass Boys that first came to the Opry was composed of Monroe, Cleo Davis (mandolin, guitar), Amos Garren (bass), and Art Wooten (fiddle). It was this group that worked weekly on the Opry and did Opry tours for the first part of 1940. Soon, though, the whole band had been replaced. That fall three new musicians emerged who would play major roles in the development of Monroe's music: singer and guitarist Clyde Moody, fiddler Tommy Magness, and bass player-comedian Bill Wesbrooks (Cousin Wilbur).

Wesbrooks was apparently the first to join. He had been born in the flatlands of western Tennessee, in Gibson County, about 1910. One of his local pals was young Eddy Arnold, and Wesbrooks played in the late 1930s in one of Arnold's first bands. Soon he had graduated to working with Uncle Henry Warren's Kentucky Mountaineers in Louisville. In July 1940, after a health crisis, he moved to Nashville. "I asked Judge George D. Hay if he knew anybody who needed anyone," he recalled. "He told me that Bill Monroe needed a comedian—so I called Bill up in West Virginia. Bill told me, 'I'll be in the first part of the week.'"[16] They met, and Monroe invited him to travel with the band the next week and "see how it works out." It seemed to, but, Wesbrooks recalled, "Bill never did hire me. He would just drive up and I'd get in the car." For the next four years Wesbrooks was a regular with the Blue Grass Boys; "I sung all the parts on the quartet, sung some, played bass fiddle, and did comedy."[17]

The second new member was Tommy Magness (1916–72), who would emerge as one of the most influential fiddlers of the 1940s. He was a native of Mineral Bluff, Georgia, a mountain community not far from the Tennessee line. Learning from local players—including a band led by the Chauncey Brothers—and his father, Magness was playing in public by the time he was nine. As a young man he was determined to make a living with his instrument. "When he left home," his sister recalled, "he took only his fiddle and some clothes. He got so hungry he couldn't stand it, and took his fiddle into a cafe. They asked him to play a tune. He did, and said he got steaks or biscuits or anything he wanted."[18] By the time he was sixteen, Tommy's family had moved to North Carolina, where he sought work in the mills around Canton and tried to get on Asheville radio.

By 1938 he had met a native of nearby Waynesville, Roy Hall, who was organizing a band called the Blue Ridge Entertainers, and Hall invited him to join. The band quickly moved from Asheville to Greenville (WBIG) and then to Winston-Salem (WAIR). Within months Hall would become the most popular singer in the Carolinas.[19]

At the band's first recording session—for ARC in November 1938—Magness played tasty back-up and also recorded the first version of a fiddle tune that would become perhaps the best-known display tune in the country: "The Orange Blossom Special." Even the Rouse Brothers, who owned the copyright on the song, had not yet recorded it. Somehow they found out about the recording and sought to block its release. On the original recording ledger, ARC boss Art Satherley wrote, "Don't release—Pub. promises trouble." The record was never released, and its master was melted for scrap in World War II. Soon the band moved again, to Roanoke, where Magness

delighted audiences with his other specialties, "Natural Bridge Blues" and "Polecat Blues."

It's not clear how Monroe heard of Magness, but it seems likely that he had crossed paths with Hall's band somewhere in the Carolinas. Monroe was at once attracted to Magness's drive and loose, bluesy style. "Now Tommy Magness," Monroe said, "had been playing with Roy Hall and they were trying to play off of bluegrass. He'd heard the way we played when Art Wooten was with me, so it was right down his alley to get somebody behind him with that, because with that kind of little bow he worked, he could move you right along."[20]

Monroe's reference to Magness's "little bow" is revealing. It suggests that even though Monroe respected "long bow" artists like Arthur Smith and Clayton McMichen he also saw a place in his music for the older mountain "jiggy bow" style— and Magness was one of the very best. And it turned out to be Magness who backed Monroe on his first solo recording, "Mule Skinner Blues," in Atlanta in 1940. "He had that fine old-time touch," Monroe reflected, "rich and pure, but he was able to put a touch of blues to it. He was the first man I ever heard play 'Orange Blossom Special,' and he could put a lot more to it than they do today."[21]

Magness's stay with the Blue Grass Boys only lasted a little over a year. By late 1941 Roy Hall offered him a better salary than the $25 a week he was getting with Monroe, and soon he had rejoined that band in Roanoke. In later years Magness would play with Roy Acuff, where he helped to popularize "Black Mountain Rag," and in 1950 he formed his own band that brought together two young musicians who would go on to form one of the most influential early bluegrass bands, banjo-ist Don Reno and guitarist Arthur Lee "Red" Smiley.

The third new Blue Grass Boy was singer and guitarist Clyde Moody (1915–89). A tall, hawk-faced man with an easy smile, Moody came from Cherokee, North Carolina, and was part Native American. He gained experience playing with the brother of Roy Hall, Jay Hugh Hall, and as a singer with Wade Mainer's band, the Sons of the Mountaineers. He was also an avid baseball fan and played professional ball for a season in Asheville. Such a background appealed to Monroe, a serious baseball fan who later would have his band dress out in uniforms and play local sand-lot teams before concerts. From 1937 to 1939 Moody played with Mainer's band over WIS Columbia, WWNC Asheville, and WPTF Raleigh—all stations the Monroes had played as well. He also made numerous Bluebird records with the band and even recorded one session with J. E. Mainer.

Moody remembered joining Monroe on September 6,

1940, in Bluefield, West Virginia. By then the band included Wesbrooks and Magness and also Mac McGar, a fiddler and mandolin player who worked with various Opry bands. Moody found himself onstage with the group even before they had a chance to rehearse, but by now he was a seasoned professional and able to make the adjustment. He would remain with the Blue Grass Boys off and on throughout the war, eventually emerging as a solo singer on the Opry and, after the war, a successful artist on King Records. His "Shenandoah Waltz" would become a major hit in 1946.[22]

ATLANTA 1

Bill Monroe's first solo recording session—and the first session to be released with the name "Blue Grass Boys"—occurred in Atlanta on October 7, 1940, at a temporary studio in the Kimball House Hotel at 30 North Pryor Street. By now Eli Oberstein had left the company and been replaced by Frank Walker (1889–1963). A native of rural upstate New York, Walker had pioneered field recording in the 1920s when he worked for Columbia and discovered groups like the Skillet Lickers, Charlie Poole, Smith's Sacred Singers, the Leake County Revellers, and dozens of others from old-time music's golden age. He joined RCA Victor in the 1930s and helped establish the Bluebird series; by 1940 he had risen to vice president in the company. A few years later he would become head of the new MGM company and play a key role in the development of Hank Williams.

Atlanta had been Walker's main headquarters in the 1920s, the place where he held biannual sessions and recorded hundreds of masters. Now he and Victor were hoping that history would repeat itself. Walker had been doing sessions in Atlanta since August 1939. For the October sessions (both in 1940 and 1941) he looked up his former assistant from the Columbia days, Dan Hornsby. The handsome son of a well-to-do Atlanta family, Hornsby was best known in town as a radio announcer and pop singer. He had recorded several pop-flavored songs for Columbia in the 1920s, but his most important job had been to line up and rehearse talent for the Columbia sessions. Indeed, at times Hornsby was running some of the sessions. By 1940 he was still active in local radio and more than happy to help Walker. Among the other acts scheduled for this session were Fiddlin' Arthur Smith and Roy Hall.

Thus Bill Monroe and his band, along with Arthur Smith, piled into his Hudson Country Club Eight, strapped Wesbrook's bass fiddle to the top, and set out for Atlanta in early October. Like Oberstein, Frank Walker was crowding several sessions

into a day's work, and little else had happened to change recording technology. Bill Wesbrooks has left a revealing account of what it was like in the studio after they arrived.

> They rented two rooms together with big sliding doors and they took and hung quilts on the walls to make the sound a little better. All the instruments recorded on one microphone. The lights would come on and you knew it was time to start recording. You'd do your tune. Then you cut 'em on about a two-inch-thick—something like beeswax. . . . It was thick to keep it from breaking so easy. . . . [Y]ou might have to make four or five masters. They put each one in a trunk—in a big steamer trunk—so that if one got broke, they'd still have a chance of having two or three more masters left. It would just fit right into these slots in these trunks. And they'd send each, like if you cut four or five masters of one tune, they'd put one in each trunk, and they'd ship these trunks separately on the train.[23]

Their destination, of course, was the Victor plant in Camden, New Jersey; there, after metal plates were made from the wax masters, the wax was shaved, smoothed, and used again. According to the original session sheets, only two selections had two takes: "Mule Skinner Blues" and "Tennessee Blues." The session ran from 1 to 3:15 P.M. Monroe was set up to receive royalties, but sidemen got a flat fee of $5 per side. Wesbrooks, who wound up playing bass on two other sessions that day, was astounded to receive a total of $120 for a hard day's work.

Even that early, "Mule Skinner Blues" was the money song from the session, the one Walker most wanted, and the one that had helped Monroe establish himself on the Opry. It was the first record released from the session (Bluebird 8568–A) and almost certainly the best-selling disc from the session. It was also issued on a Montgomery Ward disc and reissued in 1948 on the Victor label itself. And it remained in the Monroe repertoire throughout his career. With its driving rhythm, bluesy fiddle, and high, soaring vocal, it is by many standards the first record to really exhibit what would come to be called bluegrass.

Some of the other cuts from the session were not all that unique. "No Letter in the Mail" features a Monroe Brothers–like duet between Clyde Moody and Monroe. It had been written by radio veteran Bill Carlisle back in 1938 and recorded by him on Decca with his brother Cliff as Bill Carlisle's Kentucky Home Boys. It quickly became a favorite with radio singers, and Clyde Moody recorded it with a trio called the Happy-Go-Lucky Boys for Bluebird in February 1940. Just why Frank Walker would permit the Blue Grass Boys to record a number he had recorded eight months earlier is a bit of a mystery, but he might have considered the Monroe version to be better. It had been in Monroe's repertoire since he began singing with Cleo Davis in Greenville, South Carolina.[24] It's also quite likely that it was Moody who brought the song to the session.

Another of Moody's contributions was his original blues "Six White Horses," which entered bluegrass tradition through this recording. He had been doing the song since 1936 or 1937 and sang it as a solo on the record. Many stanzas seemed derived from country blues verses. The lines "The train I'm riding / Is sixteen coaches long" is, of course, the opening stanza of Elvis Presley's legendary "Mystery Train." Moody also joins Monroe on another duet with "I Wonder If You Feel the Way I Do," composed by western swing king Bob Wills. Supposedly, Wills wrote the song soon after his wife left him; he had recorded a hit version of it on ARC in the fall of 1938. "Dog House Blues," replete with impromptu yapping and whining, was an early number by Pee Wee King and his manager J. L. Frank. Moody must have helped arrange it, for on the original session sheet he shares composer credits.

Even this early, one of the most popular parts of Monroe's Opry act was his gospel quartet. In later years Monroe would claim that his was the first secular group on the Opry to have a gospel quartet, and early Opry rosters seem to bear him out. Although the show, and WSM in general, had featured various versions of the Vaughan Quartets from Lawrenceburg, Tennessee, those groups used piano accompaniment and did nothing but gospel—usually singing-convention tunes. The early quartets used a lot of the afterbeat or echo techniques that were so popular with the Monroe brothers, but the use of four voices—lead, tenor, baritone, and bass accompanied only by guitar or mandolin—opened even more possibilities.

Monroe knew and liked many African American gospel quartets of the time and was on Charlotte's station WBT at the same time as the popular Golden Gate Quartet. "Cryin' Holy Unto the Lord" is the Carter Family song known as "On the Rock Where Moses Stood," which they had recorded in 1930. Even before then, though, the song was widespread in black tradition. Since 1924 various black jubilee groups and quartets had recorded it, including the Norfolk Jubilee Quartet, the Birmingham Jubilee Singers, and the Biddleville Quartet. Later Roy Hall picked up the song, which might have been how it came to Monroe. His version does vary in several stanzas from the Carter Family version.

The session concluded with two instrumentals. One, "Tennessee Blues," a fast blues in A, was a showcase for Bill's mandolin. Wesbrooks took bass breaks on it as well, but fiddler Magness sat out on this tune, which has the distinction of being the first song with formal published composer credits to Bill Monroe. "Katy Hill" was Tommy Magness's masterpiece, played at an unheard-of speed and defining the nature of bluegrass fiddling. Monroe was proud of the recording. He said, "'Katy Hill' had a lot more in it when we recorded [it] than it ever had before. Those old-time fiddlers didn't have anybody to shove them along."[25] Magness did—Monroe's surging mandolin, Moody's strong guitar, and Wesbrook's bass. The tune itself is often seen as a variant of "Sally Johnson," which Texas fiddler Eck Robertson recorded in 1922. The former Skillet Licker fiddler Lowe Stokes was the first to record it under the name "Katy Hill" in 1928.

Another curious facet of the "Katy Hill" track is the way band members shout out old square dance calls like "Swing your partner!" and "Promenade your partner!" along with bursts of exuberance ("Oo-wee!" and "Aw, play it!"). The shouts might seem truly spontaneous, but they come at regular intervals, every strophe or so, and could well have been coached and cued by Walker and Hornsby. Such calls were staples of many early fiddle band records from the 1920s, reflecting the fact that the records were used for dances. Frank Walker adapted the actual calls to all kinds of scripted asides when he produced a long series of popular discs by the Skillet Lickers in the 1920s. As late as 1956 Monroe was still using the calls in recordings like "Tall Timber," but by then—and for a couple of decades—calls were more decorative than functional, self-conscious references to the old-time feel of the tune.

ATLANTA 2: 1941

During 1941, as America moved ever closer to involvement in the war in Europe, Bluebird released the fruits of the first Monroe session at regular intervals. Bluebird 8568 ("Mule Skinner" and "Six White Horses") came out in December 1940, only weeks after the session. Bluebird 8611 ("No Letter in the Mail" and "Crying Holy Unto the Lord") came out in February 1941, and Bluebird 8692 ("Dog House Blues" and "Katy Hill") followed in May. The last coupling, Bluebird 8813 ("I Wonder if You Feel the Way I Do" and "Tennessee Blues"), did not emerge until November 1941. By that time the Blue Grass Boys had returned for a second session with Walker and Hornsby in Atlanta.

By October 2, 1941, almost a year to the day of their first session, the Blue Grass Boys once again drove down to Atlanta and reported to the Kimball Hotel. There were some important changes in personnel, however. Art Wooten was back, replacing Tommy Magness, who had rejoined Roy Hall. In place of Clyde Moody was a new member, Pete Pyle. Born in 1920 and a native of Burnsville, Mississippi, Pyle came to fame as a performer on Memphis powerhouse station WMC in 1939 and 1940. He began writing original songs with a mandolin player and singing buddy named Edwin Crowe and soon attracted the attention of RCA Victor. On October 11, 1940, he and Crowe traveled to the same Atlanta field session at which Monroe had recorded some five days before and did a series of original songs for Bluebird. None of them attained much fame—Bluebird was betting on "Home Sweet Home in the Rockies"—and none had any kind of a bluegrass feel. But they did feature Pyle's appealing singing at a time when solo singers were coming into their own. A second Bluebird session followed on September 30, 1941, where eight more originals were cut, including a popular honky-tonk number, "Beer Drinker's Blues."

In the meantime, Pyle had gotten a job on the Grand Ole Opry as a solo singer. Although he was young—twenty-one—and inexperienced, the Opry was impressed with his Bluebird contract and looking for someone to follow Roy Acuff as a solo singing star. Pyle got a spot on the show but traveled with Monroe's band when they did personal appearances. He was soon comfortable working with the band, often singing harmony with Bill, and planned on recording with them at the October 1941 session. One song they had rehearsed, "Live and Let Live," was popularized by Wiley Walker and Gene Sullivan; another was Jimmie Davis's hit "Sweethearts or Strangers." When the group appeared at the studio, however, Walker told them that Pyle could not sing on the Monroe session. Pyle recalls the reason given as being that he was "an exclusive RCA artist" and could not sing on another's session. That in itself makes little sense because both Monroe and Pyle had recorded on the same label, Bluebird. A more likely reason was that Pyle had just finished his own second session three days earlier, and Walker was nervous about overusing him. Whatever the case, it caused a serious disruption of recording plans as Monroe scrambled to find material to replace Pyle's songs. He finally settled on a novelty song by Bill Wesbrooks, "The Coupon Song," and a fiddle tune, "Back Up and Push."

Shortly after the session, as Pearl Harbor occurred and America joined the war, Pyle was drafted and left Monroe. He later worked as the lead singer for Pee Wee King and had his own band on the Opry, the Mississippi Valley Boys. Throughout the late 1940s he worked with Jamup and Honey, Uncle Dave Macon, Robert Lunn, and gospel singer Wally Fowler. He continued to write good songs, three of which were later recorded by Monroe: "True Life Blues," "Highway of Sorrow," and "Don't Put Off Until Tomorrow." For a few weeks he even rejoined the Blue Grass Boys in late 1953 as a guitarist and then led the house band at Monroe's Brown County Jamboree. In the 1960s he had a major hit as a songwriter when Don Gibson and Jimmy Dickens each recorded versions of his "Lovin' Lies."

The session began with two gospel quartet numbers, the first being "Shake My Mother's Hand for Me." This was a 1932 work by the famed black composer Thomas A. Dorsey, known for "Peace in the Valley" and "Precious Lord, Take My Hand." After winning national fame and a small fortune as "Georgia Tom" and writing and recording double-entendre blues like "It's Tight Like That," Dorsey began writing pop-flavored gospel songs in Chicago in the early 1930s. He often worked with gospel singer Mahalia Jackson, and his songs were unique in that they were issued not in gospel books but as sheet music. He himself recorded "Shake My Mother's Hand" in 1932, but a skeptical record company, more used to Dorsey's blues, never released it.[26] The song, however, soon became popular with white gospel groups as well, and in 1939 it was printed in *Favorite Radio Songs Number Two,* compiled by V. O. Stamps and published by the huge Stamps-Baxter Music Company of Dallas.

By this time, Stamps-Baxter was making a concerted effort to get its songs heard on the radio, and it hired song pluggers to travel to various stations and try to interest singers in Stamps-Baxter songs. A next step was to issue songbooks of material specifically designed for radio use, songs that could be adopted, or songs that had already proven popular. Most of the time the songs, originally written or arranged for four parts, were redesigned for duet singing by acts like the Blue Sky Boys or the Delmore Brothers. The Blue Grass Quartet, with its use of the full four voices, was an exception to the common practice in country radio even though gospel music had featured male quartets for years. The other gospel song was "Were You There?" a familiar spiritual that had been featured by, among others, the Golden Gate Quartet, which Monroe heard during his WBT days.

A natural follow-up to Monroe's success with "Mule Skinner Blues" was "Blue Yodel No. 7 (Anniversary Blue Yodel)." Curiously, it was the only song from the session to feature Monroe singing solo. The original Rodgers song, also recorded in Atlanta in 1929, was called the "Anniversary" yodel because it was cut on the one-year anniversary of Rodgers's original "T for Texas" blue yodel. Rodgers used six stanzas in his original, from which Monroe used three: number one, number three ("I'm so lonesome"), and number six ("I like Mississippi, I'm a fool about Tennessee"). Monroe's singing is, naturally, more driving and forceful than Rodgers's, and at times he uses a sky-high falsetto rather than an actual yodel. It was the first record released from this session and in stores by December 1941. Its original B side was "In the Pines," a traditional lyric with a hugely complicated history; Monroe learned the song by hearing it on the radio as he traveled through Georgia.[27] On shows, Pete Pyle sang it with Monroe, but when he was not allowed to record, bass player Bill Wesbrooks stepped in and sang the lead to Monroe's tenor.

"The Coupon Song" was another last-minute Wesbrooks addition. He had been singing it as part of his comedy for years but never claimed to have written it. "Somebody gave me a little sheet of paper with the words on it," he recalled.[28] Ironically, one of the earlier popularizers of the song had been Boyden Carpenter, the former Monroe Brothers comedian from Raleigh. He called it "I'm Saving Up Coupons" and printed it in his own songbook. Composed in 1914 by Joe Weston, Billy James, and Abe Wilsky, it had been released on four hillbilly 78s, the first being Peg Moreland's 1929 version.[29]

"The Orange Blossom Special" had become a real crowd-pleaser in Monroe's shows when featured by Tommy Magness. Its composers, Ervin Rouse and his brother, Gordon, had recorded the piece for Bluebird in New York on June 14, 1939. Monroe's is a much more rousing version, though, and much closer to the later versions of bluegrass's best-known train piece.[30] Throughout the 1941 session there are shouted asides on many cuts, following the lead set by the earlier session. This, too, was probably at the instigation of producer Frank Walker. In "The Orange Blossom Special" the trait morphed into a comedy routine, a little skit between Wooten and other members of the band. Today "The Orange Blossom Special" is mostly done as an instrumental, but this version has singing in the middle. In the 1920s and 1930s dozens of fiddle songs imitated trains, and most had the same two-part structure: a slow, getting-started-from-the-station section followed by a train-rolling-at-full-tilt section. "The Orange Blossom Special" follows that pattern but differs in that the tempo does not change but the key does. The first part is in the key of E (in which the duet is sung) and the second part modulates to A. Thus the tension/release is created not by tempo change but by harmonic shift. This became one of the most reissued of the recordings from Monroe's 1940–41 period.

"Honky Tonk Swing" is Monroe's mandolin showcase for the session. His second recorded original piece, its title, which may well have been foisted on the tune by Walker or Hornsby, reflects the fact that this blues in C is, in the words of Rich Kienzle, "a remarkable twelve-bar tour-de-force with a boogie beat and licks that anticipate blues or even rockabilly guitar."[31] It includes bass breaks by Wesbrooks, but, like Bill's blues instrumental from the first session, no fiddle. "Back Up and Push" is the familiar fiddle tune recorded to show off Wooten's hot and "greasy" style.

SUMMARY

The Bluebird sides Monroe made during 1940 and 1941 would be the last records he would make until 1945, and as a body they represent his first attempt to articulate the new kind of music he wanted for himself. Yet there are signs of uncertainty in this vision. For one thing, Monroe was hesitant about featuring his own singing. Of these first crucial sixteen sides, Monroe sings solo on only three ("Mule Skinner," "Dog House Blues," and "Blue Yodel No. 7"); he sings duets with Moody or Wesbrooks on four. On two, someone else in the band sings lead ("Six White Horses" and "The Coupon Song"), and vocals are by the gospel quartet on three. Four are instrumentals. Moody's comment that Monroe was shy about singing too many solos seems borne out. His solo singing would emerge much more forcefully in records he would make a few years later for Columbia. But for now, he seemed to be interested in the sound of the band as a whole, and he seemed to view the group as a sort of repertory company united by a certain musical style and tempo.

Another interpretation, however, is that Monroe saw his band as something more than just a back-up for his singing. He seemed willing to share the spotlight with other members and saw the group as a synergistic whole. This, after all, was the way he had to work day-to-day when touring and making personal appearances. At rural schools, tent shows, small-town auditoriums, and outdoor picnic concerts it was absolutely necessary to spotlight all the band members and give the audience variety and a show worth their money. Monroe had worked with his brother for years, managing an entire evening's entertainment with only the two of them or with them and a comedian. Now—with Clyde Moody, who was a competent singer, an experienced comedian like Wesbrooks, and exciting fiddlers like Magness and Wooten—he could drop back from the spotlight from time to time. Within a year or two Monroe would adapt this package format for his Wallrite Opry segment, and other Opry bands of the time, like Pee Wee King and Roy Acuff, were doing similar things for their segments.

Although the three duet numbers might be seen as a lingering reminder of the old Monroe Brothers music, the rest of the sixteen, both in style and provenance, can be seen as a distinct change from that fare. The Monroes did many gospel duets that originated with the songbooks as quartets, but they were never able to use four voices in an arrangement, as Monroe did here. There were no instrumentals in the brother duets and no original mandolin instrumentals like found in "Tennessee Blues" and "Honky Tonk Swing." Although the brothers would occasionally do new songs that were current up to three or four years before the recording, here Monroe did no fewer than seven current songs, from "Orange Blossom Special" to "No Letter in the Mail." This is almost half his recorded 1940–41 repertoire. The list that follows provides the other sources for the sixteen Atlanta sides.

Original Bill Monroe compositions: two
Recently composed songs: seven
Songs from gospel songbooks: one
Traditional or African American gospel: two
Traditional instrumental: two
Traditional folk ("Mule Skinner" and "In the Pines"): two

Comparing this listing with the one for the Monroe Brothers' sixty recordings (chapter 1), several trends seem apparent. The percentage of traditional material, both gospel and secular, is obviously lower; the material taken from gospel songbooks is very much lower. The percentage of new songs is much higher, perhaps reflecting Monroe's attempt to position himself as no longer a "Carolinas" act but one that could compete with the wide range of acts on radio in the whole South or Midwest. Even the title to his mandolin piece, "Honky Tonk Swing," seems a concession to the new music of artists like Ted Daffan and Al Dexter, who were by the late 1930s starting to use the term *honkey tonk* to describe a new type of jukebox music.

The two Atlanta sessions would help to define Monroe's new music and would yield archetypal versions of songs that would remain in his repertoire and become keystones of his music. The foremost, of course, is "Mule Skinner Blues," which would remain in the core repertoire until the very end. "Cryin' Holy Unto the Lord" and "Shake My Mother's Hand for Me" would remain radio favorites through the 1940s, and "Katy Hill" was a favorite fiddle tune. "In the Pines" became a Monroe standard, as did "Orange Blossom Special." Most of the others, though, do not appear in the later recorded repertoire.

The shelf life of the records themselves can be seen by consulting the "Numerical Listings of Releases." Bluebird 8568 ("Mule Skinner") bounced out within weeks of the recording session and was issued in December 1940. Others of the sixteen emerged at normal intervals until May 1942. In October 1948 Victor reissued "Mule Skinner" backed by "Blue Yodel No. 7" on an actual Victor label. A couple of months later they did the same with two fiddle tunes, "Katy Hill" and "Back Up and Push." In 1962 a number of the cuts were put on a RCA Camden LP, and in 1991 the set was issued for the first time on compact disc. All in all, most of the sixteen recordings have been remarkably available to the public for much of five decades, a feat matched by few other performers from the era.

Notes

1. The information about Monroe's 1938 band comes from Tom Ewing, "Bob Jamieson and the Original Blue Grass Boys," *Bluegrass Unlimited* 40 (July 2005): 48–51.
2. Another mystery concerning the Rock Hill recordings is that Bill Monroe, in a conversation with a fan and record collector from Rock Hill, perked up at the mention of the town and said he had done some recording there. The Victor files show nothing—not even an unreleased session—under Bill's name, but could he have possibly played on some of Charlie's sides? If so, the files do not show it.
3. Five of the twelve tracks on the first Monroe Brothers reissue, *Early Blue Grass Music,* Camden CAL 774 (1964), were by Charlie Monroe, as were three of the twenty-five tracks on *The Essential Bill Monroe and the Monroe Brothers*, RCA 07863–67450–2 (1997).
4. The most detailed account of Cleo Davis's career is Wayne Erbsen's "Cleo Davis: The Original Blue Grass Boy," in *Bluegrass Unlimited* (Feb. 1982): 28–30 and (March 1982): 59–64. Also useful are John Rumble's liner notes to *The Music of Bill Monroe from 1936 to 1994* (MCAD 4–11048, 1994).
5. Charles K. Wolfe, "Bluegrass Touches: An Interview with Bill Monroe," *Old Time Music* 16 (Spring 1975): 8.
6. Douglas B. Green, "The Charlie Monroe Story, Part 2: The Monroe Brothers," *Muleskinner News* 4 (Feb. 1973): 11.
7. Charles K. Wolfe, notes to *Bill Monroe: Blue Moon of Kentucky* (Bear Family BCD 16399, 2002), 27.
8. John Rumble, notes to *The Music of Bill Monroe.*
9. James Rooney, *Bossmen: Bill Monroe and Muddy Waters* (New York: Dial Press, 1971), 33.
10. Bill Monroe, quoted in Charles K. Wolfe, *A Good-Natured Riot: The Birth of the Grand Ole Opry* (Nashville: Country Music Foundation Press and Vanderbilt University Press, 1999), 259. The National Life and Accident Insurance Company owned WSM, the Nashville radio station that broadcast the Grand Ole Opry.
11. Douglas B. Green, "Pete Pyle: Bluegrass Pioneer," *Bluegrass Unlimited* 12 (March 1978): 22.
12. Information on these recorded antecedents to Rodgers's composition comes from various correspondents to the list-serv "t-list" in June 2000.

13. Wolfe, "Bluegrass Touches," 7.

14. Rooney, *Bossmen,* 33.

15. This appears to have been the first example of a pattern that would occur later with Monroe's repertoire, as in 1947 when the Stanley Brothers recorded "Molly and Tenbrooks" and Wilma Lee and Stoney Cooper copied "Wicked Path of Sin" and in 1950 when Flatt and Scruggs recorded their version of "Pike County Breakdown."

16. Cousin Wilbur [Bill Wesbrooks] with Barbara McLane and Sandra Grafton, *Everybody's Cousin* (New York: Manor Books, 1979), 121–22.

17. Wesbrooks, *Everybody's Cousin,* 122.

18. Charles K. Wolfe, *Classic Country: Legends of Country Music* (New York: Routledge, 2001), 133.

19. Wolfe, *Classic Country,* 122.

20. Rooney, *Bossmen,* 36. Monroe's comments about Hall were made long after the fact in a 1970 interview.

21. Wolfe, notes to *Blue Moon of Kentucky,* 33.

22. Ivan M. Tribe and John W. Morris, "Clyde Moody: Old-Time Bluegrass and Country Musician," *Bluegrass Unlimited* (July 1975): 28–32.

23. Wesbrooks, *Everybody's Cousin,* 122–33.

24. Wayne Erbsen, "Cleo Davis: The Original Blue Grass Boy," in *The Bill Monroe Reader,* edited by Tom Ewing (Urbana: University of Illinois Press, 2000), 134–35.

25. Rooney, *Bossmen,* 35.

26. Details on Thomas Dorsey's music and career come from Charles Wolfe's personal correspondence with Ray Funk.

27. Judith McCulloh, "'In the Pines': The Melodic-Textual Identity of an American Lyric Folksong Cluster," Ph.D. diss., Indiana University, 1970, 451.

28. Wolfe, notes to *Blue Moon of Kentucky,* 38.

29. Guthrie T. Meade with Dick Spottswood and Douglas S. Meade, *Country Music Sources: A Biblio-Discography of Commercially Recorded Traditional Music* (Chapel Hill: Southern Folklife Collection, University of North Carolina Libraries in Association with the John Edwards Memorial Forum, 2002), 455.

30. Randy Noles, *The Orange Blossom Boys: The Untold Story of Ervin T. Rouse, Chubby Wise and the World's Most Famous Fiddle Tune* (Centerstream: n.p., 2002).

31. Notes to *RCA Country Legends: Bill Monroe* (BMG 07863 65120 2, 2002).

DISCOGRAPHY, 1939–41

391125   MCA reissue of a radio broadcast on WSM
Grand Ole Opry, Nashville, Tenn.
Nov. 25, 1939

[1]   MULE SKINNER BLUES (Jimmie Rodgers-George Vaughn)   MCAD 4-11048, MCA3P-3256
Monroe-L

Johnnie Cleo "J.C." Davis: m   Bill Monroe: g   Art Wooten: f
                                       Walter Franklin "Amos" Garren: sb

401007   RCA Victor Bluebird session; "Mr. Frank Walker & Mr. Dan Hornsby present"   (RCA 07863-67450-2 notes)
Kimball Hotel, 30 N. Pryor St., Atlanta, Ga.
Oct. 7, 1940, 1–3:15 P.M.

BS 054518-1   MULE SKINNER BLUES (Rodgers)   BB-8568, MW-8861,   CAL 719, APM-0568, ACL-7059,
Monroe-L   20-3163   RO 25, RCA 2494-2-R,
                                                                  RCA 07863-67450-2,
                                                                  WW-1017 (CD 8),
                                                                  BMG 75517 43600 2,
                                                                  BMG 07863 65120 2, BF16399,
                                                                  C4K 90628

BS 054518-2   MULE SKINNER BLUES   [RCA Victor ledger sheet marked "HOLD"]

BS 054519-1   NO LETTER IN THE MAIL (Carlisle) BB-8611, MW-8862   CAL 719, RCA 2494-2-R,
Moody-L, Monroe-T   ACL-7059, RCA 07863-67450-2,
                                                                  BMG 07863 65120 2, BF16399

BS 054520-1   CRYIN' HOLY UNTO THE LORD (—)   BB-8611, MW-8862   LPV 569, RCA 2494-2-R,
Monroe-L, Wesbrooks-T, Magness-B, Moody-BS   MCAD 4-11048, BMG 2100-2-R
                                                                  RCA 07863-67450-2,
                                                                  BMG 07863 65120 2, BF16399

BS 054521-1   SIX WHITE HORSES (Moody)   BB-8568, MW-8861   CAL 719, ACL-7059, RCA 2494-2-R,
Moody-L   RCA 07863-67450-2, JAS 3519,
                                                                  BMG 75517 43600 2,
                                                                  BMG 07863 65120 2, BF16399

BS 054522-1   DOG HOUSE BLUES (Moody-King-Frank) BB-8692, MW-8863   CAL 719, ACL-7059, RCA 2494-2-R,
Monroe-L   RCA 07863-67450-2,
                                                                  BMG 07863 65120 2, BF16399

BS 054523-1	I WONDER IF YOU FEEL THE WAY I DO (—) Moody-L, Monroe-T	BB-8813, MW-8864	CAL 719, ACL-7059, RCA 2494-2-R, RCA 07863-67450-2, BMG 07863 65120 2, BF16399
BS 054524-1	KATY HILL (—) Instrumental	BB-8692, MW-8863, 20-3295	CAL 719, ACL-7059, RCA 2494-2-R, RCA 07863-67450-2, BMG 07863 65120 2, BF16399
BS 054525-1	TENNESSEE BLUES (Monroe) Instrumental	BB-8813, MW-8864	CAL 719, ACL-7059, RCA 2494-2-R, RCA 07863-67450-2, BMG 75517 43600 2, BMG 07863 65120 2, BF16399
BS 054525-2	TENNESSEE BLUES	[RCA Victor ledger sheet marked "spoiled"]	

Bill Monroe: m (except -18, -22): m   Clyde Moody (except Monroe   Tommy Magness (except -20, -25): f
on -18, -22): g
Bill "Cousin Wilbur" Wesbrooks (except -20): sb

411002   RCA Victor Bluebird Session; "Mr. Frank Walker & Mr. Dan Hornsby present" (RCA 07863-67450-2 notes)
Kimball Hotel, 30 N. Pryor St., Atlanta, Ga.
Oct. 2, 1941, 9:30 P.M.–12:30 A.M.

BS 071070	SHAKE MY MOTHER'S HAND FOR ME (arr. Eugene Wright) Monroe-L, Wesbrooks-T, Wooton-B, Pyle-BS[1]	BB-8953	LPV 569, RCA 2494-2-R, RCA 07863-67450-2, BMG 07863 65120 2, BF16399
BS 071071	WERE YOU THERE? (—) Monroe-L, Wesbrooks-T, Wooton-B, Pyle-BS	BB-8953	CPL 2-9507, RCA 2494-2-R, RCA 07863-67450-2, BMG 07863 65120 2, BF16399
BS 071072	BLUE YODEL NO. 7 (ANNIVERSARY BLUE YODEL) (Rodgers) Monroe-L	BB-8861, 20-3163	CAL 719, ACL-7059, RCA 2494-2-R, RCA 07863-67450-2, BMG 07863 65120 2, BF16399
BS 071073	THE COUPON SONG (—) Wesbrooks-L	BB-8893	RCA 2494-2-R, RCA 07863-67450-2, BMG 07863 65120 2, BF16399
BS 071074	ORANGE BLOSSOM SPECIAL (Rouse) Wooten-L,[2] Monroe-T	BB-8893	CAL 719, ACL-7059, CPL 2-0466, LPM 6015, RCA 2494-2-R, RCA 07863-67450-2, BMG 07863 65120 2, BF16399, SA 06076-84600-2

BS 071075	HONKY TONK SWING (Monroe) Instrumental	BB-8988	CAL 719, ACL-7059, RCA 2494-2-R, RCA 07863-67450-2, BMG 07863 65120 2, BF16399
BS 071076	IN THE PINES (McMichen) Wesbrooks-L, Monroe-T	BB-8861	CAL 719, ACL-7059, APM-0586, RCA 2494-2-R, RCA 07863-67450-2, BMG 07863 65120 2, BF16399
BS 071077	BACK UP AND PUSH (—) Instrumental	BB-8988, 20-3295	CAL 719, ACL-7059, RCA 2494-2-R, RCA 07863-67450-2, MCAD 4-11048, BMG 07863 65120 2, BF16399

Bill Monroe: m   Pete Pyle: g   Art Wooten: f (except -70, -71, -75)
                                 Bill Wesbrooks: sb (except -70 and -71)

Notes

1. The baritone and bass parts for the two hymns (-70 and -71) are speculative. They could just as well be Pyle-B, Wooton-BS. See Pete Pyle's comments in *Bluegrass Unlimited* (March 1978): 22.

2. We have followed Billy Altman's notes on voices and instrumentation on page 2 of his notes to RCA 2494-2-R, *Mule Skinner Blues,* except for "Orange Blossom Special," where we've guessed that the lead vocal is by Art Wooten (who also does most of the spoken parts). Altman lists Pyle as a vocalist, quoting Neil V. Rosenberg's *Bluegrass: A History* (Urbana: University of Illinois Press, 1985), 54, but that is an error, for Pyle indicates he sang only on the hymns because of a contract problem.

3

"TRUE LIFE BLUES": 1942–45

About two months after Bill Monroe's second Atlanta session the Japanese attacked Pearl Harbor and America was swept into World War II. Although few foresaw the full impact of the war at the time, it gave birth to several external forces that would seriously affect Monroe's developing music. His Victor producer, Frank Walker, left RCA Victor to become the head of the V-Disc program that released a long series of pop and jazz recordings designed for use in the armed forces. A shortage in shellac meant that record companies had fewer supplies with which to make records. Gasoline rationing meant that daily touring had to be curtailed or reconfigured. The draft was hanging over the heads of every musician under thirty-five (and later, forty), and many were marking time until being called up. Starting on August 1, 1942, American Federation of Musicians president James Petrillo called his union out on strike and refused to let them record. The ban, which meant that no records could be made by the major companies, Victor and Columbia, lasted, for them, until November 11, 1944.

Bill Monroe would not be able to go back into the recording studio for more than three years—years in which his music underwent crucial changes that moved it ever more toward bluegrass as we know it today. There is substantial difference between the sound of the 1940–41 Atlanta recordings and the sound of the Columbias he would start recording in 1945. During this period Monroe continued to hone his music, experiment with different instrumental combinations, write songs, and continue to develop a solo singing style. No commercial recordings document these years, and although Monroe toured and made a living during this time, and new musicians joined the band, there is little evidence of the sound of his music. The war years represent a long, dark tunnel—Monroe's 1941 Victor music went in one side and the sleek new Columbia music came out the other. Exactly what happened in that tunnel is, and perhaps should remain, one of the great mysteries of American music.

There are a few tantalizing clues. One is the commercial prewar records that remained in print and thus kept Monroe's music before the public. The June 1941 *Bluebird Complete Catalogue* listed two records by the Blue Grass Boys: B-8568 ("Mule Skinner" and "Six White Horses") and B-8611 ("No Letter" and "Cryin' Holy Unto the Lord"). Charlie Monroe, however, had five solo records listed. Even more surprising are the number of old Monroe Brothers Bluebirds still available. Under a major catalog entry, replete with photographs, are some twenty-five records (fifty titles), including such early ones as "What Would You Give?" and "My Long Journey Home." Between December 1940 and May 1942, Bluebird released Bill's new Atlanta recordings nearly every two months.[1] Although none were reviewed in the august pages of *Billboard,* they were obviously finding their way to their audiences.

When the Grand Ole Opry went on the NBC network in the fall of 1939, Monroe often appeared on the network segment, usually the Prince Albert show. We now know that Prince Albert (the R. J. Reynolds Tobacco Company) employed the William J. Esty Advertising Agency in New York to help market the Opry and monitor how the show sounded. As a result, WSM made a number of transcriptions of shows as they were being performed and sent these "air checks," as they were called, up to New York for the agency's approval. In the 1980s, a cache of them was discovered in the basement of the agency and eventually donated to the Country Music Foundation. The transcriptions, although not intended for public consumption, were commercially made recordings and offer the only real examples of the Blue Grass Boys during these years. A preliminary list includes:

11-25-39	"Mule Skinner Blues"	Bill Monroe
11-25-39	"Bile That Cabbage Down"	Bill Monroe
3-03-40	"Cumberland Gap"	
3-03-40	"Mule Skinner Blues"	
10-05-40	"Crying Holy Unto the Lord"	Bill Monroe and Blue Grass Boys
07-18-42	"Columbus Stockade Blues"	
07-18-42	"He'll Set Your Fields on Fire"	
12-12-42	"California Blues"	
12-12-42	"Did You Ever Go Sailing?"	Blue Grass Quartet
06-09-43	"Kitty Clyde"	
06-09-43	"Weary Traveler"	
06-09-43	"Were You There?"	

This list is significant because actual recordings of these tunes exist in air-check recordings of Opry shows from the specific dates indicated. In 1994 the earliest of these air checks was reissued in John Rumble's four-CD MCA Monroe retrospective. Although the others are for archival use only, they offer a glimpse into Monroe's Opry performances of the war years. With "Mule Skinner" in current release by Bluebird, it seems only natural that it would become a standard on the network portion of the Opry. "Bile That Cabbage Down" is a familiar fiddle breakdown (usually titled "Bile *Them* . . .) sometimes credited to one of Monroe's favorite fiddlers, Clayton McMichen. Monroe always liked to claim that his Blue Grass Quartet was the first gospel quartet on the Opry, which is quite likely accurate (chapter 2). The John Daniel Quartet would emerge as an all-gospel group later, but in the early 1940s Monroe had the field to himself. Two songs on the list—"Crying Holy Unto the Lord" and "Were You There?"—had been recorded at the Atlanta sessions. The Monroe Brothers recorded "He'll Set Your Fields on Fire" as a duo, but it was now offered in a full quartet arrangement. "Did You Ever Go Sailing?" was a sprightly Albert E. Brumley tune and a favorite with quartets. It had never been recorded by Monroe nor was it to be later.

Of the remaining songs featuring Monroe, "Weary Traveler," a song by Cliff Carlisle and Bobby Gregory, was one he would not get around to recording until 1975. "Columbus Stockade Blues" came from the white bluesmen Tom Darby and Jimmie Tarlton in the 1920s, was later re-popularized by Jimmie Davis, and then was recorded by Monroe in 1962. "California Blues" is Rodgers's "Blue Yodel No. 4." Monroe would record a "Blue Yodel No. 4" for Columbia in 1946, but that was in fact Rodgers's "Blue Yodel No. 3"—or at least the first three verses of it. "Kitty Clyde," another Monroe Brothers piece (they called it "Katy Cline") that Bill preserved, was a familiar North Carolina ballad that one collector described as "the national song of the highlanders."[2]

Other lists of tunes from the war years are scattered in a few copies of the actual Opry programs for specific nights. By 1940 the show was being very careful about obtaining clearances and broadcast reporting, and Vito Pellettieri kept track of what everyone sang. The schedules, which seldom permitted variation, were printed on the weekly programs sold at the show. They give Monroe's repertoire and identify the performers with him at the time. The earliest extant program listing is from June 9, 1943:

"Kitty Clyde"	Bill Monroe
"Weary Traveler"	Bill Monroe
"Were You There?"	Quartet
"My Dixie Home"	"Bill and Lester"

Monroe's set list at this performance deserves comment. "Kitty Clyde" and "Weary Traveler" have already been discussed. "Were You There?" had been recorded in Atlanta in 1941 and released by Victor in March 1942. The names of the performers of "My Dixie Home," a song the Monroe Brothers recorded as "I Am Thinking Tonight of the Old Folks" that Monroe would later do onstage with Lester Flatt and Earl Scruggs in the band, represent a puzzle. The program lists vocals by "Bill and Lester," which suggests Lester Flatt. Yet conventional history has Flatt not joining the band until late 1944 or early 1945 and working with Charlie Monroe until then. Did he come over to try out with Bill in June 1943, or did another "Lester" on the show sing an occasional duet with Monroe? No candidates immediately suggest themselves, and the reference remains a tantalizing mystery. The second program listing comes from a year later, on July 14, 1944:

"I'm Rollin' On"	Bill Monroe
"Put My Little Shoes Away"	Bill Monroe
"Big Ball in Town"	Bill Monroe
"Bile 'Em Cabbage Down"	Chubby Wise (f)
"Live and Let Live"	Curly, Bill, and Clyde
"Why Don't You Cry Little Darling?"	Sally Ann
"He'll Set Your Fields"	Bluegrass Quartet
"Hot Corn, Cold Corn"	String Beans and "Cedric"
"Kentucky Waltz"	Clyde Moody

This Opry performance includes the old Monroe Brothers pieces "I'm Rollin' On" and "He'll Set Your Fields [on Fire]." Bill sings "Put Your Little Shoes Away," which he would record for Decca in 1954, and the western-swing favorite "Big Ball's in Town," which he would record in 1962 as "Big Ball in Brooklyn." "Live and Let Live," the Wiley Walker and Gene Sullivan favorite that had been originally set for the second Atlanta session, was one Bill would re-record in 1961 although as a duet, not as the trio heard here.

Other pieces on the program from this date show that Monroe still followed the venerable tradition of spotlighting individual members of the band. "Bile Them Cabbage Down" featured fiddler Chubby Wise, "Why Don't You Cry Little Darling?"

was sung by female vocalist Sally Ann, "Hot Corn, Cold Corn" was rendered by the comic duo of String Beans and Cedric (David Akeman and Howard Watts), and "Kentucky Waltz" was performed by guitarist and lead vocalist Clyde Moody. We know that this song, long associated with Monroe, was first heard as part of Moody's repertoire in the Blue Grass Boys because the back of a souvenir photograph of Monroe's 1943 band includes the words to "Kentucky Waltz," which is described as "featured by Clyde Moody."[3]

Clearly, the personnel of the Blue Grass Boys had changed considerably by July 1944. In fact, by 1942, with the exception of the intermittent tenure of Clyde Moody and the bass playing and comedy of Bill Wesbrooks, the rest of the group from the Atlanta sessions was gone. Who were the new band members?

One, "Curly," featured in the trio on "Live and Let Live," was Curly Bradshaw, a journeyman guitarist, singer, and harmonica specialist. A native of Greensburg, Kentucky, Bradshaw gained radio experience as a member of Uncle Henry's Kentucky Mountaineers over WHAS in Louisville. When that band moved to Chicago to be on the network, Bradshaw decided not to follow and moved to WSM, where he joined Monroe in late 1941. After the war, Bradshaw followed a solo career and recorded for a Kentucky label, Acme. In the 1940s he sang duets with Monroe and even some trios with Monroe and Clyde Moody, but he was most often heard (and depicted in band photographs) as a harmonica player.[4]

By July 1944 the Blue Grass Boys had seen a dizzying array of fiddlers since Art Wooten's departure in 1942. At times Monroe used an Opry regular, including the Kentuckian Mac McGar—known for his fast, slick fiddling with Jack Shook's Missouri Mountaineers—and Dickson County veteran Floyd Ethridge, who came from the same part of west Tennessee as Fiddlin' Arthur Smith. For a time in 1942 and 1943 the fiddler's job was given to Howard "Big Howdy" Forrester, another young fiddler from the Dickson County area. Howdy had attended high school in Nashville and as a boy began playing in local square dance bands. A versatile fiddler who would later become a mainstay of Roy Acuff's band, Forrester worked with Georgia Slim Rutland over radio in Texas and Oklahoma, pioneering a fast, intricate, western-swing, twin-fiddling style. When war broke out, Forrester knew he would be drafted soon and moved back to Tennessee to bide his time. "We did, but I still had a few months left and I worked with Bill Monroe before I was drafted," Howdy recalled.[5] Several fiddlers followed Forrester, who left in March 1943. Tommy Magness filled in briefly. Also with the band briefly was a North Carolina singer and bandleader, Carl Story. Although he was later best known for his work as a guitar-playing bluegrass gospel singer, Story had a heritage of western North Carolina fiddling and was having trouble keeping his own band of draft-age musicians together. He remained with Monroe until being inducted in October 1943.

None of these various musicians made commercial records with the band so there is no way of knowing how they sounded or what effect they may have had on the Monroe sound. It is worth noting, though, that Forrester and Ethridge played the kind of intricate, long-bow style of Arthur Smith, whereas Story and McGar both favored the older, short-bow (as Monroe called it, "jiggy bow") style. Forrester's work in western swing and twin fiddles might well have planted some potent seeds.

In the spring of 1943 another fiddler, an important musician who brought new ideas into the band, had joined: Chubby Wise (1915–96). Born Robert Russell Dees in Lake City in central Florida, Chubby learned fiddling from his father although his first instrument was the banjo—"old drop-thumb style," as he recalled.[6] In his early teens he met a Florida state champion fiddler, Bryan Purcell, who played long-bow style and taught much of it to young Wise. Other influences were Clayton McMichen and Fiddlin' Arthur Smith, the reigning kings of the instrument in the late 1930s. After he married and moved to Jacksonville, Florida, Chubby also became friends with the well-known show fiddler Erwin Rouse, composer of the "The Orange Blossom Special." By 1938 he was in Gainesville, playing with the Jubilee Hillbillies. This working radio and dance band played a rich variety of music, from traditional hoedowns to current Bob Wills favorites to pop numbers like "Stardust." With them, Chubby developed a versatile and eclectic style that was part swing, part blues, and part pop.

In late March 1943, as the Jubilee Hillbillies were being decimated by the draft and defense work, Chubby heard Bill Monroe announce on his Opry slot that Howdy Forrester was leaving for the navy. Chubby took a train to Nashville and auditioned for Monroe backstage at the Opry, playing "Katy Hill" and backing Monroe on "Footprints in the Snow." Impressed with his technical ability if not his style, Monroe hired him on the spot. Monroe recalled, "He'd been in a swing band and he just couldn't fiddle. He was fighting to get it like Howdy had it. Howdy played some pretty bluegrass music."[7] Moreover, "[Howdy] was the first man with me to play double stops."[8]

Chubby had big shoes to fill, and Monroe worried whether he could adapt his swing style to the older mountain style of Art Wooten and Tommy Magness. For a time, Monroe carried other veteran fiddlers like Floyd Ethridge and Carl Story to help teach Chubby the bluegrass style, and in later years Chubby

also credited Monroe for teaching him. "I believe in giving credit where credit is due," he said, "and Mr. Bill Monroe taught me to play bluegrass. He started me down the bluegrass trail."[9] Chubby became so adept that he would remain with Monroe off and on until 1950. Years later, when asked to compare Chubby with Howdy, Monroe said, "Chubby's a little more a lonesome type of fiddler, and he plays some blues in it. . . . Chubby could beat Howdy on a song, but Howdy would have beat Chubby on a fiddle piece like 'Cotton-Eyed Joe.'"[10]

During much of this time, and for many years afterward, Chubby was associated with "The Orange Blossom Special," although a good deal of controversy exists over whether he had a role in composing it. For five decades Chubby claimed to have written or co-written the song, but more recent research by a Florida journalist, Randy Noles, has uncovered several flaws in Chubby's familiar account. Noles concludes, "While it is impossible to conclude that the 'Special' is totally devoid of Chubby's influence . . . there is no compelling evidence that his role was significant enough to earn the designation 'uncredited co-author.'"[11] No one doubts, however, that Chubby popularized the piece far more than its originators, the Rouse Brothers, did.

Before Howdy Forrester shipped out in 1943, Monroe hired his wife, Wilene Russell Forrester, who worked professionally as an accordion player and singer, using Sally Ann as her stage name. She and Howdy met in Tulsa and married in 1940, and when he took a job with Monroe, she accompanied him to Nashville. When Forrester went into the navy Sally Ann became a regular member of the band—a way, some assumed, of ensuring that Howdy returned to the band after the war although Monroe denied that charge. In the face of much speculation he explained in later years that he wanted an accordion in his band because his mother had played the instrument at Rosine while he was growing up. In all probability, however, Monroe's mother played a small one- or two-row button accordion popular in the rural Midwest and not the larger piano accordion with keys rather than buttons that was popular with so many country and western bands in the 1940s.

In adding Sally Ann, Monroe was most likely keeping up with trends he saw developing on the music scene. Accordions were rapidly becoming fixtures in country and western bands in the 1940s and were far more common with radio bands than either before or since. On the Grand Ole Opry itself, Jack Shook's Missouri Mountaineers had featured accordians since the mid-1930s, and Pee Wee King's Golden West Cowboys had spotlighted them since 1938 (and King's band, with its Camel Caravan tours to armed forces camps, was perhaps the most popular act on the show in the early 1940s). On other country shows and records, women like Hazel Cole (of Grady and Hazel fame, who wrote "Tramp on the Street") used an accordion as did the incredibly popular band of Doc and Chickie Williams over the *Wheeling Jamboree.* Even Roy Acuff's hard-core string band the Smoky Mountain Boys had recently added an accordion, played by Jimmy Riddle, around the time Monroe hired Forrester.[12]

The sources of Sally Ann's music have been explored by Murphy Henry, who found that she was born Wilene Russell in Avant, Oklahoma, near Tulsa, on December 20, 1922.[13] She took piano lessons as a girl; listened to her stepfather play the fiddle; and, at Cain's Academy in Tulsa, she also danced to Bob Wills's western swing. She attended a small religious college at Bolivar, Missouri, later home of the Ozark Jubilee, where she was remembered as the "Hillbilly singer" of the school. In May 1939, when she was sixteen, she returned to Tulsa, where she met her future husband. Soon both Forresters were appearing on the *Saddle Mountain Round-Up* over KVOO, a sort of Opry imitation started by former Opry star Herald Goodman. They eventually found their way to Nashville, where they lived with Howdy's mother and worked on the Opry tent show run by Jamup and Honey. Among the other acts were Uncle Dave Macon and Bill Monroe.

In none of these settings, however, was there anyone who might have inspired Wilene to play the accordion. She was a trained, gifted piano player and apparently applied that talent to the accordion on her own. She thus became the "girl singer" with Monroe's band, and it was probably Monroe who gave her the stage name, Sally Ann, in deference to the old fiddle tune he liked.[14] In addition to vocal solos, she sang in trios and quartets and played an occasional solo on the instrumentals like "Blue Grass Special."

Listeners today tend to think of the accordion's role in a band as keeping a gentle rhythm by using the buttons on the bass side, by playing sustained chords in the background of vocals, and occasionally, on slower numbers, a single-note solo break. But Opry bands of 1940s, especially the Missouri Mountaineers and King's Golden West Cowboys, featured the accordion with surprising effectiveness in hot, up-tempo breakdowns like "Up Jumped the Devil." The instrument, in other words, could hold its own in a circle of string-band solos. There is a good deal of evidence to suggest that Sally Ann, grounded in Tulsa swing, was capable of playing hot as well as sweet. Between 1946 and 1951, after she left Monroe, Sally Ann played numerous solos in a series of now-rare films, *Jamboree* and *Smoky Mountain Jamboree,* with Rambling Tommy Scott. On tunes like "Buffalo Gals" and "Hand Me Down My Walking Cane" she takes imaginative, jazzlike solos, often starting with a series of single-note runs and then building to a dramatic series of block chords—very much like a jazz piano player building a solo. Her solos do not parse the melody but use the song's chord pattern to create a new but related melody line. She also understood the role of dynamics in the solo and quite often created a sound at the end of hers that was not all that different from the sudden, explosive "chop" Monroe used in some solos. Sally Ann may have been one of the first of Monroe's band members to try take-off solos (ones that depart from the melody). It seems likely that she formed the technique by the time she came to Nashville from Tulsa, and it is also plausible that she might have influenced some of Monroe's technique.

By July 1944 comedy in the Blue Grass Boys, which had first been done by Cousin Wilbur Wesbrooks, was being handled by a team: "String Beans" and "Cedric." Cedric was bass player Howard Watts, who used the stage name Cedric Rainwater. "String Beans," billed in later years as "Stringbean," who introduced the five-string banjo in the Blue Grass Boys, was David Akeman, a long, tall, ungainly lad who also doubled as a baseball player and comedian. Later to win national fame on the syndicated television show *Hee-Haw,* Akeman (1914–73) was another Kentucky boy, coming from the hamlet of Annville in Jackson County in the eastern end of the state. It was a region famed for its large number of classic, Kentucky, old-time frailing banjoists like Buell Kazee, B. F. Shelton, Dick Burnett, and Lily May Ledford.

String Beans watched his father play at country dances, and when he was twelve he traded a little hen and a banty rooster for his first banjo. By 1935 he was playing for local radio star Asa Martin, learning many of his classic tunes like "Crazy War" and "Suicide Blues," and also playing semi-pro baseball around central Kentucky. "He was a pretty good ball player," recalled his brother Robert. "He was a pitcher, and one that could never be struck out. They might catch him out or they might walk him, but they never could strike him out. He'd always hit it."[15]

Baseball, String's brother Robert Akeman thinks, is what attracted Monroe to String. "Bill come up here and got him when he was playing on WLAP and living at Winchester; Bill went up there and got him to play baseball for his team. He first hired him as a baseball pitcher. As far as I know, Bill didn't even know he played banjo when he hired him. After he found out he could play, he went to playing with Bill's band."[16] In July 1942 String joined Monroe's band on the Opry.

Robert Akeman's theory presents some problems. Bill Monroe didn't begin his own tent shows, with which his baseball teams were associated, until 1943.[17] According to Tom Ewing, it was not until in 1944 that he organized the team from his show to challenge local teams before the concerts.[18] In later years Monroe would downplay the idea that he wanted String mainly because of his skills with a ball. "Stringbeans was the first banjo picker with me," he recalled. "What I wanted was the sound of the banjo, because I'd heard it back in Kentucky, and I wanted it with the fiddle and the rest of the instruments. So Stringbeans gave us the touch of the banjo, and he was a good comedian."[19]

How Akeman's banjo playing sounded in 1942 is unknown; his first published recordings are from the February 1945 session with Monroe. In that session he used his right thumb and index finger to pluck the strings—the two-finger style many of his contemporaries played in Kentucky and elsewhere in Appalachia. He would continue for the rest of his career to play some pieces in that style, but in his post-Monroe years on the Opry he also used the old "frailing" (or "clawhammer") style in which strings are brushed rather than plucked. Whether he played that way before joining Monroe is unknown, but the fact Stringbean used the style later might have been because of the immense popularity of Grandpa Jones and his frailing songs like "Old Rattler." Like Uncle Dave Macon, another banjo player on the Opry, Akeman may have known and used plucking as well as brushing styles when he joined the Blue Grass Boys. It's possible that Monroe asked Stringbean to play the two-finger style because Monroe was familiar with Wade Mainer's successful two-finger work and thought it would be appropriate for the sound he wanted in the Blue Grass Boys at the time.

Monroe appreciated good comedy, and as soon as he joined the band String and Bill Wesbrooks ("Cousin Wilbur") became a team and regularly did comedy routines during tent show performances. One involved String and Wilbur trying to outbrag each other about who grew the tallest crops or the biggest beans. To localize the joke one would pretend to be a farmer from wherever they were playing and the other from nearby. "String could never remember the name of the town we were in," recalled Wesbrooks years later:

> Right in the middle of the act, he'd get the audience laughing and then he'd ask me out of the corner of his mouth, "What's the name of this town?" and I'd tell him. One night in Arkansas I really fixed Stringbean up. The name of the town was Rector, Arkansas. And Stringbean asks me out of the corner of his mouth, "What's the name of this town?" so I told him it was Rectum, Arkansas. That's when Stringbean up and said, "Right here, folks, right here in Rectum, Arkansas." And he liked to wreck the audience—they must have laughed for fifteen minutes. And I got

so tickled that Stringbean got broke up. . . . I looked backstage, and there was Bill Monroe and Honey Wild [who often traveled with him on a tent show] and they were backstage of the tent lying down on the ground and holding their stomachs.[20]

It's not clear how much Monroe saw String as a comedian or a ball player and how much as a banjoist. He apparently continued to interview other possible banjoists, including, in 1943, Don Reno. But photographs from the era show that String seldom posed in any kind of comic garb (as did Wesbrooks, for instance) but dressed in the shirt, tie, and jodhpurs like other Blue Grass Boys. In earlier band photographs he's holding a Gibson RB-11 banjo similar to that shown with Scruggs in his first pictures with Monroe. In his final pictures with Monroe, taken after Lester Flatt joined the band in 1945, he sports the Vega Tu-ba-phone banjo that he would use for the rest of his life. Whatever the case, another banjoist took String's job in the Blue Grass Boys when he left the group.

By July 1944 Bill Wesbrooks was no longer with the Blue Grass Boys. When he left around the end of 1943, Chubby Wise had arranged for a friend from Florida, now living in Nashville, to audition as Monroe's bassist: Howard Watts. Watts (1913–70), a native of Monticello, Florida, had been playing professionally since the mid-1930s. In 1938 he took the name "Arizona Slim" and teamed with James "Tex" Willis of Moultrie, Georgia. For the next three years they played together in their own band and with Dock Williams and the Santa Fe Trailriders. It was during this time that he met Chubby Wise. Watts came to Nashville in 1941, following the example of his friend Willis, who played bass with Paul Howard and his Arkansas Cotton Pickers. By the end of 1941 he was playing guitar and doing comedy with Howard as Arizona Slim.

When Watts joined Monroe they devised a new stage name, one he would keep for the rest of his career: "C. Cedric Rainwater." Watts, a seasoned performer with three years of experience on the Grand Ole Opry, quickly proved himself not just as a gifted comedian but also as a catcher for the Blue Grass Boys baseball band. Most important, he was a skilled bass player and vocalist who did much to shape the sound of Monroe's music between 1944 and 1948.

That this was a band in which individual performers were highlighted in each show is made even more apparent by another set of song lists created Nebraskan Dick Hill.[21] This teenage Opry fan faithfully kept a detailed diary of Opry shows he could catch, listing who played what songs when. During the fall of 1944, Hill listened to WSM's live country music shows on eleven Saturday nights, typically logging the preliminary shows from 7 P.M. and the Opry proper from 8 to its end at midnight or until he "had to go to bed."[22]

On his first Saturday's log Hill gave consecutive numbers to the entire repertoire of fifty-nine separate Opry performances. In following weeks he numbered the half-hour and fifteen-minute segments as if they were separate programs, as their sponsors intended. Each segment was introduced by the sponsor's theme sung by the featured performers.[23]

During the first half hour (8–8:30) of the Opry, sponsored by Purina ("Pureena" in Hill's idiosyncratic spelling), Monroe and the Blue Grass Boys were heard regularly, usually performing three of the eleven pieces heard during that sponsor's slot. Monroe's own fifteen-minute show came on at 10 to open the WSM Opry's third hour. There are still bluegrass fans who recall Monroe's Wallrite theme, heard directly following the half-hour Prince Albert tobacco segment that was broadcast nationwide over the NBC network.[24] The network segment gave broad national exposure to those heard over it, but during the months Hill was logging the show Monroe was not heard on it. Still, his placement in the WSM broadcasts before and after it indicates Monroe's considerable stature within the Opry lineup. Hill's list shows that Monroe's band included the same performers as in July:

[October 7, 1944]
8–8:30 brought to us by Purina
  4. If I Had My Life to Live Over (song by Clyde Muttey)
  6. Role On Muddy Roll On (didn't get name)
  8. Traveler Blues (sung by Bill Monroe)
10:00–10:15 by Wallrite (wallpaper)
40. East Rains Blues (sung by Curly Bradshaw)
41. Put Me in Your Pocket (sung by Sally Ann)
42. Fox Chase (played on mouth harp by Curly Bradshaw)
43. I Heard My Mother Call My Name (Blue Grass Quartette)

[October 21, 1944]
8:00–8:30
  1. Good Ole Mountain Dew (played by Blue Grass Boys)
  4. Dog House Blues (sung by Bill Monroe)
  9. Little Liza Jane (Bill Monroe and Blue Grass Boys)
10:00–10:15
  1. Good by Ole' Pal (Bill Monroe)
  2. Put Me in Your Pocket (Sally Ann)
  3. Shine on Me (Blue Grass Quartette)
  4. I Was Wrong (Clyde Muty)
  5. Mouth harp no. (Curly Bradshaw)

[November 4, 1944]
10:00–15 by Wallrite
  1. Goodnight Soldier (Sally Ann)
  2. I Heard My Mother Call My Name in Prayer
    (B. Grass Quartette)
  3. Home in San Antoine (Clyde Mutey)
  4. Fast Train Blues "mouth harpe" (Curly Bradshaw)
  5. How Many Biscuits Can You Eat
    (Cedric Rainwater and Stringbean)

[November 11, 1944]
8:00–30 by Pureena
  1. Shady Grove (Bill Monroe and Blue G. Boys)
  4. I Traced Her Little Footprints in the Snow
    (Bill Monroe)
  9. Rollin On (B. Monroe and Bluegrass Boys)
11. I Was Wrong (Clyde Mutey)
10:00–[10:15] by Wallrite
  1. Katty Wise (fiddle tune) (Chubby Wise)
  2. I'll Have to Live and Learn (Sally Ann)
  3. Did You Ever Go a Sailing (Blue Grass Quartette)
  4. Honkey Tonkey Sween (mandolin tune) (Bill Monroe)
  5. Live and Let Live (three men sang)

[November 18, 1944]
8:00–8:30 brought to you by Pureena
  1. Old Joe Clark (Bill Monroe and Blue Grass Boys)
  4. Mule Skinner Blues (Bill Monroe) Hit tune of the week
10. John Henry (Bill Monroe and B. Grass Boys)
10:00–10:15 by Wallrite
  1. Suiside Blues (Stringbean)
  2. Bury Me Beneath the Willow (Sally Ann)
  3. Shake My Mother's Hand for Me (Blue Grass Quartette)
  4. Maple on the Hill (Curly Bradshaw) harp
  5. Goodbye Ole Pal (Bill Monroe)

[November 25, 1944]
8:00–30 Grand Ole Opry by Pureena
  1. Good Ole Mt. Dew (Bill Monroe and Blue G. Boys)
  4. The Weary Traveler (Bill Monroe) Good!!!
  8. Roll On, Muddy, Roll On (B. M. and Blue G. Boys)
8:30–9:00 by Crazy Crystals
  8. Six White Horses (Clyde Mutey) Clyde Mutey is a member
    of the Blue Grass Boys
10:00–15 by Wallrite
  1. Fiddle Tune (Bill Monroe and B.G.B.)

2. Put Me in Your Pocket (Sally Ann)

3. Where the Soul Never Dies (hymn) (Bill Monroe)

4. Harmonica Tune (Curly Bradshaw)

5. How Many Biscuits Can You Eat (Cedric and Stringbeans)

[December 2, 1944]

8:00–8:30 by Pureena

2. Fiddle Tune (Blue Grass Boys)

3. If I Had My Life to Live Over (Clyde Mutey)

5. Blue Yodel No. 7 (Bill Monroe)

9. Foggy Mt. Top (B. Monroe and B.G.B.)

10:00–10:15 by Wallrite

1. Careless Love (Harmonica) (Curly Bradshaw)

2. Sweet Is the Flowers in May Time (Sally Ann)

3. This World Is Not My Home (Bill Monroe and Coon Hunters)

4. Pretty Little Pink (Cedric Rainwater and Stringbean)

5. Molly and Cinbrook (Bill Monroe)

[December 9, 1944]

8:00–8:30 GRAND OLE OPRY by Pureena

1. Black Eyed Susan (Blue Gras [sic] Boys)

4. How Can You Be Mean to Me (Bill Monroe)

10. I Don't Love Nobody (Bill Monroe)

10:00–10:15 by Wallrite

1. The Girl in Blue Bonnet [sic] Band (Coon Hunters)

2. Sailors Plea (Sally Ann)

3. We'll Have a New Life (Blue Grass Quartette)

4. Maple on the Hill (Curly Bradshaw)

5. My Gal's a High Born Lady (Cedric R. and Stringbean)

[December 16, 1944]

10:00–15 by Wallrite

1. Mow Them Cabbage Down (Cubby Wise)

2. Burry Me Neneath the Weeping Willow Tree (Sally Ann)

3. What Would You Give in Exchange for Soul (Coon Hunters)

4. Mossuria Waltz (Curly Bradshaw)

5. Suicide Blues (Stringbeans)

Hill's diaries reflect his perceptions of the broadcasts. In the Purina segments, Monroe and his band were identified as such, and all but a few of the solos that Hill lists for Bill Monroe during his Purina appearances can be tied to his recorded repertoire. "Dog House Blues," "Honky Tonk Swing," "Mule Skinner Blues," and "Blue Yodel No. 7" were all available on then-new Bluebird records. He would soon be recording others for Columbia: "Footprints in the Snow" and "Goodbye Old

Pal" at his 1945 session.[25] In 1947, he recorded "Molly and Tenbrooks." "Travelin' Blues," another Jimmie Rodgers piece, and "Weary Traveler" would appear on Decca/MCA recordings made in 1951 and 1975.

The many performances Hill described as by Bill Monroe and the Blue Grass Boys or just the Blue Grass Boys, usually during the Purina segments, also include some material associated with recordings. "Foggy Mountain Top" had been done by the Monroe Brothers (as "On Some Foggy Mountain Top"). Bill would perform it again in 1964 with Doc Watson and record it in 1973 with his son James. Other Monroe Brothers pieces listed include "Rollin' On" and "Roll on Buddy, Roll On" (Hill's "Roll on Muddy"), which he would record for Decca in 1964. Many of the others attributed by Hill to Monroe and the band were traditional pieces that have words associated with them and may or may not have been sung. Of these, Monroe would later record for Decca "John Henry" (in 1954, with words), "Shady Grove" (in 1961, with words), and "Old Joe Clark" (in 1962, as an instrumental). Others, like "Mountain Dew," "Little Liza Jane," and Black Eyed Susan," are familiar pieces that have been recorded by many but not Monroe.

With the Wallrite segments, it is only in retrospect that we can tell that those performers he identified individually were in fact part of Monroe's band. This is not very different from the Opry programs, which also named individuals instead of the entire band. Indeed, Monroe would follow this practice to some extent for the rest of his career, carrying additional separately billed performers with the band—like his daughter Melissa, a vocalist, or dancer Jackie Christian—and individually advertising band members like Vasser Clements or Benny Williams when he thought doing so might draw a larger crowd. Their pieces did not usually become part of Monroe's recorded repertoire.

Thus the nine pieces attributed to Curly Bradshaw are well-known standards like "Careless Love" and "Maple on the Hill," mainly done as harmonica instrumentals. Sally Ann had a regular solo spot on each program, often singing venerable sentimental songs like "Bury Me beneath the Willow" and "Sweeter Than the Flowers." One particular favorite, "Put Me in Your Pocket," was about separations caused by war. Of the songs she sang during this period, only "The Sailor's Plea" would later appear (in 1951 as a vocal solo by Bill) on a Monroe recording.

Clyde Moody's ("Mutey" to Hill) solos did not appear in Monroe's later phonograph repertoire, but he did sing "Six White Horses," which he'd recorded in 1940 with Bill. Unlike other members of the band, Moody—soon to become an independent member of the Opry cast—appeared as a soloist on other sponsors' segments.

String Beans's solos and comic duets with bassist Cedric Rainwater often featured traditional frolic songs like "Pretty Little Pink" and "How Many Biscuits Can You Eat?" that were widely performed on country radio during these years. With these songs, as with the serious songs and instrumentals done by other individual band members, familiarity was an important factor.

Hill identified three pieces as being by "Bill Monroe and the Coon Hunters" or the "Coon Hunters," but where he got that band name is not known. In any case, all three pieces were eventually in Monroe's recorded repertoire. "Girl in Blue Bonnet Band" was Hill's hearing of "The Girl in the Blue Velvet Band," which Monroe would record in 1949 for Columbia. The other two are both religious pieces that had been done by the Monroe Brothers and which Bill would later record again for Decca: "What Would You Give?" and "This World Is Not My Home."

The Blue Grass Quartet and its gospel music was an important and unique part of Monroe's music and was heard on every Wallrite segment. "There wasn't a quartet on the Opry before us," he told Jim Rooney, and there had indeed been no formal gospel quartet on the show.[26] That was in in spite of the fact that quartets had been a staple in gospel music for more than a decade, with well-known radio stars like the Rangers, the Stamps-Baxter Quartet, the MacDonald Quartet, and black groups such as the Golden Gate Quartet. Although some groups sang with a piano, others (such as the Gates) were starting to sing either a capella or with a guitar. In the case of the Blue Grass Quartet, most of the time the accompaniment was a guitar or a guitar and mandolin.

Although Monroe's Blue Grass Quartet was indeed the first such exclusively gospel group on the Opry, by 1944 the John Daniel Quartet, which did nothing but gospel, was winning a nationwide reputation on that show. Daniel, who came out of the music schools of James D. Vaughan, was a formally trained singer and composer, and just what interplay occurred between his group and Monroe's is unknown. Some of the early repertoire of the Blue Grass Quartet is known, however. In 1944 their songs included "I Heard My Mother Call My Name," a 1919 convention book song by Stamps-Baxter veteran Eugene Bartlett; "Shine on Me," an old Pentecostal song popularized by Ernest Phipps and his Holiness Quartet; "Did You Ever Go Sailing? (Down the River of Memory)," a new song from the pen of Albert E. Brumley, composer of "I'll Fly Away"; "Shake

My Mother's Hand for Me," the Thomas Dorsey favorite that Monroe had already recorded; "Where the Soul Never Dies," William Golden's turn-of-the-century song that had been recorded by the Blue Sky Boys; and "We'll Have a New Life," another new song that emerged as a southern gospel standard that Monroe would soon try at his first Columbia session. Few were ever to be recorded by Monroe, although he kept some like "Did You Ever Go Sailing?" in his repertoire for years after.

When the pieces noted by Dick Hill in the fall of 1944 are totaled, there are forty-nine, excluding repetitions and nontitled items. By the end of his career Monroe would have recorded nearly half—twenty-three—but at this time only eleven had been recorded. That was soon to change. The June 1941 catalog of Victor's Bluebird records listed two by Bill but five by brother Charlie's band. Because many of Charlie's records were actually listed as "Monroe's Boys," fans easily confused the two. Some even assumed that "Monroe's Boys" was in fact the "Monroe Brothers."

Possibly because of this honest confusion—and possibly from continued jealousy of Charlie—Bill decided within weeks of his second Atlanta session that he would change record companies. He began discussions with Art Satherley, a dapper Englishman and A&R head of the American Recording Corporation, who released titles on Okeh, Columbia, Vocalion, and other labels. Born in Bristol, England, in 1889, Satherley came to the United States in his mid-twenties to work as a secretary for Thomas Edison. In 1918 he began working for Paramount, an independent record company in Wisconsin. He developed an expertise in both black and white southern music—what was then called "race and hillbilly." By 1929 he went to work for the American Record Corporation, which later became Columbia Records. In the 1930s Satherley was responsible for recording artists like Bob Wills, Cliff and Bill Carlisle, Red Foley, Gene Autry, and Roy Acuff in addition to blues artists like Ma Rainey, Josh White, Big Bill Broonzy, and Memphis Minnie. By 1942 his roster was full of smooth-singing country cowboys and country crooners, but Satherley still liked the old mountain sound. As he would tell his singers, "Sing it in the extreme. We don't care about trick ways of phrasing or hot licks; we concentrate on the emotions."[27]

Satherley had been to Nashville numerous times to deal with his popular new act Roy Acuff and other acts such as the Andrews Brothers and Slim Smith. Columbia was also home of the two biggest country recording stars of the time, Gene Autry and Bob Wills. Satherley and Monroe soon reached an agreement, and Monroe signed a one-year contract with the company on October 26, 1942. He would cut eight sides that would be released in the Okeh "Hillbilly" series, which also sported Acuff as well as Wills and Autry. Monroe would get one cent per side on 90 percent of record sales. This was about average for the time; a number of Columbia artists netted only a half cent per side. Reliable sales figures are lacking for the Monroe Columbias, which in the event did not begin to appear until 1946, but a Curly Fox number from the same time sold around fifty thousand copies and a minor Gene Autry hit ("Silver Spurs") managed to do twenty thousand. By those standards a comparable Monroe hit like "Footprints in the Snow" would have netted him royalties of around $400. His musicians were paid at the session union scale against an advance in royalties.

As it turned out, however, all these plans came to naught. The recording ban by the American Federation of Musicians had gone into effect the previous August. Satherley, like most record executives, thought the ban would be short-lived and things would soon be back to normal. He was wrong. The ban dragged on for more than two years, not ending until November 11, 1944. Satherley reactivated Monroe's contract on that very day and began making plans to record him. The war was still very much unfinished, but some travel restrictions were being eased and Satherley began moving to obtain new recordings by his biggest stars. In December he went to Chicago for a long session with Acuff, and then in late January 1945 he recorded Bob Wills and Gene Autry in Hollywood. He next reserved a large block of time—some eleven days—in Columbia's Chicago studio for a marathon session of the label's other country and blues artists. The full session of the Chicago Columbia recordings in February 1945 was:

DATE	DAY	MX NO. BLOCK	ARTIST
13	Tues.	C4354-61	Bill Monroe and Blue Grass Boys
14	Wed.	(apparently no recording)	
15	Thurs.	C4362-69	Texas Ruby and Curly Fox
16	Fri.	(apparently no recording)	
17	Sat.	C4370-79	Bailes Brothers
18	Sun.	(closed)	
19	Mon.	C4380-87	Big Bill (Broonzy), blues singer
20	Tues.	C4390-95	Curly Williams and His Georgia Peach Pickers
		C4396-99	Clyde Moody
21	Wed.	?	untraced blues or pop sides
22	Thurs.	C4400-09	Claude Sharpe and the Old Hickory Singers
		C4410-21	Various blues or jazz groups: Buster Bennett, the Big Three Trio, Big Bill, Three Brown Boys

These were, with a few exceptions, very much a series of Nashville sessions. In addition to Monroe, also from the Opry came Curly Fox, the Bailes Brothers, Curly Williams and his western-swing band that featured the remarkable steel guitar of Boots Harris, Clyde Moody (who often sang with Monroe), and the latest old-time quartet fad on the show, the Old Hickory Singers. Most had probably secured their contract with Columbia through Acuff or through the newly emerging Acuff-Rose publishing company. Monroe was first in the schedule to be recorded. Walter Bailes of the Bailes Brothers recalls meeting Monroe and his band as they left the studio when he and his group arrived late in the afternoon for rehearsals.[28]

At Columbia, recordings were made using a different technology than Monroe had experienced with Victor. Instead of 78-rpm wax masters, Columbia used "lacquers" (or "acetates")—sixteen-inch, $33\frac{1}{3}$ metal discs covered with an acetate surface. This was common radio transcription technology in the 1930s and 1940s. The Columbia lacquers were made to track from inside to out, and only one side of the disc was used.

The technology produced better-quality recordings and also left a much fuller record of the music made at each session. If a problem occurred during the recording of a master and recording was halted, or if it was decided to try again after a complete take and get a better performance, there was no way of erasing the rejected recording. When mistakes were made in the days of wax masters, the grooves could be shaved off the wax surface and recording would begin again. With sixteen-inch lacquers, however, accepted and rejected takes were together on the discs, and both versions were preserved.

Moreover, Columbia was willing to invest the time to let the band experiment with different takes. Consequently, Monroe's Columbia recordings include up to four full takes along with up to three incomplete BD ("broke down") takes of a single master. As usual, each song or instrumental at the recording session was assigned a master number (e.g., C4327 for "Nobody Loves Me"). In addition, each take of a song was assigned a take number, hyphenated after the master number (C4327-2, etc.). Take numbers were not assigned in sequence as the recordings were being made but were given after a session (presumably by Satherley in consultation with Monroe) as a way of ranking takes. Consequently, -1 was always the take issued on the original 78s; it had been judged the best performance. The ranking process meant that for some songs the sequence of take numbers was, at first glance, in random order. The chronology of takes of "Nobody Loves Me," for example, is -2, -BD, -3, and -1, which is the actual sequence in which the recordings were made. The sequence provides some idea of how the music developed at the recording sessions as the band worked on each piece.

Although a number of people have been suggested as being at this first Columbia session, the following roster is—in the absence of official session sheets—as accurate as possible. Monroe and Wise played their traditional roles. Clyde Moody had left Monroe, signing his own Columbia contract and recording a few days after Monroe in Chicago. To play rhythm guitar and sing lead and harmony, Monroe probably acted on Howard Watts's recommendation and hired Watts's old partner, Jimmy "Tex" Willis, who remained on the Opry with Howard's Cotton Pickers when Watts went with Monroe. Stringbean played his banjo throughout, Howard Watts played bass and sang on one piece, and Sally Ann Forrester played accordion and sang on three songs. The Columbia files also list Curly Bradshaw as present at the sessions, playing a second guitar.

As he did with his first Victor session, Monroe started his Columbia career with a twelve-bar blues. With its sock chords (a specialty of Tex Willis's), familiar stock blues stanzas, and take-off solos, "Rocky Road Blues" resembles the style of western swing of the day as much as anything. Cedric Rainwater takes a nifty string-bass solo, reflecting Monroe's fondness for that instrument in his new sound. (Listeners often heard the bass loud and clear on WSM broadcasts.) Although Stringbean's banjo is audible, the accordion is stronger in the mix and ends the song with an uptown chord that emphasizes the influence of contemporary swing. The fact that it was the first track recorded, nailed by the band in just one take and one of the first two released, suggests that Satherley thought highly of "Rocky Road Blues." The song was copyrighted, with words and music credited to Monroe, by Peer International in 1946 when the actual single was released. It shares its title and the first line of the first verse with bluesman Kokomo Arnold's 1937 recording.[29]

In 1980, when County-Rebel Records issued a two-LP retrospective of Monroe's Columbia sides, album annotator Doug Green, who had worked with Monroe, asked him about many early sides. About "Kentucky Waltz," Monroe said, "I had written the tune ten years before we recorded it. It was about the first tune I wrote words for. I didn't put the words to it 'til I came to Nashville in 1939."[30] For much of the war era the song was performed by Clyde Moody, who delivered it in a warm baritone. Here, though, with Moody set to do his own session for Columbia, Monroe delivered the one-stanza song himself.

Waltzes had always been a staple of the old-time fiddlers' repertoire, and many fiddling contests of the time required contestants to excel in playing a breakdown and a "waltz of choice." By grafting words to his instrumental waltz, Monroe unknowingly created a new genre: the country music waltz. Just as Monroe wrote in his first line, "We were waltzin' that night in Kentucky," these were a series of songs about dancing to specific waltzes. "Kentucky Waltz" was on the best-seller charts for six weeks (rising as high as number three), and others soon followed. Chubby Wise helped Clyde Moody do "The Shenandoah Waltz," and Redd Stewart and Pee Wee King crafted "The Tennessee Waltz." "Kentucky Waltz" was also published (copyrighted in 1946 and again, for some reason, in 1947) by Peer, with full credits to Monroe.

The sound of Monroe's best seller is distinctively different than much of what he'd done before or would do later. He sings rather softly and in a lower key than usual. The backup emphasizes the sound of the fiddle and the accordion, with the two instruments playing in harmony on the second break; the banjo can hardly be heard on either take.

"True Life Blues" was written by Pete Pyle, who had worked with Monroe in the early 1940s and played on his second Victor session. Pyle recalled that the idea for the song came from a fan letter Monroe received in which a woman described how her husband mistreated her and took her for granted. Monroe showed the letter to Pyle and suggested he try to use its details in a song. Pyle did try, but, he recalled, he "didn't think it was much of any account." He turned it over to Monroe "not too long before I got drafted" [in 1942], and the song was copyrighted by Peer that year.[31] It was done as a duet throughout, with Tex Willis singing lead to Monroe's tenor.

The recording marks the first time a banjo break is heard on a Bill Monroe record, as Stringbean takes a nice, strong solo in his two-finger style. It took the band four takes to arrive at an acceptable version of "True Life Blues," mainly because of inconsistencies in the text between Monroe and Willis. On the first take, Monroe playfully imitates the Opry banjo star Uncle Dave Macon and shouts "Hot dog!" behind Stringbean's banjo solo. Underpinning the rhythm was a sound that would be Howard Watts's trademark during his tenure with Monroe: a four-beats-to-the-measure "walking bass."

"Nobody Loves Me," composed by fellow Opry member Zeke Clements ("Smoke on the Water"), seemed to give the singers a hard time. The arrangement called for a smooth trio—Monroe, Forrester, and Willis—and three full takes were made to try to nail it. On the one that was incomplete (BD),

Monroe stopped the singing in mid-flight, saying "I missed it there." There is little of bluegrass here—the band sounds like any one of a number of smooth-singing string bands in country music in the mid-1940s. The banjo plays simple chords. Both the accordion and fiddle are subdued and at times inaudible, and Monroe takes all of the instrumental breaks on his mandolin. This song was not released on a Columbia 78 and appeared only on collector reissues beginning in the 1970s.

One of Monroe's standards on the Opry since the early 1940s was an ersatz cowboy song, "Goodbye Old Pal." Given his love of horses, this seems a natural fit for his repertoire. Monroe purchased the song from Cliff Carlisle, and his version is close to Carlisle's 1934 recording. Columbia saved at least two takes of "Goodbye, Old Pal," the unissued one being a good deal faster and more edgy. Monroe's falsetto—what a WSM souvenir book referred to as his "trick vocal"—is very much in evidence, and it is the only song in the session to include a yodel. Recorded in two takes, its second one was rearranged to begin with the guitar rather than the fiddle and was at a slower tempo than the first.

"Footprints in the Snow" is a revamped Victorian music-hall song from England. W. K. McNeil has traced it to a composer named Harry Wright, who published it sometime in the 1890s. Monroe, though, got it by a more roundabout way. "That was written by a guy with the Cumberland Ridge Runners," he said, "but I rearranged it."[32] The Ridge Runners, a large string band that John Lair organized for WLS's National Barn Dance in the early 1930s, were playing there when the Monroes were dancing with the troupe. "The guy" might well have been Lair, who was a serious collector and student of old songs; the singer was almost certainly a very young Red Foley, who played bass and did heart songs with the group. Foley recorded the song for the American Record Company in March 1934, but it does not seem to have been issued. Ernest Branch and the West Virginia Ramblers recorded it (as "Little Footprints") for Gennett in 1931, and subsequent recordings of it were made by Big Slim Aliff (Decca, 1936) and Cliff Carlisle (Decca, 1939). "Footprints in the Snow" was also in the repertoire of several other popular radio hillbillies: the team of Slim (Clere) and Tex (Tyler) and also Bradley Kincaid.[33] The Columbia composer credits describe Monroe's version as "arranged by Boyd Lane," but Monroe told Doug Green, "I don't know why Boyd Lane's name is on there as arranger—I think he had a radio show in Chicago."[34] The Columbia ledgers give the publishing affiliation as "P. Int.," probably Peer International, whereas most of the others are simply credited to Monroe. Perhaps Satherley

sensed that the song was not Monroe's. Its first take (-2) is faster and the banjo is prominent. In the final take's mix (-1), the banjo is lower and the accordion more prominent. When "Footprints in the Snow" was finally released as a single in December 1946 it quickly became Monroe's second chart hit, rising as high as number 5 and staying on top-ten charts for four weeks. It remained a staple in Monroe's repertoire, often requested, and he performed it frequently.

At this point in the recording session the band made a try at a gospel song. The Blue Grass Quartet had been doing "I'll Have a New Life" in Opry shows earlier. When Bear Family Records ordered copies of all the Monroe Columbia masters for the complete set of Monroe's 1936–49 recordings, which Bear Family published in 2002, an unissued recording of this song turned up in the Columbia files. It was never assigned a master number, and the one take shows that the band was still working to coordinate vocals. As was typical of Monroe's gospel sound into the 1960s, only guitar and mandolin are heard backing up the song. The quartet consisted of the trio of Monroe on lead, Forrester on tenor, and Willis on baritone with Watts's bass lead added. Monroe would perfect that sound in later Columbia gospel cuts.

"Blue Grass Special" is Monroe's third twelve-bar blues instrumental, this one in the key of A. Unlike the two blues he had done for Bluebird where only the mandolin and bass took solos, "Blue Grass Special" is based on a series of "chase" solos in the manner of a swing-era jazz ensemble that includes every instrument in the band. It begins with Monroe's mandolin, then to Chubby's fiddle, back to the mandolin, then to Willis's guitar, then back again to the mandolin, then bass, then mandolin, then String's banjo, back to mandolin, Sally Ann's accordion, and then out on the mandolin. Alternate takes demonstrate that the musicians had a general idea of what to play during their breaks, but Monroe, Wise, and Forrester were capable of serious improvisation. The cut, more than other until that time, shows the extent to which Monroe was making the take-off solo a part of his music.

"Come Back to Me in My Dreams," a lilting waltz lament, is significant because, as Mark Humphrey has noted, "for the first time on record, Monroe develops a theme to which he and many bluegrass artists would return, that of the dead sweetheart accessible only in dreams."[35] The song featured the same vocal trio as on "Nobody Loves Me." Satherley did not release this track either, and it languished in the Columbia files until a Library of Congress reissue of 1976. Perhaps Monroe chose not to release the songs because when Forrester left the band before Columbia starting releasing his recordings he could no longer recreate the trio sound in performances. Eventually, he redid the song as a vocal solo for Decca in 1957. Like the first song in the session, "Come Back to Me in My Dreams" was recorded in just one take. The band had been in the studio for three hours and had recorded twenty takes of nine different pieces.

Late in the summer of 1945, a few weeks after the end of the war and seven months after Monroe's first Columbia session, Opry fan Dick Hill resumed his diary. His list provides some idea of the early postwar sound of Bill Monroe and his Blue Grass Boys. The band's membership had changed somewhat. Howard Watts had just left in order to deal with a family medical crisis, and Willis and Wise were also gone, replaced by Lester Flatt and Jim Shumate. The names of these new musicians do not appear in Hill's lists, giving the impression of a more unified band rather than a group of featured soloists. The inclusion of "String" in a September show is an anomaly, for according to Ewing, he had left the band at that point to join the army.[36] Bill's brother, Birch Monroe, is listed as playing one fiddle solo. He also filled in on bass during this time and, as he would do regularly in later years, Bill invited him to play an old-time square dance tune on the shows. Hill listed the Grand Ole Opry logs for the summer of 1945 in his diary:

[August 25, 1945]
8:00–30 by Purena

4.	Blue Eyed Jane	Bill Monroe
8.	Rember Me	B. Monroe and Quartet

10:00–15

1.	Kitty Clyde	B. Monroe and Trio
2.	If Its Wrong to Love You	Sally Ann
3.	I Know My Lord Will Lead Me Out	Blue Grass Quartette
4.	Blue Moon of Kentucky	Bill Monroe

[September 1, 1945]
8:00–8:30 by Pureena

4.	The Weary Traveler	The Bill Monroe
9.	The Old Country Church	Blue Grass Boys

10:06–15

1.	You Came Back to Me in Your Dreams	Bill Monroe and Boys
2.	Tenn. Blues (Mandolin Tune)	Bill Monroe and Boys
3.	Theme	by Bill Monroe

[September 8, 1945]
8:00–8:30 by Purena

2.	Kitty Clyde	Bill Monroe and Boys
5.	Mule Skinner Blues	Bill Monroe
10.	He Set Me Free	Blue Grass Quartette.

[September 15, 1945]
8:00–8:30

2.	Shortening Bread	B. Monroe and Boys
6.	Rokie Road Blues	Bill Monroe
10.	Life's Rail Way to Heaven	Bill M. and Quartette
14.	Theme	Blue Grass Boys

10:00–10:15 by Wallrite

1.	Rosine Breakdown	Burtch Monroe
2.	Headin' Down the Rong Highway	Sally Ann
3.	I'll Have a New Life	Quartette
4.	Goodby Ole Pal	Bill Monroe
5.	Some of These Days	Bill
6.	Good Ole Mt. Dew	Stringbeans

Once again, most pieces attributed to Bill Monroe, or to Bill with the band, were those he had recorded or would record. Three were from the recent Columbia session: "Rocky Road Blues," "Goodbye Old Pal," and "Come Back to Me in My Dreams." He would soon record another, "Blue Moon of Kentucky." This is the first reference to the song that would become his most famous composition. Monroe's fondness for the music of Jimmie Rodgers was reflected in his performance of an obscure Rodgers song from 1931, "My Blue Eyed Jane."

The gospel repertoire also included material that later appeared on record, including the venerable "Life's Railway to Heaven," which Monroe would record in 1958. "I'll Have a new Life" eventually appeared on a reissue CD that included rejected material. Among the material the Blue Grass Quartet did that did not enter the recorded repertoire was "He Set Me Free," a 1939 Brumley song published by Stamps-Baxter that later became the melody for Hank Williams's "I Saw the Light."

At the time of the February Chicago sessions the old plan of releasing Monroe on the Okeh series was dropped because the Okeh label had been converted to a blues, rhythm and blues, jazz, and gospel label. In its place was the Columbia red-label thirty-five and thirty-six thousand series that intermixed some blues with country and western releases. The first coupling from the Monroe session, "Rocky Road Blues" and "Kentucky Waltz," appeared on Columbia 36907. The titles were not surprising—Monroe had been grooming each on the Opry—but the time lag was. They were not released until January 14, 1946, almost a full year after the session. It was not as though the wartime shortage of shellac caused the delay. Between February 1945 and January 1946, Satherley released no fewer than forty-seven records by other artists, including several sides by other acts that had recorded at the Chicago session. For whatever reason, he seemed to lack confidence in his new signee and did not seem eager to get his product out. To be sure, after "Kentucky Waltz" was on the charts Columbia finally released number 37151 ("True Life Blues" and "Footprints in the Snow") on October 28, 1946. By that time Monroe had done his second Columbia session (September 16, 1946), and his new music was soaring in a new direction.

Notes

1. See "Numerical Listings of Releases," 313–40.

2. Louise Rand Bascom in *The Frank C. Brown Collection North Carolina Folklore Volume 3* (Durham: Duke University Press, 1952), 293.

3. Neil V. Rosenberg, *Bill Monroe and His Blue Grass Boys: An Illustrated Discography* (Nashville: Country Music Foundation Press, 1974), 30.

4. The harmonica had long been a popular folk instrument, especially in middle Tennessee; DeFord Bailey, Humphrey Bate, and Herman Crook all were featured harmonica players on the early Grand Ole Opry.

5. Perry Harris and H. G. Roberts, "Big Howdy Forrester," *The Devil's Box,* June 1, 1974, 8.

6. Tex Logan, "A Conversation with Chubby Wise," *Muleskinner News* (Sept. 1972): 2; see also Lance Leroy, "Master of Bluegrass Soul: Chubby Wise," *Bluegrass Unlimited* (March 1996) 11–15; and Ivan M. Tribe, "Chubby Wise: One of the Original Bluegrass Fiddlers, *Bluegrass Unlimited* 11 (Feb. 1977): 10–12.

7. James Rooney, *Bossmen: Bill Monroe and Muddy Waters* (New York: Dial Press, 1971), 42.

8. Charles K. Wolfe, "Bluegrass Touches: An Interview with Bill Monroe," *Old Time Music* 16 (Spring 1975): 9.

9. Logan, "Chubby Wise," 3.

10. Wolfe, "Bluegrass Touches," 9.

11. Randy Noles, *The Orange Blossom Boys: The Untold Story of Ervin T. Rouse, Chubby Wise and the World's Most Famous Fiddle Tune* (Centerstream, n.p., 2002), 72.

12. Roy Acuff hired Jimmie Riddle as a harmonica player and accordionist around the same time as Sally Ann joined the Blue Grass Boys. Neil V. Rosenberg, *Bluegrass: A History* (Urbana: University of Illinois Press, 1993), 65n34.

13. Murphy Henry, "Sally Ann Forrester: The First Blue Grass Girl,"

in *Country Music Annual 2001,* edited by Charles K. Wolfe and James Akenson, (Lexington: University Press of Kentucky, 2001), 101.

14. At this time Charlie Monroe had a girl singer and banjoist, Helen Osborne, who used the stage name Katy Hill, the title of the first fiddle tune Bill recorded. David Freeman, notes to *Charlie Monroe on the Noonday Jamboree—1944* (Country 538, 1974).

15. Charles K. Wolfe, *Classic Country: Legends of Country Music* (New York: Routledge, 2001), 245.

16. Wolfe, *Classic Country,* 245. According to Tom Ewing, however, Monroe did not begin using baseball to attract audiences until 1944. Ewing, "Howard Watts, Better Known as Cedric Rainwater," *Bluegrass Unlimited* (May 2002): 46.

17. Rosenberg, *Bluegrass,* 57.

18. Ibid., 49–50.

19. Wolfe, "Bluegrass Touches," 11.

20. Cousin Wilbur [Bill Wesbrooks] with Barbara McLane and Sandra Grafton, *Everybody's Cousin* (New York: Manor Books, 1979), 160–61.

21. Dick Hill, "Grand Ole Opry, 1944–45: A Radio Log," *Journal of Country Music* 5 (Fall 1974): 92–122.

22. Hill, "Grand Ole Opry," 96.

23. Such themes are parodied in Garrison Keillor's film *A Prairie Home Companion* (2006).

24. Even more recall Flatt and Scruggs's Martha White Theme of the 1950s and later because of its appearance on their album *Flatt and Scruggs at Carnegie Hall* (Columbia CL 2045/CS 8845, 1962).

25. This piece became so popular that the words to it, along with those to another favorite, "Kentucky Waltz," were printed on the back of the souvenir photographs that the band sold at show dates. Rosenberg, *Bill Monroe and His Blue Grass Boys,* 30.

26. Rooney, *Bossmen,* 35.

27. Art Satherley, interview with Charles K. Wolfe and Linnell Gentry, Madison, Tenn., Oct. 24, 1972.

28. Walter Bailes, interview with Charles K. Wolfe, Murfreesboro, Tenn., July 8, 1998.

29. "Rocky Road Blues," Decca 7449.

30. Douglas B. Green, notes to *Bill Monroe and His Blue Grass Boys: The Classic Bluegrass Recordings, Volume 1* (County CCS 104, 1980).

31. Ibid.

32. Douglas B. Green, notes to *Bill Monroe and His Blue Grass Boys: The Classic Bluegrass Recordings, Volume 2* (County CSS 105, 1980).

33. Ivan Tribe, notes to *"West Virginia Hills": Early Recordings from West Virginia* (Old Homestead OHCS-141, 1982); see also Guthrie T. Meade Jr., with Dick Spottswood and Douglas S. Meade, *Country Music Sources: A Biblio-Discography of Commercially Recorded Traditional Music* (Chapel Hill: Southern Folklife Collection, University of North Carolina at Chapel Hill Libraries in Association with the John Edwards Memorial Forum, 2002), 214.

34. Green, notes to *Bill Monroe and His Blue Grass Boys, Volume 2.*

35. Mark Humphrey, notes to *The Essential Bill Monroe and His Blue Grass Boys, 1945–1949* (Columbia C2K 52478, 1992).

36. Ewing, "Howard Watts," 47.

DISCOGRAPHY, 1942–45

ABOUT THE COLUMBIA MASTERS

Bill Monroe's Columbia masters recorded between 1945 and 1949 were made on sixteen-inch, 33⅓–rpm, acetate-coated aluminum discs called lacquers. They were recorded "inside out," meaning that the needle was started next to the label/spindle hole part of the disc, creating grooves that tracked out toward its edge—the opposite of commercial phonograph records. Most pieces were recorded more than once. Typically, each disc held a number of tracks that included some incomplete performances that were labeled "BD" ("broke down"). Take numbers, the hyphenated numbers appended to the master numbers that in the days of wax masters (and also later with tape masters) were assigned at the time of recording, were in this case assigned *after* the recording was made and used to rank the takes in terms of their quality. Consequently, in all the Columbia recordings, take one ("-1") was assigned to the recording originally selected for release on a 78–rpm single. That is why the take numbers in this portion of the discography are not in a chronological sequence but follow the sequence in which the recordings actually appear on the original lacquers. Composer credits and vocal or instrumental identifications are listed only once for each piece, in the citation for the earliest take.

450213   Columbia session; producer, Art Satherly
WBBM-CBS studio in the Wrigley Building, 410 N. Michigan Ave., Chicago, Ill.
Feb. 13, 1945, 2:15–5:15 P.M.

C4354-1	ROCKY ROAD BLUES (Monroe) Monroe-L	20013, 36907	HL 7290, CS 1065, C2K 52478, V 79518-2, JAS 3519, BCD 16399, A16652, CHK 90628
C4355-2	KENTUCKY WALTZ (Monroe) Monroe-L		C2K 52478, BCD 16399
C4355-1	KENTUCKY WALTZ	20013, 36907, 52021	H 1709, H 2064, B 2804, HL 7290, CCS 104, FC 38904, CK 53908, V 79518-2, BCD 16399, A16652
C4356-4	TRUE LIFE BLUES (Monroe) Willis-L, Monroe-T		BCD 16399
C4356-3	TRUE LIFE BLUES		BCD 16399
C4356-2	TRUE LIFE BLUES		C2K 52478, BCD 16399
C4356-1	TRUE LIFE BLUES	20080, 37151	HL 7315, CCS 104, CK 53908, BCD 16399
C4357-2	NOBODY LOVES ME Monroe-L, Forrester-T, Willis-B		FC 38904,[1] BCD 16399

C4357-BD	NOBODY LOVES ME		C2K 52478, BCD 16399
C4357-3	NOBODY LOVES ME		C2K 52478, BCD 16399
C4357-1	NOBODY LOVES ME		BCD 16399
C4358-2	GOODBYE OLD PAL (Monroe) Monroe-L		C2K 52478, C4K 47911 [CK 47915], BCD 16399
C4358-1	GOODBYE OLD PAL	20370, 37888	HL 7315, CCS 104, CK 53908, MCAD 4-11048, BCD 16399
C4359-2	FOOTPRINTS IN THE SNOW (arr. Boyd Lane) Monroe-L		BCD 16399
C4359-1	FOOTPRINTS IN THE SNOW	20080, 37151, 52021	H 1709, B 2804, HL 7290, CS 1065, CCS 105, C2K 52478, V 79518-2, BCD 16399
[no mx #]	I'LL HAVE A NEW LIFE Monroe-L, Forrester-T, Willis-B, Watts-BS		BCD 16399
C4360-2	BLUE GRASS SPECIAL (Monroe) Instrumental		BCD 16399
C4360-3	BLUE GRASS SPECIAL		C2K 52478, BCD 16399
C4360-1	BLUE GRASS SPECIAL	20384, 37960, 52022	B 2804, HL 7290, CCS 104, FC 38904, CK 53908, OC-1001, V 79518-2, BCD 16399
C4361-1	COME BACK TO ME IN MY DREAMS (B. Monroe) Monroe-L, Forrester-T, Willis-B		LBC 2, CSS 105, C2K 52478, BCD 16399

Bill Monroe: m	Tex Willis: g	Robert R. "Chubby" Wise: f
David Akeman ("Stringbean"): b	Howard Staton Watts ("Cedric Rainwater"): sb	Wilene "Sally Ann" Forrester: acc
Elliott Thurman "Curley" Bradshaw: ? (2d guitar?; named in NYC Columbia files)		

Note

1. The notes to Columbia FC 38904 describe this recorded performance as take 2, the Bear Family data ca. take 3; we have followed the Bear Family attribution.

4

"HEAVY TRAFFIC AHEAD": 1946–49

World War II ended with an atomic bang in August 1945 and by 1946 the widely anticipated postwar era was in full swing. GIs were returning to their jobs and families. Business was booming as production shifted from war goods to consumer goods, new cars were available for the first time since 1942, and homes were being built at a furious pace. The baby boom was underway.

Hillbilly music was experiencing its own boom. The postwar years of country music are now viewed as a golden era. It was a time when the music became fully professionalized and Nashville became the center of a newly prosperous music "industry." New stars were emerging—singers like Hank Williams and instrumentalists like Chet Atkins—and one of the key players at the heart of the new music economy was Bill Monroe.

The recordings Monroe made for Columbia between 1946 and 1947 featured the band that came to be known as the "Original Bluegrass Band": Lester Flatt, Earl Scruggs, Chubby Wise, "Cedric Rainwater" (Howard Watts), and Monroe. The twenty-eight sides cut at four sessions in 1946 and 1947 are widely viewed as the cornerstone of bluegrass music.

Even though the records have remained in print except for a brief period during the late 1950s and early 1960s, and even though they have influenced several generations, Columbia in the 1940s was at first not at all sure what it had. Indeed, several of the classics were not released until decades after their creation. Columbia records in 1946 was the home of artists like Gene Autry, Roy Acuff, Johnny Bond, Bob Wills, and Floyd Tillman, many of whom reflected the influence of music from B-movie westerns and sang western or cowboy-flavored songs to slick arrangements featuring muted trumpets and happy accordions. To the promoters at Columbia, Monroe's acoustic music, with its high mountain harmonies, keening fiddle, and banjo, must have seemed almost anachronistic in what was coming to be known as country and western music.

Yet Monroe's music was changing at this time. The recordings demonstrate a degree of vocal and instrumental integration and arrangement not heard in his previous recordings. The popular music of the time, dominated by trends in jazz and its country cousin, western swing, affected Monroe's music just as it did Columbia's other acts. One of the most important results of the wartime recording ban was the emergence of BMI and a Nashville-based publishing industry. The availability of publishing royalties inspired country music performers to hone their composing skills, for new material was more valuable than ever before.

The fact that Columbia rushed some of the new recordings into print although half of the eight 1945 recordings were still on its shelf suggests that producer Art Satherley recognized that the new band was better than the one of 1945. Still, his release pattern relied heavily on Monroe's earlier successes. The first, two gospel duets ("Mother's Only Sleeping" and "Mansions for Me"), echoed the Monroe Brothers and revealed the fine harmony blends Monroe was achieving with his new lead singer, Lester Flatt. One side of the second release ("Blue Yodel No. 4"), echoed the Jimmie Rodgers songs Monroe had done for Victor in 1940 and 1941 (soon after, Victor reissued these). It was only on the B side of the single, Columbia 37565, "Will You Be Loving another Man?" released July 14, 1947, that the new bluegrass sound was fully unleashed and the record-buying public first heard a full-blown Earl Scruggs banjo solo. This was part of a revolutionary sound. Only those lucky enough to hear the band in person or on Opry broadcasts knew what to expect.

Lester Raymond Flatt had been born on the Cumberland plateau of Tennessee at a hamlet called Duncan's Chapel near Sparta, about sixty miles east of Nashville, on June 14, 1914. Although he grew up in a rural family with eight siblings, only his father, who played the fiddle, made much music. In 1974 Flatt told a journalist, "Most of my brothers and sisters still live around Sparta. I was the only one to go into the music business. The rest are making an honest living!"[1] Lester learned to sing by joining the church choir and going to the old-time singing schools that dotted the rural south in those days. By 1931 young Flatt was working in a silk mill at Sparta, where he stayed until a strike closed it in 1934. By now married to Gladys Stacy, Lester moved to Virginia in 1935, where he worked as a weaver in a Burlington Mills rayon plant in Covington.

In 1939 Lester decided to try his luck as a professional musician. He started with the Charlie Scott Harmonizers on WDBJ in Roanoke and two years later moved to Burlington,

North Carolina, to team with former and future Monroe associate Clyde Moody. Following a brief return to day work in Sparta at the beginning of the war, Lester received a call from Charlie Monroe, who asked that he join his band in Greensboro, North Carolina. Both Lester and Gladys joined the band and traveled with the Kentucky Partners for a year and then left music once again to return to Sparta. The next Monroe who called was Bill. Would Lester, he asked, join his band on the Grand Ole Opry in 1944?[2]

Lester was not present at the first Columbia recording sessions in 1945, but surviving Opry souvenir programs show that he returned to the band shortly thereafter and soon became a regular. Not only did he offer Monroe a solid guitar rhythm and good lead singing but he also brought songwriting experience to the band and a substantial repertoire of little-known songs. Of one, "Mother's Only Sleeping," Monroe recalled, "Lester Flatt brought this one to me. He put it in both our names, but it was the first time I'd ever heard it. We used to share some songs that way; when he first came to work for me he thought it was the most wonderful thing in the world that I could get advance money for him from BMI."[3] With publishing furnishing the incentives, Lester's flair for songwriting was a new asset for the band.

The other key member of the new band was a soft-spoken banjo player from North Carolina, Earl Scruggs. The complete history of how Scruggs developed his revolutionary three-finger (thumb, index, and middle) banjo-picking style—which many consider the seminal event in the history of bluegrass music—is beyond the scope of this study. Suffice it to say that Scruggs was born not in the mountains but in the North Carolina piedmont, the foothills of Appalachia, in Flint Hill, a small community outside Boiling Springs, on January 6, 1924. Scruggs was raised in what he called "a musical atmosphere of the fiddle, banjo, guitar, autoharp, etc."[4] Two of his brothers and three of his sisters played stringed instruments. Their father, George Elam Scruggs, who died when Earl was four, played both fiddle and banjo. "Probably no other family enjoyed music and singing more that we did," Scruggs remarked.[5]

For reasons yet to be determined, the three-finger banjo style was extremely popular in Scruggs's section of the piedmont. As a boy young, Earl admired his older brother Junie, who played that way by 1930. Other banjo players who lived near the Flint Hill community at the time included Mack Woolbright, who recorded for Columbia in the 1920s, and DeWitt "Snuffy" Jenkins, who would achieve fame playing with Homer "Pappy" Sherrill in Byron Parker's Hillbillies. Two more whom

Scruggs recalled but who apparently did not record were Smith Hammett, whose wife was a cousin of Earl's mother, and Mack Crow.

When he was thirteen, Scruggs paid $10.95 for his first banjo. He was soon playing at local fiddlers' conventions and fish fries, and by the time he was fifteen he was on Gastonia radio with a group called the Carolina Wildcats. By 1939 he was working with Wiley, George, and Zeke Morris over WSPA in Spartanburg, South Carolina, but when the war came along young Earl got a job at the Lilly Mills in Shelby, working seventy-two-hour weeks to support his widowed mother and younger sister. In 1945, after the war ended, he went to Knoxville and joined the band of Lost John Miller.

By late November 1945, banjoist Stringbean (David Akeman) had left Monroe to form a new act with comedian Lew Childre. Always on the lookout for good potential musicians ("I wanted the sound of a banjo in my group," he said years later), Monroe had offered a job to a young South Carolina banjo player named Don Reno in 1943, but Reno had been drafted.[6] As Bill cast about for a replacement, his fiddler, Jim Shumate, approached Earl Scruggs, a young banjo player he knew from North Carolina, about working with the band. Scruggs was still playing with Lost John Miller's band and doing radio shows in Knoxville and Nashville. He was happy with Miller and had "heard things" about Monroe that made him uncertain about leaving a steady job on spec. "And Bill had never had a banjo player of my type," Scruggs recalled.[7]

For several weeks Scruggs put off Shumate, but one Saturday morning Miller called the group together and told them he was leaving the road and breaking up the band. "Then I met Shumate down at the coffee shop at the Tulane Hotel," Scruggs said, "and I told him that at that point I was disgusted with show business. I was going back to North Carolina, go back to work in the factory. And he begged me to let him call Bill and let Bill hear me before I left town."[8]

Scruggs was trying to buy a home in North Carolina and continued to support his mother and sister, but he was willing to talk with Monroe. Jim Shumate called Bill, and the two men met in Shumate's Tulane Hotel room. As Scruggs recalls, "I had a couple of tunes worked up pretty good. One was 'Sally Goodin,' which was an old-time tune that I knew he could relate to because I'd heard him play it with fiddle players. I played him that tune. Then I thought I would go to the extreme with something that he possibly never heard tell of before on the banjo. And that was 'Dear Old Dixie.' So I played him those two tunes. And I put my banjo back in my case, and he asked if I would go down to the Opry and let the group hear me. Pick with the group. In other words, he just wasn't sure, in my opinion."[9]

Monroe had a difficult decision to make. His previous banjo-picker had been a comedian, a stereotyped role for the instrument and those who played it that reached all the way back to the minstrel show era of a century earlier. When Scruggs became part of Monroe's band and they traveled with Opry pioneer and banjoist-comedian Uncle Dave Macon, Macon would kid, "You play good in a band but you're not a bit funny, are you?"[10] Scruggs did, however, represent a new kind of virtuosity in country music that was becoming fashionable. A younger generation of listeners, raised on hot jazz solos and popular music, were looking for similar hot breaks in their favorite music. Scruggs could fit into a new slot with Monroe, similar to that of lead guitarist Tommy "Butterball" Paige in Ernest Tubb's band and steel guitarist Leon McAuliffe in Bob Wills's to name but two of a generation of young sidemen known not for singing but for instrumental prowess. Was there a place for such a figure in the Blue Grass Boys?

When Lost John and his group returned to Knoxville that Saturday, Scruggs remained in Nashville and went to the Ryman Auditorium that night to pick some more with Bill before Monroe did his Opry show. Lester Flatt, who'd been with Bill since earlier in the year, had not been impressed with Stringbean's musicianship and was not sure that Monroe should hire another banjo player. When he heard Scruggs, however, he was blown away. "I had never heard anybody pick a banjo like he did," Flatt recalled. "He could go all over the neck and do things you couldn't hardly believe. Bill said 'What do you think?' And I said, 'If you can hire him, get him, whatever it costs.'"[11] Scruggs remembers:

> We just played almost continuously until the last bus out of here to Knoxville and to North Carolina, which was at ten o'clock. He had never at this point asked me if I'd go to work for him or not. So I said, "Well, that's it. I've got to catch a bus." And he said, "Be back Monday morning." I believe he gave me a time. At the time I was really sick. I had the flu. I said: "There's a few things involved. Number one is, I don't even know what you pay or anything about it. Discuss that with me." And he told me and it was in line with what John had been paying me. So I told him I had to go and get my clothes at Knoxville and go back to North Carolina and get over this [flu]. I told him I could be back the next Saturday night.[12]

Ironically, when Scruggs returned to join the band in early December, Jim Shumate had left because Howard "Howdy" Forrester had returned from the navy and reclaimed his job.

Scruggs hardly had time to get used to Forrester's fiddling because Howdy and his wife Wilene planned to leave Nashville to return to Tulsa, where they'd performed before the war. By March, Chubby Wise had returned to the band. As air checks that date from March indicate, Monroe was shaping his new band's sound in order to place the banjo up front in a way it never had been. Years later he said, "I thought it would give everybody a break you see, and give 'em a chance to let the people hear them. They all deserved that. We could have just cut it down, and let the fiddle done it all. But if you're paying the banjo player, he ought to get in there and take a break too. Because I knew that the people wanted to hear him."[13]

These air checks—earliest documents of this band's sound—come from home recordings. By the war's end, home disc-cutting machines were becoming popular in households throughout the South. These were basically record players that had special stylus arms (often placed opposite the playing stylus arm) that allowed fans to cut onto small blank discs sound from either a microphone or directly from a radio signal. The blank discs ranged from five to ten inches in diameter and could hold from ninety seconds to three minutes of music. Most were based on thinly coated aluminum and were prone to separation, warping, breaking, or wearing out after several plays. Nonetheless, they represented the only way home recordings could be made in the age before tape recorders.

Fans like Dick Hill kept logs of Opry broadcasts, but others began to use disc-cutting machines to document their favorite music. Some young musicians were captivated by Bill Monroe's exciting new music and Earl Scruggs's amazing banjo solos and sought to figure out the licks by recording the band. Because such recordings were made for home use only, no one knows how many were made or how many survived in private hands. Many disc cutters used different widths of stylus, so some discs were not readily playable on regular 78-rpm machines. Even now, engineers trying to remaster them have to experiment with different size stylus points to find the one that most closely matches the original groove.

Today we recognize these recordings as the beginning of a practice that was to continue throughout Monroe's career: live recordings made from radio broadcasts and, later, with the invention of the tape recorder, at personal appearances. Most of these recordings were never made public or released commercially and are beyond the limits of this study. In the fall of 1981, however, a bootleg LP entitled *Bluegrass Classics: Radio Shows 1946–1948,* with no label identification, appeared on the bluegrass market. It contained nineteen air checks made by the Monroe band between March 1946 and March 1948.

The recordings came indirectly from Earl Scruggs, who, while with Monroe, commissioned a number of off-air recordings of the band's Opry performances. The recordings were made by Neal Matthews Sr., a West Nashville audio enthusiast whose son performed on the Opry with the Crook Brothers and later the Jordanaires. Matthews owned a disc-cutting machine and hooked it directly to the radio to get surprisingly good recordings from WSM's nearby signal. He ran a service whereby, for the modest sum of a dollar a record, Opry performers could call his house the evening of a show and request that Matthews make an air check of that evening's performance. At one point a shed in his back yard was filled with such recordings that had not been picked up or were spoiled or otherwise unusable.

About a decade later, when home tape recorders were becoming popular, Scruggs let someone transfer the discs to tape (except for a dub of "Train 45" that was cracked) and then loaned them to a fan who returned them in unplayable condition. The discs are apparently still in Scruggs's possession. Soon taped copies of the recordings began to circulate, and eventually some were published on the bootleg LP album. The jacket, which listed no publisher or place of publication, did include three photographs of the band taken from *Bill Monroe's WSM Grand Ole Opry Song Folio No. 2* and furnished dates for twelve of its nineteen tracks.[14]

The air shots make it possible to hear what was to become Monroe's most-acclaimed band as it was heard over the airwaves. The earliest dated recordings, those from March 1946, feature two traditional pieces that Monroe would not record until the 1960s: "Little Maggie" and "Careless Love." George D. "Judge" Hay, the founder of the Opry, introduces both performances as by Bill and Earl, and Scruggs's banjo breaks alternate with Monroe's vocals in both. As was evident by Hill's logs and Opry programs from the 1940s, it was not unusual for Hay to foreground individual members of the Blue Grass Boys and the bands of other Opry cast members during the broadcast. By speaking to "brother Earl here with that fancy banjo," Hay was helping to make Scruggs a recognizable part of the Opry cast.[15] Similar although undated performances combining "Earl and Bill" are included on the bootleg. "My Dixie Home" was recorded in the 1930s by the Kentucky team of Asa Martin and James Roberts and by the Monroe Brothers themselves under the title "I Am Thinking Tonight of the Old Folks." "Little Joe" was another Monroe Brothers traditional piece that Bill eventually recorded in 1960. On the latter, the audience's appreciation of Scruggs's then-novel banjo work can be heard to increase with each of the three breaks he takes. "When I started here," Scruggs commented, "no one had heard the three-finger style before. People would gather around me like I was a freak almost." Monroe's new banjo player was attracting a lot of attention.[16]

That spring, Monroe's band came together with this combination of new and veteran members. Howard Watts, who'd left to help his wife Alice convalesce after a difficult childbirth, returned to play bass, and fiddler Howdy Forrester left, to be replaced by Chubby Wise. As the new band began working, Monroe had a hit on his hands. "Kentucky Waltz" had been released in January, and by March it was on *Billboard*'s "Most-Played Juke Box Folk Records" charts. It was Monroe's first appearance on this chart, which began in 1944. Already a popular performer, he was now much in demand as an Opry star with a hit single. "We were working all the time," Scruggs recalled. "Sometimes we wouldn't see a bed from one end of the week till the other."[17]

They were practicing as well—new Monroe-Flatt duets, banjo-sparked songs with Scruggs, elaborate gospel quartets, and even a few vocal trios. The music of the creative band inspired Monroe. "He would spend a lot of time just tightening up the group," Scruggs said. "Some rehearsals we wouldn't sing a song. We would just concentrate on the sound of the band."[18]

On September 16, 1946, the new version of the Blue Grass Boys was in Chicago for its first session with Columbia. They'd been on the road almost constantly since spring—a fact reflected in the words of the first song they recorded, "Heavy Traffic Ahead." It also reflected the harsh reality of radio and touring at the time. Regardless of how far afield they traveled, they were required by the station to be back in Nashville every Saturday night for the Opry. In exchange, the Blue Grass Boys were able to announce their forthcoming dates on the air and able to use the phrase *Grand Ole Opry* in their showcards and advertising.

Arthur E. Satherley was waiting for them in Chicago, where by 1946 Columbia was concentrating much of its recording activity. Most sessions were held in a studio at the big CBS affiliate station at WBBM on the first two floors of the Wrigley Building. One of the landmark skyscrapers visible from the Chicago lakefront, it had been built by the Wrigley Chewing Gum conglomerate. With its main entrance at 410 North Michigan Avenue, the station became the point of origin for a number of popular network shows, including *Amos n' Andy* and Gene Autry's. Although WBBM had an auditorium to accommodate live audiences, Studio 12, a large space on the second floor, was reserved for Columbia recording sessions.

Like most of the sessions in Chicago, those of September 1946 that included Monroe brought together a strange assortment of blues, gospel, and country performers. Just before Monroe's session, for example, were a set of sides by Chicago bluesman Armond "Jump" Johnson, who recorded a piece called "Yancey's Blues" that was derived from the playing of legendary Chicago pianist Jimmy Yancey. Immediately following Monroe's session was one by Wiley Walker and Gene Sullivan. Wiley and Gene, the popular duet singers from Tulsa, had a hit with "When My Blue Moon Turns to Gold Again," which Monroe would later record himself. Unlike the earlier numerical series of the 1920s, the Columbia 20000 series in which the Monroe sides were released included both blues and country selections. Later sessions yielded sides by Monroe's fellow Opry star Paul Howard, the gospel singing Johnson Family, fiddler Curley Fox and his wife Texas Ruby, and blues singer Memphis Minnie.

As with Monroe's first Columbia sessions the previous year, this one used the 33 1/3-rpm, sixteen-inch transcription disc recording technology. As a result, considerable information—in the form of complete and partial (BD) alternate takes—exists to provide a glimpse of how these canonical recordings were made. Takes were evaluated during or soon after the recording sessions, and that judged best was assigned the -1 number and earmarked for commercial release on a 78-rpm disc. Although the technology of the sessions—the 33 1/3 disc—would become the basis of the new LP records in a few years, Monroe was still more than a decade away from having his music issued on LP. A few of the songs recorded at these sessions would, however, end up on rare seven-inch, 33 1/3 singles that Columbia released in 1949 in an unsuccessful attempt to compete with Victor's new, big-holed, seven-inch, 45-rpm singles.

A little more than ten years had passed since Monroe made his first recordings. Typically, he and Charlie had been given around two hours to record ten songs using the old wax masters. Now, with the new technology and the growth in country music record sales, major labels like Columbia were willing to invest more time in recording. Just four songs were recorded over no more than two hours at each of Monroe's three sessions for Satherley in 1946. The first session began at 8 on that Monday evening.

At first the band seemed stiff, nervous, and uncertain. Although it would be one of their last songs released from this session, the first on which they worked was "Heavy Traffic Ahead." The title is a metaphor for their life and music, a happy ancestor of Willie Nelson's "On the Road Again." The first take (-2) sounds more like a test than a serious effort. The instrumental introduction is messy, and Bill sings only three of the five verses of the song, repeating one verse twice. "We had been doing a whole series of one-nighters," recalls Earl Scruggs, "and we were all tired, and most of us had never made a record before. After we ran through couple of tunes, Satherley came out of the control room and began dancing a funny little sort of Irish jig. We all laughed and relaxed a little."[19] He was trying to get them to take it easy and put more drive into the songs. In their second and final take (-1) of "Heavy Traffic Ahead," the opening arrangement—the first recording of the famous Lester Flatt "G run" followed by Monroe's mandolin, Scruggs's banjo, and Wise's fiddle—is tight, crisp, punchy, and flowing, symbolic of the overall sound of the band. Monroe does the singing on the twelve-bar blues that portrays a week in the lives of the Blue Grass Boys, who are never late while traveling in their converted airport limousine, the Blue Grass Special. As in the 1945 recording of "Blue Grass Special," every member of the band except bassist Watts—whose walking bass shines throughout the cut—takes an instrumental solo, with fiddle and banjo both getting two breaks. The title was taken from a road sign near Lester Flatt's home in Sparta in middle Tennessee, where there was hardly ever traffic. Band members would tease Lester about the lack of it.

Next came "Why Did You Wander?" an up-tempo Flatt composition and the first duet the two recorded together. Both takes are similar, but the first try (-2) was marred when Bill started to sing harmony with Lester at the start of the third verse. In the second take (-1), Bill moved his second mandolin break to the final chorus. The fact that this take, too, was marred by a minor flaw in Scruggs's banjo break is probably why it was never issued on a Columbia single. At this point, what they were doing was still very new and a bit of a stretch. As an air check made of an Opry broadcast of "Why Did You Wander?" the next year shows, they'd improved their performance considerably by the time Satherley was ready to consider releasing the song. Consequently, it languished in the vaults until 1976 when it appeared on a New World Records anthology. Meanwhile, in 1952 Flatt and Scruggs recorded their version, and the song soon became a standard in their repertoire.

The next piece was another Kentucky-themed waltz meant as a sequel to Bill's current hit. About "Blue Moon of Kentucky," he told Dorothy Horstman, "Back in those days, it seems every trip we made was from Kentucky to Florida, driving back and forth. I always thought about Kentucky, and I wanted to write a song about the moon we could always see over it. The best way to do this was to bring a girl into the song. I wanted words to this because most of my songs were instrumentals. 'Kentucky Waltz' had come earlier and I knew I could write both words and music, so I wrote it in the car on the way home from one of those Florida trips."[20] After a take aborted (-BD) when an E string of Bill's mandolin became hooked underneath a fret end (the source of his one-course harmony sound that can be heard in his 1960 recording of "Blue Grass Part 1"), Monroe sailed through his new waltz.

In marvelous understatement, Satherley typed "Good" on the original session card opposite "Blue Moon of Kentucky" even though he held up its release for a year, until September 1947. The song has become the most famous in Monroe's repertoire, pushed toward fame when Elvis Presley included it on his first recording in 1954. Monroe's recording has been recognized as a heritage document through its inclusion on two national lists: the National Academy of Recording Arts and Sciences Grammy Hall of Fame and the National Recording Registry of the Library of Congress. In 1988 it replaced "My Old Kentucky Home" as the state's official song.

The session ended after an hour and twenty minutes with another fast-tempo duet by Flatt and Monroe. "Toy Heart," which features fine mandolin work by Monroe, is the first studio recording of Scruggs's banjo work in C tuning. The song was unreleased until 1949, but when issued (in both 78 and 33⅓ singles versions) it made it to number twelve on the *Billboard* charts and was his best-selling song of the year.

At 10:30, after a break of an hour and ten minutes, the band returned to the studio and began work on "Summertime Is Past and Gone." With its thirty-two-bar, pop-song melody structure (*a1/a2/b/a2*) it resembles "Blue Moon of Kentucky," and like that song it's in a ¾ tempo. It also features one of the few vocal trios this band recorded. The text follows an *abcb* form with vocal trio harmony on the a and b parts and Flatt's solo on the c or bridge section; Rainwater sings the third or baritone part below Flatt's melody and Monroe's high harmony. In his banjo solo, Scruggs uses melodic materials similar to those in his breaks on "Heavy Traffic Ahead."

It took a number of tries to get an acceptable master for "Summertime Is Past and Gone." In -BD1 the baritone was too loud, and Flatt missed his cue to start singing the bridge. The blend was better on the next take (-BD2), but the guitar was off in spots; -2 was a good performance but ruined by the audible clearing of someone's throat. The band was not together in tempo or vocal phrasing the next try (-BD3), and the take was stopped after the first chorus. Finally, an acceptable recording was made on the fifth try, -1. Like most songs the band recorded, it become a bluegrass standard. A lot of work had produced a classic, a complex integration of voices and instruments in an arrangement unlike anything Monroe had produced before.

Although the bluegrass sound included many innovations, Monroe maintained elements of the old brother duets he and Charlie had used in the 1930s. After working on the complex "Summertime," the band sailed through "Mansions for Me," capturing a fine performance in one take. Composed by Monroe, it is a Flatt-Monroe duet similar in form and melody to the Monroe Brothers career record of 1936, "What Would You Give in Exchange for Your Soul?" "Mansions for Me" is the only piece in the band's recorded repertoire that has no instrumental breaks.

This was one of the first two sides by the classic band to be issued, released on March 24, 1947, on the flip side of "Mother's Only Sleeping." The latter piece came to Monroe from Lester Flatt. Popular in the Carolinas, the song was recorded during 1946 and 1947 by Charlie Monroe, J. E. Mainer, the York Brothers, and others, all of whom used slightly differing texts and put their own names on the piece. In 1996, however, the composers were revealed as the Spencer Brothers, Lance and Maynard. They composed it, using the title "Mother's Just Sleeping," in the summer of 1941. At the time, they were members of Charlie Monroe's Kentucky Partners troupe in Greensboro, North Carolina, and working with Stringbean, who was part of the same. After they left the older Monroe to join the service during the war, Lester Flatt joined the Kentucky Partners, which was apparently where he learned the song. "Mother's Only Sleeping" was new to Monroe when Lester began performing it with him. As with the previous number, the band nailed this one in a single take.

Monroe's first vocal showpiece had been a Jimmie Rodgers blue yodel, number 8, "Mule Skinner Blues." He recorded another blue yodel, number 7, "Anniversary Blue Yodel," at his second Bluebird session. For the final cut on this Columbia session he chose a third blue yodel that was listed in the ledgers as "Blue Yodel No. 4." It was, in fact, what Rodgers called "Blue Yodel No. 3." Bill had been developing the piece, which follows the same twelve-bar format found on "Heavy Traffic Ahead," into a showpiece for his yodeling (as well as the band's instrumental work) during Opry performances and tried one of his fancier versions on the first take (-2). The second take, judged -1 and destined for release on a single the following July, took a more conservative approach to the yodel. By the end of the session it was 12:30 A.M.

The band returned to the studio at 1 the following afternoon, Tuesday, September 17, to do four more sides. The session opened with a Lester Flatt composition, "Will You Be Loving Another Man?" By 1946 divorce was becoming an inescapable reality. In 1945 one in every three marriages in America ended in divorce, a 25 percent increase. A rival hit at the time was Merle Travis's "Divorce Me C.O.D.," and other singers were filling juke boxes with music that reflected the tensions of separation brought on by the war. "Will you love me little darling / when I'm in some other land?" Flatt's lyrics ask. The musical side of the song was as contemporary as the lyrical side. "Will You Be Loving Another Man?" was the first recording released to include a Scruggs banjo break on an up-tempo tune. Chubby Wise takes two breaks, the second reflecting the jazz influences in country fiddling in the 1940s. Rainwater's four-beat bass spurs the band along while keeping them in the groove.

Monroe told Doug Green, interviewer and former Blue Grass Boy, that he bought outright the next song in the session, "How Will I Explain about You?" from the mysterious and legendary Knoxville songwriter Arthur Q. Smith. Smith, brilliant and alcoholic, would stand outside the WNOX station door with trays of songs for sale. Prices ranged from $10 to $50, depending on how new or good Smith felt a song was. His clients included Roy Acuff, Bill Carlisle, Carl Smith, Maybelle Carter, and others, and among his hits were "Wedding Bells," "If Teardrops Were Pennies," and "I Wouldn't Change You if I Could." Flatt sang the lead on "How Will I Explain about You?" and Bill joined in with tenor harmony on the choruses. The band made changes to the arrangement after the first take (-2), with the fiddle being moved to kick off the song rather than the mandolin on the second take (-3), which was marred by timing problems on the final chorus. The band nailed it on the third take.

"Shining Path" features the Blue Grass Quartet, with Monroe singing tenor, Flatt lead, Watts baritone, and Scruggs bass, a rare performance taking that part. For years the recording, which never appeared on a single, was thought to be lost, but it came to light in the mid-1980s on a Columbia reissue album in the Hall of Fame series. It had probably not been issued because Birch Monroe, who was filling in on string bass so Watts could concentrate on the complicated baritone part, played some out-of-tune notes.

By now, Monroe sought to define the quartet as an entity separate from the Blue Grass Boys. They appeared on records under their own name and even on show bills as an added feature to Monroe's package shows. One of their most popular numbers, "Wicked Path of Sin," featured Bill's tenor, Lester's lead, Earl singing baritone, and a call-and-response chorus lead by brother Birch, who sang bass with an authority born of his training in Rosine's singing schools. He leads on the first line of the chorus, adding a responsorial part on the second line ("and loved ones wait"). Bill leads on the third line, and Flatt on the fourth. On the third chorus, however, Monroe joins Flatt on a duet harmony on the line. The final line of the last chorus ("the pearly gates") is sung in turn by Bill, Earl Scruggs, and Birch.

The band made two tries at this complex quartet, with the first one (-2) being flawed when Birch hesitated briefly at the start of the final chorus, causing Flatt to alter the rhythm briefly. In the second and final take (-1) the arrangement was tightened by shortening Bill's mandolin turnarounds from eight bars to four. The session ended with this take—two hours after it had begun. Although this was the first quartet from this band released, it did not appear until the fall of 1948 and after several other quartets recorded a year later had been issued.

The 1946 sessions had produced twelve take -1 performances, half of which would be released in 1947, two in 1948, and two in 1949. Two others did not appear on singles. It would be decades before "Why Did You Wander?" and "Shining Path" would be released.

The live recordings of Bill and the Blue Grass Boys made from Opry broadcasts by Neal Matthews for Earl Scruggs between December 1946 and July 1947 (listed together under session number 461200) provide glimpses of the band's development during the year between the first Columbia sessions and the second set of sessions in the fall of 1947. All but one ("True Life Blues") of the air-check performances features pieces not yet available on records. Some had not been recorded. Thus on December 21, 1946, they did "Mother's Only Sleeping," which they'd recorded a few months earlier and would be released the following March. From the same date comes "Roll in My Sweet Baby's Arms," a Monroe Brothers song featuring Flatt singing lead with Howard Watts singing tenor and punctuated by Scruggs, who takes all the banjo breaks to the delight of the enthusiastic audience. After they left Monroe to start their own band, Lester and Earl featured "Roll in My Sweet Baby's Arms" on their radio shows from Bristol, and it became one of their most-requested pieces after they recorded it for Mercury in 1950. It is now a bluegrass standard. The following week Monroe featured a new gospel quartet, "Little Community Church," which would not be recorded until the following October and would not be available on record until a year after that.

"Wicked Path of Sin," performed the following week, on January 3, 1947, had been recorded that fall, but it, too, would not be released until October 1948. "Remember the Cross," done the following week, would not be recorded until the coming fall and would not appear in record stores until May 1949.

On a March show, Judge Hay introduced another piece by "Bill and Earl Scruggs, with that *fancy* banjo: 'Molly and Ten-brooks.'"[21] It would be recorded the coming fall, but the record would not be issued until September 1949. Bill and Earl, however, were doing it regularly on Opry broadcasts. The following month their hot version of "Will You Be Loving Another Man?" was captured, which they'd recorded the previous fall but would not be on record until that July. On Friday, April 18, Monroe performed "Why Did You Wander?" which they'd recorded in 1946. By this time the piece had developed in the band's repertoire to become more of a banjo feature, with Earl opening and playing a second break on it; Lester and Earl would record it in a similar version for Columbia in 1952. At the end of July they did another new quartet, not yet recorded, "Shine Hallelujah Shine," along with a solo featuring Lester Flatt on a song they would never record: "Love Gone Cold." Its composer, Johnny Bond, had recorded it in 1942, and Ernest Tubb cut his cover of it in 1945. In his shows, Monroe's guitarist-lead singers in the Blue Grass Boys regularly sang covers of the hits of other country stars, which is likely why Flatt performed "Love Gone Cold." The performance captures the excitement the band was generating. In addition to Flatt's smooth, distinctive vocals, there was a bluesy fiddle break by Wise, a mandolin break by Monroe that anticipates the jagged sound that would characterize his later Decca work, and a banjo break by Earl Scruggs that brought down the house. Another performance that captures the excitement Opry audiences felt for the band's music is the undated "Blue Yodel No. 4" (480300, [1]), which had outstanding performances by all the instrumentalists. Watts, Scruggs, and Monroe received ovations for their breaks, and Monroe's high yodel at the end sent the crowd to its feet.

On Sunday evening, October 26, 1947, the Blue Grass Special rolled into Chicago for Monroe's second session with the classic band. The next afternoon, October 27, they made their way to the Wrigley Building and the WBBM Studio for what would be a massive session over the next two days. They recorded sixteen sides, most of them destined to become classics. By now the members of the band had honed their skills to an even greater level of perfection, and Satherley was eager to see what they could do with the large number of new and original songs they planned to record. Like most other recording executives, he anticipated another recording ban by the American Federation of Musicians and was eager to stockpile enough recordings to see Columbia through a long strike. As it turned out, the ban would extend for fifteen months and continue through most of 1948.

The sessions that began on that Monday, again documented in detail on the sixteen-inch transcription discs, indicate a band more comfortable in the studio than on the first visit a year earlier. They would try first one piece, then another, then return to the first for still another take, and so on. The relaxed sessions mixed new numbers with those the band had played for months on the Opry and at personal appearances. Unlike the 1946 sessions, which saw ten of twelve pieces issued on 78s, every one of the masters recorded at these sessions would be issued within the next two years.

Monday's session opened with a barn-burner, "I'm Going Back to Old Kentucky," which featured Flatt singing lead with Monroe's tenor on the duet chorus. Monroe plays mandolin harmony to the fiddle during Chubby Wise's breaks, anticipating the twin-fiddle sound he would initiate in Decca recordings of the mid-1950s, and prominent melodic backup during Flatt's verses. Three takes of the song were put on acetate. The first (-1), judged the best and ultimately issued on a single, was followed by the first attempt (-2) at another barn-burner, "It's Mighty Dark to Travel," also an up-tempo duet. Then two more tries (-BD and -2) were made at "I'm Going Back to Old Kentucky." In spite of an out-of-tune guitar chord at the end of (-2), these two tries were finally released as a single track on the two-CD Monroe retrospective in 1992. But the band nailed the song on the first take.

They then returned to "It's Mighty Dark to Travel." Monroe told Doug Green how the song came about. "I was getting some barber work done down on Broadway in Nashville one time and a colored man came to the door. Somebody had been giving him an awful hard time—I don't know if it was a white man or not—and he shook his head and said, 'It's mighty dark to travel.' I had my song right there."[22] On the first take, (-2), Scruggs played his banjo break in the third position, up the neck. Now the arrangement was changed. In addition to playing his break at the first position, Scruggs played harmony to Monroe's second mandolin break. The first try (-3) using that arrangement was spoiled when Flatt sang the wrong lyrics on the final verse. On the third try, (-1), however, they produced the cut that would be issued on a single.

"I Hear a Sweet Voice Calling" is the first trio in which Monroe sang lead on the verses and tenor on the choruses,

with Flatt on lead beneath him and Watts's baritone beneath that. It would become a standard practice later in his career. Monroe described writing the song: "I could picture somebody having some little kid, a boy or a girl like I had, and then things turn out like that. Many a time it was hard for me to sing that song."[23] Only one take—that issued—was required.

A medium-tempo duet credited to Flatt and Monroe on the original labels, "Little Cabin Home on the Hill," was distinguished by Howard Watts's four-beat walking bass that created a smooth, flowing sound. Notable also on the cut was Flatt's guitar work, especially the bass runs. On his album *Bean Blossom '79* Monroe performed the song again; dedicated it to the memory of Lester Flatt, who had recently died; and confirmed that Flatt had written it. The session ended at 5:45.

After a two-hour supper break the band returned to the studio and began work on "My Rose of Old Kentucky." The folklorist William Hugh Jansen has suggested that this "Rose" is derived from or based upon an earlier minstrel or stage song with the same title and found in oral tradition in Kentucky. In 2001 it was reported that Monroe had stated that his niece, Rosetta Monroe Kiper, "was the inspiration behind the song."[24] Monroe, in turn, used it as the basis for his composition "My Little Georgia Rose" (1950). After one take (-2) of the vocal solo they moved on to try a new instrumental, "Blue Grass Breakdown." One of Monroe's earliest up-tempo instrumentals, it gave Scruggs a chance to cut loose on the banjo with a solo that anticipated "Foggy Mountain Breakdown."[25] This piece differed from that, for, as Monroe played it, it has two sections, an A section that uses a G-F chord progression and a B section that uses a G-C chord progression. The three takes give a sense of how the arrangement was polished. In the first try (-2) at the piece Monroe arranged these sections *aabb* in his first break and *aab* in the next two. Both Wise and Scruggs play only the first section, *aa*. In that take, Chubby Wise's fiddle took the second break and Scruggs's banjo the fourth.

The band then returned to make their final definitive version of "My Rose of Old Kentucky" (-1). Monroe's vocal trademarks are particularly evident in this solo performance, especially the last verse. He effortlessly slides into falsetto when he hits the word *bloom*. Once again, Flatt contributes outstanding guitar work.

Having completed work on "My Rose of Old Kentucky" they again attacked "Blue Grass Breakdown." Now the arrangement was changed, altering the sequence of breaks. In the first try (-3), Scruggs's break was moved up to follow Bill's first break, and Wise's break moved back to precede Bill's final break.

This sequence was followed in the next and final try (-1), where Monroe shortened all of his breaks, playing only one *b* section in the first two and a simple *AB* in his final break. In later years when Monroe played the piece the entire band followed the *aab* pattern. Perhaps the tinkering on its arrangement at this session, when it was obviously a new piece, was done to reduce its playing time on the record.

Although the record labels list "Sweetheart You Done Me Wrong" as a Monroe composition, Flatt consistently maintained that he was the composer and sang lead on it.[26] Performed in the key of D, it is pitched so high that Monroe, who sings only on the choruses, places his voice on the borderline between natural and falsetto tenor with the smoothness that became the model for all bluegrass tenor singers. Again, the four-beat bass and Monroe's mandolin backup work add special dimension to the sound. The band took some time to work on this recording; three takes exist as well as two false starts. After the first take (-2), the band reduced the length of the breaks from a full to a half chorus.

The final song of the evening's session was "The Old Cross Road," a duet by Flatt and Monroe. "I wrote that song coming back from Texas, when we were working the tent show," Monroe would tell Doug Green. "I wrote it in the car while everyone was asleep. When we got back to Nashville, we got to working right on it, and it's really been a good one for us."[27] No doubt Satherley welcomed another gospel duet after the success of the last year's pairing of "Mansions for Me" and "Mother's Only Sleeping," but this one took a while to work out. It appears that they began working on it without the final lyrics. There was potential for confusion over the words because the third line of the chorus begins "one leads down" while the first line of the second verse begins "one road leads up." Although their meter is slightly different, both phrases use essentially the same melody. On various takes both Lester and Bill add or omit "road" at the wrong place. As a result, no fewer than six takes were saved, including one (-BD2) in which Monroe blurts out in frustration at the end, "That ain't doin' no good like that, damn it." It's possible that they finally stopped to write out the words before the sixth try that produced take 1, and by this point a number of other parts of the text had been altered as well. The session, the longest single one the band spent in the studio, ended at 10:30 that night.

The next afternoon the band returned to the studio and carried on with three numbers by the Blue Grass Quartet. The first was "That Home Above," of which Monroe said in 1980: "I wrote that. The Blue Grass Quartet was really working fine in

those days. Cedric did the bass, Chubby played the guitar. It's really a fine sound; it gives you a better chance to try hard to get in there with that sound."[28] On this song Watts and Scruggs switch parts at different points, with Earl singing the bass lead on the chorus. Only one take was needed. Although the next quartet was credited to Monroe and Howard Watts, "Remember the Cross" was actually written by Watts and his wife, Alice. The band had been performing it live for some time.

The third quartet was "Little Community Church." "Rosine had a Methodist and a Baptist church," Monroe explained, "and I used to stand outside and hear them sing, and I kept a picture in my mind for years of someone standing outside a little church, listening to them singing inside."[29] Once again, Chubby Wise does the guitar work. The band was also familiar with this song, having included it on their repertoire on the Opry and in personal appearances for some months. After their first try, which would ultimately be chosen as -1 and released on a single to become one of Bill's best-sellers in 1949, the band turned from gospel quartets to a secular piece.

Speaking about "Along about Daybreak," a solo he wrote, Monroe recalled, "Well, there is a true story behind that song, but it don't need to be printed. It was a good song back in its day."[30] In his biography of Monroe, Richard D. Smith dates the song to the aftermath of a fight between Bill and his wife, Carolyn. The band tried one take (-2) and then returned to "Little Community Church" for two more tries that ultimately were not judged to be as good as the first. Returning to "Along about Daybreak," they altered the arrangement, dropping the fiddle turnaround at the opening in favor of a simple guitar chord leading into Bill's vocal. The session finished at 5:30.

After a long supper break the band returned to the studio at 8 to record four more songs. They only needed one take for "When You Are Lonely" another duet in which Flatt sang lead on the verses and was joined by Bill's tenor on the chorus. Like "Little Cabin Home on the Hill," it has a smooth feeling because of Watts's four-beat walking bass. Chubby Wise's fiddle work is especially prominent in his backup role, and Monroe's mandolin solo combines the fluid sound of his Monroe Brothers work with the more rough-edged sound of his later recordings.

"Molly and Tenbrooks" (subtitled "The Race Horse Song") was, in Monroe's opinion, a good banjo song, and the recorded arrangement features three banjo breaks. Bill had been featuring the song during live performances on the Opry as a showpiece for Scruggs, who took breaks after every verse. As Monroe told Alanna Nash, "A number like 'Molly and Tenbrooks' was perfect for the banjo. If it hadn't been for numbers like 'Molly and Tenbrooks,' the banjo wouldn't have had a lot to do."[31] Monroe's vocal solo was so popular that the Stanley Brothers copied it; in fact, their recording on Tennessee's small independent Rich-R-Tone label was released a year before this Columbia version was issued.

The song refers to a match race run in Louisville, Kentucky, on July 4, 1878, in which the Kentucky Thoroughbred Ten Broeck defeated California-owned Miss Mollie MacCarthy. The race was the last four-mile heat in American turf history (by modern standards, a four-mile race is an impossibly long and grueling affair). Ten Broecks's jockey was Billy Walker, a name that became "Kiper" in Monroe's version. After the race there were unfounded rumors that Ten Broeck had been doped (verse four) and Mollie had died (verse nine). The earliest collected version of "Molly and Tenbrooks" dates from the 1880s. As Monroe explained the story behind the song to an audience at Bean Blossom, Indiana, in April 1969: "It's about two horses that was run. It's run years ago. One of them was from Kentucky and I believe the other one was from Ireland. And they run three races in the United States. They run in Kentucky and Tenbrooks was the winner. They moved to California where this lady owned this mare, and they run and she won. They met half way and Tenbrooks won the third race. And I'd like to do it for you today, 'Molly and Tenbrooks, The Kentucky Race Horse Song.'"[32] One alternate take of the number survives (-2) and has a different ending, the final verse is omitted, and Scruggs comes in for his second break a bar early. Monroe's perception of the song as a banjo piece is reflected in the way in which Scruggs's breaks were miked very high in the mix.

The Blue Grass Quartet was featured for the final cuts of the session. With Flatt singing lead, Monroe tenor, Scruggs baritone, and Rainwater bass, the first song, "Shine Hallelujah Shine," a Monroe composition, features a responsorial chorus. They'd been performing the tune on the Opry since at least the previous summer. "I'm Travelin' On and On," which Monroe wrote specifically for his quartet, was intended to include both bass and tenor lead parts. These can be heard, respectively, on the first two lines and the last line of the responsorial chorus. After these two tightly arranged quartets the session ended at 10:15. The quartets, the last studio recordings the legendary lineup made, came out on January 26, 1948, and were the first from the session to be released to the public.

Nearly a month later, on February 21, 1948, the final Grand Ole Opry air check recordings of this groundbreaking group of Blue Grass Boys included Flatt singing "Sunny Side of the Mountain," the only version of this song extant on recordings

by the Blue Grass Boys. Chubby Wise had left the band by this point, and Benny Martin, Monroe's new fiddler, is heard on the performance. Monroe may have been playing on the Opry stage during the song, but neither his voice nor mandolin is audible on the recording. Later, of course, the piece became a signature song of Jimmy Martin. "Just a Little Talk with Jesus," Cleavant Derricks's gospel quartet favorite that featured Birch Monroe singing lead (as he often did on the song with Bill at Bean Blossom in later years), was recorded the same night. The performance featured finger-style lead guitar breaks rather than Monroe's customary mandolin breaks. Presumably, they're by Scruggs, who would feature a similar sound on his and Flatt's first recordings for Mercury only a few months later.

Much has been made of the impact that Flatt and Scruggs's leaving had on Monroe in early 1948. Clearly, however, Bill was able to carry on without trouble. The next recording he made, in June 1948 on the Opry's Prince Albert segment, wasn't released until 1989 when MCA included it on an album of Bill's Opry performances. Introduced by Red Foley, Monroe did a rousing performance of "Mule Skinner Blues" (inaccurately titled "New Mule Skinner Blues") to the backup of unidentified Blue Grass Boys.

The union recording ban had kept Monroe away from the studio throughout 1948 and much of 1949. In April 1949 *Billboard* carried a lengthy note on Monroe, detailing his ambitious plans to carry a baseball team with the band's forthcoming personal appearance tours. It also added that "Monroe intends to debut his new Blue Grass Quartet for his next waxing session."[33] In fact, Bill would not record any Blue Grass Quartet numbers until April of the following year, but he continued to tour extensively. In early July it was reported that he'd returned to the Opry "following two weeks of complete rest, ordered by his doctor."[34] His Columbia records were selling briskly, as a special section in *Billboard,* "Top Selling Folk Artists over Retail Counters," reported at the end of July. Monroe ranked seventeenth in sales, with seven titles listed as best-sellers for the first six months of 1949. "Toy Heart" topped the list, with "Little Community Church," "It's Mighty Dark to Travel," "When You Are Lonely," "Wicked Path of Sin," "The Old Cross Road," and "I Hear a Sweet Voice Calling" following. Unlike the artists ranked in the sales list near him, Monroe had a large number of different records that contributed to his total, reflecting a consistency of sales.[35]

By fall 1949, the time of the final Columbia session for Monroe, Columbia had decided to shift much of its country recording to Nashville. The newly opened Castle Studio, operated by two WSM engineers, was located in the same Tulane Hotel that most musicians used as regular lodging. There, on October 22, 1949, a new version of the Blue Grass Boys assembled for what would be the final Columbia session. Still present in the band were Monroe and fiddler Chubby Wise, who had returned after a stint with Clyde Moody in Washington, D.C. Taking the place of Don Reno, who had in turn replaced Earl Scruggs, was banjoist Rudy Lyle.

Lyle was from Franklin County, Virginia, where he grew up listening to his grandfather, Lomax Blankenship, a well-known local fiddler, and a Rocky Mount banjoist named Lawrence Wright, who taught him to play rolls on the banjo. As a teenager, Lyle worked with the bandleader Uncle Joe Johnson on WPAQ radio in Mt. Airy, North Carolina, the heart of the Blue Ridge Mountains and one of the strong bastions of string-band music. Lyle was also fascinated with the radio work of banjoist Snuffy Jenkins. Some time in the summer of 1949 Monroe made a personal appearance in Mt. Airy, and all the members of the WPAQ band were there. Lyle remembered:

> At that time Bill's band had just broken up. Don Reno had just left. He didn't have too many people working with him. He had two boys called The Kentucky Twins [Mel and Stan Hankinson, who had been touring with Monroe for a couple of years and had made several records] and another fellow named Bill Myrick but didn't have a banjo player, so I tuned up and went out there with him. . . . After the show I told Bill that I'd sure like to work for him and he said he would like for me to but didn't want to take me away from Uncle Joe. . . . About three weeks later we were working a show in Radford, Virginia, at the theater. The manager came back stage and said I had a long-distance call. It was Bill. He was in D.C. and asked me if I wanted to come to work. I said yes, I was ready.[36]

Lyle took the bus to Nashville and waited in the alley behind the Ryman for Monroe and the band to arrive for the night's show. "We went in and did the RC Cola show," Lyle said. "The first tune I did was 'Cumberland Gap.' I think the RC Cola show was network then, like the Prince Albert Show, so it was getting out pretty good."[37] Lyle is in many ways one of the great unsung heroes of Monroe's post-Scruggs sides, contributing a number of great innovative breaks and backup on records from 1949 to 1954. Monroe often observed that in this era everyone—even Earl Scruggs—listened closely to Lyle. He was especially good at improvising from the blues-boogie tunes of which Monroe was fond during this time, for example, "Blue Grass Special" and "Blue Grass Stomp." Years later, Monroe told Alanna Nash, "He [Lyle] was a powerful banjo player. He

could really tie Earl Scruggs up in knots. Tie Don Reno up too, because he was such a banjo player."[38]

In place of Howard Watts was string-bass player Jack Thompson, who appeared only on this session and left soon after to join the newly formed Stringbean–Lew Childre band. Replacing Lester Flatt on lead vocals and guitar was Mac Wiseman, later known to radio listeners as the "Voice with a Heart." A native of Virginia, the twenty-four-year-old Wiseman had worked briefly with Molly O'Day and with Flatt and Scruggs and had played on the first recording sessions (for Columbia and for Mercury) for both acts. Wiseman would be with Monroe for a relatively short time in 1949 before signing as a soloist with the independent Dot Records. It was for Dot that he would have such signature hits as "Jimmy Brown the Newsboy," "Shackles and Chains," and "Love Letters in the Sand." All featured his wide-ranging, rich vocal leads and fancy guitar work. Ultimately, Wiseman would become an executive with Dot and a founding member of the Country Music Association. In later years he would record again with Monroe.

By the time of the October 22, 1949, session Columbia had issued all Monroe's earlier recordings on the label, and the sound of the classic band was widely heard. This last session shows important changes to Monroe's sound as it diverged from that of the classic band toward the sound that would emerge in his great Decca sides of the early 1950s—more intense, bluesy, and on the edge. Lyle's banjo backup contributed much to this, as did Monroe's mandolin work. The first song was "Can't You Hear Me Callin'," of which Monroe said, "Mac had just come to work with me, and he could really do that song! It gave me a shove to sing that tenor. You know, it was sad days for me, and that song meant a lot to me then. But people really like it. They still do."[39] As Doug Green pointed out, "The song has presented a challenge for bluegrass lead singers ever since it was first recorded, for the lead voice must rise to a G and hit it squarely as the young Mac Wiseman does here."[40] The song's lyrics also presented a challenge because for a line in the chorus ("a million times I've loved you Bess") puzzled listeners for many years. In his biography of Monroe, which carries the same title as the song, Richard D. Smith has explained that the reference is to Monroe's companion, Bessie Lee Mauldin.

"Travelin' This Lonesome Road," is another Monroe-Wiseman duet. "I had the chorus to this song for a long time," Monroe commented, "and when Mac came with me he helped put some words in and put together the chorus."[41] In terms of pace and feeling it maintained the intensity established by the first song in the session.

"Blue Grass Stomp" is another twelve-bar blues like "Blue Grass Special" and "Heavy Traffic Ahead." Of it Monroe remembered, "Back in those days we would play a lot of dances, and we had a few tunes that was just made for dancing. People would kind of stomp while they danced, you know, and that's why I named it that. It's got a perfect time for dancing."[42] "Blue Grass Stomp" survives in no fewer than three alternates in addition to the one issued. All have significant changes and novel licks—especially Monroe's daring double time on take two—as the band expanded the arrangement to make it into a mandolin tour-de-force.

Monroe's solo voice was heard on the final song of the session, "The Girl in the Blue Velvet Band," which had been a huge hit in 1934 when Cliff Carlisle recorded it for the American Record Corporation. The grim, melodramatic story concerns a boy from San Francisco who meets a strange girl whose hair is tied in a blue velvet band. As they walk arm in arm, she slips a "diamond worth ten grand" into his pocket and frames him for robbery. He is sent to San Quentin for ten years. The song was already widely known in folk traditions, with considerable variation, when Monroe recorded it. Although a far cry from the pine trees and cabins of many of Monroe's other songs, it was successful.

These were Monroe's last recordings for Columbia. In early November, a few weeks after the session, *Billboard* reported, "Bill Monroe, for years a standby of the Columbia rustic roster, has reportedly been dissatisfied with his treatment by that waxery for months and is now dickering with several firms. It is known that Paul Cohen, of Decca, and others have made concerted pitches to the WSM, Nashville, star. Monroe's original gripe with Columbia was their inking of the Stanley Brothers, a combo which he felt sounded too much like his own work."[43]

The Stanley Brothers had been recording for Rich-R-Tone, a small independent label based in East Tennessee, and they also performed over WCYB in Bristol on the Tennessee-Virginia border. Their mandolin player, Pee Wee Lambert, was a fan of Monroe's work; he had learned to sing "Molly and Tenbrooks" by listening to Bill's version on the Opry. After Flatt and Scruggs arrived in Bristol in the spring of 1948, Ralph Stanley, who'd played a two-finger-style banjo on his first recordings with his brother, Carter, began learning Scruggs's three-finger style. As a result, the Stanley Brothers released their cover of "Molly and Tenbrooks" in September, a year before Monroe's recording appeared on Columbia.

Around the same time, Wilma Lee and Stoney Cooper, based at WWVA in Wheeling, West Virginia, released their version of Bill's "Wicked Path of Sin." It, too, was on the Rich-R-Tone label and appeared, like the Stanley's release, before Monroe's. All this happened while the union recording ban was in effect, but Art Satherley was still actively recruiting new acts for Columbia. Late in 1948 he flew to Raleigh, North Carolina, where he auditioned the Stanley Brothers and signed them to a contract with Columbia. On March 1, 1949, he and Don Law were in Nashville for the Stanley Brothers' first Columbia recording session. A month later Satherley supervised the first Columbia recording session for Wilma Lee and Stoney Cooper. By the time of Bill's next—and final—Columbia session that October, the company had released three 78s of the Stanley Brothers' recordings, including one with "Let Me Be Your Friend," a close copy of "It's Mighty Dark to Travel."

It's not surprising that Monroe was angry with Columbia. On November 26, *Billboard* reported, "Bill Monroe has switched from Columbia to Decca, and Paul Cohen cut Monroe's first sides in Nashville November 8."[44] No evidence of the recordings said to have been made on that date has been found, but it would only be a few weeks before Monroe began making the Decca recordings that would become his most famous.

Notes

1. Charles K. Wolfe, notes to *Bill Monroe: Blue Moon of Kentucky* (Bear Family BCD 16399, 2002), 53.

2. Unsigned notes to *Foggy Mountain Jamboree* (Columbia CL 1019, 1957): "Flatt . . . in 1944 joined Bill Monroe and his Blue Grass Boys, remaining with them until 1948."

3. Douglas B. Green, notes to *Bill Monroe and His Blue Grass Boys: The Classic Bluegrass Recordings, Volume 1* (County CCS 104, 1980).

4. Earl Scruggs, *Earl Scruggs and the Five-String Banjo* (New York: Peer, 1968), 147.

5. Scruggs, *Earl Scruggs and the Five-String Banjo.*

6. Wolfe, notes to *Blue Moon of Kentucky,* 54.

7. Ibid.

8. Ibid.

9. Ibid., 55.

10. Scruggs, *Earl Scruggs and the Five-String Banjo,* 156.

11. Jake Lambert, with Curly Sechler, *A Biography of Lester Flatt: "The Good Things Outweigh the Bad"* (Hendersonville: Jay-Lyn Publications, 1982), 113.

12. Wolfe, notes to *Blue Moon of Kentucky,* 55.

13. Alanna Nash, *Behind Closed Doors: Talking with the Legends of Country Music* (New York: Knopf, 1988), 335.

14. Additional dates have been obtained from documentation that circulated with copies of the tape dubs in the 1960s.

15. Session 460300, [2], introduction to "Careless Love," March 30, 1946.

16. Neil V. Rosenberg, *Bluegrass: A History* (Urbana: University of Illinois Press, 1985), 74.

17. James Rooney, *Bossmen: Bill Monroe and Muddy Waters* (New York: Dial Press, 1971), 43.

18. Rooney, *Bossmen,* 43.

19. Earl Scruggs, conversation with Charles K. Wolfe, Earl Scruggs, Hendersonville, Tenn., May 2000.

20. Dorothy Horstman, *Sing Your Heart Out, Country Boy: Classic Country Songs and Their Inside Stories by the Men and Women Who Wrote Them,* rev. ed. (Nashville: Country Music Foundation Press, 1986), 151.

21. Session 461200, [6], March 8, 1947.

22. Douglas B. Green, notes to *Bill Monroe and His Blue Grass Boys: The Classic Bluegrass Recordings, Volume 2* (County CCS 105, 1980).

23. Green, notes to *Bill Monroe and His Blue Grass Boys, Volume 2.*

24. Anon., *Special Collector's Edition: The Bill Monroe Foundation Presents the Ribbon Cutting and Free Bluegrass Show* (Rosine, Ky.: The Rosine Project, 2001), [21]. This was the souvenir program for the opening ceremonies for the restored Monroe home place on Jerusalem Ridge, "High above Rosine, Kentucky," on August 23, 2001.

25. Over the years there has been considerable speculation that Scruggs rather than Monroe was the composer of this tune. Scruggs confirmed this in a May 15, 2004, telephone interview with Tony Trischka (article in press, *Banjo Newsletter*).

26. Anon., "Winning Combination," *Country Song Roundup* 13 (1951): 18; notes to *Foggy Mountain Jamboree* (Columbia CL 1019, 1957).

27. Green, notes to *Bill Monroe and His Blue Grass Boys, Volume 1.*

28. Green, notes to *Bill Monroe and His Blue Grass Boys, Volume 2.*

29. Green, notes to *Bill Monroe and His Blue Grass Boys, Volume 1.*

30. Ibid.

31. Nash, *Behind Closed Doors,* 336.

32. Neil V. Rosenberg, notes to *Bill Monroe with Lester Flatt and Earl Scruggs, the Original Bluegrass Band* (Rounder Special Series 06, 1978). Monroe's comments were made during a show at the Brown County Jamboree in Bean Blossom, Indiana, on April 20, 1969.

33. Johnny Sippel, "Folk Talent and Tunes," *Billboard,* April 30, 1949, 35. Replacing "hillbilly," "folk" was the word *Billboard* used at this time for what would soon be called "country and western" and later "country."

34. Johnny Sippel, "Folk Talent and Tunes," *Billboard,* July 9, 1949, 35.

35. Anon., "Top Selling Folk Artists Over Retail Counters," *The Billboard NAMM [National Association of Music Merchants] Trade Show and Convention Section,* July 30, 1949, 89.

36. Doug Hutchens, "Rudy Lyle: Classic Bluegrass Man," *Bluegrass Unlimited* 19 (April 1985): 44.

37. Hutchens, "Rudy Lyle," 44.

38. Nash, *Behind Closed Doors,* 336.

39. Green, notes to *Bill Monroe and His Blue Grass Boys, Volume 1.*

40. Ibid.

41. Ibid.

42. Green, notes to *Bill Monroe and His Blue Grass Boys, Volume 2.*

43. Johnny Sippel, "Folk Talent and Tunes," *Billboard,* Nov. 12, 1949, 35.

44. Johnny Sippel, "Folk Talent and Tunes," *Billboard,* Nov. 26, 1949, 30.

DISCOGRAPHY, 1946–49

ABOUT THE COLUMBIA MASTERS

Bill Monroe's Columbia masters recorded between 1945 and 1949 were made on sixteen-inch, 33⅓-rpm, acetate-coated aluminum discs called lacquers. They were recorded "inside out," meaning that the needle was started next to the label/spindle hole part of the disc, creating grooves that tracked out toward its edge—the opposite of commercial phonograph records. Most pieces were recorded more than once. Typically each disc held a number of tracks that included some incomplete performances that were labeled "BD" ("broke down"). Take numbers, the hyphenated numbers appended to the master numbers that in the days of wax masters (and also later with tape masters) were assigned at the time of recording, were in this case assigned *after* the recording was made and used to rank the takes in terms of quality. Consequently, in all of the Columbia recordings, take one ("-1") was assigned to the recording that was originally selected for release on a 78-rpm single. That is why the take numbers in this portion of the discography are not in a chronological sequence, but instead follow the sequence in which the recordings actually appear on the original lacquers. Composer credits and vocal or instrumental identifications are listed only once for each piece, in the citation for the earliest take.

460300	Bluegrass Classics reissue of radio broadcasts on WSM[1] Grand Ole Opry, Nashville, Tenn. March 1946 airchecks		
[1] 3/23/46	LITTLE MAGGIE Monroe-L		BGC 80
[2] 3/30/46	CARELESS LOVE Monroe-L		BGC 80

Bill Monroe: m	Lester Flatt: g	(no audible fiddle)
Earl Scruggs: b	Howard Watts: sb	

460916.1	Columbia Session; Producer: Art Satherley WBBM-CBS studio in the Wrigley Building, 410 N. Michigan Ave., Chicago, Ill. Sept. 16, 1946, 8–9:20 P.M.		
CCO 4605-2	HEAVY TRAFFIC AHEAD (Monroe) Monroe-L		BCD 16399
CCO 4605-1	HEAVY TRAFFIC AHEAD	20595, 2-275	HL 7315, SS 06, FC 38904, CK 53908, MCAD 4-11048, C2K 52478, BCD 16399, C2K 90858
CCO 4606-2	WHY DID YOU WANDER? Flatt-L, Monroe-T		BCD 16399

CCO 4606-1	WHY DID YOU WANDER?		NW 225, CSS 105, C2K 52478, BCD 16399
CCO 4607-BD	BLUE MOON OF KENTUCKY (B. Monroe) Monroe-L		BCD 16399
CCO 4607-1	BLUE MOON OF KENTUCKY	20370, 37888, 52022	B 2804, HL 7290, CS 1065, CMA 101, CCS 105, CK 46237, C2K 52478, CK 67735, V 79518-2, J2K 65816, KT 30322, BCD 16399, GHD5354, A16652, C4K 90628
CCO 4608-1	TOY HEART (Monroe) Flatt-L, Monroe-T	20552, 2-151	HL 7315, SS 06, FC 38904, C2K 52478, V 79518-2, BCD 16399, A16652
CCO 4608-BD	TOY HEART		

Bill Monroe: m   Lester Flatt: g   Chubby Wise: f
Earl Scruggs: b   Howard Watts: sb

460916.2   Columbia session; producer, Art Satherley
WBBM-CBS studio in the Wrigley Building, 410 N. Michigan Ave., Chicago, Ill.
Sept. 16, 1946, 10:30 P.M.–12:30 A.M.

CCO 4609 -BD1	SUMMERTIME IS PAST AND GONE (Monroe) Flatt-L, Monroe-T, Watts-B		BCD 16399
CCO 4609 -BD2	SUMMERTIME IS PAST AND GONE		BCD 16399
CCO 4609-2	SUMMERTIME IS PAST AND GONE		C2K 52478, BCD 16399
CCO 4609 -BD3	SUMMERTIME IS PAST AND GONE		BCD 16399
CCO 4609-1	SUMMERTIME IS PAST AND GONE	20503	HL 7315, SS 06, CK 53908, BCD 16399, A16652
CCO 4610-1	MANSIONS FOR ME (Monroe) Flatt-L, Monroe-T	20107, 37294, 54013	HL 7315, CCS 105, C2K 52478, BCD 16399, MME-71007

CCO 4611-1	MOTHER'S ONLY SLEEPING (B. Monroe) Flatt-L, Monroe-T	20107, 37294, 54013	HL 7290, CCS 104, FC 38904, C2K 52478, BCD 16399, MME-71007
CCO 4612-2	BLUE YODEL NO. 4 (Rodgers) Monroe-L		FC 38904, BCD 16399
CCO 4612-1	BLUE YODEL NO. 4	20198, 37565	HL7315, C2K 52478, V 79518-2, BCD 16399, A16652

Bill Monroe: m	Lester Flatt: g	Chubby Wise: f
Earl Scruggs: b	Howard Watts: sb	

460917   Columbia session; producer, Art Satherley
WBBM-CBS studio in the Wrigley Building, 410 N. Michigan Ave., Chicago, Ill.
Sept. 17, 1946, 1–3 p.m.

CCO 4613-2	WILL YOU BE LOVING ANOTHER MAN? (Monroe-Flatt) Flatt-L, Monroe-T		BCD 16399
CCO 4613-1	WILL YOU BE LOVING ANOTHER MAN?	20198, 36907	HL 7290, CS 1065, TLCW-04, C2K 52478, BCD 16399, A16652, C4K 90628
CCO 4614-2	HOW WILL I EXPLAIN ABOUT YOU? (Monroe) Flatt-L, Monroe-T		BCD 16399
CCO 4614-3	HOW WILL I EXPLAIN ABOUT YOU?		C2K 52478, BCD 16399
CCO 4614-1	HOW WILL I EXPLAIN ABOUT YOU?	20384, 37960	CCS 104, BCD 16399
CCO 4615-1	SHINING PATH (Monroe) Flatt-L, Monroe-T, Watts-B, Scruggs-BS		FC 38904, C2K 52478, BCD 16399, MME 71007
CCO 4616-2	WICKED PATH OF SIN (Monroe) Flatt-L, Monroe-T, Scruggs-B, Birch Monroe-BS		C2K 52478, BCD 16399
CCO 4616-1	WICKED PATH OF SIN	20503	HL 7338, CS 1065, SS 06, V 79518-2, MCAD 4-11048, BCD 16399, MME-71007

Bill Monroe: m	Lester Flatt: g	Chubby Wise (-13, -14): f
Earl Scruggs (-13, -14): b	Howard Watts (-13, -14, -16); Birch Monroe (-15 only): sb	

461200   Bluegrass Classics reissue of radio broadcasts on WSM (see also Session 480300)
                  Grand Ole Opry, Nashville, Tenn.
                  Dec. 1946–July 1947 airchecks

[1]   MOTHER'S ONLY SLEEPING   BGC 80
      12/21/46   Flatt-L, Monroe-T

[2]   ROLL IN MY SWEET BABY'S ARMS   BCG 80
      12/21/46   Flatt-L, Watts-T

[3]   LITTLE COMMUNITY CHURCH   BCG 80
      12/28/46   Flatt-L, Monroe-T, Scruggs-B, Birch Monroe-BS

[4]   WICKED PATH OF SIN   BGC 80
      1/3/47   Flatt-L, Monroe-T, Scruggs-B, Birch Monroe-BS

[5]   REMEMBER THE CROSS   BCG 80
      1/12/47   Flatt-L, Monroe-T, Scruggs-B, Birch Monroe-BS

[6]   MOLLY AND TENBROOKS   BCG 80
      3/8/47   Monroe-L

[7]   WILL YOU BE LOVING ANOTHER MAN?   BCG 80
      4/12/47   Flatt-L, Monroe-T

[8]   WHY DID YOU WANDER   BCG 80
      4/18/47   Flatt-L, Monroe-T

[9]   TRUE LIFE BLUES   BCG 80
      4/19/47   Flatt-L, Monroe-T

[10]   SHINE HALLALUJAH SHINE   BCG 80
      7/26/47   Flatt-L, Monroe-T, Scruggs-B, Birch Monroe-BS

[11]   LOVE GONE COLD   BCG 80
      7/26/47   Flatt-L

Bill Monroe (except 2): m   Lester Flatt (1, 2, 4–9, 11);   Chubby Wise (7–9, 11): f
                                        Chubby Wise (2, 7): g

Earl Scruggs (except 3–5, 10): b   Birch Monroe (6–9); Howard Watts
                                        (1, 2, 11): sb

471027.1   Columbia Records session; producer, Art Satherley
WBBM-CBS studio, Wrigley Building, 410 N. Michigan Ave., Chicago, Ill.
Oct. 27, 1947, 3:30–5:45 P.M.

CCO 4874-1   I'M GOING BACK TO OLD KENTUCKY (Monroe)   20612, 2-323   HL 7338, SS 06, FC 38904,
Flatt-L, Monroe-T   CK 53908, BCD 16399

CCO 4875-2   IT'S MIGHTY DARK TO TRAVEL (Monroe)   C2K 52478, BCD 16399,
Flatt-L, Monroe-T   C4K 90628[2]

CCO 4874-BD   I'M GOING BACK TO OLD KENTUCKY   C2K 52478, BCD 16399

CCO 4874-2   I'M GOING BACK TO OLD KENTUCKY   C2K 52478, BCD 16399

CCO 4875-3   IT'S MIGHTY DARK TO TRAVEL   BCD 16399

CCO 4875-1   IT'S MIGHTY DARK TO TRAVEL   20526   HL 7338, CS 1065, CCS 105,
RO 25, CK 53908,
MCAD 4-11048,
MCA3P-3256, BCD 16399,
C2K 90858

CCO 4876-1   I HEAR A SWEET VOICE CALLING (Monroe)   20459   H 1079, HL 7338, CS 1065,
Monroe-LV/TC, Flatt-LC, Watts-B   CSS 105, C2K 52478, BCD 16399,
A16652, MME-71007

CCO 4877-2   LITTLE CABIN HOME ON THE HILL (Monroe)   C2K 52478, BCD 16399
Flatt-L, Monroe-T

CCO 4877-1   LITTLE CABIN HOME ON THE HILL   20459   HL 7338, CS 1065, SS 06,
BCD 16399

Bill Monroe: m   Lester Flatt: g   Chubby Wise: f
Earl Scruggs: b   Howard Watts: sb

471027.2   Columbia Records session; producer, Art Satherley
WBBM-CBS studio, Wrigley Building, 410 N. Michigan Ave., Chicago, Ill.
Oct. 27, 1947, 7:45–10:30 P.M.

CCO 4878-2   MY ROSE OF OLD KENTUCKY (B. Monroe)   BCD 16399
Monroe-L

CCO 4879-2   BLUE GRASS BREAKDOWN (Monroe)   C2K 52478, BCD 16399,
Instrumental   C4K 90628

CCO 4878-1	MY ROSE OF OLD KENTUCKY	20423, 38172	HL 7290, CS 1065, SS 06, C2K52478, BCD 16399
CCO 4879-3	BLUE GRASS BREAKDOWN		BCD 16399
CCO 4879-1	BLUE GRASS BREAKDOWN	20552, 2-151	HL7290, CS1065, SS06, V 79518-2 MCAD 4-11048, CK 53908, OC-1001, BCD 16399
CCO 4880-2	SWEETHEART YOU DONE ME WRONG (Monroe) Flatt-L, Monroe-T		C2K 52478, BCD 16399
CCO 4880 -BD1	SWEETHEART YOU DONE ME WRONG		C2K 52478, BCD 16399
CCO 4880 -BD2	SWEETHEART YOU DONE ME WRONG		BCD 16399
CCO 4880-3	SWEETHEART YOU DONE ME WRONG		BCD 16399
CCO 4880-1	SWEETHEART YOU DONE ME WRONG	20423, 38172	HL 7315, SS 06, CK 53908, V 79518-2, BCD 16399
CCO 4881-2	THE OLD CROSS ROAD (Monroe) Flatt-L, Monroe-T		C2K 52478, BCD 16399
CCO 4881 -BD2	THE OLD CROSS ROAD		BCD 16399
CCO 4881 -BD3	THE OLD CROSS ROAD		BCD 16399
CCO 4881-3	THE OLD CROSS ROAD		BCD 16399
CCO 4881 -BD1	THE OLD CROSS ROAD		BCD 16399
CCO 4881-1	THE OLD CROSS ROAD	20576, 2-207	HL 7315, CCS 104, CK 53908,[3] BCD 16399, MME-71007

Bill Monroe: m	Lester Flatt: g	Chubby Wise: f
Earl Scruggs: b	Howard Watts: sb	

471028.1   Columbia Records session; producer, Art Satherley
WBBM-CBS studio, Wrigley Building, 410 N. Michigan Ave., Chicago, Ill.
Oct. 28, 1947, 3:15–5:30 P.M.

CCO 4882-BD   THAT HOME ABOVE (Bill Monroe)   BCD 16399
Flatt-L, Monroe-T, Scruggs-BV/BSC, Watts-BSV/BC

CCO 4882-1   THAT HOME ABOVE   20488   CCS 105, C2K 52478,
BCD 16399, MME-71007

CCO 4883-2   REMEMBER THE CROSS (Bill Monroe–Howard Watts)   C2K 52478, BCD 16399
Flatt-L, Monroe-T, Scruggs-B, Watts-BS

CCO 4883-1   REMEMBER THE CROSS   20576, 2-207   CCS 105, CK 53908,
BCD 16399, MME-71007

CCO 4884-1   LITTLE COMMUNITY CHURCH (Monroe)   20488   HL 7338, CCS 104,
Flatt-L, Monroe-T, Scruggs-B, Watts-BS   C2K 52478, V 79518-2,
BCD 16399, MME-71007

CCO 4885-2   ALONG ABOUT DAYBREAK (Monroe)   BCD 16399
Monroe-L

CCO 4884-2   LITTLE COMMUNITY CHURCH   BCD 16399

CCO 4884-BD   LITTLE COMMUNITY CHURCH   BCD 16399

CCO 4885-BD   ALONG ABOUT DAYBREAK   BCD 16399

CCO 4885-1   ALONG ABOUT DAYBREAK   20595, 2-275   FC 38904, CCS 104,
C2K 52478, BCD 16399

Bill Monroe: m	Lester Flatt (-85), Chubby	Chubby Wise (-85): f
Earl Scruggs (-85): b	Wise (-82–84, -88–89): g	
	Howard Watts (-85): sb	

471028.2   Columbia Records session; producer, Art Satherley
WBBM-CBS studio, Wrigley Building, 410 N. Michigan Ave., Chicago, Ill.
Oct. 28, 1947, 8–10:15 P.M.

CCO 4886-1   WHEN YOU ARE LONELY (Monroe-Flatt)   20526   HL 7338, CS 1065, SS 06,
Flatt-L, Monroe-T   V 79518-2, C2K52478,
BCD 16399

CCO 4887-2	MOLLY AND TENBROOKS (Monroe) Monroe-L		BCD 16399
CCO 4887-1	MOLLY AND TENBROOKS[4]	20612, 2-323	HL 7338, CS 1065, SS 06, CK 46029, C2K52478, R2 75720, BCD 16399, GHD5354, CCRS-7001, C2K 90858, A16652, C4K 90628
CCO 4888-2	SHINE HALLELUJAH SHINE (Monroe) Flatt-L, Monroe-T, Scruggs-B, Watts-BS		C2K 52478, BCD 16399
CCO 4888-1	SHINE HALLELUJAH SHINE	20402, 38078	CCS 105, CK 53908, BCD 16399, MME-71007
CCO 4889-2	I'M TRAVELIN' ON AND ON (Monroe) Flatt-L, Monroe-T, Scruggs-B, Watts-BS		BCD 16399
CCO 4889-1	I'M TRAVELIN' ON AND ON	20402, 38078	CCS 104, C2K 52478, BCD 16399, CCRS-7002

Bill Monroe: m

Earl Scruggs (-86, -87): b

Lester Flatt (-86, -87),

   Chubby Wise (-88,-89): g

Howard Watts (-86, -87): b

Chubby Wise (-86, -87): f

480221   Bluegrass Classics reissue of radio broadcast on WSM (see also session 480300)

                 Grand Ole Opry, Nashville, Tenn.

                 Feb. 1948 airchecks

[1] 2/21/48	JUST A LITTLE TALK WITH JESUS Flatt-L, Monroe-T, Watts-B, Birch Monroe-BS	BCG 80
[2] 2/21/48	SUNNY SIDE OF THE MOUNTAIN Flatt-L	BCG 80

Bill Monroe: m (not audible on 2)

Earl Scruggs: b (2)

Lester Flatt (2);

   Earl Scruggs (1): g

Howard Watts: sb (2)

Benny Martin: f (2)

480300   Bluegrass Classics reissue of radio broadcasts on WSM

                 Grand Ole Opry, Nashville, Tenn.

                 Undated [between beginning of 1946 and March 1948] airchecks

[1] undated	BLUE YODEL #4 Monroe-L	BCG 80

| [2] | MY DIXIE HOME | BCG 80 |
| undated | Monroe-L | |

| [3] | LITTLE JOE | BCG 80 |
| undated | Monroe-L | |

| [4] | THE SHINING PATH | BCG 80 |
| undated | Flatt-L, Monroe-T, Watts-B, Scruggs-BS | |

Bill Monroe: m   Lester Flatt (1–3);   Chubby Wise (1): f
Earl Scruggs (except 4): b   Chubby Wise (4): g
                                            Birch Monroe (3),
                                            Howard Watts (1, 2): sb

---

480605   MCA reissue of a radio broadcast on WSM[5]
            Grand Ole Opry, Nashville, Tenn.
            June 5, 1948

| [1] | NEW MULE SKINNER BLUES (Jimmie Rodgers, George Vaughn) | MCAD 42286, MCA3P-3256 |
| | Monroe-L | |

Bill Monroe: m   (?): g   (Gene Christian?): f
(Don Reno?): b   (?): sb

491022   Columbia Records session; producer, Art Satherley
            Castle Studio, Tulane Hotel, 206 8th Ave. North, Nashville, Tenn.
            Oct. 22, 1949

| CO 41835-4 | CAN'T YOU HEAR ME CALLIN' (B. Monroe) | | BCD 16399 |
| NASH 738-4 | Wiseman-L, Monroe-T | | |

| CO 41835-3 | CAN'T YOU HEAR ME CALLIN' | | BCD 16399 |
| NASH 738-3 | | | |

| CO 41835-BD | CAN'T YOU YEAR ME CALLIN' | | C2K 52478, BCD 16399 |
| NASH 738-BD | | | |

| CO 41835-2 | CAN'T YOU YEAR ME CALLIN' | | C2K 52478, BCD 16399 |
| NASH 738-2 | | | |

CO 41835-1	CAN'T YOU HEAR ME CALLIN'	20676, 2-551	HL 7290, CS 1065, CCS 104,
NASH 738-1			CK 53908, MCAD 4-11048,
			BCD 16399, C4K 90628,
			CK 92965

CO 41836-2 NASH 739-2	TRAVELIN' THIS LONESOME ROAD (Monroe) Wiseman-L, Monroe-T		C2K 52478, BCD 16399
CO 41836-1 NASH 739-1	TRAVELIN' THIS LONESOME ROAD	20676, 2-551	HL 7338, CS 1065, CSS 104, CK 53908, V 79518-2, BCD 16399
CO 41837-3 NASH 740-3	BLUE GRASS STOMP (Monroe) Instrumental		BCD 16399
CO 41837-BD NASH 740-BD	BLUE GRASS STOMP		BCD 16399
CO 41837-2 NASH 740-2	BLUE GRASS STOMP		BCD 16399
CO 41837-1 NASH 740-1	BLUE GRASS STOMP	20648, 2-423	H 1709, HL 7290, CCS 105, C2K 52478, V 79518-2, BCD 16399
CO 41838-3 NASH 741-3	THE GIRL IN THE BLUE VELVET BAND (M. Foree–C.Carlisle) Monroe-L		BCD 16399
CO 41838-2 NASH 741-2	THE GIRL IN THE BLUE VELVET BAND		BCD 16399
CO 41838-1 NASH 741-1	THE GIRL IN THE BLUE VELVET BAND	20648, 2-423	HL 7290, CS 1065, CCS 105, C2K 52478, BCD 16399, A16652

Bill Monroe: m   Malcolm "Mac" Wiseman: g   Chubby Wise: f
Rudy Lyle: b   Jack Thompson: sb

Notes

1. The recordings in sessions 460300, 461200, 480221, and 480300 were made off the air from Opry broadcasts on a home disc recorder for Earl Scruggs.

2. This track is not identified as an alternate take in the notes to C4K 90628.

3. -81 is titled "Old Cross Road Is Waitin'" on CK 53908.

4. "Molly and Tenbrooks" is subtitled "(The Race Horse Song)" on singles labels.

5. Introduced by Red Foley.

"UNCLE PEN": 1950–56

Although Bill Monroe's Columbia sessions, especially those with Lester Flatt and Earl Scruggs, have been widely hailed as the cornerstone for the bluegrass sound, it was in his Decca records of the early 1950s that Monroe crystalized that sound and established most of his core repertoire. The era produced many of the classic recordings that people identify with Bill Monroe. "Uncle Pen," "Raw Hide," "Get Down on Your Knees and Pray," "The Little Girl and the Dreadful Snake," "My Little Georgia Rose," "On and On," and "Roanoke" have become standards in bluegrass music. Among Monroe's recordings from this period are remakes of his earlier hits that have become some of the most frequently reissued: "New Mule Skinner Blues," "In the Pines," "Footprints in the Snow," and "Blue Moon of Kentucky."

If it was not the most commercially successful period in Monroe's life it marked a high point in creativity. During these years he developed the harmonic aspects of his music further than ever before by creating special tunings for the mandolin that married melody to harmony; by bringing two and three fiddles into recording sessions to play harmony breaks and backup; and by creating vocal harmonies in duets, trios, and quartets that have become the benchmark for bluegrass ensemble singing. During this time as well, he wrote many of his best autobiographical songs, gospel quartets, and instrumentals. He was also responding to many changes as Nashville grew from a southern backwater town to become the focus of a vibrant music industry. Monroe's recordings from 1950 to 1956 reflect the growth of the publishing business; the beginnings of the studio system that would create the "Nashville sound"; and the impacts of television, rock and roll, and the folk music revival.

The first four Decca sessions were quite similar to the last Columbia session in that most of the tunes were Monroe's compositions although that is obscured by confusing copyright credits. "Memories of You" was written by Monroe and "I'm

Blue, I'm Lonesome" was coauthored by Monroe and Hank Williams, but both are identified as by James B. Smith. A James W. Smith is credited with "Boat of Love," and Albert Price is listed as composer for "When the Golden Leaves Begin to Fall." Monroe's reasons for using pseudonyms may have been personal, legal, or idiosyncratic. Perhaps they had to do with the fact that many of his Columbia songs had been published by Peer-Southern, an ASCAP company that sometimes demanded exclusive rights to its composers' songs, and Monroe was being pressured to place some of his new pieces with a BMI affiliate. By this time as well, he had organized his own publishing company, Bill Monroe Music, and was placing many of his new songs with it.

At the first Decca sessions Monroe reintroduced a practice he'd used only once before on "I Hear a Sweet Voice Calling": singing lead on the verse of a song and tenor on the chorus. During the 1950s and 1960s he would follow this practice frequently and take the role of lead singer more often than before. Also in the first session was Hank Williams's "Alabama Waltz," reflecting not only Monroe's friendship with Williams but also the country music fad at the time for state-named waltzes. Monroe began the fad with "Kentucky Waltz," but by 1950 "Tennessee Waltz," with a best-selling pop version by Patti Page, had become the model. Monroe continued to include waltzes in his recorded repertoire from that point on. Yet another first occurred in "Blue Grass Ramble" when Monroe introduced a special mandolin tuning on record.

The person who ushered Monroe into his lifelong association with Decca (later MCA) was producer Paul Cohen (1906–70). A native of Chicago, Cohen began work in the record business for Columbia, but after the new label, Decca, was formed in 1934 he went to work for that. For much of his time he was based in Cincinnati, where he sold records and spotted talent for the company's pop and country division. With artists like Bing Crosby and Judy Garland in its stable, Decca quickly became a major player in the record business. Cohen eventually moved to the front office in New York and began to learn even more about how the pop music scene worked.

From its beginning, Decca had a country series, the 5000 blue-label series, that had included artists like Jimmie Davis and the Carter Family. By the 1940s the label was recording the likes of Ernest Tubb and Red Foley, and, in part at behest of these singers, it started calling the "hillbilly" recordings the "Country and Western line." By the end of World War II the company had begun the black-label 46000 series on which Monroe's first Deccas would appear. About this time,

too, Cohen replaced Dave Kapp as head of the country and western division and promptly began doing regular sessions in Nashville, becoming a pioneer of the Nashville sound. The first was in August 1947 at the Castle studios in the Tulane Hotel in downtown Nashville.

Until 1958, when he moved to Nashville to start his own label, Cohen came to that city only to do sessions. His local righthand man became Owen Bradley, then the musical director of station WSM. Bradley, who had extensive Nashville contacts and a broad knowledge of different types of music, was the perfect man to set up sessions, book studios, and round up musicians. And though Cohen was the producer of record for many of the 1950s sessions, Bradley was often the one who actually did the work.

Cohen began working with Monroe in February 1950, a few days after he released what would be one of Decca's biggest chart hits, Red Foley's "Chattanooga Shoe Shine Boy" backed with "Sugarfoot Rag." The record became one of the first and biggest crossover hits, climbing both the country and pop charts, and Cohen began to see the potential for applying the lessons of pop marketing to country music. Monroe was not a particularly good candidate for that experiment. When Decca released its first Monroe single in March 1950 Cohen set up a promotional interview with a local country DJ, Hugh Cherry, so Monroe could plug the recording. "I don't think Bill Monroe had ever done an interview before," Cherry recalled. "I'd ask him something and all I'd get is a short 'Yes sir' and 'No sir.' It was like pulling teeth."[1]

Another industry practice of the time that Cohen used was the recording of "cover" versions, whereby a good song would be recorded by several different artists on different labels or in different genres. In Tin Pan Alley it had long been standard music publishing practice to place a song with several different performers in order to sell it to as many people as possible. The pop recording industry before the days of rock and roll operated under the assumption that material (i.e., the song) was more important than the performer and that it was beneficial for a company to have its artists recording the best-selling songs. Country covers were very common and profitable in the early 1950s. Decca, under Cohen's direction, no doubt was anxious to have a proven best-seller like Monroe doing covers. Thus early Decca sessions yielded "Poison Love," "Rotation Blues," "Lonesome Truck Driver's Blues," and "Sugar Coated Love." Interesting though such sides may be, none touched the charts of the time.

Paul Cohen was also responsible for the only two regular sessions Monroe did without the Blue Grass Boys—early attempts to adapt an older Opry performer to what was later to be called the Nashville sound. In terms of country music of the era, Monroe was a best-seller, and Cohen promoted the sessions in hope of expanding his market and heightening sales. In 1973 Owen Bradley reminisced about the sessions.[2] The musicians were the top Nashville studio sidemen of the period, and the concept was a sound one. The material in one session included two covers ("Kentucky Waltz" and "Angels Rock Me to Sleep") and two old standards ("Prisoner's Song" and "Swing Low Sweet Chariot"). At a second session were five Jimmie Rodgers songs and one of Monroe's collaborations with Pete Pyle. It was good material, but the attempt to fit Monroe's highly individual style to a studio formula situation with electric instruments was a failure. Monroe, Bradley said, did not like the arrangement, and most of the performances were not of marketable quality.

It was at this point, Bradley commented, that Decca realized that the sound of Monroe's band was an important part of his success as a recording artist. To Bradley, the job of the producer at a Monroe session (and he produced more Monroe sessions than anyone else) was similar to that of an A&R man working with one of the popular dance bands of the 1930s and 1940s, for example, Guy Lombardo. The bandleader produced the final sound, and the A&R man saw that it was properly recorded. He might make suggestions, but the bandleader made all the decisions. Bradley was supposed to produce one early-morning Monroe session in 1951 but had worked late the night before and asked an associate, new to Nashville, to take over. Around noon a call from the substitute producer awakened him. He'd been in the studio for an hour and a half with Monroe and had only done one song. Furthermore, the substitute said, "I can't understand a word he says!" Bradley told him not to worry, to let Monroe do what he wanted and go on to the next song when he was satisfied with a take.[3]

That became the standard recording procedure with Monroe after the studio sound sessions of March 17 and April 23, 1951, failed. Decca was learning that a policy of minimal interference worked best with his studio work, and stylistic innovations can be safely attributed to Monroe or his musicians rather than the producer involved. Of course, a sensitive producer like Bradley or Harry Silverstein was more likely to come up with a good performance on record than an insensitive producer.

One innovation, perhaps a result of the unsuccessful electric studio sessions, was the use of studio sidemen to supplement the Blue Grass Boys. Up to this point, recordings of the group represented all or part of the band as it appeared onstage at the Opry and in personal appearances. But at following sessions a Nashville studio bass player, Ernest Newton, who first appears in the discography's personnel listings for the session of March 17, 1951, was used routinely in lieu of Bessie Lee Mauldin. Monroe resisted the wholesale introduction of nonstandard instruments, although he did allow Owen Bradley to incorporate them for selected songs recorded after this point. Thus Bradley played vibes on "Christmas Time's a-Coming" and piano on "A Mighty Pretty Waltz." Generally, though, people who appeared on these early Decca recordings were regular members of Monroe's band. Thus, sessions of July 1 and 6, 1951, represent the group with which he traveled from July to October in 1951 (except for the bassist). Similarly, sessions held on July 18 and 26, 1952, represent Monroe's summer 1952 group, which included the youngest Blue Grass Boy ever to record, fourteen-year-old Sonny Osborne.

The nineteen Bill Monroe singles that Decca released between March 1950 and October 1952 represent close to a third (28 percent) of all the Monroe singles released by Decca/MCA. The recordings made during 1950–52 were among the most influential and most copied of the Blue Grass Boys repertoire, and the sidemen who went on to fame in their own right in country and bluegrass music included Jimmy Martin, Carter Stanley, Sonny Osborne, and Gordon Terry.

A serious auto accident interrupted Monroe's career in January 1953, and he did not record again until late November of that year although he performed on the road during that summer. The sessions between November 28, 1953, and January 25, 1954, mark the last appearance of Jimmy Martin as lead singer and guitarist on Monroe's recordings and are the last appearances of Rudy Lyle as banjoist with Monroe. Either or both had appeared on most of the Decca recordings to this point and gave the Blue Grass Boys as distinctive a sound on the early Decca recordings as Lester Flatt and Earl Scruggs had on the Columbia recordings. Significantly, however, neither Martin nor Lyle received the kind of publicity that Flatt and Scruggs had, whether on record or in person. By 1952, though, Monroe's sound was no longer unique on record. Almost every major label had a band using the sound of the Blue Grass Boys—Flatt and Scruggs on Mercury and Columbia, the Stanley Brothers on Columbia, Mac Wiseman on Dot, Don Reno and Arthur Lee "Red" Smiley on King, the Lonesome Pine Fiddlers on RCA Victor, and Jim and Jesse McReynolds and Carl Sauceman on Capitol.

The sessions between June 26 and December 31, 1954,

mark an important change in the sound of the Blue Grass Boys: multiple fiddles playing harmony. Monroe's mandolin harmonies foreshadowed the change. The previous year, Mac Wiseman had begun to use western swing twin fiddles on his Dot recordings and as a result sold well outside the Southeast, especially in the Southwest, and Monroe was undoubtedly aware of that. The triple-fiddle sound was typical of Monroe's innovations, however, in that it was bluesier and less sweet sounding than the western swing twin-fiddle sound. The use of the fiddles had important implications for the band's sound in other ways as well. Arrangements (especially on the first re-cordings) tended to be tighter than before, the fiddles using a responsorial backing technique behind the vocals and shorter instrumental breaks.

From the November 28, 1953, session until the early 1960s Monroe recorded very few duets and sang nothing but lead except on religious quartets, so he did not need to rely as heavily on his guitar player being a lead singer. The session on January 19, 1954, began the increased use of studio musicians. From that point on, as his recordings started to feature multiple fiddles playing harmony, Monroe tended to include musicians in the band who could play the fiddle as well as at least one other instrument. Charlie Cline, for example, was proficient on guitar, fiddle, and banjo; Bobby Hicks played banjo and fiddle; and Joe Stuart played every instrument, including mandolin. Monroe rarely carried more than one fiddler with him in per-sonal appearances. He did, however, use multiple fiddles on the Opry and on a series of television programs made by Albert Gannaway.

The harmony fiddles could also be heard occasionally at Bill's country music park in Bean Blossom, Indiana. Monroe purchased this property in southern Indiana's scenic Brown County in 1951. On it was a barnlike music hall where, on every Sunday afternoon and evening from April to November, country music shows were held. These shows were called the Brown County Jamboree, and the park came to be called by the same name. Bill added an outdoor stage and some cabins and hired his brother Birch as manager of the jamboree. Bill played there regularly and, taking advantage of his Opry connections, booked popular country acts there and promoted their shows in his broadcasts. During the 1950s Bill maintained a house band there composed of former Blue Grass Boys. Bean Blos-som was destined to become famous in the world of bluegrass, a place at which Blue Grass Boys started their careers and where Monroe's new compositions were tested before audi-ences that knew his music well.

One of the mysteries of the Decca sessions is an eigh-teen-month hiatus between September 1955 and April 1957. The company, Owen Bradley observed, had no reason to keep Monroe away from the studio—in fact, it was in both Decca's and Monroe's interest to have him record as often as possible. The eighteen-month period, however, does coincide with the height of the rock and roll revolution and the tremendous dislocation it caused in the country music industry. Monroe, like other traditional country acts unable or unwilling to add a rockabilly flavor to their music, saw bookings drop, which made it difficult to keep a decent band together. He may have considered his band not good enough to record at this time. During the 1956 season he toured with his brother Charlie. Each would do a separate show, and then they would close the performance with duets. When Monroe returned to the studio in the spring of 1957 he began recording for his first LP, *Knee Deep in Bluegrass*, sessions (chapter 6).

THE 1950 SESSIONS: NEW FACES

Another session of Monroe's school of bluegrass was about to start. With the Korean War on the horizon (hostilities would break out that summer), many young musicians Monroe was grooming would find themselves facing draft notices before their tenure in the band was up. But all of that was only a faint rumble of thunder on the distant horizon on the cold February morning when the Blue Grass Boys trouped into the old Castle studios at the Tulane Hotel.

Although only a little more than two months elapsed between Monroe's last Columbia sessions and the first Decca ones, his band had undergone serious change. Only banjoist Rudy Lyle remained from the last Columbia outing. The rest of the group—Jimmy Martin on guitar and lead vocal, Vassar Clem-ents on fiddle, and Joel Price on bass—were by and large young and willing to let Monroe form them into the kind of ensemble sound he wanted. If during Flatt and Scruggs's tenure Monroe seemed almost overshadowed by his sidemen, he was now ready to reassert control over his music. Of his principal play-ers in the new band, Jimmy Martin was twenty-three, Vassar Clements was twenty, and banjoist Rudy Lyle was only twenty. Only Joel Price had substantial show business experience.

The members of this edition of the Blue Grass Boys had come to Monroe in a variety of ways, but almost none of them via professional channels. Almost all were recruited from the ranks of amateur or grassroots music. Jimmy Martin came from around Sneedville, in the shadows of the Cumberland

Mountains in upper east Tennessee, just a few miles from the Virginia line. His mother and stepfather were gospel singers, and he grew up listening to Monroe and others on the Opry. As a teenager, he played guitar in a local string band, and by 1949 he was working as a painter and singing part-time on Morristown radio with Tex Climer and the Blue Band Coffee Boys. In the winter of 1949 Martin learned that Monroe's regular singer Mac Wiseman was returning home to Virginia for Christmas. He rode the bus into Nashville, managed to get backstage at the Opry on Saturday night, and sang a couple of songs for Monroe. Rudy Lyle heard Martin picking in the alley behind the Ryman Auditorium and got him past the doorman by insisting, "Bill wanted to try this man out."[4] Martin recalled:

> I really didn't think I was going to try out for him that night. I really didn't think that I could pick up enough nerve to go up and just say anything to a star that was as big as Bill Monroe and my idol. I'd bought his records and used many quarters and dimes in jukeboxes trying to learn the words that him and Lester was saying. I found out that some of the words that I sang when I was with Bill were the wrong words that I had heard off the jukeboxes. I'd sung two songs"—"Poor Ellen Smith," a solo, and "The Old Cross Roads," a duet—with him, the Saturday I tried out, and he had Rudy Lyle take me up to the hotel and he gave Rudy $20 for me to eat on and everything to keep me up there to take me on his show the next week.[5]

Monroe remembered that night as well: "He had a wonderful voice that would really fit with mine."[6] That was proven the following week when Monroe took Martin along for a stage show in Fort Smith, Arkansas. They sang several duets, including "Will You Be Loving Another Man?" and won a series of encores. Monroe was equally impressed with Martin's gospel background. "He was a wonderful gospel leader," he would remark years later.[7] Martin, a fine rhythm guitarist, was unafraid to push Monroe on the mandolin. Soon he had a full-time job with the band, and Mac Wiseman was organizing his own band to take to Louisiana.

Vassar Clements, another rookie, replaced Chubby Wise on fiddle. Like Wise, Vassar was from Florida, and both knew the legendary Rouse Brothers, the Floridians who, with Wise, had popularized "The Orange Blossom Special." Vassar came from Calhoun County in West Florida, where he was born in 1928. He started playing guitar in a string band with two double first cousins, Gerald and Red Clements. After Gerald, the fiddle player, married and dropped out, Vassar was forced against his judgment to learn to play. "People liked us," he recalled. "We were all playing football in a little old town like that, they like football players and they thought we were great because we could play on an instrument a little bit. . . . I played three years [football] in high school and two years semi-professional."[8] His job with Monroe, which he took in late 1949, was his first professional work as a musician.

Clements met Monroe in Florida. Later, Vassar's wife, Millie, who worked as a telephone operator, found that Chubby had left Bill and the band needed a fiddler. She encouraged her husband to apply. Vassar came to Nashville, managed to talk his way past the guard at the Opry door, and finally got to see Monroe. He asked whether Monroe remembered him. "Yes," was the reply. "But what are you doing here?"[9]

Monroe asked him to come backstage for an audition. Mac Wiseman was still there, but on notice, and Martin had joined. After Vassar played some songs, Monroe asked how he was at playing a breakdown. After Vassar responded by playing "Orange Blossom Special" Monroe gave him $20 for a hotel room and hired him. Three weeks later, when Monroe's band was on a package tour with Hank Williams, Vassar impressed Williams enough that the older singer took him aside and told him he could have a job with the Drifting Cowboys if he tired of playing with Monroe. "Vassar started with me when he was a young boy," Monroe remembered. "We had a number called 'The New Mule Skinner Blues.' Well, Vassar was powerful on that. He put some new notes in it that was fine, that every fiddler went to searching for, to do it the way Vassar done it. And Vassar is the blues fiddler, you know. Now there's fiddlers that could beat Vassar on 'Sally Goodin' or old time fiddle numbers, but Vassar would beat 'em on a number like 'The Mule Skinner'; they wouldn't touch him on that. And if you wanted some blues played, Vassar could do it."[10]

The story of Joel Price, the other new member of the band, is that least known to modern fans. A native of Lavonia, Georgia, in Franklin County, near the South Carolina line, Price spent most of the early 1940s playing bass, singing, and doing comedy in the band of Tommy Scott's medicine show. He made his first recordings with Scott. In 1947 he auditioned for Monroe. "He was playing a show in Clayton, Georgia," Price said. "I went up to see the show, went backstage, and talked to him, asked him if he could use a comedian and a bass player. I sang two or three songs and he sang tenor with me, and then he told me, 'I can't use you now, but I might sometime.' I wasn't expecting it, but in about two weeks, he called and told me to meet him in Erwin, Tennessee. That was February 1947."[11]

Price appeared in Monroe's road band, his Opry band, and his recording band. On live shows he did what he called slapstick and sang comedy songs like "There's a Hole in the Bottom of the Sea." He also sang bass in gospel quartets. Then, in 1948, he left the band to spend a year playing in the band of Opry star George Morgan, who was starting to hit big with songs like "Candy Kisses." He rejoined Monroe in the fall of 1949, doing comedy and eventually replacing Jack Thompson on bass. Price was also beginning to write songs, and he helped Monroe compose "Boat of Love." Later he would be responsible for the popular gospel tune "Insured beyond the Grave," which Jimmy Dickens and the Louvin Brothers popularized; for Stonewall Jackson's "A Broken Heart, a Wedding Band"; for Dickens's "Gonna Swim Big Sandy"; and for Polly Possum's "Sad Singin', Slow Ridin.'" By the middle of 1951 Price had left Monroe again, this time to go with Jimmy Dickens, although he continued to play bass for Monroe on the Opry even after he'd left.

By coincidence, Monroe's first Decca session, and his first done using a tape recorder, coincided with the dawn of major-label recording in Nashville. Major labels had been coming to the city since 1944, but it was only in 1950 that they determined to make the town a recording center and began using studios there in a regular manner. Paul Cohen, the country director for the label, is considered to be one of those most instrumental in the change. All Monroe's sessions, including some of the pioneering ones, were done in Nashville studios. Through November 1953, he recorded at the Castle Studio in the Tulane Hotel.

Castle was the product of three WSM engineers moonlighting from their regular jobs to do contract recordings. Aaron Shelton, Carl Jenkins, and George Reynolds moved their operation to the hotel in 1947 and remodeled a dining room and converted a bathroom into an echo chamber. Soon they were using a Scully master cutting machine and producing recordings for a variety of labels. The name *Castle* came from the publicity nickname for WSM (the "air castle of the South"). The venerable hotel on Church Street between Seventh and Eighth Avenue north was in downtown Nashville and not far from the National Life Building, owners of the Opry. In addition to being the home of Castle, it was also a place musicians liked to stay and ran charge accounts for most bandleaders. "It was known that if you needed a place to stay," recalled Earl Scruggs, "the people at the Tulane would fix you up."[12] The hotel was razed in 1956, and the location where many recordings were made is now a parking lot.

By the time of Monroe's January 1954 session through September 1954, a time that produced such classics as "White House Blues" and the post-Elvis remake of "Blue Moon of Kentucky," local engineers Owen and Harold Bradley had opened their own studio in an alley in Hillsboro Village not far from the Vanderbilt University Campus. It was a low, one-story concrete-and-brick building that the Bradleys constructed themselves and good enough to convince Cohen to do most of the Nashville Decca recording there (the building still stands and is now an art supply store). Toward the end of 1954, the Bradleys built a better studio at 804 Sixteenth Avenue South in the heart of what is now Nashville's Music Row. Owen took an old house, removed the first floor, and created an odd structure that had a narrow flight of stairs that ran from its second floor to its basement. Bradley Film and Recording Studios was where Monroe recorded great fiddle instrumentals like "Wheel Hoss" and "Roanoke" (session 541231) as well as "Wait a Little Longer, Please Jesus" and "Let the Light Shine Down on Me" (Session 550128). By the middle of 1955 Bradley had added his famous Quonset Hut, the first of the legendary Nashville studios, which he sold to Columbia Records in January 1962.

After Owen Bradley took over all the Decca recording of Monroe he would record the master tapes, listen to various takes, decide which was best, and send that master on to New York. There it was renumbered and given a New York master number. Modern MCA vaults therefore contain only the issued version of the Monroe masters; there are no alternate takes or alternate masters. If alternate takes of these pieces did exist, they were left in Nashville and presumably have been destroyed. The surviving New York masters contain an occasional false start or a bit of studio chatter but nothing of real interest to Monroe students.

For most of this time, according to Harry Silverstein, who supervised many of Monroe's sessions for Bradley, Monroe took recording rather casually and seemed to view himself as a concert or radio artist who happened to make a few records. (Less known to Silverstein was the time Monroe spent working up songs to record, trying them out in concerts, and talking about whether a song should be recorded.) Silverstein recalls having to call Monroe in order to get him into the studio for two or three cuts. Monroe had no telephone at the time, so Silverstein would have to call a nearby country store and have the storekeeper get word to Monroe to contact him. When he finally did, Silverstein would tell him it was time to record. Monroe would call the boys and come on in.

Usually, Monroe had tunes ready to record—including, apparently, some of the cover tunes. In other words, Decca did on occasion ask Monroe to record certain materials, but it would be incorrect to say that every cover song from this period was forced on him. There would be occasions, for instance, when his guitar player would start singing a current hit as part of the show and Monroe would become interested in the song. At different points during this era he tended to emphasize different types of songs.

Monroe's first Decca sessions, on February 3, 1950, began with "Blue Grass Ramble." This was the fourth in a series of instrumentals that Monroe named to advertise his band. He had recorded "Blue Grass Special" in 1945, "Blue Grass Breakdown" in 1947, "Blue Grass Stomp" in 1949, and now it was "Blue Grass Ramble." Although there is no evidence that he or any of his musicians were, at this time, calling their music "bluegrass," Monroe's frequent use of the term would ultimately bolster the identity of his music as a new American pop music form.

"Blue Grass Ramble" features a mandolin lead. "I took some time with it and put it together," recalled Monroe. "I think it's a good bluegrass number."[13] The first strain seems derived from "I Don't Love Nobody," while the bridge resembles a mandolin redaction of the B part of "Black Mountain Rag." For this, Monroe also used a novel tuning for his mandolin, different from that he would use later on "Get Up John." Instead of the standard *eadg,* he dropped one of the E strings to C sharp and raised the Ds to E and the two Gs to A. The mandolin is thus tuned to the notes of an A major chord, the key in which the tune is played. In essence Monroe added a C sharp to the well-known traditional fiddle discord tuning of *eaea,* often called "sawmill" and best known for its use in "Black Mountain Rag."

"New Mule Skinner Blues" is musically the same song Monroe recorded back in 1940—his first as a soloist—that had also been the first song he performed on the Grand Ole Opry in 1939. It had, however, a new set of lyrics for this recording, credited to "George Vaughn." That was one of the pseudonyms used by songwriter George Vaughn Horton, older brother and former musical partner of Country Music Hall of Famer Roy Horton. George, whose best-known hit was "Mocking Bird Hill" (1951), included sequel songs among his specialties as a composer. Just a few months after he placed "New Mule Skinner Blues" with Monroe, probably through brother Roy who was working as a song plugger for Peer-Southern, George's "Hillbilly Fever No. 2" was recorded by Ernest Tubb and Red Foley. Because Monroe's Victor single of "Mule Skinner Blues" was still on the market, "New Mule Skinner Blues" was a similar sequel.

Monroe does not seem to have sung the new lyrics in concert even though the recording has remained in print since 1950. Indeed, some reissues and later recordings of "Mule Skinner Blues" have been wrongly assigned the title of the sequel, while others have erroneously credited George Vaughn as a co-writer with Jimmie Rodgers. Nevertheless, this new version did have a lasting impact on Monroe's music, and he singled out Vassar Clements's fiddle work as one of the most important elements of the recording. Subsequent performances of "Mule Skinner Blues" by the Blue Grass Boys reflected Clements's reading of the piece.

Of "My Little Georgia Rose" Ralph Rinzler has observed, "One of the many songs which Bill wrote from his life experiences; the child, who had been deserted by her mother, was about twelve years of age when the song was written back in the late 1940s. Though he has not seen her for more than ten years [ca. 1956], Bill remarks that she knows the song was written about her."[14] The tune was "written off" one of Bill's earlier songs, "My Rose of Old Kentucky," itself apparently derived from an even older minstrel song from the nineteenth century. There is also an 1899 Tin Pan Alley song of the same name although it does not seem related to Monroe's.

"Memories of You" is the first of several songs that Monroe published under the pseudonym James B. Smith or James W. Smith. He seems to have used "Smith" only in 1950, a year he also published items under his own name and as Albert Price. His reasons for doing so apparently have to do with the developing publishing activity in Nashville. Partly due to the crossover success of songs by Hank Williams and Red Foley and its development as the major country recording center, by early 1950 the town was filling with publishers' representatives wanting a piece of the new country music industry. In January, a few weeks before the session, for instance, New York publisher Nat Tannen hired Boudleaux Bryant to be his full-time publishers' representative in Nashville. At about the same time, Troy Martin arrived to take charge of the Peer-Southern catalog. Hill and Range and Acuff-Rose also had agents in place trying to sign good songwriters and get songs recorded.

Monroe had been signed to Peer-Southern throughout the 1940s and apparently still maintained ties with them. By 1951, however, he was publishing songs such as "Uncle Pen" under his own name with Hill and Range and with Bill Monroe Music. Most of the James Smith titles were published with Southern Music, possibly to get around other exclusive contracts. This was by no means an unusual practice. Later in the 1950s Flatt and Scruggs would do the same thing in an effort to make different Nashville friends happy. Ralph Rinzler thinks that "Memories of You" is also autobiographical to an extent—one of Monroe's powerful confessional songs. Robert Cantwell has analyzed the arrangement: "'Memories of You,' sung by Jimmy Martin, opens a windy, cavernous space, a kind of darkness in which the singers are lost to one another; the third with which the harmony opens drops out as the tenor springs to a tiny falsetto; miles, it seems, stretch between them. A narrowing of the voice in the tenor generates a searing sensation as the highest note, like a struck match, brightens and burns out."[15] On this recording Monroe introduced a new mandolin tuning, which he would use again in "Get Up John" and "In Despair."

The February 3, 1950, session continued into the evening, beginning with "I'm on My Way to the Old Home." Many people think of western Kentucky as being flat, but the area around Rosine is filled with gently rolling hills. The Monroe family home—which has been restored as a memorial to Bill—is on a hill overlooking the town and reached by a rough road. Thus the song's references to "the hills of old Kentucky" are autobiographically accurate. Two other details are also true to life: Both of Monroe's parents died when he was young (his mother when he was ten, his father when Monroe was sixteen), and he continued to enjoy listening to the fox hounds run at night. Fiddler Bobby Hicks, who joined the Blue Grass Boys in 1953, remembers, "We'd go fox hunting together and I'd go out and sit in the woods with him at night and build a fire and we'd listen to them dogs run."[16] Throughout his later years Monroe continued to love fox hunting and was proud of his collection of old hunting horns. Many of these were made from cow horns, fitted with a trumpetlike mouthpiece inside the small end of the horn. Monroe liked to tell friends that when he was a boy, he got so proficient at the fox horn that he could play "Old Joe Clark" on one.

Two songs with connections to Hank Williams were recorded at this session: "Alabama Waltz" and "I'm Blue, I'm Lonesome." Rudy Lyle recalled how the Blue Grass Boys used to do package tours Hank Williams, reinforcing the idea that, in an age before bluegrass had become a distinct sub-genre of the music, Monroe was considered, and considered himself, a country singer. According to Lyle, "Hank Williams used to prank with us a lot, especially at the Friday Night Frolic up at old WSM on 7th Avenue. . . . He used to always kid Bill about where he got his banjo players."[17]

The two songs reflect this relationship. "Alabama Waltz" is one of Monroe's singles that was never reissued on a domestic LP, which is a shame because it is far from pedestrian. Monroe's falsetto is in fine form, and Rudy Lyle's banjo offers innovative off-beat accents. Although credited only to "Smith,"

"I'm Blue, I'm Lonesome" was written jointly by Williams and Monroe. Monroe, touring with Williams, was trying the melody backstage when Williams overheard him and set words to it. According to Ralph Rinzler, "They sang it backstage for their own amusement though they never performed it together."[18] Reno and Smiley later recorded the song.

The personnel for the second Decca session, held just two months later on April 8, 1950, was unchanged except that brother Birch Monroe was brought in to sing bass on the two gospel numbers. Only one single from the first session, "My Little Georgia Rose" and "New Mule Skinner Blues," had been issued, so Paul Cohen and his crew had little idea of how well the new Monroe band was appealing to the public. They must have felt they had a hot new song, though, in "The Old Fiddler" because it was rushed into release before any of the other sides from either session. Otherwise, they were content to let Monroe cut a couple of his gospel quartet numbers—a genre conspicuously absent from the first Decca session.

Although "I'll Meet You in Church Sunday Morning" has little of the power or imagery of Monroe's later gospel songs and never made it much beyond the original single issue after a year of being shelved, the song had considerable appeal for grassroots gospel singers. Dozens found it a wonderful theme song for their radio shows or Wednesday night singings. Monroe re-recorded it in 1964. "Boat of Love," although credited again to "James W. Smith," was allegedly co-written by Joel Price. As Monroe told Hazel Dickens and Alice Gerrard in September 1968:

> [The song was] just another way of bringing out the right side of life . . . my way of thinking about it . . . you would speak of the boatman as Jesus Christ and of course the boat's coming, you know . . . you should be ready. That leads back to the hymns that we sang in the early days and this is my way of writing a hymn off a lot of the songs that I heard back in Kentucky when I was small. . . . That was written for a bass lead and that was my brother Birch Monroe singing bass. Birch understands my kind of writing and it's easy for him 'cause he had sung stuff kind of like that years ago.[19]

"The Old Fiddler" was composed by Hugh Ashley, a well-known songwriter, singer, and music merchant from Arkansas whose father had led one of the pioneer recording bands of the 1920s, Ashley's Melody Men. In the late 1940s he was working for Eli Oberstein, the former Bluebird A&R man who recorded the Monroe Brothers in the 1930s. Oberstein now had a New York music business and was recording on his own cut-rate labels—Royale, Varsity, and Hit. "I was doing a lot of sound-alikes for him back then," recalls Ashley. "I would do cover versions of hit records for his labels, which he would then sell through Sears. I was also doing a lot of songwriting, and he was handling them through his New York publishing contacts."[20] About the same time, Ashley worked frequently with an old-time fiddler in north Arkansas, Frank Watkins:

> He was noted in this part of the country as one of the pure authentic old-time fiddlers, and back in the early radio days of KHOZ [Harrison, Arkansas] I had him on a number of programs and did quite a lot of work with him. I wrote the song around one of his fiddle tunes, where he used an old-time tuning, the old "A" tuning. Originally I recorded it with him on my own label, Hobnob. I sang on it, and had Frank playing with someone beating the strings, in the old-time way. Then Oberstein took my master and put it out on his own Hit label, and farmed out the song to one of the publishers he was working with. I imagine Oberstein got the song to Paul Cohen at Decca. But I had been going through a stage then of writing hoedown songs—five or six of them—songs that could be sung to the up tempo of a hoedown fiddle. Bill Wimberly cut one—"At the Old Town Hall," when he was doing the Red Foley Show at Springfield, and that did good for him. I wrote another one, "A Good Time Was Had By All." which Porter Wagoner cut. I had played a lot with Frank Watkins, the old-time fiddler, and I wrote these tunes in a way that they could be done by a singer, up tempo square dance tempo.[21]

Oberstein, as was the custom, cut himself in for part of the royalties under the pseudonym Ira Wright. He got the song to Cohen, who in turn interested Monroe in it. Years later Ashley met Monroe and complimented him for recording the song even though it was not much of a hit.

Ashley noticed, however, that his song contained a reference to a fiddler named Uncle Ben and that Monroe's next recording was what would be the classic "Uncle Pen." The two songs are miles apart in feeling, but Ashley wondered if his song might have inspired Monroe's effort. "When I met Bill, I mentioned that he wrote a much better tune than mine in 'Uncle Pen,'" Ashley said. "And he quickly went on the defensive, and said, 'Well, I wrote mine before you did yours!' I didn't pursue it, but just to be honest with you, I always wondered if that inspired him to write 'Uncle Pen.'"[22] Monroe set all the instrumental sections of his version of Ashley's song to the tune of "Black Mountain Rag," with young Vassar Clements using the sawmill tuning associated with that piece, presumably the same "old-time tuning" Ashley mentioned. Monroe chose not to reproduce the effect Ashley made by beating straws on the fiddle. Possibly the band was unfamiliar with that practice, or possibly Monroe considered the sound too archaic for his music. As consolation he and Lyle offered a beautiful and unusual mandolin-banjo harmony break.

Monroe's next session was on October 15, 1950, and it was here that he recorded "Uncle Pen." There may still be a few Monroe fans who do not know the story behind what is his single most popular song, and Monroe's account to Dorothy Horstman in 1974 is as succinct an explanation as any. "My Uncle Pen [Vandiver] was one of Kentucky's old-time fiddlers, and he had the best shuffle with the bow that I'd ever seen, and kept the best time. That's one reason people asked him to play for the dances around Rosine, Kentucky. In his later years he was a crippled man. He had been thrown by a mule and had to use crutches the rest of his life. My last years in Kentucky were spent with him."[23] Pen Vandiver died in June 1932 at the relatively young age of sixty-three.

"Uncle Pen" is one of a number of autobiographical songs Monroe would produce in the 1950s. As he said to Jim Rooney, "You take somebody like Uncle Pen. I think it's a wonderful thing to write a song about him and sing it. I don't think I would have done right if I didn't write a song about him. I think it's a wonderful thing."[24] Exactly when or why Monroe wrote the song is unclear. Its copyright was not filed through his publisher, Hill and Range, until 1951. Rudy Lyle remembered that Monroe wrote the song after he had joined the band, in 1949, and that it was written "in the back seat of the car up on the Pennsylvania Turnpike on the way to Rising Sun, Maryland."[25] The car, a Hudson Hornet, had a luggage rack on its roof in which the Blue Grass Boys stored their instruments. The rack blew off as they drove down the Turnpike, scattering instruments across the highway. Another member of the band, Merle "Red" Taylor, a fiddler, also remembered Monroe writing the song. His memory is by no means inconsistent with Lyle's but offers a different perspective. Taylor told *Bluegrass Unlimited*'s writer Don Cunningham in 1982:

> I remember when we were staying in a hotel up near Danville, in Virginia. Bill brought his mandolin up to my room one morning and said, "I've got a song here I'm trying to write about an uncle of mine. His name was Pendleton Vandiver." And he strummed a little bit of what he had. He said he wanted a melody with an old timey sound that would match his uncle's fiddling, 'cause Uncle Pen had been an old-time fiddle player. Well, I liked the idea and I stayed shut up in that hotel room all day long 'til I thought I had what Bill was looking for. Then I called his room and played it for him and he said, "That's exactly what I wanted!" Bill wrote the lyrics for Uncle Pen and I wrote the fiddle part of it.[26]

According to Vassar Clements, he and Bobby Hicks also helped with the melody. The vocal on the chorus is a trio, which is rather rare in Monroe records of the time, with Monroe, Jimmy Martin, and Joel Price. "That's one of the best bands Bill ever had when I was with him," recalled Martin.[27] Merle "Red" Taylor, the new fiddler from Mississippi, also impressed hundreds of fiddlers with the bowing technique he used on the piece. As Gordon Terry explains, "He did a slow bow with a lot of finger work and a funny reverse. . . . I don't think there would be the tunes there are now, had he not played fiddle because he did something nobody did."[28] Taylor, who died in 1987, played with Paul Howard, Cowboy Copas, and Hank Williams in addition to Monroe. His colleague Buddy Spicher has said that he "started a whole new style of bowing that revolutionized fiddle playing."[29] In one way "Uncle Pen" followed the example of "The Old Fiddler," as Monroe arranged it, by using an old-time fiddle tune for part of the instrumental section. Taylor plays the second half of "Jenny Lynn" at the end of the song as a kind of finale. Monroe would record the entire piece in 1971 and include it in a tribute album to his uncle.

Monroe talked to Jim Rooney about "When the Golden Leaves Begin to Fall": "I think you really have to love music to travel. You know, I love to travel. Seems like they went together with me. Some of my numbers it's helped and played a big part. Like 'When the Golden Leaves Begin to Fall.' That was right in autumn time, you know, and leaves and everything were turning and the forest and the mountains and everything was real pretty, and, you know, winter would be coming soon—and I believe Mac Wiseman was with me back in those days—and it seems the song mighty near wrote itself after it got started."[30] That implies the song was worked out in 1949 before Wiseman left the band. Ralph Rinzler has noted that "the unusual harmonies result from the fact that the tenor line follows what is mostly a high baritone part while the baritone is singing low tenor notes, for the most part."[31] Jimmy Martin sings low in the chorus. The Stanleys had used that sort of high baritone arrangement in some of their early pieces like "White Dove," and it is possible that Monroe borrowed the technique from them. He might also have picked it up from the seven-shape-note gospel singing schools of his youth.

Two gospel songs rounded out the October 15 session. Of "Lord Protect My Soul" Monroe recalled, "To start with, 'I want the Lord to protect my soul'; that meant so much to me. And then I went to getting the verses lined up to where the tenor would come on up and pick up the high lead part, and that's how I got the tune of it. I wanted the tenor to be just as high as I could reach it and then the other parts could get their part all

right. It really is one of my favorite hymns. . . . I really love that hymn."[32] In 1981 Monroe confirmed that in a talk with Johnson Mountain Boys fiddler Eddie Stubbs. Although his first gospel song was "Wicked Path of Sin" and his second was "Shining Path," he considered "Lord Protect My Soul" to be his finest gospel composition—and it was also his favorite. About "River of Death" Monroe commented:

> Now that was Jimmy Martin singing the lead on that and that's a perfect song for Jim. Seems I have written songs, you know, that would suit the people at the time that they were working with me. Jimmy knows a lot about hymn singing; his step-father, I'm pretty sure, is a singing-school teacher; anyhow, he's a lead singer in a church and Jim learned, I guess, to sing under him. . . . That "River of Death" is perfect for him. It leads back kind of like a holiness number. You speak of things different ways and lines like that mean a lot to me . . . it gets into the way I feel and touches my heart to hear words like that.[33]

"When I think of a gospel song I think of my mother passed on and my dad, when I was four years old, gone on," Martin has reflected. "I think of good things, of churches I used to go to, and right and wrong. I put my whole heart in it."[34]

According to John Hartford, "River of Death," although it gives composer credits to Monroe, was inspired by one of Don Reno's songs.[35] In 1948 Reno worked for Monroe and wrote "I Want to Live Like Christ My Savior," which Monroe liked and they often performed with the Blue Grass Quartet. Monroe liked it so well, in fact, that he offered to buy the song from Reno, who was reluctant to sell. In January 1952 Reno and Smiley recorded it for their first King sessions—one of the few sides that never made it onto LP. In the meantime Monroe borrowed Reno's tune and came up with "River of Death." He even borrowed Reno's opening lines, changing "I want to live like Christ my savior" to "I want to want to walk with Christ my savior" in the chorus.

1951: STUDIO EXPERIMENTS

On January 20, 1951, Monroe recorded three striking originals and one cover. Of "Letter from My Darling," "a true song" is all he would say to Ralph Rinzler.[36] In Monroe's parlance that could mean it was literally based on an actual event or it reflected true emotions and real-life situations. Robert Cantwell singles out this performance as one of Monroe's most intense: "With wailing harmonies, a complaining lead vocal, and a crying fiddle, the entire song seems to weep; and Monroe's heavy, impulsive mandolin break tears the melody apart."[37] "On the Old Kentucky Shore" is also autobiographical and about the death of a girl who had been romantically linked with one of Bill's brothers. A classic Monroe dirge with Jimmy Martin and Bill at full cry, the song remained in Martin's repertoire. Its refrain, with a reference to the Ohio River and the "crepe on the door," ties the song to Monroe, however, even given the lack of specific historical background.

"Raw Hide," of course, became one of the great signature pieces. Monroe would routinely play it as fast as he possibly could and use it to challenge veteran musicians and test new musicians trying out for the band. Onstage, he would talk about other mandolin players trying to do the piece right and then rip into it to show the audience how it should be done. "Raw Hide" would, in short, become the vehicle for an old-fashioned cutting contest, to borrow the jazz term. Monroe's identity as a mandolin player became tied to the piece, and he never let anyone cut him on it. No one was surprised when Ricky Skaggs and Marty Stuart played the piece at full speed at his funeral in 1996. Monroe admitted on several occasions that he named the tune—certainly not to be confused with the cowboy theme song popularized a decade later—after a 1951 Hollywood film, *Rawhide,* which starred Tyrone Power. Monroe liked the movie because it featured his old friend Max Terhune, whom he met while working at WLS in Chicago in the 1930s.

Pete Kuykendall, the distinguished editor of *Bluegrass Unlimited,* has called this recording of "Raw Hide" "the definitive mandolin tune."[38] As with "Blue Grass Ramble," Monroe built the two parts of the piece, which is in the key of C, using earlier forms. The first part follows the same chord pattern as "Lonesome Road Blues," which Monroe also did in C and recorded in 1960. The second part follows the circle of fifths chord pattern often associated with ragtime-type pieces in country music, such as "Salty Dog Blues" and "Don't Let Your Deal Go Down." The arrangement highlights the end of this section by having all instruments stop except the one taking the break. Until discographical information became available it was rumored, because of the jazzy chords Rudy Lyle played at the end of his break on the second part, that the banjo on "Raw Hide" was played by Don Reno, who was noted for his use of sophisticated chords. Monroe's ending, with the four stop chords followed by the familiar "shave and a haircut" phrase, was new at the time and has been frequently copied. Because of its extreme tempo "Raw Hide" was considered a tour de force for the mandolin. It remained in Monroe's performance repertoire for the rest of his career, and in later years he developed the arrangement to highlight its speed.

The final song of the session was a cover. Just a year before, in January 1950, Johnnie Wright and Jack Anglin had recorded "Poison Love" for RCA Victor, and by the time of Monroe's recording it was a hit for them and climbing the charts. Ernie Newton, the bass player who would play on many of Monroe's sides, added a Latin beat to the Johnnie and Jack side that gave the song a distinctive flavor. Monroe would have none of that, however, and did the song in straight bluegrass style. The problem with Monroe doing covers for Decca was that he would never consent to try to imitate the style of the original. Everything was converted into his own inimitable style, regardless of the original. They remain not so much period pieces or curiosities but testimonies to the strength and uniqueness of Monroe's music.

The session of March 17, 1951, is a landmark of sorts, for it represents the first time Monroe recorded without his regular band and used instead a cadre of crack young Nashville studio session musicians. Grady Martin, just beginning his long career as a studio expert, played guitar, and Tommy Jackson played the fiddle. Farris Coursey was on drums, Ernie Newton on bass, composer-singer Jimmy Selph was on guitar, and Owen Bradley played organ and piano, rounding out the unusual group. Decca had learned that Victor was about to release Eddy Arnold's new recording of "Kentucky Waltz" and was anxious for Monroe to do a cover immediately. It has been rumored that the studio musicians were used because Monroe was on tour and the company was unwilling to fly all the Blue Grass Boys back to Nashville. But in fact, two Blue Grass Boys were present at the session as vocalists on the session's final piece, so it's more likely that the musicians for this session were brought in to help Monroe make a cover that sounded as much like Arnold's as possible.

"Kentucky Waltz," Monroe's first try at writing lyrics, became one of his best-known pieces. The second number cut at his first Columbia session in 1945, it became his best-selling record in terms of chart sales. In March 1951, long after Monroe's Columbia version of "Kentucky Waltz" had dropped from the charts, Eddy Arnold recorded it for RCA Victor, and by April 6 it was back on the charts. Just a few days after Arnold recorded "Kentucky Waltz," however, Paul Cohen quickly got wind of Arnold's recording and rushed Monroe into the studio to cover his own song. By April 6 Arnold's version was on its way to becoming a number-one hit. Monroe's new version was out by April 21, but it failed to catch much of the Arnold action. Next at this, the first "Nashville Sound" session for Monroe, was "The Prisoner's Song," a version of the venerable chestnut that Vernon Dalhart had recorded in 1925 and the first real country million-seller. Monroe's tenor, in its strong, classic purity, echoes Dalhart's, whose records Monroe remembered hearing as a boy.

The fact that Monroe did "Swing Low Sweet Chariot" as straight as he did is a bit surprising because the vogue in the early 1950s was to follow the lead of the gospel-singing Statesmen and Blackwood Brothers and merge the song with one called "Swing Down, Chariot." Monroe seems to have resisted though, reflecting his strong and constant respect for doing songs the "right" way—especially older songs. In later years he was fond of closing performances with "Swing Low Sweet Chariot," sometimes singing it a cappella with the audience.

No composer credits are given for the gospel quartet number "Angels Rock Me to Sleep," but it was written by Thomas Ramsey and Marion W. Easterling. The latter, an Alabama native, was born 1910 and studied gospel music under teachers of the famed James D. Vaughan Company in the 1930s—the same Vaughan Company that provided the Monroe Brothers with so much material. In the late 1940s and early 1950s Easterling was active in radio work and known for introducing memorable gospel quartet songs over the air. In 1947 he published a songbook at Clanton, Alabama, *America's Favorite Radio Songs,* and "Angels Rock Me to Sleep" appears in that. Although the Blue Grass Boys did not play instruments at the session, two—Jimmy Martin and Rudy Lyle—were present and sang tenor and baritone to Monroe's lead on this song. The identity of the bass singer is uncertain, but it sounds like Culley Holt, another Nashville studio regular who would record again with Monroe at his 1958 gospel sessions. "Angels Rock Me to Sleep" became quite popular in the early 1950s. Various gospel quartets recorded it, and other country and bluegrass acts such as Johnnie and Jack and Carl Story also did versions of it.

The next two 1951 sessions featured songs associated with Jimmie Rodgers. Since the days of "Mule Skinner Blues" Monroe had been fond of doing Rodgers songs, so it was not surprising for Paul Cohen now to suggest that Monroe do an entire set of Rodgers song material, if for no other reason than as a follow-up to Monroe's successful "New Mule Skinner Blues" for Decca the year before.

In 1949 and 1950 RCA Victor reissued its first sets of old Jimmie Rodgers recordings in a series of three special album sets, each containing three Rodgers records.[39] Throughout the 1940s very little Rodgers material had been available, and fans were clamoring; the three albums were selling surprisingly well. To get a piece of this action Columbia rushed Lefty Frizzell into the studio in June 1951 to do a new album of Rodgers material, and it seems likely that Cohen decided to do the same for Decca. Monroe was Decca's primary Rodgers-styled singer, and the

fact that he cut eight Rodgers songs suggests that at one point Decca might have thought of a four 78-rpm album set of its own to counter the Victor and Columbia sets. Two, "Brakeman's Blues" and "My Carolina Sunshine Girl," had been among the Rodgers records included in the Victor reissue sets.[40]

The sessions were not very successful. Only "Brakeman's Blues" and Travelin' Blues" were issued in Decca's normal rotation. Two more, "When the Cactus Is in Bloom" and "Sailor's Plea," were held up for more than a year before coming out in June 1952. "Peach Pickin' Time in Georgia" had to wait even longer and finally appeared on a cut-rate LP issued in April 1964, thirteen years after the session. The remaining three Rodgers titles, "My Carolina Sunshine Girl," "Ben Dewberry's Final Run," and "Those Gambler's Blues," were never issued domestically although they appeared in Japanese and Dutch Monroe collections. Owen Bradley considered the cuts to be not of marketable quality, a judgment partially borne out by listeners today. They do have their moments, though. Rudy Lyle's banjo break on "Brakeman's Blues," one of the more creative of his career, was widely admired in the 1950s.

Part of the reason for the failure of the session is because Monroe, at the April 23 session at least, was forced to use Nashville studio sidemen—one of the very few times in his 1950s recording career he would do so. The musicians were of fine quality, however. Grady Martin was on electric guitar; Hal Smith was on fiddle; and Jack Shook, the rhythm guitarist, was an Opry veteran who had also done sessions with Hank Williams. Theirs was clean, well-played music, but it was not bluegrass. The first Rodgers song session, however, had the regular Blue Grass Boys Rudy Lyle, Jimmy Martin, and Joel Price, and it is perhaps no coincidence that Decca issued all of this session's sides right away.

"Highway of Sorrow," the sole non-Rodgers item from the sessions, was strong enough to redeem its weaker efforts. Pete Pyle's masterpiece has been described by writer-singer Doug Green as "that great classic bluegrass heart song, immensely moving in its terse understatement."[41] Pyle, whose 1941–42 stint as a Blue Grass Boy (he participated in the 1941 Bluebird session) is detailed in chapter 2, returned to the Opry after a stint in the army and worked with a variety of bands throughout the 1940s. These were difficult years for him, but he kept his ties with Monroe; in 1945 the Blue Grass Boys recorded Pyle's "True Life Blues." The year 1950 found him touring with Ernest Tubb and recording an unissued session for Capitol, but he suffered continually from mental illness and had drinking problems. It was during one particularly depressing string of bad luck, which climaxed when he left Tubb, that he wrote "Highway of Sorrow." Later Monroe would record other Pyle numbers, and for a short time in 1953 Pyle rejoined the Blue Grass Boys.

Two months after the unsuccessful Rodgers song sessions and the experiment with Nashville studio musicians, Cohen took Monroe back into the studio for another cover session on July 1, 1951. By this time Carter Stanley had joined the band. Ironically, it was Columbia's signing of the Stanley Brothers in 1949 that had caused Monroe to leave the label, and in the late 1940s little love was lost between him and the Stanleys, whom he for a time viewed as his chief competition. By early 1951, however, the Stanley band had run into hard times and disbanded. Monroe quickly offered Carter a job, and soon they became fast friends. Gordon Terry had replaced Merle "Red" Taylor on fiddle. Terry, a twenty-year-old musician from Decatur, Alabama, had by 1950 landed jobs on the Opry and the newly formed WSM-TV. He was an ornate, smooth, long-bow fiddler more than actual bluegrass fiddler and a protégé of sorts of Tommy Jackson. Later he went to the West Coast and appeared in films and on television, eventually winning fame as a vocalist. Terry recorded with Monroe throughout 1951, later in the mid-1950s, and again in the early 1970s.

"Rotation Blues" was a topical hit. In April 1951, Harry S. Truman relieved Gen. Douglas MacArthur of command in Korea, which made the public even more aware of the Korean conflict. Songs about the "police action" were fast becoming a new genre of country song, and early in 1951 an on-duty officer in Korea, Lt. Stewart Powell, penned one about the rotation assignment system for troops there. Elton Britt had recorded the song for RCA Victor, and Decca felt it needed a cover version. The result was one of the few topical songs in the Monroe canon. The fact that the song was published by Tannen, a New York music publisher just starting to move into Nashville, might have also swayed Monroe, who would sign a publishing contract with Tannen shortly thereafter.

In February 1951, singer Bob Newman had recorded "Lonesome Truck Driver's Blues" for King, and it had become a modest hit, perhaps the biggest of Newman's career. A Georgia native, he had carved out a radio career with his two brothers as the Georgia Crackers and was working out of Columbus, Ohio, when he began his King recording career. Although some versions of the song bore composer credits to King studio's legendary black pianist Henry Glover, proper credits should go to Lee Roberts, the pseudonym Newman used when he published songs. Sparked by Rudy Lyle's gritty, Pee Wee Russell–styled banjo solo, Monroe turns in a surprisingly strong performance here, singing in a fine falsetto voice. It is a splendid instance of how he could take a song from another idiom (in this case,

honky-tonk) and turn it into bluegrass. More surprising, the cut never made it to any domestic LP reissue of Monroe's work.

The second session Monroe made with Carter Stanley in the band, July 6, 1951, is the only one in which Carter sings with Monroe. On all four tunes Carter sings lead to Monroe's tenor. The session, Carter's last with the band, provides the only evidence of two of bluegrass music's great voices working together at the peak of their powers. Decca was not especially impressed with the pairing, though, and scattered the four numbers on singles that were unreleased for a year. "Sugar Coated Love" came out in October, and "You're Drifting Away" had to wait until March 1953. Paul Cohen apparently thought the hot song from the session was "Get Down on Your Knees and Pray," which was rushed into single release in five weeks.

"Sugar Coated Love" by Audrey Butler is one of two occasions on which Monroe and Stanley sang a duet. It is an early example of a clever Nashville sound–style song built around an elaborate metaphor—a form somewhat unusual for Monroe. The Stanley Brothers kept the song in their stage repertoire for years, however. "Cabin of Love," the other duet, was written by Birch Monroe. It had been recorded by the Shenandoah Valley Trio, a Monroe offshoot consisting of Lyle, Martin, and Price, for Columbia in August 1950 and was released in February 1951. "You're Drifting Away" appears to have been in Monroe's repertoire for some time because its text was printed by Flatt and Scruggs in their songbook of 1950. There Monroe is given credit as the composer.[42]

Monroe had specific memories of "Get Down on Your Knees and Pray" and recounted them to Hazel Dickens and Alice Gerrard in 1968. "We were playing Asheville, North Carolina, on a Sunday," he said, "and we'd left the Grand Ole Opry and we'd gotten through Tennessee and were getting into the mountains of North Carolina, and I was driving—everyone else was sleeping." The phrase "get down on your knees and pray" came to him on that lonely highway in the wee hours of the morning. "You know," he added, "I'm a great believer in lonesome numbers and blue numbers and something that will haunt you, and singing a song and speaking of you as a Christian and talking to your brother—'Oh, brother can't you hear me say'—that was in my mind when I started the song. . . . It's the kind of song that's being raised in Kentucky. . . . I know it's our type of tune and words."[43] Monroe's mandolin breaks are especially noteworthy and incorporate delicate harmonics at the end of the break.

The October 28, 1951, session marks the recording debut of one of Monroe's most important sidemen, singer-guitarist Edd Mayfield. Born around the small Texas panhandle town of Dimmitt in 1926, Mayfield came from a family of ranchers and rodeo men. With his brothers Herb and Smokey he was a member of the Mayfield Brothers bluegrass band that played locally in west Texas. The band was offered a record contract, but the boys were too involved in ranching and rodeoing to work at their music full time. Monroe, however, heard of Edd, and after Carter Stanley left the band in the summer of 1951 Monroe and Gordon Terry found themselves sitting in Monroe's room at the Andrew Jackson Hotel, wondering who could replace him. "I know a good singer from Texas," Monroe said. "I'll give him a call."

Mayfield soon arrived in Nashville, looking like the rangy working cowboy he was, and had an immediate effect on the band. "He could sing higher than a cat's back," recalls Terry. "We started moving a lot of our arrangements up a notch or two, from B to C, for instance. And he had that high nasal sound that you can hear so well on 'The First Whippoorwill.'"[44] Mayfield's voice blended very well with Monroe's, and in later years he grew able to sing amazingly like Monroe; he also became one of the sidemen of whom Monroe thought most highly. He would leave the band soon after this recording but would rejoin it in 1954 and then again in 1958.

The composer of record for "Christmas Time's a-Coming," the best-known of all bluegrass Christmas songs, was Tex Logan, a fiddle player born and reared around Coahoma, Texas, near Big Spring. As a boy, he was fascinated with Monroe's 1940 Victor recording of "Katy Hill" featuring Tommy Magness, and he developed a lifelong enthusiasm for Monroe and his music. In 1946 he went to the Massachusetts Institute of Technology to study electrical engineering and eventually received a Ph.D. He also fell in with a country band headed by a team called Jerry (Howorth) and Sky (Snow). That led to later jobs with Red Belcher, the Lilly Brothers, Hawkshaw Hawkins, and Big Slim (Harry C. McAuliffe).

Sometime in the fall of 1949, while working at WWVA in Wheeling with the Lilly Brothers, Logan wrote "Christmas Time's A-Comin'." He did so with Monroe in mind, but he had never met Monroe and had no chance to offer it to him. In the summer of 1951, however, Logan had his chance in Wheeling:

I worked those two hitches there with Wilma Lee and Stoney Cooper. After the last hitch, which was in 1951, I'd worked late into October—I'd finished my degree [at MIT]—we played a big show in Baltimore in the Coliseum there, with Lester Flatt, Earl Scruggs, Hawkshaw Hawkins, Wayne Raney, Cowboy Copas, Wilma Lee and Stoney, and Bill Monroe. I'd never met Bill before and was real thrilled. Buck Graves was working with Wilma Lee and Stoney at the time—he and I were buddies—we'd do this song I had written for Bill, "Christmas Time's A-Comin'." . . . So Buck and I went backstage after the show and did this number

for him. We started doing it and Bill joined in on the chorus right away, and after we got through said, "I'll record it." He did shortly after that.[45]

Fiddler Gordon Terry adds, "I hadn't been with Bill too long. I went with him in the latter part of 1950. . . . I think I'd cut one session with him before then and he was going to do 'Christmas Time's A-Comin'. He said, 'If you can learn this before the session I'll let you cut it, but if not I'm going to call Tex Logan. . . . I really wanted to cut the song and sat up day and night trying to play that fiddle."[46] Terry never felt, though, that he played the song in the exact way Logan did. Shorty Shehan, playing bass with the Blue Grass Boys at the time, was an old-time fiddler, and he recalled helping Terry work out the part, for which the fiddle uses the same sawmill tuning as in "Black Mountain Rag." Logan remembers, "I was going to come into Nashville, but couldn't make it and called Bill and he said, 'We're going to go ahead and cut it and I'll play it to you over the phone and if you like it, OK, and if not, well, come in next week.' And sure enough, he played it over the phone and it sounded so good."[47]

In fact, Monroe scheduled a special session to cut the song and get it out in time for Christmas sales. "Christmas Time's A-Comin'" was issued on November 24, less than a month after the recording session. Edd Mayfield shares vocal chores on the chorus, and Owen Bradley, the session producer, added his vibraphone to the sound, probably the first time that particular instrument graced a bluegrass record. For the flip side of the new Christmas piece Monroe chose one of his most intense and brooding tunes, "The First Whippoorwill." The song is sometimes confused with "The First Whippoorwill Song" as recorded by radio singer Bradley Kincaid and featured by Scott Wiseman in the 1930s, but there is little similarity in mood or melody to that older Victorian pastoral. The idea of nightbirds crying in warning, an old superstition, helps infuse the song with melancholy and fatalism. "The First Whippoorwill" has remained a favorite among younger interpreters of Monroe's music.

Oddly, the recording has a technical flaw that has become legendary among devotees: a sudden, momentary slowing and distortion in the middle of Lyle's banjo solo. It is as if someone in the studio had bumped the tape reel on the recording console, or perhaps there was a momentary power surge. Three or four notes of Lyle's solo are distorted. At the time, banjo players especially slavishly emulated the work of early bluegrass pickers like Scruggs and Lyle; more than a few even copied Scruggs's minor mistakes, as on "My Cabin in Caroline." Some assumed that Lyle was bending his notes on purpose and set out to copy him. As a joke in later years Lamar Grier grew able to reproduce the effect by bending the neck of his instrument. Another "technical flaw" that has been rumored for years about this session was that Edd Mayfield had a head cold and therefore sounds more nasal than on later recordings.

1952–54: INTERRUPTIONS AND INNOVATIONS

The session of July 18, 1952, marks the debut of two more important Monroe sidemen, the multi-instrumentalist Charlie Cline and a very young banjo player named Sonny Osborne. Cline, born in Gilbert, Virginia, in 1931, was a superb fiddle and mandolin player who learned a lot from Fiddlin' Arthur Smith, who stayed with the Cline Family from 1940 to 1941. It was Smith who taught Cline that he "could not call himself a fiddle player until you learn to use that little finger."[48] Throughout the late 1940s, Charlie played with a West Virginia radio band, the Lonesome Pine Fiddlers, a leading radio group in the area. Larry Richardson, the band's banjo player, left to join Monroe in the early 1950s, which led directly to Cline's job with Monroe: "Bill Monroe came to Bluefield [West Virginia, the home base of the Lonesome Pine Fiddlers], and Larry Richardson had gone with him, playing banjo, and they needed a fiddler, so Larry told him about me, and Bill asked me to go play a show with him that night, and then he asked me if I wanted to work with him, so I went to Nashville, and I worked with him about five years off and on."[49]

It is noteworthy that Monroe, in getting Cline, deviated from his normal method of picking rookies for musicians. Cline was an experienced professional even though he was not yet twenty. He was to emerge as one of the most versatile of the Blue Grass Boys—in fact, for a time he was the only one of the group who had played every instrument. When Monroe was recovering from a broken collar bone in 1955 Cline even played that part on the mandolin for stage shows—one of the few Blue Grass Boys to do so.

Sonny Osborne was only fourteen when he made his debut with Monroe on this session. When Jimmy Martin left Monroe in June of 1951 he'd gone to work with Sonny's older brother, Bobby Osborne, in the Lonesome Pine Fiddlers. That summer Sonny worked in the band as banjoist, and Martin joined with the two Osborne brothers and their sister Louise to record two 78s on the Kitty label. That fall Martin and Bobby Osborne recorded under their own names for King, and then Bobby was inducted into the marines. By the summer of 1952 Martin was playing with Sonny on the radio in Middletown, Ohio. According to Martin, Monroe called him and said "they wanted him

to cut an album and he didn't have nobody to help him record and asked me would I come back down and record an album with him."[50] By 1952 Sonny was an adequate Scruggs-style banjoist. Because it was summer and Sonny was out of school, Martin decided to take him along to Nashville. That summer Osborne would be able to record ten sides with Monroe.

Sonny was not in the union, and local officials were nervous about allowing him to play. Finally, they made Martin sign his card for him and promise to watch after him. Paul Cohen was glad to see Martin back in the studios, and, according to Martin, told Monroe, "You ought to keep this boy with you. You can sell records if you keep him with you. He's the best I ever heard with his guitar and lead singing."[51] Martin had plans to use Sonny in his own band once brother Bobby got out of the service, and he knew that a summer with Monroe would be good seasoning and good publicity. He agreed to stay if Monroe would also let Sonny play out the summer. Monroe, who had never found a good replacement on banjo for Rudy Lyle, agreed. "Well, he's awful young," he told Martin. "But if you want him to work, you take care of him and everything and we'll let him work."[52]

Sonny Osborne has in later years disparaged his banjo playing on these summer 1952 sessions. As Bob Artis has written, "Admittedly, the recordings they made in those July days of 1952 were not noted for their great banjo playing. Sonny was not familiar with their material, not familiar with the musicians, and was scared to death of the bigger-than-life figure of Bill Monroe. . . . He was no Earl Scruggs, to be sure, but his work with Monroe marked the professional recording debut of one of the most important recording artists in the bluegrass field."[53]

Monroe had recorded "In the Pines" in 1941 for Victor and this version is quite similar except that it adds an extra line about the "long steel rail" in the second verse. No one seems to know how Jimmie Davis's name appeared along with Monroe's on the song credits of the 1952 version. "Footprints in the Snow" was another remake of one of Monroe's 1945 recordings. The first version was done at the first Columbia session with David "Stringbean" Akeman, Wilene "Sally Ann" Forrester, Cedric Rainwater, Curly Bradshaw, Chubby Wise, and Tex Willis. It had been Monroe's second record to hit the *Billboard* charts, and after "Kentucky Waltz" it was his most successful chart record. It was thus a good prospect for a new Decca version with the new band that included Jimmy Martin, Charlie Cline, and a young Sonny Osborne. In the 1945 version of the song, composer credits were given to one Boyd Lane as arranger; in this version credits were given to Rupert Jones, which is certainly a pseudonym for Bill Monroe.

Monroe recalled to Alice (Gerrard) Foster and Ralph Rinzler in 1969 that he got "Walking in Jerusalem" in Norwood, North Carolina. "I was visiting some friends of mine and they knew these colored folks, you know, and they had been fans of mine. They had this number . . . and wanted me to learn it and record it. I went by these people's house and I talked to this man; I believe that maybe he was a preacher . . . it's been so long ago, but anyway he wanted me to record it and sing it on The Grand Ole Opry. They sang it for me there kind of the way I sing it."[54] The song had been recorded several times by black gospel quartets in the 1920s, including the Excelsior Quartet in New York for Okeh in 1922, the Sunset Four in Chicago for Paramount in 1925, and the Birmingham Jubilee Singers in 1927 for Columbia. Backed only by Jimmy Martin's guitar and Ernie Newton's bass, the Blue Grass Quartet shines. An unexpected guest voice, the bass, is that of Boudleaux Bryant, then a recently arrived songwriter and fiddle player from Atlanta. In a few years, of course, he and his wife and writing partner Felice would be best known for the great Everly Brothers hits and for "Rocky Top."

Three of the five songs cut at the unusual night session of July 18, 1952, were Monroe songs credited to Albert Price, a name Monroe used when he published with the Tannen Publishing Company. The facts that Bryant was present at the afternoon session on this date and even sang bass on "Walking in Jerusalem" suggests strongly that he was trying to acquire some of Monroe's songs for Tannen. He got three of the best. "Memories of Mother and Dad," one of the finest of the Jimmy Martin–Bill Monroe duets, seems a conventional sentimental home song, but it is actually an accurate autobiographical song born out of Monroe's grief over the early loss of his parents. The inscriptions on the tombstones at the "little lonesome graveyard" ("gone but not forgotten" and "we shall meet again someday") are almost exactly those on the stones of Monroe's parents in the cemetery at Rosine. He had been performing "The Little Girl and the Dreadful Snake" for at least a year before this recording. As Carter Stanley recalled, "That's the first song that I ever learned to sing with Bill when I went to work with him" in the spring of 1951.[55] In the summer of 1952 the Stanleys recorded it for the independent Rich-R-Tone label about the same time Monroe did. Both singers kept it in their repertoires, and Martin replaces Stanley singing lead. For the song, Monroe recast an incident from his youth in Rosine when a little girl wandered off and fell into a well. Searchers could hear her cries but couldn't find the well.[56]

The balance of the session produced little of immediate impact on Monroe's career. Decca had high hopes for "Country Waltz" and released it as a single before the other songs from the session. Pete Pyle's fine "Don't Put Off Until Tomorrow" was shelved in the vault and not issued until Ralph Rinzler rescued it for an LP, *A Voice from on High,* in 1969, seventeen years later. At that time Monroe said, "Pete Pyle wrote that number; it has a meaning, you know, like some of my hymns. It's really a good song and I'm glad that you're going to release it. I believe just the way that I was brought up, that you have got to be saved . . . and then you're ready to die."[57] "My Dying Bed" had to wait until 1966 for issue.

On July 26, 1952, just a week after the marathon session of July 18 that produced so many of Monroe's "dark" masterpieces, he was rushed back into the studio for yet another cover, "A Mighty Pretty Waltz," which was a country version of what was essentially a pop song by Al Hoffman and Norman Gimbel. Hoffman, a major pop composer, had written songs for Walt Disney's *Cinderella* as well as pieces like "Black Eyed Susan Brown," a western swing favorite; "Allegheny Moon," a Patti Page hit; a mind-numbing novelty for Perry Como called "Hot Diggity"; and such forgettable monstrosities as "Gully Gully Ochsenpfeffer Katzenellen-Bogen by the Sea." Jeri Southern and Victor Young recorded "A Mighty Pretty Waltz" for Decca, but the companies had such high hopes for it that they decided to do a country cover as well. It was all for naught. Neither the pop version nor Monroe's caught fire—in fact, Monroe's never made it onto an LP.

The other piece recorded at the session was also a cover. Monroe composed "Pike County Breakdown" several years before he recorded it. "I wanted," he said, "to write something and title it after something up in the eastern part of Kentucky. You remember 'Sweet Betsy From Pike?' I listened to that and wrote the 'Pike County Breakdown.'"[58] On another occasion he recalled how many good bookings the Blue Grass Boys had in eastern Kentucky and implied that the piece was partially inspired by a local woman, Betty Parker, who always came to the shows. He had started playing it backstage back when Flatt and Scruggs were in the band, and in May 1952 a version was released that they recorded for the rival Mercury company in 1950. Thus as with "Kentucky Waltz" Monroe was again forced into covering one of his own songs. Sonny Osborne played banjo and Charlie Cline the fiddle and, Martin recalled, "Sonny was just getting started then and he thought that when he cut that 'Pike County Breakdown' that he had his part pretty close to what Earl [Scruggs] was doing. I had to tell him, 'Sonny, you're not anywhere close.'"[59] Osborne, however, remembers things differently. He recalls that Monroe had made suggestions that led him to try not to sound too much like Scruggs on the piece.

Monroe's Decca career was interrupted in early 1953 when he was injured in an automobile accident. On the early morning of January 16, he and Bessie Lee Mauldin were returning from a late-night fox hunt north of Nashville, driving down Highway 31–W to get back to WSM for an early-morning radio show. Near the hamlet of White House their car was struck by another vehicle whose driver had been drinking. Monroe was rushed to General Hospital in Nashville, where he was treated for fractures to his back, left arm, and nose as well as other injuries. For a time he was officially listed as being in critical condition.

It was a slow and painful recovery, and other Opry stars participated in a benefit for him on February 22. Jimmy Martin tried his best to keep the band together for radio and show dates. Because Monroe's left arm had been broken it was some time before he could resume playing the mandolin, and it was May 10 before he could resume touring. There was a major hiatus in his recording schedule—one of two such periods during the 1950s—and he didn't get back into the studio until November 28, 1953, almost sixteen months later. Of the three pieces cut ("Wishing Waltz," "I Hope You Have Learned," and "Get Up John"), only the last had an impact on his music. Monroe retuned his mandolin for this driving instrumental in the key of D, as he had with "Blue Grass Ramble" and "Memories of You." The result was a tour de force. "Get Up, John" was an old Kentucky fiddle tune that Uncle Pen called "Sleepy John." Tex Atchison, the fiddler from the Prairie Ramblers, also from western Kentucky, did a popular version of the tune he called "Sleepy Eyed John" in the late 1940s, and in 1961 Johnny Horton had a major hit with his version of the same thing.

Ralph Rinzler has described in some detail the special D tuning that Monroe uses on "Get Up, John": "In order to catch the spirit of the old-time fiddle, Bill retunes his mandolin to his version of the unusual fiddle tuning used by his uncle. The mandolin is tuned as follows: high or E strings are tuned down, one to D, the other to A (in unison with the A strings, which, like the D strings, are not altered in pitch). The G strings are both changed: the first is raised one step to A, the other is lowered one half step to F#."[60] Just as the tuning for "Blue Grass Ramble" uses the notes of an A major chord, the tuning for "Get Up, John" uses the notes of a D major chord.

Other than the mandolin, there are some unusual changes to other instruments as well. Rudy Lyle put his banjo capo up on the seventh fret so he could play in open-G tuning. As Eddie Stubbs has noted, it was one of the first cases in which that occurred in bluegrass. Don Reno would do it as well on "Charlotte Breakdown," but that would be a year away. The first half of Lyle's brief break anticipates the "melodic" approach that Bill Keith developed more fully in the 1960s. Both Lyle and Charlie Cline used harmonics in their work here, which was rather novel in a Monroe session, and Cline retuned his fiddle, dropping the E string to a D.

In Nashville for the holidays, Monroe wasted no time in catching up with his studio work, recording twelve songs in three sessions over a week. The first, on January 7, 1954, yielded another set of four singles that ran the gamut from gospel to blues. The session started with two vocal trios—rather rare in Monroe circles. "On and On" was a new Monroe composition that is generally thought to be one of the autobiographical canon. It became a regular part of Monroe's live repertoire in the 1960s and has been recorded by a number of other bluegrass groups. "I Believed in You Darling" is a more formulaic love lament that did not achieve the same level of popularity with bluegrass performers.

"New John Henry Blues," Monroe's version of the widely known traditional song, was held up for single release in the United States because Decca officials were worried about his use of the phrase *little colored boy* in the first verse. This seemed not to deter them from issuing the record in England, where it appeared on the Brunswick label as a single in July 1956. It was finally issued in the United States as a single in 1963 when Monroe's new manager Ralph Rinzler discovered it while compiling Monroe's discography. Rinzler argued with nervous Decca officials in Nashville (at the height of the civil rights movement) that the phrase was nothing more than Monroe's traditional and respectful way of referring to African Americans. The song was a regular in Monroe's performance repertoire throughout his career. "White House Blues" was another traditional number likely intended as the flip side to "New John Henry Blues," but it wound up instead on the B side of "Get Up John." Years before, the Monroe brothers learned the song from an old 78—probably the 1926 version on Columbia by Charlie Poole that contains all the stanzas Monroe uses here. The song refers to the assassination of President William McKinley in 1901 and circulated in oral tradition even before Poole did it. Rudy Lyle's banjo threatens to steal the show both from Monroe's singing and his "hot chorus" (Monroe's words) on mandolin.[61] Monroe almost never took mandolin breaks on the song in personal appearances. It became one of Lyle's best-known performances as a Blue Grass Boy, and he helped make "White House Blues" a bluegrass standard that had special appeal to banjo pickers.

The next night's session, again featuring the power trio of Jimmy Martin, Rudy Lyle, and Charlie Cline, produced mixed results, with one original and three covers of earlier songs by others. "Sitting Alone in the Moonlight" is probably the best of the lot, one of Monroe's "night" songs about loneliness and despair. The title resembles a line from "Kentucky Waltz" and is a fine example of what Dave Freeman and Gary Reid call "the chilling, hard-edged loneliness of Monroe's music in the early and mid-1950s."[62] Jimmy Martin is featured on lead, with Monroe doing the tenor. "Plant Some Flowers by My Grave" originated in 1938 when it was recorded on the old Bluebird label by an Alabama group, the McClendon Brothers Trio with Georgia Dell. In 1942 Jimmie Davis recorded it again for Decca, attaching his name in the process. Although Monroe's is a strong performance, the cut was not issued for eight years, when it was used as filler for the LP entitled *My All Time Country Favorites*. Both Charlie Cline and Lyle spice the second half of their breaks with bluesy phrasing.

Everyone had high hopes for "Changing Partners," a pop song. Composed by two veteran pop writers, Joe Darion and Larry Coleman, it was recorded by Patti Page, Kay Starr, Dinah Shore, Bing Crosby, and even Pee Wee King. Darion was best known for "The Impossible Dream" and for novelties like "The Goonie Bird Song." It was Patti Page who had the hit with "Changing Partners"; no country version made the charts. Arlie Duff, the Texas honky-tonk singer with the Ozark Jubilee in 1954, had written "Y'All Come" in 1953, and his Starday version of it climbed onto the charts in January 1954. Duff's hit, which landed him a job on the Ozark Jubilee later that year, was covered by both Bing Crosby and Monroe. Monroe began using "Y'All Come" at the end of his portion of the show on personals, which no doubt helped it become somewhat of a country standard. Clearly audible on the cut is a rhythm device, a raised pad, which Ernie Newton attached to the left-front top of the bass next to the fingerboard and beat with a drum brush held in his right hand. Newton used it to create a percussive sound resembling that of a snare drum in the same way other bass players slapped their strings and fingerboard on the off-beat.[63]

A week later at another evening session devoted to gospel songs Lyle was given a rest and in his place Monroe brought in bass singer Milton Estes. For some years Estes, who won initial fame as an emcee and singer with Pee Wee King, had a popular string band over WSM, WLAC, and the Opry, the

Musical Millers, who recorded for Decca and other labels. The first of the four gospel numbers done that night was "Happy on My Way," another effort by Pete Pyle. Of "I'm Working on a Building" Monroe told Hazel Dickens and Alice Gerrard, "I believe that I heard the Carter Family sing that song, and we got requests for it on our show dates and I thought that I should learn it. It's a holiness number, I would say. You know, there's holiness singing in my music."[64] The Carter Family had recorded the song first in 1934 for Bluebird and then for radio transcriptions later on. Not surprisingly, the construction metaphor appealed to Monroe. "From the time you're a boy on you want to build something and when you get older, to think that you're working on the building like that, why, it gives you a wonderful feeling."[65]

Bill and Bessie Lee Mauldin composed "A Voice from on High." "I sure want to be ready on that day," Bill told Dickens and Gerrard. "And I speak in my writing of a song the way I really feel about it. I really want to hear that voice calling me . . . I believe a person should try to live the best life he can live and enjoy it and live a decent life. . . . I was trying to do something with the tenor, you know, and tie some words together with the tune. So I wrote the chorus to that song and I meant it for the tenor to have the high part there, and it was about as high as I could sing. Bessie Lee Maudlin helped on the verses to that song."[66]

Although credited to Wilbur Jones, a pseudonym Monroe used for traditional or public-domain songs, "He Will Set Your Fields on Fire" was a turn-of-the-century piece by H. M. Ballew and L. L. Bracket. Monroe recorded it back in 1937 with Charlie, and in the early 1950s it was also recorded and repopularized by James and Martha Carson and by Carl Story. Monroe first heard the number at old-time singing schools when he was a child in Kentucky. "They'd never heard this number at Nashville until I took it there," he said. "Country people had heard them, but entertainers didn't care about them and they had never brought them out."[67]

By the time of his next session, June 26, 1954, banjoist Rudy Lyle had been replaced by Jim Smoak, a twenty-one-year-old South Carolinian. Smoak had grown up listening to the banjo music of his grandfather, James B. Kinsey, and, later, the radio shows of DeWitt "Snuffy" Jenkins and Homer "Pappy" Sherrill. After seeing him in person, Smoak realized that Jenkins was using three fingers to get his style and set about learning how to do so as well. Before he was out of high school he had turned down a job with the WLS Prairie Ramblers in Chicago. Shortly after he graduated from high school, Smoak toured the country radio capitols of the time and auditioned for Monroe in Nashville. A few months later, Monroe called him to join the band. This was in 1952, and although Smoak performed on tours and on the Opry, Monroe did not use him on records. During the time Monroe was laid up from his accident, Smoak took a job with Little Jimmy Dickens (who had also taken on another Blue Grass Boy, bassist Joel Price). Waiting for his draft notice, he rejoined Monroe in 1954 and performed with the Louisiana fiddler Jack Youngblood (who recorded on his own for Columbia but never did with Monroe) and Edd Mayfield. It was during this time that Smoak recorded the only session he made with Monroe. Jimmy Martin had gone to Ohio to play with a young J. D. Crowe, and Mayfield, who had been with the band earlier and done the "Christmas Time's a-Coming" session, returned as a guitarist and lead singer. All the cuts from this session, though, were Monroe solos.

The most striking feature of the June 26 session lay in the novel triple-harmony fiddles of Gordon Terry, Red Taylor, and Charlie Cline. Over the next few years, and off and on for the rest of his career, Monroe would frequently feature twin or triple fiddles playing in harmony, both on recordings and at personal appearances. On this and subsequent sessions in 1954 and 1955 the fiddle parts of the Blue Grass Boys on both vocals and instrumentals were as tightly arranged—perhaps "orchestrated" although these were head arrangements not scored parts—as anything in contemporary pop music. Merle "Red" Taylor had returned to the band after stints with Cowboy Copas and Faron Young, having backed the latter on his hit record "Live Fast, Love Hard, and Die Young." Also on board was Gordon Terry, back from the army, who had been with Monroe during 1951. These two joined with Charlie Cline gave Monroe a formidable array of fiddle talent and a set of musicians who could execute nearly any complex fiddle tune he could devise.

Who in the band came up with the twin- or triple-fiddle idea is one of the more involved puzzles of Monroe's music. Mac Wiseman had been using twin fiddles on some of his Dot records and in personal appearances for about a year, and Flatt and Scruggs used Everett Lilly and Howard "Howdy" Forrester on twin fiddles on two songs at one session in 1951: "Lonesome and Blue" and "My Darling's Last Good-Bye." Monroe, who dated his interest from a much earlier period, told Jim Rooney:

I heard twin fiddles years ago, I guess, maybe with Bob Wills' Band or there was a group out of Atlanta that had twin fiddles and Clayton McMichen had twin fiddles back years ago in the twenties. It happened that I was on the Grand Ole Opry one night, you know, and there was these two fiddlers—one of them came in and he didn't even work with me—and they started playing twin fiddles and it sounded so good on numbers like "My Little Georgia Rose" that I decided I would use some twin fiddle on some stuff, and then other people around the Opry went to featuring it right quick because it was pretty and good.[68]

The three fiddlers each have a version of how the multifiddle trend started in the band. Terry dates it to mid-1954, when he and Red Taylor were experimenting with the sound at Chain of Rocks Park in St. Louis: "We started doing some twin fiddle stuff on 'Georgia Rose' and some other things. Bill said, 'I like that,' so we come back into Nashville and he had Charlie Cline playing banjo. He got another banjo picker for the session and me and Charlie and Red Taylor cut some of the first stuff he used three fiddles on like 'Blue Moon of Kentucky.'"[69] Charlie Cline recalls Monroe using the new sound to attract fans: "Bill always tried to keep something a little different, and it just so happened that me, and Red and Gordon were all in Nashville at the same time."[70] Red Taylor, however, maintains that "me and Gordon talked Bill into the three fiddle thing with us and Charlie Cline. Bill was a little reluctant to give it a try at first but after the three of us played some things like 'Blue Moon of Kentucky' and 'Put My Little Shoes Away,' he decided that he liked the sound and we decided to cut some of it."[71]

Earlier in 1954, Jimmy Martin brought to Monroe a song written by an old friend, Little Robert Van Winkle, an early member of the Sunny Mountain Boys. Van Winkle, Martin observed, "was not a midget. We'd introduce him as, 'He's not a midget or a dwarf, he's truly a world's wonder. He's thirty-nine inches tall and weighs eighty-five pounds.' He sang bass."[72] He also wrote songs and was featuring his version of "Close By" onstage. While Martin was still with the Blue Grass Boys the band went through Knoxville and found themselves lacking one band member. Monroe called Little Robert and he filled in for a week or two. The two men came to know each other during this period and soon after, at Martin's suggestion, Monroe recorded the song that would become one of his classics. He apparently liked it so much that two months after recording it Monroe helped produce a Stanley Brothers session for Mercury and arranged for them to record a duet version of "Close By."

The reasons for Monroe cutting a new version of "My Little Georgia Rose," which he had done only four years before for the same company, are obscure. Decca would occasionally wear out the master of some best-selling singles, such as those by Bing Crosby, and order a new one made. There is little evidence, however, that the 1950 record of "My Little Georgia Rose" was in that category. Moreover, the 1954 version was not released until finding its way onto an LP compilation in 1966, twelve years later. It appears that Monroe, for the first time using a band that included three fiddles, wanted to see how his old favorite sounded when dressed up in a new sound. Edd Mayfield's guitar style, with flowing bass runs played with thumb and finger picks rather than flat pick, contrasts with those of early Blue Grass Boys guitarists like Jimmy Martin and previews the distinctive guitar sound that would be heard on Bill's first gospel album, *I Saw the Light,* in 1958.

Popular as a sentimental song with country singers since the 1920s, "Put My Little Shoes Away" was composed by the successful songwriting team of Samuel Mitchell and Charles E. Pratt and first published in 1873. Pratt was one of the first songwriters to become a part of the New York publishing center known as Tin Pan Alley. The song was widespread through records and radio and popularized through Bradley Kincaid—a source Monroe has acknowledged for other items. In 1960 he would record "Put My Rubber Doll Away," a variation on the theme of this song credited, strangely, to Roy Acuff and George W. Edgens, an Arkansas string-band leader who recorded in the 1920s. The song reflects Monroe's fascination—shared by many old-time singers of the 1920s—with dying or neglected children. It is reflected in other of his songs, like "Footprints in the Snow," "My Little Georgia Rose," "The Little Girl and the Dreadful Snake," and "I Hear a Sweet Voice Calling."

1954–56: ELVIS ATTACKS

The session of September 4, 1954, was devoted to another remake of a classic Columbia side, "Blue Moon of Kentucky," which was originally recorded in 1946 with the Flatt and Scruggs band. That record had been one of Monroe's more popular ones although it never reached the charts. In the summer of 1954 the song was given new importance when young Elvis Presley released an up-tempo version for his first single on Memphis's Sun Records. Presley's version never formally reached the charts either, but it attracted attention in August 1954, and soon western swing bandleader Cliffie Stone as well as the Stanley Brothers were doing their own versions. Monroe, in fact, had been present at the Stanley session and helped produce an arrangement of the song that was quite close to Presley's. He told the Stanleys that he, too, was planning a remake of the song at an upcoming session. It seems odd that

Decca would permit Monroe to do a one-song session, but the Presley version of "Blue Moon of Kentucky" was selling regionally at an impressive rate and would eventually top out at around a hundred thousand copies. Monroe recalled that the composer royalties he received from the Sun record in those days resulted in "some powerful checks. Powerful."[73] Decca rushed the results into the stores within a month. Monroe's version did not make the charts although it apparently sold well.

The influence of the Presley arrangement was evident in Monroe's version although not as much as on the Stanleys'. He begins in the manner of his 1946 version, in a lilting $3/4$ waltz time, his voice cushioned by the triple fiddles he used in June. Halfway through he switches to $4/4$ in the manner of Presley, speeds up the tempo, and is off. When Presley played the Grand Ole Opry a little later he approached Monroe and apologized about rearranging the song; Monroe, unfazed, told the young singer that it was fine if "Blue Moon of Kentucky" worked for him in that style.[74]

The New Year's eve session of 1954 opened a new chapter in Monroe's music, one characterized by the use of multiple fiddles playing new instrumental compositions in tightly arranged harmony. He had used the new sound as a backup to his vocals since June but now began to bring it to the forefront of his music. With this session he created the first of what eventually would be a series of seven instrumentals he would record in the 1950s and were built around multiple fiddles. At a time when his vocal compositions seemed at low ebb he turned his energies and creativity to the new fiddle instrumentals. They were, as Jim Rooney has noted, "all driving, fast-tempoed numbers which alternated sections of low-pitched intricate melodic lines with stretched-out, soaring, high harmony sections."[75]

Cline was joined by Bobby Hicks on fiddle at the session, and the first instrumental recorded was "Wheel Hoss." Monroe explained to Ralph Rinzler that the "wheel hoss" of a team of horses is the one nearest the wagon wheel (as opposed to the lead) and thus the horse that pulls more of the load. The term, which Monroe appreciated and understood, is common in the upland South to refer to anyone who works hard and steadily at a job. Banjoist Don Stover remembered the way his boss integrated his music with farm work. "Sometimes he'd call over to the hotel room and say, 'Let's go,' and we'd figure we were going out to do a show. In the end, we'd be over on his farm plowing with a mule or loading hay bales."[76]

On the next tune, "Cheyenne," Monroe did a vocal segment on the introduction, and Jackie Phelps did the guitar solo, the first time a finger-style guitar lead had been used in a Monroe instrumental recording. In discussing the fiddle tunes, Bobby Hicks recalls, "Just about everyone I talk to about bluegrass says 'Cheyenne' is the one they like the best though."[77]

The lone vocal piece in the session was "You'll Find Her Name Written There." Its composer, Harold Hensley, a veteran fiddle player from White Top Mountain, Virginia, had a stint on the Opry in 1943 and 1944. Later he moved to Los Angeles, where he became a regular on the weekly television show *Town Hall Party,* a well-respected studio musician, and a songwriter. He died in the fall of 1988. The song, which dates from 1951, was recorded by Tennessee Ernie Ford for Capitol a couple of years before this session. Even more relevant was the fact that brother Charlie Monroe had done it for RCA Victor in September 1951.

For some reason Monroe introduced with "Roanoke," the final piece in the session, a new pseudonym for composer credits: Joe Ahr. "I was in Roanoke playing at the old American Theatre there," he said. "It was when I was having some tooth problems and I didn't feel like going out to eat, so I just stayed there and wrote that number."[78] Gordon Terry recalls that Monroe liked to keep his mandolin up front in the car when he traveled in order to work out new songs, and he put the finishing touches on "Roanoke" this way. As it developed, Monroe stopped the car and asked Terry to get out his fiddle and help work out the fiddle lead.

Monroe was not the only one fascinated by the twin-fiddle sound. Kenny Baker, who became Monroe's main fiddler, was stunned when he first heard "Roanoke" and its companion piece "Wheel Hoss." "I played swing fiddle until I heard 'Roanoke' and 'Wheel Hoss.' The first time I ever heard 'Roanoke,' I thought it was the prettiest piece of music I'd ever heard. I'll bet you I put three dollars worth of damn nickels in that jukebox in Knoxville."[79] The two fiddles—Cline's and Hicks's—play together on choruses but alternate solos on verses. On a Grand Ole Opry air-check dating from around January 15, 1955, two fiddles are featured in Monroe's band although personnel are unknown.

Monroe's next session, on January 28, 1955, yielded two gospel songs. Of Hazel Houser's "Wait a Little Longer, Please Jesus," he said, "Down through the years there's always somebody who will come out with a hymn that really makes a hit. . . . Well, this number was selling good and Decca wanted me to record it, so we recorded the number. I liked it all right, but after we got to singing it, I got to liking it better."[80] The recording Monroe covered must have been the original Capitol

version of the song done by Chester Smith and issued in October 1954, three months before this recording. About this same time, Columbia was rushing out a Carl Smith cover and later Tommy Collins, the Louvin Brothers, and Porter Wagoner would do their versions as well, making the song one of the more popular modern country gospel originals. Hazel Houser, the daughter of an Assembly of God minister, wrote a number of good songs in the 1950s.

"Let the Light Shine Down on Me" came from an earlier association with its composer. In the 1940s Monroe toured with an Opry tent show that, at one time, included comedian Lazy Jim Day, Cowboy Copas, and the team of Radio Dot and Smokey (originally Dot Henderson and Louis "Smokey" Swan). The Swans had gotten their start in West Virginia before making it to WSM, and Radio Dot was a pioneering woman bandleader at that time. "Dottie Swan . . . wrote this number," Monroe said. "She was working for me a good many years ago, and she wanted me to do this song."[81] She later settled in Nashville and had a prolific song-writing and singing career. She, however, listed "Let the Light Shine Down on Me" as her most popular song. Both performances are couched in the classic Blue Grass Quartet style augmented with unusual twin fiddles on "Wait a Little Longer." Jackie Phelps does the guitar work.

Monroe's next recordings marked another new twist, his first film recordings. In the fall of 1954 the Nashville establishment was becoming increasingly nervous about the plans of a young upstart rival show called the Ozark Jubilee. That show, from Springfield, Missouri, was planning to start broadcasting over network television, on ABC. Younger, more far-sighted artists saw this as the future and complained bitterly that the Opry management was missing the boat by not trying the new medium as well. National Life bosses were skeptical but agreed to allow an independent filmmaker named Albert Gannaway make a series of films for use on syndicated television. The first premiered in January 1955: *The Country Show: with Stars of the Grand Ole Opry.* They were not on a network but were popular as syndicated shows.

Gannaway signed his initial contract with the Opry on August 1954 and started filming that November. After one session at the Ryman Auditorium, shooting moved to a theater on the Vanderbilt University campus, where the now-familiar sets with bales of hay were set up. Starting in February 1955 films were shot like Hollywood movies, in color and on 35mm. stock. Before filming stopped in December 1956 some ninety-two thirty-minute shows were in the can. Each contained a wide variety of performers, including Ernest Tubb, George Morgan, the Carter Family, Little Jimmy Dickens, Jim Reeves, and others. Monroe, the only bluegrass act on the show (although there were old-time acts like the Crook Brothers, Johnnie and Jack, and Sam and Kirk McGee), was never introduced as a "blue-grass star" but rather as another Opry star. The breathtaking performance of "Roanoke" was done as accompaniment to a group of square dancers from the Opry.

Gannaway filmed the performances like regular recording sessions. For a three-hour session Monroe received a $100 leader's fee, and each sideman was paid $50. With that, they signed away all rights to the films. Monroe's six performances, mostly songs he had recently recorded, appeared in the half-hour films labeled number 17 and numbers 21, 22, 23, and 26. There's then a jump to film number 37. In later years the "Gannaway shows" (as they came to be called) were reissued and resyndicated as *Country Music Caravan* (1967) and *Classic Country* (1980s). In 1988 some twelve home video cassettes drawn from the films were released as *The Classic Country Club Collection: Tribute, Grand Ole Opry Stars of the Fifties*. Four of Monroe's performances appear on this set.

Fiddles continued to dominate the next session, held on September 16, 1955. Vassar Clements, who rejoined the group in mid-1955, recalls: "He put Bobby Hicks back on the banjo and I played fiddle . . . and I bugged him until I got him to get another banjo player and me and Bobby played twin fiddles . . . so he finally found [Joe] Stuart."[82] Hicks, whom Monroe called "the truest fiddler he had ever heard," was a child prodigy fiddler who grew up in Greensboro, North Carolina.[83] He was eleven when he won the North Carolina State Championship playing "Black Mountain Rag" and became well-known at local fiddle contests. For a time he worked professionally with Jim Eanes in Danville. When Monroe had a two-week engagement in the area, Carlton Haney, then booking for the Blue Grass Boys, asked Hicks to play bass for the band. This was in 1953. The following year Hicks found himself in Nashville working steadily for Monroe. He soon fell in with fiddler Dale Potter, an ace session man who hung out with Chet Atkins and Jethro Burns and played hot Nashville swing. Hicks had never heard complex swing fiddling like Potter did on things like "Fiddle Patch," a wild variant of the western swing flag-waver called "Oklahoma Stomp." He told Vassar Clements about Potter's music and gradually began to use some of it on the road with Monroe. To his surprise Monroe liked it. "I'm the only one that I know of that ever got away with doing that with him on the stage," said Hicks.[84] Thus, indirectly, Dale Potter may have in-fluenced the Monroe fiddle-tune period, and it is not surprising that Potter later became a Blue Grass Boy.

Although earlier versions of the discography credit three fiddles on "Tall Timber," Bobby Hicks says that Vassar was not playing on the side, it was just Hicks and Gordon Terry. Terry thinks that its title derives from the tall pines common in Georgia, where Monroe often toured. According to old-timers at Monroe's country music park in Bean Blossom, Indiana, the Brown County Jamboree, "Brown County Breakdown" was composed in the backstage room. It, too, has only two fiddlers, but this time pairs Vassar and Hicks while Gordon sits out. Both instrumentals remained unissued until Ralph Rinzler discovered them in 1963 and released them on *Blue Grass Instrumentals* (1965).

Monroe recalled writing "Used to Be" shortly after buying his farm, which could date the song as far back as the late 1940s. It was inspired by a personal experience, and, as with many songs, Monroe experimented with "Used to Be" back-stage and in jam sessions for years before deciding to do it in public or on records. Reno and Smiley recorded the song six years later, in 1961, and released it in 1962. Monroe's version was on Decca's shelf until 1964. Charlie Cline does the guitar break.

The year 1956 was one of the few in Monroe's career when he made no formal studio recordings. A handful of ephemeral recordings, however, document at least some of the sound of the band at the end of this era. ABC television filmed segments of the Purina Grand Ole Opry during that year, and one film that survives includes a black-and-white performance of "Uncle Pen" with Joe Stuart (guitar), Bobby Hicks (fiddle), Noah Crase (banjo), and an unidentified bass player.

The other live recordings come from Sunday shows at New River Ranch, a popular country music park in Rising Sun, Maryland, near Washington D.C. Recorded by Jeremy Foster and Alice Gerrard, students from Antioch College in Yellow Springs, Ohio, they reflect the beginnings of a movement that would have a profound effect on Monroe's career— folk music enthusiasts had discovered bluegrass. These recordings reflect the rise of the home tape recorder as a tool fans and enthusiasts used like a camera to collect sound images of favorite performances. Some artists refused to allow such taping, but Monroe never did, and private recordings now exist of thousands of his performances. Indeed, Monroe's followers have been recording and trading tapes of his shows since the mid-1950s, antedating similar activities often thought to have been invented by Grateful Dead followers by more than a decade.

The performances from the New River Ranch shows are the earliest such recordings of him released to date, part of a group of live recordings edited in 1993 by Ralph Rinzler for Smithsonian/Folkways. At the show of May 13, 1956, the band included Yates Green (guitar), Bobby Hicks and Joe Stuart (fiddles), Rudy Lyle (banjo), and Chick Stripling or Bessie Lee Maudlin (bass). It would be Lyle's last recorded performance with the band. By the time of Monroe's next appearance at New River Ranch on September 23, 1956, his band included completely different personnel: Edd Mayfield (guitar), Clarence "Tater" Tate (fiddle), and an unidentified banjo player. On "Blue Grass Stomp" Don Reno sat in as guest banjo picker and showed matchless command of the blues idiom on the five-string banjo.

Notes

1. Hugh Cherry, interview with Charles K. Wolfe, Nashville, March 15, 1993.

2. Neil V. Rosenberg, *Bill Monroe and His Blue Grass Boys: An Illustrated Discography* (Nashville: Country Music Foundation Press, 1974), 47.

3. Rosenberg, *Bill Monroe and His Blue Grass Boys,* 47.

4. Pete Kuykendall, "Jimmy Martin: Super King of Bluegrass: Bluegrass Music Is His Life," *Bluegrass Unlimited* 14 (Sept. 1979): 10.

5. Kuykendall, "Jimmy Martin," 10.

6. Charles K. Wolfe, "Bill Monroe," in *The Bill Monroe Reader,* edited by Tom Ewing (Urbana: University of Illinois Press, 2000), 215.

7. Wolfe, "Bill Monroe," 215.

8. Tex Logan, "Vassar Clements: A Musician's Musician," *Muleskinner News* 4 (May 1973): 11.

9. Logan, "Vassar Clements," 11.

10. Charles K. Wolfe, "Bluegrass Touches: An Interview with Bill Monroe," *Old Time Music* 16 (Spring 1975): 9–10.

11. Joel Price, telephone interview with Charles K. Wolfe, Aug. 22, 1998.

12. Earl Scruggs, conversation with Charles K. Wolfe, Hendersonville, Tenn., April 2000.

13. Doug Hutchens, notes to *Bill Monroe: Classic Bluegrass Instrumentals* (Rebel 850, 1985).

14. Ralph Rinzler, notes to *High, Lonesome Sound of Bill Monroe* (Decca DL 4780, 1966).

15. Robert Cantwell, *Bluegrass Breakdown; The Making of the Old Southern Sound* (Urbana: University of Illinois Press, 1984), 212–13.

16. Tex Logan, "Bobby Hicks: A Living Legend Returns," *Muleskinner News* 6 (June 1975): 6.

17. Doug Hutchens, "Rudy Lyle: Classic Banjo Man," *Bluegrass Unlimited* 17 (April 1985): 45–46.

18. Rinzler, notes to *High, Lonesome Sound of Bill Monroe.*

19. Alice Foster [Gerrard] and Ralph Rinzler, notes to *Bill Monroe and His Blue Grass Boys: A Voice from on High* (Decca DL 75135, 1969).

20. Charles K. Wolfe, notes to *Bill Monroe: Bluegrass 1950–1958* (Bear Family BCD 15423, 1989), 17.

21. Wolfe, notes to *Bill Monroe.*

22. Ibid.

23. Dorothy Horstman, *Sing Your Heart Out, Country Boy: Classic Country Songs and Their Inside Stories by the Men and Women Who Wrote Them,* rev. ed. (Nashville: Country Music Foundation Press, 1986), 27.

24. James R. Rooney, *Bossmen: Bill Monroe and Muddy Waters* (New York: Dial Press, 1971), 65.

25. Hutchens, "Rudy Lyle," 45–46.

26. Don Cunningham, "Hearing Red: Merle Taylor's Bed Rock Bluegrass Fiddling," *Bluegrass Unlimited* 17 (Aug. 1982): 30.

27. Kuykendall, "Jimmy Martin," 12.

28. Tex Logan, "Gordon Terry: Fiddle Talk," *Muleskinner News* 5 (Sept. 1974): 10.

29. Wolfe, notes to *Bill Monroe,* 18.

30. Rooney, *Bossmen,* 61.

31. Rinzler, notes to *High Lonesome Sound of Bill Monroe.*

32. Gerrard and Rinzler, notes to *A Voice from on High.*

33. Ibid.

34. Kuykendall, "Jimmy Martin," 17.

35. John Hartford, conversation with Charles K. Wolfe, Madison, Tenn., Dec. 26, 1995.

36. Rinzler, notes to *High Lonesome Sound of Bill Monroe.*

37. Cantwell, *Bluegrass Breakdown,* 233–34.

38. Kuykendall, "Jimmy Martin," 13.

39. The Rodgers Victor sets were issued as P-244, P-282, and P-318.

40. It was around this time, 1951, that Hank Snow and Ernest Tubb began work to establish a memorial for Jimmie Rodgers in his hometown of Meridian, Mississippi. Monroe was one of the Opry stars present at its official opening on May 26, 1953, the twentieth anniversary of Rodgers's death. Hank Snow, Jack Ownbey, and Bob Burris, *The Hank Snow Story* (Urbana: University of Illinois Press, 1994), 356.

41. Douglas B. Green, notes to *Bill Monroe and His Blue Grass Boys: The Classic Recordings, Volume 2* (County CCS 105, 1980).

42. Lester Flatt and Earl Scruggs, *Lester Flatt and Earl Scruggs and the Foggy Mountain Boys: 1950 Edition of Radio Favorites* (N.p.: N.p., [1950]), 7.

43. Garrard and Rinzler, notes to *A Voice from on High.*

44. Gordon Terry, telephone interview with Charles K. Wolfe, May 25, 1989.

45. Wolfe, notes to *Bill Monroe,* 25.

46. Logan, "Gordon Terry," 8.

47. Ibid. Gene Wiggins argues that Logan borrowed the tune for his song from a Carson recording, "Christmas Time Will Soon Be Over," recorded in Atlanta for Okeh in 1927. Although Carson sings little on the record, the word pattern is indeed similar to Logan's. Carson's piece is no doubt steeped in North Georgia fiddle tune tradition. Wiggins, *Fiddlin' Georgia Crazy: Fiddlin' John Carson, His Real World, and the World of His Songs* (Urbana: University of Illinois Press, 1987), 206.

48. Russ Cheatham, "Charlie and Lee Cline and the Lonesome Pine Fiddlers," *Bluegrass Unlimited* 15 (Feb. 1980): 19.

49. Cheatham, "Charlie and Lee Cline," 20.

50. Kuykendall, "Jimmy Martin," 13.

51. Ibid.

52. Ibid.

53. Bob Artis, *Bluegrass: From the Lonesome Wail of a Mountain Love Song to the Hammering Drive of the Scruggs-style Banjo, the Story of an American Musical Tradition* (New York: Hawthorn Books, 1975), 137.

54. Gerrard and Rinzler, notes to *A Voice from on High.*

55. Gary Reid, unsigned notes to *Stanley Series Volume 2, Number 4* (Copper Creek CCSS-V2N4, 1987).

56. Ralph Rinzler, conversation with Neil V. Rosenberg, Bloomington, Ind., June 1963.

57. Gerrard and Rinzler, notes to *A Voice from on High*.

58. Hutchens, notes to *Classic Bluegrass Instrumentals*.

59. Kuykendall, "Jimmy Martin," 13.

60. Ralph Rinzler, notes to *Bill Monroe and the Bluegrass Boys: Love Recordings 1956–1969, Off the Record Vol. 1* (Smithsonian/Folkways CD 40063, 1993), 16.

61. Wolfe, notes to *Bluegrass 1950–1958,* 31.

62. Hutchens, notes to *Classic Bluegrass Instrumentals*.

63. A photograph of Newton with this rig is on page 41 of William R. McDaniel and Harold Seligman's *Grand Ole Opry* (New York: Greenberg, 1952).

64. Gerrard and Rinzler, notes to *A Voice from on High*.

65. Ibid.

66. Ibid.

67. Ibid.

68. Rooney, *Bossmen,* 66–67.

69. Logan, "Gordon Terry," 8.

70. Cheatham, "Charlie and Lee Cline," 20.

71. Cunningham, "Hearing Red," 31.

72. Kuykendall, "Jimmy Martin," 12.

73. Bill Monroe, interview with Dan Miller, WSM-TV, Nashville, June 14, 1981.

74. Ibid.; see also Neil V. Rosenberg, *Bluegrass: A History* (Urbana: University of Illinois Press, 1985), 121.

75. Rooney, *Bossmen,* 68.

76. Jack Tottle, "Big Banjo from Boston: The Don Stover Story," *Bluegrass Unlimited* (Jan. 1973): 8.

77. Logan, "Bobby Hicks," 7.

78. Rooney, *Bossmen,* 68.

79. Alice Foster, "Kenny Baker," *Bluegrass Unlimited* 3 (Dec. 1968): 9.

80. Gerrard and Rinzler, notes to *A Voice from on High*.

81. Ibid.

82. Tex Logan, "Vassar Clements: A Musician's Musician," *Muleskinner News* 4 (May 1973): 11.

83. Logan, "Vassar Clements," 13.

84. Ibid.

DISCOGRAPHY, 1950–56

ABOUT THE DECCA AND MCA MASTER NUMBERS

Decca and MCA masters have two numbers—the first was assigned in Nashville at the time of recording and the second in New York when the master was received there.

500203.1   Decca session; producer: [Paul Cohen?]
Castle Studio, Tulane Hotel, 206 8th Ave., Nashville, Tenn.
Feb. 3, 1950, 2:30–5:30 P.M.

| NA 2076 | BLUE GRASS RAMBLE (Bill Monroe) | 46266 | BS 1, REB-850, BCD 15423 |
| 75809 | Instrumental | | |

NA 2077	NEW MULE SKINNER BLUES	46222	ED 2353, DL 4010, DL 4327,
75810	(Jimmie Rodgers–George Vaughn)		DL 7-5010, CCS-114,
	Monroe-L		MCAD 10082, BCD 15423,
			MCA 088 170 109-2,
			R142-08, M18701,
			MCA 088 112 982-2,
			MCA 088 113 207-2,
			MCA 800004424-02

| NA 2078 | MY LITTLE GEORGIA ROSE (Bill Monroe) | 46222 | BS 1, CCS-114, MCAD 4-11048, |
| 75811 | Monroe-L | | BCD 15423, MCA 088 113 207-2 |

| NA 2089 | MEMORIES OF YOU (James B. Smith) | 46266 | DL 4780, BCD 15423 |
| 75812 | Martin-L, Monroe-T | | |

Bill Monroe: m   James Henry "Jimmy" Martin: g   Vassar Clements: f
Rudy Lyle: b   Joel Price: sb

500203.2   Decca session; producer, [Paul Cohen?]
Castle Studio, Tulane Hotel, 206 8th Ave., Nashville, Tenn.
Feb. 3, 1950, 7:30–10:30 P.M.

NA 2080	I'M ON MY WAY TO THE OLD HOME	28045	VL 3702, MCAD 4-11048,
75813	(Bill Monroe)		BCD 15423, MME B0003736-02
	Monroe-LV/TC, Martin-LC		

| NA 2081 | ALABAMA WALTZ (Hank Williams) | 46236 | BS 1, BCD 15423 |
| 75814 | Monroe-L | | |

| NA 2082 | I'M BLUE, I'M LONESOME (James B. Smith) | 46254 | DL 4780, MCAD 4-11048, |
| 75815 | Monroe-TV/LC, Martin-LV | | BCD 15423, SHA 604 |

| Bill Monroe: m | Jimmy Martin: g | Vassar Clements: f |
| Rudy Lyle: b | Joel Price: sb | |

500408   Decca session; producer, [Paul Cohen?]
Castle Studio, Tulane Hotel, 206 8th Ave., Nashville, Tenn.
April 8, 1950, 1–4 p.m.

NA 2118	I'LL MEET YOU IN CHURCH SUNDAY	46351	BS 3, BCD 15423,
76141	MORNING (Bill Monroe)		MCA B0002907-2,
	Monroe-L, Martin-T, Price-B, Birch Monroe-BS		MME B0003736-02

| NA 2119 | BOAT OF LOVE (James W. Smith) | 46254 | DL 7-5135, BCD 15423 |
| 76142 | Martin-L, Monroe-T, Price-B, Birch Monroe-BS | | |

| NA 2120 | THE OLD FIDDLER (Hugh Ashley–Ira Wright) | 46236 | BS 1, BCD 15423 |
| 76143 | Monroe-L | | |

| Bill Monroe: m | Jimmy Martin: g | Vassar Clements (-20): f |
| Rudy Lyle (-20): b | Joel Price: sb | |

501015   Decca session; producer, Paul Cohen
Castle Studio, Tulane Hotel, 206 8th Ave., Nashville, Tenn.
Oct. 15, 1950, noon–3 P.M.

NA 2254	UNCLE PEN (Bill Monroe)	46283	ED 2353, DL 4090, DL 4327,
80071	Monroe-LV/TC, Martin-LC, Price-B		DL 7-5010, MCA 2-4090, CCS-114,
			MCA 1929, MCAD 10082,
			MCA 4-11048, R2 71870,
			MCA3P-3256, MCA 088 170 109-2,
			M18701, PALM CD 2075-2,
			BCD 15423, MCA 088 112 982-2,
			MCA 088 113 207-2, M19007,
			B0000303-02, C4K 90628,
			MME B0003736-02,
			MCA 80004424-02

NA 2255 80072	WHEN THE GOLDEN LEAVES BEGIN TO FALL (Albert Price) Monroe-LV/ TC, Martin-LC, Price-B	46283	DL 4780, SHA 604, BCD 15423
NA 2256 80073	LORD PROTECT MY SOUL (Bill Monroe) Martin-L, Monroe-T, Lyle-B, Price-BS	46305	DL 7-5135, MCA 4-11048, BCD 15423, MCA B0002907-2
NA 2257 80074	RIVER OF DEATH (Bill Monroe) Martin-L, Monroe-T, Lyle-B, Price-BS	46305	DL 7-5135, BCD 15423, MME B0003736-02

Bill Monroe: m	Jimmy Martin: g	Merle "Red" Taylor (-54 and
Rudy Lyle (-54 and -55 only): b	Joel Price: sb	-55 only): f

510120   Decca session; producer, [Paul Cohen?]
Castle Studio, Tulane Hotel, 206 8th Ave., Nashville, Tenn.
Jan. 20, 1951, 10:30 A.M.–2:00 P.M.

NA 2324 80434	LETTER FROM MY DARLING (Bill Monroe) Martin-L, Monroe-T	46392	DL 4780, BCD 15423, MME B0003736-02
NA 2325 80435	ON THE OLD KENTUCKY SHORE (Bill Monroe) Martin-L, Monroe-T	46298	DL 4780, BCD 15423

NA 2326
80436
	RAW HIDE (Bill Monroe)
	Instrumental
		46392	DL 4601, MCAD 4-11048,
			  BCD 15423, R142-04,
			  M18861, MCA 088 113 207-2

NA 2327 80437	POISON LOVE (Elmer Laird) Martin-L, Monroe-T	46298	DL 7-5066, BCD 15423

Bill Monroe: m	Jimmy Martin: g	Red Taylor: f
Rudy Lyle: b	Joel Price: sb	

510317   Decca session; producer, Paul Cohen
Castle Studio, Tulane Hotel, 206 8th Ave., Nashville, Tenn.
March 17, 1951, 2–5 P.M.

NA 2361 80725	KENTUCKY WALTZ (Bill Monroe) Monroe-L	46314	BS3, BCD 15423, MCA 088 113 207–2
NA 2362 80726	PRISONER'S SONG (Guy Massey) Monroe-L	46314	BS 1, BCD 15423

| NA 2363 | SWING LOW SWEET CHARIOT (-) | 46325 | BS 3, BCD 15423 |
| 80727 | Monroe-L | | |

NA 2364	ANGELS ROCK ME TO SLEEP (-)	46325	BS3, BCD 15423,
80728	Monroe-L, Jimmy Martin-T, Rudy Lyle-B,		MCA B0002907-2
	(Culley Holt?)[1]–BS		

Bill Monroe: m   Thomas Grady Martin, Jimmy Selph: g   Thomas "Tommy" Jackson: f
Ferris Coursey: drums   Ernest "Ernie" Newton: sb   Owen Bradley (-62): piano
                                                                                Owen Bradley (-61, -63, -64): organ

510329   Decca session; producer, Paul Cohen
              Castle Studio, Tulane Hotel, 206 8th Ave., Nashville, Tenn.
              March 29, 1951, 10:30 A.M.–1:30 P.M.

| NA 2371 | BRAKEMAN'S BLUES (Jimmie Rodgers) | 46380 | BS 3, MCAD 4-11048, BCD 15423 |
| 80791 | Monroe-L | | |

NA 2372	TRAVELIN' BLUES (Jimmie Rodgers–	46380	BS 1, BCD 15423, SHA 604
80792	Shelly Lee Alley)		
	Monroe-L		

NA 2373	WHEN THE CACTUS IS IN BLOOM	28183	VL 3702, BCD 15423,
80793	(Jimmie Rodgers)		MCA 088 112 982-2,
	Monroe-L		MCA 088 113 207-2,
			MCA 80004424-02

Bill Monroe: m   Jimmy Martin: g   James "Hal" Smith: f
Rudy Lyle: b   Joel Price: sb

510423.1 Decca session; producer, Paul Cohen
              Castle Studio, Tulane Hotel, 206 8th Ave., Nashville, Tenn.
              April 23, 1951, 6–9 P.M.

NA 2379	SAILOR'S PLEA (Jimmie Rodgers–	28183	VL 3702, BCD 15423
80921	Elsie McWilliams)		
	Monroe-L		

| NA 2380 | MY CAROLINA SUNSHINE GIRL (Jimmie Rodgers) | | BS 3, BCD 15423 |
| 80922 | Monroe-L | | |

| NA 2381 | BEN DEWBERRY'S FINAL RUN (Andrew Jenkins) | | BS 3, BCD 15423 |
| 80923 | Monroe-L | | |

Bill Monroe: m		Grady Martin, Loren	Hal Smith: f
		Otis "Jack" Shook: g	
Rudy Lyle: b		Ernie Newton: sb	Ferris Coursey: drums

510423.2   Decca session; producer, Paul Cohen
Castle Studio, Tulane Hotel, 206 8th Ave., Nashville, Tenn.
April 23/24, 1951, 11:15 P.M.–2:15 A.M.

| NA 2382 | PEACH PICKIN' TIME IN GEORGIA (Jimmie Rodgers–Clayton McMitchen) | | VL 3702, BCD 15423 |
| 80924 | Monroe-L | | |

| NA 2383 | THOSE GAMBLER'S BLUES (Jimmie Rodgers) | | BS 3, BCD 15423 |
| 80925 | Monroe-L | | |

NA 2384	HIGHWAY OF SORROW (Bill Monroe–	46369	BS 3, BCD 15423
80926	Pete Pyle)		
	Monroe-L		

| Bill Monroe: m | | Grady Martin, Jack Shook: g | Hal Smith: f |
| Rudy Lyle: b | | Ernie Newton: sb | Ferris Coursey: drums |

510701   Decca session; producer, Paul Cohen
Castle Studio, Tulane Hotel, 206 8th Ave., Nashville, Tenn.
July 1, 1951, 2–5 P.M.

| NA 2420 | ROTATION BLUES (Lt. Stewart Powell) | 46344 | BS 1, BCD 15423 |
| 81249 | Monroe-L | | |

NA 2421	LONESOME TRUCK DRIVER'S BLUES	46344	BS 1, BCD 15423
81250	(Lee Roberts)		
	Monroe-L		

| Bill Monroe: m | | Carter Stanley: g | Gordon Terry: f |
| Rudy Lyle: b | | Ernie Newton: sb | |

510706   Decca session; producer, Paul Cohen
Castle Studio, Tulane Hotel, 206 8th Ave., Nashville, Tenn.
July 6, 1951, 8:30 A.M.–12 noon

| NA 2422 | SUGAR COATED LOVE (Audrey Butler) | 46369 | DL 4780, MCAD 4-11048, |
| 81272 | Stanley-L, Monroe-T | | BCD 15423 |

NA 2423[2] 81273	YOU'RE DRIFTING AWAY (Bill Monroe) Stanley-L, Monroe-T, Lyle-B, Terry-BS	28608	DL 7-5066, BCD 15423
NA 2424[3] 81274	CABIN OF LOVE (Burch [sic] Monroe) Stanley-L, Monroe-T	28749	BS 1, CCS-114, BCD 15423

NA 2425
81275
	GET DOWN ON YOUR KNEES AND PRAY
	   (Bill Monroe)
	Stanley-L, Monroe-T, Lyle-B, Terry-BS
		46351	ED 3254, DL 7-5135, BCD 15423,
			   MCA 088 113 207-2,
			   MCA B0002907-2

Bill Monroe: m   Carter Stanley: g   Gordon Terry (-22, -24): f
Rudy Lyle (-22, -24): b   Howard Watts: sb

511028   Decca session; producer, Paul Cohen
               Castle Studio, Tulane Hotel, 206 8th Ave., Nashville, Tenn.
               Oct. 28, 1951, 8–11 P.M.

NA 2521 81801	CHRISTMAS TIME'S A-COMING (Tex Logan) Monroe-LV/TC, Mayfield-LC	46386	BS 3, DL 4343, BCD 15423, MCAD 4-11048

NA 2522
81802
	THE FIRST WHIPPOORWILL (Bill Monroe)
	Mayfield-L, Monroe-T
		46386, 28045	DL 7-5066, MCA 2-4090,
			   BCD 15423, CCS-114,
			   MCAD 4-11048

Bill Monroe: m   Edd Mayfield: g   Gordon Terry: f
James Garfield "Gar" Bowers: b   Oscar "Shorty" Shehan: sb   Owen Bradley (-21): vibes

---

520718.1   Decca session; producer, Paul Cohen
               Castle Studio, Tulane Hotel, 206 8th Ave., Nashville, Tenn.
               July 18, 1952, 2:15–5:15 P.M.

NA 2781
83130
	IN THE PINES (Jimmie Davis–Bill Monroe)
	Martin-L, Monroe-T
		28416, 60074	DL 7-5010, DL 4657,
			   MCAD 4-11048, CCS-114,
			   BCD 15423, R142-04,
			   MCA 60074, MCA 088 170 109-2,
			   MCA 088 112 982-2, M18861,
			   MCA 088 113 207-2,
			   B0000303-02, MME B0003736-02,
			   MCA 80004424-02

NA 2782 83131	FOOTPRINTS IN THE SNOW (Rupert Jones) Monroe-L	28416, 60074	DL 4327, DL 4549, DL 7-5010, DL 7-5281, MCA 2-4090, CCS-114, MCAD 4-11048, BCD 15423, R2 75720, MCA 088 170 109-2, R142-08, MCA 60074, M18701, MCA 088 112 982-2, MCA 088 113 207-2, B0000303-02, MCA 80004424-02
NA 2783 83132	WALKING IN JERUSALEM (Bill Monroe) Monroe-LV/TC, Martin-LC, Cline-B, Boudleaux Bryant-BS	28608	ED 2354, DL 7-5135, MCAD 10082, MCAD 4-11048, BCD 15423, MCA 088 113 207-2, MME B0003736-02

Bill Monroe: m (except on -83)   Jimmy Martin: g   Charlie Cline (except on -83): f
Sonny Osborne: b (except on -83)   Ernie Newton: sb

520718.2   Decca session; producer, Paul Cohen
Castle Studio, Tulane Hotel, 206 8th Ave., Nashville, Tenn.
July 18/19, 1952, 8:30 P.M.–12:30 A.M.

NA 2784 83133	MEMORIES OF MOTHER AND DAD (Albert Price) Martin-L, Monroe-T	28878	DL 4780, MCA 2-4090, MCAD 4-11048, BCD 15423, MME B0003736-02
NA 2785 83134	THE LITTLE GIRL AND THE DREADFUL SNAKE (Albert Price) Martin-L, Monroe-T	28878	VL 3702, MCA 2-4090, MCAD 4-11048, BCD 15423, MME B0003736-02
NA 2786 83135	COUNTRY WALTZ (Bill Monroe– Claude V. Breland) Monroe-L	28749	BCD 15423
NA 2787 83136	DON'T PUT OFF TIL TOMORROW (Bill Monroe–Pete Pyle) Monroe-L		DL 7-5135, BCD 15423
NA 2788 83137	MY DYING BED (Albert Price) Martin-L, Monroe-T		DL 4780, BCD 15423

Bill Monroe: m   Jimmy Martin: g   Charlie Cline: f
Sonny Osborne: b   Ernie Newton: sb

520726   Decca session; producer, Paul Cohen
                    Castle Studio, Tulane Hotel, 206 8th Ave., Nashville, Tenn.
                    July 26, 1952, 8–11 A.M.

NA 2801   A MIGHTY PRETTY WALTZ (Al Hoffman–   28356   BS 1, BCD 15423
83171   Norman Gimbel)
               Monroe-L

NA 2802   PIKE COUNTY BREAKDOWN (Rupert Jones)   28356   BS 1, ED 2353, BCD 15423,
83172   Instrumental   CCS-CD-19

Bill Monroe: m   Jimmy Martin: g   Charlie Cline: f
Sonny Osborne: b   Ernie Newton: sb   Owen Bradley (-01 only): piano

---

531128   Decca session; producer, Paul Cohen
                    Castle Studio, Tulane Hotel, 206 8th Ave., Nashville, Tenn.
                    Nov. 28, 1953, 2:15–5:15 P.M.

NA 3178   WISHING WALTZ (Gene Evans)   29009   BS 1, BCD 15423
85544   Monroe-L

NA 3179   I HOPE YOU HAVE LEARNED (Carrigan-Butler)   29009   BS 1, BCD 15423,
85545   Martin-L, Monroe-T   MME B0003736-02

NA 3180   GET UP JOHN (Bill Monroe)   29141   DL 4601, BCD 15423,
85546   Instrumental   MCA 088 113 207-2

Bill Monroe: m   Jimmy Martin: g   Charlie Cline: f
Rudy Lyle: b   Ernie Newton: sb

540107[4]   Decca session; producer, Paul Cohen
                    poss. Bradley Studio, Hillsboro Village, Nashville, Tenn.
                    Jan. 7, 1954, 2:30–5:30 P.M.

NA 3205   ON AND ON (Bill Monroe)   29886   DL 4780, MCAD 10082,
85733   Martin-L, Monroe-T, Cline-B   MCAD 4-11048, BCD 15423,
                                                  MCA3P-3256, MCA 088 113 207-2,
                                                  TJ-145, MME B0003736-02

NA 3206   I BELIEVED IN YOU DARLING (Bill Monroe)   29886   BCD 15423
85734   Martin-L, Monroe-T, Cline-B

NA 3207   NEW JOHN HENRY BLUES (-)   31540   VL 3702, BCD 15423
85735   Monroe-L

| NA 3208
85736 | WHITE HOUSE BLUES (Wilbur Jones)
Monroe-L | 29141 | DL 4780, MCAD 10082,
MCAD 4-11048, BCD 15423 |

Bill Monroe: m   Jimmy Martin: g   Charlie Cline: f
Rudy Lyle: b   Ernie Newton: sb

540108[5]   Decca session; producer, Paul Cohen
poss. Bradley Studio, Hillsboro Village, Nashville, Tenn.
Jan. 8, 1954, 7:50–11:20 P.M.

NA 3212 85695	SITTING ALONE IN THE MOONLIGHT (Bill Monroe) Martin-L, Monroe-T	30178	CCS-114, MCAD 4-11048, BCD 15423, MME B0003736-02
NA 3213 85696	PLANT SOME FLOWERS BY MY GRAVE (Jimmie Davis–Rupert McClendon) Monroe-L		DL 4327, CCS-114, BCD 15423
NA 3214 85697	CHANGING PARTNERS (Joe Darion– Larry Coleman) Monroe-L	29021	BCD 15423
NA 3215[6] 85698	Y'ALL COME (Arlie Duff) Monroe-L [other parts not identified]	29021	DL 4327, DL 7-5010, MCAD 4-11048, BCD 15423

Bill Monroe: m   Jimmy Martin, Grady Martin: g   Charlie Cline: f
Rudy Lyle: b   Ernie Newton: sb

540114[7]   Decca session; producer, Paul Cohen
poss. Bradley Studio, Hillsboro Village, Nashville, Tenn.
Jan. 14, 1954, 8–11:30 P.M.

| NA 3235
85750 | HAPPY ON MY WAY (Pete Pyle)   29196
Martin-L, Monroe-T, Charlie Cline-B, Milton Estes-BS | | DL 4327, DL 4881, MCAD 11082,
MCAD 4-11048, BCD 15423 |
| NA 3236
85751 | I'M WORKING ON A BUILDING (A. P. Carter)   29348
Monroe-LV/TC, Martin-LC, Charlie Cline-B, Milton Estes-BS | | ED 2354, DL 7-5135,
BCD 15423, MCA 088 170 109-2,
MCA 088 112 982-2,
MCA 088 113 207-2,
MCA 80004424-02 |

| NA 3237
85752 | A VOICE FROM ON HIGH (Bill Monroe–
    Bessie Mauldin)
Martin-L, Monroe-T, Charlie Cline-B | 29348 | DL 7-5135, MCAD 4-11048,
    BCD 15423, CD-8007,
    MCA3P-3256, R2 70290,
    R142-04, SHA 604,
    MCA B0002907-2 |
| NA 3238
85753 | HE WILL SET YOUR FIELDS ON FIRE
    (Wilber Jones)
Martin-L, Monroe-T, Charlie Cline-B, Milton Estes-BS | 29196 | ED 2354, DL 7-5135,
    BCD 15423, MCA B0002907-2 |

| Bill Monroe: m | Jimmy Martin: g
Ernie Newton: sb | |

540626   Decca session; producer, Paul Cohen
poss. Bradley Studio, Hillsboro Village, Nashville, Tenn.
June 26, 1954, 2:20–5:15 P.M.

NA 3341 86567	CLOSE BY (Monroe–Van Winkle) Monroe-L	29289	VL 3702, MCA 2-4090, CCS-114, MCAD 4-11048, BCD 15423
NA 3342 86568	MY LITTLE GEORGIA ROSE (Bill Monroe) Monroe-L		DL 4780, BCD 15423

NA 3343
86569
	PUT MY LITTLE SHOES AWAY (arr. adptd.
	    Wilbur Jones)
	Monroe-L
		29645	DL 7-5281, MCA 2-4090,
			    MCAD 4-11048, BCD 15423

| Bill Monroe: m
Jim Smoak: b | Edd Mayfield: g
Ernie Newton: sb | Gordon Terry, Red Taylor,
    Charlie Cline: f |

540904   Decca session, producer, (Owen Bradley?)
Bradley Studio, Hillsboro Village, Nashville, Tenn.
Sept. 4, 1954, 2:20–5:20 P.M.

| NA 3364
86763 | BLUE MOON OF KENTUCKY (Bill Monroe)
Monroe-L | 29289 | ED 2353, DL 4327, DL 4359,
    DL 7-5281, MCA 2-4090,
    CCS-114, MCAD 10082,
    BCD 15423, R2 71870,
    MCA 088 170 109-2, R142-08,
    M18701, MCA 088 112 982-2,
    MCA 088 113 207-2, M19007,
    B0000303-02, MCA 80004424-02 |

| Bill Monroe: m | Edd Mayfield: g
Ernie Newton: sb | Gordon Terry, Red Taylor,
    Charlie Cline: f |

541231   Decca session; producer, Paul Cohen
               poss. Bradley Studio, Hillsboro Village, Nashville, Tenn.
               Dec. 31, 1954, 1:45–4:45 P.M.

NA 3413 87242	WHEEL HOSS (Bill Monroe) Instrumental	29645	DL 4601, MCAD 4-11048, BCD 15423, V 78010-2
NA 3414[8] 87243	CHEYENNE (Bill Monroe) Instrumental (vocal segment in intro–Monroe)	29406	DL 4327, DL 4775, DL 7-5010, MCAD 4-11048, BCD 15423, OC-1001, CCS-CD-19, SHA 604
NA 3415 87244	YOU'LL FIND HER NAME WRITTEN THERE (Harold Hensley) Monroe-L	30178	DL 7-5281, MCAD 4-11048, BCD 15423
NA 3416 87245	ROANOKE (Joe Ahr) Instrumental	29406	DL 4327, DL 7-5010, MCAD 4-11048, REB-850, BCD 15423, CCS-CD-19, MCA 088 112 982-2, MCA 088 113 207-2, MCA 80004424-02

Bill Monroe: m	Claude J. "Jackie" Phelps: g	Charlie Cline, Bobby Hicks: f
Hubert Davis: b	Ernie Newton: sb	

550000   Classic Country Collection (1, 2, 4, 6), Shanachie (5), and Original Cinema (5);
               video copies of films shot for syndicated broadcasts; producer, Al Gannaway
               Vanderbilt University, Nashville, Tenn.
               Between Dec. 1954 and Dec. 1956, probably 1955

[1]	MY LITTLE GEORGIA ROSE Monroe-L	Show 17	CCC 01-V
[2]	A VOICE FROM ON HIGH Phelps-L, Monroe-T, Charlie Cline-B	Show 21	CCC 0010-V, PALM VHS 3039-3/2
[3]	SWING LOW, SWEET CHARIOT ?	Show 22	
[4]	CLOSE BY Monroe-L	Show 23	CCC 0011-V
[5]	ROANOKE BREAKDOWN [sic] Instrumental	Show 26	SHA 604, OC-1001

[6]   YOU'LL FIND HER NAME WRITTEN THERE   Show 37   CCC 0011-V
                    Monroe-L

The following data are for [1] only:

Bill Monroe: m   Jackie Phelps: g   (? multiple fiddles audible throughout): f
Bobby Hicks: b   Ernie Newton: sb

Although fiddles are audible throughout this segment, no fiddlers are visible.

The following data are for [2] only:
Bill Monroe: m   Jackie Phelps: g   Bobby Hicks: f
                                  Buddy Killen: sb

The following data are for [4] only:

Bill Monroe: m   Jackie Phelps: g   Bobby Hicks, Gordon Terry, Red Taylor: f
Charlie Cline: b   Ernie Newton: sb

The following data are for [5] only:

Bill Monroe: m   Carlos Brock: g   Bobby Hicks, Charlie Cline: f
Jackie Phelps: b   Ernie Newton: b

Phelps, who played banjo on some Grandpa Jones King recordings a few years earlier, is here playing 2-finger banjo. The original of [5] includes square dancers but the footage including these was not included on the video sequence.

The following data are for [6] only:

Bill Monroe: m   Jackie Phelps: g   Bobby Hicks, Gordon Terry: f
Charlie Cline: b   Ernie Newton: sb

550115   MCA reissue of radio broadcast on WSM
                 Grand Ole Opry, Nashville, Tenn.
                 ca. Jan. 15, 1955

[no mx]   BLUE MOON OF KENTUCKY (Bill Monroe)   MCAD 4-11048, MCA3P-3256
                 Monroe-L

Bill Monroe: m   (Jackie Phelps?): g   (perhaps Bobby Hicks, Charlie Cline): f
(?): b   (?): sb

550128   Decca session, producer, Paul Cohen
poss. Bradley Studio, Hillsboro Village, Nashville, Tenn.
Jan. 28, 1955, 7–10:30 P.M.

NA 3425   WAIT A LITTLE LONGER, PLEASE JESUS   29436   DL 7-5135, BCD 15423
87402   (Hazel Houser)
Monroe-LV/TC, Phelps-LC, Cline-B, Hicks-BS

NA 3426   LET THE LIGHT SHINE DOWN ON ME   29436   DL 7-5135, BCD 15423,
87403   (Dot Swan)   MCA B00002907-2
Phelps-L, Monroe-T, Cline-B, Hicks-BS

Bill Monroe: m   Jackie Phelps: g   Charlie Cline, Bobby Hicks: f (-25)
William O. Killen: sb

550508   MCA reissue of concert
New River Ranch, Rising Sun, Md.
May 8, 1955

[1]   THE GIRL IN THE BLUE VELVET BAND (Mel Foree–Cliff Carlisle)   MCAD 4-11048
Monroe-L

Bill Monroe: m   (?): g   Bobby Hicks: f
(?): b   Bessie Lee Mauldin: sb

550916   Decca session; producer, Paul Cohen
Bradley Film & Recording Studio, 804 16th Ave. South, Nashville, Tenn.
Sept. 16, 1955

NA 9177   USED TO BE (Bill Monroe)   VL 3702, CCS-114,
88683   Monroe-L   MCAD 4-11048, BCD 15423

NA 9178   TALL TIMBER (Bill Monroe)   DL 4601, BCD 15423
88684   Instrumental

NA 9179   BROWN COUNTY BREAKDOWN (Bill Monroe)   DL 4601, BCD 15423, CCS-CD-19
88685   Instrumental

Bill Monroe: m   Charlie Cline: g   Bobby Hicks,
Joe Stuart: b   Bessie Lee Mauldin: sb   Gordon Terry (-77, -78),
Vassar Clements (-77, -79): f[9]

560000   Opryland Video and Original Cinema copy of television broadcast
Purina Grand Ole Opry Show, Nashville, Tenn.
1956

[1]   UNCLE PEN   Show #11   JB 1916, OC-1001
Monroe-LV/TC, Stuart-LC, ?-B

Bill Monroe: m   Joe Stuart: g   Bobby Hicks: f
Noah Crase: b   (?): sb

560513   Smithsonian/Folkways reissue of show, recorded by Jeremy Foster and Alice Gerrard
New River Ranch, Rising Sun, Md.
May 13, 1956

[1]   WATERMELON HANGING ON THE VINE   SF 40063
Instrumental

[2]   ROANOKE   SF 40063
Instrumental

[3]   BRAKEMAN'S BLUES   SF 40063
Monroe-L

[4]   CLOSE BY   SF 40063
Monroe-L

[5]   BLUE MOON OF KENTUCKY   SF 40063, SF 40061
Monroe-L

[6]   I'M WORKING ON A BUILDING   SF 40063, SF 40137
Green?-LC, Monroe-LV/TC, Stuart?: B, ?: BS

[7]   ANGELS ROCK ME TO SLEEP   SF 40063
Green?-L, Monroe-T, Stuart?: B, ?: BS

[8]   WHEEL HOSS   SF 40063
Instrumental

Bill Monroe: m   Yates Green: g   Bobby Hicks, Joe Stuart: f
Rudy Lyle: b   Chick Stripling or Bessie Lee Mauldin: sb

560923   Smithsonian/Folkways Reissue of Show, recorded by Jeremy Foster and Alice Gerrard.
New River Ranch, Rising Sun, Md.
Sept. 23, 1956

[1]   KENTUCKY WALTZ   SF 40063
Monroe-L

[2]   BLUE GRASS STOMP   SF 40063
Instrumental

Bill Monroe: m   Edd Mayfield: g   Clarence E. "Tater" Tate: f
Don Reno (2), ? (1): b   ?: sb

Notes

1. The final version of the discography in BCD 15423 has, for this song, the vocal part attributions of Monroe, Martin, Lyle, and Milton Estes. However this bass singer does not sound like Estes (see session 540114) and does sound very much like Holt, who can be heard on sessions 580319, -20, and -21.

2. On the Decca Record Personnel sheet for this session, the last two digits of this master number were inked over, changing 23 to 24.

3. On the Decca Record Personnel sheet for this session, the last two digits of this master number were inked over, changing 24 to 23. The changes suggest that the two duets were recorded first and then the two quartets were recorded.

4. The recently discovered Decca Record Personnel sheet for this session gives the date of January 7, 1954. Previously, the date was thought to be January 25, 1954. This was based on the Decca logbook. We have changed the dating of this and the two following sessions to reflect the new information because the personnel sheets were created before the log entries were made and this places the Nashville masters in numerical sequence.

5. The recently discovered Decca Record Personnel sheet for this session gives the date of January 8, 1954. Previously, the date was thought to be January 19, 1954. This was based on the Decca logbook. We have

changed the dating to this, the previous, and the following sessions to reflect the new information because the sheets were created before the log entries were made and because this places the Nashville masters in numerical order.

6. Notes to MCAD 4-11048 suggest Grady Martin is not heard on -15.

7. The recently discovered Decca Record Personnel sheet for this session gives the date of January 14, 1954. Previously, the date was thought to be January 25, 1954. This was based on the Decca logbook. We have changed the dating to this and the two previous entries to reflect the new information because the personnel sheets were created before the log entries were made and because this places the Nashville masters in numerical sequence.

8. Notes to MCAD 4-11048 have Cline playing lead guitar on -14, as in Rosenberg's 1974 discography. Jackie Phelps, however, later confirmed that it was he and not Cline who played the lead guitar on "Cheyenne." *Bluegrass Unlimited* 19 (June 1985): 9.

9. According to the notes to MCAD 4-11048, all three fiddlers play on -77. The fiddle part attributions for -78 and -79 were given by Hicks in Ed Davis, "Bobby Hicks: A Living Legend Regturns," *Muleskinner News* (June 1975): 7.

6

"GOTTA TRAVEL ON": 1957–62

For reasons no one seems to remember Monroe made no studio recordings at all in 1956 and only five in 1955. The session of April 20, 1957, would mark the first of fourteen songs he recorded in 1957. There was certainly no backlog of unreleased Monroe records; Decca issued three singles in 1955 and only one in 1956. Owen Bradley could not recall any reason for the hiatus. Perhaps Decca was beginning to think that Monroe's most effective medium was not the single but the album. By 1957 most pop artists had given up trying to compete in the singles market against rock and roll and the huge teen-aged audience that had developed; most were starting to appeal to the adult music market through albums. It may not be coincidental that in 1957 Monroe began work on his first LP by doing a series of recordings expressly for an album.

KNEE DEEP IN BLUEGRASS

Many veteran Nashville singers had begun to make the switch from a singles-driven record profile to an album-driven one, and the companies seemed convinced that the "adult" country audience would soon turn its attention to LPs. Some of Monroe's earlier singles had been collected on several EP albums (45-rpm extended-play issues that contained four songs and were released in a cardboard sleeve), but he had not yet seen any of his work on the newer LP format. Rather than collect earlier singles, Paul Cohen, Monroe's longtime producer at Decca, and Bradley decided to have Monroe cut an entirely new set of pieces for the important new LP. This, too, was to become a significant first for the Monroe discography. To be sure, Decca had not yet given up on singles and would continue releasing at least two Monroe singles a year until 1970.

In short, the age of viewing Monroe as a country star who could be assigned to do covers of others' songs was about over. Decca was beginning to consider him as the unique stylist he was and react accordingly. Nonetheless, there was still time for a couple of covers on April 20. "A Fallen Star" was a version of Jimmy C. Newman's hit for Dot, which was in turn a cover of Bobby Denton's original on Tune Records that Ferlin Huskey also covered for Capitol. Decca was moving fast. Newman's record had not gotten on the charts when Monroe went into the studio. "Four Walls" was a cover of the well-known Jim Reeves RCA Victor cut that made the charts in early April. As usual, neither of Monroe's covers met success on the charts.

Don Stover, a native of the West Virginia coal mining country, had joined the band as banjoist. Stover grew up playing clawhammer banjo and then heard Earl Scruggs along with Monroe on the Opry in the late 1940s. It took three painstaking years for him to figure out how Scruggs did it. He also spent time performing with the Lilly Brothers in Boston and with Buzz Busby in Washington, D.C., where he cut a minor classic, "Me and the Jukebox." Stover joined Monroe in 1957, one of the few banjoists who came to the Blue Grass Boys during this period with any kind of real professional experience.

At the session of May 14, 1957, Monroe and Bradley began assembling a diverse cross-section of material for the LP album to be called *Knee Deep in Bluegrass*. "A Good Woman's Love" was by Cy Coben, who was a professional song writer, a New York composer, and a trumpet player who had done such pop songs as "Sweet Violets" and "Piano Roll Blues." During a stint in the navy in World War II he was introduced to country music and decided to try his hand at that genre after the war. By 1949 Coben was writing hits for Eddy Arnold, including pieces like "Lonely Little Robin" and "I Wanna Play House with You." With Arnold's support he soon became a fixture in the Nashville songwriting community. Owen Bradley may have found "A Good Woman's Love" for Monroe; it had also been a chart hit for Hank Locklin in February 1956.

"Cry Cry Darlin'" was Monroe's second cover of a Jimmy C. Newman song in less than a month. It had been Newman's first real chart hit for Dot, making the charts on May 12, 1954, three years before. Soon after, members of the Blue Grass Boys began doing a trio version of the song during the portion of Monroe's shows, where they appeared as the Shenandoah Trio. Though A&R men might well have suggested the song to Monroe, he was familiar with it, and it adapts to his voice surprisingly well. In the Decca files the song properly known as "Sittin' on Top of the World" has been confused with "I'm Sittin' on Top of the World," an Al Jolson hit of the 1920s, and incorrectly ascribed to its composers, the Tin Pan Alley team of Ray Henderson, Victor Young, and Sam Lewis. In fact, how-ever, the song is taken from a black Mississippi string band headed by Walter Vinscon and Lonnie Chatmon, who had a hit record of it in 1930. It was widespread as a blues standard and then taken into the western swing canon when Milton Brown recorded it in 1934 and Bob Wills in 1935. In the late 1940s "Sittin' on Top of the World" often was featured on the Opry by the Crook Brothers band, and it is quite likely Monroe heard it there. Bluesman Howlin' Wolf also recorded a version in 1957.

The following day, May 15, Monroe cut six more selections for the LP, continuing to mix new material with remakes of older songs. He was still fascinated with the three-fiddle sound and now carried Dale Potter—who had influenced Bobby Hicks and Vassar Clements to experiment with swing fiddling—in addition to Joe Stuart and Gordon Terry. On bass was Bessie Lee Maudlin, who'd been playing that instrument and singing with Bill on the road since the early 1950s; her first session with the Blue Grass Boys was in 1955. Monroe introduced her to audiences as "Bessie Lee, the Carolina Songbird." Mauldin, born December 28, 1920, in Norwood, North Carolina, apparently met Bill in 1937 and moved to Nashville in 1941. She would continue to play bass on his recordings through 1964, doing more sessions and songs than any other bassist who recorded with him. Guitarist Leslie Sandy, born in 1929 in Raeford, North Carolina, had worked as a comedian ("Uncle Puny") with Bill in 1953 and 1954 and then with Jim and Jesse McReynolds, playing bass on their Capitol recordings of 1955.

"Out in the Cold World" is a version of R. S. Hanna's 1894 composition "Somebody's Boy Is Homeless Tonight," which had taken root quickly in Appalachian song traditions. Generally known as "The Wandering Boy," the Carter Family popularized it in their recording from the 1927 Bristol sessions, one of the earliest of fifteen versions recorded by country artists before 1942. The Stanley Brothers had recorded the song under the title "Wandering Boy" in 1952 for Columbia, but Monroe's version differs from theirs in text as well as title and both diverge from the Carter Family version. Monroe uses again the new pseudonym, Joe Ahr, on the composer credits.

Popularly known as "The Hills of Roane County," another Appalachian standard—a traditional Tennessee murder ballad—was dubbed here "Roane County Prison." It was based on an event that occurred about the turn of the century involving a man named Willis Mayberry from the town of Spencer in the Cumberland Mountains. The song has been widely collected by folklorists and was being recorded by old-time bands as early as 1929. Both the Cope Brothers from Knoxville and the Blue Sky Boys had hit records of it in the 1940s, but Monroe learned his version from fiddler Tommy Magness, who worked for him in 1940.

"Goodbye Old Pal" was one of Monroe's featured songs on the Opry as early as 1943, and he recorded it for Columbia in 1945. He sings this version in the key of D at the very top of his range in contrast to his earlier recording. Stover plays his banjo capoed up to the seventh fret as Rudy Lyle had done on "Get Up, John." Bill's mandolin tuning from that piece is heard on the only original piece from the session, "In Despair," an emotionally charged "true-life" song that ranks with "Memories of Mother and Dad," "When the Golden Leaves Begin to Fall," and "My Little Georgia Rose" as among the more powerful and personal pieces of one of the most creative periods of Monroe's songwriting.[1] Don Stover's lead voice is heard in the trio.

Another remake of a classic Columbia side first recorded in October 1947, "Molly and Tenbrooks" is sung with slightly different words. Monroe originally designed his arrangement of the Kentucky folksong as a vehicle for Earl Scruggs's banjo (chapter 4), a role in which Don Stover shines in this version. Monroe published a version of the song in 1947 with Peer-Southern under the title "Molly and Ten Brooks (the Race Horse Song)." A legend surrounds this recording session. Don Stover cut his finger while helping unload the bass fiddle from the car's roof rack. He tried to suppress the bleeding but it began again during work on "Molly and Tenbrooks." For a time, blood was literally running down the head of Stover's banjo.

"Come Back to Me in My Dreams" is yet another song recorded on Columbia in 1945. On that early version, Monroe did it as a trio with Tex Willis and Wilene "Sally Ann" Forrester. For some reason, though, that version had not yet been released. It was finally issued on LP in 1976. Monroe must have thought enough of the song to make a second try at preserving it.

On December 15, 1957, the Cajun fiddler, guitarist, and composer Doug Kershaw did a session as a guitar player with Monroe. He and his brother Rusty, then twenty and eighteen, respectively, had been stars at the Louisiana Hayride and recorded several rockabilly sides for Acuff-Rose's Hickory label. In 1957 they were signed by the Opry, but both knew that their military service was approaching and decided to enlist together and serve together at the start of 1958. While waiting out his time, Doug played odd jobs around Nashville. The brothers had written "Sally-Jo" earlier in the year. Doug here does the impressive guitar work on Monroe's version although he never played regularly with the Blue Grass Boys.[2] All three cuts recorded at this session were designed to round out the *Knee Deep in Bluegrass* album, which was released in August 1958.

THE FIRST GOSPEL LP

On February 25, 1958, with his first LP in the can, Monroe turned almost immediately to his next, which he determined would be an all-gospel set and eventually named *I Saw the Light*. With this and the next three sessions he did nothing but gospel songs, three at a time and all but one featuring the sound of the male gospel quartet that had been so much a part of Monroe's music since his first Victor session in 1940. Surprisingly given Monroe's skill at composing new gospel songs, none of these were from his pen, and only three were composed after 1950. Five dated from the nineteenth century, and most of the rest dated from the 1930s—an era when the old Monroe Brothers act devoted more than half its recorded repertoire to gospel songs.

Banished from the sessions, which ran from late February through March, were the fiddle and the banjo, although fiddler Baker did sing baritone in the quartets. Most were done with the spare accompaniment of Monroe's mandolin, Edd Mayfield's guitar, a string bass, and an occasional organ touch by producer Owen Bradley. In fact, Mayfield's passionate lead singing and unique guitar playing are among the high points of the twelve songs on the LP. Returning to the band after another three-year absence, he sprinkled the quartet songs with spectacular guitar runs, always using the thumb pick and finger pick in place of the flat pick.

First recorded by Hank Williams for MGM in 1947, "I Saw the Light" had ten years later become a country standard although most performers did it as a solo or as an "everybody-sings" stage-show closer. Monroe's is rather unusual in its stately quartet form. The melody for the verses of Williams's song is derived from an old gospel quartet song, "He Set Me Free," which, as Monroe likely knew, was published in 1939 by Albert E. Brumley, a songwriter from the Ozarks, and often sung by the Chuck Wagon Gang. "Lord, Build Me a Cabin in Glory" is another modern song that Monroe helped introduce into the bluegrass repertoire; Edd Mayfield sings lead in the quartet. Roy Acuff used to feature the song frequently, recording it for both MGM and Hickory. Charlie Smith recalls that Edd Mayfield's guitar run on "Lord, Build Me a Cabin in Glory" impressed and baffled Opry pickers when the Blue Grass Boys first did it on the show.

In spite of the composer credits to Kenneth Tuttle, "Lord Lead Me On" is another product of Alabama gospel leader Marion W. Easterling, who also had written Monroe's "Angels Rock Me to Sleep." Easterling wrote "Lord Lead Me On" in 1933 and published it in a Stamps-Baxter songbook of that year. It was probably introduced to the bluegrass canon by Carl Story, who recorded it for Mercury in 1952.

Culley Holt was brought in to sing bass in the quartet beginning with the session of March 19 and continuing for the next two. Holt, one of the original members of the Jordanaires, had been doing studio work in Nashville since he left that group and would sing bass on the Flatt and Scruggs hit "Cabin on the Hill" the next year. Although uncredited on the original release, "Precious Memories" is the product of a Texas gospel songwriter, John B. F. Wright. He first published it in 1925 in the original *Harbor Bells,* the first book V. O. Stamps issued before he joined forces to form the Stamps-Baxter Company. The song had been recorded numerous times in the 1920s, and as the Stamps-Baxter Company expanded it actively sought to place songs with country radio entertainers. By the end of the 1930s the company had succeeded in getting "Precious Memories" into the repertoires of groups like Lonnie Mack and Roy Buchanan, the Blue Sky Boys, the McDonald Brothers Quartet, and Whitey and Hogan (Roy White and Arval Hogan).

Monroe, not alone in his appreciation of Brumley, included three of his songs on the LP. Brumley wrote "I'll Meet You in the Morning" in 1936 and was by most standards country music's best-known gospel composer. Born in Spiro, Oklahoma, in 1905, he was for years associated with Hartford Music Company of Hartford, Arkansas, before associating with Stamps-Baxter. Throughout the 1930s and 1940s he wrote dozens of songs that became country and bluegrass standards, including "I'll Fly Away," "Turn Your Radio On," "I'd Rather Be an Old-time Christian," and "Did You Ever Go Sailing?"

The original inscription for "Life's Railway to Heaven" when it appeared in Charlie D. Tillman's 1890 songbook *The Revival* was "respectfully dedicated to the railroad men." It was written in Atlanta and based on words provided to Tillman by a Baptist preacher named M. E. Abbey. Tillman, a famous evangelist of his day, used his own original gospel songs to enhance his appeal. In the 1930s white gospel composers were fond of writing ersatz black gospel songs and classifying them as spirituals. They had little to do with real spirituals, of course, but the word *spiritual* was a code that indicated to white singers that liberties could be taken with arrangements and the songs could be sung in a looser style. "I've Found a Hiding Place" was thus classified by its composer, Albert Brumley, on its first publication in a Stamps-Baxter book in 1939. It was popularized by the Swanee River Boys over Atlanta station WSB, where the group sang it every Saturday night for years. The Jordanaires later spotlighted it on their Opry segments, and Carl Story was the first to speed it to bluegrass style when he cut it for Mercury in 1947. Monroe's high falsetto lead resembles Story's 1947 performance. One of Brumley's first real gospel hits, "Jesus Hold My Hand," first appeared in a 1933 Hartford songbook, *Gems of Gladness.* The Chuck Wagon Gang recorded it for Columbia in 1941 and saw it reissued several times on LP.

"I Am a Pilgrim" is another traditional religious lyric that was codified and arranged by a modern country singer. In this case the person who recorded and popularized it was the guitarist and singer Merle Travis. "I first heard a version of this song from Lyman Rager," he remembered, "who had learned it when he was in the Elkton, Kentucky, jail. I rewrote it, arranged it, and added to it."[3] Travis was from the same general area of western Kentucky that Monroe was, and Monroe probably knew the song from oral tradition as well as from Travis. Travis was featuring the song as early as 1939, when he was on WLW's *Boone County Jamboree* with a band called the Drifting Pioneers. He later preserved it on a memorable record for Capitol in the late 1940s.

Although Burl Ives popularized "Wayfaring Stranger" in the late 1940s when he used it as his theme song, it is one of the oldest, most historically complex of nineteenth-century American hymns. Printed sources have been found as early as 1858, and there are indications that it might well go back another generation or two. There are a number of candidates for its authorship. "A Beautiful Life" is another song brought into modern country repertoires through the recordings of the Chuck Wagon Gang; in this case they did it in 1936 at their first Columbia recording session. The composer, William Golden, originally published and copyrighted the song in 1918. The Monroe Brothers recorded it at their final recording session in 1938, where Bill sang the bass lead part. Like Monroe, Hank Williams was fascinated with gospel music and wrote more of it than he recorded. Such was the case of "House of Gold," which Williams wrote and published in 1950 but which he never recorded commercially although the demo records he made of it were subsequently issued.

FIDDLES IN STEREO

On April 8, eight days after the gospel album was finished, Monroe seemed to celebrate by doing two more twin-fiddle compositions. This time, Bobby Hicks and Kenny Baker, who would emerge in the 1970s as Monroe's favorite fiddler and perhaps the genre's most imitated one, were involved. The two instrumentals were issued on a single, back to back, and, surprisingly, made the *Billboard* hit charts that fall—the first time Monroe had done so since his Columbia days.[4]

"Panhandle Country" was learned from David "Stringbean" Akeman, the comic banjo player who later won fame on *Hee-Haw,* in the early 1940s when he was the banjo player in the wartime edition of the Blue Grass Boys. Either he or Monroe—it is unclear who—thought the tune came from Texas and hence the title. Stringbean must have played "Panhandle Country" in one of his old-time banjo-picking styles. Mayfield's break, played out of an A chord formation with the guitar capoed up three frets, attracted considerable attention among bluegrass guitarists. The tune remained a favorite in Monroe's live performance repertoire for the rest of his career.

The connection between bagpipes and fiddling in Scotland is a venerable one and now is most notable in the fiddle traditions of Canada's Cape Breton region of Nova Scotia. But American fiddlers also had Scottish influences and were fond of imitating bagpipes even before the first American country fiddle record, Eck Robertson's "Sally Gooden," brought the sound to new listeners in 1922. Bill was thinking of the Monroes' Scots ancestry when he decided to create a bagpipe sound with twin fiddles to be juxtaposed against his blues-tinged mandolin. Harold Bradley, called in to produce the session when his brother Owen was delayed from returning to Nashville from New York, remembers that there were problems in doing "Scotland" (as Monroe titled his cultural tone poem). "The piece was originally longer than it is today—four or five minutes. The band was having trouble getting it to come together."[5] With some trepidation Bradley called Monroe aside and, drawing on his considerable jazz-arrangement skills, suggested revising some parts to tighten the arrangement. Monroe thought about it and decided to take his advice.

Sadly, this session would be the last for guitarist-singer Edd Mayfield. In early July 1958 he would become ill while the band was on the road in Bluefield, West Virginia; he did not know it, but he had contracted leukemia. He was rushed to a hospital, but it was too late. He died at the age of thirty-two, leaving a wife and two young sons. He was taken back to Texas for burial.

Taking Mayfield's post in the Blue Grass Boys was Jack Cooke. Today, Vernon Crawford "Jack" Cooke is known to bluegrass followers as the long-time—since 1970—bass player for Ralph Stanley and the Clinch Mountain Boys. A native of Norton in Wise County, Virginia (in 1963 he served half a term as mayor of Norton), he was one of five boys and four girls in a musical family. His father played clawhammer banjo, and Jack was brought up in a religious home, learning to sing in church at an early age. One of his cousins was the old-time singer and banjo-picker Dock Boggs. In the mid-1950s Jack and his brothers put together a band that occasionally played on the Knoxville Barn Dance radio show. Sometimes they were accompanied by fiddler Kenny Baker, who was still living in Jenkins, just across the state line from Wise county, in Letcher County, Kentucky.

Jack first met the Stanley Brothers when the Cooke Brothers entered and won a band contest sponsored by the Stanleys. "I was playing bass—learning to play bass—back then. Me and my brothers was playing in a talent contest in my hometown of Norton, Virginia, and that's how we got to know Carter and Ralph."[6] Around 1956, when he was sixteen, Cooke was hired by the Stanley Brothers, who were then working on the *Farm and Fun Time* program at WCYB in Bristol. After working for several years as a bass player with the Stanley Brothers, Jack moved on in 1958 to join the Blue Grass Boys. He would work off and on with Bill over the next several years as guitarist, lead vocalist, and bassist. "It was a good experience," he said. "Everybody likes to play for Bill. He taught me a whole lot, you know—how to keep good time and to phrase words. We'd practice right before the show, and if I'd say a wrong word, he'd tell me to 'say it this way.'"[7]

By the time of the session on December 1, 1958, Decca was starting to record some of its material in stereo. All the cuts from this session were originally issued in mono or later even in "rechannelled" stereo. In one case "No One but My Darlin'" was issued in true stereo on the album *Bill and Charlie Monroe.* In the 1980s, however, producer Richard Weize discovered that the other three tracks from the session had also been preserved on three-track tapes. They were mixed down to stereo and presented for the first time in the Bear Family set as part of the first complete session where Monroe's bluegrass was captured in stereo sound. Jack Cooke's guitar in particular shines in the new format as does Hicks's fiddle. Monroe was also using a different mandolin for the session. His regular instrument was being refurbished, and he borrowed an F-4 model as a temporary replacement.

Folksinger Paul Clayton had recorded "Gotta Travel On" as one of the first releases on Fred Foster's Monument label, then based in Washington, D.C. Clayton, who'd conducted extensive folksong research in Virginia and North Carolina in the early and mid-1950s, built the song on traditional sources. In 1959 Foster gave it to veteran Opry star Billy Grammer to record again, and it provided his biggest chart hit. Monroe's version two months later also made the charts—his only cover recording to do so—staying there for six weeks and rising to number 15. Three more originals rounded out the session. "Big Mon," Monroe remembered, "was written in South Dakota. We was playing a square dance out there and it was wrote on the stage."[8] Charlie Cline and Bobby Hicks were the fiddlers onstage that night, and it was their improvisation that generated the basis of the tune. Both men referred to Monroe as "Big Mon" (pronounced *big munn*). Monroe worked at "Monroe's Hornpipe" and played it onstage long before recording it. By the time of the session many young pickers had learned the tune and were playing it at jam sessions, especially at Monroe's Bean Blossom, Indiana, park, the Brown County Jamboree. Many old-time southern fiddlers were somewhat casual about what they called a hornpipe, but this piece has the features of a New England hornpipe, perhaps Monroe's tribute to his many Canadian fans and Canadian tours. Benny Martin maintained it was derived from a tune he used to play, "Big-Eyed Rabbit," which Martin used when he was with Roy Acuff.

THE BRADLEY ERA

The end of the 1950s saw dramatic changes in Bill Monroe's life and music. Mayfield's death had shaken him, and his recording career, aside from his interest in gospel music, had slowed. The market for singles was collapsing, and rock and roll was hurting the sale of Monroe's music as it was mainstream country's. Moreover, Cohen was retiring. Beginning with the session of January 30, 1959, Monroe's new producer was Owen Bradley, the studio genius who had been Cohen's righthand man. On the radio, Monroe could hear young, citified voices of the folk music revival singing many of his own songs like "Darling Corey." His archrivals Lester Flatt and Earl Scruggs were plugging into the new fad and appeared on CBS television and at the Newport Folk Festival in 1960. They were also watching a string of thirteen singles climb onto the *Billboard* charts compared to Monroe's sole entry "Gotta Travel On." Flatt and Scruggs were being booked in the Northeast and at folk music venues by Boston agent Manny Greenhill while Monroe remained with Jim Denny's Nashville agency. Monroe's music was as vital as ever; in fact, by many standards he was reaching the peak of his powers. He seemed to be struggling, however, to keep his band afloat and be puzzled and resentful that younger, less seasoned artists were taking the music he created into the big time.

Monroe began 1959 by going into the studio with the same basic band with which he had recorded "Gotta Travel On" in December 1958. The one new face was that of Charlie Smith, who played the fiddle part-time with Monroe while studying for a degree in electrical engineering at a college in Nashville. He also kept a diary during these years and wrote in the entry for January 30, 1959, "Recorded Decca session with Bill Monroe & Blue Grass Boys at Owen Bradley's studio on 16th Ave. . . . Monroe used Bill Thomas' F-12 mandolin since his is still at Gibson factory. We recorded 'Stoney Lonesome' (written by me and Bill. . . . I remember recording a fifth song by Bill but Decca studio records do not list it. Bill has looked for it, but he can not find any record of it)."[9] The session ran from 8:30 P.M. until midnight and was the first of Monroe's that Owen Bradley himself produced.

"Stoney Lonesome" featured the twin fiddles of Smith and Bobby Hicks. The name came from a small town in Brown County, Indiana, through which Monroe regularly drove on his way to his country music park at Bean Blossom. "Tomorrow I'll Be Gone" came from the pen of fellow Opry star Wilma Lee Cooper. She and her husband Stoney had moved to Nashville a year or so before, and she was developing as a songwriter. Curiously, she and Stoney never recorded the song themselves. "Dark as the Night, Blue as the Day" is a classic Monroe lament that never made it onto domestic LP but was issued as a single and in an EP album only. "When the Phone Rang" was a new song by Joe Hudgins that apparently impressed Monroe more than it did Bradley. It remained on the shelf for more than five years before making it to a budget-line Vocalion LP in 1964.

The year 1959 was another one of studio drought when the Blue Grass Boys got to do only two short sessions. By now, portable reel-to-reel tape recorders were becoming commonplace with fans, and many yielded surprisingly good sound when used carefully. Young fans like Mike Seeger and Ralph Rinzler who wanted to preserve far more of Monroe's music than Decca made available continued to make their own tapes at venues like New River Ranch in Rising Sun, Maryland, and Sunset Park in West Grove, Pennsylvania. One tape that did find its way to the public dated from August 2, 1959, and was from a live show at New River Ranch that included Jack Cooke on guitar, Kenny Baker on fiddle, and Joe Stuart on banjo. The driving version of "John Henry" appeared in 1994 on the four-CD set *The Music of Bill Monroe*.

Early in 1959 Monroe turned down an offer from Alan Lomax to play at *Folk Music, '59,* a Carnegie Hall concert Lomax staged in April, because he had heard Lomax was a communist. Earl Taylor and the Stoney Mountain Boys instead provided the bluegrass component for the eager audience. It would be 1963 before Monroe appeared at a folk revival event of any sort, but the popularity of his new single derived from the burgeoning consumer interest in folk music. By November, Monroe's single "Gotta Travel On" had hit the charts (a rare thing in itself for Monroe) and climbed to number fifteen in the spring and summer.

Bradley and Decca were anxious to find a follow-up, and the session of November 25 was designed to do that (only three sides were cut). The best bets seemed to be two songs by established and experienced writers who had little experience with bluegrass: harmonica virtuoso Wayne Raney and Marty Robbins, who specialized in cowboy and sentimental songs. Raney's contribution was "Lonesome Wind Blues," which he had originally recorded in 1948 for King. On Monroe's version, Benny Martin plays twin fiddles with Dale Potter. Best known in bluegrass for his fiddling on some of Flatt and Scruggs's most influential recordings of 1952–53, Martin had worked with Monroe briefly in 1948. By this time he had begun a career as a solo vocalist (he was briefly a member of the Opry's cast) but still doing studio work as a fiddler. This turned out to be his only studio recording with Monroe because Potter played solo on the other two sides at the session. Marty Robbins had not yet recorded the western love song "Come Go with Me," and Bradley chose it for the other side of the single. It is a fascinating vocal tour de force, with Monroe singing the entire bridge in a soaring falsetto. Unfortunately, the performance never made it onto domestic LP and was out of print for years. The slow waltz "Thinking about You" by Lee Fikes rounded out the session.

Banjoist Joe Drumright had played occasionally with Monroe for more than eight years by the time of this session. A native of Dallas, he had grown up in Nashville and watched Monroe develop the genre on the Opry in the 1940s. Soon he was playing with local Nashville radio bands like Carl Tipton's, and in 1951 he was asked to replace Rudy Lyle, who had left for the army, in Monroe's band. Between stints with Monroe he played and recorded with Connie Gately and Babe Lofton and with Wilma Lee and Stoney Cooper.

As Monroe entered the 1960s his recorded repertoire began to include more traditional numbers and more songs by other artists than in the 1950s. His own songwriting fell off in both vocal and instrumental categories. There were some sessions where he seemed to be fumbling for a direction and others where he rushed into the studio with new musicians

who were given only a short time to learn the songs. Decca responded to some of this uncertainty by leaving a larger percentage of songs unissued than in the 1950s. There would be no more chart hits in the 1960s, but there would be some early 1960s recordings destined to be classics, including "Linda Lou," "Blue Grass Part 1," and "Big Sandy River."

By the fall of 1960, Monroe, like most veteran country artists, was considered an "album artist" by recording companies, and specific cuts designed as single releases were becoming increasingly rare. Thus Owen Bradley set up three sessions during the week after Thanksgiving that would be devoted to material for the Blue Grass Boys' third LP, one released in July 1961 under the title *Mr. Bluegrass*. A year had passed since Monroe's last session, and of the 1959 band only fiddler Dale Potter and bassist Bessie Lee Mauldin remained. Two important new additions were guitarist Carl Butler and banjoist Curtis McPeake.

McPeake came from the west Tennessee town of Scotts Hill and grew up under the spell of not only his father's banjo playing but also the Hawaiian and steel guitar music widely popular in the area. He began playing bluegrass about 1953 and apprenticed himself to Earl Scruggs. Curtis learned Scruggs's style and songs so well that when Earl was disabled in an accident in 1955 Flatt called on McPeake to replace him in the band. Even after Scruggs returned, McPeake continued to fill in as needed. A newspaper photograph of the group was captioned "Lester Flatt, Curtis McPeake, and the Foggy Mountain Boys." It was with Monroe, though, that McPeake's first full-time break came. "I worked a couple of years for Bill Monroe," he says. "Bill helped me a lot. Bill took me on at the Opry; he took me in when I really needed a job. It was through working with Bill at the Opry that, after I left Bill, I became the only staff banjo player the Opry's ever had."[10] McPeake eventually cut eighteen sides with Monroe (he would return to sessions as a studio man) and later became a member of Danny Davis's Nashville Brass group.

Although he'd been a member of the Opry cast since 1958, Carl Butler was still best known in the fall of 1960 as a Knoxville songwriter who had some effective recordings throughout the 1950s for Capitol and Columbia that did not reach the charts. In 1961 he would start to gain fame as a honky-tonk singer with "Honky Tonkitis," and in 1962 he had a major hit with his wife, Pearl, in "Don't Let Me Cross Over." His songs, including "Crying My Heart Out over You" and "If Teardrops Were Pennies," had been recorded by Roy Acuff, Carl Smith, and Flatt and Scruggs. Butler also coauthored songs with Scruggs, such as

"Building on Sand." Although he was a superb mountain and gospel-styled singer Butler sings on none of the sides he cut with Monroe, even "Linda Lou," a lilting waltz he composed and recorded for Capitol in 1951.

In addition to "Linda Lou," three other songs were recorded at the November 30 session. Monroe sings "Linda Lou" as a solo; it was issued on a single and a 45-EP album as well as the LP and became a popular favorite that Monroe's audiences often requested throughout the 1960s. "Sold Down the River" is a clever piece from the pen of Vaughn Horton, author of "Mocking Bird Hill." According to Monroe, "You Live in a World All Your Own" was based on an earlier song by the Knoxville tunesmith Arthur Q. Smith from whom Monroe had also bought "How Will I Explain about You?" Although credited in Decca files to Monroe, "Little Joe" dates from the mid-nineteenth century. It was copyrighted by V. E. Marsten in 1866 and a decade later by Maj. Charles E. Addison. It first appeared on record in 1925, and both the Monroe Brothers (Charlie and Bill) and the Carter Family recorded it in 1938, each using the same kind of sprightly tempo found here.

Four more songs were also recorded at the December 1 session. "Put My Rubber Doll Away" is based on another Victorian parlor song popularized by Roy Acuff and a generation of earlier country singers although it was normally done much more slowly than heard here. "Seven Year Blues," an early Louvin Brothers song dating from 1949, was then very popular with other bluegrass bands and often heard on live shows. "Time Changes Everything" and "Lonesome Road Blues" are both familiar standards that Monroe made his own.

When Ralph Rinzler asked Monroe why he did a version of Johnny Cash's Sun favorite "Big River" at the December 3 recording session he answered, "When we were on tour together, John always used to joke with me about my style. I wanted him to know I could do one of his songs and make it mine."[11] Three other songs were recorded on December 3. One, "It's Mighty Dark to Travel" was another remake of a song done years before (this time, 1947, for Columbia, with Flatt singing lead), and "Flowers of Love" was another ill-fated attempt to find a hit single. "Blue Grass Part 1" (also released as "Blue Grass Twist") was a twelve-bar blues in G that captured a special sound from Monroe's mandolin, one Bill and those close to him at that time had been calling "the sound." It can be heard at the start of the second mandolin break after the fiddle solo. The sound happened when one of the two E strings hung up on the fret wire at the thirteenth fret, which was loose. At the time, the binding was gone from that part of the fingerboard, and as

a result Monroe would get unusual two-note harmonies as he fretted the E string but only for a few moments at a time.[12]

The *Mr. Bluegrass* LP had been issued in July 1961 and sold well enough to justify a follow-up, eventually called *Bluegrass Ramble,* to be issued in the summer of 1962. The album would be heavily focused on older material, the kind of material that folk groups like the Kingston Trio were starting to record—songs Monroe was quick to note he had done years earlier. The first two sessions for the album, November 9 and 10, 1961, were completely devoted to remakes of older songs. "Nine Pound Hammer" had been in the Monroe repertoire since the 1930s when he and Charlie recorded it for Bluebird at their first session in 1936. "Little Maggie" had been recorded in the 1920s by G. B. Grayson and Henry Whitter, in the 1930s by J. E. Mainer, and in the 1940s by the Stanley Brothers. The second Stanley Brothers version of the old mountain favorite had been issued on Starday in April 1961, and many bluegrass musicians were playing it. Neil Rosenberg used it as his instrumental solo the first time he played banjo with Monroe on September 24, 1961, at Bean Blossom. "Shady Grove" was a familiar old-time song. It had not been recorded by Monroe or by the Monroe Brothers, but it had been featured in the 1930s by a radio band from Chicago, one of Monroe's favorites, the Prairie Ramblers. It had been more recently featured by the Kingston Trio as well, and Monroe had featured it on the Opry in the 1940s.

According to Richard D. Smith, band members suggested these three folk favorites at the session "because audiences had been requesting them lately."[13] "I'm Going Back to Old Kentucky" and "Toy Heart" had been recorded as duets with Lester Flatt during the Columbia years, 1947 and 1946 respectively. Here the former was done as a solo and the latter a duet. "Live and Let Live" was a duet favorite created by Wiley Walker and Gene Sullivan, the Alabama duo that won fame over Oklahoma radio in the 1940s as Wiley and Gene.

On "Toy Heart" and "Live and Let Live" Monroe sings duets with Jimmy Maynard, a newcomer to the band who played guitar and sang. Born in Temperance Hall, Tennessee, he first heard Monroe when he was thirteen. After a couple of years working in Detroit and a tour of duty in the army, he moved to Nashville in 1956. Unlike some of Monroe's hirings, there was nothing sudden or dramatic about Maynard's. He gradually got to know men like Curtis McPeake and began hanging out backstage at the Opry, where he often jammed with Monroe and his band. After Edd Mayfield died Monroe hired Jimmy as a guitar player and singer.

The fiddlers included Vassar Clements and Buddy Spicher

on the November 9 session, and Horace "Benny" Williams on November 10. It was Clements's first session with Monroe since the early 1950s. He had recently returned to Nashville after a four- or five-year stint with Jim and Jesse and had played shows with Bill that fall. Spicher, who later did several stints as a regular member of the Blue Grass Boys, would soon become Nashville's premier studio fiddler. Spicher, from Pennsylvania, was brought to Nashville from Wheeling, West Virginia, recently by Johnnie Wright and Kitty Wells. He had not previously recorded with Monroe but during the next three decades would participate in more than thirty sessions and soon became Nashville's premier studio fiddler.

Benny Williams, a talented all-around musician, grew up on Dayton Mountain in rugged southeastern Tennessee. "He never saw an electric light or tasted a Coke until he was ten years old" recalled his friend Tom Morgan.[14] He sang in a gospel quartet and played fiddle on the radio and was soon working with Mac Wiseman and then Don Reno and Arthur Lee "Red" Smiley (with whom he recorded, playing mandolin and fiddle, in 1956), the Stanleys, and Flatt and Scruggs. The early 1960s found him in Nashville, rooming with Buddy Spicher at Delia "Mom" Upchurch's boardinghouse and backing country singers on the road. He would serve with Monroe off and on for five years, often filling in on guitar or fiddle and doing vocals for recording sessions and tours. He also did a comedy routine when he worked personal appearances with the band, doing imitations of popular stars.

Three weeks later, on December 1 and 4, the band was back in the studio for the remaining six numbers for *Bluegrass Ramble*. These, too, were oddly mixed. Some were doubtless Monroe's choices, and others were ones Bradley brought in as a response to the burgeoning folk revival movement. Three songs were recorded at the first session.

Of these, the most unusual was "Danny Boy," Fred Weatherly's 1913 adaptation of an old Irish folk melody. An international hit in the 1920s, "Danny Boy" became a standard in Irish song repertoires worldwide, especially for tenor singers. It had been recorded successfully by Conway Twitty in 1959 and went to number seven on the pop charts. A little later it was featured by crooner Andy Williams. Apparently Bradley thought Monroe had a chance at a country cover of it because of his high tenor voice and intense delivery. Monroe worked hard on his vocal solo, as did guitarist Benny Williams, whose ornate chordal ending also reflected the care lavished on this, the only single released from the LP. The photograph on the front of this book, of Monroe studying lyrics and music while Williams

works on his guitar part, was taken at this session and conveys the intensity of their work that day.

"Cotton Fields" was a folk revival hit by the Highwaymen, hence the composer credits given as "Arr. and Adapt. by Dave Fisher," a member of that group. In reality the song originated with bluesman Huddie Ledbetter (Lead Belly) and was given additional exposure by Odetta and her partner Larry in their much-emulated arrangement on a 1954 recording for the Fantasy label. "Cotton Fields" was also brought to the session by Bradley. The Highwaymen's United Artists version of the song had barely been released and didn't get onto the charts until the day after Monroe's session on December 1.[15] In an attempt to emulate the original he uses a trio on the vocals—an unusual feature in an age when he preferred to sing more and more solos. "Journey's End," like "Live and Let Live," was an older country standard originally recorded by Ernest Tubb in 1954. Composer credits were to Tubb and Virgil "Pappy" Stewart, a Blytheville, Arkansas singer who led the popular Stewart Family gospel group that recorded for 4–Star in the 1940s. Although not a gospel song it had the kind of starkness that appealed to Monroe, and it is quite likely that he chose it to round out the album's vocals.

The December 4 session was devoted to three instrumentals featuring a new banjoist, Tony Ellis: "John Hardy," "Bugle Call Rag," and "Old Joe Clark." Not only were these the first traditional instrumentals Monroe had recorded since 1940 but they were also the first to feature the five-string banjo as opposed to the fiddle or mandolin as lead instrument. The fact that they were featured in such a "folk-oriented" album reflects the banjo's popularity with folk music fans and how much they associated it with bluegrass. Bradley and Monroe were aware that the old Dixieland warhorse "Bugle Call Rag" was featured by Earl Scruggs on the *Foggy Mountain Banjo* LP that had been released to great acclaim earlier in the year.

Ellis was featured on both December 1961 sessions. Born at Sylva in the mountains of North Carolina in 1939, he learned music from both his grandmother, who played drop-thumb and two-finger style banjo, and his mother, a classical pianist. When he was fourteen, Tony, who then lived in Lynchburg, watched Bill Monroe do a live radio show. "It really excited me," he said, "and so the next week I decided I was going to play the banjo and eventually I was going to get a job with Bill Monroe."[16] He at once took his trumpet, which he had been playing in high school, to a pawnshop and traded it for a banjo.

A local banjoist named Swanson Walker taught Ellis the Scruggs-style basics, including the version of "John Hardy" heard on the December 4 recording. Ellis apprenticed himself to Don Reno around 1956 and began absorbing his technique. After Ellis graduated from high school and did a stint in the service, Reno encouraged him to try to make it as a professional and called Monroe to set up an audition. In January 1960 he flew from Lynchburg to Nashville, checked into the Clarkston Hotel, and prepared to meet Monroe at WSM's Studio C the following day. "The next morning when I got up and went to shave," he remembers, "I stuck my hand down in my shaving kit and the old safety razors unscrewed in those days, and the blade was sticking in there, and I just stuck the middle finger of my left hand right down on the blade and cut it right open. So I knew I was in trouble. When I went to the audition four hours later, I'd slide up the third string, and it'd go right in the cut and I'd just bear with it and go on and do it."[17] Ellis was still playing Reno-style and was unfamiliar with Monroe's repertoire:

> After we had done several numbers, Bill said that wasn't what he wanted for his particular songs. Jack Cooke was playing guitar at that time, and Bill said he was going out to eat and get his mail, and for Jack to run through some stuff with me, and he'd come back. So Jack and I worked about two hours on his music. Jack explained how Bill would want the banjo played. . . . Just straightforward and clean and clear and not chord structured things like Don did. Play the melody as close as you could and try to drive with your thumb to bring out the expression of the melody. Hit most of those melody notes with the thumb and work around that. So when Bill came back, we went [through] these tunes again, played differently. . . . And he smiled and said, "That sounds more like banjo picking." And I felt a little better then. But he also told me there were two other banjo players in town that were auditioning at the same time.[18]

Ellis was eventually hired, and within a few days he was on the road with the band to Winnipeg, where it joined a Johnny Cash package show. Ellis didn't record with the band, however, until December 3, 1960. His participation in that session as bass player happened unexpectedly, for he'd quit the Blue Grass Boys.

> About three weeks earlier and gone to Alabama to visit with Fred Richardson, Jimmy Brock and the Sauceman Brothers. On my way to go to home to North Carolina I stopped at Linebaughs [in Nashville] to get a bite to eat. When I entered the restaurant I found Bill and Bessie eating lunch in a booth. I spoke and Bessie called me over. She explained that they were in the midst of a recording session and she had some pretty bad blisters on her hands and asked if I would be willing to finish the session for her. I agreed to help out before continuing my journey home

and played on several cuts. At the conclusion of the recording Bill asked me to stay on and continue to play banjo.[19]

He would eventually make some twenty-five sides with Monroe (through May 17, 1962) and be his regular banjoist for two years. It was, he remembers, a time when Monroe's recording efforts were unorganized: "When we would go into a session we would have no idea what we were going to do. He wouldn't tell us or rehearse ahead of time."[20] In later years Ellis would play with Mac Wiseman, befriend old-time fiddler Tommy Jarrell, and in 1988 cut *Dixie Banner,* his first of a series of well-received solo albums.

END OF THE DROUGHT

The spring of 1962 was a busy time for Monroe. After years of occasional and oddly spaced sessions he was getting into the studio almost every week. In March he went into the Capitol studio with Rose Maddox and recorded his first guest appearance on the recording of another artist. Monroe had said several times that Maddox was "the only woman who could really sing bluegrass."[21] Although based for most of her career in California, Rose had spent much of her early days with a family band before embarking on a solo career in 1959 and had chart hits such as "Loose Talk." Monroe began urging her to do a fully traditional album and even volunteered his help if she would come to Nashville for that purpose. "I done the best I could to help her," he said. "She has a good voice to listen to. We've worked some shows together down through the years and she has always been a good friend."[22] As he told Maddox's biographer, "The Maddox Brothers and Rose had their own style, but you must remember their home was Alabama, and I always thought they sang a lot of the old southern style of singing. So I helped her on one of her albums; she had some great entertainers working on it and it didn't take long at all."[23]

Of the twelve songs Maddox recorded, six had publisher's credits to Monroe and a seventh ("Footprints in the Snow") was associated with him. He played mandolin on five of those tracks: "Uncle Pen," "Footprints in the Snow," "Blue Moon of Kentucky," "My Rose of Old Kentucky," and "Molly and Tenbrooks." Donna Stoneman played mandolin on the others. Reno and Smiley with their bassist John Palmer and fiddler Mack Magaha also joined in, along with studio fiddler Tommy Jackson. Because of Monroe's exclusive Decca contract he was not mentioned on the credits to *Rose Maddox Sings Bluegrass,* but his participation was well known from the album's release.

Listeners could recognize his distinctive mandolin style in the breaks he took on each of the five songs even though most were in keys other than those in which he had recorded or usually performed them. Several were pieces on which he did not normally take mandolin breaks.

Between April 25 and May 17 he recorded eighteen selections, most of them earmarked for two new LPs, *Bluegrass Special* and *I'll Meet You in Church Sunday Morning*. The first sessions were designed for the secular album and spotlighted powerful new duet singing by Monroe and an important new addition to the band, Frank Buchanan.

Hailing from Spruce Pine, North Carolina, Buchanan started his career on the old Carolina Barn Dance show in the late 1940s. With his brother Ray, he specialized in singing mandolin-guitar duets in the manner of the Blue Sky Boys, the Morris Brothers, and the Louvin Brothers. After a hitch in the army and gigs with various local bands, in 1959 Frank found himself playing on the Old Dominion Barn Dance at WRVA in Richmond, Virginia, with the Cripple Creek Boys. Other members of the group included banjoist Tony Ellis and Cotton Stanley, a cousin of Carter and Ralph Stanley. It was there that Buchanan met Monroe. "Bill and I sang a few songs backstage," he recalled, "and he told me if I ever broke up with the Cripple Creek Boys to give him a call in Nashville."[24]

When the breakup did occur in 1959, his old friend Tony Ellis joined Monroe, and a few months later Ellis called Frank and suggested he call Monroe and take him up on his offer. Buchanan did so in the autumn of 1960 and soon found himself working on the road (not yet the studio) with the Blue Grass Boys. Soon after he joined the band, Frank began playing Monroe's classic Martin D-28 herringbone guitar. "He didn't really tell me to use it, but all his guitar men had played it down through the years and it seemed to sound best with Bill's music," he said. It had an especially good bass sound that was just right for the rhythm-guitar sound the band needed. Buchanan, like many other sidemen, learned the finer points of the music from Monroe, who "straightened me out on my timing, and helped me a lot with my singing and phrasing. Monroe builds a fire under you."[25]

Buchanan's smooth, supple voice, which Doug Green has described as "the absolute best bluegrass lead singer ever," is heard doing lead on such pieces as "There Was Nothing We Could Do," "Foggy River," and "Blue Ridge Mountain Blues."[26] On others he often takes the lead on the chorus, with Monroe singing tenor. Unfortunately, the eighteen selections cut during the spring of 1962 were the only ones on which Buchanan was

able to sing; by the fall 1962 sessions he was gone. He later worked with Jimmy Martin and Earl Taylor before moving to Detroit in 1967. He then recorded solo albums for Fortune and Atteiram.

Recollections by some of the Blue Grass Boys during this time show how hard Monroe had to struggle to keep his music before the public. "Times were awfully hard for bluegrass musicians then" recalls Buddy Pendleton, who fiddled in the band in 1962. Long road trips were par for the course. "I remember I was driving Bill Monroe's old 1958 Olds station wagon that had 250,000 miles on it one time and the shock absorbers were so worn that the shimmy broke a bolt in the steering column as we crossed a railroad track."[27] Musicians were paid by the day remembers Frank Buchanan. Instead of a steady salary, they were paid only for the days they worked and then at a fixed rate that didn't vary according to the day's number of performances, whether a few songs on the Opry to several hours of shows at a park.

The bluegrass festival circuit had not yet developed, so the band traveled far and wide to find places to play. Buchanan recalls long, long road trips into Canada, where the rock and roll fever had not yet poisoned the water for older country styles. One common venue was the drive-in theater circuit, where the band would come in and play before a movie started, usually on a percentage basis. Banjoist Tony Ellis remembers that drive-ins would run primitive public address systems into the little speakers placed atop posts, and cars pulled up alongside. When the audience liked the music, "some of them would blow their horns. Some of them whistle, holler . . . some people would get out of their cars and walk down near the concession stand, which is usually where we played, on the roof."[28] When the roof was not strong enough, the band would play on a truckbed.

The most successful of the *Bluegrass Special* titles was probably the single that includes "Blue Ridge Mountain Blues" and "How Will I Explain about You?" The former was a 1920s' favorite that had been done by legends like Riley Puckett, Pop Stoneman, Vernon Dalhart, and Sid Harkreader. The latter was a remake of a Monroe cut from 1946 when Flatt and Scruggs were with him. It was one of three numbers that Monroe bought from the superb but eccentric Knoxville songwriter Arthur Q. Smith, best known for selling his composer's rights to "Wedding Bells" and "I Wouldn't Change You if I Could." The three songs by Chuck Carson—"There Was Nothing We Could Do," "I Was Left on the Street," and "Cheap Love Affair"—all solid country songs—emerged as the newest pieces on the album.

When *Blue Grass Special* was released in 1963, Del Mc-Coury was playing guitar and singing lead with Bill, and they often sang these songs. In 1987 Del recorded the latter two with his brother Jerry on their Rounder album. "When the Bees Are in the Hive," a turn-of-the-century parlor favorite, was a fixture in repertoires of acts like the Girls of the Golden West and the North Carolina Ramblers during the 1920s and 1930s. "Columbus Stockade Blues" had been initially popularized in 1928 by an Alabama duo, Tom Darby and Jimmie Tarlton. "Big Ball in Brooklyn" was a variant of another familiar piece from old-time string bands and western swing, "Big Ball in Town," "Big Ball in Memphis," or "Big Ball in Cowtown." This piece was not included on the LP and never issued commercially in the United States although it appeared on a Japanese collection and Monroe included it in his live performance repertoire during 1963. "Foggy River" was a vintage Fred Rose song that had been a minor hit for pop singer Kate Smith in 1948 and was made into a major country hit in 1968 by Carl Smith.

At the session on May 10, 1962, Monroe began work on his second gospel album, recording nine quartets in three sessions. For this he brought studio bass vocalist Culley Holt, who'd sung on his first gospel album. Singing baritone on the first was another studio veteran, guitarist Ray Edenton, whom Owen Bradley often used as his session leader, even at some later Monroe sessions. On the later two sessions Monroe drafted Harold "Red" Stanley, who had joined the band in 1962 as a fiddler, for the baritone parts. Stanley was from around Jamestown, Tennessee, where he had won a reputation playing local dances and radio shows.

"The Old Country Baptizing" was written by Verlon Bryontt and Jim Shumate, Monroe's fiddler in 1944–45. For some reason the performance was rejected for the *I'll Meet You in Church* LP and did not appear on LP until 1974, when it was used on *The Road of Life* album. "I Found the Way" is the quartet version of the song Bill and Charlie recorded in 1937 as "I Have Found the Way." It's an old gospel convention song from the catalog of the R. E. Winsett Company; its coauthor, though, was Adger M. Pace, a mainstay of the James D. Vaughan Company of Lawrenceburg. Pace had written hundreds of songs and edited the Vaughan songbooks for many years. "This World Is Not My Home," which Monroe does as a solo, had been one of the more popular Bluebird sides he did in the 1930s with his brother Charlie. More recently, it had been featured by the Opry's Old Hickory Singers, the venerable quartet that specialized in heart and gospel songs. "Drifting Too Far from the Shore" was listed by Decca as "traditional," but in fact it had

been written and copyrighted in the early 1930s by Charles E. Moody of the Georgia Yellow Hammers. The Monroe Brothers included it at their first recording session in 1936, and it was revived by the Country Gentlemen for their first album in 1960. "Way Down Deep in My Soul," written in 1942 by Floyd Hunter, was first published in a shape-note songbook entitled *Redeeming Grace* issued by the Hartford Music Company of Arkansas. "Going Home" came from the pen of Carl Tipton, a widely known radio personality and bandleader from Murfreesboro, Tennessee, near Nashville. For years Tipton led one of the most authentic and hard-driving Monroe-styled bands and wrote some of the more memorable bluegrass gospel pieces.

The sessions of May 16 and May 17, 1962, added something Monroe had not used before to the quartet sound: the banjo. Why he made the change is unclear. He might have been responding to the general fascination of the folk revival audience with the instrument, or perhaps he was in some way acknowledging that many other bluegrass bands were including the banjo in their gospel performances. Whatever the case, Tony Ellis's work makes a change from the sparse instrumentation usually heard on Blue Grass Boys' gospel quartet numbers.

"On the Jericho Road," also listed in the Decca files as "traditional," became a gospel standard in the late 1940s and early 1950s when the Blackwood Brothers and the Jordanaires both featured it. "On the Jericho Road" was written by Donald S. McCrossan in 1928, highlighted throughout the 1930s at singing conventions and on radio shows, and finally sold to Hill and Range in 1953. "We'll Understand It Better," another song of uncertain authorship, was published and arranged by Tennessee publisher R. E. Winsett. Although credited to Monroe and Harold Donny, "Somebody Touched Me" was composed by John Reedy of Corbin, Kentucky, who recorded it in 1949 for the Twin City label. In the mid-1950s a West Virginia singer and folksong collector, Betty Bush Winger, sent a version to the Library of Congress's Archive of Folk Song, noting that it was locally popular. Carl Story recorded it in 1960 for Starday, and the Stanley Brothers did as well for King in 1961. Monroe's version was not released until 1974, when it, too, finally appeared on the *Road of Life* LP.

In the meantime, Monroe continued his normal hectic touring schedule and on Labor Day found himself on a temporary stage in front of the courthouse in Hazard, Kentucky, where he gave a free concert at the Coal Carnival.[29] Nearby was John Cohen, a photographer, filmmaker, and member of the New Lost City Ramblers, a band that did much to introduce old-time and bluegrass to folk revival audiences. Cohen was finishing his pioneering documentary on Roscoe Holcomb, a classic Kentucky traditional singer. Entitled *The High Lonesome Sound,* the film included scenes of Monroe's concert in Hazard that were intended to show the links between his high singing and that of older Kentucky songsters like Holcomb. The film, whose title was the first to tie Monroe directly to the now-familiar phrase *high lonesome sound,* shows the band steaming through "John Henry," spotlighting the work of Buchanan, fiddler Benny Williams, and Ray Goins on banjo. The earliest footage of Monroe playing to an audience, *The High Lonesome Sound* was widely shown and later released in several videotape versions. It offers the earliest scenes of Monroe playing to an audience.

The sessions of November 23 are memorable for, among other things, the fact that with them Owen Bradley's righthand man, Harry Silverstein, became a full-fledged producer for Monroe. Decca files show that Bradley did the morning session and Silverstein the afternoon one. During the remainder of the 1962 sessions Bradley and Silverstein shared duties, but by 1964 Harry was doing sessions by himself. He seems to have been sensitive to Monroe's music and managed to capture some excellent performances.

Although only six months had passed since the last recordings, the Blue Grass Boys had undergone another personnel change. Tony Ellis had been married in June and needed a better way to support himself and his wife, and Frank Buchanan left that fall because "I thought I'd quit and rest up a while."[30] Fiddler Red Stanley, whom a colleague described as "just a country fiddler," may have found some of Monroe's new pieces challenging.[31] He left to tour with Mac Wiseman and Johnny Cash. Replacing them at Monroe's fall 1962 sessions were three dynamic figures who would figure greatly in Monroe's music.

The first was banjo player Lonnie Hoppers. Born in the Missouri Ozarks town of Urbana in 1935, Hoppers was part of a musical circle that included, at various times, Doug Dillard, John Hartford, Dale Sledd, and Dean Webb. He spent much of the 1950s playing at Missouri radio stations and live shows like Lee Mace's Ozark Opry and first performed with Monroe in 1957 as a last-minute substitute for banjoist Joe Stuart at a show in Newburg, Missouri. "At the end of the show," he recalled, "Bill asked me to join him as a member of his band, but I had a steady girlfriend and a good paying job at the Ozark Opry, so with regret, I turned down his first job offer."[32]

Three years later, a late army discharge prevented Hoppers from accepting a second offer from Monroe, but when he called a third time, in October 1962, Hoppers accepted. "I was just getting settled with a job and a family and a house in Kansas City," he said, "but Monroe said he needed a banjo picker for the weekend for a package tour he was doing in Omaha. So I went to Omaha where Bill took me to a nearby store and bought a western hat for me . . . and I played for him for the weekend tour. One show was especially memorable for me . . . because Roy Acuff came out on stage and sang a duet with Bill."[33] Almost immediately after he returned with the band to Nashville, Hoppers found himself in the Decca studio for the November 23 session. "I was scared to death because Owen Bradley was engineering the session himself. I made it through the session though." Hoppers only cut twelve sides with the band before he, too, left because "there wasn't enough money in playing on the road."[34] Hoppers's early recordings such as "Careless Love" feature rather subdued banjo breaks, but later efforts such as "Big Sandy River" are full of drive and unexpected turns. Hoppers would later perform with the young Dan Crary and help form his music into one of the most influential modern styles.

Both Joe Stuart and Kenny Baker, the "new" guitarist and fiddler who replaced Buchanan and Stanley, had been with Monroe on earlier occasions. Stuart, one of Nashville's all-time great bluegrass session musicians, had recorded with Monroe on banjo in 1955. He eventually would prove his versatility by recording on every instrument in the bluegrass band except for the mandolin. On the November 23 session he takes over on guitar, offering some wonderful bass runs and propelling the band almost single-handedly through a demanding variety of material. His work on December 6 on "Darling Corey," a neglected gem that never made it onto LP, shows convincingly just how fine a guitarist he was.

Kenny Baker, a fiddler and coal miner from Jenkins in eastern Kentucky, joined Monroe first in 1956 after a stint with Don Gibson's band and left in 1958. In the early 1960s he rejoined a second time and then a third, torn between the uncertainties of life on the road and the steady wages Bethlehem Steel offered for working in the mines. Although he grew up playing the complex fiddle tunes of his father and friends in Kentucky, he soon came under the spell of Marion Sumner, the jazz-influenced swing fiddler making a reputation around Knoxville in the 1950s as a hot soloist. He also listened closely to the records of Belgian guitarist Django Reinhardt and French violinist Stephane Grappelli of the Quintet of the Hot Club of France. After Baker replaced Sumner in Gibson's band he found himself playing western swing and had little real interest in bluegrass until he heard Monroe's recordings of "Roanoke" and "Wheel Hoss."

Kenny Baker thinks he first met Monroe at a package show on which Gibson and Monroe shared the bill. He noticed Monroe sitting in the audience, watching him carefully. Later Monroe made a general offer—if Baker ever needed a job, call. When Gibson lost his television show and times got hard, Kenny did. It meant making an adjustment in his music. "When I went to work for Bill, the change I had to make in the music . . . you might say it was a big challenge," he said. "I decided before I ever went there I knew just how I could play that kind of music without even thinking about it. I found I didn't know near what I thought I did. Bill explained to me after I'd worked with him for a while that he thought my fiddle would help his music some."[35] A friend was trying, without much luck, to help Kenny learn the breaks and tunes but finally gave up and went to Monroe, admitting defeat. "He said, 'Now don't listen to what somebody else is playing, you play what you feel and what you hear, that's why I want you.'"[36]

Baker was fascinated with the way Monroe ran his recording sessions during the early 1960s, and his description reveals a lot about how some sides originated. Monroe's studio procedures, as reflected in the unissued Columbia takes (chapters 3 and 4), were still being followed. "I found Bill very easy to work with in recording. He sets his music up and tells you what he wants," Baker said. If Bradley or Silverstein brought in a number they wanted the band to try, "if it was a strange number to us they'd play it for us . . . and we would listen to it and each man would figure out his break. Then we would start with it and somewhere along the line some man's gonna make a boo boo, then that gives you another chance to improvise this number as you go with it. Four times, most of the time, we generally had a pretty good cut."[37]

Baker, in fact, was responsible for the band doing "Careless Love" at the November 23 session. He was a fan of big bands and the swing era, had seen Nat "King" Cole do the number in a Hollywood film long before he met Monroe, and was impressed with the slow, deliberate way Cole sang it and played it on piano. "We was in this recording session one day and we was beatin' around trying to hunt another number. I thought, well if I show it to him just exactly like he [Cole] done it, he'll not be interested, but if I boost it up just a little bit, he might. So we tried it and we took one cut and right there and then we just recorded it. Every note I hit, this man [Cole] had it on the piano."[38]

"I'm So Lonesome I Could Cry," the familiar Hank Williams lament, was another filler for the still-incomplete *Bluegrass Special* LP. "Jimmy Brown the Newsboy," a Carter Family song

based on a nineteenth-century broadside, was cut in response to Mac Wiseman's recent hit version as well as the Flatt and Scruggs version of the previous year that was becoming popular at folk festivals. It was obviously designed for the charts because it came out on a single and never found its way onto an LP.

On the afternoon of November 23 the band returned to try to finish out the material for the new gospel album that had been started in May. For some reason, possibly because the new band was not known for its singing, no more quartets were done—just three Monroe solos. "Pass Me Not," although credited to Monroe, was a familiar nineteenth-century hymnbook favorite by Fanny J. Crosby and W. H. Doane that Monroe remembered from his youth. "The Glory Land Way," credited as "traditional" in the Decca files, was written by J. S. Torbett in the 1930s and assigned to the Winsett Company, whose books Monroe seemed to know well. "Farther Along," also credited in the files to Monroe, has a more confusing history. The song is usually credited to a Missouri songwriter and preacher, W. B. Stevens, in a 1916 songbook, but earlier versions appear in a 1911 songbook from Anderson, Indiana, and an even earlier 1894 songbook published by L. L. Pickett in Louisville. In the 1930s the song was popularized by a female gospel trio from Texas, the Burnett Sisters, who traveled, did radio work, and recorded. By 1939 it had become popular in country circles—possibly through its acquisition and promotion by R. E. Winsett—and was featured and recorded by Charlie Monroe, Roy Acuff, and others. By 1962, the date of this session, it had become a gospel standard.

Two weeks later, in Nashville for the slow holiday season, the same band returned to Bradley's studio on December 6 and 10 to try again to finish the two LPs. Two fine instrumentals by Baker, his first compositions to be recorded by the band, rounded out the *Bluegrass Special* set. "Big Sandy River," the more up-tempo of the pair, became especially popular when released on a single from the session and has remained a favorite. "Darling Corey" was the traditional mountain song recorded in the 1920s by banjo-playing songsters like B. F. Shelton. It had been one of the most popular of the Monroe Brothers's Bluebird releases; they did it in 1936 and saw it reissued on Alan Lomax's *Smoky Mountain Ballads* set in 1941. Pete Seeger's folk revival version, copied by the Kingston Trio, had renewed its popularity yet again, and Bradley probably looked on it as a good cover bet. Whatever the case, it was issued on a single the following April and never put onto an LP.

"Cindy" was another traditional number destined only for

release as a single and not on LP. Unlike most of the "shout" arrangements of the song, often featured as the opener or closer to radio shows in the 1930s, Monroe takes the vocal himself. A new gospel song, "Master Builder," and the more traditional-sounding "Let Me Rest at the End of My Journey" made further inroads to the gospel album. The latter had been recorded for Columbia in the early 1950s by the Shenandoah Valley Trio, the stage name that Bill gave the Blue Grass Boys when they played as a warm-up act. It was said to have been composed by Birch Monroe.[39]

Notes

1. Richard D. Smith gives the story of this song in *Can't You Hear Me Callin'? : The Life of Bill Monroe* (New York: Little, Brown, 2000), 142.

2. Smith describes Monroe's impromptu recruitment of the young rockabilly for the recording session (*Can't You Hear Me Callin'?* 143).

3. Dorothy Horstman, *Sing Your Heart Out, Country Boy: Classic Country Songs and Their Inside Stories by the Men and Women Who Wrote Them,* rev. ed. (Nashville: Country Music Foundation Press, 1986), 48.

4. By this time *Billboard* had increased the number of positions listed on its charts from the ten shown in the 1940s.

5. Harold Bradley, interview with Neil V. Rosenberg and Charles Wolfe, Nashville, Tenn., April 5, 1998.

6. Barry Brower, "Making the Blend: The Jack Cooke Story," *Bluegrass Unlimited* (Jan. 1987): 55.

7. Brower, "Making the Blend," 55.

8. Doug Hutchens, notes to *Bill Monroe: Classic Bluegrass Instrumentals* (Rebel 850, 1985).

9. Charles K. Wolfe, notes to *Bill Monroe: Bluegrass 1959–1969* (Bear Family BCD 15529, 1991), 4.

10. Bruce Nemerov, "Curtis McPeake: Bluegrass Banjo with Brass," *Bluegrass Unlimited* (Jan. 1978): 36.

11. Wolfe, notes to *Bluegrass 1959–1969,* 5.

12. See Smith, *Can't You Hear Me Callin'?* 156, for a more detailed description.

13. Ibid., 158.

14. Tom Morgan, conversation with Charles Wolfe, Lebanon, Tenn., Feb. 27, 2001.

15. Smith says that the song "was suggested on the spur of the moment by fiddler Bobby Joe Lester, who was performing it in a side group he had with Tony Ellis" (*Can't You Hear Me Callin'?* 158). Ellis, however, says, "It seems to me Owen Bradley suggested Bill do it as a Bluegrass rendition." Tony Ellis to Neil V. Rosenberg, email, June 6, 2003.

16. Bobby Fulcher, "Tony Ellis with Bill Ellis," *1990 Program for Tennessee Banjo Institute* (Lebanon: N.p., [1990]), 29.

17. Fulcher, "Tony Ellis with Bill Ellis."

18. Ibid.

19. Ellis to Rosenberg email.

20. Smith, *Can't You Hear Me Callin'?* 155.

21. Jonny Whiteside, *Ramblin' Rose: The Life and Career of Rose Maddox* (Urbana: University of Illinois Press, 1997), 204–6.

22. Whiteside, *Ramblin' Rose,* 205.

23. Ibid., 206.

24. Clarence H. Greene, "Frank Buchanan: The Genial Gentleman of Bluegrass," *Bluegrass Unlimited* 20 (Feb. 1986): 27.

25. Greene, "Frank Buchanan," 28.

26. Douglas B. Green, "Where Are They Now," *Pickin'* 1 (Feb. 1974): 25.

27. Ed Davis, "Buddy Pendleton," *Muleskinner News Yearbook,* (April 1975): 8.

28. Wolfe, notes to *Bluegrass 1959–1969,* 2.

29. John Cohen's photograph from this event appears with Ralph Rinzler's "Bill Monroe—'The Daddy of Blue Grass Music,'" *Sing Out!* 13 (Feb.–March 1963): 5.

30. Green, "Where Are They Now," 25.

31. Doyle Jones, interview with Charles K. Wolfe, Jamestown, Tenn, May 3, 1977.

32. Don Ginnings, "Lonnie Hoppers," *Bluegrass Unlimited* 17 (March 1983): 33.

33. Ginnings, "Lonnie Hoppers," 34

34. Ibid.

35. Alice Foster, "Kenny Baker," *Bluegrass Unlimited* 3 (Dec. 1968): 10.

36. Foster, "Kenny Baker," 10.

37. Ibid.

38. Ibid., 9.

39. Ivan Tribe, notes to *New Sounds Ramblin' from Coast to Coast: The Early Days of Bluegrass, Volume 3* (Rounder 1015, 1983), 5.

DISCOGRAPHY, 1957–62

570420   Decca session; producer, Paul Cohen
Bradley Film & Recording Studio, 804 16th Ave. South, Nashville, Tenn.
April 20, 1957, 10:45 A.M.–1:45 P.M.

| NA 9813 | A FALLEN STAR (James Joiner) | 30327 | DL 4327, BCD 15423 |
| 102328 | Monroe-L | | |

NA 9814	FOUR WALLS (Marvin Moore–	30327	DL 4327, DL 7-5010, BCD 15423
102329	George Campbell)		
	Monroe-L		

Bill Monroe: m   Joe Stuart: g   Gordon Terry, Tommy Jackson: f
Don Stover: b   Bessie Lee Mauldin: sb

570514   Decca session; producer, Paul Cohen
Bradley Film & Recording Studio, 804 16th Ave. South, Nashville, Tenn.
May 14, 1957, 1:15–4:15 P.M.

| NA 9815 | A GOOD WOMAN'S LOVE (Cy Coben) | | DL 8731, VL 7-3870, |
| 102733 | Monroe-L | | MCAD 4-11048, BCD 15423 |

| NA 9816 | CRY CRY DARLIN' (Jimmy Newman) | | ED 2585, DL 8731, VL 7-3870, |
| 102734 | Monroe-L | | MCAD 4-11048, BCD 15423 |

NA 9817	I'M SITTIN' ON TOP OF THE WORLD	30486	DL 8731, VL 7-3870,
102735	(R. Henderson, J. Young, S. Lewis)		MCAD 4-11048,
	Monroe-L		BCD 15423, MCA 088 170109-2,
			MCA 088 113 207-2

Bill Monroe: m   Joe Stuart: g   Dale Potter, Gordon Terry, Tommy Jackson: f
Don Stover: b   Bessie Lee Mauldin: sb

570515.1[1]   Decca session; producer, Paul Cohen
Bradley Film & Recording Studio, 804 16th Ave. South, Nashville, Tenn.
May 15, 1957, 1:20–4:20 P.M.

| NA 9818 | OUT IN THE COLD WORLD (Joe Ahr) | | DL 8731, VL 3702, VL 7-3870, |
| 102736 | Monroe-L | | MCA 426, BCD 15423 |

| NA 9819 | ROANE COUNTY PRISON (Joe Ahr) | | ED 2585, DL 8731, VL 7-3870, |
| 102737 | Monroe-L | | MCA 2-4090, BCD 15423 |

| NA 9820
102738 | GOODBYE OLD PAL (Bill Monroe)
Monroe-L | | DL 8731, VL 7-3870, BCD 15423,
MCA 088 112 982-2,
MCA 088 113 207-2,
MCA 80004424-02 |

| Bill Monroe: m | Leslie Sandy: g | Dale Potter, Gordon Terry, Joe Stuart: f |
| Don Stover: b | Bessie Lee Mauldin: sb | |

570515.2 Decca session; producer, Paul Cohen
Bradley Film & Recording Studio, 804 16th Ave. South, Nashville, Tenn.
May 15, 1957[2]

| NA 9821
102739 | IN DESPAIR (Joe Ahr)
Monroe-LV/TC, Stover-LC, Stuart-B | | DL 8731, VL 7-3870, BCD 15423 |

| NA 9822
102740 | MOLLY AND TENBROOKS (Bill Monroe)
Monroe-L | 30486 | ED 2585, DL 8731, DL 7-5010,
DL 7-5025, BCD 15423,
MCA 088 170 109-2,
MCA 088 112 982-2,
MCA 088 113 207-2,
MCA 80004424-02 |

| NA 9823
102741 | COME BACK TO ME IN MY DREAMS (Bill Monroe)
Monroe-L | | DL 8731, VL 7-3870, MCA 2-4090,
BCD 15423 |

| Bill Monroe: m | Leslie Sandy: g | Dale Potter, Gordon Terry, Joe Stuart: f |
| Don Stover: b | Bessie Lee Mauldin: sb | |

571215 Decca session; producer, Paul Cohen
Bradley Film & Recording Studio, 804 16th Ave. South, Nashville, Tenn.
Dec. 15, 1957, 2:15–5:15 P.M.

| NA 10045
103937 | SALLY-JO (Rusty & Doug Kershaw)
Monroe-L | 30647 | DL 8731, VL 7-3870, BCD 15423 |

| NA 10046
103938 | BRAND NEW SHOES (Lester Blackwell)
Monroe-L | 30647 | ED 2585, DL 8731, VL 7-3870,
BCD 15423 |

| NA 10047
103939 | A LONESOME ROAD (TO TRAVEL) (Joe Earl Stuart Jr.)
Monroe-L | | DL 8731, VL 3702, BCD 15423 |

| Bill Monroe: m | Douglas Kershaw: g | Joe Stuart[3], Kenny Baker: f |
| Jimmy Elrod: b | Bessie Lee Mauldin: sb | |

580225   Decca session; producer, Owen Bradley
Bradley Film & Recording Studio, 804 16th Ave. South, Nashville, Tenn.
Feb. 25, 1958, 6:30–9:30 p.m.

NA 10163
104726
	I SAW THE LIGHT (Hank Williams)
	Mayfield-L, Monroe-T, Kenny Baker-B, Gordon Terry-BS
		DL8769, BCD 15423,
		  MCA 088 170 109-2,
		  MCA 088 112 982-2,
		  MCA 088 113 207-2,
		  MCA B0002907-2,
		  MCA 80004424-02

NA 10164 104727	LORD, BUILD ME A CABIN IN GLORY (Curtis Stewart) Mayfield-L, Monroe-T, Baker-B, Terry-BS	DL8769, BCD 15423
NA 10165 104728	LORD LEAD ME ON (Kenneth Tuttle) Mayfield-L, Monroe-T, Baker-B, Terry-BS	DL8769, BCD 15423, MCA B0002907-2

Bill Monroe: m   Edd Mayfield: g
                        Bessie Lee Mauldin: sb

580319   Decca session; producer, Owen Bradley
Bradley Film & Recording Studio, 804 16th Ave. South, Nashville, Tenn.
March 19, 1958

NA 10181 104729	PRECIOUS MEMORIES (-) Mayfield-L, Monroe-T, Kenny Baker-B, Culley Holt-BS	31107	ED 2610, DL 8769, BCD 15423, M18940, MCA B0002907-2
NA 10182 104730	I'LL MEET YOU IN THE MORNING (Albert E. Brumley) Monroe-LV/TC, Mayfield-LC, Baker-B, Holt-BS		DL 8769, DL 4173, MCAD 4-11048, BCD 15423
NA 10183 104731	LIFE'S RAILWAY TO HEAVEN (-) Monroe-LV/TC, Mayfield-LC, Baker-B, Holt-BS		ED 2610, DL 8769, BCD 15423, MCA B0002907-2

Bill Monroe: m   Edd Mayfield: g
                        Bessie Lee Mauldin: sb   Owen Bradley (except -82): organ

580320   Decca session; producer, Owen Bradley
Bradley Film & Recording Studio, 804 16th Ave. South, Nashville, Tenn.
March 20, 1958, 7:45–10:45 P.M.

NA 10184 104732	I'VE FOUND A HIDING PLACE (Albert E. Brumley) Monroe-LV/TC, Mayfield-LC, Kenny Baker-B, Culley Holt-BS	ED 2610, DL 8769, BCD 15423, MCA B0002907-2

| NA 10185 | JESUS HOLD MY HAND (Albert E. Brumley) | 31107 | ED 2610, DL 8769, BCD 15423, |
| 104733 | Mayfield-L, Monroe-T, Baker-B, Holt-BS | | MCA B0002907-2 |

| NA 10186 | I AM A PILGRIM (Merle Travis) | | DL 8769, BCD 15423, |
| 104734 | Monroe-L, Mayfield-T, Baker-B, Holt-BS | | MCA B0002907-2 |

Bill Monroe: m   Edd Mayfield: g
                                   Bessie Lee Mauldin: sb

580321[4]   Decca session; producer, Owen Bradley
Bradley Film & Recording Studio, 804 16th Ave. South, Nashville, Tenn.
March 21, 1958, 8–11 P.M.

| NA 10187 | WAYFARING STRANGER (-) | | DL 8769, DL 4172, BCD 15423, |
| 104735 | Monroe-LV/ TC, Mayfield-TV/LC, Kenny Baker-B, Culley Holt-BS | | SHA 604, MCA B0002907-2 |

| NA 10192 | A BEAUTIFUL LIFE (William Golden) | | DL 8769, BCD 15423, NM 8061-1 |
| 104736 | Mayfield-L, Monroe-T, Baker-B, Holt-BS | | |

| NA 10193 | HOUSE OF GOLD (Hank Williams) | | DL 8769, BCD 15423 |
| 104737 | Monroe-L | | |

Bill Monroe: m   Edd Mayfield: g
                                   Bessie Lee Mauldin: sb   Owen Bradley (except -92): organ

580408   Decca session; producer, Harold Bradley
Bradley Film & Recording Studio, 804 16th Ave. South, Nashville, Tenn.
April 8, 1958

| NA 10221-16 | PANHANDLE COUNTRY (Bill Monroe) | 30739 | DL 4601, BCD 15423, CCS-CD-19, |
| 104835-16 | Instrumental | | MCA 088 113 207-2 |

NA 10222	SCOTLAND (Bill Monroe)	30739	DL 4134, DL 4601, MCAD 10082,
104836	Instrumental		MCAD 4-11048, BCD 15423,
			OC-1001, MCA 088 170 109-2,
			SHA 604, MCA 088 112 982-2,
			MCA 088 113 207-2,
			MCA 80004424-02

Bill Monroe: m   Edd Mayfield: g   Kenny Baker, Bobby Hicks: f
Joe Drumright: b   Bessie Lee Mauldin: sb

580426   MCA reissue of radio broadcast
                    Grand Ole Opry, Nashville, Tenn.
                    April 26, 1958

[1]   MOLLY AND TENBROOKS (Bill Monroe)   MCAD 4-11048
                    Monroe-L

Bill Monroe: m   Edd Mayfield: g   (Kenny Baker?): f
(Joe Drumright?): b   (?): sb

581201[5]   Decca session; producer, Owen Bradley
                    Bradley Film & Recording Studio, 804 16th Ave. South, Nashville, Tenn.
                    Dec. 1, 1958, 9 A.M.–12:30 P.M.

NA 10516   GOTTA TRAVEL ON (Paul Clayton)   30809   ED 2674, DL 4327, DL 7-5010,
  106200   Monroe-L   BCD 15423, MCA 088 170 109-2,
                                                                                MCA3P 2999, MCA 088 112 982-2,
                                                                                MCA 088 113 207-2,
                                                                                MCA 80004424-02

NA 10517   NO ONE BUT MY DARLIN' (Bill Monroe)   30809   ED 2674, VL 3702, DL 7-5066,
  106201   Monroe-L   BCD 15423

NA 10518   BIG MON (Bill Monroe)   DL 4601, MCAD 4-11048,
  106209   Instrumental   BCD 15423, MCA 088 113 207-2

NA 10519   MONROE'S HORNPIPE (Bill Monroe)   DL 4601, BCD 15423
  106210   Instrumental

Bill Monroe: m   Vernon Crawford "Jack" Cooke: g   Bobby Hicks: f
Robert Lee Pennington: b   Bessie Lee Mauldin: sb

590000   Unidentified broadcast released on Kemtac
                    (Radio?), (location?)
                    (Date?)

[1]   GOTTA TRAVEL ON   K 3308
                    Monroe-L

Bill Monroe: m   (Jack Cooke?): g   (Bobby Hicks?): f
(Robert Lee Pennington?): b   (Bessie Lee Mauldin?): sb[6]

590130   Decca session; producer, Owen Bradley (also listed as "leader")
                  Bradley Film & Recording Studio, 804 16th Ave. South, Nashville, Tenn.
                  Jan. 30, 1959, 8:30 P.M.–12 midnight

NA 10592   WHEN THE PHONE RANG (Joe Hudgins)   VL 3702, BCD 15529
   106539   Monroe-L

NA 10593   TOMORROW I'LL BE GONE   30944   BS 3, ED 2674, BCD 15529
   106540   (Wilma Lee Cooper)
                  Monroe-L

NA 10594   DARK AS THE NIGHT, BLUE AS THE DAY   30944   BS 3, ED 2674, MCAD 4-11048,
   106541   (Bill Monroe)   BCD 15529
                  Monroe-L

NA 10595   STONEY LONESOME (Bill Monroe)   DL4601, BCD 15529
   106542   Instrumental

Bill Monroe: m   Jack Cooke: g   Bobby Hicks, Charles Smith: f
Robert Lee Pennington: b   Bessie Lee Mauldin: sb

590802   MCA reissue of concert
                  New River Ranch, Rising Sun, Md.
                  Aug. 2, 1959

[1]   JOHN HENRY (Traditional)   MCAD 4-11048, SF 40091[7]
                  Monroe-L

Bill Monroe: m   Jack Cooke: g   Kenny Baker: f
Joe Stuart: b   (Bessie Lee Mauldin?): sb

591125   Decca session; producer, Owen Bradley (also listed as "leader")
                  Bradley Film & Recording Studio, 804 16th Ave. South, Nashville, Tenn.
                  Nov. 25, 1959, 2:30–6:00 P.M.

NA 10902   LONESOME WIND BLUES (Wayne Raney)   31031   BS 3, ED 2713, BCD 15529
   108458   Monroe-L

NA 10903   THINKING ABOUT YOU (Lee Fikes & Bill Monroe)   BS 3, ED 2713, DL 4303,[8]
   108459   Monroe-L   BCD 15529

NA 10904   COME GO WITH ME (Marty Robbins)   31031   BS 3, BCD 15529
   108460   Monroe-L

Bill Monroe: m   Jack Cooke: g   Dale Potter, Benny Martin (-02): f
Joe Drumright: b   Bessie Lee Mauldin: sb

601130   Decca session; producer, Owen Bradley (also listed as "leader")
Bradley Film & Recording Studio, 804 16th Ave. South, Nashville, Tenn.
Nov. 30, 1960, 2:30–6 p.m.

11333 109959	SOLD DOWN THE RIVER (Vaughn Horton) Monroe-L		DL 4080, MCAD 4-11048, BCD 15529
11334 109960	LINDA LOU (Carl Butler) Monroe-L	31218	ED 2713, DL 4080, BCD 15529, MCA 088 113 207-2
11335 109961	YOU LIVE IN A WORLD ALL YOUR OWN (arr. & adptd. Bill Monroe) Monroe-L		ED 2724, DL 4080, BCD 15529
11336 109962	LITTLE JOE (Bill Monroe) Monroe-L		ED 2724, DL 4080, MCAD 4-11048, BCD 15529

Bill Monroe: m   Carl Butler: g   Dale Potter: f
Curtis McPeake: b   Bessie Lee Mauldin: sb

601201   Decca session; producer, Owen Bradley (also listed as "leader")
Bradley Film & Recording Studio, 804 16th Ave. South, Nashville, Tenn.
Dec. 1, 1960, 10:30 A.M.–1:30 P.M.

NA 11341 109920	PUT MY RUBBER DOLL AWAY (Geo. W. Edgins–Roy Acuff) Monroe-L	31218	ED 2713, DL 4080, BCD 15529
NA 11342 109921	SEVEN YEAR BLUES (Ira Louvin–Charles Louvin–Eddie Hill) Monroe-L		DL 4080, BCD 15529
NA 11343 109922	TIME CHANGES EVERYTHING (Tommy Duncan) Monroe-L		DL 4080, BCD 15529, MCA 088 113 207-2
NA 11344 109923	LONESOME ROAD BLUES (Bill Monroe) Monroe-L		DL 4080, MCAD 4-11048, BCD 15529, R142-04, MCA 088 113 207-2

Bill Monroe: m   Carl Butler: g   Dale Potter: f
Curtis McPeake: b   Bessie Lee Mauldin: sb

601203   Decca session; producer, Owen Bradley (also listed as "leader")
                   Bradley Film & Recording Studio, 804 16th Ave. South, Nashville, Tenn.
                   Dec. 3, 1960, noon–3 P.M.

NA 11345   BIG RIVER (John R. Cash)   DL 4080, BCD 15529
    109924   Monroe-L

NA 11346   FLOWERS OF LOVE (Ellen Martin–   31346   DL 4080, BCD 15529
    109925   Bill Monroe)
                  Monroe-L

NA 11347   IT'S MIGHTY DARK TO TRAVEL (Bill Monroe)   DL 4080, MCA 2-4090, BCD 15529
    109926   Monroe-L

NA 11348[9]   BLUE GRASS PART I (Bill Monroe)   31346   ED 2724, DL 4080, DL 4393,
    109927   Instrumental   MCA 2-4090, BCD 15529

Bill Monroe: m   Carl Butler: g   Dale Potter: f
Curtis McPeake: b   Paul Anthony "Tony" Ellis: sb

611109   Decca session; producer, Owen Bradley (also listed as "leader")
                   Bradley Film & Recording Studio, 804 16th Ave. South, Nashville, Tenn.
                   Nov. 9, 1961, 2–5 p.m.

NA 11803   LITTLE MAGGIE (Bill Monroe)   DL 4266, BCD 15529
    111388   Monroe-L

NA 11804   I'M GOING BACK TO OLD KENTUCKY (Bill Monroe)   DL 4266, MCA 2-4090,
    111389   Monroe-L   MCAD 4-11048, BCD 15529,
                                                                                     MCA 088 112 982-2,
                                                                                     MCA 088 113 207-2,
                                                                                     MCA 80004424-02

NA 11805   TOY HEART (Bill Monroe)   31409   DL 4266, MCAD 4-11048,
    111390   Monroe-LV/TC, Maynard-LC   BCD 15529, MCA 088 112 982-2,
                                                                                     MCA 088 113 207-2,
                                                                                     MCA 80004424-02

Bill Monroe: m   James H. "Jimmy" Maynard: g   Vassar Clements, Norman "Buddy" Spicher: f
Curtis McPeake: b   Bessie Lee Mauldin: sb

611110   Decca Session; Producer: Owen Bradley (also listed as "leader")
Bradley Film & Recording Studio, 804 16th Ave. South, Nashville, Tenn.
Nov. 10, 1961, 2–5 P.M.

NA 11806	SHADY GROVE (-)		DL 4266, BCD 15529
111391	Monroe-LV/TC, Maynard-LC, Williams-B		
NA 11807	NINE POUND HAMMER (-)		DL 4266, DL 4485, MCAD 4-11058,
111392	Monroe-L		BCD 15529, M19007
NA 11808	LIVE AND LET LIVE (Wiley Walker–Gene Sullivan)		DL 4266, BCD 15529,
111393	Monroe-LV/TC, Maynard-LC		MCA 088 113 207–2

Bill Monroe: m   Jimmy Maynard: g   Horace "Benny" Williams: f
Curtis McPeake: b   Bessie Lee Mauldin: sb

611130   Decca session; producer, Owen Bradley (also listed as "leader")
Bradley Film & Recording Studio, 804 16th Ave. South, Nashville, Tenn.
Nov. 30, 1961, 2-5:30 P.M.

NA 11819	DANNY BOY (Fred E. Weatherly)	31409	ED 2753, DL 4266, DL 7-5010,
111451	Monroe-L		BCD 15529, SHA 604
NA 11820	COTTON FIELDS (arr. adptd. Dave Fisher)		DL 4266, BCD 15529
111452	Monroe-LV/TC, Lester-LC, Ellis-B		
NA 11821	JOURNEY'S END (Pappy Stewart–Ernest Tubb)		DL 4266, BCD 15529
111453	Monroe-L		

Bill Monroe: m   Benny Williams: g   Buddy Spicher, Bobby Joe Lester: f
Tony Ellis: b   Bessie Lee Mauldin: sb

611204   Decca session; producer, Owen Bradley (also listed as "leader")
Bradley Film & Recording Studio, 804 16th Ave. South, Nashville, Tenn.
Dec. 4, 1961, 6:30–11:30 P.M.

NA 11822	JOHN HARDY (-)	ED 2724, DL 4266, BCD 15529
111454[10]	Instrumental	
NA 11823	BUGLE CALL RAG (Elmer Schoebel–Billy Meyers–Jack Pettis)	DL 4266, BCD 15529
111455	Instrumental	

NA 11824   OLD JOE CLARK (-)   DL 4266, BCD 15529,
   111456   Instrumental   MCA 088 113 207-2

Bill Monroe: m   Jimmy Maynard: g   Bobby Joe Lester: f
Tony Ellis: b   Bessie Lee Mauldin: sb

620000.1   Unidentified broadcast released on Kemtac
                (Radio, probably WSM),[11] (location unknown, probably Nashville)
                (Date?)

[1]   SHADY GROVE   K 3308
                Monroe-LV/TC, Cooke-LC, ?-B

Bill Monroe: m   (Jack Cooke?): g   (?): f
(?): b   (?): sb

620000.2   Unidentified broadcast released on Kemtac
                (Radio?), (location unknown)
                (Date?)

[1]   DARK AS THE NIGHT, BLUE AS THE DAY   K 3308
                Monroe-L

Bill Monroe: m   (Jack Cooke?): g   (Kenny Baker?): f
(?): b   (?): sb

620319.1   Capitol session (#10550) for Rose Maddox; producer, Ken Nelson
                Nashville, Tenn.
                March 19, 1962

37318-18   UNCLE PEN (Bill Monroe)   T1799, BCD 15743
                Rose Maddox-L

37319-5   FOOTPRINTS IN THE SNOW (trad.: arr. Rose Maddox)   T1799, BCD 15743
                Maddox-L

37320-15   BLUE MOON OF KENTUCKY (Bill Monroe)   T1799, BCD 15743
                Maddox-L

Bill Monroe: m   Red Smiley: g   Mac Magaha, Tommy Jackson: f
Don Reno: b   John Palmer: sb   Wayne Gailey (-18, -19): esg

620319.2   Capitol session (#10551) for Rose Maddox; producer, Ken Nelson
Nashville, Tenn.
March 19, 1962

37317-17   MY ROSE OF OLD KENTUCKY (Bill Monroe)   T1799, BCD 15743,
Rose Maddox-L   Hip-O 314 564682 2

37321-17[12]   MOLLY AND TENBROOKS (Bill Monroe)   T1799, BCD 15743
Maddox-L

Bill Monroe: m   Red Smiley: g   Mac Magaha, Tommy Jackson: f
Don Reno: John Palmer: sb   Wayne Gailey: esg (not audible)

620425   Decca session; producer, Owen Bradley
Columbia Recording Studio, 804 16th Ave. South, Nashville, Tenn.
April 25, 1962, 10:15 A.M.–1:15 P.M.

NA 12025   THERE WAS NOTHING WE COULD DO   31487   DL 4382, BCD 15529
112147   (Chuck Carson)
Buchanan-L, Monroe-T

NA 12026   I WAS LEFT ON THE STREET (Chuck Carson–Bill Monroe)   DL 4382, BCD 15529
112148   Monroe-LV/TC, Buchanan-LC

NA 12027   CHEAP LOVE AFFAIR (Chuck Carson–Bill Monroe)   DL 4382, BCD 15529
112149   Monroe-LV/TC, Buchanan-LC

Bill Monroe: m   Franklin G. "Frank" Buchanan: g   Benny Williams, Harold "Red" Stanley: f
Tony Ellis: b   Bessie Lee Mauldin: sb

620426   Decca session; producer, Owen Bradley (also listed as "leader")
Columbia Recording Studio, 804 16th Ave. South, Nashville, Tenn.
April 26, 1962, 2:30–5:30 P.M.

NA 12030   WHEN THE BEES ARE IN THE HIVE (Alfred Bryan–Kerry Mills)   DL 4382, BCD 15529
112152   Monroe-L

NA 12031   BIG BALL IN BROOKLYN (Bill Monroe)   BCD 15529, CCS-CD-19
112153   Monroe-LV/TC, Buchanan-LC

NA 12032   COLUMBUS STOCKADE BLUES (-)   DL 4382, BCD 15529,
112154   Monroe-LV/TC, Buchanan-LC   MCA 088 113 207-2

Bill Monroe: m   Frank Buchanan: g   Benny Williams, Red Stanley: f
Tony Ellis: b   Bessie Lee Mauldin: sb

620503   Decca session; producer, Harry Silverstein (Owen Bradley listed as "leader")
Columbia Recording Studio, 804 16th Ave. South, Nashville, Tenn.
May 3, 1962, 10 A.M.–1 P.M.

NA 12045   BLUE RIDGE MOUNTAIN BLUES (Bill Monroe)   31456[13]   ED 2753, DL 4382, BCD 15529
112210   Buchanan-L, Monroe-T

NA 12046   HOW WILL I EXPLAIN ABOUT YOU   31456   ED 2753, DL 4382, BCD 15529
112211   (Bill Monroe)
Monroe-LV/TC, Buchanan-LC

NA 12047   FOGGY RIVER (Fred Rose)   DL 4382, BCD 15529
112212   Buchanan-L, Monroe-T

Bill Monroe: m   Frank Buchanan: g   Benny Williams, Red Stanley: f
Tony Ellis: b   Bessie Lee Mauldin: sb

620510   Decca session; producer, Harry Silverstein (Owen Bradley listed as "leader")
Columbia Recording Studio, 804 16th Ave. South, Nashville, Tenn.
May 10, 1962, 2–5 P.M.

NA 12052   THE OLD COUNTRY BAPTIZING (Jim Shumate Sr.–Verlon Bryontt)   MCA 426, BCD 15529
112226   Buchanan-L, Monroe-T, Raymond O. "Ray" Edenton-B, Culley Holt-BS

NA 12053   I FOUND THE WAY (Rev. L. E. Green–Adger M. Pace)   DL 4537, BCD 15529
112227   Buchanan-L, Monroe-T, Edenton-B, Holt-BS

NA 12054   THIS WORLD IS NOT MY HOME (-)   MCA 426, BCD 15529
112228   Monroe-LV/TC, Buchanan-LC, Edenton-B, Holt-BS

Bill Monroe: m   Frank Buchanan: g
Bessie Lee Mauldin: sb

620516   Decca session; producer, Harry Silverstein (Owen Bradley listed as "leader")
Columbia Recording Studio, 804 16th Ave. South, Nashville, Tenn.
May 16, 1962, 10 A.M.–1 P.M.

NA 12067   WAY DOWN DEEP IN MY SOUL (-)   DL 4537, BCD 15529
112252   Buchanan-L, Monroe-T, Red Stanley-B, Culley Holt-BS

NA 12068   DRIFTING TOO FAR FROM THE SHORE (-)   DL 4537, BCD 15529,
112253   Buchanan-L, Monroe-T, Stanley-B, Holt-BS   MCA 088 113 207-2

NA 12069   GOING HOME (Carl Tipton)   31943   ED 2792, DL 4537, BCD 15529
   112254 Buchanan-L, Monroe-T, Stanley-B, Holt-BS

Bill Monroe: m   Frank Buchanan: g
Tony Ellis: b   Bessie Lee Mauldin: sb

620517   Decca session; producer, Harry Silverstein (Owen Bradley listed as "leader")
                Columbia Recording Studio, 804 16th Ave. South, Nashville, Tenn.
                May 17, 1962, 6:30–9:30 P.M.

NA 12073   ON THE JERICHO ROAD (-)   ED 2792, DL 4537, BCD 15529
   112258 Buchanan-L, Monroe-T, Red Stanley-B, Culley Holt-BS

NA 12074   WE'LL UNDERSTAND IT BETTER (-)   DL 4537, BCD 15529
   112259 Monroe-LV/TC, Buchanan-LC, Stanley-B, Holt-BS

NA 12075   SOMEBODY TOUCHED ME (Bill Monroe–Harold Donny)   MCA 426, BCD 15529,
   112260 Buchanan-L, Monroe-T, Stanley-B, Holt-BS   MCA 088 113 207-2

Bill Monroe: m   Frank Buchanan: g
Tony Ellis: b   Bessie Lee Mauldin: sb

620903   Shanachie video reissue of shot from movie *High Lonesome Sound;* producer, John Cohen
                County Courthouse, Hazard, Ky.
                Sept. 3, 1962

[1]   JOHN HENRY   [movie]   SHA 1404, PALM VHS 3039-3/2
                Monroe-L

Bill Monroe: m   Frank Buchanan: g[14]   Benny Williams: f
Ray Goins: b   Melvin Goins: sb

621123.1   Decca session; producer, Harry Silverstein (Owen Bradley listed as "leader")
                Columbia Recording Studio, 804 16th Ave. South, Nashville, Tenn.
                Nov. 23, 1962, 11 A.M.–2 P.M.

NA 12234   CARELESS LOVE (-)   DL 4382, DL 4469, BCD 15529
   112800 Monroe-L

NA 12235   I'M SO LONESOME I COULD CRY (H. Williams)   DL 4382, BCD 15529,
   112801 Monroe-L   MCA 088 113 207-2

NA 12236   JIMMY BROWN THE NEWSBOY (A. P. Carter)   31802   BCD 15529, MCA 088 112 982-2,
   112802   Monroe-L   MCA 088 113 207-2,
                                                                                    MCA 80004424-02

Bill Monroe: m   Joe Stuart: g   Kenny Baker: f
Lonnie Hoppers: b   Bessie Lee Mauldin: sb

621123.2   Decca session; producer, Harry Silverstein (Owen Bradley listed as "leader")
                Columbia Recording Studio, 804 16th Ave. South, Nashville, Tenn.
                Nov. 23, 1962, 3–6 P.M.

NA 12237   PASS ME NOT (Bill Monroe)   MCA 426, BCD 15529
   112803   Monroe-L

NA 12238   THE GLORY LAND WAY (-)   DL 4537, BCD 15529
   112804   Monroe-L

NA 12239   FARTHER ALONG (Bill Monroe)   ED 2792, DL 4537, BCD 15529
   112805   Monroe-L

Bill Monroe: m   Joe Stuart (-38, -39),   Kenny Baker, Joe Stuart (-37): f
Lonnie Hoppers (-38, -39): b   Lonnie Hoppers (-37): g
                                     Bessie Lee Mauldin: sb

621206   Decca session; producer, Harry Silverstein (Owen Bradley listed as "leader")
                Columbia Recording Studio, 804 16th Ave. South, Nashville, Tenn.
                Dec. 6, 1962, 10 A.M.–1 P.M.

NA 12257   BIG SANDY RIVER (Bill Monroe–   31487   ED 2753, DL 4382, MCAD 4-11048,
   112859   Kenny Baker)   BCD 15529, CCS-CD-19
              Instrumental

NA 12258   BAKER'S BREAKDOWN (Bill Monroe–Kenny Baker)   DL 4382, BCD 15529
   112860   Instrumental

NA 12259   DARLING COREY (Bill Monroe)   31596   MCAD 4-11048, BCD 15529
   112861   Monroe-L

Bill Monroe: m   Joe Stuart: g   Kenny Baker: f
Lonnie Hoppers: b   Bessie Lee Mauldin: sb

621210 Decca session; producer, Harry Silverstein (Owen Bradley listed as "leader")
Columbia Recording Studio, 804 16th Ave. South, Nashville, Tenn.
Dec. 10, 1962, 10 A.M.–1 P.M.

NA 12269	CINDY (arr. adptd. Bill Monroe)	31802	BCD 15529
112922	Monroe-L		
NA 12270	MASTER BUILDER (J. W. Wilson-Wes Martin)	31943	ED 2792, DL 4537, BCD 15529
112923	Monroe-L		
NA 12271	LET ME REST AT THE END OF MY JOURNEY (-)		DL 4537, MCA 2–4090, BCD 15529
112924	Monroe-L		

Bill Monroe: m   Joe Stuart: g   Kenny Baker: f
Lonnie Hoppers: b   Bessie Lee Mauldin: sb

Notes

1. More recently discovered Decca Record Personnel sheets show that the six tunes recorded at this and the following session, previously listed in a single session, were in fact recorded at two sessions. The information on the sheets, however, contains confusing anomalies. The date given for this session is May 5. The same date was typed on the sheet for the following session, then the 5 was typed over and the number 15 substituted. We hypothesize that 15 is the correct date and 5 is a mistake for this session, as that chronology preserves the numerical sequence of the masters.

2. The times given on the Decca Record Personnel sheet for this session present a further confusing anomaly because they are 1:30–4:30, completely overlapping with the times presented for the previous session. It's most likely that this was an evening session.

3. The Decca Record Personnel sheet lists Stuart, Baker, Elrod, and Kershaw as playing guitar; Monroe was on mandolin, and Mauldin on bass. Previous versions of this discography listed Dale Potter as being on fiddle and did not include Mauldin on bass.

4. The change in the date of this session, the change of the Nashville master number for "Wayfaring Stranger," and the identification of Mauldin as bassist for this and the previous two sessions reflect new information in recently discovered Decca Record Personnel sheets.

5. This appears to have been the first Decca stereo session. Only the first two masters were issued by Decca in stereo mixes; only the Bear Family reissue has all four in stereo (see notes to MCAD 4–11048).

6. Personnel conjecture, but the sound of this recording is very close to that of the recording as released on Decca.

7. See note 14 below.

8. The release of -03 on DL 4303, a simulated "live" LP, includes an added applause track.

9. -48 is entitled "Blue Grass Twist" on ED 2724 and MCA 2-4090.

10. Some MCA information lists 111459, -60, and -61 as New York master numbers for these recordings.

11. T. Tommy Cutrer introduces the performance, suggesting that this is a live recording from the Grand Ole Opry.

12. There is a break in master numbers here, but the recordings are consecutive.

13. When Decca first released this single, the band was identified on its labels as "Bill Monroe and The Bluegrass Ramblers." The error was corrected in later pressings.

14. In his notes to Smithsonian/Folkways SF CD 40091, John Cohen describes the band seen in the brief segment of his movie as being the Lonesome Pine Fiddlers. However two of the musicians listed here—Buchanan and Williams—were regular members of the Blue Grass Boys at this time and are visible in Cohen's movie and photo images from this date. Brothers Ray and Melvin Goins were members of the Lonesome Pine Fiddlers at this time, which explains Cohen's comment. In his still photos from the same event—*Sing Out!* 13 (Feb.–Mar. 1963): 5 and *There Is No Eye: John Cohen Photographs* (New York: Powerhouse, 2001)—it is Bessie Lee Mauldin rather than Melvin Goins playing bass. Evidently, Ray Goins played the entire show with Monroe while Melvin Goins played only part of it. Cohen's film (1964, distributed by Brandon Films) and the video releases of it do not include Monroe's sound at this event. According to Mike Seeger, "That brief Monroe footage is not synchronized. The sound is from one of my New River Ranch tapes, I think" (email to Sandy Rothman, Jan. 29, 2004). The track of Monroe on SF CD 40091 is from session 590802. It is not the same as the sound track in this segment of Cohen's film, which remains untraced.

7

"DEVIL'S DREAM": 1963–72

As late as mid-1962 Bill Monroe had not appeared at a folk revival event of any sort. By this time other leading bands, particularly those of Flatt and Scruggs and the Stanley Brothers, were familiar figures at folk festivals and college concerts. Monroe's late entry into this market began in the late summer of 1962 when he was interviewed by Ralph Rinzler, a key figure in the folk revival movement through his work with the New York City club, the Friends of Old Time Music, and membership in the best-known folk revival bluegrass band, the Greenbriar Boys. Rinzler had deep appreciation of Monroe's music. He had been attending Blue Grass Boys concerts at New River Ranch, a country music park near Washington, D.C., since the mid-1950s, and knew more than most young fans of the movement just how important Monroe was.

Monroe's aversion to writers was such that he once threatened to break his mandolin over one's head if his name were mentioned in a book, so Rinzler's article, based on his interview, was the first serious piece on the artist. It appeared in the January 1963 issue of *Sing Out!* magazine. That same month Rinzler helped Monroe get his first folk festival booking, at the University of Chicago's Folk Festival on February 1 and 2, and his first solo concert in New York City on February 8. Rinzler continued to use his extensive contacts and credibility to find Monroe revival jobs, including a stint at the Ash Grove in Hollywood and an appearance at the Newport, Rhode Island, Folk Festival. Monroe was impressed with the new bookings, and in May 1963 Rinzler moved to Nashville to take over his management.

At the time Rinzler came to Nashville, Monroe was being booked by Jim Denny's talent agency, which handled most of the industry's hottest stars. Much of the work Denny found for Monroe, though, was on package tours with people like Johnny Cash.[1] He hadn't, for example, thought enough of Monroe to place a display advertisement on his behalf in the 1963 issue of *Billboard* that featured country music. Rinzler, however, had contacts, and to some extent credibility, and began to set up a series of bookings to supplement Denny's efforts.

Monroe was grateful to Rinzler for opening new areas of booking and sensed that Denny's people didn't have much of a handle on the folk revival business. He was content, therefore, to have Rinzler and Denny both booking for him, each dealing with different parts of his audience. Rinzler opened an office—Bill Monroe Associates—with himself as manager and WSM veteran Ken Marvin as "exclusive agent." Monroe took Rinzler on a tour of the offices on what was then the developing Music Row so he could meet song publishers and other bookers curious about the folk revival and Rinzler's role in it. Rinzler was also concerned with revitalizing Monroe's country music park at Bean Blossom, Indiana, and exploring talent possibilities there.

Soon Rinzler also began to take a hand in planning Monroe's recordings. When a session was being planned he would meet with Monroe, the Decca A&R man Harry Silverstein, and usually someone from Denny's publishing company, Cedarwood, to talk over possible tunes. His concern was to push Silverstein and Monroe toward material better-suited to Monroe's style, songs that his new, college-age, urban audiences would appreciate. "Bill was quick to figure out how to work the college audiences," Rinzler recalled. "He was such an experienced showman to start with." Although Silverstein, Denny's representative, or Rinzler himself would often suggest items for Monroe to record, the final decision was always Monroe's. "Bill did what he wanted. There was no imposing of material on him."[2] For his part, Rinzler suggested Monroe re-record some of his classics that had been out of print for years, and some of those suggestions he accepted. Others, such as a joint studio LP with guitarist Doc Watson, with whom Rinzler also worked, did not bear fruit.

Rinzler was successful in finding new venues, for example, the Newport Folk Festival, but bookings were not always lucrative and it was not easy to keep the band together. By September 1963, beset by pressures from his own band and from his work with the Newport Folk festival, Rinzler returned to New York, where he continued to manage Monroe for the folk music circuit. He also began to work on a series of well-planned reissue LPs of Monroe's earlier work.

Working through Decca's New York office and their senior producer, jazz legend Milt Gabler, Rinzler was able to explore the backlog of unissued Monroe tapes in the New York files—tapes sent from Nashville before the office there began to retain them. At first, he said, the albums were designed to show Harry Silverstein the kind of material Monroe could do best and help him in designing the repertoires of new albums. The tapes were meant to be models. Thus as Monroe continued to work on new sets in Nashville, Decca also issued several influential compilations Rinzler had done of well-selected material, some of which had not appeared before. "New John Henry Blues," done in 1954 but unissued, was such a strong performance that Rinzler convinced Decca to issue it on a single, the flip side of Bill Keith's showcase "Devil's Dream." The albums Rinzler edited included *Bill Monroe Sings Country Songs* (1964), *Bluegrass Instrumentals* (1965), *The High Lonesome Sound* (1966), *Bill and Charlie Monroe* (1969), *A Voice from On High* (1969), and *Bill Monroe's Country Music Hall of Fame* (1971).

Such albums coupled with Rinzler's continuing efforts to expose Monroe to a younger, more national audience soon had an effect. While he maintained his base and bookings through his longtime country music channels, Monroe was also getting work through the developing bluegrass and, after 1965, festival circuit. His schedule was becoming fuller and more complex, and by 1964 he was touring to all parts of the country. He spent so much time on the road that he finally bought a bus to make life a little easier for himself and the band.

During the 1960s Monroe took advantage of the geographical spread of bluegrass to new regions—a trend that continued after the folk revival movement petered out—to draw into his working band young musicians from many locations. They included Bill Keith and Peter Rowan from Boston; Lamar Grier from Washington; Byron Berline from Oklahoma; Sandy Rothman, Richard Greene, and Roland White from California; and Del McCoury from Pennsylvania. When he was between full-time band members, which happened a lot in the 1960s, he drew on a second pool of musicians for gigs and recording sessions. These Nashville-area musicians, slightly older and more seasoned, tended to be from the Upper South and had grown up with the music firsthand. They included Joe Stuart, Benny Williams, Buddy Spicher, Jimmy Maynard, and others. There was not so much a North-South or urban-rural distinction between the two groups as there was one of age and educational background. Many younger ones were college students, graduates, or dropouts such as Bill Keith, Richard Greene, Byron Berline, and Don Lineberger. In addition, Bill's son, James William Monroe, became a band member during this period. As Monroe worked with the new Blue Grass Boys he continued, as ever, to teach and challenge them, and he learned from them as well.

Monroe was soon involved in festivals devoted exclusively to bluegrass. He was the central figure at the first festival promoted by Carlton Haney, the Roanoke Blue Grass Festival in Fincastle, Virginia, in 1965, and he continued to be instrumental in helping the nascent bluegrass festival movement.[3] He soon developed his own festival at Bean Blossom in 1967, which became the best known and best attended of such events. New visibility and new audiences also brought new honors. In 1969 Monroe was made an honorary Kentucky Colonel, and in the fall of 1970 he was elected to the Country Music Hall of Fame.

Monroe's recorded repertoire in this period contains older, more traditional numbers and more songs by other artists than his earlier recordings. His own songwriting slacked off, both in vocal and instrumental categories. Much "new" material is also a reworking of older tunes such as those he learned from his Uncle Pen. There were sessions when he seemed to fumble for direction, and on other occasions he rushed into the studio with new musicians who had been given only a short time to learn the songs. Decca responded to some of this uncertainty by leaving unissued a much larger percentage of his work than in the 1950s. There would be no more chart hits during this period, but some recordings were destined to be classics: "Roll On, Buddy, Roll On," "There's an Old, Old House," "Blue Night," "The Gold Rush," "Walls of Time," "Crossing the Cumberlands," "Walk Softly on My Heart," "With Body and Soul," and others. For an era that began with such uncertainty it turned out to be another rich chapter in one of the most distinctive forms of American music.

ROMANCING THE FOLK

The growing impact of the northern urban interest in bluegrass began to affect Monroe in the three months following his last session, yet despite Rinzler's efforts he was still lagging behind Flatt and Scruggs in festival appearances.[4] They had been at the first Newport festival in 1959, and in December 1962 they were achieving national fame through the *Beverly Hillbillies* television show and its theme, "The Ballad of Jed Clampett." Rinzler had known and admired Monroe's music since 1954 and was a member of a young band, the Greenbriar Boys, that emulated much of it, but he did not get to know him well until August 1962, when he began to interview him for an article in *Sing Out!* magazine, the leading journal of the folk revival movement. After gaining Monroe's confidence, Rinzler began talking with him at length about his music and helping set up dates for the band at folk venues.

Although Monroe was being managed by Jim Denny's Nashville agency, Denny's people were still geared to putting him on traditional country shows and package shows. "Jim Denny's crew was not doing well with the college people," Rinzler recalled.[5]

During one of their telephone conversations early in 1963, Rinzler suggested with some trepidation that Monroe might want to listen to a young banjo player named Bill Keith. In almost every way Keith was a product of the folk revival. Born in Boston in 1939, he grew up playing tenor and plectrum banjo and performed with a Dixieland band. In 1957 he got his first five-string banjo, and he immediately bought Pete Seeger's instruction book when he heard Seeger perform with the Weavers. He heard his first Earl Scruggs record in 1958. As Keith continued to develop his skills around New England he began playing with a local fiddler from Nova Scotia, June Hall. "I would go down there Wednesday nights," he remembers, "and play banjo to her fiddle, and it just occurred to me that it might be possible" to work out what would eventually be called a "chromatic" style. Following the fiddle-tune patterns he heard June Hall play, he worked out a version of "Devil's Dream." "Then for a long time I didn't put it to use in any other tunes," but he finally worked up an arrangement of "Sailor's Hornpipe," another venerable New England fiddle tune.[6]

Playing those two songs in a medley, Bill Keith won the Philadelphia Folk Festival banjo contest in September 1962, and he soon was playing with Red Allen, Frank Wakefield, and Tom Morgan in the Washington area. One night he met Earl Scruggs and showed him some tablatures of Scruggs's tunes that he had written out while learning the style. Scruggs, impressed, invited Keith to come to Nashville and visit backstage at the Opry. According to Jim Rooney, Monroe and Kenny Baker heard Keith playing "Devil's Dream" and "Sailor's Hornpipe" and were impressed as well. Thus when Rinzler called, Monroe was familiar with Keith's name. Monroe told Rinzler, though, that he had invited Jack Cooke's banjo player, Del McCoury, to come to Nashville to try out for the Blue Grass Boys. Rinzler suggested to Monroe, who had been especially impressed with Del's singing, that the solution to the problem of having two banjo pickers in the band was to bring in Keith as his new banjo star and switch Del to guitar so as to take advantage of his singing.

McCoury was born in 1939 in Bakersville, North Carolina, and grew up in York County, Pennsylvania, an area with a surprisingly strong country and bluegrass scene. Learning to play the banjo from Scruggs's records, he'd also developed into a good straight-ahead singer and after an apprenticeship with local bands was discovered by Monroe while playing in a club in Baltimore with Jack Cooke's Virginia Playboys. It was January 1963, and Monroe needed a guitarist and a banjoist for the Blue Grass Boys at his February 8 concert in New York for the Friends of Old Time Music; knowing Cooke, he invited him and McCoury to come along. Afterward, Monroe suggested that McCoury come to Nashville for a full-time job but then asked that he switch to guitar. Monroe needed Bill Keith as his new banjo player and he also needed a strong singer to help him on vocal choruses. "Up until that time [joining Monroe]," Del recalls, "I had never really seriously tried to do anything with a guitar because I wasn't interested that much in it. But Bill said, 'No, I'll tell you what. If you can make the grade in two weeks, I'll hire you.' I knew I was on a trial basis so I really had to work at it. I had played with plenty of guitar players that played behind the beat—they just couldn't get on top of it. So I think the biggest thing on my mind was to play on top of the beat and play to Bill's mandolin; to his rhythm lead."[7]

The deal was done. Within ten days after joining Monroe, Keith joined the band in the studio for the session on March 20, 1963. Because Monroe didn't like the idea of having two Bills in the band, he insisted on calling Keith "Brad," a shortening of his middle name, Bradford. With Benny Williams and then Jackie Phelps brought in as studio substitutes for McCoury (unable to play at the March sessions because he was not yet in the union), and Kenny Baker, with the band since the previous fall, still playing fiddle, the band ripped into a hot new set of instrumentals. "Devil's Dream" and "Sailor's Hornpipe" were the two specialties that Keith had already developed for his new style. Indeed, he sometimes played them together as a medley in the key of A. For this session, however, "Sailor's Hornpipe" was moved up to B flat to accommodate Baker, who found his fiddle solo worked better in that key. "Salt Creek" was another that Bill Keith brought to the band; he had learned it in Boston from another of his banjo mentors, the former Blue Grass Boy Don Stover. A traditional fiddle tune known as "Salt River" once recorded by Clark Kessinger in the 1920s, its name was changed for the March 20 recording because Monroe's latest single was "Big Sandy River," and the company feared customers would confuse the two. The piece has become a favorite in bluegrass banjo repertoires and has been often recorded.

At the March 27 recording session, "Pike County Breakdown" dramatized more than any how different Keith's style was from that of Scruggs. Along with the other sides from this session, it marked the beginning of a major shift in bluegrass banjo playing from the classic three-finger style Scruggs had established a generation before. "Pike County" had first been recorded by Bill in 1952, but now he wanted to do a new version of it. In the first part Keith duplicates Scruggs's version of the tune and then goes on to do it in his own style. This was the way Monroe had asked him to play it. Possibly because it seemed to be a deliberate parody the version was not issued until a Japanese set included it years later.

"Santa Claus" is a version of another old fiddle tune, "I Don't Love Nobody." Bill had learned it from an old-time fiddler who lived in the northern Kentucky–southern Indiana region. Keith remembered that Monroe usually played the tune in a different way from that of the March 27 recording. "Every other time he played it, except the time it was recorded, it was up-beats he was playing it in, and I copied the rhythm in my banjo break from what he was doing on the mandolin; and then so did the fiddle; and so when we got to the studio, he said, 'Well, I'm not going to do it, everybody else is doing it.'"[8]

"Were You There?" was a remake of a quartet version of an old spiritual Bill had done in 1941 and often performed on the Opry. It was intended for the new gospel album but for some reason not used and would not be issued for five years. Monroe's "Shenandoah Breakdown," like "Salt Creek," was destined to become another favorite with young banjo pickers seeking to emulate Bill Keith's style, but it was not issued on LP until 1985 and appeared only as a single in September 1964.

In this year of festival jobs the band did not get into Nashville studios for any formal recordings between March 27 and the end of the year. Fortunately, a series of live tapes, not the least of which was made at Newport, provide a chronicle of the band's sound that year. Keith sparked the buzz about Bill Monroe's new band in the spring of 1963, but listeners also noticed Del McCoury's fine voice as he become familiar with Bill's repertoire and began singing the old duets. Kenny Baker's reputation as a hot fiddler also helped. High-quality portable tape recorders, open-reel machines, were widely available (the cassette era didn't begin until the 1970s). Monroe's fans and followers set up microphones onstage next to the public address mike (multi-mike public address technology was rare) or plugged them into soundboards at Monroe appearances. Some recordings from the period were released years later in two packages Rinzler edited for Smithsonian/Folkways, and others were published on bootleg albums.

In May 1963 Monroe traveled to California to appear at a number of venues that were new to him. He appeared with the

Blue Grass Boys at the UCLA Folk Festival from May 3 through 5, an event organized by folklore professor D. K. Wilgus, a pioneer in the study of country music. Monroe and the band stayed in southern California after the festival except for a trip on May 10 and 11 to the Bay Area for concerts in Santa Clara and Berkeley. Returning to Hollywood, they began a week-long engagement on May 14 at the Ash Grove, the West Coast's premier folk venue, where the producer of *The Beverly Hillbillies* "discovered" Flatt and Scruggs. They followed Doc Watson, whom Rinzler booked to appear there the previous week with Clarence Ashley and Roscoe Holcomb.

It was at the Ash Grove that Monroe, at Rinzler's suggestion, first began doing duets with Watson. The two worked so well together that Rinzler tried to work out a contract agreement between Decca and Watson's label, Vanguard, so the pair could do an album, but he never succeeded. Informal recordings of the two of them survive, however, and have been released commercially. Two cuts from what may have well have been their first public performance together on May 14 at the Ash Grove, "You Won't Be Satisfied That Way" and "Memories of You," were released on Smithsonian/Folkways. The Monroe-Watson duets at the Ash Grove were a nightly feature. Five more pieces from May 17 were also issued on Smithsonian/Folkways. Four further duets by Bill and Doc, also recorded during the week, were released on a bootleg LP album.

Also recorded at the Ash Grove stand were a few cuts of Bill with the Blue Grass Boys, later released on Smithsonian/Folkways. These include versions of "True Life Blues" and "Raw Hide." On May 19 Bill and Doc appeared at the Monterey Folk Festival in a workshop moderated by D. K. Wilgus that included a version of "Get Up John" by Bill and Doc as well as Monroe's introduction of the tune.

Del McCoury remembers bruising cross-country trips to California, including one when "we played one club in California for two or three weeks and the owner gave him a bad check or something," which caused several band members to quit for steadier day jobs.[9] Whether McCoury is describing the trip in May or the other in December is beside the point because members left the band after both gigs. Kenny Baker left the Blue Grass Boys when they returned to Nashville from California at the end of May. During June the band sometimes played without a fiddler. Benny Williams or Buddy Pendleton filled in on some dates; a friend of Del's, Billy Sage, played some others; and then Del brought in another friend from his Baltimore days, Billy Baker, Kenny's cousin and a fine fiddler himself. Monroe tried to hire Baker on a permanent basis, but

he didn't want to move to Nashville. Fortunately, he performed at several venues that were recorded and from which releases eventually came.

Not long after they returned to Nashville from California, Decca released Bill's latest LP, *Blue Grass Special,* which featured recordings made in 1962. There would not be another LP featuring contemporary secular recordings by Bill Monroe and the Blue Grass Boys released again until 1967, but significant recordings were being made.

Of all the festival dates, perhaps the most symbolic was the prestigious Newport Folk Festival, which Monroe played for the first time in July 26, 1963, sharing the stage with Doc Watson and Bob Dylan. On the way up to Newport the band stopped off in New York to tape a spot for Oscar Brand's transcribed radio show, *The World of Folk Music,* and did versions of "Devil's Dream," "I Am a Pilgrim," and "Mule Skinner Blues" before moving on to Newport.

At the time, Vanguard Records was taping all the Newport concerts, and tapes were made of all of the shows by the Blue Grass Boys that year. Although the Vanguard files showed the tapes as existing, a search of the tape files could not turn them up; for years it was assumed they had been destroyed, lost, or stolen. Finally, in the summer of 2002, Bear Family owner Richard Weize discovered the tape boxes misfiled in the Los Angeles archives of MCA. Notes on the boxes indicate that they had for some reason been sent to the American Federation of Musicians local office in Nashville. Puzzled, the AFM forwarded them to MCA, where Monroe was still under contract. The tapes, seventeen tunes and some engrossing stage chatter, were finally leased by Bear Family and released on a CD in the spring of 2003.

The tapes document one of Monroe's best bands and one that never recorded commercially. Enhanced by David Gahr's remarkable and seldom seen photographs of the band on-stage, the album includes both complete shows. Del McCoury plays guitar and sings, Bill Keith is on the banjo, Billy Baker is on fiddle, and Bessie Lee Mauldin is on bass. Both Keith and McCoury recorded with Monroe but were never in the studio together with him. They did record later with Baker for the Rebel label.[10]

On the first show the Blue Grass Boys are introduced by Sen. Claiborne Pell of Rhode Island, a testimony to the importance the Newport organizers placed on the appearance. The predictable standards "Muleskinner" and "Uncle Pen" follow, with McCoury and Keith singing on the latter's chorus. Then came Keith's "Devil's Dream," which he recorded some four months earlier and was about to be released as a single. After a drag-race version of "Molly and Tenbrooks," another predictable standard that was also a favorite with folk audiences, Monroe introduces his "new bass singer" for the Blue Grass Quartet: Ralph Rinzler. They do a fine quartet version of "I Am a Pilgrim," winning the biggest hand of the night. The set concludes with a blistering version of "Raw Hide" on which Keith's breathtaking solo shows how well he absorbed some of the older Scruggs style in addition to creating his own.

The set of the following day, July 27, was a workshop rather than a concert. It began with Monroe complaining that he was nervous because he hadn't had much breakfast. Then Billy Baker needs to replace a string on his fiddle, and to kill time Monroe does a solo version of "Paddy on the Turnpike." Keith then comes forward for another of his specialties, "Pike County Breakdown," and all join in for a second version of "Raw Hide." After a couple of other standards, an unusual segment occurs when Rinzler comes out to coordinate a question-and-answer session between Bill and the audience. When someone asks Monroe if he ever sings ballads, he segues into a haunting solo version (accompanied by guitar) of "Pretty Fair Maiden in the Garden," an old ballad he had not yet recorded. "Salt Creek," already a Keith favorite even though the recording hadn't been released, follows and shows how impressed Monroe was with his new banjo player. "Lonesome Road Blues" concludes the set.

Although Monroe tried to convince Billy Baker to stay on with him, Baker didn't wish to relocate to Nashville. So after the band returned from Newport at the end of July, Joe Stuart, who'd played off and on as a Blue Grass Boy since 1955, rejoined as fiddler. Monroe toured all fall with this band. A recording of one of their shows, done November 16 in Wooster in western Massachusetts, was released by Acoustic Disc in 2004. The setting was the venerable old Mechanics Hall, an 1857 music hall that billed itself as "one of the world's finest concert halls" and "the nation's finest pre–Civil War concert hall." Although it had seen the likes of Enrico Caruso and Antonín Dvorak, by the 1970s it was also used for shows by Mel Torme, Ella Fitzgerald, and the Paul Butterfield Blues Band. On November 16 Monroe and the Blue Grass Boys were the headliners at a bluegrass-themed country show along with Grandpa Jones and the Lilly Brothers.

Monroe's portion of the show was recorded by young David Grisman, later to win fame for his innovative "dawg" music and also a devoted disciple of Monroe. At the time, Grisman was playing mandolin with the New York Ramblers. His tape would not be released to the public until forty-one years later, but it captures the band in fine form. Monroe was very aware that his star that night was the local boy, Bill Keith. As he introduced him he said, "I know you're acquainted with him in this part of the country. I know he's glad to be back in his home state." True to his word, Monroe let Keith shine on "Devil's Dream" and an expanded version of "John Henry." The regular song set was enhanced by two vocals by Bill's daughter, Melissa, who sang the modern Buck Owens song "Love's Gonna Live Here" and "Dreaming of a Little Cabin." Toward the end, Bill summoned Bea Lilly back to the stage and told him, "Bea, get that guitar there and help on this song, if you don't mind." The two then did a fine version of the old Monroe Brothers song "What Would You Give in Exchange for Your Soul?" Responding to an audience request, Monroe closed the show with a driving version of "Blue Ridge Mountain Blues."

HARRY'S PLAN

Keith's tenure with the band lasted only about nine months, ending just before Christmas in 1963. It was an electrifying time, and his presence rejuvenated Monroe and the band. As writer-musician Jim Rooney recalls, "There was no question that Monroe responded to Keith, and vice versa. Everybody on the Opry was talking about it."[11] Ironically, though, during Keith's actual tenure only one record on which he played was released. "Devil's Dream" came out as a single in September 1963. "Sailor's Hornpipe," Keith's other masterpiece, was not released for more than two years, when it appeared on the *Bluegrass Instrumentals* LP in June 1965. "Salt Creek" came out more than three months after Keith left, in March 1964, and "Shenandoah Breakdown" appeared September 1964. Although Monroe, the band, and serious fans seemed to recognize the importance of Keith's new style, Decca did not.

Keith left for several reasons, one of them musical. He began to feel that his style was not entirely appropriate for the Blue Grass Boys' sound. "It's funny," he says, "the more I played with him, the less it seemed that some of the stuff worked to use as ornaments to a tune. I mean it was great to use for leads, but just to throw in this stuff and splash it up seemed wrong. So I was using less and less of that as time went on."[12] In addition, Keith had joined the Air Force Reserve, and his regular meetings got in the way of touring. Then there was the problem of Monroe agreeing to appear on the ABC television program *Hootenanny,* which had blacklisted several folk performers, including Pete Seeger, who had been Keith's banjo influence when he was young. As Keith remembers it, Bob Dylan had circulated a letter mentioning a boycott and suggesting other performers join in. It was one dramatic instance where the older values of Nashville and country music conflicted directly with those of the folk revival. Keith did not want to appear on *Hootenanny,* and one solution was to leave the band.

By the end of 1963 Joe Stuart and Del McCoury remained. Del was establishing himself as a fine singer and guitarist but almost missed the sessions of January 27 and 28, 1964, entirely. He'd been playing with Billy Baker, who was not a member of the Blue Grass Boys at that time. "We come in off the road one day," he recalls, "and I didn't know we had a session the next day. I think Harry Silverstein might have called him for a session after we got in . . . Billy and me figured we didn't have nothing to do for a few days so we went to Knoxville and got on the Cas Walker show, just to have something to do. We came back on Tuesday and found they'd done a session on Monday."[13]

Monroe improvised for that January 27 session by moving Joe Stuart to guitar and bringing in two of his local standbys, Joe Drumright (banjo) and Benny Williams (fiddle). With little time for rehearsal, all three numbers on Monday were vocal solos. The first, "I'll Meet You in Church Sunday Morning," was a remake of the piece Monroe had recorded for Columbia in 1950 and would be one of the final numbers (and eventually title song) for the new gospel LP. "Mary at the Home Place," a ballad by Florida bluegrasser Ken Clark, found its way onto a single and entered the regular repertoire for much of the decade. "Highway of Sorrow," written by 1940s' Blue Grass Boy Pete Pyle, had been one of Monroe's best-sellers for the thirteen years since he first cut it in 1951.

McCoury rejoined the band for the January 28 session and helped create one of the all-time classic bluegrass duets, "Roll On Buddy, Roll On." Although credited to fellow Opry stars the Wilburn Brothers in the Decca files, the song was a venerable "shout" tune recorded in the 1920s by Charley Bowman, the Carolina Tar Heels, and others. Monroe waxed it for Bluebird with brother Charlie in 1936. A second powerful duet, "Legend of the Blue Ridge Mountains," was never issued in the United States. "One of God's Sheep" by the flamboyant gospel singer and promoter Wally Fowler, creator of the Oak Ridge Quartet, finally gave Owen Bradley enough titles for the gospel album.

A time lag seems to have developed between the sessions of February 3 and April 9, 1964, which followed McCoury's departure, and the decision of Decca's front office to release sides from them. A number of the recordings from the period were not issued in any form until years later when they appeared on a Japanese set following publication of the 1974 version of this discography. Many others were scattered on miscellaneous LPs and 45s. It seems to be another of those periodic episodes where Monroe tended to give in to the Nashville system. Many of the recordings featured his coterie of bluegrass studio men from Nashville—Jackie Phelps, Joe Drumright, Buddy Spicher, and others—and they did not normally play with him on the road.

Similarly, several songs recorded at this time reflect relationships with band personnel. "Last Old Dollar," for instance, came from Ken Marvin, who handled bookings for Bill Monroe Associates after Rinzler left for New York. Marvin had polished, recorded, and copyrighted the old folksong when he and Rollin Sullivan were doing their Lonzo and Oscar act on the Grand Ole Opry. "Never Again," written in the 1950s by fiddler Benny Williams and sung by him and Monroe, had been recorded in 1963 by the Stanley Brothers, who'd learned it from Williams when he worked for them in 1958. "Louisville Breakdown" and "Bill's Dream" were two solid new instrumentals; the latter, based on sounds in a dream he'd had of hearing foxhounds at the bottom of a well, was not issued in the United States until 1994, and the former, with its fine banjo solo by Joe Stuart, would find a home in 1969 on the *Bill and Charlie Monroe* LP. "I tried to write the kind of number the people in Louisville would like," recalled Monroe, in one of his more expansive comments.[14] "(We're Going) Just Over in the Glory Land" was a Texas gospel warhorse penned in 1906 by Emmett Dean and James W. Acuff. A favorite of the old New Orleans jazz bands, many folk revival bands had picked it up as well. "Fire on the Mountain" was Monroe's tribute to the Atlanta fiddlers of the 1920s he admired, like Clayton McMichen and Lowe Stokes. As with the previous year, these winter sessions marked the end of Monroe's formal studio work throughout 1964. As in the previous year, however, enthusiasts taped bookings that included college and festival venues arranged by Ralph Rinzler. Many tapes feature Doc Watson as a special guest star and often spotlight more duets between Monroe and him.

The new combination seemed to inspire creative magic in Monroe. At a concert at Oberlin College in Ohio on April 18, the men performed two new numbers, "Kentucky Mandolin" and "Lonesome Moonlight Waltz," that would not be recorded in the studio for several years. Another performance was taped at New London, Connecticut, on August 31, and another undated appearance was included in a Watson bootleg LP on the Los Angeles–based Intermedia label in 1982.[15]

In the spring of 1964 Decca released two new albums. *I'll Meet You in Church Sunday Morning* was Bill's second gospel effort and would be his last album using only contemporary recordings until 1967. *Bill Monroe Sings Country Songs,* released on Decca's budget label, Vocalion, was a retrospective—the first new release to reflect Rinzler's research into Monroe's earlier recordings. It included gems from the 1950s that had never been released, "John Henry," "Used to Be," and "When the Cactus Is in Bloom."

The personnel of the Blue Grass Boys shifted considerably in 1964. When Jerry Garcia recorded Bill's opening show at Bean Blossom in May, Benny Williams was back on fiddle, Jimmy Maynard was playing guitar, and a Nashville-based musician named Bruce Withers filled in on banjo. During the summer, Californian Sandy Rothman played guitar, and a New Yorker, Steve Arkin, a protégé of Keith's, played banjo. By the fall Jimmy Maynard was back again on guitar and Bill had a new banjoist, Don Lineberger from Valdosta, Georgia. Don was Monroe's first banjo picker from the South to play the chromatic style associated with Keith. A left-hander, he'd learned from Bobby Thompson and worked out other licks on his own.

Moreover, after nearly a decade and a half Bessie Lee Mauldin was gone—a shock to many who'd followed Bill's music. In her place was another person with close ties to Bill—his son, James William Monroe. Born in 1941 to Bill and wife Carolyn, James Monroe grew up listening to his father on the Opry and watching home rehearsal sessions with guitarists like Clyde Moody and Lester Flatt polishing the famous G run. He grew up in Nashville and shared his father's love of baseball. "I played Little League and pitched in high school, too," he said. "I was interested in football. I played left end when I was in high school. I got a motorcycle, too, but I had a wreck with it and broke my leg and nose and that ended my motorcycle days." As a young man he worked at a number of jobs unrelated to music. "I worked in construction, hanging sheet rock, and worked at Rudy's sausage company and then at a machine company in Nashville." He also tried his hand at booking shows, but in 1964 he decided to start working with his father's band—not that it was all so carefully planned:

> When I first started I was going on the road with daddy some, just to sell books and help drive. He worked a show in Atlanta, Georgia, one time . . . I didn't even know what a chord change was. I couldn't even hear one. But I could keep time, and that's what I did on that show. At the last minute the bass man couldn't make it and the contract called for five men, so [daddy] said, "Just get up on stage and hold it and play rhythm." That's

exactly how I got into music. If it hadn't have been for that problem, I may never have got into it. I got to where I could get the chords and make some runs on the bass and started liking it. . . . Back when I started I had all of Bill's records and some of the other artists, too, I would practice three or four hours a day with those records. When I first went out, other artists would laugh because I didn't know what I was doing. That gets to you and I was determined to learn to play the bass and I did. I didn't have any teacher. I did watch the other bass men like (Junior) Huskey and Joe Zinkan. I had a hard time even though I had pretty good timing. Daddy will hit off and on beats and then turn around and do it on and off. He'll do it on purpose but it makes it hard to keep the right beat going.[16]

A few weeks later that fall Jimmy Maynard was replaced by Jimmy Elrod, another Nashville veteran who'd recorded on banjo at one session with Bill in 1957 and with Wilma Lee and Stoney Cooper later in the 1950s. Benny Williams remained on fiddle.

Ralph Rinzler's activities as Bill's agent for the Northeast brought new gigs that sometimes led to booking complications. When Ralph arranged a Boston concert for Bill and the Blue Grass Boys along with Doc Watson on Saturday, October 31, Bill had already advertised that he and the Blue Grass Boys would be at Bean Blossom the next day. Bill's solution was to send the current Blue Grass Boys—Williams, Lineberger, Elrod, and James Monroe—to substitute for him at Bean Blossom. He flew to Boston and put together another set of Blue Grass Boys. The pickup band included some special musicians. Sitting in on fiddle was a key figure in the Boston-area bluegrass scene, Tex Logan, who wrote Monroe's perennial favorite "Christmas Time's a-Coming" and had been in the Boston area since the early 1950s. He moved there to attend graduate school and convinced the Lilly Brothers, Everett and Bea, and Don Stover to join him. Filling out the band on bass was Everett Alan Lilly, son of the mandolin player in the Lilly Brothers and a member of another Boston-area bluegrass group, the Charles River Valley Boys. Bill Keith, on banjo, brought with him Peter Rowan, who played mandolin in a band Keith and Jim Rooney had put together. It was Rowan's first experience playing guitar and singing lead with Monroe. In the coming week he would go to Nashville, Tennessee, and then travel with Monroe to perform with him at a show in Bean Blossom.

Late in 1964 Monroe took part in the filming of his first Hollywood feature, a music-heavy potboiler called *Second Fiddle to a Steel Guitar.* It was little more than a series of musical performances by most Nashville heavyweights of the time: Little Jimmy Dickens, Kitty Wells, Curly Fox, Minnie Pearl, Webb

Pierce, Lefty Frizzell, Connie Smith, Sonny James, and others. Headliners included veteran slapstick team of Leo Gorcey and Huntz Hall, famous as the Bowery Boys. The film, and others like it featuring gospel and rock and roll, was designed to appeal to rural drive-in movie audiences who had often heard their favorite singers but never seen them on-screen in those days of monolithic network television run from New York and Los Angeles. Monroe performed "Mule Skinner Blues" and "Blue Moon of Kentucky," putting down the sound track at Owen Bradley's new studio, Bradley's Barn, in the Nashville suburb of Mount Juliet, Tennessee. At this session were Blue Grass Boys Don Lineberger, Jimmy Elrod, and James Monroe, along with Buddy Spicher, who was filling in for Benny Williams. Two days later the visuals were filmed in the same studio, with everyone playing along to the earlier day's recordings. It was a challenge for Williams to match Spicher's unusual fiddle parts.

One complete concert from this period was released on a bootleg LP under the Stack-O-Hits label. It has been reissued subsequently on a number of other labels, and cuts from it remain in print. Details of its exact location and personnel are unknown, but research suggests that it was the same band Monroe used for *Second Fiddle to a Steel Guitar:* Don Lineberger on banjo, Jimmy Elrod on guitar, Benny Williams on fiddle, and James Monroe on bass. The twelve issued songs are pretty much the usual fare except for the seldom heard "Prisoner's Song" and "Nine Pound Hammer." Williams contributes most vocal leads in the songs for which Bill sings tenor.

The band Monroe brought to the session of March 16, 1965, had played together since the previous fall: Elrod, Lineberger, Williams, and James Monroe. Buddy Spicher, now a much-used Nashville session musician, was also present. Starting with this session Harry Silverstein is officially listed on Monroe's albums as producer, a job he had been doing for two years. Decca files also show ace studio guitarist Ray Edenton as "session leader," although it is not clear what that means. Normally, Nashville studio parlance defines a session leader as the one who organizes a band, gets it together, and usually plays with it. Edenton appears as "leader" from March 1965 through January 1967, however, and it is possible that he was given that role because of some studio tie-in with Bradley, given that his rhythm guitar is not audible. It is our opinion that Edenton does not actually play on recordings from this period.

"The Long Black Veil" was a version, although not a cover one, of the song Lefty Frizzell made so popular in 1959, six years earlier. Composed by two veteran Music Row songwriters, Marijohn Wilkin and Danny Dill, the song was picked up by many young folksingers who mistakenly thought it to be an ancient ballad. The Country Gentlemen introduced it to bluegrass listeners in 1960, and it had subsequently been recorded by the Kingston Trio, Burl Ives, and Joan Baez. Bill recorded it at Silverstein's suggestion. It was not released until 1970, when it appeared on the *Kentucky Blue Grass* LP.

"I Live in the Past" was written by Virginia Stauffer, who would later contribute "With Body and Soul" for the April 1969 session and was becoming a familiar name in the Monroe repertoire (and Monroe's life). A native of Michigan, dark-haired Virginia Mai Stauffer came to Nashville and met Bill in the mid-1960s. Much taken with her good looks, he nicknamed her "Gypsy" and sometimes introduced her songs onstage by saying they were written "by an old gypsy woman." She often traveled with the band but did not perform. Stauffer provided "I Live in the Past" in March 1965, "With Body and Soul" in April 1969, and "Road of Life." In September 1970, as their relationship deepened, Monroe moved in with her at a trailer park she managed. "There's an Old, Old House," released on the other side of the single that contained "I Live in the Past," was written by George Jones and Hal Bynum. Charlie Smith recalls Jones pitching the song to Monroe backstage at the Opry in August 1962. Jones's United Artists single had been issued in July 1963. Monroe liked "There's an Old, Old House" very much and started doing it at concerts. The song remained a favorite of his over the years. In 1964 the New York Ramblers released a version of "There's an Old, Old House" on a single issued on the Silver Bell label.[17] Monroe thus found himself in a situation similar to that of his earlier days, when "Mule Skinner Blues" and "Molly and Tenbrooks" had been covered by Roy Acuff and the Stanley Brothers before Monroe could get out his own version. The New York Ramblers' cover of "There's an Old, Old House" showed that young bluegrass bands in the North were watching Monroe as closely as they had once followed Scruggs.

In April 1965, shortly after this session, Peter Rowan joined the Blue Grass Boys. Rowan grew up in eastern Massachusetts listening to country music on Boston's Hayloft Jamboree and Elvis Presley on the jukebox. After hearing folksingers like Eric von Schmidt and Joan Baez in Boston, he became interested in older forms of music. Rowan discovered the Country Gentlemen and the Stanley Brothers in college, which led him to bluegrass and eventually to Monroe's work. He found in Monroe's classic sides the same kind of blues he heard in the folk movement and auditioned for him in the fall of 1964 through Bill Keith's offices. As guitarist, Rowan was lead vocalist for the band, and he sang lead to Bill's tenor in duets. Like Keith, Rinzler, and the other folk music enthusiasts who'd come recently to bluegrass, he was serious about the idea that Bill Monroe was the father of the genre, and he worked to learn the music in depth: "I learned all his old duets . . . everything he'd ever sung with anyone else," Rowan recalled. "At one time or another, we did 'em all live on the Opry."[18]

About a month later there was another change in the Blue Grass Boys when Gene Lowinger, a Brooklyn native from the New York Ramblers, signed on as fiddler. Although there had been much interest in bluegrass banjo on the part of northern folk music followers, the fiddle was still an exotic item to most, and Lowinger was a pioneer in that regard. Monroe, proud of the diverse backgrounds of his current band, took to introducing him as "the only Jewish bluegrass cowboy in the country."

At the same time, Decca released *Blue Grass Instrumentals*. Not only was it Monroe's first instrumental album it was also the first one for which Ralph Rinzler provided notes that named the musicians on each tune and quoted Monroe discussing the history and meaning of the music. Some of the tunes Keith recorded in 1963 were included, and all other tracks were from the 1950s.

SOUND BITES

Throughout his career Monroe was obligated to make regular appearances on the Opry, although by 1965 the earlier rule about members appearing every week had been relaxed. Other well-known country shows, especially on the West Coast, had for years been on television, but the Opry had only an occasional flirtation with TV. In 1955–56 ABC picked it up for a prime-time slot, and in June 1965 the Opry's owners decided to start *National Life Grand Ole Opry,* which would be syndicated. The films were not made at live Opry shows on the Ryman Auditorium stage but in the studios of Nashville WSM, which produced the show. Each show featured four or more performers on a rustic, country-porch-and-flowers set. Jud Collins did the announcing, and John Cameron Swaze, a well-known reporter and watch pitchman, did the National Life commercials.

By 1967 the show was being seen in eighteen cities, including unusual country music markets like San Francisco, Detroit, and St. Louis as well as Atlanta, Oklahoma City, Dallas, Kansas City, and Louisville. Indeed, it was so popular that on certain weeks it was ranked number one in Detroit and number two in San Francisco. The films had a second lease on life when in

1969 the Ralston Purina Company bought them and renamed the series *That Good Ole Nashville Music*. The shows continued until 1977 although some later episodes were newly filmed performances done when the original series of National Life shows had been exhausted. The second series was by 1969 reaching as many as fifty markets. Thus Monroe's performances on these films had a surprisingly wide circulation, probably greater than many of his albums. Oddly, the shows have never been packaged together in one anthology. All in all, there seems to be no way to determine exactly how many videos Monroe made for the syndicated television show. The only ones known are those released in some commercial way, and they have come to light as various independent filmmakers and video producers have drawn upon them over the years for use in documentaries about Monroe. The earliest program to be so mined for old images was number seven, taped in June or July 1965, which Rachel Liebling used in her documentary *High Lonesome* that Shanachie released on home video format in 1994 (chapter 9). The Blue Grass Boys recorded at least two numbers for the show: "Bluegrass Breakdown" and "Uncle Pen." The band included Rowan, Lowinger, Don Lineberger, and James Monroe.

It would be more than a year before Monroe returned to the Decca studio, October 1966, but fans and promoters continued to make dozens of informal tapes of concerts, workshops, and jam sessions, and in the 1990s many of these began to find their way out on various CD reissues, thereby qualifying them for this discography. One collection that includes assorted live recordings from the period is an anthology Rinzler put together for Smithsonian/Folkways, *Off the Record: Live Recordings 1956–69,* which was issued in September 1993. On June 17, 1965, Rinzler recorded a "barbecue picking party" at Tex Logan's home in Madison, New Jersey. Logan, who'd moved to New Jersey from Boston when he began working for Bell Labs, regularly hosted such events, to which he invited members of the bluegrass and old-time music community in the Northeast. Performers at this event included not only members of the current Blue Grass Boys like Rowan but also former members like Bill Keith and young local musicians like David Grisman, who played bass on "Cotton-Eyed Joe." Rinzler noted that the recording "represents the first time I heard Bill play and sing lead with Tex."[19]

In 1965 the band traveled north to the Newport Folk Festival again, where on July 24, a Saturday afternoon, Monroe joined Logan and Rowan for a "Fiddle and Mandolin Workshop." After Monroe's few introductory remarks, the occasion became a mini-concert, with Rowan and Monroe singing their new co-composition "Walls of Time," Logan and Monroe doing the same "Cotton-Eyed Joe" they'd tried a month earlier at Logan's, Monroe and Rowan singing "Shady Grove," and all three doing "Grey Eagle." At the formal concert that evening the whole band, including banjoist Don Lineberger, bass player James Monroe, and fiddler Gene Lowinger, did a set of seven familiar tunes: "Mule Skinner Blues," "Blue Moon of Kentucky," "Walls of Time," "Blue Yodel No. 4," "Molly and Tenbrooks," "Somebody Touched Me" (with Rinzler again joining on bass), and "Blue Grass Breakdown." On two numbers a triple-fiddle sound was created when Lowinger was joined by Tex Logan and Byron Berline, another fiddler playing with Bill for the first time. A twenty-one-year-old Oklahoma contest fiddler who'd beaten his father, also a contest fiddler, at his first contest eleven years earlier, Byron had discovered bluegrass via the Dillards, and earlier in the year he was featured on the first bluegrass album to foreground old-time fiddle tunes with bluegrass backup, the Dillards' *Pickin' and Fiddlin'*. Ralph Rinzler had written the liner notes, so it's not surprising that Byron and his father were invited to appear at Newport. But Byron's appearance with Monroe was a last-minute thing, a sign of Monroe's recognition of his ability.

Because Monroe's Decca contract was still in force and he was very careful not to endanger it, the Newport recordings Vanguard made remained in the vaults for years. They began appearing on various Vanguard CD sets in 1992, and some have appeared in more than one.

Rinzler was a central behind-the-scenes figure in the creation of Carlton Haney's Roanoke Blue Grass Festival at Fincastle Virginia.[20] He documented the Labor Day weekend 1965 event with three recordings made at a workshop with Peter Rowan: "Get Up, John," "Kansas City Railroad Blues" (an instrumental not previously recorded), and "Walls of Time." Also recorded were three numbers from the "Story of Blue Grass," a concert at which Rinzler used all the discographical data he'd assembled on Monroe to help Haney recreate various versions of the Blue Grass Boys. This particular segment included Monroe's 1949 band with Mac Wiseman, Benny Martin, and Don Reno.

By the time of the first Roanoke Festival, September 1965, Don Lineberger had left the Blue Grass Boys. His place was taken by Lamar Grier, who was a seasoned veteran from the lively Washington, D.C., bluegrass scene and had played and recorded with such performers as Buzz Busby. At the time he joined Monroe he'd just finished working on Hazel Dickens and Alice Gerrard's first Folkways album. Over the winter there

was another change as Gene Lowinger left and was replaced by Richard S. Greene. Trained as a classical violinist in Los Angeles where he grew up, Greene's real mentors were Scott Stoneman and Dale Potter, two rather different fiddlers who both pushed the envelope of fiddling styles by incorporating elements of jazz, blues, and improvisation. "What Scott did was to play 'violinistically' on the fiddle," Greene said. "That made him different from all the others. He played with a certain fire and intensity that really communicated. That's when I wanted to be a fiddler! He made the fiddle do as much as it could do sound-wise."[21]

By 1966 Greene was playing fiddle and bass for the Greenbriar Boys, the band of which Ralph Rinzler had been a part. That connection put him in touch with Monroe. "Ralph Rinzler, who was in the band, left to manage Bill's career," he remembered. "He recommended me when Bill needed a fiddler in an emergency. I very much wanted to do that more than anything in life. I kept myself moving in those circles in order for that to happen. A few months later, Bill offered me a full-time job." Greene was one of the band's more unusual fiddlers. "Just the way I held my hands on the instrument gave me a little different look, a classical look," he observed. Monroe soon learned to appreciate the technical abilities of his new twenty-four-year-old star. "He would do a phrase on the mandolin and I would do the same phrase on the fiddle doubling whatever notes he doubled. He appreciated the way I was able to capture his meaning."[22]

James Monroe, who'd been playing bass for less than two years, remembers the group with Rowan, Greene, and Grier as including some of Monroe's most adventuresome musicians: "They were doing a lot of different things with the timing," he laughs. "It was all I could do just to hang on."[23] To hone his skills James spent about a year working off and on with another Nashville band, an informal group that included Jerry Munday and played at a place called King Henry's Lodge.

The first sound snapshot of this band in action dates from May 4 through 6, 1966, at the Gaslight Cafe in New York City. They are represented in three numbers—two familiar instrumentals, "Watermelon Hangin' on the Vine" and "Fire on the Mountain," and a version of Bill's latest single "I Live in the Past." Another of Tex Logan's "barbecue and pickin'" parties on June 20 yielded "White House Blues" and "Roll in My Sweet Baby's Arms," the latter with a guest tenor in the form of Hazel Dickens. "Wayfaring Stranger," also done at this session, demonstrates the phrase-copying Richard Greene mentions as well as Monroe's unique mandolin technique. Yet another party at

Logan's home on August 26 preserved a pair of duets between Monroe and Doc Watson, "Watson's Blues" and "Turkey in the Straw." It is the earliest version of the former, which MCA did not record in the studio until the mid-1970s.

In June 1966 Decca released *The High Lonesome Sound*, Rinzler's second annotated retrospective LP. With it, the phrase *high lonesome sound*, which John Cohen used to title his obscure documentary film four years earlier, became widely associated with Bill Monroe and bluegrass music. With its focus on the classic duets of the early 1950s by Jimmy Martin and Carter Stanley the album was acclaimed as one of Bill's best. It set the bar high for the contemporary Blue Grass Boys, who still had not been in the recording studio.

BLUEGRASS TIME?

On November 3, 1966, Monroe finally began work on his first fully new LP since his *Meet You in Church* gospel set was released in the spring of 1964. It would eventually be called *Blue Grass Time*, and tracks would be completed in a series of five closely spaced sessions throughout the winter. After several years of often being between full-time regulars, Monroe's current band had worked together for some time. If in earlier groups, both for recording and touring, he drew heavily on a pool of older Nashville-area musicians from the upland South, he now found himself with Blue Grass Boys from Los Angeles (Greene), from Boston (Rowan), and from Washington (Grier). These younger musicians figured not only in the folk revival but also in the nationalization of bluegrass music, and many had spent at least some time in college. They had middle-class suburban backgrounds, another distinction from older Blue Grass Boys.

Rowan, with him the longest, had not only learned all his old duets but also co-composed "Walls of Time" with him, a piece they did on almost every show. At sessions for the record, though, James Monroe took most of the leads and Rowan got the leftovers, whether a third baritone part as in "When My Blue Moon Turns to Gold Again" and "I Wonder Where You Are Tonight" or a rare duet such as "Midnight on the Stormy Deep" in the December 16, 1966, session.

Although Rowan was Monroe's lead singer and strongest duet partner since Frank Buchanan in 1962 the repertoire of these sessions hardly reflects that. Indeed, he did not record "Walls of Time" with him. One reason for this, according to Rowan, was that Monroe was letting Silverstein call too many shots in selecting material, and sessions were laced with

songs the band had not performed regularly. "On that album *Blue Grass Time*," Rowan observed, "it's all stuff the producer said to record. Bill was just going along with the producer. He wasn't sticking behind the vision of the band."[24] Thus the October 14, 1966, session produced a version of a 1940 chestnut by Wiley Walker and Gene Sullivan, "When My Blue Moon Turns to Gold Again," by then a standard country duet and even an Elvis Presley favorite. "I Wonder Where You Are Tonight" had been written for cowboy singer Gene Autry's radio show in 1941 by Johnny Bond. It was originally designed as a trio, as Monroe does it here. "Log Cabin in the Lane," although credited on the label to bluegrass composer Jim Eanes, was a version of Will S. Hays's nineteenth-century hit song "The Little Old Log Cabin in the Lane," which Fiddlin' John Carson recorded in 1923 at country music's first real recording session. "Turkey in the Straw" and "Paddy on the Turnpike" are familiar traditional fiddle tunes. "Pretty Fair Maiden in the Garden," the traditional English broadside ballad that Monroe sang solo at Newport 1963, had been cast into string-band form by the revivalist New Lost City Ramblers and was picked up for an album by the Stanley Brothers in 1963. In Bill's version, which came from his mother, the Napoleonic-era soldier of the original broadside had changed to a cowboy.

More standards, again probably suggested by Harry Silverstein, appeared in the sessions of December 6 and 16, 1966, and January 23, 1967, all devoted to *Blue Grass Time*. Autry Inman's 1953 Decca hit "That's All Right," with its oddly breaking chorus, receives a new reading by Monroe as a soloist that spotlights Greene's tough, bluesy fiddle. "It Makes No Difference Now" had been penned in 1938 by western writer Floyd Tillman, and hit versions by Cliff Bruner and even Bing Crosby helped make it a standard. "Dusty Miller" and "Soldier's Joy" are two venerable pieces featuring Greene's innovative style. The former was one of the most widely copied performances on the album, and the latter was not included on the final version of the album but was in John Rumble's four-CD MCA retrospective of 1994. "All the Good Times Are Past and Gone," done here as a trio, is a remake of the Monroe Brothers' 1937 recording. "Midnight on the Stormy Deep," another radio favorite from the duet era of the 1930s, which Monroe learned from the singing of Mac and Bob, marks the only studio duet featuring Monroe and Rowan. Fiddler Richard Greene has special memories of his solo on this piece: "That was one of my favorite solos, but that wasn't improvised in the normal sense—I would organize my licks just before the take. I never played it quite like that before or after."[25]

"Blue Night," from a surprising source, the pen of Kirk McGee, a longtime Opry veteran and Uncle Dave Macon crony, is the recording that has endured from this session. Monroe continued to use it and later bands such as Hot Rize picked it up as well. Greene's intense double stops add surprising passion to the performance. "Grey Eagle," however, was the third fiddle tune from this group of sessions to remain on the shelf until years later when a Japanese reissue included it.

Within a month of completing the album both Greene and Rowan had left Monroe, and Byron Berline joined in March of 1967. Although Berline was a country boy he was also a college graduate who had come into bluegrass through the folk revival and represented a new generation of "Texas-style" or "contest-style" fiddling. Monroe had earlier employed musicians familiar with techniques and tunes of southwestern fiddling (such as Chubby Wise, Howard "Howdy" Forrester, and Kenny Baker), but Berline was the first actual native fiddler from the region to join the band. He only recorded three tunes during his tenure, two of which, "The Gold Rush" and "Sally Goodin," found their way into the canon as classic bluegrass fiddling performances.

An April tour to the West Coast led to the hiring of Roland White as guitarist and lead singer. White, of course, became best known for his work with his brother, Clarence. The brothers were Acadian French Canadian (their family name was originally LeBlanc), but the family had moved to Los Angeles in 1954, where Clarence and Roland grew up. In 1960 they formed the Country Boys, a progressive young band that changed its name to the Kentucky Colonels in 1963. The band split after a number of appearances on the folk revival circuit and a well-done album called *Appalachian Swing,* with Clarence going with the Byrds and Roland joining Monroe. Roland, known primarily as a mandolin player, naturally switched to guitar in Monroe's group.

When Lamar Grier left following the return to Nashville, Bill hired Joseph C. "Butch" Robins, eighteen, as banjoist. Robins, who would join Bill again a decade later, left in June, not long after Decca released *Blue Grass Time,* Monroe's first album with all recent recordings since 1964. Now, however, he had a new band. The latest to join was banjoist Vic Jordan. A New Jersey native who grew up in Virginia listening to Scruggs and Reno and working with Allen Shelton, Jordan moved to Nashville in 1964. There he started what would be a long and productive studio career doing everything from bluegrass session work to commercial advertising jingles. He began by performing with Jimmy Martin, where he replaced J. D. Crowe, and then, starting in January 1965, worked with Wilma Lee and Stoney

Cooper for eighteen months. Not long after that he received another call: "Jim Monroe called me and said Lamar Grier had left and daddy wanted to know if I still wanted the job. I said, 'Yeah, tell him I'm free,'" recalled Jordan. He dug out some of the old Monroe records and worked with Kenny Baker to learn the repertoire "because I wasn't too sure of the melody. He's [Monroe] a stickler for melody. When it's instrumental time he wants to hear tone, time, and melody. No razzmatazz. Now when he's singing, he wants pretty good solid drive and good fill behind him; good pretty stuff, but don't get flaky back there. When it's your turn to play, then let them have it."[26] Jordan would record with the band from August 1967 through November 1968, for nine tunes, and eventually leave Monroe to take a better-paying job with Lester Flatt. He would, in fact, be Flatt's first banjoist after the break with Scruggs.

Of this band, Berline was the first to leave. His tenure extended from March to September, when he was inducted into the army. That is why Monroe scheduled a summer session for August 23, 1967, in the midst of the busy festival and touring season, the first time in his career he would do so. He was anxious to record with Berline before the younger man left the band. The session, like Monroe's with Keith in March 1963, featured the instrumental work of his prodigy.

"The Gold Rush" was a Monroe original that followed the form of a traditional fiddle tune. It was relatively simple and catchy, and Berline plays it with little ornamentation or variation in the style of southeastern fiddlers. Long-time rumors that Berline rather than Monroe composed it have been addressed by Byron: "Bill had the idea and was picking on it when we were on the bus traveling, and he asked me to help him with it to give it a more old-time fiddle sound. We worked on it for some time before we recorded it, and I came up with the third part at the end of the tune. So, no I did not write the entire tune, but I did help." Berline recalled that Monroe chose the name after he'd left the Blue Grass Boys and was in basic training: "Bill called me when I was in basic training at Ft. Polk, Louisiana, and asked if I thought 'The Gold Rush' would be a good name, and I of course said yes. I could just see an old covered wagon heading west and rolling over a rock on the second part of the tune where it goes from D to A."[27] Released on a single in fall of 1968, more than a year after it was recorded, it quickly became a standard in bluegrass and old-time fiddle repertoires.

"Sally Goodin" has had special significance to Texas fiddling ever since Eck Robertson introduced it to record in 1922. On that occasion he wove a series of melodic variations into the music, ones so popular that they have become part of the tune. It was this tradition within a tradition that Berline, who had also learned variations from Benny Thomasson, another legendary contest-style fiddler, recorded with Monroe. By introducing the techniques of southwestern contest fiddling into a bluegrass instrumental, Monroe's recording of "Sally Goodin" did for southwestern fiddle style what "Devil's Dream" had done for Keith's banjo work. It gave a "new old-time" dimension to bluegrass and represented a balance of personal innovation (Berline's) with regional traditions.

"Virginia Darlin'," originally issued on the flip side of the "Gold Rush" 45-rpm single and much later on a Rebel LP, is an up-tempo piece Monroe derived from an older Kentucky fiddle tune and has echoes of "Durham's Bull." Named in honor of Virginia Stauffer, it spotlights more of Berline's work as well as a rare bass solo by James Monroe.

Starting with the next session, November 9, 1967, the Decca files finally list Monroe as the "leader" of the session bands. Berline's place at fiddle was taken by Benny Williams. By now the band was working on the *Kentucky Blue Grass* LP and having trouble finding time for the sessions. This first was at night and demonstrated the problems of using studio musicians on Monroe's recordings. Session fiddler Vassar Clements was playing regularly at a local club in Nashville and had to leave the studio early to get there on time. He and Benny Williams had carefully worked out a twin-fiddle part for "Kentucky Mandolin," a new instrumental Bill had finished. All these plans went by the board, however, and Williams, slated for the tenor fiddle part, had to scramble to do a lead solo in a matter of minutes. "Train 45 (Heading South)" is Monroe's reading of an old fiddle tune known to some as "Reuben's Train." It was first popularized in the 1920s by Tennessee fiddler G. B. Grayson who, with Henry Whitter, recorded as Grayson and Whitter, and again in the 1930s by J. E. Mainer, whose version seems the immediate source for Monroe's. It is a fine, driving arrangement that features the two fiddlers before Clements left the session. "Is the Blue Moon Still Shining?" is one of the few songs written by Bill's daughter, Melissa, who had a brief recording career in the 1950s, and is sort of an "answer song" to "Blue Moon of Kentucky."

Shortly after the November 9, 1967, session, Benny Williams was injured in a hunting accident, and Kenny Baker rejoined the band on fiddle. He had been with the group for a full year—the start of a stint that would extend into 1984—when they next recorded on November 14, 1968. Although Roland White had been present at the sessions of August 23 and

November 9, 1967, White did not sing until this session, when he joined James and Bill for the trio (throughout, as in "On and On") of "I Want to Go with You" and did a duet with Bill on "Walls of Time." The band also did one of the three sides set aside for the new LP; another, "Crossing the Cumberlands," appeared only on a single; and the third, "Walls of Time," was not released in the United States until 1994, when John Rumble included it on his four-CD Monroe retrospective for MCA. It was re-done in 1972 with James Monroe singing lead.

Both "Crossing the Cumberlands" and "Walls of Time," two of Monroe's finest later compositions, had been developed with the earlier 1966 band that included Lamar Grier and Peter Rowan. Of the haunting banjo feature "Crossing the Cumberlands," Vic Jordan recalls, "[It] was really Lamar Grier's piece. He really did that one beautifully, a lot better than I did, but he left and I was in the band, so it was up to me to do it."[28] "Walls of Time" had been worked out with Peter Rowan singing lead, but Roland White gave it a credible shot. To be level with Monore at the microphone, Jordan remembers, White had to stand on a soft-drink box.

On December 20, 1968, the band was featured on *National Life Grand Ole Opry* and did a version of "Train 45 Headin' South," a performance subsequently issued commercially on a train song compilation by Opryland Home Video.

In March 1969 the bluegrass world was shaken by the announcement that Flatt and Scruggs were splitting up. The breakup also had a direct impact on Monroe's band because Flatt hired Vic Jordan as banjoist and Roland White as mandolinist for his new band, which would eventually be called the Nashville Grass.

With White gone, Bill turned the job of guitarist over to his son James, who'd played bass with the group for nearly five years. As he observes, "I never had done much with the guitar. Oh, I had done one number as a part of the show, but that was all. I knew the job was going to be hard. Especially with tunes like 'Raw Hide' and 'John Henry' and 'Mule Skinner,' with a guitar part in it, and 'Uncle Pen' with the guitar kick-off. I was ready singing-wise, but just had not done that much guitar playing. Right when Roland quit, the festivals and summer season were about three weeks away and I had to really get onto it. I wanted the opportunity to get that job."[29]

Banjoist Rual Yarbrough replaced Vic Jordan. A native of Lawrenceburg, Tennessee, home of James D. Vaughan and his song publishing company—the company that defined modern gospel quartet music—Yarbrough had heard Monroe on the radio since boyhood. He represented a return to the basics, being totally from within the southeastern bluegrass tradition, as were most of Monroe's sidemen during the 1950s. Yarbrough's first break was with an Alabama band, the Dixie Gentlemen, which included Jake Landers and Herschel Sizemore and recorded for United Artists and Time Records. They also did one of the legendary Tommy Jackson square dance albums for Dot. When the Dixie Gentlemen split up, Rual worked for a time with Jimmy Martin in Nashville and then with Flatt and Scruggs, Jim and Jesse McReynolds, and Bobby Smith and the Boys from Shiloh. One night when he was with the Boys from Shiloh, Rual stopped in Columbus, Ohio:

> Bill Monroe was working a small club there. So we stopped over to visit with them a little while. Vic Jordan had just left Bill, and they had another boy from Springfield, Ohio filling in that night. I mentioned to Kenny Baker that I'd like to have the job. I had no idea they would consider me because Vic was such a good banjo player I didn't think I could take up anywhere close to where he left off. Kenny told me he thought I could get the job if he wanted it. So I went back to the dressing room and told Bill. Bill came out and talked to me and told me to call him on my way back from Wheeling on Monday. I did, got the job that Monday, and we went in for a recording session on Wednesday![30]

The session of March 26, 1969, marked the first time in which James Monroe played guitar instead of bass and was one of the first that featured him on a strong solo vocal. "I Haven't Seen Mary in Years" was an old-sounding but new song written by Damon Black, author of "Tall Pines" and "Sweet Mary and the Miles in Between." Baker's fiddling is augmented on this and others from the session by Joe Herman "Red" Hayes, the veteran Texas fiddler and songwriter responsible for "Satisfied Mind." "Fireball Mail" had the distinction of being one of the band's first stereo singles and was the 1942 hit by Roy Acuff that had been written by Fred Rose under the pen name Floyd Jenkins. Monroe follows Acuff's original arrangement by soaring into falsetto on the third line of the verse. The last track that day was "The Dead March," the first of Uncle Pen Vandiver's fiddle tunes Monroe recorded although he was planning an album that would feature all of them. It would be called *Uncle Pen*.

PENDLETON'S LEGACY

One last piece was needed for the *Kentucky Blue Grass* LP and that was the first concern for the next studio session of April 29, 1969. It turned out to be "Cripple Creek" featuring Yarbrough's banjo in a Monroe version of a song that had been used for

decades as a closing theme for the Stanley Brothers. The traditional song was familiar to bluegrass audiences in an arrangement that opened with a verse sung in a slow vocal trio followed by a fast banjo and fiddle instrumental—originated by Flatt and Scruggs but first recorded by Sonny Osborne and then Jimmy Martin, Earl Taylor, and others. "What about You?" features a solo by James and is a haunting favorite associated with Kitty Wells and also Johnnie Wright and Jack Anglin. "This was Jim Anglin's favorite song," recalls Wright. "He had written it about his first wife. Jack and I recorded it as a waltz a year later for RCA."[31] It had also been recorded by Jim and Jesse McReynolds in 1963. "With Body and Soul," a love song of the first order, was written by Virginia Stauffer. Monroe's version became popular in the early 1970s, and that popularity was bolstered when two of the most successful younger groups, the Seldom Scene and the Newgrass Revival, recorded versions. "Methodist Preacher," another of Uncle Pen's tunes, has overtones of "Leather Britches" and is well known to Kentucky fiddlers even now. Kenny Baker is featured exclusively on the piece.

In June 1969 Decca released *A Voice from on High,* Ralph Rinzler's latest retrospective LP. A few months earlier another reissue set he'd edited was also released: *Bill Monroe and Charlie Monroe.* On it were some of Bill's classics from the 1950s along with sides Charlie cut for Decca, also in the 1950s. The brothers were not actually featured performing together on that album, but Rinzler had a plan to bring them together to perform. He had started working as a folklore specialist with the Smithsonian Institution, and for the July 4 Festival of American Folklife on the Mall in Washington, D.C., he arranged for a reunion of the three Monroe Brothers, Charlie, Birch, and Bill, who had his full band, including Baker, Yarbrough, James, and bassist Doug Green. Birch joined them to fiddle on "How Old Are You My Pretty Little Miss?" and sing bass on "He Will Set Your Fields on Fire" and "I Know My Lord's Gonna Lead Me Out." Charlie sang on the two gospel numbers as well and played on "Durang's Hornpipe." These live recordings were later released on a Smithsonian/Folkways CD.

In the fall of 1969 "With Body and Soul" was released on a single. A performance of it, probably at the Ryman Auditorium, was broadcast on the *National Life Grand Ole Opry* and was used in Rachel Liebling's *High Lonesome* and released as well as a track on the CMH CD based on the film.

The period from 1969 to 1972 was a relatively stable time for the Blue Grass Boys, with Kenny Baker beginning his longest tenure with the band and James Monroe settling into a regular role as guitarist and lead singer. On October 28 the crew gathered at Bradley's Barn to put down another single and work more on the *Bill Monroe's Uncle Pen* album. The choice for single was a new song by Monroe and Jake Landers, "Walk Softly on My Heart." Landers, a young singer from rural northwestern Alabama, cut his teeth in the Dixie Gentlemen with Rual Yarbrough, Vassar Clements, and Herschel Sizemore. By the mid-1960s he often toured with Monroe when needed although he never made it into a studio session. When they traveled, he and Monroe wrote songs together, the best known of which were "Walk Softly on My Heart" and "Beyond the Gate," which Monroe would also record later. Monroe's version, released as a single the following March, had little impact on the hit charts, but in 1990 a country rock band, the Kentucky Headhunters, did a new version that became one of the biggest records of the year. By the end of its run on the charts (which included a CMT video with Monroe as a guest), the Headhunters' version was declared gold and eventually double platinum. In 2001 it received another lease on life when recorded by Ricky Skaggs and the Dixie Chicks, winning a Grammy nomination. Landers became one of the most successful bluegrass composers, placing songs with the likes of the Osborne Brothers, the Nashville Bluegrass Band, Vassar Clements, and the Bluegrass Cardinals.

"Tall Pines" features Monroe's soaring tenor on the chorus in a performance issued on a single in 1973 and included on the *Bill Monroe and James Monroe: Father and Son* album. "Candy Gal," another Uncle Pen tune, is a twin-fiddle arrangement of the piece credited to Uncle Bunt Stephens, the Tennessee fiddler who won a 1926 fiddle contest that Henry Ford, who was campaigning to revive old-time fiddling and dancing and the preindustrial values of family and home he believed to be associated with them, organized in the mid-1920s. Because there are no other recordings of the piece, it is possible that Pendleton Vandiver learned it from one of Stephens's radio performances.

More work on the *Bill Monroe's Uncle Pen* set took place about a month later on November 25. The first tried was "Land of Lincoln," an instrumental Monroe had been playing frequently at the time in concerts. Unfortunately, the master tape for this particular performance, which featured Baker's fiddling, was shelved and subsequently lost in the Decca-MCA-Universal vaults. "Going Up Caney," however, as well as "The Lee Weddin Tune," both made it into the *Uncle Pen* album, and both were learned from Pendleton Vandiver years before. The challenge

that Monroe and Harry Silverstein faced with the *Uncle Pen* album was how to season the collection of old fiddle tunes with enough modern bluegrass sounds to make it commercial. One way was to work out arrangements with twin fiddles and another was to create intricate vocal parts for old dance tunes, such as with "Going Up Caney."

The final session for the decade occurred on December 17 and was officially listed as a James Monroe session, the resulting single issued under James Monroe's name. Bill does sing tenor on "Bonny," an original song with something of a folk sound, but James sings a solo on "Sweet Mary and the Miles in Between." At this session he deviated from his usual practice of recording "stereo live" and followed the lead of other Nashville studio stars by recording via overdubs. The vocal parts to these songs were not recorded until the following session of January 19, 1970.

The year began with an unexpected setback. On January 8, during one of Nashville's bitterest cold spells, producer Harry Silverstein suffered a heart attack and was rushed to St. Thomas Hospital, where he died. The native of Cincinnati was only thirty-eight but had been with Decca for fifteen years as a producer and promotion specialist. For several years before his death he was Owen Bradley's assistant, Bradley by then being Decca's vice president. In a statement released to the media, Bradley described Silverstein as "my right hand man and best friend."[32] Silverstein, who produced a number of sessions that bore Bradley's name, had recently begin to be credited under his own name. He was returned to Cincinnati for burial.

Bradley had no immediate replacement for Silverstein, so he apparently supervised the next *Uncle Pen* session, done the evening of January 19, 1970, at Bradley's Barn, himself. James Monroe was still playing guitar, and Tommy Williams joined Kenny Baker. Williams would later help Baker to create the distinctive twin-fiddle sound on several studio sessions in the early 1970s. Originally from Florida, Williams was by now a crack Nashville studio musician who had played for a time with Charley Pride's band, the Pridesmen, and had been a regular on *Hee-Haw*.

"McKinley's March," in spite of its formal composer credits, is an old Kentucky fiddle tune still played in Adair County. "Now 'McKinley's March' is an old timer," Monroe said, "no telling how old it is. I learned it from my uncle up in Kentucky."[33] Despite that pedigree, the tune did not make it onto the final *Uncle Pen* album and was released only as a single. "Texas Gallop" was also associated with the western Kentucky fiddle tradition that produced Uncle Pen, and it did make it onto the tribute album that was still two years away from release. A gallop is a familiar type of fiddle tune, often played in $^2/_4$ time. The tune itself was recorded by Tommy Jackson under the name "Rachel" and featured as a mandolin piece by Ronnie Reno, who called it "Texas Quick-Step."

ROAD OF LIFE

For the next session, March 26, Owen Bradley talked his younger brother Harold into trying producing. The job at hand was the start of a new gospel set that would be called *Road of Life* although not released until 1974. The liner notes to the album contained tributes to the Monroe gospel sound from members of the Lewis Family and the Sullivan Family, the two best-known bluegrass gospel family groups. One of the more revealing came from Roy "Pop" Lewis: "Bill is one of the main reasons why our gospel music has a bluegrass sound. I've said several times that if we're on the wrong road with bluegrass gospel, then Bill is responsible for it." Wallace Lewis remarked that Monroe's songwriting "probably had an influence on my own songwriting," and Polly Lewis echoed, "Gospel songs are a basic part of Bill's original style, because I've never heard him put on a show without doing a sacred number." "Little Roy" Lewis, a banjoist, added that "Bill really was the start of what they call 'Gospel Grass' today."[34]

The quartet on the four songs is classic Monroe gospel that features James Monroe as well as banjoist Rual Yarbrough and bass singer Culley Holt. Holt, a native of Oklahoma, came to fame as the bass singer for the original Jordanaires in the early 1950s but left them in 1954 to pursue a freelance career in the Nashville studios. He recorded some with Johnnie and Jack and with Flatt and Scruggs ("Cabin on the Hill") in addition to working on various Monroe gospel LPs, among them *I Saw the Light* (1958) and *I'll Meet You in Church Sunday Morning* (1962). He died in 1980.

The title song, "Road of Life" was yet another gem from the hand of Virginia Stauffer," and "It's Me Again Lord" is from the fine western Kentucky gospel songwriter Dottie Rambo. A native of Camp Breckenridge, Kentucky, Rambo began writing songs when she was twelve and soon attracted the attention of gospel giant Jimmie Davis, who began popularizing her work. Although not specifically a gospel songwriter she produced such favorites as "One More Valley" and "Build My Mansion (Next Door to Jesus)," often used by gospel bluegrass bands. By the time "It's Me Again Lord" was cut in 1970, Dottie Rambo,

her husband, Buck, and their daughter, Reba, had formed the Singing Rambos and become a well-established force in country gospel. "Beyond the Gate" was the second song co-written by Monroe and Jake Landers, and "I Will Sing for the Glory of God" is attributed to "B. F. Logan"—that is, Benjamin Franklin "Tex" Logan Jr., Monroe's longtime fiddler friend and writer of the "Christmas Time's a-Coming."

The spring of 1970 saw Bill reunited briefly with one of his most influential Blue Grass Boys when he and his current band jammed backstage at the Opry with Earl and Randy Scruggs. In the jam, Monroe led everyone through one of his characteristic medleys. It was filmed by National Educational Television and broadcast the following January on a ninety-minute special, *Earl Scruggs: His Family and Friends,* but was not included in the album of the same title that Columbia released later that year.

In June 1970 Decca released *Kentucky Blue Grass,* his first album of newly recorded material in three years. Ralph Rinzler's notes stated that the recordings had been made over a five-year period, and he named the many Blue Grass Boys who played on the album and described at length how Monroe instilled musical passion in them. He discussed Carlton Haney's festivals and Bill's appearance at the 1969 Newport Folk Festival and called bluegrass music "the direct result of one man's creative genius."[35] Bill's recent musical activities were bringing the recognition that had eluded him.

In October 1970 Bill Monroe was elected to the Country Music Hall of Fame—naturally enough, its first bluegrass member—and Decca decided to celebrate the occasion with a new LP. The set, which Rinzler probably programmed, was a mixture of old and new, and in the notes Rinzler lauded Monroe as "one of our nation's leading musical figures."[36] Some cuts went as far back as 1952, but six were new and done specifically for the occasion. Two came from the session of December 2, 1970. The Monroe standard "Kentucky Waltz" had first been recorded for Columbia in 1945 and was redone in 1951, soon after he signed with Decca. For this occasion Monroe was able to enhance his lilting melody with three fiddles (Red Hayes, Kenny Baker, and Gordon Terry). Hayes (or as it is sometimes spelled, Hays) grew up in the Texas-Louisiana music scene and for a time was in Nashville doing session work and occasionally writing songs and publishing them. "The Girl in the Blue Velvet Band" had been recorded for Columbia in 1949. Young bluegrass bands heard and liked it, and in 1969 a young country band featuring Bill Keith and Richard Greene even adopted the title for its name: the Blue Velvet Band. A third side from this session, a remake of "My Little Georgia Rose," was unissued, and the tapes have been lost.

Starting with this session Monroe was working with a new producer: Walter Haynes. Owen Bradley, who had taken over Monroe from Paul Cohen, was becoming a living legend in Nashville (indeed, he was only four years away from being elected to the Hall of Fame). With the loss of Harry Silverstein, it became necessary for a new generation, represented by Haynes, who would do most of Monroe's LPs through the 1970s, to take over.

A native of Kingsport, in east Tennessee, Haynes came to Nashville as a young man in 1949 to try to make it as a fiddler. He found work on the Opry with Paul Howard and his Arkansas Cotton Pickers and roomed with Howard's steel guitar player, Billy Bowman. Bowman, who went on to even greater fame with Bob Wills, was beginning to master the new pedal steel guitar, and Haynes grew interested. After a stint in the service he returned and began playing steel for Jimmy Dickens. During the next decade he continued to work with Dickens and then as a member of the Opry staff band before drifting into song publishing and studio work. It was through the latter that Haynes grew to know Owen Bradley, and in 1969 he joined the Kapp Record Company. Because the Kapp division was to be transferred to the West Coast, Bradley, who needed a replacement, offered the job to Haynes.

Bradley continued to produce the label's giant stars like Conway Twitty, Loretta Lynn, Brenda Lee, and Ernest Tubb, but he assigned Haynes to take some of the bluegrass acts and younger, up-and-coming artists such as Cal Smith and Jeannie Pruett. Included on the bluegrass roster were Bill Monroe and Jimmy Martin. Haynes had difficulties with Martin but found he enjoyed working with Monroe. Like Silverstein, he learned that the best approach was to leave him alone and let him call the shots for his albums:

> When he got ready to record, he would come by the office and we would talk for ten or fifteen minutes—that's usually all it would take to work it out—and I'd have my secretary set up the recording date. Bill would choose all the songs and the musicians. We would never really have to find any studio musicians. A typical Monroe LP in those days would sell around twenty-five to thirty thousand copies, but we never ran into the red with him, because it didn't really cost anything to record him. He would use just four or five men, and he always got in and out of the studio quickly, and we never had much in the mixing or production charges. We would budget a typical Monroe album at eight or nine thousand dollars—a far cry from the $150,000 budget we got to having for other MCA albums just a few years later.[37]

Monroe would often sit just behind Haynes in the studio when they were mixing the album, occasionally making suggestions.

The sessions of December 2 and 3, 1970, mark the first time Monroe recorded with the ace studio banjoist Bobby Thompson, who was a founder of the so-called chromatic style and doing up to ten sessions a week in the Nashville studios, from Hank Snow to *Hee-Haw*. Monroe had long been aware of Thompson's abilities on fiddle tunes. He was an innovative stylist who had solid credentials in bluegrass history and was highly respected in the contemporary studio scene. From the area around Converse, South Carolina, a region that also produced banjoist Buck Trent and guitarist Hank Garland, Thompson's first notable job was with Carl Story and the Rambling Mountaineers. There a chance conversation with former Flatt and Scruggs fiddler Benny Sims, who was working with Bonnie Lou and Buster, a group with which Story often shared showbills, encouraged him to "play fiddle tunes note-for-note" on the banjo."[38] He began to develop a version of what came to be called the chromatic style. After two years, Thompson moved on to the band of Jim and Jesse, who wanted him to play the then- popular Scruggs style rather than his new style. Of his own music, he recalled, "I just let it slide."[39] A further interruption from the draft and a stint in the army delayed his work even more, and when Thompson came out of the service he took a day job and put his musical career on hold. When he heard that Bill Keith, then playing with Monroe, was getting all the credit for the "new" chromatic style he was surprised. In 1966 Thompson moved to Nashville to work with Jim and Jesse again but found he could make better money doing studio work. To counter the fact that the "Nashville sound" of the day didn't have much work for a banjo player, he also became adept at the rhythm guitar. By the early 1970s he'd become a member of a band composed of top-flight Nashville studio men, Area Code 615, that made two highly acclaimed LPs.

The triple-fiddle session continued the next day, December 3, with three more instrumentals. About "Lonesome Moonlight Waltz," Monroe told Vic Gabany that he kept the tune "thirty-six years before I recorded it. It's a good waltz number."[40] That would make the song's composition date around 1934, even before the Monroe Brothers made their first Bluebird recordings. Although it was originally issued only as a single and did not appear on an LP until 1985, the piece has remained popular and was recorded by a trio of three mandolin players, David Grisman, Jethro Burns, and Tiny Moore, in the late 1970s. "Tallahassee" has also been continuously popular with younger bands since its similar appearance on a Decca single. "Now 'Tallahassee,'" Monroe stated, "I was in Ashland, Kentucky, and I wrote 'The Ashland Breakdown,' 'The Call of the Shepherd,' and 'Tallahassee' I wanted to title that number from Florida."[41] On the remake of "Get Up, John," Gordon Terry switches to guitar and only two fiddles are featured. This was the only one of the three tunes from this session to find its way onto the *Country Music Hall of Fame* LP in 1971. It was, of course, based on the fiddle tune called "Sleepy John" that Uncle Pen used to play.

Two weeks later, on January 13, 1971, Bill Monroe returned to the studio. Apparently, Bobby Thompson was booked so the call went to banjoist Earl Snead, who played bass for Lester Flatt after Jake Tullock left and was a fixture on the Nashville bluegrass scene. In later years he drove the tour bus for Lester Flatt and his band.

The session yielded a series of remakes. "Summertime Is Past and Gone," first recorded by Monroe in the 1940s' Columbia era, was again done as a trio vocal. This time Monroe was joined by son James and the versatile Joe Stuart. "Katy Hill," however, was a fiddle tune not especially associated with Uncle Pen. Monroe recalled learning it from the fiddling of former Skillet Lickers leader Clayton McMichen and maintained that McMichen derived the tune from an older one called "Sally Johnson." Whatever the case, Monroe often featured the piece on the Opry and recorded it at one of his first Victor solo sessions in 1940. Two other remakes from days past included "Rocky Road Blues" and the old 1939 Opry opener "Mule Skinner Blues."

Two days later, on January 15, 1971, three tunes associated with Uncle Pen were recorded. The hero of the tribute was, of course, Kenny Baker, the fiddler most closely associated with Monroe over the years. Baker remembers that Monroe told him of his plans for such an album as early as 1957: "After I got to playing his stuff a little bit, he told me about these old numbers of his Uncle Pen's. He said he was saving them back for the right fiddler, the man he thought could play them and do them right."[42] And a few months after the cuts were completed Monroe told Jim Rooney, "And to remember them numbers! I don't think there's been many got away from me."[43] To preserve them Monroe would regularly take them out once or twice a year and play over them to make sure he still had them.

"Poor White Folks" was one Monroe mentioned to Rooney as "White Folks Ain't Treating Me Right," a tune also associated with the famed black musician Arnold Shultz. "The Old Gray Mare Came Tearing Out of the Wilderness," a reasonably familiar tune in western Kentucky, was commercially recorded in the 1920s by Ted Sharp and others, and "Kiss Me Waltz" was

well known to many early fiddlers and had also been recorded in the 1920s.

Three more instrumentals were cut at the last *Uncle Pen* session on January 20, 1971, although only the first two would make it into the album. Of the three, "Jenny Lynn" is the most interesting. The tune is mentioned prominently in Bill's song "Uncle Pen" ("The greatest of all was 'Jenny Lynn' / To me that's where fiddlin' begins"). And at the end of the original 1950 recording of "Uncle Pen," Monroe taught fiddler Red Taylor how to play part of the tune and had him ride out the end of the song with it. In years thereafter Monroe would tell all his new fiddlers to find the original record and learn "Jenny Lynn" from it so they could duplicate the arrangement onstage. Presumably, for this "full" version of the song he taught the other half of the tune to Kenny Baker. Guthrie T. Meade dates the song to before 1846, crediting it to an obscure composer named Wallerstein, and further notes that it was often danced to as "Heel and Toe Polka."

There's no doubt that "Jenny Lynn" was one of Pen Vandiver's showpieces, probably a western Kentucky tune he adapted and made his own. Even Birch Monroe knew and played it. Whether it is named after Jenny Lind, the Swedish singer who toured America under P. T. Barnum's promotion in the 1850s, is an open question. A "Jenny Lind Polka" was known and played widely during the Civil War, but the tune that was recorded is not that one. Curiously, the next tune, which Monroe calls "Heel and Toe Polka," is far closer to the old "Jenny Lind Polka." It, too, presumably, was known to Pen Vandiver and dozens of other fiddlers.

"Milenberg Joy" was an old New Orleans jazz tune popularized in Chicago in the 1920s by entertainers such as Jelly Roll Morton and by bands like the New Orleans Rhythm Kings. The name should properly be "Milenburg Joys," named after an old dance hall near Lake Pontchartrain in New Orleans. During the 1920s the young jazz musicians on Chicago's South Side made the tune into a jazz standard, as it remains today with many Dixieland musicians. Although young Bill and Charlie Monroe arrived toward the end of this scene, they apparently did not learn the tune directly from a jazz band. Bill recalled that they picked it up from a novelty band they heard over WLS, the Hoosier Hotshots, who featured it and recorded it in the early 1930s. Far from bluegrass (the Hotshots used a washboard, clarinet, slide whistle, and guitar), yet the band was skilled at adapting pop instrumentals to a small-group format. This version of the tune appeared on *Bill Monroe Sings Bluegrass Body and Soul* in 1977.

Monroe didn't return to the studio for fourteen months; meanwhile, James decided to move on. In June 1971 he played his first show on his own at his father's festival in Bean Blossom, Indiana. James continued to work occasionally with the Blue Grass Boys, however. That December a *Martha White Opry* television show documented him playing guitar as Bill sang "Little Cabin Home on the Hill" with Lester Flatt along with the Blue Grass Boys and the Nashville Grass. In addition to James, the line-up included Roland White (mandolin), Haskell McCormick (banjo), and Paul Warren (fiddle) from Flatt's group and James (guitar), Kenny Baker and Joe Stuart (fiddles), and Jack Hicks (Bill's new banjoist) from the Blue Grass Boys. In the early 1990s filmmaker Steve Gebhardt would use the footage for his documentary on Monroe that was later issued as a commercial video.

The next actual studio session, set for March 14, 1972, was designed to begin work on the first album that would feature James, *Bill Monroe and James Monroe: Father and Son*. Since 1964 Monroe had used James as a sideman on albums, first as a bass player and since 1969 as a guitarist; he had also used him as a lead singer on gospel quartets and in vocal trios. Now that James had started his own band, the Midnight Ramblers, it was time to feature him on a series of duets.

The first two songs done for the album were old chestnuts: "Sweetheart You Done Me Wrong" dated from a 1947 Columbia session in which Monroe sang tenor to Lester Flatt's lead, and "Banks of the Ohio" was an authentic traditional murder ballad the Monroe Brothers did in 1936. "Tall Pines," a new addition to the canon, was written by young Damon Black from Missouri, who wrote long distance for Nashville publishing companies. "He understands the type of songs that would go into bluegrass," says James. "He wrote 'Sweet Mary and the Miles in Between,' 'Tall Pines,' and 'I Haven't Seen Mary in Years.' He's a wonderful writer. He can write bar songs that country singers have cut, but he understands bluegrass and can write for it, too. He can write either way."[44] "Tall Pines" was released as a single, and although it did not get on the charts it did become very popular with fans and parking-lot pickers.

The second *Father and Son* session, held the following day, March 15, 1972, featured identical personnel and reflected some important changes in the Blue Grass Boys. As of the March 14 recordings, Jack L. Hicks had come onboard to play banjo. The most chromatic of Monroe's melodic-style banjoists, he wound up spending almost four years with the band.

A native of Ashland, Kentucky, Hicks grew up with banjos around his house. His father, Pat, played them, repaired

them, and built them. When he felt that Jack was old enough to have one for his own, Pat Hicks took an old RB-100, fitted a new neck and tone ring to it, and presented it to the boy. Earl Scruggs's style, the father suggested, was the way to go. Young Jack already knew that. In 1955, when he was only three, he had attended the weekly show that Flatt and Scruggs played in Grayson, Kentucky. Although his father provided demanding lessons in the Scruggs style, Jack eventually discovered other methods as well. Listening to LPs by the Country Gentlemen, he became fascinated with the more progressive work of Eddie Adcock. "Some things just strike your fancy," he said later. "Up until a year before I moved to Nashville, I played nothing but his style."[45]

Both of Jack's parents were big bluegrass fans and were regulars on the festival circuit. Young Jack, reputed to be more than another parking-lot picker, soon attracted the attention of Monroe himself: "At Bean Blossom, Bill Monroe told me that when Rual Yarbrough quit, I could have his job. I was at one of Bill's festivals and Jim and Jesse were there. I told them I was looking for a job and went to work for them the next week. I think I was 17 or 18 at the time."[46] Before he knew it Jack Hicks was playing the Opry for the first time. He arrived early for the show, even before Jim and Jesse, and in his backstage wanderings encountered Stringbean (David Akeman). "You pick that thing, boy?" String asked. "I try," Jack answered. Impressed, Stringbean took him under his wing and stayed with him until the band arrived.

Hicks's Opry connections led to a series of other jobs with a variety of acts: Del Reeves, Buck White, Lester Flatt, Sonny James, and, finally, Conway Twitty, with whom he remained for some nine years and played not banjo so much as steel guitar. He is now out of music entirely, working as a farrier and in a trucking business. "I enjoyed the four years playing with Monroe more than anybody," he recalls. "I had more freedom to pick."[47]

Another change that began with the session of March 15, 1972, was the addition of Monroe Fields on bass. A true journeyman sideman, Fields played mandolin with Carl Sauceman in the 1960s and bass with Jim and Jesse during the same decade. He even sang baritone on that pair's *Old Country Church* album. Both "Foggy Mountain Top" and "What Would You Give in Exchange?" are from the old Monroe Brothers repertoire; in fact, both were substantial hits on the Bluebird label. "Mother's Only Sleeping" is a remake of a Monroe-Flatt duet from the Columbia days, 1946. The odd one here is "Love Please Come Home," a 1961 hit for Reno and Smiley that had originally been recorded by its composer, Leon Jackson, for King in the late 1950s. It had become a parking-lot favorite by 1972, and Monroe took a liking to it. He was still doing it onstage into the 1990s.

The last duet session with James, on March 21, 1972, is noteworthy for the inclusion of the powerful "Walls of Time," which Monroe and Peter Rowan coauthored in 1965 when James was just starting out in the band and recorded (with Roland White singing lead) in 1968, but that version was not released. In the meantime the song had gotten around, and other groups were doing it frequently. On this version, James sings lead. "My Old Kentucky and You" was written by Monroe for a woman named Jewel Breeding, whose first name appears in the lyrics. The summer after this recording, when this song had been released as a single, he would invite her onstage at festivals to stand by him as he sang "My Old Kentucky and You" to her.[48] James does not sing on this cut; it is Monroe Fields who takes the lead, Joe Stuart sings baritone, and Monroe the tenor. The cut did not make it onto LP until five years later, when it surfaced on the *Body and Soul* set. The single issued in the summer of 1972 backed it with "Lonesome Moonlight Waltz. "When the Golden Leaves Begin to Fall," credited to one of Monroe's pseudonyms, Albert Price, was also cut.

In June 1972 the *Uncle Pen* album was released. It was Monroe's first "concept" album, one for which he developed the repertoire, created the arrangements, and wrote the liner notes. It was a widely acclaimed milestone in his recording career. It was also the first album in which Ralph Rinzler did not play a direct role. When Rinzler became involved with Monroe in 1963, Bill had five albums on Decca—four newly recorded in the past five years and the other a recently released retrospective of uneven quality. Two albums represented Monroe's earlier recordings. One from Camden in 1962 contained all but a few of the 1940–41 Victors and was great-sounding. But for most who listened to bluegrass in 1962 it sounded different than other early bluegrass, more "old-timey" and bluesy. Moreover, there was no banjo to be heard on these cuts. The 1946–47 Columbias with Flatt, Scruggs, Wise, and Watts were, however, recognized as definitive bluegrass. A 1961 Harmony album contained only a few of them, however, along with some from 1945 and others from 1949. The vast majority of Bill Monroe's best recordings were, in 1963, either out of print or available only on 45-rpm singles.

Rinzler represented a generation of bluegrass fans who favored the LP as a recording medium, and he saw that part of his task in selling Monroe to new listeners was to place Bill's best recordings on albums that included explanatory notes. One, *Blue Grass Special,* was close to release when Rinzler began working with Decca to improve their Monroe products. The first album in which he had any say was a 1964 Vocalion (Decca's bargain label) retrospective that included previously unissued material Rinzler discovered during the course of his discographical research. The following year *Blue Grass Instrumentals* was released, the first of four retrospectives with extensive notes that included interview material from Bill and detailed who was playing and singing on each cut.

As Monroe gained new audiences beyond his familiar venues within earshot of the Opry he began to tour more widely. He also began attracting new musicians from afar. His band of the mid-1960s, represented on *Bluegrass Time,* was the result. It was the only album consisting entirely of newly made recordings that would be released until *Kentucky Blue Grass.* The four retrospectives released between 1965 and 1969 came at a time when bluegrass festivals were proliferating, part of the groundswell that helped Bill get elected to the Country Music Hall of Fame in 1970. By 1972, when the brilliant *Uncle Pen* album was released, Bill's stature as a country and folk music icon had been established, and the recordings testifying to that status were available on LP. He was hosting the nation's biggest bluegrass festival and helping his son promote a separate career. Both endeavors would be represented by recordings in 1973.

Notes

1. Ralph Rinzler, telephone interview with Charles K. Wolfe, Murfreesboro, Tenn., Jan. 1991.

2. Ibid.

3. For more on the bluegrass festival movement, see Neil V. Rosenberg, *Bluegrass: A History* (Urbana: University of Illinois Press, 1985), chs. 7, 10.

4. For the term *romancing the folk,* see Benjamin Filene, *Romancing the Folk: Public Memory and American Roots Music* (Chapel Hill: University of North Carolina Press, 2000).

5. Ralph Rinzler, telephone interview with Charles K. Wolfe.

6. Tony Trischka, "Bill Keith," *Bluegrass Unlimited* (Dec. 1975): 12.

7. Charles K. Wolfe, notes to *Bill Monroe: Bluegrass 1959–1969* (Bear Family BCD 15529, 1991), 15.

8. Wolfe, notes to *Bill Monroe: Bluegrass 1959–1969.*

9. Del McCoury, interview with Charles K. Wolfe, Nashville, March 1991.

10. Some of these recordings were issued by Rebel, others appeared on the Rebel subsidary, Zap.

11. Wolfe, notes to *Bill Monroe: Bluegrass 1959–1969.*

12. Trischka, "Bill Keith," 13.

13. Gwen Taylor, "Del McCoury," *Bluegrass Unlimited* 7 (June 1973): 18.

14. Doug Hutchens, notes to *Bill Monroe: Classic Bluegrass Instrumentals* (Rebel 850, 1985).

15. The unsigned notes to *Doc Watson: Out in the Country* (Intermedia QS 5031, 1982) state, in part, "This album presents an even dozen early recordings by Doc that have never been made available previously. Recorded by noted folk and blues producer Norman Dayron, they represent some of the finest and purest work yet committed to disc by the traditional master." Dayron was associated with the Chicago blues scene.

16. Pete Kuykendall, "James Monroe," *Bluegrass Unlimited* 8 (July 1973): 9.

17. The band included mandolin player David Grisman, Jim Field and Jody Stecher on guitars, Gene Lowinger on fiddle, and Winnie Winston on banjo. Field learned the song from Sandy Rothman, who'd worked as a Blue Grass Boy in the summer of 1964.

18. Alan Steiner, "Peter Rowan: Wandering Boy Returns to His Roots," *Bluegrass Unlimited* 13 (Feb. 1979): 13.

19. Ralph Rinzler, notes to *Bill Monroe and the Bluegrass Boys: Live Recordings 1956–1969, Off the Record Volume 1* (Smithsonian/Folkways CD 40063, 1993), 16.

20. Haney chose to describe the musical genre as "blue grass," following Monroe's name for his band. Rosenberg, *Bluegrass,* 206.

21. Richard J. Brooks, "An Interview with Richard S. Greene, Virtuoso Violinist," *Bluegrass Unlimited* 19 (Nov. 1984): 19.

22. Brooks, "An Interview with Richard S. Greene."

23. Kuykendall, "James Monroe," 10.

24. Steiner, "Peter Rowan," 13.

25. On April 3, 1966, in a show at the Brown County Jamboree in Bean Blossom, Indiana, Monroe spoke of learning this song from Mac and Bob (Lester McFarland and Bob Gardner), the popular blind duet act of the 1930s.

26. David Robinson, "Vic Jordan," *Pickin'* 1 (Aug. 1974): 6.

27. Byron Berline to Neil V. Rosenberg, email, March 25, 2005.

28. Robinson, "Vic Jordan," 6.

29. Kuykendall, "James Monroe," 9.

30. Patricia Glenn, "Rual Yarbrough," *Bluegrass Unlimited* 13 (Oct. 1978): 11. The Springfield banjo player was Howard Aldridge.

31. Wolfe, notes to *Bill Monroe: Bluegrass 1959–1969..*

32. Owen Bradley, notes to *Bill Monroe: The Weary Traveler* (MCA 2173, 1976).

33. Charles K. Wolfe, notes to *Bill Monroe: Bluegrass 1970–1979* (Bear Family BCD 15606, 1994), 4. One suspects that "McKinley's March" dates to the time of President McKinley; Meade notes several variants in aural tradition from Adair County in south central Kentucky and associates them with the tune known widely as "Chinese Breakdown." Guthrie T. Meade Jr., with Dick Spottswood and Douglas S. Meade, *Country Music Sources: A Biblio-Discography of Commercially Recorded Traditional Music* (Chapel Hill: Southern Folklife Collection, University of North Carolina at Chapel Hill Libraries in Association with the John Edwards Memorial Forum, 2002), 871.

34. Roy Lewis, notes to *Road of Life* (MCA 426, 1973).

35. Ralph Rinzler, notes to *Kentucky Blue Grass* (Decca DL 75213, 1970).

36. Ralph Rinzler, notes to *Bill Monroe's Country Music Hall of Fame* (Decca DL 75281, 1971).

37. Wolfe, notes to *Bill Monroe: Bluegrass 1970–1979*, 5.

38. Bobby Thompson, telephone interview with Tony Trischka, Fairlawn, N.J., 1998.

39. Ted Belue, "Legacy of Bobby Thompson," *Bluegrass Unlimited* 25 (Sept. 1990): 36.

40. Wolfe, notes to *Bill Monroe: Bluegrass 1970–1979*, 6.

41. Ibid.

42. Kenny Baker, notes to *Kenny Baker Plays Bill Monroe* (County CO 761, 1976).

43. Rooney, *Bossmen,* 96.

44. Kuykendall, "James Monroe," 11.

45. Wolfe, notes to *Bill Monroe: Bluegrass 1970–1979*, 10.

46. Ibid.

47. Ibid.

48. Carl Fleischhauer and Neil V. Rosenberg, *Bluegrass Odyssey* (Urbana: University of Illinois Press, 2001), 156–57.

DISCOGRAPHY, 1963–72

630208   Smithsonian/Folkways Reissue of Concert
Friends of Old Time Music, NYU School of Education, 35 W. 4th St., New York, NY
Feb. 8, 1963, 8:30 P.M.–?

[1]   WALKIN' THE DOG (Tex Grimsley-Cliff Grimsley)   SFW 40160
Cooke-L

[2]   LIVE AND LET LIVE (Wiley Walker-Gene Sullivan)   SFW 40160
Monroe-LV/TC, Cooke-LC, McCoury-B

[3]   GREY EAGLE   SFW 40160
Instrumental

[4]   I SAW THE LIGHT (Hank Williams)   SFW 40160
Cooke-L, Monroe-T, McCoury-B

[5]   LORD, BUILD ME A CABIN IN GLORY   SFW 40160
Cooke-L, Monroe-T, McCoury-B

[6]   SHADY GROVE   SFW 40160
Monroe-Lv/TC, Cooke-LC

[7]   THE BRAKEMAN'S BLUES (Jimmie Rodgers)   SFW 40160
Monroe-L

Bill Monroe: m	Jack Cooke: g	Kenny Baker: f
Delano F. "Del" McCoury: b	Bessie Lee Mauldin: sb	

630320   Decca session; producer, Harry Silverstein (Owen Bradley listed as "leader")
Columbia Recording Studio, 804 16th Ave. South, Nashville, Tenn.
March 20, 1963, 10 A.M.–1 P.M.

NA 12434   SALT CREEK (Bill Monroe–Bradford Keith)   31596   MCAD 4-11048, REB-850,
   113295   Instrumental   BCD 15529, CCS-CD-19

NA 12435   DEVIL'S DREAM (Bill Monroe)   31540   REB-850, BCD 15529,
   113296   Instrumental   MCA 088 113 207-2

NA 12436   SAILOR'S HORNPIPE (Bill Monroe–Bradford Keith)   DL 4601, MCAD 4-11048,
   113297   Instrumental   BCD 15529

| NA 12437 | WERE YOU THERE (Bill Monroe) | | DL 4896, MCA 426, BCD 15529, |
| 113298 | Monroe-L | | M18940 |

| Bill Monroe: m | Benny Williams: g | Kenny Baker: f |
| William Bradford "Bill/Brad" Keith: b | Bessie Lee Mauldin: sb | |

630327   Decca session; producer, Harry Silverstein (Owen Bradley listed as "leader")
Columbia Recording Studio, 804 16th Ave. South, Nashville, Tenn.
March 27, 1963, 7–10 P.M.

| NA 12450 | PIKE COUNTY BREAKDOWN (Bill Monroe) | | REB-850, BCD 15529 |
| 113313 | Instrumental | | |

| NA 12451 | SHENANDOAH BREAKDOWN (Bill Monroe) | 31658 | REB-850, BCD 15529, CCS-CD-19 |
| 113314 | Instrumental | | |

| NA 12452 | SANTA CLAUS (Bill Monroe) | | DL 4601, BCD 15529 |
| 113315 | Instrumental | | |

| Bill Monroe: m | Jackie Phelps: g | Kenny Baker: f |
| Bill Keith: b | Bessie Lee Mauldin: sb | |

630514.1[1]   Smithsonian/Folkways reissue of concert
The Ash Grove, Hollywood, Calif.
May 14, 1963

| [1] | YOU WON'T BE SATISFIED THAT WAY | SF 40064 |
| | Watson-L, Monroe-T | |

| [2] | MEMORIES OF YOU | SF 40064 |
| | Watson-L, Monroe-T | |

| Bill Monroe: m | Arthel Lane "Doc" Watson: g |

630514.2   Smithsonian/Folkways and FBN reissues of concert
The Ash Grove, Hollywood, Calif.
May 1963[2]

| [1] | TRUE LIFE BLUES—BILL & BOYS | FBN-210, SF 40063 |
| | McCoury-L, Monroe-T | |

| [2] | RAWHIDE—BILL & BOYS | FBN-210 |
| | Instrumental | |

| [3] | WHAT DOES THE DEEP SEA SAY? | FBN-210 |
| | Watson-L, Monroe-T | |

| [4] | FEAST HERE TONIGHT—BILL & DOC | FBN-210 |
| | Watson-L, Monroe-T | |

| [5] | MIDNIGHT ON THE STORMY DEEP | FBN-210 |
| | Watson-L, Monroe-T | |

| [6] | YOU WON'T BE SATISFIED THAT WAY | FBN-210 |
| | Watson-L, Monroe-T | |

Bill Monroe: m   Del McCoury (1–2): g,   Kenny Baker (1–2): f
                                  Doc Watson (3–6): g
Bill Keith: b (1–2)   Bessie Lee Mauldin: sb (1–2)

630517   Smithsonian/Folkways and FBN reissues of concert
The Ash Grove, Hollywood, Calif.
May 17, 1963

| [1] | WHAT WOULD YOU GIVE IN EXCHANGE FOR YOUR SOUL | SF 40064, SF 40137 |
| | Watson-L, Monroe-T | |

| [2] | WHERE IS MY SAILOR BOY? (WHAT DOES THE DEEP SEA SAY?) | SF 40064 |
| | Watson-L, Monroe-T | |

| [3] | BANKS OF THE OHIO | FBN-210, SF 40064 |
| | Watson-L, Monroe-T | |

| [4] | FIRE ON THE MOUNTAIN | SF 40064 |
| | Instrumental | |

| [5] | CHICKEN REEL | SF 40064 |
| | Instrumental | |

Bill Monroe: m   Doc Watson: g

630519   FBN reissue of concert
Monterey Folk Festival—workshop hosted by D. K. Wilgus, Monterey, Calif.
May 19, 1963, 11:30 A.M.

| [1] | BILL'S INTRO & GET UP JOHN | FBN-210 |
| | Instrumental | |

Bill Monroe: m   Doc Watson: g

630723   Kemtac pirate of Oscar Brand's The World of Folk Music, radio transcription session;
show #109, master XGPB-1004
(Radio Station studio?), New York City
ca. July 23, 1963

[1]   DEVIL'S DREAM   K 3308
Instrumental

[2]   I AM A PILGRIM   K 3308
Monroe-LV/TC, McCoury-LC, Keith-B, Ralph Rinzler-BS

[3]   MULE SKINNER BLUES
Monroe-L

| Bill Monroe: m | Del McCoury: g | Billy Baker-f |
| Bill Keith: b | Bessie Lee Mauldin: sb | |

630726   Recordings made by Vanguard, owned by MCA, leased by Bear Family; producer, Ralph Rinzler
Newport Folk Festival, concert, Newport, R.I.
July 26, 1963 (evening)

[1]   WATERMELON HANGING ON THE VINE [theme]   ACD 25001
Instrumental

[2]   MULE SKINNER BLUES   ACD 25001
Monroe-L

[3]   UNCLE PEN   ACD 25001
Monroe-LV/TC, McCoury-LC, Keith-B

[4]   DEVIL'S DREAM   ACD 25001
Instrumental

[5]   MOLLY AND TENBROOKS   ACD 25001
Monroe-L

[6]   I AM A PILGRIM   ACD 25001
Monroe-LV/TC, McCoury-LC, Keith-B, Ralph Rinzler-BS

[7]   RAWHIDE   ACD 25001
Instrumental

Bill Monroe: m	Delano F. "Del" McCoury: g	Billy Baker: f
Bill Keith: b	Bessie Lee Mauldin (1–6),	
	Ralph Rinzler (7): sb	

630727   Recordings made by Vanguard, owned by MCA, leased by Bear Family; producer, Ralph Rinzler
                  Newport Folk Festival, workshop, Newport, R.I.
                  July 27, 1963 (morning)[4]

[1]   PADDY ON THE TURNPIKE   ACD 25001
           Instrumental

[2]   PIKE COUNTY BREAKDOWN   ACD 25001
           Instrumental

[3]   RAWHIDE   ACD 25001
           Instrumental

[4]   GET UP JOHN   ACD 25001
           Instrumental

[5]   WILL YOU BE LOVING ANOTHER MAN   ACD 25001
           McCoury-L, Monroe-T

[6]   CONVERSATION WITH RALPH RINZLER   ACD 25001
           Monroe, Rinzler

[7]   PRETTY FAIR MAIDEN IN THE GARDEN   ACD 25001
           Monroe-L

[8]   SALT CREEK   ACD 25001
           Instrumental

[9]   LONESOME ROAD BLUES   ACD 25001
           Monroe-L

Bill Monroe (except 6): m   Del McCoury (except 6): g   Billy Baker (except 1, 6, 7): f
Bill Keith (except 6, 7): b   Bessie Lee Mauldin (except 6): sb

---

631116   Recordings made by David Grisman, leased to Acoustic Disc
                  Mechanic's Hall, Worcester, Mass.
                  Nov. 11, 1963

[1]   WATERMELON HANGING ON THAT VINE [theme]   ACD-59
           Instrumental

[2]   BAND INTROS   ACD-59
           Monroe

[3]	PANHANDLE COUNTRY Instrumental	ACD-59
[4]	DARK HOLLOW McCoury-L	ACD-59
[5]	ON AND ON McCoury-L, Monroe-T, Keith-B	ACD-59
[6]	DEVIL'S DREAM Instrumental	ACD-59
[7]	LOVE'S GONNA LIVE HERE Melissa Monroe-L	ACD-59
[8]	DREAMING OF A LITTLE CABIN Monroe-L	ACD-59
[9]	MULE SKINNER BLUES Monroe-L	ACD-59
[10]	FOOTPRINTS IN THE SNOW Monroe-L	ACD-59
[11]	BLUE MOON OF KENTUCKY Monroe-L	ACD-59
[12]	RAW HIDE Instrumental	ACD-59
[13]	JOHN HENRY Monroe-L	ACD-59
[14]	I SAW THE LIGHT McCoury-L, Monroe-T, Keith-B, Stuart-BS	ACD-59
[15]	WAITING FOR BEA Monroe	ACD-59
[16]	WHAT WOULD YOU GIVE? Lilly-L, Monroe-T	ACD-59
[17]	UNCLE PEN Monroe-LV/TC, McCoury-LC, Keith-B	ACD-59
[18]	BLUE RIDGE MOUNTAIN BLUES McCoury-L, Monroe-T	ACD-59

[19]   Y'ALL COME   ACD-59
                Monroe-L

Bill Monroe: m   Del McCoury, Mitchell "Bea"   Joe Stuart: f
Bill Keith: b   Lilly (16): g
                                  Bessie Lee Mauldin: sb

640000   Intermedia reissue of concert
                 Venue, place?
                 Date? (before 1982 [date of album's publication], probably 1963 or 1964)

[1]   WHAT WOULD YOU GIVE IN EXCHANGE FOR YOUR SOUL (trad: arr. Watson)   QS 5031
                Watson-L, Monroe-T

Bill Monroe: m   Doc Watson: g

640127   Decca session; producer, Harry Silverstein (Owen Bradley listed as "leader")
                 Columbia Recording Studio, 804 16th Ave. South, Nashville, Tenn.
                 Jan. 27, 1964, 6–9 P.M.

NA 12798   I'LL MEET YOU IN CHURCH SUNDAY MORNING (-)   DL 4537, BCD 15529
   114410   Monroe-L

NA 12799   MARY AT THE HOME PLACE (Ken Clark)   31651   DL 4671, BCD 15529
   114411   Monroe-L

NA 12800   HIGHWAY OF SORROW (Bill Monroe–Pete Pyle)   DL 4539, DL 4780, MCA 2-4090,
   114412   Monroe-L   BCD 15529, MCA 088 113 207-2

Bill Monroe: m   Joe Stuart: g   Benny Williams: f
Joe Drumright: b   Bessie Lee Mauldin: sb

640128   Decca session; producer, Harry Silverstein (Owen Bradley listed as "leader")
                 Columbia Recording Studio, 804 16th Ave. South, Nashville, Tenn.
                 Jan. 28, 1964, 6–9 P.M.

NA 12801   ONE OF GOD'S SHEEP (Wally Fowler)   DL 4537, BCD 15529
   114413   Monroe-L

NA 12802   ROLL ON BUDDY, ROLL ON (Teddy Wilburn–Doyle Wilburn)   DL 4896, MCAD 4-11048,
   114414   Monroe-LV/TC, McCoury-LC   BCD 15529, MCA 088 112 982-2,
                                                                                      MCA 088 113 207-2

NA 12803[5] 114415	LEGEND OF THE BLUE RIDGE MOUNTAINS (Horace Scarlet) Monroe-LV/TC, McCoury-LC	BCD 15529

Bill Monroe: m Joe Drumright: b	Del McCoury: g Bessie Lee Mauldin: sb	Benny Williams, Joe Stuart: f

640203 Decca session; producer, Harry Silverstein (Owen Bradley listed as "leader")
Columbia Recording Studio, 804 16th Ave. South, Nashville, Tenn.
Feb. 3, 1964, 6–9 P.M.

NA 12814 114490	LAST OLD DOLLAR (Lloyd George & Rollin Sullivan) Monroe-L	DL 7-5213, BCD 15529

NA 12815 114491	BILL'S DREAM (Bill Monroe) Instrumental	MCAD 4-11048, BCD 15529

Bill Monroe: m Joe Stuart: b	Jimmy Maynard: g Bessie Lee Mauldin: sb	Benny Williams, Buddy Spicher: f

640409 Decca session; producer, Harry Silverstein (Owen Bradley listed as "leader")
Columbia Recording Studio, 804 16th Ave. South, Nashville, Tenn.
April 9, 1964, 6–9 P.M.

NA 12904 114772	LOUISVILLE BREAKDOWN (Bill Monroe) Instrumental	DL 7-5066, REB-850, BCD 15529, CCS-CD-19

NA 12905 114773	NEVER AGAIN (Benny Williams) Monroe-LV/TC, Williams-LC	DL 7-5213, MCAD 4-11048, BCD 15529

NA 12906 114774	(WE'RE GOING) JUST OVER IN THE GLORY LAND (-) Monroe-L	MCA 426, BCD 15529, MCA 088 113 207-2

NA 12907 114775	FIRE ON THE MOUNTAIN (Bill Cody–Carl Eugster) Monroe-L	DL 7-5213, BCD 15529, MCA 088 113 207-2

Bill Monroe: m Joe Stuart: b	Jackie Phelps: g Bessie Lee Mauldin: sb	Benny Williams, Buddy Spicher: f

640418 Smithsonian/Folkways reissue of concert
Finney Chapel, Oberlin College, Oberlin, Ohio
April 18, 1964

[1]	KENTUCKY MANDOLIN Instrumental	SF 40064

| [2] | LONESOME MOONLIGHT WALTZ
Instrumental | SF 40064 |

Bill Monroe: m   Doc Watson: g

640831   Smithsonian/Folkways reissue of concert
[venue?], New London, Conn.
Aug. 31, 1964

| [1] | FOGGY MOUNTAIN TOP
Watson-L, Monroe-T | SF 40064 |

Bill Monroe: m   Doc Watson: g

641031   Smithsonian/Folkways Reissue of Concert
Jordan Hall, Boston, Mass.
Oct. 31, 1964

| [1] | KATY HILL
Instrumental | SF 40063 |

| [2] | BLUE GRASS BREAKDOWN
Instrumental | SF 40063 |

| [3] | RAW HIDE
Instrumental | SF 40063 |

| [4] | Y'ALL COME
Monroe-L, band-response | SF 40063 |

| [5] | SOLDIER'S JOY
Instrumental | SF 40064 |

| [6] | EAST TENNESSEE BLUES
Instrumental | SF 40064 |

| [7] | MIDNIGHT ON THE STORMY DEEP
Watson-L, Monroe-T | SF 40064 |

| [8] | HAVE A FEAST HERE TONIGHT
Watson-L, Monroe-T | SF 40064, SF 40061 |

Bill Monroe: m   Peter Rowan (1–4),   Benjamin "Tex" Logan (1–4): f
                                  Doc Watson (5–8): g
Bill Keith (1–4): b   Everett Alan Lilly (1–4): sb

641100   [Movie, reissued on Vic Lewis Video]; producer, Vic Lewis
Bradley's Barn, Nashville, Tenn.
Late fall 1964

[1]   MULE SKINNER BLUES   VLV 008-96820
Monroe-L

[2]   BLUE MOON OF KENTUCKY   VLV 008-96820
Monroe-L

Bill Monroe: m	Jimmy Elrod: g	Buddy Spicher, Benny Williams: f[6]
Don G. Lineberger: b	James William Monroe: sb	

650000   Concert recording bootlegged on Stack-O-Hits and Hollywood[7]
(Venue), (location?)
(Date?) (probably fall 1964 but definitely before 1981)

[1]   ORANGE BLOSSOM SPECIAL   A. G. 9001, HCD-409, PS 80246
Instrumental

[2]   UNCLE PENN [sic]   A. G. 9001, HCD-409, PS 80246
Monroe-LV/TC, Williams-LC, (?)-B

[3]   FOOTPRINTS IN THE SNOW   A. G. 9001, HCD-409
Monroe-L

[4]   BLUEGRASS BREAKDOWN   A. G. 9001, HCD-409
Instrumental

[5]   I SAW THE LIGHT   A. G. 9001, HCD-409
Williams-L, Monroe-T, (?)-B, (?)-BS

[6]   SHADY GROVE   A. G. 9001, HCD-409
Monroe-LV/TC, Williams-LC

[7]   SHENANDOAH BREAKDOWN   A. G. 9001, HCD-409
Instrumental

[8]   MULE SKINNER BLUES   A. G. 9001, HCD-409
Monroe-L

[9]   PRISON SONG [sic for PRISONER'S SONG]   A. G. 9001, HCD-409
Monroe-L

[10]   BLUE MOON OF KENTUCKY   A. G. 9001, HCD-409, PS 80246
Monroe-L

[11]   CAN'T YOU HEAR ME CALLING   A. G. 9001, HCD-409, PS 80246
            Williams-L, Monroe-T

[12]   NINE POUND HAMMER   A. G. 9001, HCD-409
            Monroe-L

Bill Monroe: m   Jimmy Elrod: g   Benny Williams: f
Don Lineberger: b   James Monroe: sb

650316   Decca session; producer, Harry Silverstein (Ray Edenton listed as "leader")
               Columbia Recording Studio, 804 16th Ave. South, Nashville, Tenn.
               March 16, 1965, 6–9 P.M.

NA 13373   THE LONG BLACK VEIL (Marijohn Wilkin–Danny Dill)   DL75213, BCD 15529,
   115841   Monroe-L   MCA 088 113 207-2

NA 13374   I LIVE IN THE PAST (Virginia Stauffer)   31878   DL75213, MCA 2-4090,
   115842   Monroe-L   BCD 15529

NA 13375   THERE'S AN OLD, OLD HOUSE (Hal Bynum–   31878   BCD 15529
   115843   George Jones)
            Monroe-L

Bill Monroe: m   Jimmy Elrod: g   Benny Williams, Buddy Spicher: f
Don Lineberger: b   James William Monroe: sb

650400   Shanachie Video reissues of National Life Grand Old Opry program #7, originally broadcast on CBS.
               Grand Ole Opry, Nashville, Tenn.
               Between April and Aug. 1965.

[1][8]   BLUEGRASS BREAKDOWN   SHA 604
            Instrumental

[4]   UNCLE PEN   SHA 604
            Rowan-L, Monroe-T, Lowinger-B

Bill Monroe: m   Peter Rowan: g   Gene Lowinger: f
Don Lineberger: b   James Monroe: sb

650617   Smithsonian/Folkways reissue of party
                  Tex Logan's home, Madison, N.J.
                  June 17, 1965

[1]   COTTON-EYED JOE   SF 40063
           Monroe-L, Logan-T

Bill Monroe: m   Peter Rowan: g   Tex Logan: f
Bill Keith: b   David Grisman: sb   (unidentified): other instruments

---

650724.1   Vanguard session at concert
                  Newport Folk Festival, workshop ("Fiddle & Mandolin"), Newport, R.I.
                  July 24, 1965, (1:30–3 P.M.)

[1]   INTRODUCTION   V77012-2
           Monroe

[2]   WALLS OF TIME   V 77012-2, V 187/89-2
           Rowan-L, Monroe-T

[3]   GREY EAGLE   V 77012-2, V 187/89-2
           Instrumental

[4]   COTTON-EYED JOE   V 77012-2, V 187/89-2
           Logan-L, Monroe-T

[5]   SHADY GROVE   V 77012-2, V 187/89-2,
           Monroe-LV/TC, Rowan-TC   V 77007-2

Bill Monroe (2–5): m   Peter Rowan (2–5): g   Tex Logan (3, 5): f

---

650724.2   Vanguard session at concert
                  Newport Folk Festival, concert, Newport, R.I.
                  July 24, 1965, evening (8–)

[1]   MULE SKINNER BLUES   VCD77006
           Monroe-L

[2]   BLUE MOON OF KENTUCKY   VCD77006, V 77007-2
           Monroe-L

[3]   WALLS OF TIME   VCD77006
           Rowan-L, Monroe-T

[4]   BLUE YODEL #4   V 77012-2, V 187/89-2,
        Monroe-L   V 208/10-2

[5]   MOLLY AND TENBROOKS   V 77012-2, V 187/89-2
        Monroe-L

[6]   SOMEBODY TOUCHED ME   VCD77006
        Rowan-L, Monroe-T, (Lowinger?)-B, (Ralph Rinzler?)-BS

[7]   BLUE GRASS BREAKDOWN   VCD77006, V 78003-2,
        Instrumental   V 187/89-2

Bill Monroe: m   Peter Rowan: g   Gene Lowinger, Tex Logan (2, 3),
Don Lineberger: b   James Monroe: bs   Byron Berline (2, 3): f

---

650905   Smithsonian/Folkways and Shanachie Video reissues of concert
                Roanoke Bluegrass Festival, Cantrell's Horse Farm, Fincastle Va.
                Sept. 5, 1965

[1]   GET UP JOHN   SF 40063, SF 40092
        Instrumental

[2]   KANSAS CITY RAILROAD BLUES   SF 40063
        Instrumental

[3]   WALLS OF TIME   SF 40063, SF 40163
        Rowan-L, Monroe-T

[4]   WHEN HE REACHED DOWN HIS HAND FOR ME   SF 40063, SF 40092,
        Wiseman-L, Monroe-T, Don Reno-B, Benny Martin-BS   SF 40137

[5]   TRAVELING DOWN THIS LONESOME ROAD   SHA 604
        Wiseman-L, Monroe-T

[6]   RAW HIDE   SHA 604
        Instrumental

Bill Monroe: m   Peter Rowan (1–3),   Benny Martin (5–6): f
Don Reno (5–6): b   Mac Wiseman (4–6): g
                                      James Monroe (5–6): sb

660504   Smithsonian/Folkways reissue of concert
                 Gaslight Cafe, New York, N.Y.
                 May 4–6, 1966

[1]   WATERMELON HANGING ON THE VINE   SF 40063
                 Instrumental

[2]   I LIVE IN THE PAST   SF 40063
                 Monroe-L

[3]   FIRE ON THE MOUNTAIN   SF 40063, SF 40149
                 Instrumental

Bill Monroe: m   Peter Rowan: g   Richard Greene, Tex Logan (3): f
Lamar Grier: b   James Monroe: sb

660620   Smithsonian/Folkways reissue of party
                 Tex Logan's home, Madison, N.J.
                 June 20, 1966

[1]   WAYFARING STRANGER   SF 40063, ACD-46
                 Rowan-L, Monroe-T

[2]   WHITE HOUSE BLUES   SF 40063, SF 40080[9]
                 Monroe-L

[3]   ROLL IN MY SWEET BABY'S ARMS   SF 40063
                 Monroe-L, Hazel Dickens-T

Bill Monroe: m   Peter Rowan (1, 2, 3): g   Richard Greene (1, 2, 3?),
(Lamar Grier?): b   (Hazel Dickens, 1?,   Tex Logan (2): f
                                    James Monroe, 2–3?): sb

660826   Smithsonian/Folkways reissue of party
                 Tex Logan's home, Madison, N.J.
                 Aug. 26, 1966

[1]   WATSON'S BLUES   SF 40064, SF 40163
                 Instrumental

[2]   TURKEY IN THE STRAW   SF 40064
                 Instrumental

Bill Monroe: m   Doc Watson: g

661014   Decca session; producer, Harry Silverstein (Ray Edenton listed as "leader")
Columbia Recording Studio, 804 16th Ave. South, Nashville, Tenn.
Oct. 14/15, 1966, 10 P.M.–1 A.M.

NA 14302   WHEN MY BLUE MOON TURNS TO   32075   DL 4896, BCD 15529
118062   GOLD AGAIN (Wiley Walker–Gene Sullivan)
Monroe-LV/TC, J. Monroe-LC, Rowan-B

NA 14303   I WONDER WHERE YOU ARE TONIGHT (Johnny Bond)   DL 4896, BCD 15529,
118063   Monroe-LV/TC, J. Monroe-LC, Rowan-B   MCA 088 113 207-2

NA 14304   TURKEY IN THE STRAW (Traditional)   DL 4896, BCD 15529
118064   Instrumental

Bill Monroe: m   Peter Rowan: g   Richard Greene: f
Lamar Grier: b   James Monroe: sb

661103   Decca session; producer, Harry Silverstein (Ray Edenton listed as "leader")
Columbia Recording Studio, 804 16th Ave. South, Nashville, Tenn.
Nov. 3/4, 1966, 10 P.M.–2:30 A.M.

NA 14324   PRETTY FAIR MAIDEN IN THE GARDEN   32075   DL 4896, MCA 2-4090,
118149   (Bill Monroe)   BCD 15529
Monroe-L

NA 14325   LOG CABIN IN THE LANE (Jim Eanes)   DL 7-5213, BCD 15529
118150   Monroe-L

NA 14326   PADDY ON THE TURNPIKE (Bill Monroe)   REB-850, BCD 15529
118151   Instrumental

Bill Monroe: m   Peter Rowan: g   Richard Greene, Buddy Spicher
Lamar Grier: b   James Monroe: sb   (except -26): f

661206   Decca session; producer, Harry Silverstein (Ray Edenton listed as "leader")
Columbia Recording Studio, 804 16th Ave. South, Nashville, Tenn.
Dec. 6, 1966, 6–9:30 P.M.

NA 14394   THAT'S ALL RIGHT (Autry Inman)   DL 4896, BCD 15529
118287   Monroe-L

NA 14395   IT MAKES NO DIFFERENCE NOW (F. Tillman–J. Davis)   DL 4896, BCD 15529
118288   Monroe-L

NA 14396	DUSTY MILLER (Traditional)	DL 4896, MCAD 4-11048,
118289	Instrumental	BCD 15529, MCA 088 113 207-2,
		M18983

Bill Monroe: m
Lamar Grier: b

Peter Rowan: g
James Monroe: sb

Richard Greene: f

661216   Decca session; producer, Harry Silverstein (Ray Edenton listed as "leader")
Columbia Recording Studio, 804 16th Ave. South, Nashville, Tenn.
Dec. 16/17, 1966, 10 P.M.-1:30 A.M.

NA 14421	MIDNIGHT ON THE STORMY DEEP (Traditional)	DL 4896, MCAD 10082,
118347	Rowan-L, Monroe-T	MCAD 4-11048, BCD 15529,
		MCA 088 112 982-2,
		MCA 088 113 207-2,
		MCA 80004424-02

NA 14422	ALL THE GOOD TIMES ARE PAST AND GONE (Traditional)	DL 4896, BCD 15529
118348	J. Monroe-L, Monroe-T, Rowan-B	

NA 14423	SOLDIER'S JOY (Bill Monroe)	MCAD 4-11048, BCD 15529
118349	Instrumental	

Bill Monroe: m
Lamar Grier: b

Peter Rowan: g
James Monroe: sb

Richard Greene: f

670123   Decca session; producer, Harry Silverstein (Ray Edenton listed as "leader")
Columbia Recording Studio, 804 16th Ave. South, Nashville, Tenn.
Jan. 23, 1967, 6-9 P.M.

NA 14474	BLUE NIGHT (Kirk McGee)	DL 4896, MCAD 4-11048,
118524	Monroe-L	BCD 15529

NA 14475	GREY EAGLE (Bill Monroe)	BCD 15529
118525	Instrumental	

Bill Monroe: m
Lamar Grier: b

Peter Rowan: g
James Monroe: sb

Richard Greene: f

670823   Decca session; producer, Harry Silverstein (Bill Monroe listed as "leader")
Columbia Recording Studio, 804 16th Ave. South, Nashville, Tenn.
Aug. 23, 1967, 6–9 P.M.

NA 14784   THE GOLD RUSH[10] (Bill Monroe)   32404   DL 7-5281, MCA 2-4090,
119363   Instrumental   BCD 15529

NA 14785   SALLY GOODIN (Bob Wills–Tommy Duncan)   DL 7-5213, MCAD 4-11048,
119364   Instrumental   BCD 15529, MCA 088 113 207-2

NA 14786   VIRGINIA DARLIN' (Bill Monroe)   32404   REB-850, BCD 15529
119365   Instrumental

Bill Monroe: m   Roland Joseph White: g   Byron Berline: f
Victor Howard "Vic" Jordan: b   James Monroe: sb

671109   Decca session; producer, Harry Silverstein (Bill Monroe is listed as "leader")
Columbia Recording Studio, 804 16th Ave. South, Nashville, Tenn.
Nov. 9, 1967, 6–9 P.M.

NA 14837   IS THE BLUE MOON STILL SHINING?   32245   DL 7-5213, MCA 2-4090,
119587   (Melissa Monroe)   BCD 15529
Monroe-L

NA 14838   TRAIN 45 (HEADING SOUTH) (Bill Monroe)   32245   BCD 15529
119588   Monroe-L

NA 14839   KENTUCKY MANDOLIN (Bill Monroe)   DL 7-5213, MCA 2-4090,
119589   Instrumental   MCAD 10082, MCAD 4-11048,
    BCD 15529, CCS-CD-19

Bill Monroe: m   Roland White: g   Benny Williams, Vassar Clements
Vic Jordan: b   James Monroe: sb   (except -39): f

681114   Decca session; producer, Harry Silverstein (Bill Monroe listed as "leader")
Columbia Recording Studio, 804 16th Ave. South, Nashville, Tenn.
Nov. 14, 1968, 6–9:30 P.M.

NA 15330   I WANT TO GO WITH YOU (Bill Monroe)   DL 7-5213, BCD 15529
120936   J. Monroe-L, Monroe-T, White-B

NA 15331   CROSSING THE CUMBERLANDS (Bill Monroe)   32502   BCD 15529, CCS-CD-19
    Instrumental

| NA 15332
120938 | WALLS OF TIME (Bill Monroe)
White-L, Monroe-T | | MCAD 4-11048, BCD 15529,
MCA 088 112 982-2,
MCA 088 113 207-2,
MCA 80004424-02 |

| Bill Monroe: m | Roland White: g | Kenny Baker: f |
| Vic Jordan: b | James Monroe: sb | |

681220   Opryland Home Video reissue of live radio/television syndicated broadcast for *National Life*
Grand Ole Opry, Nashville, Tenn.
Dec. 20, 1968

| [1] | TRAIN 45 HEADING SOUTH
Monroe-L | | JB 1914 |

| Bill Monroe: m | Roland White: g | Kenny Baker: f |
| Vic Jordan: b | James Monroe: sb | |

690326   Decca session; producer, Harry Silverstein (Joe Zinkan listed as "leader")
Columbia Recording Studio, 804 16th Ave. South, Nashville, Tenn.
March 26, 1969, 6–9 P.M.

| NA 15500
121370 | I HAVEN'T SEEN MARY IN YEARS
(Damon Black)
J. Monroe-L, Monroe-T | 32502 | MCA 310, MCAD 4-11048,
BCD 15529, MCA 088 113 207-2 |

| NA 15501
121371 | FIREBALL MAIL (Floyd Jenkins)
Monroe-L | 7-32574 | BCD 15529 |

| NA 15502
121372 | THE DEAD MARCH (Bill Monroe)
Instrumental | | DL 7-5348, MCAD 4-11048,
BCD 15529 |

| Bill Monroe: m | James Monroe: g | Kenny Baker, Joe Herman "Red" Hayes: f |
| Rual Yarbrough: b | Joe Zinkan: sb | |

690429   Decca session; producer, Harry Silverstein (Joe Zinkan listed as "leader")
Columbia Recording Studio, 804 16th Ave. South, Nashville, Tenn.
April 29, 1969, 6–9 P.M.

| NA 15591
121591 | CRIPPLE CREEK (arr. Bill Monroe)
Instrumental | | DL 7-5213, BCD 15529 |

| NA 15592
121592 | WHAT ABOUT YOU?[11] (Johnny Wright–Jack Anglin)
J. Monroe-L | | BCD 15529 |

NA 15593	WITH BODY AND SOUL (Virginia Stauffer)	7-32574	MCA 2251, MCAD 4-11048,
121593	Monroe-L		BCD 15529, MCA 088 113 207-2

NA 15594	METHODIST PREACHER (Bill Monroe)	DL 7-5348, BCD 15529
121594	Instrumental	

Bill Monroe: m James Monroe: g Kenny Baker, Thomas "Tommy" Williams: f
Rual Yarbrough: b Joe Zinkan: sb[12]

690704   Smithsonian session at Smithsonian Folkways reissue of concert
Festival of American Folklife, Washington, D.C.
July 4, 1969 (Smithsonian Folkways gives this as July 3, 1969)

[1]   PADDY ON THE TURNPIKE   SF 40063
Instrumental

[2]   HOW OLD ARE YOU MY PRETTY LITTLE MISS?   SF 40063
Instrumental

[3]   HE WILL SET YOUR FIELDS ON FIRE   SF 40063
C. Monroe-L, Bill Monroe-T, Birch Monroe-BS

[4]   DURANG'S HORNPIPE   SF 40063
Instrumental

[5]   I KNOW MY LORD'S GONNA LEAD ME OUT (Traditional)   FAF Vol. 1, SF 40063
C. Monroe-L, Bill Monroe-T, Birch Monroe-BS

[6]   UNCLE PEN (Bill Monroe)   FAF Vol 1
B. Monroe-LV/TC, J. Monroe-LC, Yarbrough-B

Bill Monroe: m Charlie Monroe (2–5), Birch Monroe (2, 4),
Rual Yarbrough (6): b James Monroe (6): g Kenny Baker (6): f
Douglas B. "Doug" Green (6): sb

691000   Shanachie Video and CMH CD reissue of live radio/television broadcast
Grand Ole Opry, Nashville, Tenn.
Fall 1969

[1]   WITH BODY AND SOUL   SHA 604, CD 8007,
Monroe-L   CD-1788, CD-6294
CD-8421, CD-8933

Bill Monroe: m James Monroe: g Kenny Baker, (Tommy Williams?): f
Rual Yarbrough: b (not visible but most likely Bill Yates): sb

691028   Decca session; producer, Harry Silverstein
Bradley's Barn, Mount Juliet, Tenn.
Oct. 28, 1969, 6–9:00 P.M.

NA 15821 122181	WALK SOFTLY ON MY HEART[13] (Jake Landers–Bill Monroe) Monroe-LV/TC, J. Monroe-LC, Yarbrough-B	32654	MCA 2251, MCAD 10082, MCAD 4-11048, BCD 15529, MCA 088 112 982-2, MCA 088 113 207-2, M19007, MCA 80004424-02
NA 15822[14] 122182	TALL PINES (Damon Black) J. Monroe-L, Monroe-TC		
NA 15823 122183	CANDY GAL (Bill Monroe) Instrumental		DL 7-5348, BCD 15529

Bill Monroe: m   James Monroe: g   Kenny Baker, Red Hayes: f
Rual Yarbrough: b   Bill Yates: sb

691125   Decca session; producer, Harry Silverstein (Bill Monroe listed as "leader")
Bradley's Barn, Mount Juliet, Tenn.
Nov. 25, 1969, 6–9 P.M.

NA 15846 122251	LAND OF LINCOLN (Bill Monroe) Instrumental		
NA 15847 122252	GOING UP CANEY (Bill Monroe) Yates-L, Monroe-T, Yarbrough-B	32827	DL 7-5348, DL 7-1916, MCAD 4-11048, BCD 15529, MCA3P-3256, CCS-CD-19, SHA 604
NA 15848 122253	THE LEE WEDDIN TUNE (Bill Monroe) Instrumental		DL 7-5348, MCAD 10082, BCD 15529

Bill Monroe: m   James Monroe: g   Kenny Baker: f
Rual Yarbrough: b   Bill Yates: sb

691217   Decca session; producer, Harry Silverstein (Joe Zinkan listed as "leader") (Session
listed under James Monroe)
Bradley's Barn, Mount Juliet, Tenn.
Dec. 17, 1969, 6–9 P.M.

NA 15869 122326	BONNY[15] (Juanita Southern) J. Monroe-L, Monroe-T	32645	MCA 310, BCD 15529

NA 15870   SWEET MARY AND THE MILES IN BETWEEN   32645   BCD 15529
    122327   (Damon Black)
             J. Monroe-L

Bill Monroe: m   James Monroe: g   Kenny Baker, Tommy Williams: f
Rual Yarbrough: b   Joe Zinkan: sb

700119[16]   Decca session; producer, ? (Bill Monroe listed as "leader")
              Bradley's Barn, Mount Juliet, Tenn.
              Jan. 19, 1970, 6–9 P.M.

15898   McKINLEY'S MARCH (Bill Monroe)   32654   REB-850, BCD 15606
    122426   Instrumental

15899   TEXAS GALLOP (Bill Monroe)   DL 7-5348, BCD 15606,
    122427   Instrumental   CCS-CD-19

Bill Monroe: m   James Monroe: g   Kenny Baker, Tommy Williams: f
Rual Yarbrough: b   Joe Zinkan: sb

700326   Decca session; producer, probably Harold Bradley (Bill Monroe listed as "leader")
              Bradley's Barn, Mount Juliet, Tenn.
              March 26, 1970, 6–10 P.M.

NA 15976   ROAD OF LIFE (Virginia Stauffer)   MCA 426
    122600   Monroe-LV/TC, J. Monroe-LC, Yarbrough-B, Culley Holt-BS

NA 15977   IT'S ME AGAIN LORD (Dottie Rambo)   MCA 426
    122601   J. Monroe-L, Monroe-T, Yarbrough-B, Holt-BS

NA 15978   BEYOND THE GATE (Bill Monroe–Jake Landers)   MCA 426
    122602   J. Monroe-L, Monroe-T, Yarbrough-B, Holt-BS

NA 15979   I WILL SING FOR THE GLORY OF GOD (B. F. Logan)   MCA 426
    122603   J. Monroe-L, Monroe-T, Yarbrough-B, Holt-BS

Bill Monroe: m   James Monroe: g   Kenny Baker: f
Rual Yarbrough: b   (unknown; overdubbed later): sb

700500   NET broadcast, released by Varied Directions Inc. on DVD; director, David Hoffman;
sound track acquired by Columbia[17]
Ryman Auditorium dressing room, Nashville, Tenn.
Ca. May 1970

NCO 108787   MEDLEY (with Bill Monroe): TRAIN 45 / LITTLE MAGGIE /   J9
MY LITTLE GEORGIA ROSE /NINE POUND HAMMER
Monroe-L

Bill Monroe: m   James Monroe, Randy Scruggs: g   Kenny Baker: f
Rual Yarbrough, Earl Scruggs: b   Skip Payne: sb

701202   Decca session; producer, Walter Haynes (Bill Monroe listed as "leader")
Bradley's Barn, Mount Juliet, Tenn.
Dec. 2, 1970, 6–9 P.M.

NA 16262   KENTUCKY WALTZ (Bill Monroe)   DL 7-5281, MCAD 10082,
123259   Monroe-L   MCAD 4-11048, BCD 15606,
R142-08, MCA 088 112 982-2,
MCA 80004424-02

NA 16263   THE GIRL IN THE BLUE VELVET BAND (Cliff Carlisle–Mel Foree)   DL 7-5281, BCD 15606
123260   Monroe-L

NA 16264   MY LITTLE GEORGIA ROSE (Bill Monroe)
123261   Monroe-L

Bill Monroe: m   James Monroe, Gordon Terry   Kenny Baker, Red Hayes,
Robert C. "Bobby" Thompson: b   (-63): g   Gordon Terry (except on 63): f
Joe Stuart: sb

701203   Decca session; producer, Walter Haynes (Bill Monroe listed as "leader")
Bradley's Barn, Mount Juliet, Tenn.
Dec. 3, 1970, 6–9 P.M.

NA 16269   LONESOME MOONLIGHT WALTZ   32966   REB-850, MCAD 4-11048,
123266   (Bill Monroe)   BCD 15606
Instrumental

NA 16270   TALLAHASSEE (Bill Monroe)   32827   REB-850, BCD 15606, CCS-CD-19
123267   Instrumental

| NA 16271 | GET UP JOHN (Bill Monroe) | DL 7-5281, MCAD 4-11048, |
| 123268 | Instrumental | BCD 15606 |

Bill Monroe: m	James Monroe,	Kenny Baker, Red Hayes
Bobby Thompson: b	Gordon Terry (-71): g	Gordon Terry (except on -71): f
	Joe Stuart: sb	

710113   Decca session; producer, Walter Haynes (Bill Monroe listed as "leader")
Bradley's Barn, Mount Juliet, Tenn.
Jan. 13, 1971, 6–9 P.M.

| NA 16300 | SUMMERTIME IS PAST AND GONE (Bill Monroe) | DL 7-5281, BCD 15606 |
| 123353 | Monroe-LC/TV, J. Monroe-LV, Stuart-B | |

| NA 16301 | ROCKY ROAD BLUES (Bill Monroe) | DL 7-5281, MCAD 4-11048, |
| 123354 | Monroe-L | BCD 15606, B0000303-02 |

| NA 16302 | MULE SKINNER BLUES (Jimmie Rodgers–George Vaughn) | DL 7-5281, BCD 15606 |
| 123355 | Monroe-L | |

| NA 16303 | KATY HILL (Bill Monroe) | |
| 123356 | Instrumental | |

| Bill Monroe: m | James Monroe: g | Kenny Baker: f |
| Earl Snead: b | Joe Stuart: sb | |

710115   Decca session; producer, Walter Haynes (Bill Monroe listed as "leader")
Bradley's Barn, Mount Juliet, Tenn.
Jan. 15, 1971, 6–9 P.M.

| NA 16310 | POOR WHITE FOLKS (Bill Monroe) | DL 7-5348, BCD 15606 |
| 123350 | Instrumental | |

NA 16311	THE OLD GRAY MARE CAME TEARING OUT OF THE WILDERNESS	DL 7-5348, BCD 15606
123351	(Bill Monroe)	
	Instrumental	

| NA 16312 | KISS ME WALTZ (Bill Monroe) | DL 7-5348, BCD 15606 |
| 123352 | Instrumental | |

| Bill Monroe: m | James Monroe: g | Kenny Baker: f |
| Bobby Thompson: b | Joe Stuart: sb | |

710120   Decca session; producer, Walter Haynes (Bill Monroe listed as "leader")
Bradley's Barn, Mount Juliet, Tenn.
Jan. 20, 1971, 6–9 P.M.

NA 16316	JENNY LYNN (Bill Monroe)	DL 7-5348, MCAD 4-11048,
123381	Instrumental	BCD 15606
NA 16317	HEEL AND TOE POLKA (Bill Monroe)	DL 7-5348, BCD 15606
123382	Instrumental	
NA 16318	MILENBURG JOY (Bill Monroe)	MCA 2251, BCD 15606
123383	Instrumental	

Bill Monroe: m   James Monroe: g   Kenny Baker, Buddy Spicher: f
Bobby Thompson: b   Joe Stuart: sb

711200   Grand Ole Opry broadcast, guest appearance on Martha White portion, issued by Original Cinema
Grand Ole Opry, Nashville, Tenn.
Dec. 1971

[1]	LITTLE CABIN HOME ON THE HILL	OC-1001
	Flatt-L, Monroe-T	

Bill Monroe, Roland White: m   James Monroe, Lester Flatt,   Kenny Baker, Joe Stuart,
Jack Hicks, Haskell McCormick: b   Howard G. "Johnny" Johnson: g   Paul Warren, (?): f
                                         Billy Linneman: sb   Harold Weakly: snare drum; (?): piano

720314   MCA session; producer, Walter Haynes (Bill Monroe listed as "leader")
Bradley's Barn, Mount Juliet, Tenn.
March 14, 1972, 6–9 P.M.

NA 16730	SWEETHEART YOU DONE ME WRONG (Lester Flatt–Bill Monroe)		MCA 310, BCD 15606
123907	J. Monroe-L, Monroe-T		
NA 16731	BANKS OF THE OHIO (arr. & adapt. B. Welch–J. Farrar)		MCA 310, BCD 15606
123908	J. Monroe-L		
NA 16732[18]	TALL PINES (Damon Black)	40006	MCA 310, BCD 15606
123909	J. Monroe-L, Monroe-T		

Bill Monroe: m   James Monroe: g   Kenny Baker, Tommy Williams: f
Jack Hicks: b   Monroe Fields: sb

720315   MCA session; producer, Walter Haynes (Bill Monroe listed as "leader")
Bradley's Barn, Mount Juliet, Tenn.
March 15, 1972, 6–9 P.M.

NA 16733	MOTHER'S ONLY SLEEPING (Bill Monroe)		MCA 310, BCD 15606
123910	Monroe-LV/TC, J. Monroe-LC		
NA 16734	FOGGY MOUNTAIN TOP (A. P. Carter)	40006	MCA 310, BCD 15606
123911	Monroe-LV/TC, J. Monroe-LC		
NA 16735	LOVE PLEASE COME HOME (Leon Jackson)		MCA 310, BCD 15606
123912	J. Monroe-L, Monroe-T		
NA 16736	WHAT WOULD YOU GIVE IN EXCHANGE? (J. H. Carr–F. J. Barry)		MCA 310, BCD 15606
123913	J. Monroe-L, Monroe-T		

Bill Monroe: m   James Monroe: g   Kenny Baker, Tommy Williams: f
Jack Hicks: b   Monroe Fields: sb

720321   MCA session; producer, Walter Haynes (Bill Monroe listed as "leader")
Bradley's Barn, Mount Juliet, Tenn.
March 21, 1972, 6–9 P.M.

NA 16737	WHEN THE GOLDEN LEAVES BEGIN TO FALL (Albert Price)		MCA 310, BCD 15606
123914	Monroe-LV/TC, J. Monroe-LC		
NA 16738	WALLS OF TIME (Bill Monroe)		MCA 310, BCD 15606,
123915	J. Monroe-L, Monroe-T		Hip-O 314 564682 2
NA 16739	MY OLD KENTUCKY AND YOU (Bill Monroe)	32966	MCA 2251, MCAD 4-11048,
123916	Fields-L, Monroe-T, Stuart-B[19]		BCD 15606

Bill Monroe: m   James Monroe,   Kenny Baker,
Jack Hicks: b   Joe Stuart (-39 only): g   Joe Stuart (except -39),
                                Monroe Fields: bs   Tommy Williams: f

Notes

1. In his notes to Smithsonian/Folkways SF 40064 Ralph Rinzler dates this performance as April 14, 1963, which is almost certainly off by a month. Monroe did not travel to California until May. Watson was at the Ash Grove along with Clarence Ashley. Contemporary advertising gives them equal billing, along with Roscoe Holcomb, for May 7–12; Monroe and the Blue Grass Boys were advertised for May 14–19. Monroe also appeared with the Blue Grass Boys at the UCLA Folk Festival on May 3–5 and at concerts in Santa Clara and Berkeley on May 10 and 11. His appearance at the Monterey Folk Festival with Watson on the May 19 is listed in session 630519.

2. This date is uncertain; some of these masters may have been recorded on different nights. In the notes to SF 40063 Rinzler gives "April-May" for [1], while the producer of FBN-210 states that all were recorded in May. Although Monroe's spoken introductions to the two

releases of [1] differ, the music portions of each are the same. "Where Is My Sailor Boy?" is the title of the original Monroe Brothers version of [3], recorded at session 361012. For Monroe's California dates, see note 1 above.

3. Introduction by Sen. Claiborne Pell of Rhode Island.

4. Emcee was Bill Clifton.

5. -03 was entitled "Young Girl Dressed in Blue" on the original session data; that was crossed out and the present title substituted at a later date. AFofM sheets list Stuart as guitarist.

6. Only one fiddler is seen in the movie *Second Fiddle to a Steel Guitar,* for which these recordings were made. According to Lineberger, Spicher, who often played a second fiddle with them on recording sessions, at the Opry and at other Nashville gigs during this period, took Benny Williams's place at the audio recording session because Williams wasn't available for the recording session. It was done in the afternoon, and both tunes were in one take. Two days later the visuals were done at the same studio; Williams was fiddling as the band played along with the recordings.

7. This material was also issued in Europe in 1984 on the Astan label.

8. Assigned master numbers refer to the sequence of the performances on the original recording. Other performances are by Bob Luman, Skeeter Davis, Bobby Bare, and Curley Fox. On SHA 604 [1] cycles from this visual to others and back, and segues into the Columbia master of this instrumental part way through.

9. SF 40080 has a CD-ROM feature; in it this track is linked to an "Archive" with three brief excerpts of Rinzler's interview recordings of Monroe: "getting older," "singing for the first time," and "becoming a mandolin player."

10. The title "Fiddle Time" was originally given to this piece on the Decca Record Personnel sheet.

11. This song is earmarked on the Decca Record Personnel sheet to be a James Monroe release. It would have been his first recording under his name rather than Bill's. It was, however, never released by Decca.

12. Decca session records NVR saw listed Robert B. "Bill" Yates as bass player; all other sources, including the liner notes to DL 7-5348, BCD 15529, and MCAD 4-11048, list Zinkan.

13. The original title of -21 was "Walk Softly on This Heart of Mine," and the song has subsequently become better known under that title.

14. Master -22 ("Tall Pines") was extensively altered by the re-recording of several tracks at session 720314 and renumbered to master 16732.

15. The vocal parts to this and the following song were recorded at the following session, 700119.

16. Also recorded at this session were the vocal parts for masters -69 ("Bonny") and -70 ("Sweet Mary and the Miles in Between"), tracks for which were recorded at the previous session, 691217. Producer Harry Silverstein died on January 8, 1970.

17. This recording was made for the National Educational Television network's ninety-minute special *Earl Scruggs: His Family and Friends,* which was broadcast on January 19, 1971. On April 28, 1971, it, along with other recordings selected from the special's soundtrack, was assigned a Columbia master number. All of these recordings except this Monroe performance were released later that year on Columbia C 30584, *Earl Scruggs: His Family and Friends.*

18. 16732 is an extensively revised version of master 15822, recorded at session 691028.

19. The notes to MCAD 4-11048 have L and B parts reversed for -39, but that represents a mistake in Neil V. Rosenberg's 1974 discography. Monroe's mandolin is not audible on -39.

8

"JERUSALEM RIDGE": 1973–80

By 1973 Bill Monroe was fully in control of his revitalized career. In addition to his hugely successful festival at Bean Blossom, Indiana, he was promoting festivals at a number of other venues. Earlier, he'd been a proud loner; now, he exploited his new role as "father of bluegrass music" by joining with Lester Flatt, Jim and Jesse McReynolds, and James Monroe—who started his own band in 1971—to promote the Bluegrass Express tour that traveled extensively doing shows throughout 1972. During the rest of the 1970s and beyond, Bill's recording career would reflect these trends as he was more and more frequently a guest of other bluegrass and country stars. As at festivals and on tour, he appeared frequently with James in the recording studio for the next five years, helping promote his son's solo career.

Bill Monroe and James Monroe: Father and Son was released in March of 1973, with liner notes by Roy Acuff, who said, "This would have to be an outstanding album because the two perform well together as a father and son duo, as I have heard them on many occasions on the Grand Ole Opry."[1] Not coincidentally, it was about this time that Monroe allegedly began circulating a petition to friends in the Opry cast, asking that the Opry management make James a member. A number of people agreed to sign, but others—including Lester Flatt—supposedly had doubts. Acuff's liner notes certainly suggest that he would have had no problem in James becoming a member.

Exactly how well the set sold is not clear, but years later James referred to it as "a monster in the bluegrass field."[2] A review in *Bluegrass Unlimited* said that James's leads were "a joy to hear" and his voice was "distinctively Monroe, yet much softer than that to which we have become accustomed." The duets were so impressive, the reviewer maintained, that "at times one wonders whether MCA is not just putting us on with dubbing."[3]

THE OTHER NASHVILLE

In June of 1973 MCA was focused on live recordings, not dubs, as its staff packed a truck containing a portable sixteen-track studio and drove north out of Nashville toward another Nashville—the county seat of Brown County, Indiana, near the site of Monroe's annual Bean Blossom festival. The result was one of Monroe's best-selling albums, the two-LP collection called simply *Bean Blossom*. The first sessions described in this chapter are all from June 17, 1973, and appeared on that album. They represent not only Monroe and his band but also a number of the guest artists and jam sessions from Bean Blossom, which in 1973 was riding the crest of popularity for bluegrass festivals.

Bluegrass festivals, many featuring Monroe, gained popularity in 1965 and 1966. In June 1967 Monroe started what he first called his "Blue Grass Celebration" (the following year it became a "festival") at Bean Blossom, Indiana, site of his country music park, "the Brown County Jamboree." Within four years the annual event was attracting some twelve thousand people, a cross-section of fans from California to New York, and national coverage from *Newsweek*. Although Bean Blossom was by no means the only bluegrass festival, it probably had the highest profile, and Monroe was always anxious to promote it. By now he was thoroughly enjoying his role as a patriarch of the music.

It was, Walter Haynes recalls, Monroe's idea to record the Bean Blossom show live. "He came in one day and we got to talking about the fact that he had never done a live album. That was getting to be the big thing back in the early 1970s, and we decided the best kind of live show to do would be to tape up at Bean Blossom."[4] Monroe scheduled members of the Bluegrass Express tour—James Monroe, Jim and Jesse, and Lester Flatt—to join him on the album. Also included was Jimmy Martin, then riding a wave of popularity following a recent appearance on the Nitty Gritty Dirt Band's hit set *Will the Circle Be Unbroken*. The 1973 festival was planned to be the biggest "yet at Bean Blossom, with nine days of music," and it would attract an impressive seventy-five thousand people.

The original *Bean Blossom* set opened with Monroe and his regular band in full cry, doing a set of familiar standards: "Mule Skinner Blues," "Uncle Pen," and "Blue Moon of Kentucky." The unusual cut, one Monroe had not recorded formally before, was "You Won't Be Satisfied That Way." In 1963 he brought the song to a rehearsal session with Doc Watson, and the two of them added it to their repertoire for a series of shows they did

that year and the next. The song originated with Jimmie Davis, the singing governor of Louisiana, whose location in Shreveport made him a powerful figure for spreading good songs. Jack Hicks was still on banjo at this time and almost stole the show with his fierce picking. Bob Fowler joined the band on guitar.

A highlight of festivals at Bean Blossom and elsewhere was informal stage jam sessions, especially those in which Monroe sang with various other bands. That happened a lot at Bean Blossom, and the MCA set was criticized because its producers didn't include more. They did, however, feature Monroe, Jim, and Jesse doing "I Wonder Where You Are Tonight." "Roll On Buddy" is a duet with James that recreates the earlier version in which Del McCoury sang lead in 1964 and Charlie Monroe did as well on the Monroe Brothers' Bluebird cut in the 1930s. The fiddle standard "Orange Blossom Special" is done by Carl Jackson, a young banjoist who was winning a huge following through his work on Glen Campbell's television show.

Another type of festival jam session, often used to close shows, involved Monroe getting together an ensemble of his favorite fiddlers. It grew out of the various recreations of his band and the on-stage jams that started with Carlton Haney's first festival. With Bill these got increasingly baroque, with the number of fiddlers going up each year. All three numbers ("Down Yonder," "Soldier's Joy," and "Grey Eagle") featuring this festival's group of twelve fiddlers made the cut for the LP. Some had long and close associations with Monroe and his music; others were best known for their work with others. At the event, which was probably more interesting to watch in person than hear on a recording, Monroe briefly calls the roll to start things off and mentions his current fiddler, Kenny Baker, and then Howard "Howdy" Forrester, best known for his work with Roy Acuff but an alumnus of an early Monroe band from the 1940s.

The others involved in one of the most impressive gatherings of fiddling talent in recent history were Jim Brock, the current fiddler for Jim and Jesse; Randall Collins, the current fiddler for James Monroe's band; and Paul Warren, best known for his work with Flatt and Scruggs and at the time the fiddler for Lester Flatt. Tex Logan played informally with Bill at parties that began in the 1960s and contributed "Christmas Time's a-Coming" to the Monroe repertoire; Gordon Terry did some of his best fiddle work with Monroe; and Buck Ryan, at the time playing with Don Reno and Bill Harrell, was best known for carving out a career on his own. The former Lonesome Pine fiddler Curly Ray Cline was well known for his work with Ralph Stanley, and Tater Tate had been a fixture in bluegrass bands since the 1950s and was currently playing with the Shenandoah Cutups, who were also on the bill at the festival. Tate would later become fiddler and bassist for the Blue Grass Boys. Monroe closed the show, as he often did in those days, with a sing-along-styled "Swing Low Sweet Chariot," a performance winning enough to get MCA to try it as a single.

The two-LP result, *Bean Blossom,* stirred some controversy with bluegrass fans, especially over its cover festooned with flowers, butterflies, and frogs and because of the fact that the faces of the parking-lot pickers pictured inside the jacket had, for legal reasons, been airbrushed out. *Bean Blossom* flew out of the stores, however, and for a time roosted on the charts of best-selling country albums. It was able to capture much of the enthusiasm generated by the burgeoning festival scene and introduced thousands to classic traditional bluegrass. It stayed in print for years, and although it might not have captured what veteran fans considered to be the high points of the festival, it was a good, solid album that pleased Monroe and encouraged MCA to do even more of his music—including another two-LP set, *Greatest Hits,* in 1975.

In September 1973 Monroe returned to his birthplace, Rosine, Kentucky, for the first of what would become annual Homecoming Festivals featuring his music. He stood, hat off, as a monument to his uncle Pendleton Vandiver was unveiled, an ornate gravestone honoring Uncle Pen for being an "Outstanding Kentuckian." It was just one of the festivals he was promoting as he took advantage of the popularity of Bean Blossom. The event also reflected the success of the *Uncle Pen* album.

On Monday, March 18, 1974, not quite a year after the Bean Blossom recordings, Monroe took part in a concert by Lester Flatt and the Nashville Grass at Vanderbilt University in Nashville—the same venue at which Flatt and Scruggs recorded one of their great live albums in 1964. RCA producer Bob Ferguson set up his recording gear in Neely Auditorium and captured the entire concert, which ran from 8 to 9:30 P.M. Songs featuring Monroe included "Uncle Pen," "Blue Moon of Kentucky," "Used to Be," "Will You Be Lovin' Another Man," "Little Cabin Home on the Hill," "Crying Holy Unto the Lord," "Sally Goodin'," and "Muleskinner Blues." Flatt's band included Marty Stuart on mandolin, Curly Seckler on guitar and vocals, Paul Warren on fiddle, Kenny Ingram on banjo, Johnny Montgomery on bass, and Charlie Nixon on Dobro. The Blue Grass Boys featured Bill Box on guitar, James Moratto on banjo, Gregg Kennedy on bass, and Kenny Baker on fiddle. Flatt joined Monroe to re-create some of their classics like "Will You Be Lovin' Another Man" and "Little Cabin Home on the Hill."

It was almost two years before Monroe went into the MCA studios again, and when he did it was with a substantially new band. Kenny Baker was still onboard, but the rest of the line-up was new. There was vocalist and guitarist Ralph Lewis (no relation to Wayne Lewis, who would join in 1976), banjoist Bob Black, and bass player-baritone singer Randy Davis. Joining the regular Blue Grass Boys were Joe Stuart and James Monroe. In a characteristic flurry of three back-to-back sessions in early March 1975 this crew recorded one of Monroe's most interesting albums, *Bill Monroe: The Weary Traveler.*

The key to many of these changes was veteran singer Ralph Lewis, who was born on April 25, 1928, in the Big Laurel area of Madison County, North Carolina, north of Asheville. This was the same Madison County legendary for great ballad singers, the same Madison County that produced the Crowder Brothers, the Callahan Brothers, and a dozen other radio singers from the 1930s. Ralph's older brothers Ervin and Blanco were professional musicians who worked with the likes of Wiley and Zeke Morris and even helped Fred Kirby record some of his RCA Bluebird sides just before the war. Soon Ralph was old enough to join the band, and he moved north to do so around Niagara Falls, New York, where they were playing. After the war he returned to Asheville, where he led his own band at WLOS, Ralph Lewis and the Carolina Pals. Through the 1960s and 1970s the band continued to play at Asheville conventions, dances, and country clubs. Featured with the group were Dewey and Woolsey Shelton, first cousins to Jack and Curly Shelton and from Madison County as well. "I had kept a good band over the years," Lewis recalls:

I had stayed in the music, even while holding down a day job. The word was in Nashville, if somebody was seeking a banjo picker or fiddle player or whatever, in the bluegrass end of it, if they said they'd picked with me, they'd just have 'em come on, already hired. Good credentials. Marc Pruett and Steve Sutton and Don Humphries, the songwriter, and Orville Freeman, who was always my fiddle player. From time to time we would do shows with Monroe, booked at the same place, and we always kind of hit it off and liked to jam with each other. Just sit around, the two of us. Mutual respect. Kenny and I had jammed a lot, too. In fact, I played twin fiddle with him on his Grassy Fiddle Blues album.

So in 1974 Bill got to Kenny to give me a call and asked me if I wanted to come down and go to work with him. They had asked before, but this was kind of an urgent case; Kenny told me that Bill had fired everybody [including guitarist Bill Box and banjoist Dwight Dillman] except him. So he asked if I could bring a banjo player and a bass player and go to work with him. So I got Marc Pruett and Randy Davis; they wanted me to bring them down and get together, so we went down and got with them and picked most of a day and part of a night, picked and talked. They were excited about us becoming members of the Blue Grass Boys.[5]

Pruett decided not to sign on, preferring instead to run his music store in Asheville. Dillman stayed another three months, and then Kenny got Bob Black onboard as a banjoist. Ralph Lewis remembers joining the Blue Grass Boys formally on July 4, 1974; he would remain until "May or June" of 1976.

Lewis's memories of Monroe's recording sessions are similar to those of Pete Rowan and others. There was virtually no rehearsal, and Monroe seldom announced ahead of time what the group would record:

> We had no earthly idea of what we were going to record when we went in for that *Weary Traveler* album. There were a couple of songs we pretty much knew were going to happen—that "Mary Jane" and "Watson Blues." They were pretty much cut and dried at the time. But he had a bunch of tapes and scribbles and this and that and the other, ideas for songs, where he'd have the words down. The song "Weary Traveler" itself, we had never run over that at all, nobody knew nothing of that. It was an old Cliff Carlisle tune he had an idea on. But on a lot of them, we'd get it on the first take, it would suit him.[6]

The habit of not rehearsing before a session went back at least to the mid-1960s because Richard Greene and Lamar Grier also remember it. Monroe said on several occasions that his idea was to keep a band of musicians good enough to nail songs they hadn't heard before and by not rehearsing the band kept its spontaneity.

The session of March 10, 1975, began with "Clinging to a Saving Hand," which was written by Bill Mack, who had recorded some things on the D label. Now Mack was DJ on a midnight-to-early-morning radio show in the Dallas–Ft. Worth area. In late 1974, while the Monroe band was on tour through Texas, the group appeared on the show, and what was supposed to be a half-hour stop-over turned into an all-night stand as the band played, answered questions, and spun records. When they were ready to leave, Mack gave Monroe a demo tape containing "Clinging to a Saving Hand." "Show Me the Way" is another contribution from Virginia Stauffer.

"Jerusalem Ridge," Kenny Baker's showpiece, was one of the best-known and most-played Monroe tunes from the 1970s. In 1978 he explained the tune to writer Don Rhodes, saying that the title did indeed refer to the Jerusalem Ridge near his hometown of Rosine. "That's where we fox-hunted when I was growing up. I have loved that area ever since I was a kid. I wanted

to write a song about it, and I wanted to go back in time with the music to reflect the Scottish and Irish sounds. It has been five years since I wrote it, with the song having four parts to it. I think it is one of my best numbers."[7] As usual when Monroe wanted what he liked to call a "stout" guitar he called on Joe Stuart, a veteran who mainly played fiddle at these sessions, and it is Stuart who drives this performance.

Monroe and Ralph Lewis worked out "Ashland Breakdown" one evening in a motel in Ashland, Kentucky. Lewis recalls:

> When we were traveling, Kenny and I would room together in motels, and Bob [Black] and Randy (Davis) usually bunked together, and Bill had a room by himself. Bill called me one night; he had had the idea on that tune, asked me to bring my guitar over. When he'd get an idea of something, he'd want me to have some input on it; sometimes if he'd get stuck on something, he'd want me to play mandolin too; he'd hand me the mandolin and get me to try it and see where it would go. So he worked that ["Ashland Breakdown"] out just before we did the session.[8]

The second day of the *Weary Traveler* sessions, March 11, 1975, continued with no changes in personnel. James Monroe was again present to add his background guitar, and, again, he did not sing; the singing was shared by Monroe, Lewis, and Davis. Bill had played "Mary Jane, Won't You Be Mine" when Carter Stanley worked with him in 1951. He "gave" it to Stanley, who reworked it into a song the Stanley Brothers recorded in 1953 as "Say Won't You Be Mine." That recording had a good deal of airplay in the 1970s. "Farther On," more commonly "Better Farther On," is a popular gospel tune from the early 1950s that was not issued from the session; its master tapes have apparently been lost.

"Old, Old House" was taught to Monroe one night backstage at the Opry by its co-composer, George Jones, who felt Monroe should try it. Monroe loved the song and sang it publicly for the first time on his set at the Opry; he first recorded it under the title "There's An Old, Old House" for a Decca single in 1965. In the years since it became a permanent part of his repertoire. This recording was the first time the song appeared on an album, which is probably why he recut it. Onstage, Monroe would sing the song with great emotion—so great that some observers thought he was choking up. Sidemen, however, report that Monroe could crack his voice in such a way as to make a listener think he was in tears when in reality he was dramatizing the sentiment in the song.

"Watson Blues" had been around as an untitled instrumental since about 1963 and was apparently derived from the tune of Bill's "You'll Find Her Name Written There" (Decca, 1954). Ralph Rinzler has reported that "this song emerged during Doc and Bill's first rehearsal [in 1963]. Bill suggested trying the tune; Doc immediately came up with the tasteful introductory guitar run, prompting Bill to say, 'Since you've added to this, why don't we call it "Watson Blues"?'"[9] With Doc Watson not around for this studio session, Monroe again called for driving guitar work from Joe Stuart.

The other new member of the band during these March sessions was banjo player Bob Black. A native of Des Moines, he learned much of his music from an Iowa City fiddler, Alan Murphy, and grew adept at playing fiddle tunes on the banjo. He also developed a style that was part chromatic, part Scruggs. Black was skilled in creating backup arrangements and breaks for almost any fiddle tune he encountered. His early models were the Dillards, but after he started coming to Bean Blossom in 1970 he found himself camped next to Jimmy Arnold and Tommy Jarrell, each of whom impressed him. Soon he was playing frequently with Kenny Baker, even recording with him, and Black's chromatic style and fondness for playing high on the neck impressed Monroe. Baker recruited him to replace Dwight Dillman in the Blue Grass Boys, and from the fall of 1974 until the fall of 1976 he was the regular banjoist for that band, including the extensive tours of Japan in 1974 and 1975 and Europe in 1975. In 1984 Monroe observed, "I believe Bob Black is the best at playing the old-time fiddle numbers of any banjo players."[10]

After leaving Monroe, Black played with Buck White and the Down Home Folks for a couple of years and recorded three LPs with them; he also continued to record with Kenny Baker and eventually played on no fewer than five of his County albums. In 1979 he issued an influential solo album on Ridge Runner, *Ladies on the Steamboat*. Today he continues to work and teach in the Midwest. In 2005 he published *Come Hither to Go Yonder* with the University of Illinois Press, a biography that focuses on his days with Monroe. At that time *Ladies on the Steamboat* was republished in a CD version expanded to include five tracks from a December 1974 show by Monroe in Osaka, Japan. All instrumentals, these tracks predate the first MCA recording session by this group of Blue Grass Boys and demonstrate Black's mastery of such Monroe standards as "Raw Hide" and "Blue Grass Breakdown."

Three more pieces were recorded on March 12, 1975. The first, "Thank God for Kentucky," was originated by journalist Hazel Smith, who worked in Monroe's office and by the 1990s wrote a column for *Country Music* magazine. Ralph Lewis

recalls Hazel being in the studio on the day of the session with a demo of "Thank God for Kentucky" on tape. Monroe liked the words but thought a new melody was necessary, so he and Lewis went to a corner of the studio and worked out a new one on the spot, bit by bit, phrase by phrase. When Monroe was satisfied they taught the new music to the band and at once began to record. The resulting cut was not issued as a single but did have a lot of airplay. The next song, "Reasons Why," was on another tape, this one brought into the studio by a songwriter named Juanita Southern, who was a friend of Hazel Smith. Finally, "Weary Traveler," the title song of the LP, was coauthored by two country veterans, Cliff Carlisle and Bobby Gregory. Monroe liked Carlisle's music and recorded several of his other songs; on occasion, he even bought songs from him, such as "Goodbye Old Pal." Carlisle had written and recorded the song for Decca in 1938, and Monroe performed it frequently on the Opry during the war years but not much since then. The album was released in January 1976, its cover illustrating the song (Monroe was pictured standing at an old train station) and also reproducing the lyrics.

CONCERT RECORDINGS

In April 1975, Bill and the Blue Grass Boys began a twenty-five-day European tour. It was not his first appearance outside the United States, for in addition to many shows in Canada since the 1940s he'd performed in Europe in 1966 and during December 1974 had done a series of concerts in Japan with this particular group of Blue Grass Boys. But this was his most extensive trip abroad so far, with performances in England, Scotland, Ireland, the Netherlands, Belgium, and Germany. In 2004 Bear Family Records issued *Bill Monroe in Germany: Far Across the Blue Water,* a boxed set that includes recordings made near the end of this tour at the Neusüdende Country and Bluegrass Meeting, Germany's oldest and largest festival of this type.

Two shows are included in the recording. Taken together, they show how Monroe shaped his standard patterns of repertoire and performance to fit these special circumstances as well as how this particular group of Blue Grass Boys sounded in concert. The first show, presented in entirety, includes Ralph Lewis's version of "Roust-A-Bout," which Flatt and Scruggs recorded in 1967, and several pieces in which Bob Black's banjo work shines. His break on "Grey Eagle," a fiddle tune few banjo pickers attempt, is particularly notable.

In the second show, Bill Clifton, the American bluegrass pioneer who'd been living in England since 1963 and had done much to introduce and promote bluegrass in Europe, joined Monroe onstage. The principal organizer of the tour, he sang four duets with Monroe. Except for this portion, the entire second show is included in the Bear Family set. It reflects well the audience's enthusiasm for Monroe. Following "Orange Blossom Special," with its two encores, Bill called for audience requests and, after doing several of those and an audience sing-along on "Swing Low Sweet Chariot" and "I Saw the Light," responded with further encores. He closed with one he'd worked up especially for the tour—Bobby Helms's hit of the 1950s, "Fraulein." Later, Bill and Ralph Lewis joined in at a jam session with a local group, the Emsland Hillbillies.

Bill's final public recording made in 1975 was a reunion with Ralph Stanley at the Fifth Annual Carter Stanley Memorial Festival at McClure, Virginia, on May 25. Monroe sang tenor to Stanley's lead on "I'm on My Way Back to the Old Home" and "Can't You Hear Me Callin'?" backed by Stanley's band.

FAMILY CIRCLE

In 1975 the senior musician in the Monroe family, Birch, was celebrating his seventy-fourth birthday. Birch had worked as a fiddler and bassist with both Bill and Charlie in the 1940s. When Bill purchased the Brown County Jamboree in the early 1950s, Birch moved to nearby Martinsville, Indiana, and spent most of the next three decades managing Bill's Bean Blossom venue, where, in addition to the annual festivals that began in 1967, Saturday night dances and regular Sunday shows were still held. Birch was a capable old-time fiddler who played for the square dances at Bean Blossom on Saturday nights and always made guest appearances with Bill when the Blue Grass Boys were at the Jamboree. Just before the 1975 festival he joined the current edition of the Blue Grass Boys in Nashville for a real studio album: *Brother Birch Monroe Plays Old Time Fiddle Favorites*.

It was recorded for Atteiram, a new independent company owned by Carl Queen and operated from Marietta, Georgia. Begun in 1972, the label had a number of good bluegrass albums in its catalog, ones by Randall Collins, banjoist Vic Jordan, Jesse McReynolds, Carl Story, and Joe Stuart. James Monroe had done his LP *Something New* for Atteiram in 1974 and would make two more with that label in 1976.

Identified on the album cover as the "Blue Grass Boys," the group included Birch on fiddle, Bill Monroe on mandolin, Bob Black on banjo, Ralph Lewis on guitar, and Randy Davis on string bass. Bill takes significant breaks on "Carroll County

Blues" and the misspelled "Durang's Hornpipe," both of which he'd played frequently with Birch at Bean Blossom. The tunes did include the familiar "Cumberland Gap," "Flop Eared Mule," and "Down Yonder" as well as such lesser-known pieces as the acerbic "Natural Bridge Blues" composed by Tommy Magness, who played on Monroe's first solo Bluebird session; two by the Opry fiddler Arthur Smith, "Dixon County Rag" and "Florida Blues"; and the Mississippi tune "Carroll County Blues" popularized by Willie Narmour and Shell Smith in the 1920s. "Comin' Down from Boston" is an even rarer tune, often called "Take Me Back to Georgia" in the 1920s and "Rattlesnake Bit the Baby" in the Upland South. "The Beautiful Red Rose Waltz" was Birch's composition.

Charlie Monroe died on September 27, 1975, at the age of seventy-two in his home at Reidsville, North Carolina. He had been in and out of the music for twenty years before but appeared frequently at festivals and reunion shows during his final few years. Just a few days before he died, he played a show in Rosine. In February 1976 James went into the Fireside Studio in Nashville to cut a tribute album for his uncle on Atteiram. Called *James Monroe Sings Songs of "Memory Lane" of His Uncle Charlie Monroe,* the album included Bill on all sides as well as Vic Jordan on banjo; Gerald Sullivan on bass; and, at various times over the three-day session, fiddlers Joe Stuart, Kenny Baker, and Jim Brock. Many of the songs were Charlie's well-loved favorites from the 1940s and 1950s that he recorded for RCA: "The Red Rocking Chair," "Down in the Willow Garden," "Bringing in the Georgia Mail," and "It's Only a Phonograph Record." Bill and James recreated some of the old Monroe Brothers duet sound on the album's title song, "Down Memory Lane," as well as on "I'm Coming Back but I Don't Know When" and "Rolling in My Sweet Baby's Arms" (Bill sings tenor). "When the Angels Carry Me Home" is a gospel trio with Joe Stuart singing bass, and "I'm Old Kentucky Bound" and "What Became of That Beautiful Picture" are solos by James. Twin fiddles are heard throughout.

The original Atteiram liner notes list all three fiddlers. Jim Brock played only on the first day's session, February 9, at which four pieces were recorded. Kenny Baker was not present that day; Joe Stuart was the other fiddler. Brock did not sing. That explains why "When the Angels Carry Me Home" is the only one on which twin-harmony fiddles are not heard as Stuart sang in the trio on that track. Jordan overdubbed a banjo harmony part on "I'm Coming Back but I Don't Know When." In 1999 four of these recordings were reissued along with six from another session Bill made with James in 1978.

Kenny Baker, in addition to recording regularly with Monroe, also recorded six albums on his own for County, an independent old-time and bluegrass label in Floyd, Virginia. Starting in 1968 with *High Country* and in 1969 with *Portrait of a Bluegrass Fiddler,* the albums were some of the best-selling releases in County's catalog and solidified Baker's role as the most influential bluegrass fiddler. On March 29 and 30, 1976, he recorded his seventh effort, *Kenny Baker Plays Bill Monroe,* a collection of all-Monroe tunes. Three of its selections were ones for which Baker had played on the original Monroe recordings: ""Big Sandy River," "Ashland Breakdown," and "Lonesome Moonlight Waltz." Some others were tunes Monroe had written earlier but never recorded, taught to Baker for use on the album: "Road to Columbus," "Mississippi Waltz," and "Fiddler's Pastime." Also included were classics like "Cheyenne," "Jerusalem Ridge," "Brown County Breakdown," "Wheel Hoss," "Stoney Lonesome," and "Monroe's Hornpipe."

Monroe made an impromptu appearance. "Bill happened in on the session, Kenny asked him to play a bit if he would, and to everyone's surprise, Bill got out his mandolin and recorded the entire session."[11] MCA granted permission for Monroe to appear on the Country label, and the album was released to overwhelmingly good reviews.

A few weeks after the County session the band was back in a Nashville studio to record a set for radio broadcast for the Canadian Broadcasting Corporation's series *Country Roads.* The show was transcribed, and LP copies were made available to the public in limited edition. One of the session's unique features is the dialog between host and DJ Vic Mullen and Monroe. Although banded like a typical LP, the disc contains two complete radio broadcast transcriptions. Side one, with selections one to four, is set up as the first segment; side two, selections five to eight, is set up as the second. Personnel includes James Monroe and Bob Jones on guitar; Kenny Baker, fiddle; Bob Black, banjo; Randy Davis, bass; and Vic Mullen, emcee. James was again a guest with Bill, helping out on guitar; Jones was trying out with the Blue Grass Boys. The tunes are the obligatory standards: "Uncle Pen," "Footprints in the Snow," "I'm Working on a Building," "Dear Old Dixie," "Blue Moon of Kentucky," and "It's Me Again Lord." "Jerusalem Ridge" and "Mary Jane, Won't You Be Mine" were favorites from the new *Bill Monroe: The Weary Traveler* album.

During the 1960s the Kentuckian Tom T. Hall established an enviable reputation in Nashville with original songs like "The Year That Clayton Delaney Died," "Homecoming," "A Week in a County Jail," and "Harper Valley PTA." Many reflected the Nashville sound, but he was genuinely fond of bluegrass. In fact, he'd begun his career playing with the Kentucky Travelers, a bluegrass band that recorded in the late 1950s for Starday, and in July 1976 he went into the studio to do a bluegrass tribute, *The Magnificent Music Machine.* Backed by some of the music's best performers and sidemen, Hall recorded a version of "Molly and Tenbrooks," with Monroe playing mandolin but not singing and a crack studio team: banjoist Bobby Thompson, guitarists Charlie Collins and Ray Edenton, fiddlers Kenny Baker and Buddy Spicher, bassist Bob Moore, Dobroist Gene Bush, and—a rare occasion for Monroe—drummer Buddy Harman. It is the only cut on the album that includes Monroe.

BILL MONROE SINGS BLUEGRASS, BODY AND SOUL

More than eighteen months passed before Monroe got into the regular MCA studio again, in part because of MCA's release of his well-annotated *Greatest Hits* package and in part because of his extensive tours to the Far East and Europe. By October 1976, however, he was ready to begin work on what would be his next album, *Bill Monroe Sings Bluegrass, Body and Soul.* By now, ten cuts on an LP had replaced the standard twelve of earlier years. Six pieces for this album would be new cuts made while Monroe was in town for the annual Opry birthday celebration and DJ convention; the remaining four would be drawn from recordings made in the early 1970s.

The first session, October 20, 1976, started with two remakes. The first, "My Cabin in Caroline," was from the first Flatt and Scruggs Mercury session in 1949. In his notes to the album Monroe said: "Lester thought it would be a great song for me and was, and sung in the key of C." The second, "No Place to Pillow My Head," dates from the Monroe Brothers era but is credited here to Monroe and Flatt. It had, however, been earlier recorded by Chicago-based singers Karl and Harty (Karl Davis and Hartford Connecticut Taylor). "An old song by two Great men," Monroe wrote of it in his liner notes.[12] Both older songs, associated with Flatt, reflected again the improved relationship between the two bluegrass patriarchs.

"My Sweet Blue-Eyed Darling" was the new song from the set, one Monroe described merely as "what beautiful eyes." Along with "Jerusalem Ridge" it likely qualifies as the best-known Monroe classic from the 1970s. It has become a favorite jam session tune, and Monroe often used it to open his shows, even in later years. He redid it in the 1980s with Ricky Skaggs, and in the 1990s young groups such as California and the

Lonesome River Band were busy recording it, giving "My Sweet Blue-Eyed Darling" an even longer lease on life. It was one of the few Monroe cuts from the era to be released on a single, in this case MCA 40675, the flip side of "Monroe's Blues," which he recorded the following day.

Important new additions to the Blue Grass Boys, starting with this session, included guitarist and lead singer Wayne Lewis (no relation to Ralph Lewis) and banjo player Bill Holden. Lewis's background included gospel music as well as a stint with Ralph Stanley; he would remain a mainstay in the band into the mid-1980s. Lewis was born in Sandy Hook in eastern Kentucky on March 17, 1943. Both parents were good singers, and as a young boy he first sang publicly in church with his sisters. It was the start of his long and deep-seated love of gospel music. Wayne was five when his family moved to New Boston, Ohio, above the Ohio River, and as a young man he spent some thirteen years working a day job at the steel mill there. By 1965 he was living in the Portsmouth, Ohio–Ashland, Kentucky, area and playing with a group called the Kentuckians (not to be confused with Red Allen's band of the same name). For the next six years that band, Wayne playing guitar and singing lead, appeared at clubs and bluegrass barns in eastern Kentucky, West Virginia, and Ohio.

In the process they cut an EP for the Jalyn label and an LP with Paul "Moon" Mullins, the Middletown fiddler and DJ. They also swapped sets with J. D. Crowe and Doyle Lawson in Lexington and jammed with banjoists like Tim Spradlin and Jack Hicks (who would later also join Monroe). After the Kentuckians finally parted ways, Lewis had a brief stint with Ralph Stanley in 1974. A few months later he joined Lillimae Whitaker and the Dixie Gospel-Aires and was still with them when he was asked to join Monroe in May 1976. In addition to recording on a regular basis with Monroe as a lead singer, Lewis also did a solo album for Old Homestead, backed by Kenny Baker, Joseph C. "Butch" Robins, and Bobby Osborne. "I have no desire to leave the Blue Grass Boys," he said in 1981. "I am living a country boy's dream of being with Bill Monroe on the Grand Ole Opry."[13] Lewis would remain with Monroe for just under a decade and was the next-to-last guitarist and lead singer in the Blue Grass Boys.

Bill Holden, born in 1950 in Fort Worth, came into bluegrass through his sister's interest in the folk revival of the early 1960s. Like so many other younger banjoists, his first real instruction came not from an aged grandfather or uncle but from Pete Seeger's little manual How to Play the Five-String Banjo. After an apprenticeship that included a job with a local band, the Brazos River Ramblers, and its leader Steven Bruton, who went on to work with Kris Kristofferson, Bob Dylan, and Bonnie Raitt, Holden left for Nashville and the big time. "I left Texas strictly looking for Bill Monroe," he recalls. "I called the Blue Grass Talent Agency and said, 'Look, do you need a banjo player with Bill Monroe?' And he said, 'No,' and I said, 'That's OK, I'm coming anyway.' I got to Nashville and found a place to live and joined the union, and the only band that needed a banjo player at that time was James Monroe. I had the Father and Son album and had listened to that, but I didn't really know a lot about their music. I just wanted to play. So James took me. I auditioned for him and Vic Jordan and that was it. He said, 'Get a white pair of pants and you're hired.'"[14] It was March 1974.

Holden performed with the Midnight Ramblers for nearly six months and then joined the Washington, D.C.–based Country Gentlemen. He stayed there for two years, cutting the Joe's Last Train album with them and learning a lot about banjo playing from Doyle Lawson. He also sang with the group, usually bass. "During my two years with the Country Gentlemen, Doyle Lawson erased all my bad habits, and taught me how to play right," he remembers. In September or October 1976 he quit the group and decided to return to Texas, but on his way home he stopped in Nashville and decided to call Monroe. "He knew me because of all the time I had spent with James," Holden said, "playing on all those shows." As it turned out, Monroe did need a banjo player, and he hired Holden. Eagerly, Holden explained to Monroe how much he had improved and how Lawson helped him do so:

> It didn't make an impression on him. Bill wanted me to play a certain way, and I said, "No, no, Doyle said to play it this way." And basically, it was Scruggs style playing. . . . Bill can't tell you how to play. He thinks in terms of mandolin and fiddle, but he really doesn't think in terms of a five-string banjo. He said Earl Scruggs had a wonderful roll, but that's all he would ever say about Earl Scruggs. He liked the way Jack Hicks played, and Bobby Thompson, but he can't tell you how to play. He would play notes for you, but he can't play the banjo.[15]

Holden was one of the few sidemen who had experience with Monroe and one of the young progressive bands, and his comparison is instructive. The casual way in which Monroe taught the band a new tune bothered Holden:

> If he wanted to teach you a new song, he would play it for you. He wouldn't even tell you, he'd just play it. He'd play something right before you'd be going on stage, but he would never sit

down and say, "Look, we're rehearsing this for an album." He would play a few tunes for you to see if you could pick it up, and the next thing you know you're going in there to record it. We never knew what we were going to be recording until we got there. That's the way it's always been with him. Every Blue Grass Boy will agree with this. You get the idea that he wants you to kind of learn it, but you'll never hear anything out of him. And you'll do that maybe three or four months, and when he thinks it's right, then he goes into the studio and BAM! you do it. He'll never say, "Look, work on your part till you like it and then we'll record it." We never had that choice.[16]

The session of October 21, 1976, began with "Monroe's Blues." Timed at three minutes, fifty seconds, it was one of the longest studio cuts in the recorded canon; it was also issued as a single, on the flip side of "My Sweet Blue-Eyed Darling." "To me," Monroe says in his often cryptic notes for the original LP, "this is a great number. I've had the blues and I love the blues."[17]

"The First Whippoorwill," a remake of his 1951 recording, was not used on the *Body and Soul* album but appeared for the first time on a Bear Family boxed set. "Lucky Lady," according to Bill Holden, was the name of a ranch Monroe owned north of the Dallas–Ft. Worth area. The property was named after a woman friend in the region. In his notes Monroe mentions "a song about a Texas lady named Luckie."[18] "My Louisiana Love," another new song, was notable in that bassist Randy Davis sings lead. "That's the only one Bill gave him a shot on," says Holden. "The rest of the time he sang baritone."[19] The three fiddles on this session and the one the day before include Stuart and Baker and also mark some of the earliest work of Blaine Sprouse who worked as a session player at the time after starting with Jimmy Martin. *Bill Monroe Sings Bluegrass, Body and Soul* was released in January 1977 to generally favorable reviews.

Six months later, work began on the next album, *Bill Monroe: Bluegrass Memories*, which was recorded on July 25, 27, and 28, 1977, at Bradley's Barn. In spite of its title, which suggests a tour of older songs that had special memories for the singer, the album was remarkable in that it included only one remake and one older song. The balance of the material consisted of eight new songs, reflecting Monroe's continuing burst of creativity in the mid-1970s. Also noteworthy is the absence of Kenny Baker, who had been replaced by Buddy Spicher. Baker severely cut his hand with a hunting knife and was sidelined for some time. The wound was bad enough to end his guitar playing although he eventually regained his mastery of the fiddle. Spicher had played on Monroe sessions since 1961

and was well known around Nashville as a premier studio session fiddler and soloist.

Producer Walter Haynes sensed that the new album would be out just in time for the Christmas buying season (it was set for release in October) and encouraged Monroe to add two seasonal songs, a stereo remake of the old favorite "Christmas Time's a-Coming" and a new song by Virginia Stauffer, "That's Christmas Time to Me." Although its sentimental catalog of things Christmas seems un-Monroe-like, he apparently liked the song and kept it in his repertoire through the 1980s and 1990s. "The Sunset Trail" and "Texas Blue Bonnet" demonstrated Monroe's continued interest in Texas. Bill Holden remembers him spending some time trying to teach "The Sunset Trail" to the band, but for some reason it seemed to give them trouble. Its subject, however, surprised no one; "Bill Monroe has this fixation with the West and cowboys, and he still loves Texas."[20] In fact, rumors persist that Monroe even filmed a cameo role in a made-for-television western during this time—a film that was never released.

"Pinewood Valley" is a rarity in Blue Grass Boys history, a banjo instrumental that the composer was able to record himself and for which he could receive full composer credit. "I wrote that one," Holden stated. "He did that as a favor to me. I think it was my birthday when we recorded that. As a matter of fact, I told him, and these were my exact words, 'Bill, that song's not ready; I'm not through with it.' And he said, 'Well, why'd you write it, boy?' But he needed something to fill in. It was named after Buddy Spicher's ranch—Buddy had thought he might try to record it later on. Where the tune came from—I stole part of it from an old *Hee Haw* song, when they first used to introduce *Hee-Haw*."[21] Holden also has vivid memories of "Blue Goose," another instrumental: "I don't know a damn thing about where he got it, except that I wish I could record it over again. That's one he pulled out on us. If you listen real close, when I finish my part on it, you can hear the frustration because I rake the strings with my thumb—cause I assumed we were gonna re-do it. I wasn't satisfied with it because I was kind of behind that beat. I finally fumbled through it and raked across the strings." A number of the sidemen were upset at Monroe's habit of not doing retakes and fixes in the studio. "You'd like to do a retake," Holden said, "but he won't do it. It would be done once or twice. If you didn't like your part, it was too bad; if he liked it, it was on wax. I'd like to re-do all of them (the sides we cut with Monroe). There's only one song that I did that I thought was OK, and that was 'Texas Blue Bonnet.'"[22]

Holden left the Blue Grass Boys before *Bill Monroe: Blue-*

grass *Memories* came out, and his dilemma seems typical of many musicians Monroe hired during the 1970s. "My salary the best month I ever worked for Monroe was $700; the worst was $300. I had joined the union in 1973, and when I joined Monroe you get a flat $50 a day when you worked—whether it was one or a hundred shows."[23] On days when the band didn't work, there was no pay. The Opry paid $25 for each appearance, which were now fairly frequent, and recording an album netted about $200 extra. For much of the time he was with Monroe, Holden kept a day job to supplement his income. Ralph Lewis recalled getting $65 each day he worked with Monroe, and more when he and Baker worked as back-up bands in the ten to fifteen festivals Monroe ran annually during the 1970s. Holden and Randy Davis were also assigned to work the record table at shows, and many times he volunteered to help Monroe with farm work. "I didn't mind doing the work, and at lunch we'd go up to the house and have bologna sandwiches, and that's about the only time Monroe would really relax. He'd sit around and tell stories about the old days." Eventually, though, Holden became discouraged. "I knew the kind of competition that was out there," he observed, "and I couldn't see any future in it."[24] He eventually returned to Texas and left the music business entirely, working construction and eventually owning his own company.

One of the more durable songs from the session is "She's Young and I'm Growing Old." Al Jones and Frank Necessary did it for a time, and then the Johnson Mountain Boys added it to their repertoire. The July 27 session also included "My Sweet Memory," a Monroe original; "My Florida Sunshine," another original, was done at the July 28 session, as was A. P. Carter's classic "Wabash Cannon Ball."

By January 1978, Bill's band included a new banjo picker, Butch Robins. His first recorded appearance was on January 11, when NBC taped a special, *Fifty Years of Country Music*, for which Monroe performed "Blue Moon of Kentucky" and sang a duet with Dolly Parton on "Mule Skinner Blues." The show was broadcast on January 22, and videos from it have found their way to several documentaries. The Opry duet on "Mule Skinner" by Monroe and Parton "for a time became a regular feature of the program," notes Robert Cantwell, who reflected on its "sexual tension."[25]

January had always been a time for Monroe to get in off the road and tend to recording projects, and the sessions of January 24 and 30, 1978, were dedicated to a follow-up album with son James. *Bill and James Monroe: Together Again* would be released in the fall of 1978 and mark another first in that

Monroe was recording in the studio with a group larger than the Blue Grass Boys. The Midnight Ramblers, James Monroe's band, joined them. As James observed, "Both his Band and mine were used to play on the session. It was a first for Bill and myself to record this way. I think the record will do well, and I hope the DJs will give it plenty of play."[26] Fortunately, both groups contained superb bluegrass musicians, and the project turned into far more than just another Bean Blossom–style jam session.

The big change in Bill Monroe's band came with the addition of banjo player Butch Robins, who joined in late 1977. Born Joseph Calvin Robins in Lebanon, Virginia, in 1949, Robins learned to play from his father, an employee of the Tennessee Valley Authority, and was attending local fiddlers' conventions by the time he was thirteen. When he worked briefly as a Blue Grass Boy at the first Bean Blossom festival he absorbed what he could from players like Lamar Grier, whose place he took. Another mentor emerged when Butch was drafted. DeWitt "Snuffy" Jenkins and Homer "Pappy" Sherill played in Columbia, South Carolina, near Ft. Jackson, where Robins was stationed. Butch began to join them for area shows, playing guitar and banjo when Jenkins played washboard, and added Jenkins's sharp, pre-Scruggs style to his own. After the army, jobs with Charlie Moore, Robert "Tut" Taylor, Wilma Lee and Stoney Cooper, Jim and Jesse, Buck White, and Leon Russell followed. Robins, relocated to Nashville, next played electric bass with the New Grass Revival. He eventually found a job with Monroe and stayed with him for a month less than four years, from 1977 to 1981. Like many banjo players who worked with Monroe, Robins loved the blues, could translate fiddle melodies to a five-string banjo, and appreciated shape-note harmonies. In 2003 Robins published his musical autobiography, which covers many aspects of his career but is dominated by his experiences with Monroe, whom he describes as "a human artist who seemed to transcend earthly bounds."[27]

James Monroe's band had two new additions who would make names for themselves. Banjoist Alan O'Bryant was a founder of the Nashville Bluegrass Band and a bluegrass songwriter. Fiddler James Bryan, an Alabama native, enjoyed a long association with Norman and Nancy Blake as well as a set of fine old-time solo fiddle albums for Rounder.

The session included two new songs by one of James Monroe's favorite writers, Damon Black, who contributed "Tall Pines" to the earlier father and son collaboration and "Sweet Mary and the Miles in Between" to one of James's 1969 singles. Black was a Missouri farmer whose land had been in his family for generations, but his real passion lay in songwriting. About 1975 he moved to Nashville to try writing songs full time. Although he had a number of good cuts he eventually gave up and returned to Missouri, where in later years he sold a parcel of land to the retail giant Wal-Mart and suddenly became wealthy enough to retire from farming. Returning to songwriting, he sent a tape of new songs to his old friend Porter Wagoner, who in 2000 used them in his well-received "comeback" album, *The Best I've Ever Been.* For James Monroe in 1978 Black contributed "Hard Times Have Been Here" and "Jake Satterfield," both sung by James with Bill's harmony voice on the choruses.

Bill Monroe was responsible for what was probably the biggest hit of the album, given its airplay and the number of other bands that picked it up. He had performed "Six Feet under the Ground" for some time before recording it. "Who's Gonna Shoe Your Pretty Little Feet," a traditional mountain favorite, has a lyric derived from a long Scottish ballad, "The Lass of Roch Royal," and is from the days of the Monroe Brothers, quite likely even earlier. "Muddy Waters" bears composer credits to the guitar player for the Seldom Scene, Phil Rosenthal. The group was big in 1978 and recorded the song. The familiar blues and western swing number "Corrina, Corrina," popularized originally in the 1930s, features a twin-banjo break. The band took advantage of the doubled instrumentation to work out an arrangement featuring Alan O'Bryant doing the lead and Butch Robins the harmony.

On February 8, 1978, the same personnel assembled in Bradley's Barn to finish *Together Again.* Two classics were recut: "Have a Feast Here Tonight," a hit for the old Monroe Brothers, and "I'm Going Back to Old Kentucky," which Bill first performed in 1947 with Lester Flatt and again in 1962 with Frank Buchanan. "Golden River" was by the author of "This Ole House," Stuart Hamblen. The most enduring, however, turned out to be "Those Memories of You," Alan O'Bryant's remarkable effort to write a "Monroesque" tune. It was eventually recorded by the Nashville Bluegrass Band, but even more impressive was its inclusion on the *Trio* album by Dolly Parton, Linda Ronstadt, and Emmylou Harris. Its release as a single, and the spectacular success of the *Trio* album, helped make the song a modern bluegrass favorite.

About five weeks later, on March 17, James produced yet another session of himself and his father, this time for his own Raintree label. Six sides were cut, all featuring duet vocals by James and Bill Monroe: "Nine Pound Hammer," the Wiley

Walker–Gene Sullivan hit "Live and Let Live," "I Haven't Seen Mary in Years," "Bonny," "When the Bees Are in the Hive" (popularized in the 1930s by Roy Harvey), and a duet version of "When the Angels Carry Me Home." Alan O'Bryant continued to do banjo work, Buddy Spicher did the fiddle parts, and Billy Linneman the string bass. The cuts were released in September 1999 on an album entitled *Bluegrass Special Memories,* along with four songs from the recordings Bill made in 1976 for the memorial album for Charlie Monroe. It was the last recording session in which James would participate with his father until 1994.

It was natural for MCA to want a follow-up to the hugely successful *Bean Blossom* album of 1973, and in June 1979 they sent a team of engineers north again to record, at concerts on June 12 and 15, what would be Monroe's final album of the decade, *Bean Blossom '79.* Some historians consider the album to be a better version of a live Monroe concert than the earlier one was. Especially interesting is the "Molly and Tenbrooks Medley," which includes "Little Maggie," "Train 45," and what MCA's design staff insisted on calling "Blue Moon on Kentucky." Monroe was fond of creating such medleys, usually to answer requests for certain songs. He had the uncanny knack of being able to play back the items requested in the medley in the order they had been requested.

With the exception of "The Old Mountaineer," new at the time, the rest of the tunes are familiar ones that date from the 1950s or earlier. Among them are "Rocky Road Blues," "Dog House Blues," and "Orange Blossom Special" from the 1940s and "The Little Girl and the Dreadful Snake," "In Despair," "John Henry," and "Y'All Come" from the 1950s. Especially noteworthy are Monroe's comments introducing Lester Flatt's anthem "Little Cabin Home on the Hill." Flatt died barely a month before, and grief was still fresh in the bluegrass community. For Monroe, it was a sign that things were changing and old times were indeed past and gone. With his own health uncertain, he ended the 1970s by looking back over his achievements and what bluegrass had become. Its success was epitomized by a concert at the White House on August 7, 1980, where Jimmy Carter introduced Monroe. The event and performance were recorded by the Smithsonian and later included on Ralph Rinzler's Smithsonian/Folkways *Off the Record* set and a video by Homespun Tapes. With seven years of recordings in his newfound role as the music's elder statesman, Bill Monroe forged into the 1980s. His band was intact, his reputation was at a peak, and his music was as challenging as ever.

Notes

1. Roy Acuff, notes to *Bill Monroe and James Monroe: Father and Son* (MCA 310, 1973).

2. Don Rhodes, "Monroe the Father, Monroe the Son," *Bluegrass Unlimited* 12 (Feb. 1978): 17.

3. George B. McCeney, *Bluegrass Unlimited* 7 (May 1973): 17.

4. Charles K. Wolfe, notes to *Bill Monroe Bluegrass 1970–1979* (Bear Family BCD 15606 DI, 1994), 12.

5. Wolfe, notes to *Bill Monroe Bluegrass 1970–1979*, 16.

6. Ibid.

7. Rhodes, "Monroe the Father," 15.

8. Wolfe, notes to *Bill Monroe Bluegrass 1970–1979*, 16.

9. Ralph Rinzler, notes to *Bill Monroe and Doc Watson: Live Duet Recordings 1963–1980, Off the Record Volume 2* (Smithsonian/Folkways SF CD 40064, 1993), 10.

10. Bill Monroe, notes to *Bob Black: Ladies on the Steamboat* (Ridge Runner RRR 0018, 1984).

11. Douglas B. Green, notes to *Kenny Baker Plays Bill Monroe* (Country CO 761, 1976).

12. Bill Monroe, notes to *Bill Monroe Sings Bluegrass, Body and Soul* (MCA MCA-2251, 1977).

13. Paul Morris, "Wayne Lewis," *Bluegrass Unlimited* (Sept. 1981): 43.

14. Wolfe, notes to *Bill Monroe Bluegrass 1970–1979*, 20.

15. Ibid.

16. Ibid.

17. Monroe, notes to *Bill Monroe Sings Bluegrass, Body and Soul.*

18. Ibid.

19. Wolfe, notes to *Bill Monroe Bluegrass 1970–1979*, 20.

20. Ibid., 21.

21. According to Tom Ewing, it was three days after Holden's twenty-seventh birthday; he was born on July 25, 1950.

22. Wolfe, notes to *Bill Monroe Bluegrass 1970–1979*, 21.

23. Ibid.

24. Ibid.

25. Robert Cantwell, *Bluegrass Breakdown* (Urbana: University of Illinois Press, 1984), 223–24.

26. James Monroe, notes to *Bill and James Monroe: Together Again* (MCA MCA-2367, 1978).

27. Butch Robins, *What I Know 'bout What I Know* (Bloomington, Ind.: First Books Library, 2003), vii.

DISCOGRAPHY, 1973–80

730616.1[1]   MCA session; producers, Walter Haynes and Snuffy Miller (Bill Monroe listed as "leader")
Bill Monroe's 7th Annual Bluegrass Festival at Bill Monroe's Brown County Jamboree, Bean Blossom, Ind.
June 16, 1973

NA 17233	MULE SKINNER BLUES (BLUE YODEL NO. 8) (Jimmie Rodgers–	MCA 2-8002, BCD 15606
MC 1979	George Vaughn)	
	Monroe-L	

| NA 17234 | YOU WON'T BE SATISFIED THAT WAY (Jimmie Davis–Lloyd Ellis) | MCA 2-8002, |
| MC 1980 | Monroe-L | MCAD 4-11048, BCD 15606 |

| NA 17235 | UNCLE PEN (Bill Monroe) | MCA 2-8002, BCD 15606 |
| MC 1981 | Monroe-LV/TC, Fowler-LC, Hicks-B | |

| NA 17236 | BLUE MOON OF KENTUCKY (Bill Monroe) | MCA 2-8002, BCD 15606 |
| MC 1982 | Monroe-L | |

Bill Monroe: m   Robert "Bob" Fowler: g   Kenny Baker: f
Jack Hicks: b   Guy Stevenson: sb

730616.2   MCA session; producers, Walter Haynes and Snuffy Miller (Bill Monroe listed as "leader")
Bill Monroe's 7th Annual Bluegrass Festival at Bill Monroe's Brown County Jamboree, Bean Blossom, Ind.
June 16, 1973

| NA 17237 | ROLL ON BUDDY (P.D.) | MCA 2-8002, BCD 15606 |
| MC 1983 | J. Monroe-L, B. Monroe-T | |

| NA 17238 | I WONDER WHERE YOU ARE TONIGHT (J. Bond) | MCA 2-8002, BCD 15606 |
| MC 1984 | Jim McReynolds-L, Bill Monroe-T, Jesse McReynolds-B | |

| NA 17239 | ORANGE BLOSSOM SPECIAL (P.D.) | MCA 2-8002, BCD 15606 |
| MC 1985 | Instrumental | |

Bill Monroe, Jesse   Bob Fowler, James Monroe (-37 only),   Kenny Baker: f
  McReynolds (-38 only): m   Jim McReynolds (-38 only): g
Jack Hicks (except -39),   Guy Stevenson: sb
  Carl Jackson (-39 only): b

730617   MCA session; producers, Walter Haynes and Snuffy Miller (Bill Monroe listed as "leader")
Bill Monroe's 7th Annual Bluegrass Festival at Bill Monroe's Brown County Jamboree, Bean Blossom, Ind.
June 17, 1973

NA 17240 MC 1959	DOWN YONDER (P.D.) Instrumental	40220	MCA 2-8002, BCD 15606
NA 17241 MC 1960	SOLDIER'S JOY (P.D.) Instrumental		MCA 2-8002, BCD 15606
NA 17242 MC 1961	GREY EAGLE (P.D.) Instrumental		MCA 2-8002, BCD 15606
NA 17243 MC 1962	SWING LOW SWEET CHARIOT (P.D.) Monroe-L, with audience	40220	MCA 2-8002, BCD 15606

Bill Monroe: m   Bob Fowler: g   Kenny Baker and guests:[2]f
Jack Hicks: b   Guy Stevenson: sb

740318   RCA session at concert for Lester Flatt and the Nashville Grass; producer, Bob Ferguson
Neely Auditorium, Vanderbilt University, Nashville, Tenn.
March 18, 1974, 8–9:30 P.M.

DWA5-0885	UNCLE PEN (Bill Monroe) Monroe-LV/TC, Box-LC, Kennedy-B	BCD 15975, BCD 16614
DWA5-0586	BLUE MOON OF KENTUCKY (Bill Monroe) Monroe-L	APL1-0588, BCD 15975, BCD 16614
DWA5-0587	USED TO BE (Bill Monroe) Monroe-L	BCD 15975, BCD 16614
DWA5-0588	WILL YOU BE LOVIN' ANOTHER MAN (Lester Flatt–Bill Monroe) Flatt-L, Monroe-T	APL1-0588, BCD 15975, BMG 74465 99002 2, BCD 16614
DWA5-0589	LITTLE CABIN HOME ON THE HILL (Lester Flatt–Bill Monroe) Flatt-L, Monroe-T	APL1-0588, BCD 15975, BMG 74465 99002 2, BCD 16614
DWA5-0590	CRYING HOLY UNTO THE LORD Flatt-L, Monroe-T, ?-B, Warren-BS	BCD 15975, BCD 16614
DWA5-0591	SALLY GOODIN' Instrumental	BCD 15975, BCD 16614

DWA5-0592   MULESKINNER BLUES (Jimmie Rodgers)   BCD 15975
             Monroe-L

Bill Monroe, Marty Stuart	Bill Box, Lester Flatt (-88 to -91),	Kenny Baker, Paul Warren (-88 to -91): f
(-88 to -91): m	Curly Seckler (-88, -89): g	
James Moratto, Kenny Ingram	Gregg Kennedy, Johnny	Charlie Nixon (-88 to -91): Dobro
(-88 to -91): b	Montgomery (-88 to -91): sb	

741213   Green Valley Records release of concert
              Mainichi Hall, Osaka, Japan
              Dec. 13, 1974

[1]   DEAR OLD DIXIE (Traditional)   GV 147
       Instrumental

[2]   TRAIN 45 (Traditional)   GV 147
       Instrumental

[3]   BLUE GRASS SPECIAL (Bill Monroe)   GV 147
       Instrumental

[4]   BLUE GRASS BREAKDOWN (Bill Monroe)   GV 147
       Instrumental

[5]   RAWHIDE (Bill Monroe)   GV 147
       Instrumental

| Bill Monroe: m | Ralph Lewis: g | Kenny Baker: f |
| Robert W. "Bob" Black: b | Stephen Randall "Randy" Davis: sb | |

750310   MCA session; producer, Walter Haynes (Bill Monroe listed as "leader")
              Bradley's Barn, Mount Juliet, Tenn.
              March 10, 1975, 6–9 P.M.

NA 17638   CLINGING TO A SAVING HAND (Bill Mack)   MCA 2173, BCD 15606
  MC 3949   Monroe-L

NA 17639   SHOW ME THE WAY (Virginia Stauffer)   MCA 2173, BCD 15606
  MC 3950   Monroe-LV/TC, Lewis-LC, Davis-B

NA 17640   JERUSALEM RIDGE (Bill Monroe)   MCA 2173, BCD 15606
  MC 3951   Instrumental

NA 17641 MC 3952	ASHLAND BREAKDOWN (Bill Monroe) Instrumental		MCA 2173, BCD 15606, CCS-CD-19
Bill Monroe: m Bob Black: b		James Monroe, Ralph Lewis (except -40), Joe Stuart (-40): g Randy Davis: sb	Kenny Baker, Joe Stuart (except -40): f

750311   MCA session; producer, Walter Haynes (Bill Monroe listed as "leader")
Bradley's Barn, Mount Juliet, Tenn.
March 11, 1975, 6–9 P.M.

NA 17642 MC 3953	MARY JANE, WON'T YOU BE MINE (Bill Monroe) Monroe-LV/TC, Lewis-LC, Davis-B	MCA 2173, BCD 15606
NA 17643 MC 3954	FARTHER ON (R. E. Winsett) Monroe-L	
NA 17644 MC 3955	OLD, OLD HOUSE (George Jones–Hal Bynum) Monroe-L	MCA 2173, BCD 15606
NA 17645 MC 3956	WATSON BLUES (Bill Monroe) Instrumental	MCA 2173, BCD 15606

Bill Monroe: m Bob Black: b	James Monroe, Ralph Lewis (except -45): g Randy Davis: sb	Kenny Baker, Joe Stuart: f

750312   MCA session; producer, Walter Haynes (Bill Monroe listed as "leader")
Bradley's Barn, Mount Juliet, Tenn.
March 12, 1975, 6–9 P.M.

NA 17646 MC 3957	THANK GOD FOR KENTUCKY (Hazel Smith) Monroe-LV/TC, Lewis-LC, Davis-B	MCA 2173, BCD 15606
NA 17647 MC 3958	REASONS WHY (Juanita Southern) Monroe-L	MCA 2173, BCD 15606
NA 17648 MC 3959	WEARY TRAVELER (Cliff Carlisle–Bobby Gregory) Monroe-L	MCA 2173, BCD 15606

Bill Monroe: m Bob Black: b	James Monroe, Ralph Lewis: g Randy Davis: sb	Kenny Baker, Joe Stuart: f

750517.1   Recordings made by Hartmut Lang, released by Bear Family; Bill Monroe listed as "producer"
Gasthof Lindenhof, Neusüedende, Germany
May 17, 1975, 6–7:15 P.M.

[1]   INTRODUCTION   BCD 16624/1
      Ekkehard Schumann, Monroe

[2]   ROUST-A-BOUT (B. Graves)   BCD 16624/1
      Lewis-L

[3]   BLUE GRASS BREAKDOWN (Bill Monroe)   BCD 16624/1
      Instrumental

[4]   MULE SKINNER BLUES (P.D.)   BCD 16624/1
      Monroe-L

[5]   FOOTPRINTS IN THE SNOW (P.D.)   BCD 16624/1
      Monroe-L

[6]   KENTUCKY MANDOLIN (Bill Monroe)   BCD 16624/1
      Instrumental

[7]   I'M WORKING ON A BUILDING (A. P. Carter)   BCD 16624/1
      Monroe-LV/TC, Lewis-LC, Black-B, Davis-BS

[8]   THE ROAD OF LIFE (Virginia Stauffer)   BCD 16624/1
      Monroe-LV/TC, Lewis-LC, Black-B, Davis-BS

[9]   GREY EAGLE (P.D)   BCD 16624/1
      Instrumental

[10] FESTIVAL WALTZ (Kenny Baker)   BCD 16624/1
      Instrumental

[11] UNCLE PEN (Bill Monroe)   BCD 16624/1
      Monroe-LV/TC, Lewis-LC, Davis-B

[12] THE TRUCK DRIVIN' MAN (Terry Fell)   BCD 16624/1
      Lewis-L

[13] IN THE PINES (Clayton McMichen)   BCD 16624/1
      Lewis-L, Monroe-T

[14] SHUCKIN' THE CORN (Earl Scruggs)   BCD 16624/1
      Instrumental

| Bill Monroe: m | Ralph Lewis: g | Kenny Baker: f |
| Bob Black: b | Randy Davis: sb | |

750517.2   Recordings made by Hartmut Lang, released by Bear Family; Bill Monroe listed as "producer"
Gasthof Lindenhof, Neusüedende, Germany
May 17, 1975, 9–10:30 P.M.

[1]   ROLL IN MY SWEET BABY'S ARMS (P.D.)   BCD 16624/1
Lewis-L, Monroe-T, Davis-B

[2]   DOIN' MY TIME (Jimmie Skinner)   BCD 16624/1
Lewis-L

[3]   FLINT HILL SPECIAL (Earl Scruggs)   BCD 16624/1
Instrumental

[4]   LITTLE JOE (Bill Monroe)   BCD 16624/1
Monroe-L

[5]   YOU WON'T BE SATISFIED THAT WAY (Jimmie Davis–Lloyd Ellis)   BCD 16624/1
Monroe-L

[6]   WALKING IN MY SLEEP
Clifton-L, Monroe-T

[7]   SWEETHEART YOU DONE ME WRONG
Clifton-L, Monroe-T

[8]   WILDWOOD FLOWER
Instrumental

[9]   BLUE RIDGE MOUNTAIN BLUES
Clifton-L, Monroe-T

[10]   LITTLE CABIN HOME ON THE HILL
Clifton-L, Monroe-T

[11]   MCKINLEY'S MARCH (Bill Monroe)   BCD 16624/2
Instrumental

[12]   I SAW THE LIGHT (Hank Williams)   BCD 16624/2
Lewis-L, Monroe-T, Black-B, Davis-BS

[13]   ORANGE BLOSSOM SPECIAL (Ervin Rouse)   BCD 16624/2
Instrumental

[14]   ORANGE BLOSSOM SPECIAL (Ervin Rouse)   BCD 16624/2
Instrumental

[15]   ORANGE BLOSSOM SPECIAL (Ervin Rouse)   BCD 16624/2
Instrumental

[16]	BLUE MOON OF KENTUCKY (Bill Monroe) Monroe-L	BCD 16624/2
[17]	MY LITTLE GEORGIA ROSE (Bill Monroe) Monroe-L	BCD 16624/2
[18]	DOWN YONDER (P.D.) Instrumental	BCD 16624/2
[19]	WABASH CANNONBALL (A. P. Carter) Monroe-L	BCD 16624/2
[20]	YOU'LL FIND HER NAME WRITTEN THERE (Harold Hensley) Monroe-L	BCD 16624/2
[21]	SWING LOW SWEET CHARIOT/I SAW THE LIGHT (P.D.) Monroe-L	BCD 16624/2
[22]	JOHN HENRY (P.D.) Monroe-L	BCD 16624/2
[23]	MOLLY AND TENBROOKS (Bill Monroe) Monroe-L	BCD 16624/2
[24]	FRAULEIN (Lawton Williams) Monroe-L	BCD 16624/2

Bill Monroe: m   Ralph Lewis, Bill Clifton (6–10): g   Kenny Baker: f
Bob Black: b   Randy Davis: sb

750517.3   Recordings made by Hartmut Lang, released by Bear Family; Bill Monroe listed as "producer"
Gasthof Lindenhof, Neusüedende, Germany
May 17, 1975

[1]   ROLL IN MY SWEET BABY'S ARMS
[vocal parts not known]

[2]   TRUCK DRIVING MAN
[vocal parts not known]

[3]   MEDLEY (SITTIN' ON TOP OF THE WORLD / HAND ME   BCD 16624/2
        DOWN MY WALKIN' CANE / GOOD OLD MOUNTAIN DEW /
        CARELESS LOVE / BLUE MOON OF KENTUCKY) (Henderson–
        Young–Lewis[23] / P.D. / Lunsford–Wiseman /P.D. / Bill Monroe)
      Monroe, Lewis-L; Monroe-TC; Emsland Hillbillies-L [?]

Bill Monroe: m   Ralph Lewis: g
Emsland Hillbillies:
  Kalli Buskohl: lead eg   Ronnie Seffinga: eg   Ronnie Seffinga: accordian
  Emmo Doden: drums   Hermann Lammers Meyer: esg

750525   Rebel session at concert for Ralph Stanley and the Clinch Mountain Boys; producer, Charles R. Freeland
             5th Annual Carter Stanley Memorial Festival, McClure, Va.
             May 25, 1975

[1]   I'M ON MY WAY BACK TO THE OLD HOME   SLP 1554
      Stanley-L, Monroe-T

[2]   CAN'T YOU HEAR ME CALLING   SLP 1555
      Stanley-L, Monroe-T

Bill Monroe (2): m   Keith Whitley, Ricky Lee: g   Curley Ray Cline: f
Ralph Stanley: b   Jack Cook: sb   (?) (2): Dobro

750600   Atteiram session for Birch Monroe; producer, Bill Monroe
             Glaser Brothers Recording Studio, Nashville, Tenn.
             Ca. May 1975[4]

[1]   BOATIN' UP SANDY (Birch Monroe)   API-L-1516
      Instrumental

[2]   DIXON COUNTY RAG (Arthur Smith)   API-L-1516
      Instrumental

[3]   FLOP EARED MULE (arr. Birch Monroe)   API-L-1516
      Instrumental

[4]   DOWN YONDER (L. W. Gilbert)   API-L-1516
      Instrumental

[5]   FLORIDA BLUES (Arthur Smith)   API-L-1516
      Instrumental

[6]	COMIN' DOWN FROM BOSTON (Birch Monroe) Instrumental	API-L-1516
[7][5]	CUMBERLAND GAP (arr. Birch Monroe) Instrumental	API-L-1516
[8]	CARROLL COUNTY BLUES (arr. Birch Monroe) Instrumental	API-L-1516
[9]	THE BEAUTIFUL RED ROSE WALTZ (Birch Monroe) Instrumental	API-L-1516
[10]	DURANE'S[6] HORNPIPE (arr. Birch Monroe) Instrumental	API-L-1516
[11]	NATURAL BRIDGE BLUES (Tommy Magness) Instrumental	API-L-1516

Bill Monroe: m[7]   Ralph Lewis g[8]   Birch Monroe: f
Bob Black: b   Randy Davis: sb

760209 Atteiram session for James Monroe; producers, James Monroe, Carl Queen
Fireside Studios, Nashville, Tenn.
Feb. 9, 10, and 11, 1976, 6 P.M. daily

[1]	DOWN IN THE WILLOW GARDEN (Charlie Monroe) J. Monroe-L	API-L-1532
[2]	BRINGING IN THE GEORGIA MAIL (Fred Rose) J. Monroe-L, B. Monroe-T	API-L-1532, RR-599D
[3]	THE RED ROCKING CHAIR (J. Duffy) J. Monroe-L	API-L-1532
[4]	WHEN THE ANGELS CARRY ME HOME[9] (Charlie Monroe) J. Monroe-L, B. Monroe-T, Stuart-BS	API-L-1532
[5]	DOWN MEMORY LANE (Marvin Enloe) J. Monroe-L, B. Monroe-T	API-L-1532, RR-599D
[6]	I'M OLD KENTUCKY BOUND (Charlie Monroe) J. Monroe-L	API-L-1532
[7][10]	I'M COMING BACK BUT I DON'T KNOW WHEN (Charlie Monroe) J. Monroe-L, B. Monroe-T	API-L-1532, RR-599D

[8]	ROLLING IN MY SWEET BABY'S ARMS (Lester Flatt) J. Monroe-L, B. Monroe-T	API-L-1532, RR-599D[11]
[9]	WHAT BECAME OF THAT BEAUTIFUL PICTURE (Mel Butler–Shep Sessions) J. Monroe-L	API-L-1532
[10]	IT'S ONLY A PHONOGRAPH RECORD (Charlie Monroe) J. Monroe-L	API-L-1532

Bill Monroe: m	James Monroe: g	Joe Stuart (except 4),
Vic Jordan: b	Gerald Sullivan: sb	Kenny Baker (5–10),
		Jim Brock (1–4): f[12]

760329.1   County session for Kenny Baker; producer, David Freeman
Nashville, Tenn.
March 29 or 30, 1976

[1]	ROAD TO COLUMBUS Instrumental	CO 761
[2]	LONESOME MOONLIGHT WALTZ Instrumental	CO 761
[3]	MONROE'S HORNPIPE Instrumental	CO 761
[4]	CHEYENNE Instrumental	CO 761
[5]	BIG SANDY RIVER Instrumental	CO 761
[6]	STONEY LONESOME Instrumental	CO 761
[7]	WHEEL HOSS Instrumental	CO 761
[8]	FIDDLER'S PASTIME Instrumental	CO 761

Bill Monroe: m	Joe Stuart: g	Kenny Baker: f
Vic Jordan: b	Randy Davis: bs	

760329.2   County session for Kenny Baker; producer, David Freeman
Nashville, Tenn.
March 29 or 30, 1976

[1]   BROWN COUNTY BREAKDOWN   CO 761
Instrumental

[2]   JERUSALEM RIDGE   CO 761, CD-8007,
Instrumental   SHA 604, RO 25

[3]   MISSISSIPPI WALTZ   CO 761
Instrumental

[4]   ASHLAND BREAKDOWN   CO 761, MCAD 4-11048
Instrumental

Bill Monroe: m   Joe Stuart: g   Kenny Baker: f
Bob Black: b   Randy Davis: bs

760504   Country Road reissue of radio broadcast session for CBC;[13] producer, Ira Stewart
Nugget Studios, Nashville, Tenn.
May 4, 1976

[1]   UNCLE PEN   CR-02
Monroe-LV/TC, Jones-LC, Davis-B

[2]   FOOTPRINTS IN THE SNOW   CR-02
Monroe-L

[3]   JERUSALEM RIDGE   CR-02
Instrumental

[4]   I'M WORKING ON A BUILDING   CR-02
Monroe-LV/TC, Jones-LC, Black-B, Davis-BS[14]

[5]   MARY JANE, WON'T YOU BE MINE (My Little Sweetheart   CR-02
    of the Mountains)
Monroe-LV/TC, Jones-LC,[15] Davis-B

[6]   BLUE MOON OF KENTUCKY   CR-02
Monroe-L

[7]   DEAR OLD DIXIE   CR-02
Instrumental

[8]   IT'S ME AGAIN LORD   CR-02
               Jones-L, Monroe: T, Black-B, Davis-BS

Bill Monroe: m   James Monroe, Bob Jones: g   Kenny Baker: f
Bob Black: b   Randy Davis: sb   Vic Mullen: mc

760713   Mercury session for Tom T. Hall; producer, Jerry Kennedy
               U.S. Recording Studios, Inc., Nashville, Tenn.
               July 13, 1976, 10 P.M.–1 A.M.

52445   MOLLY AND TENBROOKS (Bill Monroe)   SRM-1-1111
               Tom T. Hall-L

Bill Monroe: m[16]   Charlie Collins, Ray Edenton: g   Kenny Baker, Buddy Spicher: f
Bobby Thompson: b   Bob Moore: sb
Buddy Harman: dr   Gene Bush: Dobro

761020   MCA session; producer, Walter Haynes (Bill Monroe listed as "leader")
               Bradley's Barn, Mount Juliet, Tenn.
               Oct. 20, 1976, 6–9 P.M.

NA 17907   MY CABIN IN CAROLINE (Lester Flatt–Earl Scruggs)   MCA 2251, BCD 15606
  MC 5809   Monroe-L

NA 17908   NO PLACE TO PILLOW MY HEAD (Bill Monroe–Lester Flatt)   MCA 2251, BCD 15606
  MC 5810   Monroe-LV/TC, Lewis-LC, Davis-B

NA 17909   MY SWEET BLUE-EYED DARLING   MCA 40675   MCA 2251, BCD 15606
  MC 5811   (Bill Monroe)
               Lewis-L, Monroe-T, Stuart-B

Bill Monroe: m   James Monroe, Wayne Lewis: g   Kenny Baker, Joe Stuart,
William O'Neal "Bill" Holden: b   Randy Davis: sb   Blaine Sprouse: f

---

761021   MCA session; producer, Walter Haynes (Bill Monroe listed as "leader")
               Bradley's Barn, Mount Juliet, Tenn.
               Oct. 21, 1976, 6–9:30 P.M.

NA 17910   MONROE'S BLUES (Bill Monroe)   MCA 40675   MCA 2251, BCD 15606
  MC 5812   Instrumental

NA 17911   THE FIRST WHIPPOORWILL (Bill Monroe)   BCD 15606
  MC 5813   J. Monroe-L, Monroe-T, Stuart-B[17]

NA 17912 MC 5814	LUCKY LADY (Bill Monroe) Instrumental	MCA 2251, BCD 15606
NA 17913 MC 5815	MY LOUISIANA LOVE (Bill Monroe) Davis-L, Monroe-T, Stuart-B	MCA 2251, BCD 15606

Bill Monroe: m Bill Holden: b	James Monroe, Wayne Lewis: g Randy Davis: sb	Kenny Baker, Joe Stuart, Blaine Sprouse: f

770725   MCA session; producer, Walter Haynes (Bill Monroe listed as "leader")
Bradley's Barn, Mount Juliet, Tenn.
July 25, 1977, 6–9 P.M.

NA 18005 MC 6754	CHRISTMAS TIME'S A-COMING (Tex Logan) Monroe-LV/TC, J. Monroe-LC, Davis-B	MCA 2315, BCD 15606
NA 18006 MC 6755	TEXAS BLUE BONNET (Bill Monroe) Instrumental	MCA 2315, BCD 15606
NA 18007 MC 6756	THE SUNSET TRAIL (Bill Monroe) Monroe-LV/TC, Lewis-LC, Davis-B	MCA 2315, BCD 15606

Bill Monroe: m Bill Holden: b	James Monroe, Wayne Lewis: g Randy Davis: sb	Buddy Spicher: f

770727   MCA session; producer, Walter Haynes (Bill Monroe listed as "leader")
Bradley's Barn, Mount Juliet, Tenn.
July 27, 1977, 6–9 P.M.

NA 18008 MC 6757	MY SWEET MEMORY (Bill Monroe) Lewis-L, Monroe-T, Davis-B	MCA 2315, BCD 15606
NA 18009 MC 6758	SHE'S YOUNG (AND I'M GROWING OLD) (Bill Monroe) Monroe-LV/TC, Lewis-LC, Davis-B	MCA 2315, BCD 15606
NA 18010 MC 6759	BLUE GOOSE (Bill Monroe) Instrumental	MCA 2315, BCD 15606

Bill Monroe: m Bill Holden: b	James Monroe, Wayne Lewis: g Randy Davis: sb	Buddy Spicher: f

770728   MCA session; producer, Walter Haynes (James Monroe listed as "leader")
Bradley's Barn, Mount Juliet, Tenn.
July 28, 1977, 6–9:30 P.M.

NA 18011   THAT'S CHRISTMAS TIME TO ME (Virginia Stauffer)   MCA 2315, BCD 15606
  MC 6760   Monroe-L

NA 18012   PINEWOOD VALLEY (William Holden)   MCA 2315, BCD 15606
  MC 6761   Instrumental

NA 18013   MY FLORIDA SUNSHINE (Bill Monroe)   MCA 2315, BCD 15606
  MC 6762   Lewis-L, Monroe-T, Davis-B

NA 18014   WABASH CANNON BALL (A. P. Carter)   MCA 2315, BCD 15606
  MC 6763   Monroe-L

Bill Monroe: m   James Monroe, Wayne Lewis: g   Buddy Spicher: f
Bill Holden: b   Randy Davis: sb   Walter Haynes: bells (-11 only)

780111   NBC broadcast *Fifty Years of Country Music,* published on Original Cinema and ABC-CLIO
Grand Ole Opry, Nashville, Tenn.
Probable recording date, Jan. 11, 1978; broadcast date, Jan. 22, 1978.

[1]   BLUE MOON OF KENTUCKY   ABC-CLIO
  Monroe-L

[2]   MULE SKINNER BLUES   OC-1001
  Monroe-L, Dolly Parton-T

Bill Monroe: m   Wayne Lewis: g   Kenny Baker: f
Joseph C. "Butch" Robins: b   Randy Davis: sb

780124   MCA session; producer, Walter Haynes (James Monroe listed as "leader")
Bradley's Barn, Mount Juliet, Tenn.
Jan. 24, 1978, 6–9 P.M.

NA 18020   HARD TIMES HAVE BEEN HERE (Damon Black)   MCA 2367, BCD 15606
  MC 7265   J. Monroe-L, Monroe-T

NA 18021   SIX FEET UNDER THE GROUND (Bill Monroe)   MCA 2367, BCD 15606
  MC 7266   Monroe-LV/TC, J. Monroe-LC

NA 18022   WHO'S GONNA SHOE YOUR PRETTY LITTLE FEET (P.D.)   MCA 2367, BCD 15606
    MC 7267   J. Monroe-L, Monroe-T

Bill Monroe: m   James Monroe, Wayne Lewis: g   Kenny Baker, James Earl Bryan: f
Butch Robins, Alan O'Bryant: b   Randy Davis: sb

780130   MCA session; producer, Walter Haynes (James Monroe listed as "leader")
                   Bradley's Barn, Mount Juliet, Tenn.
                   Jan. 30, 1978, 6–9 P.M.

NA 18023   JAKE SATTERFIELD (Damon Black)   MCA 2367, BCD 15606
    MC7268   J. Monroe-L, Monroe-T

NA 18024   MUDDY WATERS (Phil Rosenthal)   MCA 2367, BCD 15606
    MC 7269   J. Monroe-L, Monroe-T

NA 18025   CORRINA, CORRINA (P.D)   MCA 2367, BCD 15606
    MC 7270   J. Monroe-L, Monroe-T

Bill Monroe: m   James Monroe, Wayne Lewis: g   Kenny Baker, James Bryan: f
Butch Robins, Alan O'Bryant: b   Randy Davis: sb

780208   MCA session; producer, Walter Haynes (James Monroe listed as "leader")
                   Bradley's Barn, Mount Juliet, Tenn.
                   Feb. 8, 1978, 6–9 P.M.

NA 18033   HAVE A FEAST HERE TONIGHT (Charlie Monroe)   MCA 2367, BCD 15606
    MC 7286   J. Monroe-L, Monroe-T

NA 18034   GOLDEN RIVER (Stuart Hamblen)   MCA 2367, BCD 15606
    MC 7287   J. Monroe-L, Monroe-T

NA 18035   I'M GOING BACK TO OLD KENTUCKY (Bill Monroe)   MCA 2367, BCD 15606
    MC 7288   Monroe-LV/TC, J. Monroe-LC

NA 18036   THOSE MEMORIES OF YOU (Alan O'Bryant)   MCA 2367, BCD 15606
    MC 7289   J. Monroe-L, Monroe-T

Bill Monroe: m   James Monroe,[18] Wayne Lewis: g   Kenny Baker, James Bryan: f
Butch Robins, Alan O'Bryant: b   Randy Davis: sb

780317   Raintree Records, James Monroe session
Hilltop Studio, Nashville, Tenn.
March 17, 1978

[1]   NINE POUND HAMMER   RR-599D
J. Monroe-L, B. Monroe-T

[2]   LIVE AND LET LIVE   RR-599D
J. Monroe-L, B. Monroe-T

[3]   I HAVEN'T SEEN MARY IN YEARS   RR-599D
J. Monroe-L, B. Monroe-T

[4]   BONNY   RR-599D
J. Monroe-L, B. Monroe-T

[5]   WHEN THE BEES ARE IN THE HIVE   RR-599D
J. Monroe-L, B. Monroe-T

[6]   WHEN THE ANGELS CARRY ME HOME[19] (Charlie Monroe)   RR-599D
J. Monroe-L, B. Monroe-T

Bill Monroe: m   James Monroe: g   Buddy Spicher (except 6): f
Alan O'Bryant (except 6): b   Billy Linneman (except 6): sb

790612   MCA session; producer, Walter Haynes, coproduced by Ron Chancey (Wayne Lewis listed as "leader")
Bill Monroe's 13th Annual Bluegrass Festival, Bill Monroe's Brown County Jamboree, Bean Blossom, Ind.
June 12, 1979

MC 9711   ROCKY ROAD BLUES (Bill Monroe)   MCA 3209, BCD 15606
Monroe-L

MC 9712   THE LITTLE GIRL AND THE DREADFUL SNAKE (A. Price)   MCA 3209, BCD 15606
Lewis-L, Monroe-T

MC 9713   IN DESPAIR (Joe Arr [sic]-Juanita Pennington)   MCA 3209, BCD 15606
Monroe-LV/TC, Lewis-TC

MC 9714   MOLLY AND TENBROOKS MEDLEY: LITTLE MAGGIE / TRAIN 45 /   MCA 3209, BCD 15606
   BLUE MOON OF KENTUCKY (Bill Monroe)
Monroe-L

Bill Monroe: m   Wayne Lewis: g   Kenny Baker: f
Butch Robins: b   Randy Davis: sb

790616   MCA session; producer, Walter Haynes, coproduced by Ron Chancey (Wayne Lewis listed as "leader")
Bill Monroe's 13th Annual Bluegrass Festival, Bill Monroe's Brown County Jamboree, Bean Blossom, Ind.
June 16, 1979

MC 9705   INTRO (WATERMELON HANGIN' ON THE VINE) / JOHN HENRY (P.D.)   MCA 3209, BCD 15606
Monroe-L

MC 9706   DOG HOUSE BLUES (Bill Monroe)   MCA 3209, BCD 15606
Monroe-L

MC 9707   THE OLD MOUNTAINEER (Bill Monroe)   MCA 3209, BCD 15606
Instrumental

MC 9708[20]   LITTLE CABIN HOME ON THE HILL (Bill Monroe–Lester Flatt)
Lewis-L, Monroe-T

MC 9709   ORANGE BLOSSOM SPECIAL (Ervin Rouse)   MCA 3209, BCD 15606
Monroe-L

MC 9714   Y'ALL COME (Arlie Duff)   MCA 3209, BCD 15606
Monroe-L, Audience

Bill Monroe: m   Wayne Lewis: g   Kenny Baker: f
Butch Robins: b   Randy Davis: sb

790900   MCA session; producer, Walter Haynes
Nashville, Tenn.
Between June 17, 1979, and Feb. 1980; probably fall 1979

MC 9708   LITTLE CABIN HOME ON THE HILL (Bill Monroe–Lester Flatt)   MCA 3209, BCD 15606
Lewis-L, Monroe-T

Bill Monroe: m   Wayne Lewis: g   Kenny Baker: f

800807   Smithsonian/Folkways, Homespun Tapes (video) reissue of concert
The White House, Washington, D.C.
Aug. 7, 1980

[0]   Introduction   VD-MON-MN01
President Jimmy Carter

[1]   UNCLE PEN   VD-MON-MN01
Monroe-LV/TC, Lewis-LC, Robins-B

[2]   BLUE MOON OF KENTUCKY   VD-MON-MN01
Monroe-L

[3]	RAW HIDE Instrumental	VD-MON-MN01
[4]	RABBIT IN THE LOG [FEAST HERE TONIGHT] Watson-L, Monroe-T	VD-MON-MN01
[5]	PADDY ON THE TURNPIKE Instrumental	VD-MON-MN01, SF 40064

Bill Monroe (1–5): m
Butch Robins (1–3): b

Wayne Lewis (1–3),
Doc Watson (4–5): g
Mark G. Hembree (1–3): sb

Kenny Baker (1–3): f

Notes

1. The entries for sessions 730616 and 730617 represent the 1973 Bean Blossom Festival recordings in which Bill Monroe participated. In Neil V. Rosenberg, *Bill Monroe and His Blue Grass Boys: An Illustrated Discography* (Nashville: Country Music Foundation Press, 1974), 97, is the statement "the performances recorded at this and sessions 83–87 [numbers assigned in that book] took place over a period of several days. MCA assigned a single date to all the sessions for convenience in record-keeping." Subsequently it was determined that all of the performances occurred on June 16 and 17.

2. The guest fiddlers were Jim Brock, Lonnie Pierce, Ralph "Joe" Meadows, Randall Collins, Arnold "Buck" Ryan, Gordon Terry, Howard "Howdy" Forrester, Tex Logan, Curley Ray Cline, Paul Warren, and Tater Tate.

3. This composer attribution follows that of the 1957 recording and, like it, is incorrect.

4. On March 6, 1999, Atteiram owner Carl Queen told Tom Ewing that the recording session took place "just before Bean Blossom." Ewing, email to Rosenberg, March 7, 1999.

5. Overdubbed ending by Birch Monroe on this track.

6. The first word of this title should be *Durang's.*

7. Bill takes breaks on masters [8] and [10].

8. Personnel identified on the album as "The Blue Grass Boys"; names supplied by Bob Black.

9. According to Lance LeRoy's notes to RR-599D, that CD, released in September 1999, includes five songs "from February 10, 1976, sessions." Perhaps he arrived at that conclusion because "When the Angels Carry Me Home" is on both albums. However the recordings are not the same. [4] is a trio with a full band in the key of B with a playing time of 1:35, while the version on RR-599D, which is listed below in session 780317, is a duet with just Bill and James in the key of A with a playing time of 1:44.

10. Vic Jordan overdubbed a banjo harmony part on this track.

11. The title for this track is given as "Roll in My Sweet Baby's Arms" on RR-599D.

12. The liner notes list all three fiddlers. According to Jim Brock, who spoke with Tom Ewing on November 13, 1999, he played only on the first day's session, at which tracks [1]-[4] were recorded. Baker was not present; Joe Stuart was the other fiddler. Brock did not sing. This explains why track [4] is the only one on which twin-harmony fiddles are not heard, as Stuart sang in the trio on that track.

13. Recorded for the CBC Radio Network Series "Country Road." Although banded, this recording contains two complete radio broadcast transcriptions with dialog between Mullen and Monroe. Side one, with selections [1–4], is set up as the first segment; side two, with selections [5–8], is set up as the second.

14. The singers' names but not their vocal parts are announced by Monroe for this track.

15. As Bob Black comments concerning the lead singer on the choruses of this track, "I think this is correct but it's possible it could be James Monroe" (Black to Rosenberg, Feb. 12, 1997).

16. According to union session data, four songs were cut at this session. Monroe took part only in the first song. The other three songs recorded were "Rank Stranger," "Fox on the Run," and "I Think I'll Just Lay Around Drunk." Personnel present but not performing on this cut included Donna Stoneman and Jody Drumright, mandolins, and Earl J. T. Gray and Arthur Malmin, harmony vocals.

17. The vocal parts on this track are Rosenberg's guess after listening to Bear Family reissue and comparing with -13.

18. James Monroe plays the lead guitar breaks on "Golden River" and "Those Memories of You."

19. It is not certain if this track was recorded at this session or at session 760209; see note 9, above.

20. This track was re-recorded later in the studio with just mandolin, guitar, and fiddle (see next session).

9

"MY LAST DAYS ON EARTH": 1980–96

During the last sixteen years of his life Bill Monroe continued to write new songs, perform regularly on the Grand Ole Opry, maintain a hectic touring schedule, and record at a pace that surpassed even that of his earlier years. Yet there were significant changes in his recording methods. A string of new young producers for MCA began to take a more hands-on approach to studio sessions and encouraged the singer to do a series of special projects with invited guests in order to bolster sales. He also continued to do guest appearances on other albums, some more acknowledged than others. Although his sessions were still done in what the old producers called "stereo live," which is now called "from the floor" (the entire band in the studio to make the master recording), Monroe gradually became more familiar with the multitrack studio environment. He continued to maintain control over all the final product but seemed to welcome input from younger producers like Walter Haynes, Emory Gordy Jr., and Vic Gabany.

"THE MANDOLIN ALBUM"

In February 1981 Monroe and the band were in the Music Mill Studio on downtown Nashville's Music Row to complete work on the album that would become *Bill Monroe: Master of Bluegrass*. Walter Haynes was still producing Bill's albums, as he'd done for the past decade.

Monroe referred to *Master of Bluegrass* as "the mandolin album . . . the first one I've ever made" and singled out as his favorites two originals, "Old Ebenezer Scrooge" and "Come Hither to Go Yonder."[1] He also often spoke of how instrumentals could be as evocative as lyrics in calling up an image or a sense of the past. Named after the town of Daingerfield, Texas, "Old Danger Field," said Monroe, "goes back a long time, how the people would have danced and listened to the music."[2] "Evening Prayer Blues" was his tribute to DeFord

Bailey, the legendary black harmonica player from the early days of the Opry. Bailey wrote and began playing the piece in the 1920s as a tribute to a famed Nashville preacher, Zema W. Hill.[3] "DeFord was the best harmonica player, when it came to playing the blues," Monroe observed, "of any man, I thought, that ever lived."[4] On June 23, 1983, a little over two years after he recorded his mandolin version of "Evening Prayer," Monroe played it as a solo over Bailey's grave at a service dedicating a monument to him.

During the time he was recording *Master of Bluegrass* Monroe was diagnosed with colon cancer, and barely three weeks after he finished the sessions he underwent surgery for it. His illness loomed over the recording process—at one point he was seriously concerned about whether he would survive long enough to see the album to completion—and it played a part in creating the most controversial and the most discussed tune from the set, "My Last Days on Earth." A strange, haunting, and evocative lament, it was unlike anything else Monroe had written for the mandolin. He recorded it on the final day of the session, asking his regular band to sit out and using only the backing of Mark Hembree's bass and Norman Blake's parlor-style guitar. Blake, a superb instrumentalist and songwriter from Georgia, won his reputation as an ace studio musician with Johnny Cash and later with John Hartford's pioneer "new-grass" backup band on the album *Aereo-Plain*. By the time "My Last Days on Earth" was recorded he had established his own solo career.

The tune was another Monroe piece that required putting the mandolin into a cross-tuning, something he had done earlier with "Blue Grass Ramble," "Get Up John," and "In Despair." Here, however, he created a different tuning that changed the strings from lowest to highest course. As Tom Ewing explains: "Both G strings up to A; D strings are unchanged; first A string up to C, the other unchanged; first E string up to F and the other down to D."[5] Monroe provided a number of accounts of how he came to write the piece. One of the best was to journalist Alanna Nash:

Well, one night along in the morning, around two or three o'clock, I couldn't sleep and it was as cold as it could be, boy. So I thought I'd get up and get my mandolin, and I'd just see what I could come up with. I'd see what different style I could tune. Something new. So I got my mandolin, and I went to coming up with tuning a different style, where it would harmonize. You could play two strings and one would be harmony for the other string, you see. So I got it tuned up the way I wanted it, and then I went to playin' some on it. . . . But it seemed like

when I started on it, "My Last Days on Earth" just wrote itself, like it was there already. I was going along with it, and it was really sad.[6]

When he heard the "Last Days" master and began to notice the effect it had on people—some in the studio that night were in tears after the take was completed—producer Walter Haynes decided to do something he had never tried with a Monroe recording, augment and "sweeten" it with discrete background tracks. He sold Monroe on the idea, and six weeks later, on April 7, a trio of background singers was brought in for an overdub session. The delay might have been occasioned by Monroe's surgery at Baptist Hospital and his recovery. He apparently discussed the new album with Haynes in the hospital, and suggested some wordless oohs and ahs when asked about which words might fit. Haynes pushed his luck further and suggested adding a string section, which he did in a second overdub session on April 28, three weeks later.

Monroe, present in the studio for the April 28 session, was impressed with the six members of the Sheldon Kurland Strings and how they read the arrangements for his song. "They wrote their parts," he told an interviewer. "They play by notes, by music, is the way they do, so they didn't have any trouble following the notes and everything."[7] Haynes also had Monroe in the studio during the final mixing. "He would always sit right behind me while I did the mixing, and at one point Bill heard the deep sound of a cello, and excitedly whispered, 'What is that?' 'It's a cello, Bill,' I said. Bill said nothing else for a while, but he heard it again later, and asked, 'Can you bring that sello [sic] up a little more?'"[8]

"My Last Days on Earth" became the showpiece of the new album, and fans widely assumed that Monroe had written it as a sort of last will and testament, an acknowledgement of his illness and eventual mortality. MCA issued it as a single, and although it never appeared on *Billboard*'s singles' charts it did receive a great deal of airplay. It was also used in a popular Hollywood film, *All the Pretty Horses*. Monroe's Nashville memorial service in 1996 began with the famed F-5 mandolin standing on an empty stage while "My Last Days on Earth" softly played through the sound system.

THE CATHEDRAL CAVERNS GOSPEL ALBUM

In the spring of 1982, after he started touring again, Monroe decided he wanted to do a live gospel album and use some of the old favorites that he liked to sing but had never gotten around to recording. Rather than go into a rural church, he wanted to record at Cathedral Caverns on U.S. Highways 72 and 431 between Woodside and Grant in northeastern Alabama, not far from Huntsville. In those days the cave was privately owned and a successful attraction that drew some twenty-four thousand tourists a year. Discovered in 1952, it had a massive entrance and one of the largest known stalagmites, called Goliath. To boost attendance, the owner staged gospel music concerts in the cavern, which was advertised as being naturally air-conditioned. On several occasions Monroe was booked for a show. He liked the reverberations created by the acoustics in the cave's huge room and decided he wanted to record there.

Thus it came to be that Monroe approached his friend Vic Gabany, whom he'd long known as a sound man at the Opry and an engineer who'd sat in on his recording sessions since 1971, at the Opryland Hotel one afternoon and said, "I want you to help me talk to Walter Haynes" about the idea of a live gospel album. Appreciating the problems from an engineer's perspective, Gabany nonetheless agreed and spoke to Haynes, who had no problem with the idea and told Vic to go ahead and set up the session.[9]

In the meantime, though, Monroe had to solve a major personnel problem in his band. The driving banjoist Joseph C. "Butch" Robins had given notice, and it was necessary to find a replacement. The prime candidate was Blake Williams, a twenty-six-year-old musician from Benny Martin's hometown, Sparta, Tennessee. When barely a teenager, Blake began performing with a popular teen-aged band, Blades of Bluegrass, which did many local television shows and appearances in Nashville. By the time he was seventeen he had moved on to full-time work with Bobby Smith and the Boys from Shiloh, and by 1978 he was playing with the band of another Sparta native, Lester Flatt. After Flatt died, Williams began to fill in with James Monroe's band. In July 1981 Williams heard that Robins was leaving the Blue Grass Boys:

> We were playing a festival in North Carolina. I was going over there with James Monroe. Alan Phelps told me, "Did you hear that Butch quit?" And James at the time was doing some country music things and trying to slow down and quit. So I say, "I may just go and try out." So I went to Bill when we got to the festival, and I said, "I'm going to come down and pick with you tonight." And he said, "Okay, be ready." So I came out and we did "Cryin' Holy" and I think I played "Shuckin' the Corn." That night when we were all getting ready to leave, I said, "Are you gonna hire somebody right away?" And he said, "Probably so." And that's all he would tell me. I came back to [James's] bus,

and we were getting ready to leave, and I told James, "James, he's not gonna consider me because he don't want you to quit playing bluegrass music." James said, "Well, I'll take care of that." He went off the bus and came back in a while and said, "You got that job if you want it." So Bill called me the next week, and he had four dates that weekend. He told me what they were and then said, "Can you help me on that?" I said, "Does this mean I got the job?" And he said, "I guess so." And that's the way it stood for ten years.[10]

During his early days with the band Monroe featured many of the new instrumentals from *Master of Bluegrass*, and for Williams it was a baptism in fire. "They were numbers I didn't really know, but that proved to be good," he said. "A lot of those new numbers used so many of the positions and rolls he continued to use, and a lot were in minor keys, so I got in there and learned them. Bill was such a great teacher."[11]

It turned out that Blake's first recording session with the band would be the live gospel album at Cathedral Caverns. But from the beginning, things went wrong; in Gabany's words, it turned out to be "a thrash."[12] The cavern's oddly shaped entrance made it difficult to get MCA's equipment inside, and some of the gear wasn't working right. Then there was the fact that bassist Mark Hembree and his wife Georgia were momentarily expecting a baby, and Mark alerted Monroe to the possibility that he might well have to fly back to Nashville should she go into labor. As a hedge against Hembree's absence, Monroe decided to find a "reserve" singer and called the Nashville union and asked whether it could send someone who could sing bass. Williams recalled that instead of one singer, the union sent two: "One was a bass singer, but the other was a baritone. So Bill sorta felt inclined to use both of these. Neither had ever sung with us before."[13] Consequently, half of the regular Blue Grass Quartet vocal team was sidelined that day.

Monroe also brought along a stack of old hymnbooks for reference, and the singers took some material, such as "What a Friend We Have in Jesus," directly from the books. "And all this," recalls Gabany, "was being done in one take. This was an actual show; what you get is what you get."[14] None of the repertoire was planned ahead of time. Some unusual songs were included, one of which was "Baptize Me in the Cumberland River," an original by Monroe. It was "a tune he wrote about two people that used to come around a lot," Williams remembered. "They were really good friends of his. Their names were Clarence and Armalee Green. They were real sweet people. Bill actually wrote the song about Clarence when he was baptized.

I had heard him sing it a couple of times before we recorded it, but I don't know how old it was."[15] Another unusual selection was a haunting Kenny Baker solo identified as "Little Shepherd." Others included somewhat lengthy versions of such standards as "Precious Memories," "I'll Fly Away," "Wayfaring Stranger," and "Shouting on the Hills of Glory."

Although Monroe liked the cavern's booming echo, Haynes and Gabany had to place the vocal and instrumental microphones so close that little of the echo was caught on the main tapes. Additional microphones were aimed out into the cavern as a remedy in order to capture ambient sound that would later be mixed in.

Walter Haynes took the tape back to Nashville, where he began to work on it at his studio in Burns, Tennessee. Somewhere along the way—and without consulting Monroe—he decided to sweeten one of the vocals by having studio musician Kurt Storey come in and add yet another voice to the master. When Monroe finally came to the studio to hear the finished master of what everyone was calling "the cavern album," Gabany ran the board while Haynes and Monroe listened. Haynes tried to signal the necessity of fading the new track for the song with the added voice, but Gabany couldn't locate that specific track. The cat was out of the bag. "What was that voice?" Monroe snapped. "Back up the tape." Furious, he asked why Haynes had done such a thing. "I just thought it would help the song, Bill," was the reply.[16]

Possibly because of that incident the album was shelved. In 1985 Bill's new producer, Emory Gordy Jr., was given the opportunity to work further with it. After listening to the recording he informed MCA that he was not interested in doing so. It remained unissued until its inclusion in Bear Family's complete set of Monroe's 1981–94 MCA recordings.

THE ALL-STAR SESSIONS

In 1979 Jim Fogelsong took over as head of Nashville's MCA. A native of West Virginia, Fogelsong was a graduate of the Eastman School of Music and had toured with Fred Waring's choir. In New York he worked with such pop greats as Julie Andrews and Robert Goulet before coming to Nashville as head of Dot Records and working with Roy Clark, Donna Fargo, and others. When he arrived at MCA he was distressed to learn that Bill Monroe's recent album sales had dropped "down to three or four thousand copies each." *Bill Monroe Sings Bluegrass, Body and Soul,* and *Bluegrass Memories* were both released in 1977. *Bill and James Monroe: Together Again* came out in 1978. "In

spite of these sales," Fogelsong recalls, "I was determined to keep Bill on the label—as was Jimmy Bowen after me. But we felt that Bill's voice was pretty much shot. It was OK for concerts, not for the recording studio."[17] *Bean Blossom '79,* was, like the album with James, an attempt to repeat earlier successes. The fact that *Master of Bluegrass* was an all-instrumental effort probably reflected Fogelsong's judgment concerning Bill's vocal work.

During Fogelsong's tenure (1979–84), Monroe only asked to meet with him twice. Once was to inform him that Rod Stewart had called Monroe, wanting him to be on Stewart's new album. "That's great, Bill," Fogelsong replied, "great that he thinks so much of you." "Yes," Monroe responded. "But I don't want my fans to think I've gone rock on them."[18] He had no such reservations, however, about working with contemporary country music stars.

One possible solution to slumping sales, as well as the perceived voice problem, was an album for which Monroe would be joined by special guests, not particularly bluegrass artists but mainstream country stars. Vic Gabany met with Monroe, and they began making a list of Bill's ideal duet partners: Willie Nelson, Johnny Cash, the Oak Ridge Boys, John Hartford, Waylon Jennings, Larry Gatlin and the Gatlin Brothers, Emmylou Harris, and Charley Pride. In the end, only Pride was unable to join the project because he was still under contract to RCA and they weren't inclined to release him. Monroe then wanted to invite Loretta Lynn, but that didn't work out either. Finally Haynes recruited, as a last-minute replacement, fellow MCA artist Barbara Mandrell. The substitution is reflected in the Monroe-Mandrell dialog that prefaces "My Rose of Old Kentucky" when Bill expresses gratitude: "You helped me complete the album and I thank you so much."

The sessions were held, one track at a time, over a six-month period at the Burns Station Studio in Burns, Tennessee, near Dickson and west of Nashville, starting in mid-December 1982. Gabany recalls it as the first session on which Monroe was coaxed into using headphones and the first time they did overdubs on a Monroe session at which he was present. As Blake Williams observes:

> I think the point that sticks in my mind most about those sessions is how much respect each of those country music artists had for Bill Monroe. I remember Mel Tillis coming in and saying he used to go out to the old pump in the backyard and splash water on his face—so he could stay awake long enough to hear Bill on the Opry. I heard Emmylou Harris tell him that she would sing the phone book with him just to sing with him.

The one thing I do remember, Bill Monroe always had a presence about him, onstage or whatever; he attracted attention. He had a demeanor that had a real strong presence. The first time I ever seen two people in the same room with an equally strong presence was when Johnny Cash came into the session. It was almost like at that point Bill asked Johnny what he would like to sing.[19]

In fact, Cash's duet, "I Still Miss Someone," was the only song in the project that Monroe had not previously recorded. As the project came together his enthusiasm for it grew. Gabany recalls that on February, 22, 1983, Monroe called the studio and asked if it was free that afternoon. Willie Nelson was in town, and he wanted to rush in and cut the duet with him. Fortunately, it was. Moreover, the Blue Grass boys were all available, and Haynes was able to round up studio musicians Charlie Collins and Buddy Spicher.

Although many of the tracks are of interesting music, each is preceded by dialog between Monroe and his guest. It's surprising that Monroe, a man of few words at most times, decided to make these introductory statements. In recent years he had been called upon to talk in public more than ever but tended to give rather brief stock answers to standard questions. The often stilted and mawkish dialogs represent Monroe's public persona of the time. Some, such as those between Monroe and John Hartford and Monroe and Ricky Skaggs, sound genuine and sincere. Others are full of obsequious Music Row gush.

The Mandrell duet, "My Rose of Old Kentucky," features Mandrell playing an overdubbed Dobro break, the first time a Dobro appears on a Monroe recording, and the song is rewritten slightly to make it a male-female duet. The Gatlin Brothers track "Is The Blue Moon Still Shining" features a complex harmony arrangement, with Larry Gatlin singing lead and Monroe tenor on the first verse; Monroe doing lead, with all three Gatlins singing backup on the second verse; Gatlin and Monroe again on the second chorus; and all four singing on the fourth chorus. The blistering duet with Ricky Skaggs, then at the height of his popularity as the leader of the "new traditionalists" in contemporary country music, marked the first of several collaborations between the two. It's the only piece on the album that has been reissued—in John Rumble's detailed and carefully edited four-CD set but without the introductory dialog. Willie Nelson's "The Sunset Trail" features Nelson's guitar break and also includes unusual fiddle backup by Baker and Buddy Spicher that sounds like it came from the soundtrack of a Hollywood western. On "Kentucky Waltz" Joe

Stuart was called in to help play guitar, the last in a long series of recordings he made with Monroe.

Bill Monroe and Friends had the effect for which the MCA bosses had hoped: It rejuvenated Monroe's sales. After it was released on January 12, 1984, it spent six weeks on the country album charts. Curiously, no single was pulled from it—the June 1981 single of "My Last Days on Earth" backed with "Come Hither to Go Yonder" would be Bill's last MCA single of new material. Moreover, bluegrass fans were less than happy with the album. The leading magazine in the field, *Bluegrass Unlimited,* did not review it because its editors did not want to print negative comments about the "father" of their music.

Monroe did not return to the studio that year, but on December 15, 1983, he was recorded live in concert at the Bottom Line in New York. Originally broadcast on January 28, 1984, as one of the Silver Eagle Cross Country Music radio shows, the concert was released on a King Biscuit Flour Hour CD under the title *Bill Monroe: Lookin' Back* in 1999.

Done with Monroe's regular road band, the session is a good sampling of what a typical Monroe set was like at the time. A number of notables were in the audience—Roy Horton, Roland White, former *Pickin'* editor Doug Tuchman, and Doug Dillard. All the tunes were old favorites with the exception of "Ebenezer Scrooge" from the *Master of Bluegrass* set. As of this writing, these are Kenny Baker's last published recordings with Monroe. It was a brilliant end to a complex and rewarding relationship that endured for more than two decades.

By 1983 Ricky Skaggs had been with the major label CBS/ Epic for two years and had a string of number-one singles and three hit albums on that major label. Early in 1984 he began work on the album *Country Boy,* which would win even more sales and awards, and asked Monroe to perform as a special guest on his country version of Monroe's 1950s' composition "Wheel Hoss." Monroe readily agreed. The Skaggs studio band, which included drums, electric steel, and Bobby Hicks's fiddle, laid down the basic tracks, and the Monroe came in at a later date and did his mandolin part as an overdub—another first for him. The track would win Skaggs, by then a newly inducted Grand Ole Opry regular, a Grammy in 1984 for Best Instrumental Performance.

During this same time, Skaggs talked Monroe into traveling to New York to appear in a video of the version of "Uncle Pen" from the album. "We were in New York twenty-four hours and we worked twenty-two of them," quipped Monroe later.[20] In the video Monroe plays his own Uncle Pen who makes a trip to New York with his recording star nephew (Skaggs). There were rumors at the time that Monroe also played an electric mando-lin on the recording of "Uncle Pen," but he vehemently denied that.[21]

By 1983 Walter Haynes, with whom Monroe had not always gotten along, left MCA and a new team headed by Jimmy Bowen emerged. The key player in the new group, as far as Monroe was concerned, was Emory Gordy Jr., a well-known Georgia producer and musician. Cutting his teeth by playing bass on studio sessions in the 1960s, Gordy in 1971 moved to the West Coast to become a key musician in the band of pop singer Neil Diamond. Further famous sessions followed; he played the prominent bass line in Elvis Presley's "Burning Love," for instance. In 1975 he was a charter member of Emmylou Harris's Hot Band, and in 1982 he joined Vince Gill, a fellow member of Rodney Crowell's band, the Cherry Bombs, in *Here Today,* a much-acclaimed bluegrass album project with David Grisman, Herb Pedersen, and Jimmy Buchanan. By 1983, however, Gordy had decided to make a change in his life. He recalls:

> I had retired from show-biz in '83 and moved from L.A. to the little town of Dallas, Georgia (my home town) to become a land surveyor. I was talked into getting back into the business by Tony Brown [also in Crowell's band] when he left RCA to go with the new Bowen regime at MCA. Bowen wanted all production to be in-house and I was called up to Nashville for a meeting with him (at the request of Tony Brown) in '84. He asked me to go back home and think about how much I needed to be a member of the new team. I figured up a generous figure and then doubled it. He didn't blink an eye, and in an instant, I was back in the music bizz.[22]

Bowen and Brown soon called a meeting to decide which producers would work with which MCA artists. Gordy wasted no time. "Monroe's name was called, [and] I got up and raised my hand toward the ceiling as high as I could get it." He then began to assess Monroe's latest work, *Bill Monroe and Friends.* "I listened to it . . . tried to like it . . . listened to it . . . tried to like it . . . it was awful." Next he met with Monroe. "I asked him what he'd like to do next. He said that a lot of people that weren't on the last album wanted to sing with him." In other words, a sequel to *Friends.* Gordy shuddered. "I thought, 'I've got to get him back to being himself.' I said, 'Bill, how would it be if we got some of these guys you taught how to play blue-grass, like Sonny Osborne, Ralph Stanley (he had played on the road with Bill at one time, as well as Carter). . . . I kept naming bluegrass artists, all of whom had been greatly influenced by Monroe. Bill thought for a second and said, 'That'll be wonder-ful . . . and we'll call it the *Bluegrass Hall of Fame.'"*[23] The tim-

ing was excellent. Monroe had opened his own Bluegrass Hall of Fame and Museum in Nashville, Tennessee, in June 1984, and opportunities for mutual publicity were obvious.

Gordy wasted little time. On May 2, 1985, he set up the first sessions at Sound Stage, one of Music Row's premier facili-ties, to start work on what would be known as *Bill Monroe and the Stars of the Bluegrass Hall of Fame.* The regular Blue Grass Boys were on hand for all the sessions, although when a guest banjo player was present Blake Williams would play what he called "backup banjo."

Replacing Kenny Baker was twenty-eight-year-old Glen Carl-ton Duncan from Columbus, Indiana. Duncan had discovered bluegrass as a young man when he heard Baker play with Mon-roe at Bean Blossom. A student of fast, jazzy-styled instrumen-talists like Benny Martin and Bobby Hicks, he worked on the road for various bands, singing tenor and playing fiddle, and in 1983 moved to Nashville. There he filled in on the Opry and started to establish himself as a session player. Eventually, he would become one of the most sought-after backup fiddlers not only in bluegrass but also for mainstream singers. Dun-can would play on albums ranging from gospel singer Doyle Lawson to pop singer Shania Twain and from the Kendalls to Barbara Mandrell. In 1983, however, shortly after he arrived in town, he heard that Monroe was seeking a replacement for Kenny Baker. Singer Kathy Chiavola found out and introduced him to Monroe. On Duncan's first Opry appearance with the Blue Grass Boys, Monroe asked what he wanted to fiddle. "Wheel Hoss," he answered, and kicked into it at a ferocious tempo that surprised even Monroe. As he struggled to keep up with his new fiddler, Monroe lost his pick and had to resort to doing a buck dance on the last chorus.[24] Ironically, the *Hall of Fame* set would be the only one to feature Duncan's fiddling.

INTO THE DIGITAL AGE

As work started on the new album, producer Emory Gordy Jr., "consulting engineer" Vic Gabany, and the entire MCA team found themselves in the middle of a momentous shift in recording technology, away from the older analog style to the new digital style.[25] "I was a big proponent of digital," recalls Gordy. "I had done the first digital project in Nashville, albeit just a mix-down to two tracks for a Vince Gill RCA album in 1983. Bowen [the new head of MCA] was definitely a digital, forward-looking guy, so he backed me 100 percent. He also gave me enough rope to hang myself, including some decent bucks to do the Monroe recordings."[26]

A note on the back of the *Hall of Fame* album states that it was "recorded digitally using the Mitsubishi X-800 thirty-two track system, without overdubs or the use of earphones. Every effort was made to capture these songs 'live,' as they were performed [,] without alteration." Editing was not easy during the early days of digital technology. Gordy recalls that "there was no multi-track editing available; during mixdowns we had to mix to the edits—shifting from one take to the other—comparing the 'ends' and 'outs.' It was very difficult, but the engineers were up to the challenge, especially since the project was so different from the day-to-day grind. It was a breath of fresh air for them. My biggest regret is the amount of reverb used. But then all the product done in country music during that time sounded that way."[27]

The first day's work on the album yielded sides with the Osborne Brothers and, at a second session, by Carl Story. The former was the Osbornes' trio vocal version of "I Hear a Sweet Voice Calling." Bill sang tenor to Bobby, a reprise of their legendary version of it on the Sunday morning gospel concert in 1966 at Carlton Haney's second bluegrass festival in Roanoke, Virginia, which was a show-stopping performance that fans still talked about. Story did "True Life Blues" as a duet, Monroe singing tenor, a piece he had done with Monroe back in the 1940s.

The next session, on May 6, brought in the current edition of the Country Gentlemen, who, with Monroe singing lead on the choruses and tenor to Charlie Waller's lead on the verses, formed a vocal quartet on "Lord, Protect My Soul," which Monroe recorded with Jimmy Martin on lead in 1950. That evening Mac Wiseman came in to do "Travelin' This Lonesome Road," a duet he sang with Monroe on their classic Columbia recording from 1949. The following afternoon, May 7, Jim and Jesse McReynolds recorded "I'm on My Way Back to the Old Home" and "Mighty Dark to Travel." Both had originally been done as duets, and here Monroe sang the tenor part in trio versions. "Mighty Dark to Travel" was a Columbia favorite, and "I'm on My Way Back to the Old Home" was from Monroe's first Decca session some thirty-five years before. The latter was shelved for the time being and would be released a couple of years later in the *Bluegrass '87* album. That evening the Seldom Scene arrived—at least John Duffey and Mike Aldridge from the group did—and with Clarence "Tater" Tate filling in on bass vocals did the quartet "Remember the Cross," another Columbia song that had been largely written by bassist Howard Watts in the 1940s. Again, Bill sang tenor, this time to John Duffey's lead.

The only song recorded for this album that wasn't a familiar favorite, and the only one not done with a guest artist, was Monroe's new "Let the Gates Swing Wide," which was recorded on the afternoon of June 10 with the regular band singing as the Blue Grass Quartet. "I needed some additional songs," Gordy says, "especially a gospel quartet, to finish the *Bluegrass Hall of Fame* project, and just happened to tune in the Grand Ole Opry, and recorded Monroe and the Boys doing 'Let the Gates Swing Wide' live sans the last two verses. I thought that the song was too short and immediately contacted Bill to encourage him to add another verse or two. I think that I also talked to a few of the guys in the band about it."[28] "He wrote the last verse the day we recorded it," notes Blake Williams. "He needed another verse. He sat down and sang a little there, put some words together. Someone wrote it on a piece of paper and we did it."[29] The song alternates a traditional gospel "coming home" refrain with choruses that describe Monroe's childhood in Kentucky—"those memories still remain." The second verse takes an unusual turn, starting with references to "back in the hills of old Kentucky" and suddenly bringing in the line, "Bluegrass music belongs to America." The final verse is more autobiographic: "All through the years / I've sung the gospel."[30]

That evening Ralph Stanley came in and did two tracks, "Can't You Hear Me Callin'" and "Pike County Breakdown" but had problems with the latter. "Ralph took me to the side during the session," Gordy remembered, "and told me he had not played the song very much and was not comfortable with his performance. I promised him it 'would never see the light of day.' I never mixed or edited it. I should have burned the original multitracks. I respect Ralph that much." After completing "Can't You Hear Me Callin'" with Monroe singing tenor to Ralph's lead, Gordy grew curious about how Stanley alone would sound on the song. "I told Ralph we were having a technical problem and asked him to sing all of the song, solo. There was no technical problem. I have that performance on tape . . . he's amazing."[31] True to his word, Gordy shelved "Pike County Breakdown," and it remains unissued.

A week later another former Blue Grass Boy, fiddler Bobby Hicks, joined Bill in the studio. In 1981 Skaggs hired the legendary fiddler who'd recorded on many of Bill's best recordings in the 1950s to play in his band, Kentucky Thunder. Increasingly, Hicks took on the role of the patriarchal bluegrass fiddler that Baker had previously held. At this session he cut two instrumentals with Bill and the Blue Grass Boys, doing twin fiddle with Glen Duncan, "The Golden West" and "Old Brown County Barn." The latter was held and later used on *Bluegrass*

'87. "'Golden West,' I'm pretty sure he had that instrumental for some time," maintains Williams. "I think I recall Butch Robins playing that at a festival. 'The Old Brown County Barn' was a fairly recent tune when we recorded it."[32] The title of the latter referred to the barn at Bill's Brown County Jamboree, a structure that had been on the Bean Blossom park site since the early 1940s. Bill and James had recently razed it by fire in order to make renovations at the property.

Hicks stuck around for the concluding session for the album that evening, when Del McCoury came in. McCoury, who'd worked with Bill in 1963 and 1964, recorded extensively in the 1970s but more recently carried on his performance career at a relatively low level. Now things were heating up for him—a new album, *Sawmill* (Rebel 1636), was about to be released. His first new studio album in four years, it included his teenaged son, Ronnie, who'd recently joined Del's band as mandolinist. Del was not as obvious a choice to fill in on the album as he would be in the 1990s, when he and his band were putting out an album a year and sweeping the awards at the International Bluegrass Music Association (IBMA). The choice did reflect, however, the high esteem in which many in the inner circles of bluegrass held him for his powerful singing and dynamic rhythm-guitar work. Del sang two songs at the session. The one used on the *Hall of Fame* set was "I'm Going Back to Old Kentucky," another chestnut from Monroe's glory years at Columbia, with McCoury singing lead to Monroe's tenor. The other track, a new song called "Bluest Man in Town," was held for *Bluegrass '87*, Bill's next release.

The result of the sessions was a group of songs in which Monroe sang lead on just one—thereby addressing, albeit unintentionally, earlier concerns about his singing voice.[33] At the same time, he sang tenor with many of the most highly regarded singers in bluegrass music in a series of duets, trios, and quartets. Gordy at once got to work mixing and editing the album, and it was on the street barely two months later, on August 19, 1985.

Early in the new year work began on the album that would be entitled *Bluegrass '87*. Three tracks that would be on it had been recorded during the *Hall of Fame* sessions: "The Bluest Man in Town," "Old Brown County Barn," and "Mighty Dark to Travel." The first new sessions for the album, that of March 17, 1986, yielded two new instrumentals, "Dancin' in Brancin'" and "Jekyll Island." Both featured the twin fiddles of Bobby Hicks and Buddy Spicher. The word *Brancin'* was supposed to be *Branson*, a reference to the Missouri country music watering hole. "In an effort to get a jump on the artwork," Gordy says,

"I had given the liner notes orally over the phone to the art department at MCA." That, coupled with several further production steps, altered the song's true title, "Dancing in Branson." "By the time I caught the error, it was too late," Gordy remembers, "and I certainly didn't want to wait for the next release opportunity on the MCA schedule."[34]

A later session that same day resulted in two Monroe vocals, "Stay Away from Me" and "Music Valley Waltz." The latter, co-written with Monroe's new friend John Hartford, was named for the area near Briley Parkway to the north of the Grand Ole Opry where Monroe's Bluegrass Hall of Fame was originally located.

Other new tunes came from the band's experience and touring. "Jekyll Island," remembers Williams, was written in honor of a festival held there that Monroe used to attend. "Texas Lone Star," written one night before Monroe took the stage at a concert in Houston, was in honor of a local band, Lonestar, that had been opening for Monroe. The first version of the tune was unissued, but it would be redone in 1988. "Stay Away from Me" was one Bill had written earlier but had been reluctant to record. "Bill used to sing this once in a while," Williams observed. "He said, 'That's a country song. That's why I never recorded that.' And that was one of those incidents where we all got in the studio and all suggested to him that it would make a real fine bluegrass song. Got him to record it."[35]

The sessions also produced a mystery: "I Love the State of Virginia." The only detail about it is Tom Ewing's recollection that it was a Monroe vocal solo. "Angels Rock Me to Sleep," the first crack at a gospel number for the new album, was one Monroe first cut in 1951. Blue Grass Boys bass player Tater Tate was concentrating on his bass vocal for the quartet, so Gordy stepped in to play string bass. This was standard practice during his tenure as producer; he had first done so on the session of May 7, 1985, when Bill recorded "Remember the Cross" with members of the Seldom Scene. "The Long Bow" was another new fiddle tune, the title deriving from the "long bow" fiddle style that was so popular in Texas and with Monroe's radio heroes of the 1930s, Arthur Smith and Clayton McMichen. The session was the last with Monroe for Wayne Lewis, who'd been with him since 1976.

Bill's new guitarist was Tom Ewing. Born on September 1, 1946, in Columbus, Ohio, Ewing told an interviewer in 1983, "I think my bluegrass roots go back a long way, because my grandfather liked to play the fiddle. My parents were small-town folk. And they both worked. So I spent a lot of time at the homes of the folks who liked country music."[36]

Drawn to folk music in the early 1960s he learned about Bill Monroe from Ralph Rinzler's liner notes to a Greenbrier Boys album. In August 1963 he saw Monroe for the first time at a show in Delaware, Ohio. Inspired by the Monroe-McCoury duets, he bought a Martin D-28 like he'd seen Del playing and began working on bluegrass. Starting college at Ohio State in 1964, he hung out in downtown bars of Columbus, where there was a vibrant bluegrass scene, and he was able to hear bluegrass pioneers like Pee Wee Lambert, Sid Campbell, John Hickman, and Landon Rowe.

After a two-year stint in the Naval Reserve, a trip to Monroe's 1969 Bean Blossom Festival recharged Tom's interest in bluegrass. The following year he met former Blue Grass Boy Sandy Rothman, and for the next few years while he was finishing his journalism degree at Ohio State they performed together with mandolinist Lake Brickey as the B Natural Boys. As Ewing's involvement in Monroe's music deepened, he sought out and transcribed "every Monroe recording that featured a lead voice beside Monroe's."[37]

Following his graduation in 1973, Ewing began playing with the Cincinnati-based band of bluegrass pioneer Earl Taylor and the Stoney Mountain Boys. It was during this time, July 1974, that he first auditioned for Bill Monroe. Monroe had just hired Ralph Lewis but told Ewing that he'd keep him in mind. Two years later, when Lewis left, Bill tried without success to contact Ewing in Columbus. At the time, Ewing lived in Cincinnati, still working with Earl Taylor (he played on Taylor's final Vetco album). That year, Tom returned to Columbus to begin work on a second degree, in education, at Ohio State.

He began teaching elementary school in 1978 but kept active on the Columbus bluegrass scene as a dj on WOSU-AM and in a series of bands, including one with former Blue Grass Boy Tony Ellis. In May 1986, after Wayne Lewis had given Monroe his notice, Ewing went to Nashville. On May 23 he began his career as a Blue Grass Boy, singing "I'm on My Way Back to the Old Home" with Monroe on the Opry. He would be the final lead singer and guitarist in the Blue Grass Boys, remaining with the group until Monroe's death a little more than a decade later.

The final session for *Bluegrass '87* did not take place until several months later, on August 19, 1986, and was devoted to trying to achieve more gospel numbers. The first try was a remake of an old Monroe Brothers tune, "God Holds the Future in His Hands." It was another song Monroe had taken from a James D. Vaughan songbook and was written by Vaughan and his leading lyricist, James Rowe, in 1922.

"Farther On"—not to be confused with the more familiar "Farther Along"—had been cut in 1975 by Monroe himself, but this version, like the earlier one, remained unissued. The song is credited to R. E. Winsett, another influential Tennessee publisher-composer. "The Old Crossroads," the only number issued from the session, is a remake of the Monroe-Flatt duet recorded for Columbia in 1947. It is a Monroe original and not the same as a song with a similar title that the Monroe Brothers recorded in the 1930s.

Even though recording technology was undergoing extensive changes, Monroe continued to follow his earlier ideas about how his band should set up in the recording studio. He wanted everyone to stand in a semicircle. There were no headphones or sound baffles (except occasionally one for the bass that went up only three or four feet), and everyone had eye contact. "No one ever sat down," recalls Vic Gabany. "Once Mark Hembree got a stool over behind his bass, and was just leaning it a little bit to play. Bill saw this and got furious. He went over and ripped Mark unmercifully."[38] Blake Williams adds, "Most of the time we recorded in a sort of semicircle, with the microphone pointed away from the center, such that we wouldn't get so much bleed-over. It was all basically done live. And in the studio, as with most of his playing, he concentrated a lot on what the fiddle players were doing. He loved twin- and triple-fiddle players. And he spent a lot of time giving them instructions on how he thought things should go. He was a little bit nervous about recording. But he took suggestions pretty well in the studio too."[39]

Bluegrass '87 was released the following spring. One of the songs on it reflected an on-going facet of Monroe's music of which many fans were only slightly aware: he was a working Nashville songwriter. Not only did he continue to write new songs but he also lobbied people to record them. Blake tells a story about "Bluest Man in Town" that illustrates the extent to which the "old man" would go to pitch a song:

We were on our way to California one time. We were going through Las Vegas and somebody suggested we drive down the strip. And we saw Ray Charles's name up on the MGM Grande Hotel. And Bill said, "Can we go see him?" We just pulled Bill's bus up in front. And we get off and we go in and we run into some guys with radios in their hands. And one thing led to another and before you know it, we are all walking down this hallway underneath the MGM Grande. Here comes Ray Charles, and he is singing "Blue Moon of Kentucky" before he even gets to Bill. He obviously knows that we are there and we go into his dressing room. Bill sang him this song, and he said, "This will make you a powerful number." And we had a good visit. And then we went and got back on the old bus and took off. I always felt that was so bizarre.[40]

Another song Monroe was pitching to other musicians in the late 1980s was a guitar solo he called "Ozark Rag." He had been playing it on the guitar informally, and once at a Nashville party he grabbed a pink Fender Telecaster and played it replete with amplifier. He finally found a taker in the young guitarist for Porter Wagoner's new "all-girl" band, the Right Combination. Glenda Faye Kniphfer, known professionally as Glenda Faye, was a superb flat-top guitarist and a friend of Wanda Vick, the Alabama instrumentalist who was the band's cornerstone. Wagoner agreed to produce at his own successful Fireside Studio a bluegrass album featuring the guitar of Glenda Faye for the independent Flying Fish label and recruited a number of established names in bluegrass for the project, including Jesse McReynolds, Vassar Clements, and Bobby Thompson. Monroe, whose only previous publicly acknowledged guest appearances had been with Ralph Stanley, Tom T. Hall, and Ricky Skaggs, agreed to lend his mandolin to "Ozark Rag" and "Down Yonder." Released in 1987 as *Flat Pickin' Favorites,* the album remained available for some time and was reissued on CD in 1992.

A most unusual guest appearance came in September 1987 when Monroe, in California on tour, was asked to come to Hollywood and record some music for the soundtrack to a new film, *Planes, Trains, and Automobiles* starring John Candy and Steve Martin. Martin, himself a banjo player (he later guested on an Earl Scruggs album), loved bluegrass and idolized Monroe. Emory Gordy Jr. went along to produce the sessions, as did a full complement of Blue Grass Boys. The sessions were held on September 7 at the Enterprise Recording Studio in Burbank on behalf of Paramount Pictures, which produced the film. None of the tracks, however, were ever to see the light of day. They did not appear anywhere in the film nor on its soundtrack album. One that featured Monroe and Candy singing "Blue Moon of Kentucky" in unison "didn't work out too well" in the words of Blue Grass Boys guitarist Tom Ewing.[41] The only trace of this enterprise is a scene in the latter half of the film when Martin and Candy, driving down the highway in a battered convertible, sing a couple of verses of "Blue Moon of Kentucky."

In January 1988 work began on what was to be Gordy's masterpiece with Monroe, *Southern Flavor.* He had discovered the ideal way to adapt Monroe's music to the new digital technology. One of the main advantages of the digital system

(aside from sharper sound) is its ability to take parts of one performance and seamlessly patch them into another. Gordy recalls:

> What I did with Monroe was to do a test take and have the band come in and listen. We'd discuss what needed to be done and then they'd go back out and play several takes in a row. I'd keep notes on each take as it went down, starring the good stuff and putting x's beside the bad parts. When I figured I had enough good stuff (anywhere from three to ten takes), I'd call them in and we'd go onto the next song. Then I had the engineer make a copy of all the takes, including false starts, and I took them home, reassessed the data, and wrote out each instrument a bar or so before an edit, and bar after an edit. I write music notes on a staff, not tablature. . . . I've been reading and writing music since I was about six or seven. I've still got all those notes and manuscripts somewhere.
>
> I didn't have to do any tempo correcting. Amazingly, when the band got comfortable with the arrangement, they were very consistent from take to take. There were a considerable number of edits on each tune—sometimes thirty to forty per song! After I finished, I gave a copy to Blake Williams, and he couldn't hear the edits. I figured a banjoist could hear any contrivances before other players. I can still hear three or four edits, but only because I labored over them. I don't think anyone else can hear them.[42]

Although Richard D. Smith describes Gordy's technique as focused on dealing with intonation problems in Bill's voice, it was, in fact, used for many aspects of the performances he produced at these sessions.[43]

The band gathered at Sound Stage studio on January 4 and 5 to start the new album. Bill's new fiddler, Mike Feagen, along with veterans Bobby Hicks and Buddy Spicher, created a triple-fiddle trio sound for the album reminiscent of Bill's mid-1950s' recordings. One of the more unusual tunes was "Stone Coal," for which Monroe used a new cross-tuning on his mandolin. "It's something like what I used on 'My Last Days on Earth,' but it's different," he said. The tune itself, he explained to journalist Thomas Goldsmith, was "put together up in the eastern part of Kentucky. Ricky Skaggs and his father were there and his father came up with that name, 'Stone Coal.'"[44] Another cut was a second version of "Texas Lone Star," one with three fiddles and one that, unlike the first version, was released. "Sugar Loaf Mountain, done on January 8, was a tune that originated in New England. "Is it Maine?" Blake Williams asked. "We were playing a show there and he wrote it backstage. It felt a little like 'Clinch Mountain Backstep' almost. And it came down to the end of the session and he said, 'Why don't we put a banjo tune on here?' And I said, 'What about "Sugar Loaf Mountain"? And Bill said, 'How does that go?' So we actually worked that up on the spot a couple of times and recorded it."[45]

One tune that didn't make it out of the session was "Blue Savannah Waltz," written by a fiddler from Savannah (in west Tennessee) named Wayne Jerrolds. At various times Jerrolds would come up to the Opry and play with Monroe, and apparently he once gave Monroe a pair of mules. To return the favor Monroe instructed his producers to "get him on one of my albums" but that never happened.[46] Monroe did, however, decide to record Jerrolds's signature song even though he didn't know it all that well. "Bill didn't really know how it went," recalls guitarist Tom Ewing. "There were some strange time changes and producer Emory Gordy told them to just let Bill go ahead and do it and get it over [with] rather than trying to work it out with him, as they had tried to do."[47]

"What a Wonderful Life," the first of the gospel quartets from the session, was written by Monroe's old friend and campsite picker Raymond Huffmaster, who drove the Osborne Brothers' tour bus. It took two tries to get the song right (the first, unissued version was on January 8, and the take that was used was on January 14). "The Days Gone By" was a trio, another new song, the first verse of which had been written by Tom Ewing. "I reminded Bill of this later," he said, "and he eventually arranged to give me one-fourth credit on the lyrics."[48] "White Rose," done as a Monroe solo, was an early Carl Butler song and different from the older "White Rose" widely recorded in the 1920s. "Life's Highway," another trio, was a song banjoist Blake Williams had often performed with Bobby Smith and the Boys from Shiloh. "Take Courage Un' Tomorrow" was a song Monroe remembered being sung at the funeral of Uncle Pen's son Cecil. "Give Me Wings," Williams thinks, was a new song that Gerald Evans, its composer, had pitched to Bill at a festival somewhere.

Southern Flavor was well-received when it was released later in 1988 and even attracted the attention of the National Recording Arts and Sciences (NARAS), the national all-genre music trade organization that bestows the annual Grammy Award. In 1987 at the thirtieth competition, "Old Brown Country Barn," Monroe's track from *Bluegrass '87,* had been a final nominee in the Best Country Instrumental Performance category but lost out to the western swing group Asleep at the Wheel's "String of Pearls." For the 1988 awards, NARAS responded to the activities of the new International Bluegrass Music Association and created a new category: Best Bluegrass Recording. *Southern Flavor* made the list of five final nominees,

as did albums by Bela Fleck, David Grisman, Peter Rowan and the Nashville Bluegrass Band, and the Seldom Scene. On February 22, 1989, the academy announced that *Southern Flavor* had indeed won the first-ever Bluegrass Grammy. Everyone agreed that it was a good choice in symbolic terms as well as for musical value.

A GALAXY OF LIVE RECORDINGS

On Thursday, March 2, 1989, Monroe's old friend and long-time Blue Grass Boy Tater Tate drove him to the Home Place Studio in Nashville for a guest appearance on Jim and Jesse's new album *Music among Friends.* Backed by Jim and Jesse's band, the group did a quartet version of "Wicked Path of Sin" on which Tate sang bass to Monroe's tenor, Jim McReynolds's lead, and Jesse's baritone. Tate had been fiddler with Lester Flatt's Nashville Grass and continued with that group after Curly Seckler took it over. He rejoined the Blue Grass Boys in 1985, however, replacing Mark Hembree on bass.

Tate would play an important role in the music of Monroe's later years. Fans would later claim, with justification, that he had worked with Monroe for more consecutive years than any other musician. Unlike many of the other younger Blue Grass Boys, he was a genuine old-time mountain fiddler who had worked his way up through many first-generation bluegrass bands in the 1950s. Born on February 4, 1931, at Gate City, Virginia, in the "golden triangle" of Virginia, Tennessee, and Kentucky, Tate heard his first bluegrass when he heard Flatt and Scruggs over WCYB in Bristol and was impressed by the overall sound of the band and especially liked the rapid-fire fiddling of Jim Shumate on show-off pieces like "Train 45." By 1950, still a teenager, he was playing professionally with the Bailey Brothers' Happy Valley Boys and then went on to spend time with Carl Story, the Sauceman Brothers, Hylo Brown, Red Smiley, Jim Eanes, Herschel Sizemore, and Lester Flatt. By 1956 he was playing with Monroe on live shows although he would not record with him for another seventeen years. Overall, Tate appeared on more than sixty albums by a wide variety of classic bluegrass figures.

Tate was not as slick or fancy a fiddler as Kenny Baker, Glen Duncan, Bobby Hicks, or Buddy Spicher. His was a slightly more archaic sound, with rich double stops and a clear, mellow tone. Tate was originally hired to play bass for the Blue Grass Boys and only later became their fiddler. He also developed into a fine bass singer and became a fixture in gospel quartets. In addition, he frequently drove the band's bus. According to a familiar story, a friend once asked Tate why he didn't play fiddle more for the group. The reason, he explained, was so he could get some rest on the bus. Monroe would routinely ask his fiddler to come up front with him to work out new tunes. As much as Tate enjoyed doing so, it became wearisome for a veteran in his sixties with a sore back.

In October 1989 Monroe would celebrate his fiftieth year on the Grand Ole Opry, and both the Opry and MCA felt it would be a good idea to celebrate with a new set of live Opry recordings. The producers at MCA continued to worry about the deterioration of Monroe's voice, his intonation being uncertain and sometimes high notes would be flat. A series of live recordings in which the best performance could be selected seemed a solution.

By early 1989 Emory Gordy Jr. had moved on, and a new producer was found in Steve Buchanan, the marketing director for the Opry working under General Manager Hal Durham. He had come to the job from his earlier work at Top Billing, a leading Nashville firm. As the idea for a live Opry album developed, he found himself working as liaison between MCA and the Opry and soon evolved into the role of producer. According to Blake Williams, the arrangement began when Monroe ran into Buchanan one night at the Opry and said, "Would you help me with my new album?"[49]

In the spring of 1989, MCA started recording the band live on the Saturday night Opry. With the Opry sound system already in place and Monroe in a familiar environment, the project at first seemed a sure thing. Problems, however, soon developed. "They were taping the Opry live," said Blake Williams. "For one reason or another, it was becoming impossible to get something we really wanted. Either something was out of tune, somebody missed something, or there was a technical problem. So we actually went into the Grand Ole Opry House empty one night after a *Nashville Now* show and recorded some of those numbers. I think 'Pike County Breakdown' and 'Working on a Building' were two of the numbers we did that night to finish that album. I'm not sure any of them [the songs] were actually recorded at a live Opry show," laughs Williams.[50]

In those days the Opry also had a summer matinee on Tuesdays and Thursdays, and some tracks were recorded then. Tom Ewing, who kept detailed notes on many appearances, is sure that two of the matinee performances were on June 13 and June 27. He also recalls recording "Precious Memories" in an empty auditorium. The official American Federation of Musicians union sheets for the album give a range of dates in May and June accompanied by a note that directs "see attached list." No list, however, is attached, and thus the exact dates are guesswork.

There were no new songs on *Live at the Opry* nor any radically different arrangements of older ones. With favorites like "Molly and Tenbrooks," "Footprints in the Snow," "Rawhide," "In the Pines," and "Pike County Breakdown" it was almost a greatest hits package—a fact that could have been by design. In 1989, with CDs rapidly replacing LPs, much of Monroe's classic MCA material was out of print, and reissues of his older recordings demonstrated a serious interest in seeing the prime Monroe sides out on the new CD technology.

One anomaly in *Live at the Opry* was the little-publicized addition of a superb 1948 air check from the *Prince Albert Show* as host Red Foley introduces Monroe doing "Mule Skinner Blues." Although mistakenly listed on the CD as "New Mule Skinner Blues," it is a sterling performance, Monroe at the height of his powers, of the old, original "Mule Skinner Blues" with the same basic lyrics as the Jimmie Rodgers song.

Monroe's onstage celebration of fifty years with the show was covered live by the Nashville Network, and *Live at the Opry* was released in the fall of 1989 in time for the Opry's birthday celebration in October. The album itself marked another milestone. It was his first MCA album not issued on LP. It came out only on CD and "HiQ" cassette.

Although these were Monroe's last "live" recordings for MCA, they came at a time when his live performances were being more and more carefully recorded elsewhere. The recordings—including several from influential documentary films—were not released right away but have become available more recently and help provide a fuller picture of Monroe's music during his last years of performing. During the summers of 1989 and 1990 as well, several filmmakers were working on documentaries that would help solidify the canonization of Monroe and make him an icon of American music. One by-product of their work was the production of a substantial number of recordings of Monroe's live appearances.

On May 11, 1989, the band had played a show at a trendy folk music venue, the Mountain Stage, at Charleston, West Virginia. Performances there were routinely recorded for a radio show, and Monroe's was no exception. A CD entitled *Bill Monroe: Live from the Mountain Stage* on the Blue Plate Music label was released on May 11, 1999. This was Monroe's portion of the actual radio show, intact and with little or no editing. Once again, "Mule Skinner" was mistakenly titled "New Mule Skinner Blues." In fact, there's no evidence that Monroe ever sang the latter's new lyrics anywhere except on his frequently reissued 1950 recording. In "Blue Moon of Kentucky" he invites the audience to sing along, which he enjoyed doing in later years. Monroe's traveling companion Diana Christian sings one of her own songs, "My Blue Eyes from Heaven," and the band introduces a new instrumental, "Northern White Clouds." Blake Williams does most of the emcee work, and the band overall was satisfied with the experience. As Tom Ewing says, "The Mountain Stage people provided us with one of the best sound situations I've ever experienced. Everyone could hear everyone else, and their own selves perfectly."[51]

Between May and July 1990, sandwiched in between live appearances typical of his work at festivals and other venues that were being recorded for a documentary film, were six studio recordings for his new gospel album, *Crying Holy Unto the Lord*. The project came about one day when Monroe telephoned MCA to announce "I want to do a gospel album with Steve."[52] He had enjoyed working on the Opry album with Buchanan. Although the younger man didn't have much producing experience, MCA's Tony Brown agreed to sign off on the project and appeared at some of the sessions to watch the group at work.

Ten cuts were planned for the album. On half of these, Bill and the Blue Grass Boys were joined by guest bluegrass artists. At the first session, held in the Reflections Studio on May 15, Mac Wiseman joined Bill for a version of the Monroe Brothers' career duet "What Would You Give in Exchange?" This recording was deemed not usable, and Wiseman would return to sing with Bill at the final session.

Also recorded but judged not acceptable at the first session was a version of the title song, "Cryin' Holy Unto the Lord." It is for some reason credited to "Irene Amburgey," the veteran Kentucky performer of the 1930s who with her sisters worked as the Sunshine Sisters, for a time with the Coon Creek Girls, and for a time over WSB as Mattie, Martie, and Minnie. She had no doubt known the song all her life because her parents traveled the South, appearing at singing conventions. The song is certainly older than that, however. Most country fans associate it with the Carter Family's 1930 recording, which they called "On the Rock Where Moses Stood," but black jubilee quartets were recording it as early as 1924 and Monroe had recorded it at his second Bluebird session in 1941. Monroe would record a strong version of it at the album's final session.

Thus the only issued recording from this session was Cleavant Derricks's "Just a Little Talk with Jesus." Derricks was nearly the only African American to write songs for the Stamps-Baxter tradition, and when he wrote "Just a Little Talk" for a 1937 Stamps-Baxter book it immediately became a favorite of gospel quartets, both black and white. Air-checks reveal the Blue Grass Quartet doing it on the Opry as early as 1948. This bass lead number was a favorite of Birch Monroe, who regularly sang that part with Bill and the Blue Grass Quartet whenever they visited the Brown County Jamboree in Bean Blossom. Tater Tate singing bass is featured on this version.

The following week the second session began with Monroe's own song, "Shine Hallelujah Shine," another performance that would be redone at a later session. For the session's second song, guest singers Ralph Stanley and Ricky Skaggs helped out on the old Stanley Brothers favorite "Harbor of Love." Although Monroe had never performed the song, it was familiar to him, for he'd helped produce the Stanley Brothers original 1954 Mercury recording.

Blake Williams recalls an experience from this session that illustrates Monroe's remarkably open mind about the way non-bluegrass groups such as the Kentucky Headhunters covered his songs. He seemed as delighted with the Headhunters' success (chapter 7) as he had been with that of Elvis Presley with "Blue Moon of Kentucky" decades earlier:

> He came into the studio to record with Ricky Skaggs that day and we would rehearse the song and we made a few cuts and we were fine tuning everything. And Bill kept saying, "I got to be somewhere at six o'clock." We would play some more, and he would say, "What time is it? I've got to be somewhere at six o'clock." And Ricky said, "Bill, where are you going?" And he said, "Well, the Kentucky Headhunters are having an album party and I'm invited." And finally it got down to where he was going to leave, and he had on a pretty nice suit. He asked Ricky, "How do I look?" And Ricky said, "Well, I'm sure you will look a good deal better than anything they'll be wearing down there at the party."[53]

The next session was held on the evening of June 12 and began with guest artists Jim and Jesse McReynolds, who helped on the first song, a quartet arrangement of their "Are You Lost in Sin?" Jimmy Campbell was paired with Tater Tate to give a twin-fiddle effect, and Jesse played mandolin harmonies with Monroe. Jim McReynolds also played guitar but was not miked. The second song was a new number by young Nashville bluegrass musician and songwriter Billy Smith (He had played with Curly Seckler's versions of the Nashville Grass), "He'll Take You In." Another bass lead number, it featured Tater Tate's vocal work.

The fourth session, on June 27, began with a quartet featuring as guests the Osborne Brothers. "Just Over in the Glory Land," a 1906 classic by Emmett S. Dean and James W. Acuff, had been recorded by Mainer's Mountaineers in Charlotte in 1938, when the Monroe Brothers were there. For this quartet version, Bobby Osborne sang lead while his brother, Sonny, did the baritone part, with Monroe and Tate rounding out the harmony. As with the previous session, harmony instrumentals were featured, with Bill and Bobby doing twin mandolins while Blake and Sonny did a banjo duet. The session's second song featured Bill singing "Baptize Me in the Cumberland River," one of his compositions that had been on the Cathedral Caverns set.

"You're Drifting Away," which Monroe had originally recorded with Carter Stanley in 1951, was done at the fifth session of July 17 as a quartet, Ricky Skaggs singing lead. It was also a first of sorts for the Monroe recording history because he was not present at the original recording. According to guitarist Tom Ewing, Skaggs had already come in and recorded his lead, and on a separate occasion Ewing and Tate recorded the baritone and bass parts. At a third studio date Monroe dubbed in his tenor and mandolin parts.

Mac Wiseman returned on July 24 to sing lead on "This World Is Not My Home," a vintage song incorrectly credited to J. R. Baxter Jr. The song had been recorded by an African American singer, Sam Jones (some of whose recordings were marketed under the name Stovepipe Number One) as early as 1924 and was widely waxed throughout the 1920s and 1930s—including a version by the Monroe Brothers. Following this, the band recorded the versions of "Cryin' Holy Unto the Lord" and "Shine Hallalujah Shine" that appear on the album.

This session at the Reflections Studio was to be the last official MCA session in Monroe's forty-year association with the company. Shortly thereafter he was quietly dropped from the roster—a fact he never knew—although MCA head Tony Brown continued to insist that the company would still be interested in new projects. They would, however, be "on spec" and done by independent producers like Vic Gabany.

Cryin' Holy Unto the Lord was not released until April 30, 1991, ten months after its completion. It was Monroe's last official studio album.

FILMS AND VIDEOS

Between 1989 and 1992 no fewer than four major motion picture projects were done on Bill Monroe and his music. It appears that filmmakers were realizing that he was entering his eighth decade and might only be a presence for a few more years. Filmmaker Rachael Liebling was surprised that so many of Monroe's contemporaries were still around but were, like Monroe, beginning to show their age. "I undertook the

project with a sense of urgency," she recalled.[54] A rush began to capture on film and tape as much of Monroe's rich legacy as possible, and for a time, camera crews followed him everywhere. Monroe, traditionally hesitant to appear in television or movies, was surprisingly cooperative. The result was not only the films and videos but also a number of spin-offs, including many field recordings of the band in action, several albums, and a book.

The first of these projects, *High Lonesome: The Story of Bluegrass Music,* was directed by Liebling, a New York resident who had first seen Monroe at a 1987 concert at the Lone Star Roadhouse in New York City. For this, her first full-length film, she assembled a support staff. Andrew Serwer, an associate editor at *Fortune* magazine, played an important role as associate producer. A regular commentator on National Public Radio and PBS, Serwer was a former resident of the Washington, D.C., area, where he first heard bluegrass. Rachel's senior consultant was her father, Jerome Liebling, a well-known film historian at Hampshire College in Massachusetts who won his reputation as a still photographer and documentarian at the University of Minnesota before relocating to Hampshire College to start a film program. Other consultants included Neil Rosenberg, Ralph Rinzler, Yale historian Alan Trachtenberg, folklorist and later director of the National Endowment for the Humanities William Ferris, and filmmaker Ken Burns. Working through Northside Films and Hampshire College, Liebling put together funding from a number of sources, including the National Endowment for the Arts.

High Lonesome was about bluegrass music as a whole but focused substantially on Monroe and the ways his music embodied developments in twentieth-century southern culture and history. Liebling, building on the techniques of Ken Burns, made considerable use of archival images—whether still photographs or films—in constructing her narrative. In a similar way, for the sound track she used excerpts from sixteen of Monroe's earlier recordings, ranging from the Monroe Brothers' "This World Is Not My Home" of 1936 to "Sugar Loaf Mountain" from 1988. Liebling also used archival film footage of Monroe's performances, including the Ganaway "Roanoke" of 1955, a performance of "Uncle Pen" in 1965, several pieces from Carlton Haney's "Story of Blue Grass" concert at the first festival of 1965, and an Opry performance of "With Body and Soul" from 1969.

In June 1989, Liebling and her crew traveled to Monroe's Bean Blossom Festival and filmed four Monroe performances that were included in the final cut of the film. Directly after the festival they went with Monroe to his old home place at Rosine. From this visit came a solo version of the old Kentucky fiddle tune "Going Across the Sea," which Monroe learned from Uncle Pen and never recorded before. Later they accompanied him and the Blue Grass Boys to a show at the Bell Cove Club in Hendersonville, Tennessee, to celebrate Monroe's seventy-eighth birthday. "I'm Going Back to Old Kentucky," "Uncle Pen," and "Mule Skinner Blues" in the film all date from that show.

Liebling interviewed and filmed a number of other bluegrass performers during the summer of 1989 as well, including Ralph Stanley, Jim and Jesse McReynolds, Jimmy Martin, the Osborne Brothers, the Seldom Scene, Alison Krauss, the Nashville Bluegrass Band, and Mac Wiseman, who also served as the narrator for the film. In the fall of 1990, just as work was finishing on the film, Liebling interviewed Monroe again and recorded him as he recited the words to "I'm on My Way to the Old Home," "Uncle Pen," and "Old Old House." "I had to rendezvous with the band upstate New York somewhere," said Liebling, "in a parking lot while they were heading for a gig, and record on the bus. I had the lyrics written out on paper, but I got some wrong for 'Old Old House' so Bill started singing in order to remember. . . . I do recall it was cold outside, waiting in that parking lot."[55]

Monroe's spoken lyrics frame the film, opening it and closing it. The finished film had its premier a number of times, first in November 1991 at the Anthology Film Archives in New York City and then in September 1992 at the annual convention of the International Bluegrass Music Association in Owensboro, Kentucky. Shown at a number of festivals, it won six awards, including a Gold Plaque Award at the Chicago International Film Festival, Best Feature Documentary at the Atlanta Film Festival, a Silver Award for Independent Feature at the Houston International Film Festival, a Red Ribbon at the American Film Festival, an Indie Award from the National Association of Independent Record Distributors and Manufacturers, and a CINE Golden Eagle Award. It went into limited national release in 1994 through Tara Releasing, appearing at a number of art theaters that year, and was released as a home video by Shanachie in August 1994. The wide circulation of the film, and Liebling's presentation of it at a number of film festivals, helped spread bluegrass to thousands who had only fleeting knowledge of who Monroe was.

A few of Monroe's performances from the movie were selected for release on the soundtrack album issued on the CMH label in 1994. Only two of the new tracks were included, the solo "Going Across the Sea" and "I'm on My Way to the Old

Home" from Bean Blossom. The band was Bill's regular Blue Grass Boys lineup for that summer: Blake Williams, Tom Ewing, Billy Rose, and Tater Tate. Other cuts by Monroe on the album included the live 1969 "With Body and Soul" and two of the sixteen pieces taken from his earlier recordings used on the soundtrack. The rest of the CD featured other artists from the movie in a mixture of recordings from earlier sources and from recordings made for the movie.

In the summer of 1989, a second motion picture document was created when Reinhard Pietsch videotaped Monroe's July 30 concert at Streekermoor in northern Germany. Although Liebling and Steve Gebhardt (discussed subsequently) documented portions of Bill's live performances around this time, this is the only complete and unedited Monroe concert published in this format to date. Even though the lighting is somewhat poor, the show offers glimpses into the theatrics of Monroe's late-career performances as he reshaped his most popular recordings to fit the stage context.

One example was rapping with his knuckles on the top of the mandolin at the end of his break in "Blue Grass Breakdown," something he'd done since the mid-1960s. "Blue Moon of Kentucky" is another example. Monroe had performed the song for almost every show in the final four decades of his career. By July 1989 he would mention that the piece was Elvis Presley's first recording and urge the audience to clap and sing along. He'd also devised a new ending to one of his most frequently performed numbers, "Uncle Pen." At the song's end he would stop playing the mandolin and, as the fiddle played, begin to dance.

Monroe intensified and illustrated the meaning of several other pieces in various ways. "Raw Hide" had from the beginning been a tour de force, a virtuoso instrumental that he often played. Eventually, he shaped the arrangement to focus on that fact. Here we see him calling out "Are you ready?" as he stops and then speeds up several times at the end of the piece, dramatizing the challenge its speed presented to the Blue Grass Boys. On "Southern Flavor" he took his final break with the microphone lowered so he had to bend down very low in order to play in front of it. Although there was no accompanying dialog, band members would on occasion ask what he was doing. "I'm getting down," Monroe would reply, alluding to the era's slang for soulful intensity. Acting out the meaning of the lyrics to "There's an Old, Old House," Monroe performed this "sad song" (as he said afterward) by singing in weeping tones and lowering his hat and bowing his head at the tune's end.

This lengthy, intense, and dramatic concert performance

contrasts with the brief and rather formulaic interview with Jim Skurdall that was typical of Monroe's interviews in later years. Skurdall, an American who lived in Germany and worked as a teacher, translator, and musician, recorded the interview the day after the concert for broadcast on the West German radio network. Pietsch had taken Monroe shopping just before the interview. "Bill had bought gifts in Bremen for his daughter," Skurdall said, "and he was in good spirits. We went into a room of the inn and ordered two glasses of orange juice. Bill, who was wearing his hat, apologized for being without a tie." The radio director told Skurdall "to keep it basic, to ask questions that would help German listeners who had no prior knowledge of bluegrass music understand the music a little better."[56] Both the interview and the concert were included on a DVD in the Bear Family set *Bill Monroe in Germany: Far Across the Blue Water* (2004).

A third filmmaker was University of Cincinnati film professor Steve Gebhardt, who began work on his project before Liebling began hers. Unlike Liebling's *High Lonesome,* which followed bluegrass from Monroe to a broader music culture, Gebhardt's *Bill Monroe, Father of Bluegrass Music* focused more on its subject. Between June 1990 and September 1991 Gebhardt's crew followed and filmed Monroe extensively. During that time they recorded and videotaped more than 130 songs, by far the largest body of Monroe's daily working repertoire yet captured in this way. The venues included scenes aboard the tour bus, the Blue Grass Special; at the Frontier Ranch Park in Reynoldsburg, Ohio; at Monroe's home at Goodlettsville, Tennessee (including a fox hunt); at the Grand Ole Opry; and at the Long Hollow Jamboree in Goodlettsville. Most of the recordings were done at Monroe's Bean Blossom park. Gebhardt was able to use only a fraction of his material, but in 2002 a large number of the recordings were released on the first of two double-CD sets planned by the independent label Copper Creek, distributed on the Rural Rhythm label. This first set, *Bill Monroe and the Blue Grass Boys Live, Volume 1,* appeared in May 2002. In 2004 plans for the second set were shelved following difficulties in obtaining permissions from some of the artists involved.

Among Gebhardt's work is a remarkable intensive sequence in which he documented four successive live shows at Bean Blossom throughout June 15 and 16, 1990. They featured occasional guests such as Emmylou Harris on a couple of numbers and are remarkable in that they provide some idea of what a typical Monroe show repertoire was like in those days. Monroe was drawing on a repertoire of almost sixty years and on

songs beloved by three generations of fans. From his recorded career alone, in 1990 he could draw on almost five hundred pieces, but many had fallen completely out of his current set lists. Like most major musical performers who have long careers (Frank Sinatra, Elvis Presley, Muddy Waters, Odetta, Bob Dylan), Monroe evolved a core repertoire, a group of songs to which he returned again and again. The Gebhardt recordings provide information about how that worked in the early 1990s.

A typical Bean Blossom set would usually include from a dozen to fifteen tunes. Often five or six would be instrumentals, ranging from the old favorites like "Dusty Miller" and "Blue Grass Breakdown" to newer pieces like "Southern Flavor" and the unrecorded "Tombstone Junction." Lead singer Tom Ewing was usually given a solo, sometimes doing traditional songs like the murder ballad "Willie Moore" from the repertoire of Kentucky performers Dick Burnett and Leonard Rutherford. Their 1926 recording on Harry Smith's Folkways *Anthology of American Folk Music* had introduced it to folk revivalists. Tom had learned it from one such group, Tom Paley's Old Reliable String Band, who'd recorded it for Folkways. There were regular choices from the 1940–41 period of Monroe's first solo recordings ("Dog House Blues" and "Mule Skinner Blues") and favorites from mid-1940s Columbia classics ("Kentucky Waltz," My Rose of Old Kentucky," "Blue Moon of Kentucky," "Rocky Road Blues," and "It's Mighty Dark to Travel"). The early Decca period is represented by "I'm on My Way to the Old Home," "Raw Hide," and "Uncle Pen." The songs and tunes from this era were among Monroe's most requested and copied numbers. The new material of the 1960s and 1970s is not as well represented in the set lists. "Love, Please Come Home," a 1972 song with James Monroe and long a regular in his performances, was a bluegrass classic when Bill recorded it because of Don Reno and Red Smiley's 1961 hit version. Many newer instrumentals from more recent years ("Sugar Loaf Mountain," "Tombstone Junction," and "Northern White Clouds") are included as well. In some instances the older songs were rearranged. "It's Mighty Dark to Travel" and "I'm on My Way [Back] to the Old Home" were originally recorded with duet choruses but were now being done with trio choruses.

Although only twenty-seven of the Gebhardt recordings were released on Copper Creek/Rural Rhythm set, the entire collection is archived at the Country Music Foundation in Nashville, where it will be available to researchers. In the meantime, the list presented in the discography for this chapter will provide documentation of what "working" or "core" repertoire Monroe used at this point in his career.

Gebhardt's film, which premiered on the Nashville Network in 1993 and was released at the same time on video by Original Cinema, did not receive the same exposure in film festivals that Liebling's work did. It also differed in focus. Liebling had stressed Monroe's connections with the past and his efforts to maintain the integrity of the rural culture from which he'd come by developing a musical form true to it, but Gebhardt used interviews and performances by younger, high-profile country stars like Marty Stuart, Ricky Skaggs, and Emmylou Harris. Rock stars such as Paul McCartney and Jerry Garcia testified to Monroe's broad influence on popular music. Gebhardt's preface to *Bill Monroe: Father of Bluegrass, a Bilingual Handbook*, an annotated transcription of the film by Hisae and Taisuke Nishigauchi, explains how his thinking about making the film was shaped by extensive interaction with Harry Smith, to whom the film is dedicated.[57]

The fourth video project on Monroe was in some ways less ambitious but in others the most rewarding. This was a two-video-tape set done at one marathon session at a Nashville studio, Imagemaker, on March 3, 1992. The project was developed by Ralph Rinzler and John Hartford (who had become especially close to Monroe when both found themselves fighting cancer). The idea was to produce a quality video tape that could be used as a teaching tool for younger musicians wanting to learn Monroe's style. Hartford and Rinzler sold the idea to Homespun Tapes, an old and respected publisher of instructional videos and tapes of traditional music. Founded by singer-songwriter Happy Traum and his wife Jane in 1967, by the early 1990s the company had a catalog of some four hundred tapes, ranging from jazz to old-time fiddling. The catalog was especially rich in bluegrass and included tapes by a number of former Blue Grass Boys such as Vassar Clements and Bill Keith as well as the respected veterans Sonny Osborne, Norman Blake, Mark O'Connor, Doc Watson, Pete Wernick, Jesse McReynolds, and Mike Seeger.

Some thirty tracks were recorded that day, and all of them released on the first volume of a two-part home video. The entire band was present in the studio—Dana Cupp on banjo, Tom Ewing on guitar, Tater Tate going back on bass, and young Jimmy Campbell replacing him on fiddle. Many of the songs are familiar, but several, like the instrumentals "Frog on a Lilly Pad" and "Galley Nipper," were new to the recording studio. Other performances gained in nuance, like the vocal associated with "Poor White Folks," one of Uncle Pen's tunes that Bill recorded as an instrumental in 1971.

The original plan had called for Monroe to play each tune at normal speed and then play it more slowly, explaining and showing exactly what he was doing. Monroe, however, found that virtually impossible to do, so the producers sought out Sam Bush. For six months the younger player carefully analyzed everything Monroe did and then made a separate "explanatory instructional tape" to accompany the originals.

REISSUES

At about the same time that video and filmmakers were embarking on a flurry of activity designed to create documentary retrospectives of Bill Monroe's music, various record companies suddenly became aware of their obligations to explore the Big Mon's rich audio heritage. The lightning change from vinyl to CD—even though many bluegrass fans, among the most traditional in the business, still preferred vinyl—gave Monroe enthusiasts a certain leverage with various companies anxious to start repackaging back catalogs in the newer format. In Monroe's case that meant a dramatic sea change. Within five years a great percentage of his classic recordings were back in print.

MCA/Decca had not assembled any sort of retrospective package since *The Best of Bill Monroe* in June 1975. All of their releases since then—some twelve sets—were of newly recorded material. But if MCA was hesitant about recycling classic material, independent labels were not. The first new, well-annotated reissue of Decca/MCA material came from the independent Rebel of Canada. In 1985 their *Classic Bluegrass Instrumentals* brought back into the marketplace a basic collection of classic instrumentals. Two years later, County Records compiled *In the Pines*, described as containing "intense and expressive recordings from the early 1950s."

Some reissues from the late 1970s and 1980s like these were subsequently republished on CD, but as LPs were quickly being phased out of the market the new reissues took advantage of the new format's potential for increased contents. The most dramatic entry in the historic reissue sweepstakes came not from an American company but from Germany's Bear Family. In the early 1980s, Bear Family initiated a series of elegant boxed-set reissues that typically included a complete chronological range of an artist's work along with lavishly illustrated booklets or books containing song notes and discographies. Most boxes focused on mainstream country acts like Lefty Frizzell, Johnny Cash, and Hank Snow.

When Bear Family owner Richard Weize was approached about doing his first bluegrass box—devoted to Monroe—he was skeptical, fearing there was not a large enough audience to make a bluegrass set break even. In October 1989, however, Bear Family, leasing the masters through MCA and remastering from original tapes, released *Bill Monroe—Bluegrass, 1950–58*, a set of four CDs with an extensive booklet that included all Monroe's Decca recordings for the first eight years. It was the largest and most comprehensive set yet devoted to a bluegrass figure, and in spite of its hefty price tag the initial pressing of a thousand boxes quickly sold out. It was reprinted and soon became one of the top-sellers in the Bear Family catalog. It was followed in 1991 by a second chronological Monroe set, *Bluegrass 1959–69*; in 1995 by a third, *Bluegrass 1970–79*; in 2002 by a fourth, *Blue Moon of Kentucky, 1936–49*; and finally in 2006 by *Bluegrass 1981–94*. For the first time, all of Monroe's Bluebird, Columbia, and Decca/MCA sides—the famous as well as the obscure—were available to people who wanted to study the complete works without editorial interference.

When BMG released *Mule Skinner Blues* in the RCA Heritage Series in 1991 it was the first of Monroe's complete RCA Victor Bluebird sessions of 1940–41, including one piece, "The Coupon Song," that had previously only appeared on 78s. Researched, compiled, and produced by Billy Altman, it included a detailed introduction and song notes to Monroe's first sixteen commercial recordings.

Monroe's Columbia recordings from the second half of the 1940s, long considered his most influential, had never been completely available, even on LP, although many appeared on Harmony and Columbia reissues in the 1960s. In 1978 Rounder Records addressed that lack with *Bill Monroe with Lester Flatt and Earl Scruggs: The Original Bluegrass Band*. With extensive notes, the album presented twelve cuts from Monroe's 1946–47 sessions. In 1980 County Records released a two-volume set, *Bill Monroe and His Blue Grass Boys: The Classic Bluegrass Recordings*. Douglas B. Green's detailed notes included important interview materials from Monroe, and the twenty-four cuts included material from Monroe's 1945 and 1949 sessions. There was no overlap with the Rounder set. Two songs in volume 2 had not been released in the 1940s: "Why Did You Wander?" and "Come Back to Me in My Dreams." In 1984 Columbia stepped into the picture with a Monroe set in the well-publicized Columbia Historic Edition series. Well annotated and edited by discographer Bob Pinson, the Historic Edition set only had ten songs but included three previously unissued takes: "Nobody Loves Me," "Shining Path," and an alternate take of "Blue Yodel No. 4." These were still in print when Sony decided to exploit Monroe's Columbia catalog in the CD format.

Thus Monroe's domestic boxed-set reissues got under way with an odd and controversial Columbia set entitled *The Essential Bill Monroe,* a two-CD, box released in October 1992. It was edited and produced by Columbia's dean of vernacular reissues, Lawrence Cohn, who two years earlier shocked the record world with his excellent set of bluesman Robert Johnson's complete recordings, a boxed set that included every known alternate take and became a surprise best-seller. Its success helped Cohn launch the highly acclaimed Blues and Roots Series of CBS archival material from the 1920s and 1930s. His plan was to repeat the Johnson set using the legendary masters Monroe cut for Columbia between 1945 and 1949. They would be released on the Legacy label.

When his search for masters was finished, Cohn had some fifty-six (we now know of ninety-nine) performances, including alternate takes, false starts, and several performances that Columbia never officially released. By then, however, the Legacy reissue market was going soft, and CBS executives felt there was not enough of a market to support a three-CD set. Cohn was convinced to cut back the project to a forty-track, two-CD set. That permitted one take of all forty Monroe Columbias but no multiple takes. Hesitant to throw away the only chance he might have to let the alternate takes see the light of day, Cohn dropped a number of the "original" takes and replaced them with alternates.

Such a philosophy might make good sense with jazz and blues, in which alternate takes often mean different solos, but bluegrass fans didn't see it that way. Most had grown up memorizing the original Columbias note for note, and they howled in protest when they heard different, at times even inferior, versions of beloved classics. Listening to one such inferior alternate, one contemporary bluegrass musician quipped, "It's hard to imagine a group of musicians who were so good play[ing] so badly."[58]

It was widely felt that *The Essential Bill Monroe* was a prime example of a collector's discographical mentality overriding the cause of good music. Adding to the confusion was the fact that the notes to the set incorrectly identified one song, "Heavy Traffic Ahead," as an alternate take when it was not and failed to identify three others—"How Will I Explain about You," "Wicked Path of Sin," and "Little Cabin Home"—as alternate takes. After three years of fussing, CBS/Legacy finally let Cohn issue the remaining "original" takes as a supplementary single CD, *Sixteen Gems,* in 1996. These sets, along with the Bear Family boxes, finally made most of Monroe's greatest music available for the first time in his life although several key

Columbia tracks remained unissued because of their mistaken labeling on *The Essential Bill Monroe.*

For those who wanted a less inclusive sample of Monroe's music, the Country Music Hall of Fame began a long-term project that eventually resulted in a four-CD set, *The Music of Bill Monroe,* which was released on July 19, 1994. Drawing on rare illustrations from the Country Music Foundation's archives and working with Monroe himself, producer John Rumble put together a unique retrospective ninety-eight-song collection. Because the project was issued through MCA, cross-licensing expenses prevented the set from being a true retrospective; only five Columbias are included, as are two Monroe Brothers and two of the Atlanta Bluebirds. The rest are primarily from the Decca catalog with the exception of a number of live recordings. One, a Grand Ole Opry air-shot of "Mule Skinner Blues," is from 1939, Monroe's first year on the Opry; another is an Opry shot of "Blue Moon of Kentucky" from 1955. Also from 1955 is a live recording of "Girl in the Blue Velvet Band" from one of Mike Seeger's recordings at New River Ranch, and from 1958, an Opry track of "Molly and Tenbrooks" and another New River Ranch performance of "John Henry." From Monroe's 1994 sessions for a never-released instrumental album comes a version of "Boston Boy." Rumble's comprehensive notes added considerably to the value of the wide-ranging set.

The Music of Bill Monroe was heavily promoted and has remained in print as of this writing. Monroe went into the studio with Marty Stuart in mid-1994 and cut a promotional album for radio use only. In addition to reproducing nine tracks from the boxed set, *The Radio Album* featured six unique Monroe instrumental recordings. On four Stuart provided guitar accompaniment; the other two, "Never Leave the 'A' String" and "Sally Goodin," were mandolin solos.

GUEST SPOTS

During these years Monroe continued his round of guest appearances on others' albums—indeed, he intensified them. In 1992 he appeared on two cuts from Ralph Stanley's critically acclaimed *Saturday Night and Sunday Morning* for Dick Freeland's independent Rebel label. Monroe sang tenor to Stanley's lead on "Letter from My Darling" and tenor in the quartet that sang the Albert Brumley favorite "I'll Meet You in Church Sunday Morning." According to Freeland, an attempt was made to do a third selection, "Can't You Hear Me Callin'?" That didn't work out, however, and the tape was junked. In March 1992 Monroe guested on one cut from Larry Cordle

and Glen Duncan's CD *Lonesome Standard Time.* Cordle wrote "Kentucky King" as a tribute to Monroe; the song features the mandolin as well as a tag verse of Monroe's theme "Watermelon Hangin' on the Vine." The band's regular mandolin player, Butch Baldassari, has said, "I played on 'Kentucky King'—Bill played on 'The Watermelon.'"[59]

That fall, Bill sat in on a session for Mark O'Connor's album *Heroes,* playing his composition "Gold Rush" with a hot band that included Byron Berline, Dan Crary, and John Hickman. Another session with a taste of Bill's mandolin sound came in January 1994, when he made an unscheduled guest shot on Pam Tillis's *Sweetheart's Dance.* According to the well-circulated press release that accompanied the album, Monroe was finishing a session at Imagine Studio and Tillis was set to record next. When the two met, Tillis invited Monroe to play on her cut "Til All the Lonely's Gone," which he did as an overdub. A member of the Blue Grass Boys who heard the cut, however, thinks that most of the audible mandolin on the track is by Sam Bush, who was at the session as well.

In June, Bill and the Blue Grass Boys returned to the studio at the request of Emory Gordy Jr., who was producing an album by Shawn Camp for Warner Brothers. They furnished background vocals, doing answer lines to Shawn's lead in quartet fashion for one song, "Worn Through Stone." Unfortunately, Camp, who came from a bluegrass background and had worked as a fiddler with the Osborne Brothers, was dropped by Warner Brothers, and the album was never released.

A more substantial guest appearance came on Kathy Chiavola's CD *The Harvest,* a collection that featured the popular Nashville singer with stars such as Chet Atkins, Emmylou Harris, Vince Gill, Tony Rice, Bela Fleck, and Randy Howard. Growing up singing rock, blues, and folk music in Kansas City, Chiavola studied music formally at Oberlin College's Conservatory of Music and trained for a time with Metropolitan Opera star Eileen Farrell. She sang opera professionally for a time before coming to Nashville, discovering bluegrass, and working with the likes of Doug Dillard, Vassar Clements, and Jerry Douglas. Monroe was impressed enough with her talents to offer her a job in the band, but she declined. One July afternoon in 1994 at his farmhouse, the two of them recorded a basic track to "Stay Away from Me," which Monroe had earlier done on his *Bluegrass '87* album. A few months later a full band was brought in to overdub the track, which became one of the more successful on the album released on Chiavola's My Label.

An even more substantial involvement came when former Blue Grass banjoist Butch Robins decided to cut his own album on the Hay Holler label. Session notes and interviews with Robins indicate that Monroe was on five instrumental numbers recorded on October 28 and 30, 1994, at two different studios. One venue was Vic Gabany's studio at John Overton High School, where Robins recalls Monroe enjoying being with the students. By now he tired easily and was good for only three or four hours at a time. For each tune, mandolin player Mike Compton—long a close student of Monroe's style—sat in front of Monroe and played along with him to help him remember. Quite a bit of separate tracking was done digitally so Robins could cut and paste from various takes. All of the tunes except "The Golden West" were previously unrecorded. During the sessions, Robins called Monroe historian Doug Hutchens, who asked, "Did you get 'Tanyards'?"[60] This was a favorite of Robins's father, and Monroe liked to play it backstage at Bean Blossom. All Monroe played on that tune, Robins admitted, was some rhythm. Mike Compton played most of the finished cut. The CD was released as *Butch Robins: Grounded, Centered, Focused.*

In November, as he was completing work on the Robins CD, Monroe took time out for two other guest appearances. On November 8 he worked on a version of "Sally Goodin" for Byron Berline's Sugar Hill set *A Fiddle and a Song.* The cut turned out to be a double father-and-son reunion because it featured Monroe and his son James as well as Earl and Randy Scruggs. Later that month Monroe recorded two tracks for *Gary Brewer Guitar,* a Copper Creek set. One was another version of "Ozark Rag," which he'd first recorded in 1987 with Glenda Fay, and the other, "The Old Kentucky Blues," featured Monroe and Dobro pioneer Josh Graves together in the studio for the first time. These seem to have been the only tunes Monroe wrote specifically for the guitar.

ON-SPEC SESSIONS

After Monroe was released from his MCA contract in the early 1990s Vic Gabany began to produce a series of sessions at his own expense with the understanding that MCA might be interested in leasing them. Gabany had begun his career in 1971, working with Joe Mills at the fabled Bradley's Barn and then as a sound man for the Grand Ole Opry. The first Monroe project on which he worked was the *Country Music Hall of Fame* set and then on the *Uncle Pen* album. "By '83 I was sort of Bill's regular engineer" he recalled.[61] "I was dedicated to his music, and did a lot of freelance business with him." His first actual "on spec" project was a collection of fresh Monroe instrumen-

tals, the first installment of which had taken place at Imagine Studios on November 14, 1993. Four pieces were cut, most in four takes: "Friday Night at the Opry" (which Bill improvised one night backstage and the band played several times, including at the Opry, just before the session); "Tombstone Junction" (written on September 22, 1974, at Tombstone Junction, a western-themed amusement park in Parker's Lake, Kentucky, where Bill was doing a show); "Northern White Clouds" (written on the bus en route north to Ohio); and "Slow and Easy Blues." Bill had wanted "Northern White Clouds" to have twin fiddles—preferably Kenny Baker and Bobby Hicks—but that never worked out. Nor was he satisfied with some of the set's mixes for the band. Most of the group—Tom Ewing, Dana Cupp, and Tater Tate (on bass)—were regulars, but he was breaking in a new fiddler, Robert Bowlin, from Pocahontas, Arkansas. "Northern White Clouds" had been recorded at the Mountain Stage broadcast in 1989. It and "Tombstone Junction" were recorded by Steve Gebhardt in 1990 for his documentary and subsequently released on the first volume of the Copper Creek/Rural Rhythm set.

A second session for the instrumental CD took place a few weeks later, on January 9, 1994. The same band was in place, but Jimmy Campbell was brought in to add a second fiddle to a redone version of "Tombstone Junction." A second version of "Slow and Easy Blues" was done as well as five new instrumentals: "Jack Across the Way," "Frog on the Lily Pad," "Smoky Mountain Schottische," "Roxanna Waltz," and "Boston Boy," which Birch Monroe and Uncle Pen liked to play. A final session in May yielded five more masters, including "Land of Lincoln," which Monroe had recorded in 1969 but the master of which was lost. This last instrumental set was one of Monroe's finer late efforts, but Tony Brown passed on it. Only "Boston Boy," which was included on John Rumble's four-CD anthology *The Music of Bill Monroe,* has been released.

Another project Gabany pitched to Tony Brown was a new live Bean Blossom album to help celebrate the festival's thirtieth year. Brown considered the idea but felt it was too soon to do another live album so close to the release of the *Live at the Grand Ole Opry* CD. Gabany held off for a few months. "Then I sent Tony a letter and said that because of Bill's continuing interest in the project, and due to his health, that I would go ahead and record the project on my own, and give MCA first refusal. I took Kurt Storey and one other engineer and a multitrack digital system, and recorded some twenty hours worth of material off the stage in June 1994."[62] He also returned in June 1995 for even more material. Although the tapes contain some historic moments such as a reunion on stage of Monroe and Kenny Baker ("Bill, I've been waiting on this since 1984"), MCA still showed no interest. The tapes remain, as of 2006, in raw unmixed form in Gabany's personal collection.

BILL'S LAST SESSIONS

Fiddler Jimmy Campbell had played for Monroe a few years earlier and always wished to have him on one of his own sessions. Monroe would routinely tell Campbell that he was under contract to MCA and his bosses would never approve, but Campbell attended the Butch Robins session in a little studio in the basement of a duplex called Top of the Hill Studio. Between takes, he again approached Monroe about being on his album and found the patriarch to be quite cordial. Sure, he'd be glad to. They did the session a few weeks later, recording twelve good instrumentals that included the first studio recordings of Monroe originals "Lonesome Old Farmer," "Woodstock Hornpipe," "Fiddlers Blues," and "Chilly Winds of Shannon." The album was released under the title *Pieces of Time* on a Japanese label, Red Clay, in 1996.

There would be time for one last session. Monroe's old friend Hazel Smith had two sons, Billy and Terry, who had turned into fine songwriters and top-notch traditional bluegrass musicians. In the early months of 1996 they wanted to do a tribute album to the man who had inspired them so much. They got a deal with K-Tel, a direct-mail company that was starting to branch out from its repackaging format, and on February 21 they invited Monroe to join them for a session at the Tracking Station Recording Studio at 50 Music Square West on Music Row. Brought in to help out were Robert Bowlin on fiddle and ace banjo picker Charlie Cushman. Monroe played on a version of "Mule Skinner Blues" and sang a little harmony on the last chorus of "Walk Softly on This Heart of Mine." He then did a solo on "Blue Moon of Kentucky" and that was it. His recording career was over, sixty years and four days after the Monroe Brothers sang "My Long Journey Home" for Eli Oberstein in Charlotte. Fittingly, it ended with a final version of the haunting song that had become his best-known work—his signature song for three generations. On September 9, forty-one days after the Smith CD was released, Bill Monroe was gone.

Notes

1. Ray Edlund, "Bill Monroe—the Master Speaks" in *The Bill Monroe Reader,* edited by Tom Ewing (Urbana: University of Illinois Press, 2000), 143.

2. Richard D. Smith, "Bill Monroe—His Best Days on Earth," in *The Bill Monroe Reader,* edited by Tom Ewing (Urbana: University of Illinois Press, 2000), 175. Julia LaBella told Sandy Rothman that the tune was named for the town of Daingerfield in northeastern Texas. Bill had visited there and met Julia's grandmother, who lived nearby. Tom Ewing to Neil V. Rosenberg, email, Dec. 10, 2003.

3. Monroe quoted in David C. Morton with Charles K. Wolfe, *DeFord Bailey: A Black Star in Early Country Music* (Knoxville: University of Tennessee Press, 1991), 67.

4. Morton with Wolfe, *DeFord Bailey,* 6.

5. Ewing, ed., *The Bill Monroe Reader,* 106.

6. Alanna Nash, *Behind Closed Doors; Talking with the Legends of Country Music* (New York: Knopf, 1988), 338.

7. Edlund, "Bill Monroe—the Master Speaks," 145.

8. Walter Haynes, interview with Charles K. Wolfe, Pigeon Forge, Tenn., Nov. 11, 1993.

9. Vic Gabany, interview with Neil V. Rosenberg, Nashville, Tenn., March 10, 2001.

10. Blake Williams, interview with Charles K. Wolfe, Sparta, Tenn., March 12, 2001.

11. Interview with Blake Williams.

12. Interview with Vic Gabany.

13. Interview with Blake Williams.

14. Interview with Vic Gabany.

15. Interview with Blake Williams.

16. Interview with Vic Gabany.

17. Jim Fogelsong, interview with Charles Wolfe, July 13, 1999.

18. Interview with Jim Fogelsong.

19. Interview with Blake Williams.

20. Nash, *Behind Closed Doors,* 341.

21. Ibid.

22. Emory Gordy Jr. to Neil V. Rosenberg, email, Sept. 10, 2001.

23. Ibid.

24. Richard D. Smith, *Can't You Hear Me Callin'? The Life of Bill Monroe* (New York: Little, Brown, 2000), 255.

25. Gabany was "hired as a technical consultant (Vic knew a lot of old tricks of the trade that some of the newer engineers didn't), and as a familiar face to Monroe. I wanted to make Bill as comfortable as possible, and Vic fulfilled that requirement with grace to spare." Emory Gordy Jr. to Neil V. Rosenberg, email, Sept. 23, 2003.

26. Emory Gordy Jr. to Neil V. Rosenberg, Sept. 10, 2001.

27. Ibid.; see also Emory Gordy Jr., "Recording a Bluegrass Album: Part 3," *International Bluegrass* 2 (July–Aug. 1987): 5.

28. Emory Gordy Jr. to Neil V. Rosenberg, Sept. 23, 2003.

29. Interview with Blake Williams.

30. "I (and, I think Glen Duncan, and Blake) was disappointed with the new lyrics, but felt that if Bill wanted to talk about bluegrass belonging to America, then the lyrics should stand. It was sort of like Bill turning over the estate of his creation of a whole genre of American music to its rightful heirs, and in retrospect, I appreciate those words. They were very appropriate, and I was very grateful that he was still writing songs." Emory Gordy Jr. to Neil V. Rosenberg, Sept. 23, 2003.

31. Emory Gordy Jr. to Neil V. Rosenberg, email, Aug. 9, 2001.

32. Interview with Blake Williams.

33. Gordy writes, "I didn't take Bill's 'perceived voice problem' into consideration of *Bill Monroe and the Stars of the Bluegrass Hall of*

Fame. The concept of that album made the consideration moot, but it never entered my mind as an obstacle." Emory Gordy Jr. to Neil V. Rosenberg, Sept. 23, 2003.

34. Ibid.

35. Interview with Blake Williams.

36. Don Jaccaud, "Four on a Ramble," *Bluegrass Unlimited* (Nov. 1987): 34.

37. Michelle H. Putnam, "Tom Ewing: Destination—Blue Grass Boy," *Bluegrass Unlimited* (Nov. 1987): 34.

38. Vic Gabany, interview with Charles K. Wolfe, Hillsboro, Tenn., March 9, 2001.

39. Interview with Blake Williams.

40. Ibid.

41. Tom Ewing to Neil V. Rosenberg, email, Feb. 9, 2001.

42. Emory Gordy Jr. to Neil V. Rosenberg, email, Sept. 10, 2001.

43. Smith, *Can't You Hear Me Callin'?* 264.

44. Thomas Goldsmith, "Recording the Grammy Winner: Bill Monroe in the Studio," in *The Bill Monroe Reader,* edited by Tom Ewing (Urbana: University of Illinois Press, 2000), 199.

45. Interview with Blake Williams.

46. Vic Gabany interview with Charles K. Wolfe.

47. Tom Ewing, telephone interview with Neil V. Rosenberg, Sept. 1, 1998.

48. Tom Ewing to Neil V. Rosenberg, Aug. 19, 1998.

49. Interview with Blake Williams.

50. Ibid.

51. Tom Ewing to Neil V. Rosenberg, email, April 29, 1999.

52. Vic Gabany, interview with Charles K. Wolfe.

53. Interview with Blake Williams.

54. Rachel Liebling, notes to *High Lonesome: The Story of Bluegrass Musie* (CMH CD8007, 1994).

55. Rachel Liebling to Neil V. Rosenberg, email, Aug. 13, 2002.

56. Jim Skurdall to Neil V. Rosenberg, Nov. 16, 2004.

57. Steve Gebhardt, "Preface," in *Bill Monroe: Father of Bluegrass, a Bilingual Handbook,* edited by Hisae Nishigauchi and Taisuke Nishigauchi (Takarazuka, Japan: B.O.M., 1997), iii–v.

58. Jack Tottle, conversation with Charles K. Wolfe, Murfreesboro, Tenn., March 16, 1999.

59. Butch Baldassari to Neil V. Rosenberg, March 1, 1997.

60. Butch Robins, telephone interview with Neil V. Rosenberg, March 6, 2001.

61. Vic Gabany interview with Charles K. Wolfe.

62. Ibid.

DISCOGRAPHY, 1981–96

810203　　　MCA session; producer, Walter Haynes
Music Mill Studio, Nashville, Tenn.
Feb. 3, 1981, 6–9 P.M.

MC 11414　　OLD EBENEZER SCROOGE (Bill Monroe)　　　　　　　　　　MCA-5214, BCD 16637
Instrumental

MC 11415　　GO HITHER TO GO YONDER[1] (Bill Monroe)　　51129　　　MCA-5214, MCAD 4–11048
Instrumental　　　　　　　　　　　　　　　　　　　　　　　　　BCD 16637

MC 11416　　RIGHT, RIGHT ON (Bill Monroe)　　　　　　　　　　　　MCA-5214, BCD 16637
Instrumental

Bill Monroe: m　　　　　　　Wayne Lewis: g　　　　　　Kenny Baker (except on -14): f
Butch Robins: b　　　　　　Mark Hembree: sb

810204　　　MCA session; producer, Walter Haynes
Music Mill Studio, Nashville, Tenn.
Feb. 4, 1981, 6–9 P.M.

MC 11417　　LOCHWOOD (Bill Monroe)　　　　　　　　　　　　　　MCA-5214, BCD 16637
Instrumental

MC 11418　　OLD DANGER FIELD[2] (Bill Monroe)　　　　　　　　　　MCA-5214, BCD 16637
Instrumental

MC 11419　　FAIR PLAY (Bill Monroe)　　　　　　　　　　　　　　MCA-5214, BCD 16637
Instrumental

Bill Monroe: m　　　　　　　Wayne Lewis: g　　　　　　Kenny Baker: f
Butch Robins: b　　　　　　Mark Hembree: sb

810219　　　MCA session; producer, Walter Haynes
Music Mill Studio, Nashville, Tenn.
Feb. 19, 1981, 6–10:30 P.M.

MC 11420　　MELISSA'S WALTZ FOR J.B. (Bill Monroe)　　　　　　　MCA-5214, BCD 16637
Instrumental

MC 11421　　LADY OF THE BLUE RIDGE (Bill Monroe)　　　　　　　MCA-5214, BCD 16637
Instrumental

MC 11422	MY LAST DAYS ON EARTH[3] (Bill Monroe) Instrumental with vocal backing	51129	MCA-5214, MCAD-10082, MCAD 4–11048, MCA3P-3256, MCA 088 112 982–2, MCA 088 113 207–2, MCA 80004424–02, BCD 16637
MC 11423	EVENING PRAYER BLUES (arr. Bill Monroe) Instrumental		MCA-5214, BCD 16637

Bill Monroe, Larry Sledge (except -22),   Norman Lee Blake, Wayne Lewis   Kenny Baker (except -22): f
   Jesse McReynolds   (except -22): g
   (except -22): m   Mark Hembree: sb
Butch Robins (except -22): b

810407   MCA session; producer, Walter Haynes
Music Mill Studio, Nashville, Tenn.
April 7, 1981, 6–9 P.M.

MC 11422   MY LAST DAYS ON EARTH—additional tracks recorded on existing master tape
Background vocals: Arlene Hardin, Curtis Young, Cindy Nelson

                 Norman Blake: g
                 Mark Hembree: sb

810428   MCA session; producer, Walter Haynes; strings arrangements, William K. McElhiney
Music Mill Studio, Nashville, Tenn.
April 28, 1981, 6–9 P.M.

MC 11422   MY LAST DAYS ON EARTH—additional tracks recorded on existing master tape

Sheldon Kurland Strings: Carl Gorodetzky, George Binkley III, Marvin D. Chantry, Roy Christensen,
   Conni L. Ellisor, Dennis W. Molchan

820703   Festival of American Folklore/NEA Folk Arts Program, National Heritage Fellowship Awards
   Ceremony; producers, Ralph Rinzler (FAF), Bess Hawes (NEA)
Departmental Auditorium, Constitution Ave., Washington, D.C.
July 3, 1982

[1]   DUSTY MILLER   ABC-CLIO
     Instrumental

| [2] | UNCLE PEN | ABC-CLIO |
| | Monroe-LV/TC, ?-LC, ?-BC | |

| Bill Monroe: m[4] | Barry Mitterhoff, Hazel Dickens: g | Dan Goldman: f |
| Frank Necessary: b | (Jim Duke?): sb | |

820704   MCA recording of live concert; producer, Walter Haynes[5]
Cathedral Caverns near Huntsville, Ala.
July 4,[6] 1982, 2–5 P.M., 6–9 P.M.

| MC 13414 | PRECIOUS MEMORIES | BCD 16637 |
| | Lewis-L, Monroe-T, (?)-B,[7] Jon Mohr-BS[8] | |

| MC 13415 | LITTLE SHEPHERD [CALL OF THE SHEPHERD] | BCD 16637 |
| | Instrumental | |

| MC 13416 | THE OLD CROSSROADS | BCD 16637 |
| | Lewis-L, Monroe-T, (?)-B, Mohr-BS | |

| MC 13417 | WAYFARING STRANGER | BCD 16637 |
| | Monroe-L | |

| MC 13418 | IN THE GLORYLAND WAY | BCD 16637 |
| | Monroe-LV/TC, Lewis-LC, (?)-B, John Mohr-BS | |

| MC 13419 | WHAT A FRIEND WE HAVE IN JESUS | BCD 16637 |
| | Lewis-L, Monroe-T, (?)-B, Mohr-BS | |

| MC 13420 | SHOUTING ON THE HILLS OF GLORY | BCD 16637 |
| | Lewis-L, Monroe-T, (?)-B, Mohr-BS | |

| MC 13421 | BAPTIZE ME IN THE CUMBERLAND RIVER (Bill Monroe) | BCD 16637 |
| | Monroe-L | |

| MC 13422 | WICKED PATH OF SIN | BCD 16637 |
| | Lewis-L, Monroe-T, (?)-B, Mohr-BS | |

| MC 13423 | I'LL FLY AWAY | BCD 16637 |
| | Lewis-L, Monroe-T, (?)-B, Mohr-BS | |

| Bill Monroe: m | Wayne Lewis: g | Kenny Baker, Buddy Spicher: f |
| Blake Williams: b | Mark Hembree: sb | |

821006   WSM-TV production, Nashville Alive 1982; released on video by Gabriel Communications
                Opryland Hotel; Nashville, Tenn.
                Oct. 6, 1982

[1]   BLUE MOON OF KENTUCKY   G 8010FR-2
                Monroe-L

Bill Monroe: m   Wayne Lewis: g   Kenny Baker: f
Blake Williams: b   Mark Hembree: sb

821216   MCA session; producer, Walter Haynes
                Burns Station Sound, Burns, Tenn.
                Dec. 16, 1982, 3–4 P.M.

MC 13873   MY LOUISIANA LOVE (Bill Monroe)   MCA-5435, BCD 16637
                Mel Tillis-L, Monroe-T[9]

Bill Monroe: m   Wayne Lewis: g   Kenny Baker: f[10]
Blake Williams: b   Mark Hembree: sb

821222   MCA session; producer, Walter Haynes
                Burns Station Sound, Burns, Tenn.
                Dec. 22, 1982, 6–9 P.M.

MC 13874   IS THE BLUE MOON STILL SHINING (Bill Monroe)   MCA-5435, BCD 16637
                Monroe-T, L; Larry, Rudy, and Steve Gatlin—various harmony parts[11]

Bill Monroe: m   Wayne Lewis, Dale Sellers: g   Kenny Baker, Hoot Hester: f
Blake Williams: b   Mark Hembree: sb

821223   MCA session; producer, Walter Haynes
                Burns Station Sound, Burns, Tenn.
                Dec. 23, 1982, 6–9 P.M.

MC 13875   MY SWEET BLUE-EYED DARLIN' (Bill Monroe)   MCA-5435,[12] MCAD 10082,
                Skaggs-L, Monroe-T[13]   MCAD 4–11048,
                                                                            MCA 088 170 109–2, BCD 16637

Bill Monroe: m   Wayne Lewis, Dale Sellers,   Kenny Baker, Buddy Spicher: f
Blake Williams: b   Ricky Skaggs: g[14]
                                Mark Hembree: sb

830106   MCA session; producer, Walter Haynes
                    Burns Station Sound, Burns, Tenn.
                    Jan. 6, 1983 9 A.M.–1 P.M.

MC 13894   OLD RIVERMAN (Bill Monroe-John Hartford)   MCA-5435, BCD 16637
                    Hartford-L, Monroe-T;[15] overdubbed voices behind first break.

Bill Monroe: m   Wayne Lewis: g   Kenny Baker, Buddy Spicher: f
Blake Williams, John Hartford: b   Mark Hembree: sb

830126   MCA session; producer, Walter Haynes
                    Burns Station Sound, Burns, Tenn.
                    Jan. 26, 1983, 3–6 P.M.

MC 13950   WITH BODY AND SOUL (Virginia Stauffer)   MCA-5435, BCD 16637
                    Waylon Jennings-L, Monroe-T[16]

Bill Monroe: m   Wayne Lewis, Gary Scruggs: g   Kenny Baker, Buddy Spicher: f
Blake Williams: b   Mark Hembree: sb

830127   MCA session; producer, Walter Haynes
                    Burns Station Sound, Burns, Tenn.
                    Jan. 27, 1983, 10 A.M.–1 P.M.

MC 13951   I STILL MISS SOMEONE (Johnny Cash–Roy Cash Jr.)   MCA-5435, BCD 16637
                    Johnny Cash-L, Monroe-T[17]

Bill Monroe: m   Wayne Lewis: g   Kenny Baker, Buddy Spicher: f
Blake Williams: b   Mark Hembree: sb

830201   MCA session; producer, Walter Haynes
                    Burns Station Sound, Burns, Tenn.
                    Feb. 1, 1983, 6:30–9:30 P.M.

MC 13988   BLUE MOON OF KENTUCKY (Bill Monroe)   MCA-5435, BCD 16637
                    Monroe-L, Oak Ridge Boys quartet parts[18]

Bill Monroe: m   Wayne Lewis, Joe Stuart:[19] g Kenny Baker,[20] Buddy Spicher: f
Blake Williams: b   Mark Hembree: sb

830222   MCA session; producer, Walter Haynes
                   Burns Station Sound, Burns, Tenn.
                   Feb. 22, 1983, 2–5 P.M.

MC 14043   THE SUNSET TRAIL (Bill Monroe)   MCA-5435, BCD 16637
                   Nelson-L, Monroe-T and L[21]

Bill Monroe: m   Wayne Lewis, Charlie Collins,   Kenny Baker, Buddy Spicher: f
Blake Williams: b   Willie Nelson:[22] g
                                Mark Hembree: sb

8300420   MCA session; producer, Walter Haynes
                   Burns Station Sound, Burns, Tenn.
                   April 20, 1983, 8–11 P.M.

MC 14264   KENTUCKY WALTZ (Bill Monroe)   MCA-5435, BCD 16637
                   Monroe-L, Emmylou Harris-T and L[23]

Bill Monroe: m   Wayne Lewis, Joe Stuart: g   Kenny Baker, Buddy Spicher: f
Blake Williams: b   Mark Hembree: sb

830504   MCA session; producer, Walter Haynes
                   Burns Station Sound, Burns, Tenn.
                   May 4, 1983, 8–11 P.M.

MC 14333   MY ROSE OF OLD KENTUCKY (Bill Monroe)   MCA-5435, BCD 16637
                   Monroe-L, Mandrell-T[24]

Bill Monroe: m   Wayne Lewis, Kenneth W. Lewis: g   Kenny Baker, Buddy Spicher: f
Blake Williams: b   Mark Hembree: sb   Barbara Mandrell: Dobro

---

831215   *Silver Eagle Cross Country Music Show* (radio program), released on Silver Eagle CC label, with
                       a box consumer mail reply survey card addressed to King Biscuit Flower Hour Records,
                       P.O. Box 6700, FDR Station, NY 10150
                   The Bottom Line,[25] New York City, N.Y.
                   Dec. 15, 1983[26]

[1]   ON MY WAY BACK HOME[27] (Charlie Monroe)[28]   SEA-CD-70007
                   Monroe-LV/TC, Lewis-LC

[2]   I'VE LIVED A LOT IN MY TIME (Jim Reeves/Dick Reynolds/Jack Rhodes)   SEA-CD-70007
                   Lewis-L

[3]   FOOTPRINT [sic] IN THE SNOW (traditional, arr. Bill Monroe)   SEA-CD-70007
        Monroe-L

[4]   THE OLD, OLD HOUSE (traditional, arr. Bill Monroe)   SEA-CD-70007
        Monroe-L

[5]   EBENEZER SCROOGE (traditional, arr. Bill Monroe)   SEA-CD-70007
        Instrumental

[6]   WAYFARING STRANGER (traditional, arr. Bill Monroe)   SEA-CD-70007
        Monroe-L

[7]   BLUE MOON OF KENTUCKY (Bill Monroe)   SEA-CD-70007
        Monroe-L

[8]   CLOSE BY (Bill Monroe)   SEA-CD-70007
        Monroe-L

[9]   FOGGY MOUNTAIN BREAKDOWN (Earl Scruggs)   SEA-CD-70007
        Instrumental

[10]   SHUCKIN' THE CORN (Earl Scruggs)   SEA-CD-70007
        Instrumental

[11]   ROCKY ROAD BLUES (Bill Monroe)   SEA-CD-70007
        Monroe-L

[12]   MULE SKINNER BLUES (traditional, arr. Bill Monroe)   SEA-CD-70007
        Monroe-L

[13]   ROLLIN' IN MY SWEET BABY'S ARMS (Roy Acuff)   SEA-CD-70007
        Lewis-L, Monroe-T

Bill Monroe: m   Wayne Lewis:[29] g   Kenny Baker: f
Blake Williams: b   Mark Hembree: sb

840322?[30]   CBS/Epic sessions for Ricky Skaggs; "Production crew," Phil Somers, Mike Blake, John Ristoff,
        Larry Frazier, and Mike Morgan
        Audio Media, 808 19th Ave South, Nashville, Tenn.
        March 21, 1984, 10 A.M.–1 P.M., 2–5 P.M.
        April 17, 1984, 10 A.M.–1 P.M.
        May 15, 1984, 2–5 P.M.

135338   WHEEL HOSS   FE 49410
          Instrumental

Bill Monroe: m   Ricky Skaggs: g ("guitars")   Bobby Hicks: f ("fiddles")
Bruce Boulton: esg   Jesse Chambers: sb   George Grantham: dr
                                Gary Smith: pno

850502.1   MCA session; producer, Emory Gordy Jr.
          Sound Stage Studio, Nashville, Tenn.
          May 2, 1985, 3–6 P.M.

MC 18233   I HEAR A SWEET VOICE CALLING (Bill Monroe)   MCA-5625, BCD 16637
            Bobby Osborne-L, Bill Monroe-T, Sonny Osborne-B

Bill Monroe, Bobby Osborne: m   Wayne Lewis: g   Glen Duncan: f
Blake Williams, Sonny Osborne: b   Tater Tate: sb

850502.2   MCA session; producer, Emory Gordy Jr.
          Sound Stage Studio, Nashville, Tenn.
          May 2, 1985, 7–10 P.M.

MC 18234   TRUE LIFE BLUES (Bill Monroe)   MCA-5625, BCD 16637
            Carl Story-L, Monroe-T

Bill Monroe: m   Wayne Lewis, Carl Story: g   Glen Duncan: f
Blake Williams: b   Tater Tate: sb

850506.1   MCA session; producer, Emory Gordy Jr.
          Sound Stage Studio, Nashville, Tenn.
          May 6, 1985, 3–6 P.M.

MC 18235   LORD, PROTECT MY SOUL (Bill Monroe)   MCA-5625, BCD 16637
            Charlie Waller-L, Monroe-T/LC, Jimmy Gaudreau-B, Bill Yates-BS

Bill Monroe, Jimmy Gaudreau: m   Wayne Lewis, Charlie Waller: g   Glen Duncan: f
Blake Williams: b   Tater Tate: sb

850506.2   MCA session; producer, Emory Gordy Jr.
Sound Stage Studio, Nashville, Tenn.
May 6, 1985, 7–10 P.M.

MC 18236   TRAVELIN' THIS LONESOME ROAD (Bill Monroe)   MCA-5625, MCAD 4–11048,
Mac Wiseman-L, Monroe-T   BCD 16637

Bill Monroe: m   Wayne Lewis, Mac Wiseman: g   Glen Duncan: f
Blake Williams: b   Tater Tate: sb

850507.1   MCA session; producer, Emory Gordy Jr.
Sound Stage Studio, Nashville, Tenn.
May 7, 1985, 3–6 P.M.

MC 18237   I'M ON MY WAY BACK TO THE OLD HOME (Bill Monroe)   MCA-5625, BCD 16637
Jim McReynolds-L, Monroe-T, Jesse McReynolds-B

MC 18238   MIGHTY DARK TO TRAVEL (Bill Monroe)   MCA-5970, BCD 16637
Jim McReynolds-L, Monroe-T, Jesse McReynolds-B

Bill Monroe, Jesse McReynolds: m   Wayne Lewis, Jim McReynolds: g   Glen Duncan: f
Blake Williams: b   Tater Tate: sb

850507.2   MCA session; producer, Emory Gordy Jr.
Sound Stage Studio, Nashville, Tenn.
May 7, 1985, 7–10 P.M.

MC 18239   REMEMBER THE CROSS (Bill Monroe and Howard Watts)   MCA-5625, BCD 16637
Monroe-L, T; John Duffey-L, T; Mike Auldridge-B; Tater Tate-BS

Bill Monroe, John Duffey: m   Wayne Lewis: g   Glen Duncan: f
Blake Williams: b   Emory Gordy Jr.: sb   Mike Auldridge-Dobro

---

850610.1   MCA session; producer, Emory Gordy Jr.
Sound Stage Studio, Nashville, Tenn.
June 10, 1985, 2–5 P.M.

MC 18479   LET THE GATES SWING WIDE (Bill Monroe)   MCA-5625, BCD 16637
Lewis-L, Monroe-T, Duncan-B, Tater Tate-BS

Bill Monroe: m   Wayne Lewis: g   Glen Duncan: f
Blake Williams: b   Emory Gordy Jr.: sb

850610.2   MCA session; producer, Emory Gordy Jr.
Sound Stage Studio, Nashville, Tenn.
June 10, 1985, 6–9 P.M.

MC 18476   CAN'T YOU HEAR ME CALLIN' (Bill Monroe)   MCA-5625, BCD 16637
Ralph Stanley-L, Monroe-T

MC 18490   PIKE COUNTY BREAKDOWN
Instrumental

Bill Monroe: m   Wayne Lewis: g   Glen Duncan: f
Blake Williams, Ralph Stanley: b   Tater Tate: sb

850617.1   MCA session; producer, Emory Gordy Jr.
Sound Emporium, Nashville, Tenn.
June 17, 1985, 3–6 P.M.

MC 18477   THE GOLDEN WEST (Bill Monroe)   MCA-5625, BCD 16637
Instrumental

MC 18491   OLD BROWN COUNTY BARN (Bill Monroe)   MCA-5970, MCAD 4–11048,
Instrumental   BCD 16637

Bill Monroe: m   Wayne Lewis: g   Glen Duncan, Bobby Hicks: f
Blake Williams: b   Tater Tate: sb

850617.2   MCA session; producer, Emory Gordy Jr.
Sound Emporium, Nashville, Tenn.
June 17, 1985, 8–11 P.M.

MC 18478   I'M GOING BACK TO OLD KENTUCKY (Bill Monroe)   MCA-5625, BCD 16637
Del McCoury-L, Monroe-T

MC 18492   BLUEST MAN IN TOWN (Bill Monroe)   MCA-5970, BCD 16637
Del McCoury-L, Monroe-T

Bill Monroe: m   Wayne Lewis, Del McCoury: g   Glen Duncan, Bobby Hicks: f
Blake Williams: b   Tater Tate: sb

860317.1   MCA session; producer, Emory Gordy Jr.
Sound Emporium, Nashville, Tenn.
March 17, 1986, 2–5 P.M.

MC 22693   DANCIN' IN BRANCIN'[31] (Bill Monroe)   MCA-5970, BCD 16637
Instrumental

MC 22687   JEKYLL ISLAND (Bill Monroe)   MCA-5970, BCD 16637
Instrumental

Bill Monroe: m[32]   Wayne Lewis: g   Buddy Spicher: f
Blake Williams: b   Tater Tate: sb

860317.2   MCA session; producer, Emory Gordy Jr.
Sound Emporium, Nashville, Tenn.
March 17, 1986, 6–9 P.M.

MC 22690   STAY AWAY FROM ME (Bill Monroe)   MCA-5970, MCAD 4–11048,
Monroe-L   BCD 16637

MC 22686   MUSIC VALLEY WALTZ (Bill Monroe and John Hartford)   MCA-5970, BCD 16637
Monroe-L

Bill Monroe: m   Wayne Lewis: g   Bobby Hicks, Buddy Spicher: f
Blake Williams: b   Tater Tate: sb

860318.1   MCA session; producer, Emory Gordy Jr.
Sound Emporium, Nashville, Tenn.
March 18, 1986, 2–5 P.M.

[1]   TEXAS LONE STAR (Bill Monroe)
Instrumental

[2]   I LOVE THE STATE OF VIRGINIA
[?]

Bill Monroe: m   Wayne Lewis: g   Bobby Hicks, Buddy Spicher: f
Blake Williams: b   Tater Tate: sb

860318.2   MCA session; producer, Emory Gordy Jr.
Sound Emporium, Nashville, Tenn.
March 18, 1986, 6–10 P.M.

MC 22692   ANGELS ROCK ME TO SLEEP (Thomas Ramsey–Marion Easterling)   MCA-5970, BCD 16637
Lewis-L, Monroe-T, Williams-B, Tate-BS

MC 22684   THE LONG BOW (Bill Monroe)   MCA-5970, MCAD 4–11048,
Instrumental   BCD 16637

Bill Monroe: m   Wayne Lewis: g   Bobby Hicks, Buddy Spicher: f
Blake Williams: b   Tater Tate (-84),
                                                   Emory Gordy Jr. (-92): sb

---

860819   MCA session; producer, Emory Gordy Jr.
Sound Stage Studios, Nashville, Tenn.
Aug. 19, 1986, 2–6 P.M.

[1]   GOD HOLDS THE FUTURE IN HIS HANDS   BCD 16637
Ewing-L, Monroe-T, Williams-B, Tate-BS

[2]   FARTHER ON
Monroe-L

MC 22688   THE OLD CROSSROADS[33] (Bill Monroe)   MCA-5970, MCAD 4–11048,
Ewing-L, Monroe-T, Williams-B, Tate-BS   BCD 16637

Bill Monroe: m   Thomas Dollison "Tom" Ewing: g   Buddy Spicher, Clarence "Tater" Tate: f
Blake Williams: b   John Montgomery: sb

870000A   Flying Fish session for Glenda Faye; producer, Porter Wagoner[34]
Fireside Studio, Nashville, Tenn.
(1987?)

[1]   DOWN YONDER   FF 432
Instrumental

Bill Monroe, Jesse McReynolds: m   Glenda Faye (Kniphfer): g   Vassar Clements: f
Bobby Thompson: b   Roy Huskey Jr.: sb   Nancy Given: snare dr

870000B   Flying Fish session for Glenda Faye; producer, Porter Wagoner
Fireside Studio, Nashville, Tenn.
[1987?]

[1]   OZARK RAG   FF 432
Instrumental

Bill Monroe, Jesse McReynolds: m   Glenda Faye (Kniphfer): g   Vassar Clements: f
Bobby Thompson: b   Roy Huskey Jr.: sb   Nancy Given: snare dr

870907   Paramount Pictures session for the movie *Planes, Trains and Automobiles*;
producer, Emory Gordy Jr., eng., Chuck Ainlay
Enterprise Recording Studio, Burbank, Calif.
Sept. 7, 1987 afternoon[35]

[1]   ROANOKE
Instrumental

[2]   BLUE MOON OF KENTUCKY
instrumental

[3]   BLUE MOON OF KENTUCKY
Monroe, John Candy-L[36]

Bill Monroe: m   Tom Ewing: g   Mike Feagan: f
Blake Williams: b   Tater Tate: sb

880104   MCA session; producer, Emory Gordy Jr.[37]
Sound Stage, Nashville, Tenn.
Jan. 4, 1988 1–4 P.M.

MC 25361   SOUTHERN FLAVOR (Bill Monroe)   MCA-42133, MCAD 10082,
Instrumental   MCAD 4–11048, BCD 16637

Bill Monroe: m   Tom Ewing: g   Bobby Hicks, Buddy Spicher,
Blake Williams: b   Tater Tate: sb   Mike Feagan: f

880105   MCA session; producer, Emory Gordy Jr.[38]
Sound Stage, Nashville, Tenn.
Jan. 5, 1988, 1–4 P.M.

MC 25359   STONE COAL (Bill Monroe)   MCA-42133, BCD 16637
Instrumental

MC 25358   TEXAS LONE STAR (Bill Monroe)   MCA-42133, BCD 16637
Instrumental

| Bill Monroe: m | Tom Ewing: g | Bobby Hicks, Buddy Spicher, |
| Blake Williams: b | Tater Tate: sb | Mike Feagan: f |

880108   MCA session; producer, Emory Gordy Jr.
Sound Stage, Nashville, Tenn.
Jan. 8, 1988, 1–4 P.M.

[1]   WHAT A WONDERFUL LIFE (Raymond Huffmaster)
Ewing-L, Monroe-T, Williams-B, Tate-BS

MC 25356   SUGAR LOAF MOUNTAIN (Bill Monroe)   MCA-42133, SHA 604,
Instrumental   BCD 16637

| Bill Monroe: m | Tom Ewing: g | Bobby Hicks, Buddy Spicher, |
| Blake Williams: b | Tater Tate: sb | Mike Feagan: f |

880112   MCA session; producer, Emory Gordy Jr.
Sound Stage, Nashville, Tenn.
Jan. 12, 1988, 7–10 P.M.

[1]   BLUE SAVANNAH WALTZ[39] (Wayne Jerrolds)
Monroe-L

MC 25354   THE DAYS GONE BY (Bill Monroe[40])   MCA-42133, BCD 16637
Ewing-L, Monroe-T, Williams-B

MC 25353   WHITE ROSE (Carl Butler)   MCA-42133, BCD 16637
Monroe-L

| Bill Monroe: m | Tom Ewing: g | Bobby Hicks, Buddy Spicher, |
| Blake Williams: b | Tater Tate: sb | Mike Feagan: f |

880113   MCA session; producer, Emory Gordy Jr.
Sound Stage, Nashville, Tenn.
Jan. 13, 1988, 7–10 P.M.

MC 25360   LIFE'S HIGHWAY (Bobby Smith)   MCA-42133, BCD 16637
Ewing-L, Monroe-T, Williams-B

[2]   TAKE COURAGE UN' TOMORROW (arr. Bill Monroe)
                        Ewing-L, Monroe-T, Williams-B, Tate-BS

Bill Monroe: m   Tom Ewing: g   Bobby Hicks, Buddy Spicher,
Blake Williams: b   Tater Tate (-60),   Mike Feagan: f
                                       Emory Gordy Jr. (2): sb

880114   MCA session; producer Emory Gordy Jr.
                          Sound Stage, Nashville, Tenn.
                          Jan. 14, 1988, 7–10 P.M.

MC 25355   GIVE ME WINGS (Gerald Evans)   MCA-42133, BCD 16637
                          Ewing-L, Monroe-T, Williams-B, Tater Tate-BS

MC 25357   WHAT A WONDERFUL LIFE (Raymond Huffmaster)   MCA-42133, BCD 16637,
                          Ewing-L, Monroe-T, Williams-B, Tater Tate-BS

MC 25362   TAKE COURAGE UN' TOMORROW[41] (arr. Bill Monroe)   MCA-42133, MCAD 4–11048,
                          Ewing-L, Monroe-T, Williams-B, Clarence "Tater" Tate-BS   BCD 16637

Bill Monroe: m   Tom Ewing: g   Bobby Hicks, Buddy Spicher,
Blake Williams: b   Emory Gordy Jr.: sb   Mike Feagan: f

890302   Rounder session for Jim and Jesse and the Virginia Boys; producer, Carl Jackson
                          Home Place Studio, Nashville, Tenn.
                          March 2, 1989

[1]   WICKED PATH OF SIN   Rdr 0279
                          Jim McReynolds-L, Monroe-T, Jesse McReynolds-B, Tater Tate-BS

Bill Monroe, Jesse McReynolds: m   Jim McReynolds, Carl Jackson: g   Jim Buchanan: f
Vic Jordan: b   Roy Huskey: sb

890505   MCA sessions; produced by Steve Buchanan and Bill Monroe[42]
                          Grand Ole Opry, Nashville, Tenn.
                          May 5,[43] June 13 [14?], and June 27, 1989

[1]   MOLLY AND TENBROOKS (Bill Monroe)   MCAD-42286, BCD 16637
                          Monroe-L

[2]   FOOTPRINTS IN THE SNOW (Roy Carter)   MCAD-42286, BCD 16637
                          Monroe-L

[3]	SITTIN' ALONE IN THE MOONLIGHT (Bill Monroe) Ewing-L, Monroe-T	MCAD-42286, BCD 16637
[4]	PRECIOUS MEMORIES (traditional, arr. Bill Monroe) Ewing-L, Monroe-T, Williams-B, Tate-BS	MCAD-42286, BCD 16637
[5]	RAWHIDE (Bill Monroe) Instrumental	MCAD-42286, BCD 16637
[6]	MY SWEET DARLIN'[44] (Bill Monroe) Ewing-L, Monroe-T, Williams-B	MCAD-42286, BCD 16637
[7]	IN THE PINES (Clayton McMichen, Slim Bryant) Ewing-L, Monroe-T	MCAD-42286, BCD 16637
[8]	LOVE, PLEASE COME HOME (Leon Jackson) Ewing-L, Monroe-T, Williams-B	MCAD-42286, BCD 16637
MC 30116 [6/14/89]	PIKE COUNTY BREAKDOWN (Bill Monroe) Instrumental	MCAD-42286, MCAD 4–11048, BCD 16637
MC 30117 [6/14/89]	I'M WORKING ON A BUILDING (traditional, arr. Bill Monroe) Monroe-LV/TC, Ewing-LC, Williams-B, Tate-BS	MCAD-42286, MCAD 4–11048, BCD 16637
[9]	WATERMELON HANGING ON THE VINE [theme] Instrumental	MCAD-42286, BCD 16637

Bill Monroe: m   Tom Ewing: g   Tater Tate: f
Blake Williams: b   Billy Rose: sb

890511   Blue Plate Music reissue of radio broadcast[45]
Live from the Mountain Stage, Charleston, W.V.
May 11, 1989

[1]	MY SWEET BLUE EYED DARLIN' Ewing-L, Monroe-T, Williams-B	BPM-400
[2]	NEW MULE SKINNER BLUES[46] Monroe-L	BPM-400
[3]	SOUTHERN FLAVOR Instrumental	BPM-400
[4]	BEAUTIFUL LIFE Ewing-L, Monroe-T, Williams-B, Tate-BS	BPM-400

[5]	MY BLUE EYES FROM HEAVEN Diana Christian-L	BPM-400
[6]	NORTHERN WHITE CLOUDS Instrumental	BPM-400
[7]	UNCLE PEN Monroe-LV/TC, Ewing-LC, Williams-B	BPM-400
[8]	BLUE MOON OF KENTUCKY[47] Monroe-L	BPM-400
[9]	SUGAR LOAF MOUNTAIN Instrumental	BPM-400
[10]	THE OLD HOME TOWN Ewing-L	BPM-400
[11]	I'M WORKING ON A BUILDING Monroe-LV/TC, Ewing-LC, Williams-B, Tate-BS	BPM-400
[12]	RAWHIDE Instrumental	BPM-400
[13]	ROLLIN' IN MY SWEET BABY'S ARMS[48] Ewing-L, Monroe-T, Williams-B	BPM-400

Bill Monroe: m   Tom Ewing: g   Tater Tate: f
Blake Williams:[49] b   Billy Rose: sb

890615/18   Shanachie (video) and CMH reissue of movie soundtracks/visuals; producer, Rachel Liebling and Andrew Serwer
Bill Monroe's 23d Annual Bluegrass Festival at Bill Monroe's Brown County Jamboree, Bean Blossom, Ind.
June 15–18, 1989

[1][50]	THE OLD BROWN COUNTY BARN Instrumental	SHA 604
[2][51]	SOUTHERN FLAVOR Instrumental	SHA 604
[3][52]	SOUTHERN FLAVOR Instrumental	SHA 604

| [4][53] | I'M ON MY WAY TO THE OLD HOME | SHA 604, CD-8007 |
| | Ewing-L, Monroe-T, Williams-B | |

| Bill Monroe: m | Tom Ewing: g | Tater Tate: f |
| Blake Williams: b | Billy Rose: sb | |

890619   Shanachie (video) and CMH reissue of movie soundtracks/visuals; producers Rachel Liebling and Andrew Serwer
Monroe family home, Rosine, Ky.
June 19, 1989

| [1] | GOING ACROSS THE SEA | SHA 604, CD-8007, CD-6297 |
| | Instrumental | |

Bill Monroe: m

890730.1   Recordings made by Pieter Groenveld and Liz Meyer (BCD 16624/3 and /4); video made by Reinhard
Pietsch (BCD 16624/5), released by Bear Family
Zur Neuen Heimat (restaurant), Streekermoor, Germany
July 30, 1989

| [0] | INTRODUCTION | BCD 16624/5 |
| | Klaus Grotelüschen | |

| [1] | MY SWEET BLUE EYED DARLING (Bill Monroe) | BCD 16624/3, /5 |
| | Ewing-L, Monroe-T, Williams-B | |

| [2] | THE OLD HOME TOWN (Carter Stanley)[54] | BCD 16624/3, /5 |
| | Ewing-L | |

| [3] | SUGAR LOAF MOUNTAIN (Bill Monroe) | BCD 16624/3, /5 |
| | Instrumental | |

| [4] | MULESKINNER BLUES (P.D.) | BCD 16624/3, /5 |
| | Monroe-L | |

| [5] | BLUE MOON OF KENTUCKY (Bill Monroe) | BCD 16624/3, /5 |
| | Monroe-L | |

| [6] | SOUTHERN FLAVOR (Bill Monroe) | BCD 16624/3, /5 |
| | Instrumental | |

| [7] | A BEAUTIFUL LIFE (William Golden) | BCD 16624/3, /5 |
| | Ewing-L, Monroe-T, Williams-B, Tate-BS | |

[8]	THE OLD BROWN COUNTY BARN (Bill Monroe) Instrumental	BCD 16624/3, /5
[9]	UNCLE PEN (Bill Monroe) Monroe-LV/TC, Ewing-LC, Williams-B	BCD 16624/3, /5
[10]	CHEYENNE (Bill Monroe) Instrumental	BCD 16624/3, /5
[11]	FOOTPRINTS IN THE SNOW (P.D.) Monroe-L	BCD 16624/3, /5
[12]	MY LITTLE GEORGIA ROSE (Bill Monroe) Monroe-L	BCD 16624/3, /5
[13]	WALLS OF TIME (Bill Monroe) Ewing-L, Monroe-T	BCD 16624/3, /5
[14]	JERUSALEM RIDGE (Bill Monroe) Instrumental	BCD 16624/3, /5
[1]	RAW HIDE (Bill Monroe) Instrumental	BCD 16624/4, /5
[2]	DOWN YONDER (P.D.) Instrumental	BCD 16624/4, /5
[3]	IN THE PINES (Clayton McMichen) Ewing-L, Monroe-T	BCD 16624/4, /5
[4]	BLUEGRASS BREAKDOWN (Bill Monroe) Instrumental	BCD 16624/4, /5
[5]	THERE'S AN OLD, OLD HOUSE (George Jones) Monroe-L	BCD 16624/4, /5
[6]	I SAW THE LIGHT (Hank Williams) Ewing-L, Monroe-T, Williams-B, Tate-BS	BCD 16624/4, /5
[7]	ON AND ON (Bill Monroe) Ewing-L, Mnroe-T, Williams-B	BCD 16624/4, /5
[8]	SOLDIER'S JOY (P.D.) Instrumental	BCD 16624/4, /5
[9]	WAYFARING STRANGER (P.D.) Monroe-L	BCD 16624/4, /5

[10]	MOLLY AND TENBROOKS (Bill Monroe) Monroe-L	BCD 16624/4, /5
[11]	ROLL IN MY SWEET BABY'S ARMS (P.D.) Ewing-L, Monroe-T, Williams-B	BCD 16624/4, /5
[12]	SALLY GOODIN (P.D.) Instrumental	BCD 16624/4, /5
[13]	[SO LONG AND GOODBYE (Mark Fourner)][55] WATERMELON HANGING . . . Instrumental	BCD 16624/4, /5
[14]	JOHN HENRY (P.D.) Monroe-L	BCD 16624/4, /5
[15]	WHEEL HOSS (Bill Monroe) Instrumental	BCD 16624/4, /5

Bill Monroe: m	Tom Ewing: g	Tater Tate: f
Blake Williams: b	Billy Rose: sb	

890731   Video recording of interview for WDR (Westdeutscher Rundfunk) made by Reinhard Pietsch, released by
        Bear Family
    Zur Neuen Heimat (restaurant), Streekermoor, Germany
    July 31, 1989

["Bonus"]	INTERVIEW[56] Monroe interviewed by Jim Skurdall	BCD 16624/5

890913.1   Shanachie (video) reissue of movie soundtracks/visuals; producers, Rachel Liebling and Andrew Serwer
    Blue Grass Special (Monroe's bus), vicinity of Hendersonville, Tenn.
    Sept. 13, 1989

[1]	I'M GOING BACK TO OLD KENTUCKY Ewing-L, Monroe-T[57]	SHA 604

890913.2   Shanachie (video) and CMH reissue of movie soundtracks/visuals; producers Rachel Liebling and Andrew Serwer
    Bell Cove Club, Hendersonville, Tenn.
    Sept. 13, 1989

[1]	I'M GOING BACK TO OLD KENTUCKY Ewing-L, Monroe-T	SHA 604

[2]   UNCLE PEN   SHA 604
                   Monroe-LV/TC, Ewing-LC, Williams-B

[3]   MULE SKINNER BLUES   SHA 604
                   Monroe-L

Bill Monroe: m   Tom Ewing: g   Tater Tate: f
Blake Williams: b   (Billy Rose?): sb

900515   MCA session; producer, Steve Buchanan
                     Reflections Studio, Nashville, Tenn.
                     May 15, 1990, 2–5 P.M.

[1]   WHAT WOULD YOU GIVE IN EXCHANGE?
                   Wiseman-L, Monroe-T

[2]   CRYIN' HOLY UNTO THE LORD (Irene Amburgey)
                   Ewing-L, Monroe-T, Williams-B, Tate-BS

MC 35226   JUST A LITTLE TALK WITH JESUS (Cleavant Derricks)   MCAD-10017, BCD 16637
                   Ewing-L, Monroe-T, Williams-B, Tate-BS

Bill Monroe: m   Tom Ewing, Mac Wiseman (1): g   Tater Tate: f
Blake Williams: b   Billy Rose: sb

900521   MCA session; producer, Steve Buchanan
                     Reflections Studio, Nashville, Tenn.
                     May 21, 1990, 2–5 P.M.

[1]   SHINE HALLELUJAH SHINE (Bill Monroe)
                   Ewing-L, Monroe-T, Williams-B, Tate-BS

MC 35223   HARBOR OF LOVE (Carter Stanley)   MCAD-10017, BCD 16637
                   Ralph Stanley-L, Monroe-T, Ricky Skaggs-B, Tate-BS

Bill Monroe: m   Tom Ewing, Ricky   James R. "Jimmy" Campbell,
Blake Williams: b   Skaggs (-23): g   Tater Tate: f
                                  Billy Rose: sb

900612   MCA session; producer, Steve Buchanan
                  Reflections Studio, Nashville, Tenn.
                  June 12, 1990, 6–9 P.M.

MC 35231   ARE YOU LOST IN SIN? (Jim McReynolds–Jesse McReynolds)   MCAD-10017, BCD 16637
                 Jim McReynolds-L, Monroe-T, Jesse McReynolds-B, Tate-BS

MC 35228   HE'LL TAKE YOU IN (Billy Smith–Steffan Baker)   MCAD-10017, BCD 16637
                 Ewing-L, Monroe-T, Williams-B, Tate-BS

Bill Monroe, Jesse   Tom Ewing: g[58]   Jimmy Campbell, Tater Tate: f
   McReynolds (-31): m   Billy Rose: sb
Blake Williams: b

900615.1   Original cinema (video) reissue of movie soundtracks/visuals; producer, Steve Gebhardt
                  On the Blue Grass Special, en route to Bean Blossom, Ind.
                  June 15, 1990

[1]   BLUE MOON OF KENTUCKY   OC-1001
                 Monroe-L

Bill Monroe: m
Blake Williams: b

900615.2   Original Cinema (video) and Copper Creek reissue of movie soundtracks/visuals; producer, Steve Gebhardt[59]
                  Brown County Jamboree Park, Bean Blossom, Ind.
                  June 15, 1990, afternoon show

[1]   LOVE, PLEASE COME HOME   RHY-1015
                 Ewing-L, Monroe-T, Williams-B

[2]   WILLIE MOORE   RHY-1015
                 Ewing-L

[3]   BLUEGRASS BREAKDOWN   RHY-1015
                 Instrumental

[4]   MULE SKINNER BLUES   RHY-1015
                 Monroe-L

[5]   KENTUCKY WALTZ   RHY-1015
                 Monroe-L

[6]   SOUTHERN FLAVOR   RHY-1015
                 Instrumental

| [7] | THE OLD CROSS ROAD | RHY-1015 |
| | Ewing-L, Monroe-T, Williams-B, Tate-BS | |

| [8] | NORTHERN WHITE CLOUDS | |
| | Instrumental | |

| [9] | WALK SOFTLY ON THIS HEART OF MINE | |
| | Diana Christian-L | |

| [10] | Y'ALL COME | |
| | Diana Christian-L | |

| [11] | OLD JOE CLARK | |
| | Instrumental | |

| [12] | THEME: WATERMELON ON THE VINE | RHY-1015 |
| | Instrumental | |

Bill Monroe: m   Tom Ewing: g   Tater Tate: f
Blake Williams: b   Billy Rose: sb

900615.3   Original Cinema (video) and Copper Creek reissue of movie soundtracks/visuals. Producer: Steve Gebhardt[60]
Brown County Jamboree Park, Bean Blossom, Ind.
June 15, 1990, 11 P.M. show

| [1] | I'M ON MY WAY BACK TO THE OLD HOME | OC-1001, RHY-1015 |
| | Monroe-LV/TC, Ewing LC, Williams-B | |

| [2] | O-HIO | |
| | Ewing-L | |

| [3] | SUGARLOAF MOUNTAIN | RHY-1015[61] |
| | Instrumental | |

| [4] | MY ROSE OF OLD KENTUCKY | |
| | Monroe-L | |

| [5] | BLUE MOON OF KENTUCKY | |
| | Monroe-L | |

| [6] | THE OLD, OLD HOUSE | RHY-1015 |
| | Monroe-L | |

| [7] | TOMBSTONE JUNCTION | OC-1001, RHY-1015 |
| | Instrumental | |

| [8] | TAKE COURAGE UN' TOMORROW | RHY-1015 |
| | Ewing-L, Monroe-T, Williams-B, Tate-BS | |

| [9] | THE LONG BOW | |
| | Instrumental | |

| [10] | RAGTIME ANNIE | |
| | Instrumental | |

| [11] | SHENANDOAH BREAKDOWN | RHY-1015 |
| | Instrumental | |

| [12] | DOG HOUSE BLUES | RHY-1015[62] |
| | Monroe-L | |

| [13] | RAW HIDE | OC-1001, RHY-1015 |
| | Instrumental | |

| [14] | WATERMELON ON THE VINE | |
| | Instrumental | |

| [15] | JOHN HENRY/MULE SKINNER BLUES | |
| | Monroe-L | |

Bill Monroe: m   Tom Ewing: g   Tater Tate: f
Blake Williams: b   Billy Rose: sb

900616.1   Original Cinema (video) and Copper Creek reissue of movie soundtracks/visuals; producer, Steve Gebhardt[63]
Brown County Jamboree Park, Bean Blossom, Ind.
June 16, 1990, afternoon show

[1]   WHY DID YOU WANDER?
Monroe-L

[2]   THE OLD HOME TOWN
Ewing-L

[3]   BLUEGRASS BREAKDOWN
Instrumental

[4]   BLUE MOON OF KENTUCKY
Monroe-L

[5]   SOUTHERN FLAVOR
Instrumental

[6]   A BEAUTIFUL LIFE
             [Ewing-L, Monroe-T, Williams-B, Tate-BS]

[7]   WHEEL HOSS   RHY-1015
             Instrumental

[8]   I WANT TO GO WITH YOU
             Diana Christian-L

[9]   SOLDIER'S JOY
             Instrumental

[10]   UNCLE PEN   OC-1001, RHY-1015
             Monroe-LV/TC, Ewing-LC, Williams-B

[11][64]   THEME [WATERMELON ON THE VINE]   RHY-1015
             Instrumental

Bill Monroe: m   Tom Ewing: g   Tater Tate: f
Blake Williams: b   Billy Rose: sb

900616.2   Original Cinema (video) and Copper Creek reissue of movie soundtracks/visuals; producer, Steve Gebhardt
                Brown County Jamboree Park, Bean Blossom, Ind.
                June 16, 1990, evening show

[1]   MY SWEET BLUE EYED DARLING
             Ewing-L, Monroe-T

[2]   TAKE ME HOME   RHY-1015
             Ewing-L

[3]   CROSSING THE CUMBERLANDS
             Instrumental

[4]   MY ROSE OF OLD KENTUCKY
             Monroe-L, Emmylou Harris-T

[5]   KENTUCKY WALTZ   OC-1001
             Monroe-L, Emmylou Harris-T

[6]   COME HITHER TO GO YONDER   RHY-1015
             Instrumental

[7]   CRYIN' HOLY UNTO THE LORD   RHY-1015
             Ewing-L, Monroe-T, Williams-B, Tate-BS

[8]	NORTHERN WHITE CLOUDS Instrumental	RHY-1015
[9]	WALK SOFTLY ON THIS HEART OF MINE Diana Christian-L	
[10]	ROCKY ROAD BLUES Diana Christian-L	
[11][65]	SOLDIER'S JOY Instrumental	
[12]	IT'S MIGHTY DARK TO TRAVEL Ewing-L, Monroe-T, Williams-B	OC-1001, RHY-1015
[13]	DOG HOUSE BLUES Monroe-L	
[14]	WATERMELON ON THE VINE Instrumental	
[15]	UNCLE PEN Monroe-LV/TC, Ewing-LC, Williams-B	OC-1001
[16]	DUSTY MILLER Instrumental	RHY-1015
[17]	HAPPY BIRTHDAY Monroe-L	RHY-1015
[18]	ROLL IN MY SWEET BABY'S ARMS Ewing-L, Monroe-T, Williams-B	RHY-1015

Bill Monroe: m	Tom Ewing: g	Tater Tate: f
Blake Williams: b	Billy Rose: sb	

900624.1   Original Cinema (video) and Copper Creek reissue of movie soundtracks/visuals; producer, Steve Gebhardt
Frontier Ranch Park, Reynoldsburg, Ohio
June 24, 1990, 6 P.M., part 1

[1]	MY SWEET BLUE-EYED DARLING Ewing-L, Monroe-T, Williams-B
[2]	O-HIO Ewing-L

| [3] | PIKE COUNTY BREAKDOWN | OC-1001 |
| | Instrumental | |

| [4] | MULE SKINNER BLUES | |
| | Monroe-L | |

| [5] | BLUE MOON OF KENTUCKY | |
| | Monroe-L | |

| [6] | SOUTHERN FLAVOR | |
| | Instrumental | |

| [7] | I'M WORKING ON A BUILDING | OC-1001 |
| | Ewing-L, Monroe-T, Williams-B, Tate-BS | |

| [8] | THE GOLD RUSH | |
| | Instrumental | |

| [9] | WALK SOFTLY ON THIS HEART OF MINE | |
| | Diana Christian-L | |

| [10] | Y'ALL COME | |
| | Diana Christian-L | |

Bill Monroe: m   Tom Ewing: g   Tater Tate: f
Blake Williams: b   Billy Rose: sb

900624.2   Original Cinema (video) and Copper Creek reissue of movie soundtracks/visuals; producer, Steve Gebhardt
Frontier Ranch Park, Reynoldsburg, Ohio
June 24, 1990, 6 P.M., part 2

| [1] | FOOTPRINTS IN THE SNOW | OC-1001 |
| | Monroe-L | |

| [2] | CAN'T YOU HEAR ME CALLING | OC-1001 |
| | McCoury-L, Monroe-T | |

| [3] | DEVIL'S DREAM | OC-1001 |
| | Instrumental | |

| [4] | I'M GOING BACK TO OLD KENTUCKY | OC-1001 |
| | McCoury-L, Monroe-T | |

| [5] | ORANGE BLOSSOM SPECIAL | |
| | Instrumental | |

[6]   WHISPERING HOPE
            Instrumental

[7]   TRUE LIFE BLUES
            McCoury-L, Monroe-T

[8]   SHENANDOAH BREAKDOWN
            Instrumental

[9]   MOLLY AND TENBROOKS MEDLEY:
            [a]   MOLLY AND TENBROOKS
                   Monroe-L

            [b]   BLUE MOON OF KENTUCKY
                   Monroe-L

            [c]   SWING LOW SWEET CHARIOT
                   Monroe-L

            [d]   I'LL FLY AWAY
                   Monroe-L

            [e]   I SAW THE LIGHT
                   [Quartet]

[10]   WATERMELON ON THE VINE
            Instrumental

[11]   WILL YOU BE LOVING ANOTHER MAN
            McCoury-L, Monroe-T

Bill Monroe: m	Del McCoury: g	Chubby Wise, Tater Tate (6, 9–11): f
Bill Keith, Blake Williams (9–11): b	Billy Rose: sb	

900627   MCA session; producer, Steve Buchanan
            Sound Emporium, Nashville, Tenn.
            June 27, 1990, 6–9 P.M.

MC 35225   JUST OVER IN THE GLORY LAND (arr. Bill Monroe)   MCAD-10017, BCD 16637
            Bobby Osborne-L, Monroe-T, Sonny Osborne-B, Tate-BS

MC 35230   BAPTIZE ME IN THE CUMBERLAND RIVER (Bill Monroe)   MCAD-10017, BCD 16637
            Monroe-L

Bill Monroe, Bobby Osborne (1): m	Tom Ewing: g	Tater Tate: f
Blake Williams, Sonny Osborne (1): b	Billy Rose: sb	

900700.1   Original Cinema (video) and Copper Creek reissue of movie soundtracks/visuals; producer, Steve Gebhardt
Inside Bill Monroe's house, Goodlettsville, Tenn.
July 1990

[1]   NEVER LEAVE THE "A" STRING
Instrumental

[2]   SOLDIERS JOY   OC-1001
Instrumental

[3]   POCAHONTAS   OC-1001
Instrumental

[4]   CARROLL COUNTY BLUES   OC-1001
Instrumental

[5]   LONESOME MOONLIGHT WALTZ
Instrumental

Bill Monroe: m

900700.2   Original Cinema (video) and Copper Creek reissue of movie soundtracks/visuals; producer, Steve Gebhardt[66]
Bill Monroe's farm, "Fox Hunt," Goodlettsville, Tenn.
July 1990

[1]   OLD GRAY EAGLE   OC-1001
Instrumental

[2]   TOMBSTONE JUNCTION   OC-1001
Instrumental

[3]   HALFWAY TO MOREHEAD
Instrumental

[4]   POCAHONTAS
Instrumental

[5]   UNCLE PEN   OC-1001
Monroe-LV/TC, Skaggs-LC

Bill Monroe: m   Ricky Skaggs: f

900706   Original Cinema (video) reissue of movie soundtracks/visuals; producer, Steve Gebhardt
Bill Monroe's farm, Goodlettsville, Tenn.
July 6, 1990

[1]   TOMBSTONE JUNCTION   OC-1001
Instrumental

[2]   SLOW AND EASY BLUES   OC-1001
Instrumental

Bill Monroe: m   John Hartford (1): f
John Hartford (2): b

900707.1   Original Cinema (video) and Copper Creek reissue of movie soundtracks/visuals;
producer, Steve Gebhardt
Grand Ole Opry, Nashville, Tenn.
July 7, 1990, afternoon show

[1]   IN DESPAIR
Monroe-LV/TC, Ewing-LC, Williams-B

[2]   FAREWELL BLUES   OC-1001
Instrumental

[3]   JUST A LITTLE TALK WITH JESUS
Ewing-L, Monroe-T, Williams-B, Tate-BS

[4]   JOHN HENRY
Monroe-L

[5]   TOMBSTONE JUNCTION   OC-1001
Instrumental

Bill Monroe: m   Tom Ewing: g   Tater Tate: f
Blake Williams: b   Billy Rose: sb

900707.2   Original Cinema (video) reissue of movie soundtracks/visuals; producer, Steve Gebhardt
Grand Ole Opry, Nashville, Tenn.
July 7, 1990, 7:30 P.M. show

[1]   WATERMELON ON THE VINE   OC-1001
Instrumental

[2]   MARY JANE, WILL YOU BE MINE
Monroe-LV/TC, Ewing-LC, Williams-B

[3][67]   TELLICO PLAINS
               Instrumental

[4]   FOOTPRINTS IN THE SNOW
               Monroe-L

[5]   RAW HIDE   OC-1001
               Instrumental

Bill Monroe: m   Tom Ewing: g   Tater Tate: f
Blake Williams: b   Billy Rose: sb

900717   MCA session; producer, Steve Buchanan
               Digital Recorders, Nashville, Tenn.
               July 17, 1990, 6–9 P.M.

MC 35227[68]   YOU'RE DRIFTING AWAY (Bill Monroe)   MCAD-10017, MCAC/D411048,
               Ricky Skaggs-L, Monroe-T, Tom Ewing-B, Tater Tate-BS   BCD 16637

Bill Monroe: m   Ricky Skaggs: g
                               Billy Rose: sb

900724   MCA session; producer, Steve Buchanan
               Reflections, Nashville, Tenn.
               July 24, 1990, 6–9 P.M.

MC 35229   THIS WORLD IS NOT MY HOME (J. R. Baxter Jr.)   MCAD-10017, BCD 16637
               Mac Wiseman-L, Monroe-T, Tate-B

MC 35222   CRYIN' HOLY UNTO THE LORD (Irene Amburgey)   MCAD-10017, BCD 16637
               Ewing-L, Monroe-T, Williams-B, Tate-BS

MC 35224   SHINE HALLELUJAH SHINE (Bill Monroe)   MCAD-10017, BCD 16637
               Ewing-L, Monroe-T, Williams-B, Tate-BS

Bill Monroe: m   Tom Ewing: g   Tater Tate: f
Blake Williams: b   Billy Rose: sb

900919   Original Cinema (video) and Copper Creek reissue of movie soundtracks/visuals; producer, Steve Gebhardt
Bill's 79th birthday party, Longhollow Jamboree,[69] Goodlettsville, Tenn.
Sept. 19, 1990

[1]   UNCLE PEN
Monroe-LV/TC

[2]   MULE SKINNER BLUES
Monroe-L

[3]   BLUE MOON OF KENTUCKY
Monroe-L

[4]   TOMBSTONE JUNCTION   OC-1001
Instrumental

[5]   WALK SOFTLY ON THIS HOUSE [sic] OF MINE
Monroe-L

[6]   BLUEGRASS BREAKDOWN
Instrumental

[7]   THE WAYFARING STRANGER
Monroe-L (?)

[8][70]   OLD PAL OF MINE
?

Bill Monroe: m	Wayne Lewis, Tom Ewing: g	John Hartford, Jimmy Campbell: f
Blake Williams: b	Tater Tate: sb	

901028   Shanachie (Video) reissue of movie soundtracks/visuals; producers, Rachel Liebling and Andrew Serwer
Blue Grass Special (Monroe's Bus), parking lot, Piermont, N.Y.
Oct. 28, 1990

[1]   I'M ON MY WAY TO THE OLD HOME   SHA 604
Monroe recites lyrics

[2]   UNCLE PEN   SHA 604
Monroe recites lyrics

[3]   OLD OLD HOUSE   SHA 604
Monroe-L

No instruments used.

910913   Original Cinema (video) and Copper Creek reissue of movie soundtracks/visuals;
producer, Steve Gebhardt
Brown County Jamboree Park, Bean Blossom, Ind.
Sept. 13, 1991, evening show

[1]   UNCLE PEN
Monroe-LV/TC, Ewing-LC, Williams-B

[2]   THE OLD OLD HOUSE
Monroe-L

[3]   SOUTHERN FLAVOR   OC-1001
Instrumental

Bill Monroe: m   Tom Ewing, Marty Stuart (3): g   Jimmy Campbell: f
Blake Williams: b   Tater Tate: sb

920000   Freeland session for Ralph Stanley; producer, Charles R. Freeland[71]
Music Row Audio, Nashville, Tenn.
1992

[1]   LETTER FROM MY DARLING   CRFRC CD-9001
Stanley-L, Monroe-T

[2]   I'LL MEET YOU IN CHURCH SUNDAY MORNING   CRFRC CD-9001
Stanley-L, Monroe-T, Cooke-B, Shelton Faezell-BS

Bill Monroe: m   Ernie Thacker, Junior Bankenship: g   Curly Ray Cline, Art Stamper: f
Ralph Stanley: b   Jack Cooke: sb

920300   Sugar Hill session for Larry Cordle, Glen Duncan, and Lonesome Standard Time; producers,
Glen Duncan and Larry Cordle
Music Row Audio, Nashville, Tenn.
March 1992

[1]   KENTUCKY KING[72] (L Cordle, J. Rushing)   SH-CD-3802
Cordle-L, Duncan-T, Southards-B

Bill Monroe, Butch Baldassari: m   Larry Cordle: g   Glen Duncan: f (including
Mike Bub: b   Wayne Southards: esb   overdub harmonies)

920303   Homespun Tapes (Video) session; producer, "From a concept developed by Homespun Tapes in Collaboration with Ralph Rinzler and John Hartford"[73]
Imagemaker Productions (video studio), Nashville, Tenn.
March 3, 1992

[1]   SWEET BLUE EYED DARLING   VD-MON-MN01
       Ewing-L, Monroe-T, Cupp-B

[2]   POOR WHITE FOLKS   VD-MON-MN01
       Monroe-L

[3]   FROG ON A LILY PAD   VD-MON-MN01
       Instrumental

[4]   GALLEY NIPPER   VD-MON-MN01
       Instrumental

[5]   LONESOME MOONLIGHT WALTZ   VD-MON-MN01
       Instrumental

[6]   DUSTY MILLER   VD-MON-MN01
       Instrumental

[7]   SALLY GOODIN   VD-MON-MN01
       Instrumental

[8]   JENNY LYNN   VD-MON-MN01
       Instrumental

[9]   KATY HILL   VD-MON-MN01
       Instrumental

[10]   SMOKY MOUNTAIN SCHOTTISCHE   VD-MON-MN01
       Instrumental

[11]   MULE SKINNER BLUES   VD-MON-MN01
       Instrumental

[12]   OZARK RAG   VD-MON-MN01
       Instrumental

[13]   SLOW AND EASY BLUES   VD-MON-MN01
       Instrumental

[14]   TENNESSEE BLUES   VD-MON-MN01
       Instrumental

[15]   ROCKY ROAD BLUES   VD-MON-MN01
             Monroe-L

[16]   MEMORIES OF MOTHER AND DAD   VD-MON-MN01
             Ewing-L, Monroe-T

[17]   TOMBSTONE JUNCTION   VD-MON-MN01
             Instrumental

[18]   KENTUCKY WALTZ   VD-MON-MN01
             Instrumental

[19]   I'M ON MY WAY BACK TO THE OLD HOME   VD-MON-MN01
             Monroe-LV/TC, Ewing-LC, Cupp-B

[20]   PIKE COUNTY BREAKDOWN   VD-MON-MN01
             Instrumental

[21]   NEVER LEAVE THE "A" STRING   VD-MON-MN01
             Instrumental

[22]   GET UP JOHN   VD-MON-MN01
             Instrumental

[23]   SOUTHERN FLAVOR   VD-MON-MN01
             Instrumental

[24]   WHEEL HOSS   VD-MON-MN01
             Instrumental

[25]   ROANOKE   VD-MON-MN01
             Instrumental

[26]   RAW HIDE   VD-MON-MN01
             Instrumental

[27]   BLUE GRASS BREAKDOWN   VD-MON-MN01
             Instrumental

[28]   A CONVERSATION WITH BILL MONROE   VD-MON-MN01
             Monroe, John Hartford

[29]   OLD JOE CLARK   VD-MON-MN01
             Monroe-L

[30]   MY LAST DAYS ON EARTH   VD-MON-MN01
        Instrumental

Bill Monroe (except 11, 12,   Tom Ewing (except 28, 29),   Jimmy Campbell (except 28, 29): f
  28, 29): m   Bill Monroe (11, 12): g
Dana Cupp (except 28, 29): b   Tater Tate (except 28, 29): sb

---

920920   Recording made for Warner Brothers; producer, Mark O'Connor
               The Sound Emporium, Nashville, Tenn.
               Sun., Sept. 20, 1992

[1]   GOLD RUSH (Bill Monroe)   W 9 45257–2, M18983,
        Instrumental   SA 06076–8G420–2

Bill Monroe: m   Dan Crary: g   Mark O'Connor, Byron Berline: f
John Hickman: b   Roy Huskey Jr.: sb

931114   On-spec session; producer, Vic Gabany
               Imagine Studios, Nashville, Tenn.
               Nov. 14, 1993

[1]   FRIDAY NIGHT AT THE OPRY
(4 takes)   Instrumental

[2]   TOMBSTONE JUNCTION
(4 takes)   Instrumental

[3]   NORTHERN WHITE CLOUDS
(3 takes)   Instrumental

[4]   SLOW AND EASY BLUES
(4 takes)   Instrumental

Bill Monroe: m   Tom Ewing: g   Robert Bowlin: f
Dana Cupp: b   Tater Tate: sb

940109.1   On-spec session; producer, Vic Gabany[74]
                 Imagine Studios, Nashville, Tenn.
                 Jan. 9, 1994, 2–5 P.M.

[1]   TOMBSTONE JUNCTION
(1 take)   Instrumental

[2]   JACK ACROSS THE WAY
(1 take)   Instrumental

[3]   FROG ON THE LILY PAD
(5 takes)   Instrumental

MC 42973   BOSTON BOY (traditional, arr. Bill Monroe)   MCAC/D4–11048, BCD 16637
                 Instrumental

[5]   SMOKEY MOUNTAIN SCHOTTISCHE
(2 takes)   Instrumental

[6]   ROXANNA WALTZ
(3 takes)   Instrumental

[7]   SLOW & EASY BLUES
(1 take)   Instrumental

Bill Monroe: m   Tom Ewing: g   Robert Bowlin, Jimmy Campbell (1): fl
Dana Cupp: b   Tater Tate: sb

940109.2   Arista session, overdub, for Pam Tillis; producer, Pam Tillis and Steve Fishell
                 Imagine Studios, Nashville, Tenn.
                 Jan. 9, 1994, 5–7 P.M.[75]

[1]   TIL ALL THE LONELY'S GONE (Pam Tillis, Bob DiPiero,   AR 07822 18758–2
                    John Scott Sherrill)
                 Pam Tillis, Mel Tillis-L; Cindy Tillis Westmoreland,
                    Connie Tillis Howden, Carrie Tillis, Mel Tillis Jr. backup vocals

Bill Monroe: m[76]   John Jorgenson, Biff Watson,   Sam Bush: f
John Jarvis: pno   Dan Dugmore: g[77]   Greg Leisz: Dobro
                                  Willie Weeks: sb
                                  Milton Sledge: dr. & percussion

940522   On-spec session; producer, Vic Gabany[78]
                 Imagine Studios, Nashville, Tenn.
                 May 22, 1994

[1]   POCAHONTAS[79]
(2 takes)   Instrumental

[2]   OLD FARM BLUES
(3 takes)   Instrumental

[3]   TWO FINGER WALTZ
   (2 takes)   Instrumental

[4]   LAND OF LINCOLN
   (5 takes)   Instrumental

[5]   WATERMELON HANGING ON THE VINE[80]
   (1 take)   Instrumental

Bill Monroe: m   Tom Ewing: g   Robert Bowlin: f
Dana Cupp: b   Tater Tate: sb

940600   On-spec album project; producer, Vic Gabany
                  Bill Monroe's Blue Grass Festival, Bean Blossom, Ind.
                  June 1994

[data not yet obtained]

940606   Overdub session for Warner Brothers for a Shawn Camp album; producer, Emory Gordy Jr.
                  Woodland Studio, Nashville, Tenn.
                  June 6, 1994

[1]   WORN THROUGH STONE (Shawn Camp and John Scott Sherrill)
                Tom Ewing-L, Bill Monroe-T, Dana Cupp-B, Tater Tate-BS

[no instruments used at session]

940700   MCA session for *The Music of Bill Monroe: The Radio Special;*[81] producer, Tim Riley
                  Audio Productions, Nashville, Tenn.
                  Mid-1994

[1]   SOUTHERN FLAVOR   MCA3P-3256, BCD 16637
                Instrumental

[2]   NEVER LEAVE THE "A" STRING   MCA3P-3256, BCD 16637
                Instrumental

[3]   TENNESSEE BLUES   MCA3P-3256, BCD 16637
                Instrumental

[4]   I'D LOVE TO BE OVER YONDER   MCA3P-3256, BCD 16637
                Instrumental

[5]	RAWHIDE Instrumental	MCA3P-3256, BCD 16637

[6]	SALLY GOODIN Instrumental	MCA3P-3256, BCD 16637

Bill Monroe, m   Marty Stuart (1, 3–5): g

940727   My Label session for Kathy Chiavola; producer, Kathy Chiavola[82]
(Bill Monroe's cabin), Goodletsville, Tenn./Top of the Hill Studio, Nashville, Tenn.
July 27, 1994/ca. Oct. 21, 1994

[1]	STAY AWAY FROM ME (Bill Monroe) Monroe L, Chiavola-T	KCP 1001 CD

Bill Monroe: m   Kathy Chiavola: g   Randy Howard: f
Butch Robins: b   Kurt Storey: sb

941028   Hay Holler session for Butch Robins; producers, Joseph C. Robins and Kerry Hay
Hillsboro High School Vocational Studio, Nashville, Tenn.
Oct. 28, 1994[83]

[1]	I'D LIKE TO BE OVER YONDER (Bill Monroe) Instrumental	HHH-CD-108

[2]	THE GOLDEN WEST (Bill Monroe) Instrumental	HHH-CD-108

Bill Monroe, Mike Compton: m   David Grier: g   Jimmy Campbell: f
Butch Robins: b   Marvin Cockram, Mike Bub (2): sb[84]

941030   Hay Holler session for Butch Robins; producers, Joseph C. Robins and Kerry Hay
Top O' The Hill Recorders, Nashville, Tenn.
Oct. 30, 1994[85]

[1]	MY FATHER'S FOOTSTEPS (Bill Monroe) Instrumental	HHH-CD-108

[2]	OLD LONESOME WALTZ (Bill Monroe) Instrumental	HHH-CD-108

[3]   TANYARDS (Bill Monroe)   HHH-CD-108
       Instrumental

Bill Monroe, Mike Compton: m   David Grier: g   Jimmy Campbell (2, 3), Buddy
Butch Robins: b   Marvin Cockram (3),   Spicher (3): f
                                       Mike Bub (1, 2): sb

941108   Sugar Hill session for Byron Berline; producer, Byron Berline
              Champagne Studios, Nashville, Tenn.
              Nov. 8, 1994

[1]   SALLY GOODIN (traditional, arr. Byron Berline)   SH CD 3838
       Instrumental

Bill Monroe: m   Randy Scruggs: g   Byron Berline: f
Earl Scruggs: b   James Monroe: sb

941130   Copper Creek session for Gary Brewer; producers, Gary Brewer and Stretchgrass Productions
              Falk Recording Studio, Louisville, Ky./Fox Farm Recording, Nashville, Tenn.
              Nov. 30[86]/Dec. 8,[87] 1994

[1]   THE OZARK RAG (Bill Monroe)   CCCD-0137
       Instrumental

[2]   THE OLD KENTUCKY BLUES (Bill Monroe)   CCCD-0137
       Instrumental

Bill Monroe, Gary Brewer (1): m   Gary Brewer: g   Ron Stewart (1, 2): f
Ron Stewart (1): b   Dale "Punch" Taylor: sb   Josh Graves (2): d

---

950320   Red Clay session for Jimmy Campbell; producer, Jimmy Campbell
              Top of the Hill Studio, Nashville, Tenn.
              March 20, 1995

[1]   DOWN YONDER (Old Time)   RC 113
       Instrumental

[2]   WATSONS BLUES (B. Monroe)   RC 113
       Instrumental

[3]   TEXAS QUICKSTEP (Old Time)   RC 113
       Instrumental

[4]	LONESOME OLD FARMER (B. Monroe) Instrumental	RC 113
[5]	WOODSTOCK HORNPIPE (B. Monroe) Instrumental	RC 113
[6]	JENNY LYNN (Old Time) Instrumental	RC 113
[7]	FIDDLERS BLUES (B. Monroe) Instrumental	RC 113
[8]	OLD TENNESSEE RIVER (J. Campbell, B. Monroe, B. Williams) Instrumental	RC 113
[9]	CHILLY WINDS OF SHANNON (B. Monroe) Instrumental	RC 113
[10]	SOLDIERS JOY (Old Time) Instrumental	RC 113
[11]	EBENEZER SCROOGE (B. Monroe) Instrumental	RC 113
[12]	BLUES FOR CASEY C. Campbell, B. Monroe) Instrumental	RC 113

Bill Monroe, Mike
  Compton (5, 11): m
Dana Cupp: b
	Ronny McCoury: g
	Mike Bub: sb
		Buddy Spicher (4),
		  Robert Bolin (7, 11),
		  Jimmy Campbell: f

950600   On-spec album project; producer, Vic Gabany
Bill Monroe's Blue Grass Festival, Bean Blossom, Ind.
June 1995

960221   K-Tel session for Billy and Terry Smith; producers, Billy and Terry Smith
Tracking Station Recording Studio, Nashville, Tenn.
Feb. 21, 1996

[1]	MULE SKINNER BLUES (Rogers/Vaughn) B. Smith-L	KT 3642–2

[2]	WALK SOFTLY ON THIS HEART OF MINE (Landers/Monroe)	KT 3642–2
	B. Smith-L, T. Smith-B and T, except Monroe-T last chorus	

[3]	BLUE MOON OF KENTUCKY (Monroe)	KT 3642–2
	Monroe-L	

Bill Monroe: m	Billy Smith: g	Robert Bowlin: f
Charlie Cushman: b	Terry Smith: sb	

Notes

1. The proper title of this piece is "Come Hither to Go Yonder."

2. The proper title of this piece is "Old Daingerfield."

3. See the following two sessions for vocal and string section overdub data.

4. Monroe was backed in this performance, on the occasion of being awarded the National Heritage Fellowship, by Hazel Dickens and Friends.

5. According to Vic Gabany, postproduction was done at Burns Station Sound, Burns, Tenn., by Jack Barlow.

6. Gabany dated this session as taking place on July 3, but according to Jeff Place of the Smithsonian, Monroe was in Washington at an awards ceremony on July 3 (see previous entry). *Bluegrass Unlimited*'s personal appearances listings for July 1982 have Monroe at a festival in Cathedral Caverns, Woodville, Ala., from July 2–5. According to Tom Ewing, "on the 2nd [Monroe] was part of a . . . show near Alvord, Texas. He flew . . . to DC on the . . . 3rd, then flew to Alabama on the 4th for the session" (email to Neil V. Rosenberg, Aug. 26, 2003).

7. According to Blake Williams, Monroe asked the union for a bass singer, and they also sent a baritone vocalist. Both sang these parts on the recording; Williams and Hembree, who usually sang those parts, did not sing on this session.

8. Gabany notes that an additional singer, John Mohr, was present. Monroe got him for this engagement because bassist Hembree, who sang bass in the quartet, was uncertain about the gig as his wife was pregnant and due around this date. Although Hembree was present, Mohr sang all bass vocal parts.

9. Dialog between Monroe and Tillis at start of recording.

10. Baker overdubbed a second fiddle part.

11. Dialog between Monroe and Larry Gatlin at start of recording. Tom Ewing writes, "No one will ever know for sure concerning vocal parts. Larry usually sings lead, Steve the low harmony parts, and Rudy the high harmonies." Ewing to Rosenberg, March 2000.

12. Title given as "My Sweet Darlin'" on the jacket of MCA-5435.

13. Dialog between Monroe and Skaggs at start of recording.

14. Skaggs takes the guitar break.

15. Dialog between Monroe and Hartford at start of recording.

16. Dialog between Monroe and Jennings at start of recording. Monroe's vocal is barely audible in mix on lines 1–2 of the verses.

17. Dialog between Monroe and Cash at start of recording.

18. Dialog between Monroe and one member of the Oak Ridge Boys at start of recording. The Oak Ridge Boys provide dialog over the final fade-out. The Oak Ridge Boys at this time consisted of Duane Allen, lead; Joe Bonsall, tenor; William Lee Golden, baritone; and Richard Sterban, bass.

19. Stuart takes the guitar break.

20. Baker takes last fiddle break solo.

21. Dialog between Monroe and Nelson at start of recording.

22. Nelson takes the guitar break.

23. Dialog between Monroe and Harris at start of recording.

24. Dialog between Monroe and Mandrell at start of recording.

25. The liner notes identify this as a performance "at a showcase club" on January 28, 1984, but Monroe did not play in New York City on that date, and Roland White, who was driving bus for Monroe that fall, identified the club as the Bottom Line and time as the fall of 1983.

26. Monroe's performance at the Bottom Line is listed in *The New Yorker*, Dec. 12, 1983, 6; the January 1984 date given in the liner notes was probably the date on which it was broadcast.

27. The proper title is "I'm on My Way to the Old Home."

28. The composer credit is for the incorrect title; the correct composer credit is Bill Monroe.

29. Only Lewis is introduced; Williams is mentioned; Baker is identified on the basis of style. Hembree confirmed his presence (telephone conversation to Rosenberg, Aug. 8, 2006).

30. The date of this recording is approximate because it consists of overdubs. Ricky Skaggs stated in an interview that Monroe "did it as an overdub" (*Frets*, March 1985, 37). We have found records of three sessions at which Skaggs and band worked on this tune. At the first, all of the musicians listed above except Monroe are listed. "Something in My Heart" (135337) and "I'm Ready" (135339) were also worked on at that time. At the second session Skaggs and Bouton worked on these three tunes plus "I'll Take the Blame." At the third session Smith and steel guitarist Lloyd Green worked on "Wheel Hoss," "I'm Ready," and "Rendezvous." It is not known when Monroe did his overdub.

31. The correct title is "Dancin' in Branson."

32. This is the first session at which Bill played his newly repaired F-5. It had been vandalized on November 13, 1985, and was repaired and returned to him on February 25, 1986. Tom Ewing, *The Bill Monroe Reader* (Urbana: University of Illinois Press, 2000), 182–83.

33. This is the same song as the one entitled "The Old Cross Road" on Monroe's original Columbia recording.

34. According to producer Porter Wagoner, this and the following

were overdub sessions; only Monroe was present "on the floor." Interview with Emory Gordy Jr., Oct. 23, 2001.

35. MCA files were found by Richard Weize at the company's archives in Los Angeles; date of safety master edit reel: September 11, 1997 (Richard Weize to Charles Wolfe, fax, March 9, 2001).

36. Tom Ewing has observed that "Bill and John Candy attempted to sing 'Blue Moon of Kentucky' in unison, it didn't work out too well" (email to Rosenberg, Feb. 9, 2001).

37. This is the first session for the *Southern Flavor* album. Vic Gabany says he was a "consultant" engineer on the album because at this time MCA required an in-house engineer for its projects. He'd been sitting in on Monroe sessions as an engineer since 1971. Album credits, however, suggest that the "consultant" label came earlier.

38. This session is described in detail in Thomas Goldsmith, "Bill Monroe in the Studio," *Bluegrass Unlimited* 23 (April 1989): 46–48. The article includes photographs by Raymond Huffmaster.

39. Tom Ewing has said, "This was 'very strange'—Bill didn't really know how it went. There were strange time changes and producer Emory Gordy told them to just let Bill go ahead and do it and get it over rather than trying to work it out with him, as they had tried to do" (Ewing to Rosenberg, telephone conversation, Sept. 1, 1998).

40. "I wrote the first verse of 'The Days Gone By' and reminded Bill of this later. Eventually he arranged to give me one-fourth credit on the lyrics." Ewing to Wolfe.

41. "Bill told me that this last one [-62] was sung at the funeral for Uncle Pen's son Cecil." Ewing to Rosenberg, March 2000.

42. Introductions by Grant Turner.

43. The AFofM sheet for this session gives these three dates and states, "See attached list," but no list was attached. The two pieces reissued on MCAD 4–11048 are said in the notes to that set to have been recorded on June 14. May 5 was a Friday, June 13 a Tuesday, June 14 a Wednesday, and June 27 a Tuesday. Tom Ewing notes, "Some of this was recorded at Opry Matinees on June 13th and 27th, but not all. Some was recorded on Friday and Saturday nights, but I have no firm notes on this. I recall recording "Precious Memories" one weekday evening without an audience." (Ewing to Rosenberg, March 2000).

44. In his introduction to this performance, Monroe states, "The title is 'My Sweet Blue Eyed Darlin.'"

45. Although each tune has its own track number on the CD, there has been little or no editing done to the radio progam.

46. In spite of its title, this performance has Rodgers's original lyrics.

47. Monroe invites the audience to sing and clap along with this song, something he'd done occasionally for several decades.

48. Monroe introduces this song with a joke he frequently used about its title.

49. Williams does some of the emcee work.

50. A fragment, shot from behind Monroe. This and the three shots from 890913 come at the same point in the film.

51. Filmed at the Bean Blossom sunset jam; many other musicians in addition to Monroe and the Blue Grass Boys are seen and heard.

52. Filmed onstage at Bean Blossom, with the camera focusing on dancers.

53. Filmed onstage at Bean Blossom on Sunday, June 18th.

54. The composer credit is incorrect; this is a Lester Flatt composition.

55. Although Monroe says "so long and goodbye," that is not the title of the piece; it is "Watermelon Hanging on the Vine," Monroe's theme song, which is why the title has been placed in brackets.

56. The interview was broadcast on WDR from Cologne on the night of October 20, 1989, and interspersed with recordings from the concert of July 30, 1989.

57. Monroe and Ewing sang while the Blue Grass Boys played cards. Tom Ewing recalls that "the bus sequence was shot on Wednesday, 9/13/89, prior to Bill's birthday party that evening at the Bell Cove Club in Hendersonville. (We were all a little disgruntled at having to do this since we'd just gotten back from Sunset Park [Sept. 10] and were heading to MO and IL in a couple of days [Sept. 15 and 16], then leaving for Japan on 9/19)." Ewing to Rosenberg, March 2002.

58. "Jim McReynolds played guitar on (-31)," Ewing remembers, "but it wasn't miked." Ewing to Rosenberg, March 2002.

59. Jacky Christian dances; Wayne Lewis does the introductions.

60. Jacky Christian dances; Wayne Lewis does the introductions.

61. The notes to RHY-1015 incorrectly date this as being on June 16.

62. The notes to RHY-1015 incorrectly date this as being on June 16.

63. Jacky Christian dances; Wayne Lewis does the introductions.

64. Ewing writes: "2nd 'set'" (Ewing to Rosenberg, March 2000).

65. Jacky Christian dances to this piece.

66. The Copper Creek notes state "with Ricky Skaggs and Steve Buchanan." Buchanan was Monroe's producer at the time; it is not known what his role was in this session.

67. Monroe introduces this as a "number he wrote last night, in about thirty seconds."

68. Although this is listed here as a single session, it is in fact the product of three separate sessions. According to Tom Ewing, "Bill was not present. Ewing and Tate recorded harmony vocals with Skaggs' already-recorded lead, and Rose added string bass. Bill dubbed in tenor and mandolin later, date unknown." Ewing to Rosenberg, March 2000

69. The personnel on this session is conjectural.

70. This piece is cut to while in progress. It is probably "Goodbye Old Pal."

71. On September 15, 1997, Dick Freeland wrote to Neil V. Rosenberg, "An attempt was made at another tune—"Sweetheart of Mine Can't You Hear Me Calling." The initial quality was not acceptable and the recording was never completed, and to the best of my recollection nothing remains of that attempt."

72. This song about Monroe ends with an instrumental chorus version of his longtime theme "Watermelon Hanging on the Vine." "I played on 'Kentucky King'—Bill played on 'The Watermelon,'" Butch Baldassari recalled (Baldassari to Rosenberg, March 1999).

73. The cover of the video package describes it as "produced by Smithsonian/Folkways and Homespun Video." The program opens with an introduction by Ralph Rinzler and Sam Bush that was not recorded at the same time as Monroe's performance. John Hartford is present throughout the session with Monroe, asking questions and engaging in dialog with him. At several points Rinzler can be heard speaking to Monroe off-camera. The video closes with the White House concert recording described in session 800807.

74. The data are taken from the notes of Vic Gabany; Tom Ewing writes, "Bill should be listed as composer of all tunes except 'Boston Boy' of course." Ewing to Rosenberg, March 2000.

75. Date from Vic Gabany.

76. Only Monroe played at the overdub session. "Dana Cupp has heard recording and says that most of the audible mandolin is by Bush." Ewing to Rosenberg, March 2000.

77. Jorgenson, lead electric guitar; Watson, acoustic guitar; and Dugmore, electric guitar.

78. Data are from the notes of Vic Gabany.

79. "Bill is composer of [1] through [4]." Ewing to Rosenberg, March 2000.

80. A short rendition of Monroe's theme.

81. This hour-long promotional album's six tracks, narrated by Stuart, included nine earlier ones from MCAD 4–11048: "What Would You Give in Exchange for Your Soul," "Mule Skinner Blues," "It's Mighty Dark to Travel," "Blue Moon of Kentucky," "Uncle Pen," "On and On," "Going Up Caney," "A Voice from on High," and "My Last Days on Earth." All except the first are heard in their entirety. Numbers [1] and [6] from this session are heard under the narration.

82. Monroe and Chiavola recorded at Monroe's home; the other parts were overdubbed in Nashville.

83. Date and sequence from Butch Robins, *What I Know 'bout What I Know* (Bloomington, Ind.: First Books Library, 2003).

84. Liner notes credit Cockram with bass on both [1] and [2]; Robins (*What I Know,* 199) credits Mike Bub with bass on [2].

85. Dates, sequence from Robins, 198–99.

86. Bed tracks recorded November 30 in Louisville: Brewer (g), Stewart, and Taylor.

87. Overdubs recorded on December 8 in Nashville: Monroe, Brewer (g, m), and Graves.

NUMERICAL LISTING
OF RELEASES

Following the title and composer credit of every master listed in the discographies come the catalog descriptors: a set of symbols, either numbers or a combination of letters and numbers, used by a recording company to identify a published recording in their catalog. Each of these denotes a specific publication on which the recording has been released—a 78, 45, EP, LP, CD, or video. What follows lists those releases in full and gives their date of publication if known.

The list is organized alphabetically by company (company names in bold face) and by chronological or numerical order within companies, using the *catalog descriptors* printed on record or disc labels and/or on album containers. The list includes two basic types of publication: singles and albums.

A *single* is any recording that includes no more than two masters. In the discographical entries for individual masters, singles are in the first column to the right of the song copyright credit. Monroe's first singles on Victor's Bluebird label were ten-inch discs that were played on turntables revolving at the speed of 78-rpm (revolutions per minute). In the late 1940s microgroove technology enabled record manufacturers to issue singles on seven-inch records. At first there were competing seven-inch formats. Columbia championed $33\frac{1}{3}$-rpm singles, while Victor and other manufacturers favored 45-rpm singles with large center holes. The latter format won out. For a short time, however, Monroe's Columbia singles were released in three different singles formats: ten-inch, 78-rpm; 7–inch, $33\frac{1}{3}$-rpm; and seven-inch, 45-rpm. The $33\frac{1}{3}$-rpm singles had their own numerical series. Otherwise, the same numbers were used for singles whether on 78- or 45-rpm format. During the early 1950s his Decca singles were released on both 78-rpm and 45-rpm singles, but by 1956 the 78s were discontinued.

Monroe's singles were released by three companies: Columbia, Decca/MCA, and Victor. In the entries for those companies, each single's number appears on the left, followed by the titles of the two masters it contains, one on the same line as the number, the other directly beneath it. To the far right comes the date of publication:

| 20552 2–151 | TOY HEART | March 14, 1949 |
| | BLUE GRASS BREAKDOWN | |

In the late 1930s and early 1940s Montgomery Ward issued all of the Monroe Brothers and Bill Monroe Bluebird recordings on their label. Some of these paired the same two masters as the Bluebird releases while others mixed the masters in different combinations. A concordance that shows these pairings is included in the Victor section of the list.

An *album* is any recording that includes more than two masters. In the discographical entries for individual masters, catalog descriptors for albums and videos are in the second column to the right of the song's copyright credit. The earliest phonograph albums collected ten-inch or twelve-inch, 78-rpm singles in a binding like that of a photograph album (hence the name). When long-playing (LP) microgroove ten- or twelve-inch, 33⅓-rpm records were introduced in the late 1940s, they, too, were called albums. During the 1950s microgroove technology was also applied to singles, resulting in seven-inch, 45-rpm extended play (EP) albums. Between the 1970s and the 1990s some albums were also issued on cassettes. These are not listed separately because as far as we know all cassette publications used the same numbers and had the same contents as the LPs and CDs they paralleled. During the 1980s compact disc (CD) technology began to replace the earlier phonograph records, and for a period albums were released in both LP and CD formats. We use the word *album* to refer to all of these technologies. Although, technically speaking, videos are not albums, they are listed here in the same place as albums because they, too, can contain more than two masters.

Bill Monroe's recordings have appeared in all album formats, from a single Monroe Brothers 78 in a Victor album, a number of EP albums, through twelve-inch LP albums (we know of no ten-inch albums) and, in his final decade, CD albums.

Most of the companies in this list have issued only albums. In the entries for those companies, each album's catalog descriptor is on the left, followed by the title of the album. To the far right comes the date of publication. Annotative information (like the series title) is placed beneath the catalog descriptor on the left, indented. Here is an example from the Copper Creek listings:

| CCRS-7001 | Wildwood Flower: Classic Country Performances | 2003 |
| Roots Series Volume 1 | | |

In the 1970s, MCA republished Monroe's earlier Decca albums unchanged except for new MCA catalog descriptors. A concordance that shows the relationships between the two sets of descriptors is included in the Decca/MCA section of the list.

All album catalog descriptors in this list were published with or have been assigned by us a set of letters that precede their number in the discographical entries for individual masters. These letters function as abbreviated symbols for the full names of the publishers. "Abbreviations: Recording Publishers," an alphabethical index of these letter prefixes along with the name of the companies associated with them, is given below.

Wherever possible, we have provided dates of publication. The primary source has been the publisher. Publishers' dates come from company files, from catalogs, and from copyright information included on labels and album covers or boxes. When other sources for dates have been consulted, an abbreviation follows the date. "Abbreviations: Release Date Publishers," a brief list of these, is given below.

USING THE LIST WITH THE DISCOGRAPHY

What follows is how to trace the recordings on which a master in the discography was published. The example, "Danny Boy," is the song on which Monroe was working at the session of November 30, 1961, session 611130 (when the photograph on this book's jacket was taken). The song is listed in the discography section at the end of chapter 6 (p.139).

NA 11819	DANNY BOY (Fred E. Weatherly)	31409	ED 2753, DL 4266,
11451	Monroe-L		DL 7–5010,
			BCD 15529, SHA 604

The first catalog descriptor to the right of the copyright credit identifies the single on which the song was published. Session 611130 was a Decca session, so this single is listed under Decca/MCA as follows:

| 31409 | TOY HEART | July 2, 1962, July 7 1962B |
| | DANNY BOY | |

These lines indicate that the single paired "Danny Boy" with "Toy Heart," that it was published by Decca in early July 1962, and that it was reviewed soon after in *Billboard*.

The rest of the catalog descriptors in the discographical listing for "Danny Boy" are in the album column. Checking the abbreviation in "Abbreviations: Recording Publishers" for the first three album catalog descriptors—ED and DL—shows that they, too, are listed under Decca/MCA:

ED 2753	DANNY BOY	November 25, 1963
	BLUE RIDGE MOUNTAIN BLUES	
	HOW WILL I EXPLAIN ABOUT YOU	
	BIG SANDY RIVER	
DL 4266	*Blue Grass Ramble*	June 11, 1962, June 16, 1962B
DL 7–5010	*Bill Monroe's Greatest Hits*	June 17, 1968

These lines indicate that the first album in which "Danny Boy" was included came out about a month before the single, that the song was published a year later in an EP with three pieces from another album and then republished in a "Greatest Hits" album in 1968.

Checking the abbreviation for the final two album catalog descriptors—BCD and SHA—leads to two other companies. The first is Bear Family:

| BCD 15529 | *Bill Monroe: Bluegrass 1959–1969* | 1991 |

The second is Shanachie:

| SHA 604 | *High Lonesome* | 1994 |

Bear Family's four-CD boxed set includes all of Monroe's recordings from the period covered in chronological order along with a detailed brochure by Neil Rosenberg and Charles Wolfe. In Shanachie's video, Rachel Liebling combined "Danny Boy" in the sound track with visual shots of rural scenes to evoke a romantic memory of Monroe's youth.

ABBREVIATIONS: RECORDING PUBLISHERS

The following letters or combinations of letters preface some single and all album numbers to the right of tune titles and composer credits in the discography. Full information, including title and, where known, date of release, is listed under the company name.

A	Sony Music Special Products		ED	Decca/MCA
ABC-CLIO	ABC-CLIO and Documentary Arts			
ACD	(with two-digit number) Acoustic Disc		FAF	Smithsonian Institution
ACD	(with five-digit number): . . . And More Bears (Bear		FBN	FBN
	Family subsidiary)		FC	Columbia
ACLI	Victor		FE	Epic, *see* Columbia
A.G.	Stack-O-Hits		FF	Flying Fish
API	Atteiram			
APL	Victor		G	Gabriel Communications
APM	Victor		GHD	Green Hill
AR	Arista		GV	Green Valley Records
AXM	Bluebird; *see* Victor			
			H	Harmony, *see* Columbia
B	Harmony, *see* Columbia		HCD	Hollywood
BB	Bluebird; *see* Victor		HHH	Hay Holler
BCD	Bear Family		Hip-O	Hip-O
BGC	Bluegrass Classics		HL	Harmony, *see* Columbia
BMG	Victor			
BO	Universal Special Products		J	Varied Directions Inc.
BPM	Blue Plate Music		J2K	Columbia
BS	Blue Grass Special		JAS	Bear Family
			JB	Opryland Home Video
C2K	Columbia			
C4K	Legacy; *see* Columbia		K	Kemtac
CAL	Camden; *see* Victor		KCP	My Label
CC	Copper Creek		KT	K-Tel
CCC	Classic Country Collection			
CCCD	Copper Creek		LBC	Library of Congress
CCRS	Copper Creek Roots Series		LPM	Victor
CCS	County		LPV	Victor
CD	CMH			
CK	Columbia		M	Time-Life
CMA	Country Music Association		MCA	Decca/MCA
CO	County		MCA3P	Decca/MCA
CPL	Victor		MCAD	Decca/MCA
CR	Country Road		MME	Music Mill Entertainment
CRFRC	Freeland Records		MW	Montgomery Ward; *see* Victor
CS	Columbia			
			NH	New Haven
DD	Dust-to-Digital		NW	New World
DL	Decca/MCA			

OC	Original Cinema	SF	Smithsonian/Folkways
		SH	Sugar Hill
P	Victor	SHA	Shanachie
PALM	Palm Pictures	SLP	Rebel
PS	Park South Records	SRM	Mercury
PV	Paramount Pictures	SS	Rounder
QS	Intermedia	T	Capitol
		TJ	Thrill Jockey
R	Time-Life	TLCW	Time Life
R2	Rhino		
RC	Red Clay	V	Vanguard
RCA	Victor	VCD	Vanguard
Rdr	Rounder	VD	Homespun Tapes
REB	Rebel of Canada	Vi	Victor
RHY	Rural Rhythm	VL	Vocalion, *see* Decca/MCA
RO	Smithsonian Institution	VLV	Vic Lewis Video
RR	Raintree		
RVN	Revenant	W	Warner
		WW	West Hill Audio Archives
SA	Sanctuary		
SEA	Silver Eagle		

ABBREVIATIONS: RELEASE DATE PUBLISHERS

The following letters are placed at the end of dates to indicate the source of a date. *Billboard* and *Schwann* are music trade publications; Meade et al. is a research discography. Dates that do not have an abbreviation following them come from the company that published the recording.

B   *Billboard* (weekly magazine)

M   Guthrie T. Meade Jr., with Dick Spottswood and Douglas S. Meade, *Country Music Sources: A Biblio-Discography of Commercially Recorded Traditional Music* (Chapel Hill: Southern Folklife Collection, University of North Carolina at Chapel Hill Libraries in Association with the John Edwards Memorial Forum, 2002)

S   *Schwann* (monthly magazine)

NUMERICAL LISTING

ABC-CLIO & Documentary Arts (DVD-ROM):

ABC-CLIO	*Masters of Traditional Arts* (ISBN 1-57607-962-7)	2002

Acoustic Disc:

ACD-46	*Jerry Garcia & David Grisman: Grateful Dog*	2001
ACD-59	*Bill Monroe and the Blue Grass Boys: Live at at Mechanic's Hall*	2004
(Archive Series)		

Arista:

AR 07822 18758-2	*Pam Tillis: Sweetheart's Dance*	1994

Atteiram:

API-L-1516	*Brother Birch Monroe Plays Old Time Fiddle Favorites*	1976
API-L-1532	*James Monroe Sings Songs of "Memory Lane" of His Uncle Charlie Monroe*	ca. 1976

Bear Family; . . . and More Bears (ACD—and More Bears):

BCD 15423	*Bill Monroe—Bluegrass 1950–1958*	1989
BCD 15529	*Bill Monroe: Bluegrass 1959–1969*	1991
BCD 15743	*Rose Maddox—The One Rose: The Capitol Years*	1993
BCD 15606	*Bill Monroe: Bluegrass 1970–1979*	1994
BCD 15975	*Flatt on Victor Plus More*	2000
JAS 3519	*Tennessee Saturday Night*	2001
BCD 16399 FL	*Bill Monroe: Blue Moon of Kentucky 1936–1949*	2002
BCD 16614	*Live at Vanderbilt*	2002
ACD 25001 AA	*Bill Monroe: July 1963: Two Days at Newport*	2003
BCD 16624 EK	*Bill Monroe in Germany: Far Across the Blue Water*	2004
BCD 16673	*Bill Monroe: Bluegrass 1981–1994 My Last Days on Earth*	2006

Bluebird: see Victor

Bluegrass Classics:

BGC 80	*Bluegrass Classics Radio Shows 1946–1948: Bill Monroe & the Bluegrass [sic] Boys*	Fall 1981

Blue Grass Special:

BS 1	*Bill Monroe Blue Grass Special*	ca. 1975
BS 3	*Bill Monroe Blue Grass Special*	ca. 1975

Blue Plate Music:

BPM-400	*Bill Monroe Live from the Mountain Stage*	May 11, 1999

BMG: see Victor

Camden: see Victor

Capitol:

T 1799	*Rose Maddox Sings Bluegrass*	Dec. 1962
Reissued on CD in 1998 as Capitol 7243-8-35160-2-5		

Classic Country Collection (video):

CCC 01-V	*Tribute: Opry Stars of the 50's, Vol. 1*	1988
CCC 0010-V	*Tribute: Opry Stars of the 50's, Vol. 10*	1988
CCC 0011-V	*Tribute: Opry Stars of the 50's, Vol. 11*	1988

CMH:

CD-8007	*High Lonesome: The Story of Bluegrass Music*	1994
CD-1788	*The Original Stars of Bluegrass Music*	1997
CD-6294	*Great Ballads of Bluegrass*	2002
CD-6297	*The World's Greatest Bluegrass Live*	2003
CD-8421	*American Gothic: Bluegrass Songs of Death and Sorrow*	2003
CD-8933	*Twentieth Century Bluegrass Masters*	2005

Columbia/SONY/CBS/-Harmony:

Columbia singles are in numerical order, with date of release. The 2- numbers represent seven-inch, $33\frac{1}{3}$-rpm singles released at the same time as the ten-inch, 78-rpm singles:

20013, 36907	KENTUCKY WALTZ ROCKY ROAD BLUES	Jan. 14, 1946
20080, 37151	TRUE LIFE BLUES FOOTPRINTS IN THE SNOW	Oct. 28, 1946, Oct. 19, 1946B
20107, 37294	MANSIONS FOR ME MOTHER'S ONLY SLEEPING	Mar. 24, 1947, Mar. 15, 1947B
20198, 37565	WILL YOU BE LOVING ANOTHER MAN? BLUE YODEL NO. 4	July 14, 1947, July 26, 1947B
20370, 37888	GOODBYE OLD PAL BLUE MOON OF KENTUCKY	Sept. 22, 1947, Sept. 20, 1947B
20384, 37960	HOW WILL I EXPLAIN ABOUT YOU? BLUE GRASS SPECIAL	Nov. 3, 1947, Nov. 15, 1947B
20402, 38078	SHINE HALLELUJAH SHINE I'M TRAVELING ON AND ON	Jan. 26, 1948
20423, 38172	MY ROSE OF OLD KENTUCKY SWEETHEART YOU DONE ME WRONG	April 12, 1948, April 17, 1948B
20459	I HEAR A SWEET VOICE CALLING LITTLE CABIN HOME ON THE HILL	July 12, 1948, July 3, 1948B
20488	LITTLE COMMUNITY CHURCH THAT HOME ABOVE	Oct. 25, 1948
20503	SUMMERTIME IS PAST AND GONE WICKED PATH OF SIN	Oct. 4, 1948, Oct. 2, 1948B
20526	WHEN YOU ARE LONELY IT'S MIGHTY DARK TO TRAVEL	Dec. 27, 1948, Jan. 1, 1949B

| 20552, 2-151 | TOY HEART | Mar. 14, 1949 |
| | BLUE GRASS BREAKDOWN | |

| 20576, 2-207 | REMEMBER THE CROSS | May 2, 1949 |
| | THE OLD CROSS ROAD | |

| 20595, 2-275 | ALONG ABOUT DAYBREAK | July 18, 1949 |
| | HEAVY TRAFFIC AHEAD | |

| 20612, 2-323 | I'M GOING BACK TO OLD KENTUCKY | Sept. 12, 1949 |
| | MOLLY AND TENBROOKS | |

| 20648, 2-423 | BLUE GRASS STOMP | Dec. 12, 1949 |
| | THE GIRL IN THE BLUE VELVET BAND | |

| 20676, 2-551 | TRAVELIN' THIS LONESOME ROAD | Mar. 13, 1950 |
| | CAN'T YOU HEAR ME CALLIN'? | |

The following singles were issued on October 9, 1954B, in Columbia's Hall of Fame series:

| 52021 | KENTUCKY WALTZ |
| | FOOTPRINTS IN THE SNOW |

| 52022 | BLUE MOON OF KENTUCKY |
| | BLUE GRASS SPECIAL |

| 54013 | MANSIONS FOR ME |
| | MOTHER'S ONLY SLEEPING |

Columbia EPs in numerical order:

H 1709	KENTUCKY WALTZ	July 25, 1953
	FOOTPRINTS IN THE SNOW	
	I HEAR A SWEET VOICE CALLING	
	BLUE GRASS STOMP	

| H 2064 | KENTUCKY WALTZ |
| | BLUE MOON OF KENTUCKY |

B 2804	Hall of Fame Series
	KENTUCKY WALTZ
	FOOTPRINTS IN THE SNOW
	BLUE GRASS SPECIAL
	BLUE MOON OF KENTUCKY

Columbia (etc.) albums in chronological order with dates of release where known.

HL = Harmony, and FE = CBS/Epic; all other are Columbia or CBS/Sony or are specified in the listing:

HL 7290/HL 11335	The Great Bill Monroe	Mar. 20, 1961B
HL 7315	The Best of Bill Monroe	June 6, 1964B
HL 7338	Original Bluegrass Sound	June 1965S
CS 1065	Sixteen All-Time Greatest Hits	Aug. 1970S
FE 49410	Ricky Skaggs: Country Boy	1984
FC 38904	Bill Monroe: Columbia Historic Edition	1984
CK 46029	Columbia Country Classics, Volume 1: The Golden Age	1990
CK 46237	Uncle Art Satherley: American Originals	1991
C4K 47911 Legacy	Roots n' Blues—the Retrospective (1925–1950)	1992
C2K 52478	The Essential Bill Monroe and His Blue Grass Boys, 1945–1949	1992
CK 53908 Legacy	Bill Monroe: 16 Gems	1996
CK 67735	Bluegrass Super Hits	1996
J2K 65816 Columbia/Epic/Legacy	Country: The American Tradition	1999
C4K 90628 Columbia/Legacy	Can't You Hear Me Callin': Bluegrass, Eighty Years of American Music	Sept. 21, 2004
C2K 90858	The Essential Earl Scruggs	2004
CK 92965 Columbia/Legacy	The Best of Can't You Hear Me Callin': Bluegrass, Eighty Years of American Music	

Copper Creek:

CCCD-0137	Gary Brewer, Guitar	1995
CCRS-7001 Roots Series Volume 1	Wildwood Flower: Classic Country Performances	2003
CCRS-7002 Roots Series Volume 2	Brother I'm Getting Ready to Go	2003
CCRS-7007 Roots Series Volume 7	Tom T. Hall, The Magnificent Music Machine	2004

Country Music Association:

CMA 101	Here Lives Country Music	June 1973

Country Road (Sutton West, Ontario):

CR-02	Bill Monroe: Live Radio	1982

County:

CO 761	Kenny Baker Plays Bill Monroe	1976
CCS 104	Bill Monroe and His Blue Grass Boys: The Classic Bluegrass Recordings, Volume 1	1980
CCS 105	Bill Monroe and His Blue Grass Boys: The Classic Bluegrass Recordings, Volume 2	1980
CCS-114 reissued on CD in 1993 as CCS-CD-114	Bill Monroe and His Blue Grass Boys: In the Pines	1987
CCS-CD-19	Bill Monroe & His Blue Grass Boys: American Traveler	2000

Decca/MCA:

Singles (78- and 45-rpm discs) in numerical order, with date of release:

46222	MY LITTLE GEORGIA ROSE NEW MULE SKINNER BLUES	Mar. 13, 1950
46236	THE OLD FIDDLER ALABAMA WALTZ	May 15, 1950, May 6, 1950B
46254	I'M BLUE, I'M LONESOME BOAT OF LOVE	July 31, 1950, Aug. 5, 1950B
46266	MEMORIES OF YOU BLUE GRASS RAMBLE	Oct. 9, 1950, Oct. 14, 1950B
46283	WHEN THE GOLDEN LEAVES BEGIN TO FALL UNCLE PEN	Dec. 18, 1950, Dec. 23, 1950B
46298	POISON LOVE ON THE OLD KENTUCKY SHORE	Mar. 5, 1951, Feb. 24, 1951B
46305	RIVER OF DEATH LORD PROTECT MY SOUL	April 9, 1951, April 21, 1951B
46314	PRISONER'S SONG KENTUCKY WALTZ	May 5, 1951, April 21, 1951B
46325	SWING LOW SWEET CHARIOT ANGELS ROCK ME TO SLEEP	June 25, 1951, June 16, 1951B
46344	ROTATION BLUES LONESOME TRUCK DRIVER'S BLUES	July 23, 1951, July 21, 1951B
46351	GET DOWN ON YOUR KNEES AND PRAY I'LL MEET YOU IN CHURCH SUNDAY MORNING	Sept. 4, 1951, Aug. 25, 1951B
46369	SUGAR COATED LOVE HIGHWAY OF SORROW	Oct. 15, 1951, Oct. 13, 1951B
46380	BRAKEMAN'S BLUES TRAVELIN' BLUES	Nov. 24, 1951B
46386	THE FIRST WHIPPOORWILL CHRISTMAS TIME'S A-COMING	Nov. 26, 1951, Nov. 24, 1951B
46392	RAW HIDE LETTER FROM MY DARLIN'	Jan. 21, 1952, Jan. 19, 1952B

28045	I'M ON MY WAY TO THE OLD HOME THE FIRST WHIPPOORWILL	Mar. 13, 1952
28183	WHEN THE CACTUS IS IN BLOOM SAILOR'S PLEA	June 2, 1952, May 24, 1952B
28356	A MIGHTY PRETTY WALTZ PIKE COUNTY BREAKDOWN	Aug. 18, 1952
28416	FOOTPRINTS IN THE SNOW IN THE PINES	Oct. 13, 1952
28608	YOU'RE DRIFTING AWAY WALKING IN JERUSALEM	Mar. 23, 1953
28749	CABIN OF LOVE COUNTRY WALTZ	July 13, 1953
28878	THE LITTLE GIRL AND THE DREADFUL SNAKE MEMORIES OF MOTHER AND DAD	Nov. 30, 1953
29009	I HOPE YOU HAVE LEARNED WISHING WALTZ	Mar. 8, 1954
29021	Y'ALL COME CHANGING PARTNERS	Feb. 8, 1954
29141	GET UP JOHN WHITE HOUSE BLUES	May 13, 1954
29196	HAPPY ON MY WAY HE WILL SET YOUR FIELDS ON FIRE	Aug. 2, 1954
29289	CLOSE BY BLUE MOON OF KENTUCKY	Oct. 4, 1954
29348	A VOICE FROM ON HIGH I'M WORKING ON A BUILDING	Dec. 5, 1954
29406	CHEYENNE ROANOKE	Feb. 7, 1955
29436	WAIT A LITTLE LONGER, PLEASE JESUS LET THE LIGHT SHINE DOWN ON ME	Feb. 28, 1955
29645	WHEEL HOSS PUT MY LITTLE SHOES AWAY	Oct. 17, 1955

29886	ON AND ON I BELIEVED IN YOU DARLING	April 30, 1956
30178	YOU'LL FIND HER NAME WRITTEN THERE SITTIN' ALONE IN THE MOONLIGHT	Jan. 7, 1957
30327	A FALLEN STAR FOUR WALLS	May 13, 1957
30486	I'M SITTIN' ON TOP OF THE WORLD MOLLY AND TENBROOKS	Nov. 4, 1957
30647	BRAND NEW SHOES SALLY JO	May 5, 1958, May 5, 1958B
30739	SCOTLAND PANHANDLE COUNTRY	Sept. 29, 1958, Aug. 22, 1958B
30809	GOTTA TRAVEL ON NO ONE BUT MY DARLIN'	Dec. 28, 1958, Dec. 22, 1958B
30944	TOMORROW I'LL BE GONE DARK AS THE NIGHT, BLUE AS THE DAY	Oct. 19, 1959, Oct. 26, 1959
31031	LONESOME WIND BLUES COME GO WITH ME	Jan. 11, 1960, Jan. 4, 1960B
31107	PRECIOUS MEMORIES JESUS HOLD MY HAND	June 20, 1960, June 27, 1960B
31218	LINDA LOU PUT MY RUBBER DOLL AWAY	Feb. 27, 1961, Feb. 27, 1961B
31346	BLUE GRASS PART I FLOWERS OF LOVE	Jan. 1, 1962, Dec. 25, 1961B
31409	TOY HEART DANNY BOY	July 2, 1962, July 7, 1962
31456	BLUE RIDGE MOUNTAIN BLUES HOW WILL I EXPLAIN ABOUT YOU?	Jan. 14, 1963, Jan. 12, 1963B
31487	THERE WAS NOTHING WE COULD DO BIG SANDY RIVER	April 29, 1963, April 27, 1963B
31540	NEW JOHN HENRY BLUES DEVIL'S DREAM	Sept. 23, 1963

31596	DARLING COREY SALT CREEK	Mar. 9, 1964, Mar. 7, 1964B
31658	MARY AT THE HOME PLACE SHENANDOAH BREAKDOWN	Aug. 31, 1964
31802	JIMMY BROWN THE NEWSBOY CINDY	June 7, 1965, June 12, 1965B
31878	THE OLD OLD HOUSE I LIVE IN THE PAST	Dec. 13, 1965, Dec. 18, 1965B
31943	MASTER BUILDER GOING HOME	April 25, 1966
32075	WHEN MY BLUE MOON TURNS TO GOLD AGAIN PRETTY FAIR MAIDEN IN THE GARDEN	Dec. 7, 1966
32245	IS THE BLUE MOON STILL SHINING? TRAIN 45 (HEADING SOUTH)	Jan. 1, 1968
32404	THE GOLD RUSH VIRGINIA DARLING	Oct. 26, 1968
32502	CROSSING THE CUMBERLANDS I HAVEN'T SEEN MARY IN YEARS	May 19, 1969
32574	FIREBALL MAIL WITH BODY AND SOUL	Oct. 6, 1969, Oct. 18, 1969B
32645	BONNY SWEET MARY AND THE MILES IN BETWEEN	ca. Mar., 1970
32654	McKINLEY'S MARCH WALK SOFTLY ON MY HEART	Mar. 9, 1970
32827	GOING UP CANEY TALLAHASSEE	May 3, 1971
32966	LONESOME MOONLIGHT WALTZ MY OLD KENTUCKY AND YOU	May 15, 1972
40006	TALL PINES FOGGY MOUNTAIN TOP	Jan. 29, 1973
40220	SWING LOW, SWEET CHARIOT DOWN YONDER	Mar. 25, 1974

| 40675 | MY SWEET BLUE-EYED DARLING | Jan. 17, 1977 |
| | MONROE'S BLUES | |

| 51129 | COME HITHER TO GO YONDER | June 12, 1981 |
| | MY LAST DAYS ON EARTH | |

| 60074 | IN THE PINES | July 30, 1973 |
| | FOOTPRINTS IN THE SNOW | |

Decca EPs (seven-inch, 45discs) in numerical order:

ED 2353	NEW MULE SKINNER BLUES	April 30, 1956
	UNCLE PEN	
	BLUE MOON OF KENTUCKY	
	PIKE COUNTY BREAKDOWN	

ED 2354	GET DOWN ON YOUR KNEES AND PRAY	April 30, 1956
	WALKING IN JERUSALEM	
	I'M WORKING ON A BUILDING	
	HE WILL SET YOUR FIELDS ON FIRE	

ED 2585	CRY CRY DARLIN'	June 23, 1958
	ROANE COUNTY PRISON	
	MOLLY AND TENBROOKS	
	BRAND NEW SHOES	

ED 2610	PRECIOUS MEMORIES	Aug. 11, 1958
	LIFE'S RAILWAY TO HEAVEN	
	I'VE FOUND A HIDING PLACE	
	JESUS HOLD MY HAND	

ED 2674	GOTTA TRAVEL ON	Dec. 21, 1959
	NO ONE BUT MY DARLIN'	
	TOMORROW I'LL BE GONE	
	DARK AS THE NIGHT, BLUE AS THE DAY	

ED 2713	LONESOME WIND BLUES	Mar. 26, 1962
	LINDA LOU	
	THINKING ABOUT YOU	
	PUT MY RUBBER DOLL AWAY	

ED 2724	YOU LIVE IN A WORLD ALL YOUR OWN	Oct. 8, 1962
	LITTLE JOE	
	BLUE GRASS TWIST	
	JOHN HARDY	

ED 2753   DANNY BOY   Nov. 25, 1963
                 BLUE RIDGE MOUNTAIN BLUES
                 HOW WILL I EXPLAIN ABOUT YOU?
                 BIG SANDY RIVER

ED 2792   GOING HOME   May 3, 1965
                 ON THE JERICHO ROAD
                 FARTHER ALONG
                 MASTER BUILDER

Decca (DL), Vocalion (VL), and MCA (MCA) albums are in chronological order, with dates of release where known. Release numbers beginning with *7* denote stereo recordings. The first album known to be issued in both mono and stereo is DL 7-4266. In the 1970s the Decca albums were republished with MCA numbers. A concordance is at the end of this list.

DL 8731	*Knee Deep in Blue Grass*	June 23, 1958, July 14, 1958B
DL 8769	*I Saw the Light*	Aug. 11, 1958, Aug. 4, 1958B
DL 7-8769	*I Saw the Light*	Mar. 18, 1968
DL 4010	*All Time Country & Western-Original Hit Performances*	May 16, 1960
DL 4080	*Mr. Blue Grass*	May 29, 1961, May 8, 1961B
DL 4090	*All Time Country & Western-Original Hit Performances, Volume 2*	Dec. 5, 1960
DL 4134	*All Time Country & Western-Original Hit Performances, Volume 3*	May 28, 1961, May 8, 1961B
DL 4172	*Country Jubilee*	Aug. 7, 1961
DL 4266	*Blue Grass Ramble*	June 11, 1962, June 16, 1962B
DL 4303	*Grand Ole Opry, Saturday Night*	Aug. 8, 1962
DL 4327	*My All Time Country Favorites*	Oct. 8, 1962, Oct. 13, 1962B
DL 4343	*A Country Christmas*	Oct. 29, 1962
DL 4359	*All Time Country & Western-Original Hit Performances, Volume 4*	
DL 4382	*Blue Grass Special*	June 17, 1963, June 8, 1963B
DL 4393	*On Stage at the Grand Ole Opry*	Feb. 11, 1963
DL 4469	*All Time Hootenanny Favorites*	Nov. 4, 1963
DL 4485	*All Time Hootenanny Folk Favorites, Volume 2*	Jan 20, 1964, Jan. 25, 1964B
VL 3702	*Bill Monroe Sings Country Songs*	Mar. 2, 1964, Mar. 7, 1964B
DL 4537	*I'll Meet You in Church Sunday Morning*	June 15, 1964, June 12, 1964B
DL 4539	*Saturday Night at the Grand Ole Opry, Volume 2*	Nov. 23, 1964
DL 4549	*All Time Country & Western-Original Hit Performances, Volume 5*	June 15, 1964
DL 4601	*Bluegrass Instrumentals*	June 14, 1965, June 12, 1965B
DL 4657	*All Time Country & Western-Original Hit Performances, Volume 6*	June 14, 1964
DL 4671	*Saturday Night at the Grand Ole Opry, Volume 3*	Aug. 9, 1965
DL 4775	*All Time Country & Western-Original Hit Performances, Volume 7*	
DL 4780	*The High Lonesome Sound*	June 13, 1966, June 11, 1966B
DL 4881	*All Time Country & Western Original Hit Performances, Volume 8*	June 12, 1967
DL 4896	*Blue Grass Time*	June 12, 1967
DL 7-5010	*Bill Monroe's Greatest Hits*	June 17, 1968
DL 7-5025	*All Time Country & Western Original Hit Performances, Volume 9*	Sept. 30, 1968
DL 7-5066	*Bill Monroe and Charlie Monroe*	Feb. 24, 1969
DL 7-5135	*A Voice from on High*	June 30, 1969
VL 7-3870	*Bluegrass Style*	Dec. 30, 1969

DL 7-5213	*Kentucky Blue Grass*	June 29, 1970
DL 7-5281	*Bill Monroe's Country Music Hall of Fame*	April 26, 1971
DL 7-5348	*Bill Monroe's Uncle Pen*	June 1, 1972
MCA 310	*Bill Monroe and James Monroe: Father & Son*	Mar. 1, 1973
MCA 2-8002	*Bean Blossom*	Nov. 1, 1973
MCA 426	*Road of Life*	Nov. 4, 1973
MCA 2-4090	*The Best of Bill Monroe*	June 9, 1975
MCA 1929	*Country Sides: The Great MCA "Twofer" Sampler*	June 9, 1975
MCA 2173	*Bill Monroe: The Weary Traveler*	Jan. 5, 1976
MCA 2251	*Bill Monroe Sings Bluegrass, Body and Soul*	Jan. 10, 1977
MCA 2315	*Bill Monroe: Bluegrass Memories*	Oct. 3, 1977
MCA 2367	*Bill & James Monroe: Together Again*	June 15, 1978
MCA 3209	*Bill Monroe: Bean Blossom '79*	Feb. 15, 1980
MCA 5214	*Bill Monroe: Master of Bluegrass*	July 2, 1981
MCA 5435	*Bill Monroe and Friends*	Jan. 12, 1984
MCA 5625	*Bill Monroe and Stars of the Bluegrass Hall of Fame*	Aug. 19, 1985
MCA 5970	*Bluegrass '87*	1987
MCA 42133	*Southern Flavor*	1988
MCA 42286	*Bill Monroe and the Blue Grass Boys Live at the Opry*	1989
MCA 10017	*Cryin' Holy Unto the Lord*	1991
MCAD 10082	*Bill Monroe: Country Music Hall of Fame Series*	1991
MCAD 4-11048	*The Music of Bill Monroe from 1936 to 1994*	1994
MCA3P-2999	*Decca Historical Sampler*	1994
MCA3P-3256	*The Music of Bill Monroe: The Radio Special*	1994
MCA 088 170 109-2	*20th Century Masters, The Millennium Collection: The Best of Bill Monroe*	1999
MCA 088 112 982-2	*The Very Best of Bill Monroe and His Blue Grass Boys*	2001
MCA/Decca 088 113 207-2	*Bill Monroe Anthology*	2003
MCA Nashville B0002907-2	*Bill Monroe and His Blue Grass Boys: The Gospel Spirit*	2004
MCA 800004424-02	*Bill Monroe and His Blue Grass Boys: The Definitive Collection*	2005

"Replaces *The Very Best of Bill Monroe and His Blue Grass Boys* 088 112 982-2"

Concordance: Decca albums republished with MCA numbers:

MCA 17	=	DL 7-5010
MCA 82	=	DL 4080
MCA 88	=	DL 4266
MCA 97	=	DL 4382
MCA 104	=	DL 4601
MCA 110	=	DL 4780
MCA 116	=	DL 4896
MCA 124	=	DL 7-5066
MCA 131	=	DL 7-5135
MCA 136	=	DL 7-5213

MCA 140	=	DL 7-5281
MCA 226	=	DL 4537
MCA 527	=	DL 8769

Dust-to-Digital:

| DD 01 | *Goodbye, Babylon* | 2003 |

Epic: see Columbia

FBN:

| FBN-210 | *Bill & Doc Sing Country Songs: Limited Club Edition* | ca. 1978 |

Flying Fish:

| FF 432 | *Glenda Faye: Flat Pickin' Favorites* | 1987 |

Freeland:

| CRFRC CD-9001 | *Ralph Stanley: Saturday Night & Sunday Morning* | 1992 |

Gabriel Communications (video):

| G 8010FR-2 | *Opry Family Reunion, Volume 2* | 2001 |

Green Hill:

| GHD5354 | *Country Legends: Bluegrass* | 2003 |

Green Valley Records:

| GV 147 | *Bob Black: Ladies on the Steamboat* | 2005 |

Harmony: see Columbia

Hay Holler:

| HHH-CD-108 | *Butch Robins: Grounded, Centered, Focused* | 1995 |

Hip-O:

| Hip-O 314 564682 2 | *Bluegrass Essentials Vol. 2* | 1999 |

Hollywood:

| HCD-409 | *Bill Monroe at His Best* | 1989 |

Homespun Tapes (video):

| VD-MON-MN01 | *The Mandolin of Bill Monroe, Video One* | 1992 |

K-TEL:

| KT 30322 | *Best of Bluegrass* | 1991 |
| KT 3642 | *Billy & Terry Smith, Bill Monroe Tribute* | 1996 |

KEMTAC:
K 3308   *The Stars of Country Music on the Air*   Dec. 1973

Intermedia:
QS 5031   *Doc Watson: Out in the Country*   1982

Legacy: see Columbia

Library of Congress:
LBC 2   *Folk Music in America, Vol. 2: Songs of Love, Courtship & Marriage*   1976

MCA: see Decca/MCA

Mercury:
SRM-1-1111   *Tom T. Hall: The Magnificent Music Machine*   1976

Montgomery Ward: see Victor

Music Mill Entertainment:
MME-71007   *Bill Monroe & His Blue Grass Boys: Mansions for Me*   2001
   Sony Music Special Products
MME B0003736-02   *Bill Monroe & His Bluegrass Boys, Featuring Jimmy Martin:*   2004
                                   The King & the Father
   Universal Music Special Markets

My Label:
KCP 1001 CD   *Kathy Chiavola: The Harvest*   1995

New Haven:
NH 8061-2   *Bluegrass Top Twenty Gospel Songs of the Century*   2006

New World Records:
NW 225   *Hills & Home: Thirty Years of Bluegrass*   1976
NW 287   *Country Music: South and West*   1977

Opryland Home Video (video):
JB 1914   *Greats of the Grand Ole Opry, Vol. 1, Train Songs*
JB 1916   *Greats of the Grand Ole Opry, Vol 3, Moving Home*

Original Cinema (video):
OC-1001   *Bill Monroe, Father of Bluegrass Music*   1993

Palm Pictures (video, CD):
PALM VHS 3039-3/2   *American Roots Music, Episode Two*   2001
PALM CD 2075-2   *American Roots Music*   2001

Paramount Pictures (video):

PV-32063   *Planes, Trains, and Automobiles*   1987

Park South Records:

PS 80246 90655 2 7   *The Golden Treasure Series of Bluegrass*   2002

Raintree:

RR-599D   *James & Bill Monroe: Bluegrass Special Memories*   Sept. 1999

RCA Victor: see Victor

Rebel:

SLP 1554/55   *Ralph Stanley & the Clinch Mountain Boys, Live!*   1976
                               at McClure, Virginia

Rebel of Canada:

REB-850   *Classic Bluegrass Instrumentals*   1985

Red Clay:

RC CD 113   *Jimmy Campbell: Pieces of Time*   1996

Revenant:

RVN 211   *Harry Smith's Anthology of American Folk Music, Volume 4*   2000

Rhino:

R2 70290   *Great Gospel Performances, Vol. 3: Country Gospel* 1992
R2 71870   *Appalachian Stomp: Bluegrass Classics*   1995
R2 75720   *Appalachian Stomp: More Bluegrass Classics*   1999

Rounder:

SS 06   *Bill Monroe with Lester Flatt and Earl Scruggs:*   1978
                               "The Original Bluegrass Band"
Rdr 1026   *Poor Man, Rich Man: American Country Songs of Protest*
Rdr 1073   *The Monroe Brothers: What Would You Give in Exchange*   2000
                               for Your Soul, Volume One
Rdr 1074   *The Monroe Brothers: Just a Song of Kentucky, Volume Two*   2001
Rdr 0279   *Jim and Jesse McReynolds, Music among Friends*   1991

Rural Rhythm:

RHY-1015   *Bill Monroe & the Blue Grass Boys: Live, Volume One*   May 2002

Sanctuary:

SA 06076-84600-2   *Americana Series: The Best of Bluegrass*   2003
SA 06076-86420-2   *Americana Series: The Best of Bluegrass, Volume 2*   2006

Shanachie (video):

SHA 604	*High Lonesome*	1994
SHA 1404	*That High Lonesome Sound*	1996

Silver Eagle Cross Country Music:

SEA-CD-70007	*Bill Monroe: Lookin' Back*	1999

Smithsonian Folkways:

SF CD 40061	*American Roots Collection*	1996
SF CD 40063	*Bill Monroe and the Bluegrass Boys:*	
	Live Recordings 1956–1969, Off the Record Vol. 1	1993
SF CD 40064	*Bill Monroe and Doc Watson:*	1993
	Live Duet Recordings 1963–1980, Off the Record Vol. 2	
SF CD 40080	*Crossroads: Southern Routes, Music of the American South*	1996
includes CD-ROM		
SF CD 40091	*There Is No Eye: Music for Photographs* (ed. John Cohen)	2001
SFW CD 40092	*Classic Bluegrass from Smithsonian Folkways*	2002
SFW 40137	*Classic Southern Gospel from Smithsonian Folkways*	2005
SFW 40149	*Back Roads to Cold Mountain*	2004
SFW 40160	*Friends of Old Time Music*	2006
SFW 40163	*Classic Bluegrass Vol. 2 from Smithsonian Folkways*	2005

Smithsonian Institution:

FAF Vol. 1	*Festival of American Folklife, Vol. 1*	1969
RO25/P8 15640	*The Smithsonian Collection of Classic Country Music*	1981

Sony: see Columbia

Sony Music Special Projects:

A16652	*Bill Monroe: Blue Moon of Kentucky*	1993

Stack-O-Hits:

A. G. 9001	*Orange Blossom Special—Bill Monroe & Bluegrass Boys*	1981

Sugar Hill:

SH-CD-3802	*Larry Cordle, Glen Duncan & Lonesome Standard Time:*	1992
	Lonesome Standard Time	
SH-CD-3838	*Byron Berline: A Fiddle and a Song*	1995

Thrill Jockey:

TJ-145	*Jimmy Martin: Don't Cry to Me*	2004

Time Life:

TLCW-04	*Country & Western Classics: Flatt & Scruggs*	1982
TLCW-05	*Country & Western Classics: Duets*	ca. 1982
R142-08	*Time-Life's Treasury of Bluegrass*	2000

R142-04	*Time-Life's Treasury of Bluegrass, Vol. 2*	2001
M18701 314541804-2	*Time-Life's Treasury of Bluegrass*	2002
M18861 440069432-2	*The Time-Life Treasury of Bluegrass: America's Music*	2002
M18940 A70207	*Heaven Bound: The Best of Bluegrass Gospel*	2003
M18983 OPCD-8544	*Pure Pickin': Classic Bluegrass Instrumentals*	2004
M19007 B0002395-02	*Legends of Bluegrass*	2004

Universal Special Products:

B0 000303-02	*Flatt & Scruggs, Bill Monroe: Winning Combinations*	2003

Vanguard:

VCD 77006	*"Newport Folk Festival Classics": Bluegrass Breakdown*	1992
V 77007-2	*Folk Music at Newport, Part One*	1995
V 77012-2	*"Newport Folk Festival Classics": Bluegrass Masters*	1996
V 78003-2	*Generations of Bluegrass, Vol. 1: Pickers & Fiddlers*	1998
V 78010-2	*Generations of Bluegrass, Vol. 3: Legendary Pickers*	1999
V 79518-2	*Bill Monroe and His Blue Grass Boys: The Early Years*	1998
V 187/89-2	*Newport Folk Festival: Best of Bluegrass 1959–66*	2001
V 208/10-2	*Roots of the Blues*	2002

Varied Directions Inc.:

J9	*The Complete Earl Scruggs Story* (DVD)	2004

Vic Lewis Video:

VLV 008-96820	*Second Fiddle to a Steel Guitar*	1991

Victor, RCA Victor, Bluebird, Camden, BMG:

Bluebird singles are in numerical sequence, with release dates given where known.

By the Monroe Brothers:

BB-6309	WHAT WOULD YOU GIVE IN EXCHANGE?	May 1936M
	THIS WORLD IS NOT MY HOME	
BB-6363	WHAT IS A HOME WITHOUT LOVE?	July 1936M
	DRIFTING TOO FAR FROM THE SHORE	
BB-6422	MY LONG JOURNEY HOME	Aug. 1936M
	NINE POUND HAMMER IS TOO HEAVY	
BB-6477	GOD HOLDS THE FUTURE IN HIS HANDS	Oct. 1936M
	YOU'VE GOT TO WALK THAT LONESOME VALLEY	
BB-6512	SIX MONTHS AIN'T LONG	Oct. 1936M
	DARLING COREY	
BB-6552	JUST A SONG OF OLD KENTUCKY	Nov. 1936M
	DON'T FORGET ME	

BB-6607	ON SOME FOGGY MOUNTAIN TOP	Dec. 1936M
	IN MY DEAR OLD SOUTHERN HOME	
BB-6645	LITTLE RED SHOES	Jan. 1937M
	NEW RIVER TRAIN	
BB-6676	THE OLD CROSS ROAD	Feb. 1937M
	WE READ OF A PLACE THAT'S CALLED HEAVEN	
BB-6729	MY SAVIOR'S TRAIN	
	DREAMED I SEARCHED HEAVEN FOR YOU	
BB-6762	WHERE IS MY SAILOR BOY?	Mar. 1937M
	THE CARTER FAMILY AND JIMMIE RODGERS IN TEXAS,	
	by Jimmie Rodgers and the Carter Family	
BB-6773	I AM THINKING TONIGHT OF THE OLD FOLKS	Mar. 1937M
	ROLL IN MY SWEET BABY'S ARMS	
BB-6820	WILL THE CIRCLE BE UNBROKEN	April 1937M
	THE SAINTS GO MARCHING IN	
BB-6829	WATERMELON AM HANGIN' ON THAT VINE	May 1937M
	THE FORGOTTEN SOLDIER BOY	
BB-6866	I AM READY TO GO	May 1937M
	SOME GLAD DAY	
BB-6912	WHAT WOULD THE PROFIT BE?	
	I HAVE FOUND THE WAY	
BB-6960	KATY CLINE	July 1937M
	ROLL ON, BUDDY	
BB-7007	I AM GOING THAT WAY	Aug. 1937M
	I'LL LIVE ON	
BB-7055	DO YOU CALL THAT RELIGION?	Sept. 1937M
	I'M GOING	
BB-7093	WEEPING WILLOW TREE	Oct. 1937M
	OH, HIDE YOU IN THE BLOOD	
BB-7122	WHAT WOULD YOU GIVE IN EXCHANGE	Oct. 1937M
	FOR YOUR SOUL—PART 2	
	WHAT WOULD YOU GIVE IN EXCHANGE—PART 3	

BB-7145	ON MY WAY TO GLORY HE WILL SET YOUR FIELDS ON FIRE	Nov. 1937M
BB-7191	LET US BE LOVERS AGAIN ALL THE GOOD TIMES ARE PASSED AND GONE	Dec. 1937M
BB-7273	ON THAT OLD GOSPEL SHIP MY LAST MOVING DAY	
BB-7326	WHAT WOULD YOU GIVE IN EXCHANGE—PART 4 SINNER YOU BETTER GET READY	Feb. 1938M
BB-7385	ON THE BANKS OF THE OHIO FAME APART FROM GOD'S APPROVAL, by Uncle Dave Macon	Mar. 1938M
BB-7425	THE OLD MAN'S STORY I'VE STILL GOT NINETY-NINE	April 1938M
BB-7460	PEARLY GATES ON MY WAY BACK HOME	
BB-7508	HAVE A FEAST HERE TONIGHT GOODBYE MAGGIE	June 1938M
BB-7562	A BEAUTIFUL LIFE WHEN OUR LORD SHALL COME AGAIN	July 1938M
BB-7598	ROLLING ON LITTLE JOE	July 1938M

By Bill Monroe and His Blue Grass Boys:

BB-8568	MULE SKINNER BLUES SIX WHITE HORSES	Dec. 1940
BB-8611	NO LETTER IN THE MAIL CRYIN' HOLY UNTO THE LORD	Feb. 1941M
BB-8692	DOG HOUSE BLUES KATY HILL	May 1941, July 1941M
BB-8813	I WONDER IF YOU FEEL THE WAY I DO TENNESSEE BLUES	Oct. 1941, Nov. 1941M
BB-8861	BLUE YODEL NO. 7 (ANNIVERSARY BLUE YODEL) IN THE PINES	Dec. 1941, Jan. 1942M

BB-8893	THE COUPON SONG ORANGE BLOSSOM SPECIAL	Feb. 1942M
BB-8953	SHAKE MY MOTHER'S HAND FOR ME WERE YOU THERE?	April 1942, Mar. 28, 1942B
BB-8988	HONKY TONK SWING BACK UP AND PUSH	May 15, 1942B

Montgomery Ward (MW)-Bluebird (BB) numerical concordance and release list for the Monroe Brothers:

MW-4745	=	BB-6309
MW-4746	=	BB-6363
MW-4747	=	BB-6422
MW-4748	=	BB-6645
MW-4749	=	BB-6607
MW-5026	=	BB-6477

MW-7010   WATERMELON AM HANGIN' ON THAT VINE
             ON THE BANKS OF THE OHIO

MW-7011	=	BB-6552
MW-7012	=	BB-6512
MW-7086	=	BB-6729
MW-7087	=	BB-6676

MW-7140   THE FORGOTTEN SOLDIER BOY
             WHERE IS MY SAILOR BOY?

MW-7141   I AM THINKING TONIGHT OF THE OLD FOLKS
             I AM GOING THAT WAY

| MW-7142 | = | BB-6820 |
| MW-7143 | = | BB-7055 |

MW-7144   I'LL LIVE ON
             OH, HIDE YOU IN THE BLOOD

MW-7145   ROLL IN MY SWEET BABY'S ARMS
             WEEPING WILLOW TREE

MW-7312   WHAT WOULD YOU GIVE IN EXCHANGE FOR YOUR SOUL—PART 2
             ON THE OLD GOSPEL SHIP

MW-7313   WHAT WOULD YOU GIVE IN EXCHANGE—PART 3
             ON MY WAY TO GLORY

MW-7314   WHAT WOULD YOU GIVE IN EXCHANGE—PART 4
                    MY LAST MOVING DAY

MW-7315   HE WILL SET YOUR FIELDS ON FIRE
                    SINNER YOU BETTER GET READY

MW-7316	=	BB-7191
MW-7447	=	BB-7508
MW-7448	=	BB-7425
MW-7449	=	BB-7460
MW-7450	=	BB-7562
MW-7451	=	BB-7598
MW-8453	=	BB-6866
MW-8454	=	BB-6912
MW-8455	=	BB-6960

Montgomery Ward (MW)-Bluebird (BB) numerical concordance list for Bill Monroe and the Blue Grass Boys:

MW-8861	=	BB-8568
MW-8862	=	BB-8611
MW-8863	=	BB-8692
MW-8864	=	BB-8813

Monroe Brothers Victor single:

27493   DARLING COREY   see album Victor P-79

Bill Monroe and the Blue Grass Boys RCA Victor singles in numerical order;
the labels include the statement "Reissued by Popular Request":

20-3163   MULE SKINNER BLUES   Oct. 23, 1948
                    BLUE YODEL NO. 7 (ANNIVERSARY BLUE YODEL)

20-3295   KATY HILL   Dec. 25, 1948
                    BACK UP AND PUSH

Albums are in chronological order; unless otherwise indicated, the album is Victor:

P-79   *Smoky Mountain Ballads*   July 1941
 78-rpm album set; includes five discs: Victor 27493-27497

CAL 719   *The Father of Bluegrass Music*   Aug. 4, 1962B
  Camden
CAL 774   *Early Blue Grass Music*   1964
  Camden
LPV 507   *Smoky Mountain Ballads*   1964
  Vintage
LPV 532   *The Railroad in Folksong*   1966
  Vintage

LPM 6015	*Stars of the Grand Ole Opry*	1967
LPV 569	*Early Blue Grass*	Nov. 1969S
Vintage		
CPL 2-0466	*Stars of the Grand Ole Opry—1926–1974*	May 1974
ACLI-0535(e)	*The Sound of Bluegrass*	1974
Camden		
APM-0568	*Bluegrass for Collectors*	June 1974
APL 1-0588	*Lester Flatt Live! Bluegrass Festival,* *with Guest Bill Monroe*	1974
AXM2-5510	*Feast Here Tonight: Monroe Brothers*	1975
Bluebird		
ACL-7059	*Bill Monroe and His Blue Grass Boys*	1978
CPL 2-9507	*Sixty Years of Grand Ole Opry*	1986
RCA 8417-2-R	*Are You from Dixie? Great Country Brother Teams*	1988
BMG 2100-2-R	*Something Got a Hold of Me: A Treasury of Sacred Music*	1990
RCA 2494-2-R	*Mule Skinner Blues*	1991
RCA 07863-67450-2	*The Essential Bill Monroe & the Monroe Brothers*	1997
BMG 75517 43600 2	*Bona Fide Bluegrass and Mountain Music*	2002
BMG 07863 65120 2	*Bill Monroe: RCA Country Legends*	2002
BMG 74465 99002 2	*More Bona Fide Bluegrass & Mountain Music*	2002

Vocalion: see Decca/MCA

Warner Brothers:

| W 9 45257-2 | *Mark O'Connor, Heroes* | 1993 |

West Hill Audio Archives:

| WW-1017 | *American Pop: An Audio History. From Minstrel*
 to Mojo: On Record, 1893–1946, Vol. 3 | 1997 |

Appendix A

PERFORMERS' NAMES IN THE DISCOGRAPHIES

The numbers in this index denote recording session numbers based on the date of the session. The first two digits represent the year; the next two, the month; and the final two, the day. When more than one session took place on a single day, a decimal point, followed by a number, indicates the sequence of sessions on that day.

Appendix B

PRODUCERS' NAMES IN THE DISCOGRAPHIES

The numbers in this index indicate recording session numbers based on the date of the session. The first two digits represent the year; the next two, the month; and the final two, the day. When more than one session took place on a single day, a decimal point, followed by a number, indicates the sequence of sessions on that day.

Appendix C

TITLES IN THE DISCOGRAPHIES

The numbers in this index indicate recording session numbers based on the date of the session. The first two digits represent the year; the next two, the month; and the final two, the day. When more than one session took place on a single day, a decimal point followed by a number indicates the sequence of sessions on that day.

"Blue Moon of Kentucky," *in medley,* 750517.3, 790612, 900624.2

"Blue Night," 670123

"Blue Ridge Mountain Blues," 620503, 631116, 750517.2

"Blue Savannah Waltz," 880112

"Blues for Casey C.," 950320

"Bluest Man in Town," 850617.2

"Blue Yodel No. 4," 460916.2, 480300, 650724.2

"Blue Yodel No. 7" ("Anniversary Blue Yodel"), 411002

"Boat of Love," 500408

"Boatin' Up Sandy," 750600

"Bonny," 691217, 700119, 780317

"Boston Boy," 940109.1

"Brakeman's Blues," 510329, 560513, 630208

"Brand New Shoes," 571215

"Bringing in the Georgia Mail," 760209

"Brown County Breakdown," 550916, 760329.2

"Bugle Call Rag," 611204

"Cabin of Love," 510706

"Call of the Shepherd" *see* "Little Shepherd"

"Candy Gal," 691028

"Can't You Hear Me Callin'," 491022, 650000, 750525, 850610.2, 900624.2

"Careless Love," 460300, 621123.1

"Careless Love," *in medley,* 750517.3

"Carroll County Blues," 750600, 900700.1

"Changing Partners," 540108

"Cheap Love Affair," 620425

"Cheyenne," 541231, 760329.1, 890730.1

"Chicken Reel," 630517

"Chilly Winds of Shannon," 950320

"Christmas Time's a-Coming," 511028, 770725

"Cindy," 621210

"Clinging to a Saving Hand," 750310

"Close By," 540626, 550000, 560513, 831215

"Columbus Stockade Blues," 620426

"Come Back to Me in My Dreams," 450213, 570515.2

"Come Go with Me," 591125

"Come Hither to Go Yonder," 900616.2. *See also* "Go Hither to Go Yonder"

"Comin' Down from Boston," 750600

"Corrina, Corrina," 780130

"Cotton-Eyed Joe," 650617, 650724.1

"Cotton Fields," 611130

"Country Waltz," 520718.2

"The Coupon Song," 411002

"Cripple Creek," 690429

"Crossing the Cumberlands," 681114, 900616.2

"Cry Cry Darlin'," 570514

"Cryin' Holy Unto the Lord," 401007, 740318, 900515, 900616.2, 900724

"Cumberland Gap," 750600

"Dancin' in Brancin'" (*properly* "Dancin' in Branson"), 860317.1

"Danny Boy," 611131

"Dark as the Night, Blue as the Day," 590130, 620000.2

"Dark Hollow," 631116

"Darling Corey," 360621, 621206

"The Days Gone By," 880112

"The Dead March," 690326

"Dear Old Dixie," 741213, 760504

"Devil's Dream," 630320, 630723, 630726, 631116, 900624.2

"Dixon County Rag," 750600

"Dog House Blues," 401007, 790616, 900615.3, 900616.2

"Doin' My Time," 750517.2

"Don't Forget Me," 360621

"Don't Put Off Til Tomorrow," 520718.2

"Down in the Willow Garden," 760209

"Down Memory Lane," 760209

"Down Yonder," 730617, 750517.2, 750600, 870000A, 890730.1, 950320

"Do You Call That Religion," 360621

"Dreamed I Searched Heaven for You," 361012

"Dreaming of a Little Cabin," 631116

"Drifting Too Far from the Shore," 360217, 620516

"Durang's Hornpipe," 690704, 750600

"Dusty Miller," 661206, 820703, 900616.2, 920303

"East Tennessee Blues," 641031

"Ebenezer Scrooge," 831215, 950320. *See also* "Old Ebenezer Scrooge"

"Evening Prayer Blues," 810219

"Fair Play," 810204

"A Fallen Star," 570420

"Farewell Blues," 900707.1

"Farther Along," 621123.2

"Farther On," 750311, 860819

"Feast Here Tonight," 630514.2. *See also* "Have a Feast Here Tonight," "Rabbit in the Log"

"Festival Waltz," 750517.1

"Fiddlers Blues," 950320

"Fiddler's Pastime," 760329.1

"Fire on the Mountain," 630517, 640409, 660504

"Fireball Mail," 690326

"The First Whippoorwill," 511028, 761021

"Flint Hill Special," 750517.2

"Flop Eared Mule," 750600

"Florida Blues," 750600

"Flowers of Love," 601203

"Foggy Mountain Breakdown," 831215

"Foggy Mountain Top," 640831, 720315. *See also* "On Some Foggy Mountain Top"

"Foggy River," 620503

"Footprints in the Snow," 450213, 520718.1, 620319.1, 631116, 650000, 750517.1, 760504, 831215, 890505, 890730.1, 900624.2, 900707.2

"The Forgotten Soldier Boy," 361012

"Four Walls," 570420

"Fraulein," 750517.2

"Friday Night at the Opry," 931114

"John Henry," *in medley,* 790616, 900615.3
"Journey's End," 611130
"Just a Little Talk with Jesus," 480221, 900515, 900707.1
"Just a Song of Old Kentucky," 360621
"Just Over in the Glory Land," 900627. *See also* "(We're Going) Just Over in the Glory Land"

"Kansas City Railroad Blues," 650905
"Katy Cline," 370215
"Katy Hill," 401007, 641031, 710113, 920303
"Kentucky King," 920300
"Kentucky Mandolin," 640418, 671109, 750517.1
"Kentucky Waltz," 450213, 510317, 560923, 701202, 830420, 900615.2, 900616.2, 920303
"Kiss Me Waltz," 710115

"Lady of the Blue Ridge," 810219
"Land of Lincoln," 691125, 940522
"Last Old Dollar," 640203
"The Lee Weddin Tune," 691125
"Legend of the Blue Ridge Mountains," 640128
"Let Me Rest at the End of My Journey," 621210
"Letter from My Darling," 510120, 920000
"Let the Gates Swing Wide," 850610.1
"Let the Light Shine Down on Me," 550128
"Let Us Be Lovers Again," 370803
"Life's Highway," 880113
"Life's Railway to Heaven," 580319
"Linda Lou," 601130
"Little Cabin Home on the Hill," 471027.1, 711200, 740318, 750517.2, 790616, 790900
"Little Community Church," 461200, 471028.1
"The Little Girl and the Dreadful Snake," 520718.2, 790612
"Little Joe," 380128, 480300, 601130, 750517.2
"Little Maggie," 460300, 611109
"Little Maggie," *in medley,* 700500, 790612
"Little Red Shoes," 360217
"Little Shepherd," 820704
"Live and Let Live," 611110, 630208, 780317
"Lochwood," 810204
"Log Cabin in the Lane," 661103
"Lonesome Moonlight Waltz," 640418, 701203, 760329.1, 900700.1, 920303
"Lonesome Old Farmer," 950320
"A Lonesome Road," 571215
"Lonesome Road Blues," 601201, 630727
"Lonesome Truck Driver's Blues," 510701
"Lonesome Wind Blues," 591125
"The Long Black Veil," 650316
"The Long Bow," 860318.2, 900615.3
"Lord, Build Me a Cabin in Glory," 580225, 630208
"Lord Lead Me On," 580225
"Lord, Protect My Soul," 501015, 850506.1
"Louisville Breakdown," 640409
"Love Gone Cold," 461200
"Love, Please Come Home," 720315, 890505, 900615.2

"Love's Gonna Live Here," 631116
"Lucky Lady," 761021

"Mansions for Me," 460916.2
"Mary at the Home Place," 640127
"Mary Jane, Won't [Will] You Be Mine," 750311, 760504, 900707.2
"Master Builder," 621210
"McKinley's March," 700119, 750517.2
Medleys:
   Intro ("Watermelon Hangin' on the Vine") / "John Henry," 790616
   "John Henry" / "Mule Skinner Blues," 900615.3
   "Molly and Tenbrooks" Medley: "Little Maggie" / "Train 45" / "Blue Moon of Kentucky," 790612
   "Molly and Tenbrooks" Medley: "Molly and Tenbrooks" / "Blue Moon of Kentucky / "Swing Low Sweet Chariot" / "I'll Fly Away" / "I Saw the Light," 900624.2
   "Sittin' on Top of the World" / "Hand Me Down My Walkin' Cane" / "Good Old Mountain Dew" / "Careless Love" / "Blue Moon of Kentucky," 750517.3
   "Swing Low Sweet Chariot" / "I Saw the Light," 750517.2
   "Train 45" / "Little Maggie" / "My Little Georgia Rose" / "Nine Pound Hammer," 700500
"Melissa's Waltz for J.B.," 810219
"Memories of Mother and Dad," 520718.2, 920303
"Memories of You," 500203.1, 630514.1
"Methodist Preacher," 690429
"Midnight on the Stormy Deep," 630514.2, 641031, 661216
"Mighty Dark to Travel," 850507.1, 900616.2. *See also* "It's Mighty Dark to Travel"
"A Mighty Pretty Waltz," 520726
"Milenburg Joy," 710120
"Mississippi Waltz," 760329.2
"Molly and Tenbrooks," 461200, 471028.2, 570515.2, 580426, 620319.2, 630726, 650724.2, 750517.2, 760713, 890505, 890730.1
"Molly and Tenbrooks," *in medley,* 790612, 900624.2
"Monroe's Blues," 761021
"Monroe's Hornpipe," 581201, 760329.1
"Mother's Only Sleeping," 460916.2, 461200, 720315
"Muddy Waters," 780130
"Mule Skinner [Muleskinner] Blues (Blue Yodel No. 8)," 391125, 401007, 480605 (*mistitled* "New Mule Skinner Blues"), 630723, 630726, 631116, 641100, 650000, 650724.2, 710113, 730616.1, 740318, 750517.1, 780111, 831215, 890511 (*mistitled* "New Mule Skinner Blues"), 890730.1, 890913.2, 900615.2, 900624.1, 900919, 920303, 960221
"Mule Skinner Blues," *in medley,* 900615.3
"Music Valley Waltz," 860317.2
"My Blue Eyes from Heaven," 890511
"My Cabin in Caroline," 761020
"My Carolina Sunshine Girl," 510423.1
"My Dixie Home," 480300. *See also* "I Am Thinking Tonight of the Old Folks"
"My Dying Bed," 520718.2
"My Father's Footsteps," 941030

750517.2, 750517.3, 760209, 831215, 890511, 890730.1, 900616.2

"Rolling On," 380128

"Roll On, Buddy (, Roll On)," 370215, 640128, 730616.2

"Rotation Blues," 510701

"Roust-a-Bout," 750517.1

"Roxanna Waltz," 940109.1

"Sailor's Hornpipe," 630320

"Sailor's Plea," 510423.1

"The Saints Go Marching In," 361012

"Sally Goodin," 670823, 740318, 890730.1, 920303, 940700, 941108

"Sally-Jo," 571215

"Salt Creek," 630320, 630727

"Santa Claus," 630327

"Scotland," 580408

"Seven Year Blues," 601201

"Shady Grove," 611110, 620000.1, 630208, 650000, 650724.1

"Shake My Mother's Hand for Me," 411002

"Shenandoah Breakdown," 630327, 650000, 900615.3, 900624.2

"She's Young and I'm Growing Old," 770727

"Shine Hallalujah Shine," 461200, 471028.2, 900521, 900724

"Shining Path," 460917, 480300

"Shouting on the Hills of Glory," 820704

"Show Me the Way," 750310

"Shuckin' the Corn," 750517.1, 831215

"Sinner You Better Get Ready," 370803

"Sittin' on Top of the World," *in medley,* 750517.3. *See also* "I'm Sittin' on Top of the World"

"Sitting Alone in the Moonlight," 540108, 890505

"Six Feet under the Ground," 780124

"Six Months Ain't Long," 360621

"Six White Horses," 401007

"Slow and Easy Blues,", 900706, 920303, 931114, 940109.1

"Smoky Mountain Schottische," 920303, 940109.1

"Sold Down the River," 601130

"Soldier's Joy," 641031, 661216, 730617, 890730.1, 900616.1, 900616.2, 900700.1, 950320

"So Long and Goodbye" ("Watermelon Hangin' on the Vine"), 890730.1

"Somebody Touched Me," 620517, 650724.2

"Some Glad Day," 370215

"Southern Flavor," 880104, 890511, 890615/18, 890730.1, 900615.2, 900616.1, 900624.1, 910913, 920303, 940700

"Stay Away from Me," 860317.2, 940727

"Stone Coal," 880105

"Stoney Lonesome," 590130, 760329.1

"Sugar Coated Love," 510706

"Sugar Loaf Mountain," 880108, 890511, 890730.1, 900615.3

"Summertime Is Past and Gone," 460916.2, 710113

"Sunny Side of the Mountain," 480221

"The Sunset Trail," 770725, 830222

"Sweet Blue Eyed Darling," 920303. *See also* "My Sweet Blue-Eyed Darling"

"Sweetheart You Done Me Wrong," 471027.2, 720314, 750517.2

"Sweet Mary and the Miles in Between," 691217, 700119

"Swing Low Sweet Chariot," 510317, 550000, 730617

"Swing Low Sweet Chariot," *in medley,* 750517.2, 900624.2

"Take Courage un' Tomorrow," 880113, 880114, 900615.3

"Take Me Home," 900616.2

"Tallahassee," 701203

"Tall Pines," 691028, 720314

"Tall Timber," 550916

"Tanyards," 941030

"Tellico Plains," 900707.2

"Tennessee Blues," 401007, 920303, 940700

"Texas Blue Bonnet," 770725

"Texas Gallop," 700119

"Texas Lone Star," 860318.1, 880105

"Texas Quickstep," 950320

"Thank God for Kentucky," 750312

"That Home Above," 471028.1

"That's All Right," 661206

"That's Christmas Time to Me," 770728

"There's an Old, Old House," 650316, 890730.1. *See also* "Old, Old House"

"There Was Nothing We Could Do," 620425

"Thinking about You," 591125

"This World Is Not My Home," 360217, 620510, 900724

"Those Gambler's Blues," 510423.2

"Those Memories of You," 780208

"Til All the Lonely's Gone," 940109.2

"Time Changes Everything," 601201

"Tombstone Junction," 900615.3, 900700.2, 900706, 900707.1, 900919, 920303, 931114, 940109.1

"Tomorrow I'll Be Gone," 590130

"Toy Heart," 460916.1, 611109

"Train 45 (Heading South)," 671109, 681220, 741213

"Train 45," *in medley,* 700500, 790612

"Travelin' Blues," 510329

"Travelin' (Down) This Lonesome Road," 491022, 650905, 850506.2

"Truck Driving Man," 750517.1, 750517.3

"True Life Blues," 450213, 461200, 630514.2, 850502.2, 900624.2

"Turkey in the Straw," 660826, 661014

"Two Finger Waltz," 940522

"Uncle Pen," 501015, 560000, 620319.1, 630726, 631116, 650000, 650400, 690704, 730616.1, 740318, 750517.1, 760504, 800807, 820703, 890511, 890730.1, 890913.2, 900616.1, 900616.2, 900700.2, 900919, 901028, 910913

"Untitled Instrumental," 920303

"Used to Be," 550916, 740318

"Virginia Darlin'," 670823

"A Voice from on High," 540114, 550000

"Wabash Cannonball," 750517.2

"Wabash Cannon Ball," 770728

"Wait a Little Longer, Please Jesus," 550128

"Walking in Jerusalem," 520718.1

"Walking in My Sleep," 750517.2

"Walkin' the Dog," 630208

"Walk Softly on My (This) Heart (of Mine)," 691028, 900615.2, 900616.2, 900624.1, 900919, 960221

"Walls of Time," 650724.1, 650724.2, 650905, 681114, 720321, 890730.1

"Watermelon Hangin' on (That) the Vine," 360621, 560513, 630726, 631116, 660504, 890505, 890730.1 (*mistitled* "So Long and Goodbye"), 900615.2, 900615.3, 900616.1, 900616.2, 900624.2, 900707.2, 940522

"Watermelon Hangin' on the Vine," *in medley,* 790616

"Watson Blues," 660826, 750311, 950320

"Way Down Deep in My Soul," 620516

"Wayfaring Stranger," 580321, 660620, 820704, 831215, 890730.1, 900919

"Weary Traveler," 750312

"Weeping Willow Tree," 370215

"We'll Understand It Bettter," 620517

"We Read of a Place That's Called Heaven," 361012

"(We're Going) Just Over in the Glory Land," 640409. *See also* "Just Over in the Glory Land"

"Were You There?" 411002, 630320

"What about You?" 690429

"What a Friend We Have in Jesus," 820704

"What a Wonderful Life," 880108, 880114

"What Became of That Beautiful Picture," 760209

"What Does the Deep Sea Say?" 630514.2. *See also* "Where Is My Sailor Boy"

"What Is Home without Love?" 360217

"What Would the Profit Be?" 370215

"What Would You Give in Exchange (for Your Soul)?" 360217, 630517, 640000, 631116, 720315, 900515

"What Would You Give in Exchange for Your Soul—Part 2," 370803

"What Would You Give in Exchange—Part 3," 370803

"What Would You Give in Exchange—Part 4," 370803

"Wheel Hoss," 541231, 560513, 760329.1, 840322?, 890730.1, 900616.1, 920303

"When He Reached Down His Hand for Me," 650905

"When My Blue Moon Turns to Gold Again," 661014

"When Our Lord Shall Come Again," 380128

"When the Angels Carry Me Home," 760209, 780317

"When the Bees Are in the Hive," 620426, 780317

"When the Cactus Is in Bloom," 510329

"When the Golden Leaves Begin to Fall," 501015, 720321

"When the Phone Rang," 590130

"When You Are Lonely," 471028.2

"Where Is My Sailor Boy," 361012, 630517. *See also* "What Does the Deep Sea Say?"

"Whispering Hope," 900624.2

"White House Blues," 540107, 660620

"White Rose," 880112

"Who's Gonna Shoe Your Pretty Little Feet," 780124

"Why did You Wander?" 460916.1, 461200, 900616.1

"Wicked Path of Sin," 460917, 461200, 820704, 890302

"Wildwood Flower," 750517.2

"Willie Moore," 900615.2

"Will the Circle Be Unbroken," 361012

"Will You Be Loving Another Man?" 460917, 461200, 630727, 740318, 900624.2

"Wishing Waltz," 531128

"With Body and Soul," 690429, 691000, 830126

"Woodstock Hornpipe," 950320

"Worn Through Stone," 940606

"Y'All Come," 540108, 641031, 790616, 900615.2, 900624.1

"You Live in a World All Your Own," 601130

"You'll Find Her Name Written There," 541231, 550000, 750517.2

"You're Drifting Away," 510706, 900717

"You've Got to Walk That Lonesome Valley," 360621

"You Won't Be Satisfied That Way," 630514.1, 630514.2, 730616.1, 750517.2

General Index

Song Title Index

NEIL V. ROSENBERG is professor emeritus of folkore at Memorial University of Newfoundland, where he taught from 1968 to 2004, and a fellow of the American Folklore Society. He did his undergraduate work in history at Oberlin College and his graduate work in folklore at Indiana University. Among his books are *Bill Monroe and His Blue Grasss Boys: An Illustrated Discography* (1974); *Bluegrass: A History* (1985); *Transforming Tradition* (1993); and, with Carl Fleischhauer, *Bluegrass Odyssey* (2001). He has also written extensively about aspects of folk and country music in Atlantic Canada and edited and written notes for many recordings. His contribution to Smithsonian/Folkways' *Anthology of American Folk Music* won a Grammy in 1997 for best album notes. A musician since childhood, he played as a substitute member of Bill Monroe's Blue Grass Boys in 1961 and 1965 and managed Monroe's Brown County Jamboree in Bean Blossom, Indiana, in 1963.

CHARLES K. WOLFE taught at Middle Tennessee State University in Murfreesboro, retiring in 2005. A student of English literature, he did his undergraduate degree at Southwest Missouri University and his graduate work at the University of Kansas. The recipient of numerous awards for many recordings, articles, and books about southern American folk and popular music, he was often consulted by national and international media. Among his work are *The Devil's Box: Masters of Southern Fiddling* (1997), *A Good-Natured Riot: The Birth of the Grand Ole Opry* (1999), which won two national book awards, and *Classic Country: Legends of Country Music* (2002). His book with David Morton, *DeFord Bailey: A Black Star in Early Country Music* (1991), led to Bailey's induction into the Country Music Hall of Fame in 2005. He was also active in the Tennessee Valley Old-Time Fiddler's Association, the Tennessee Folklore Society, and the International Bluegrass Music Association, serving two terms on its board of directors. In 1990 the association presented him with its Distinguished Achievement Award.

The University of Illinois Press
is a founding member of the
Association of American University Presses.

Composed in 9/13.5 Meta Normal
with Meta display
by Jim Proefrock
at the University of Illinois Press
Designed by Paula Newcomb
Manufactured by Sheridan Books, Inc.

University of Illinois Press
1325 South Oak Street
Champaign, IL 61820-6903
www.press.uillinois.edu